A History of
American Civilization

A History of American Civilization

MERLE CURTI
UNIVERSITY OF WISCONSIN

RICHARD H. SHRYOCK
JOHNS HOPKINS UNIVERSITY

THOMAS C. COCHRAN
UNIVERSITY OF PENNSYLVANIA

FRED HARVEY HARRINGTON
UNIVERSITY OF WISCONSIN

Essay Index Reprint Series

BOOKS FOR LIBRARIES PRESS
FREEPORT, NEW YORK

STANDARD BOOK NUMBER:

8369-1031-1

LIBRARY OF CONGRESS CATALOG CARD NUMBER:

68-29199

PRINTED IN THE UNITED STATES OF AMERICA

Contents

ing Capital: Foreign Loans, Banking, The Corporation—Manufacturing—The Problem of Competition—The Working Classes—Industry and Culture

Eastern Theater—Dividing the Confederacy—The Last Cam-
paigns—Raising Troops—The Soldier's War—War Finance—The
War Economy, North and South—Politics in the Confederacy—
Politics in the Union—Ending Slavery—The Election of 1864

The Role of Technology—Business and the Market—Advertising
—Managerial Enterprise—The Standard of Living—The Decline
of Trade Unionism—The New Labor Movement—Organizing
Office Workers—The Self-Employed—Farmers in the Twenties—
Farmers and Depression—War Brings Boom Years—Advance of
Science—The General Welfare: A New Conception

Maps

Preface

This book is designed to meet the needs of those who want a one-volume American history text which emphasizes social and intellectual as well as political and economic trends.

In preparing this abridged edition of our two-volume text, we have tried to retain the distinctive features of the longer work. That is, we have dealt with institutions as well as events, in order to give readers an understanding of the forces that have created American civilization. We have departed from the purely chronological approach, so as to put stress on the development of political democracy, on ideas, on science and technology, on economic change, and on the place of the American republic in the larger world pattern.

This volume divides American history into six time periods. Part I deals with the colonial era, from Columbus through the French and Indian War. Part II centers on the transition from colony to republic, 1763–1815. Part III spans the years from 1815 to 1850, a period of great economic progress. Parts IV and V both concern the years 1850–96, Part IV treating the sectional conflict (1850–77), while Part V covers the transition from a farm to a factory civilization (1850–96, with emphasis on the later years). Part VI (1896–1919) stresses concentration of economic power, the progressive movement, and emergence of the United States as a world power. Part VII is on the years since 1919, in which the United States has faced the domestic and foreign problems of a mature industrial nation.

The maps were prepared by James J. Flannery of the University of Kansas, Arthur H. Robinson of the University of Wisconsin acting as general adviser on map problems.

M. C.
R. H. S.
T. C. C.
F. H. H.

January, 1953

Part I

The Foundations of
American Culture
(1492-1763)

American civilization is based on European culture as modified by the American environment. It is important, therefore, to begin the study of American history with the colonial era. It was then that the economic, political, and cultural institutions of Europe first made their impact felt in the New World. It was then that American conditions began to change these European institutions, and to create what would in time become an American culture.

1

The Background
and the Environment

The First Americans

One could begin with Christopher Columbus. But America was settled several thousand years before 1492, by primitive Asiatic peoples who moved across the Bering Strait into Alaska, then spread slowly over the two continents. The descendants of these immigrants were the American Indians, whom the first European explorers found long established in the "new world." To the red man, America was a very old world indeed.

There is little exact knowledge about the first invasion of the Western Hemisphere. Did a change in climate produce famine and drive these people into the Americas? Were they expelled from their Asiatic homeland by military conquerors? Was love for adventure involved? We do not know. There is no written record of these migrations. Nor did the story survive in oral tradition; the very fact of the migration was forgotten.

The people who crossed the Bering Strait were in the hunting-fishing stage of development. They had the bow and arrow and a throwing stick. They could make nets and baskets and knew how to chip stone. They painted and tattooed themselves and had a crude mythology. As they became adjusted to their new environment, these first settlers improved their culture. But their attainments were their own. Out of contact with Old World progress, the Indians had no knowledge of many basic elements of Eastern Hemisphere civilization: the wheel, plow, iron implements, livestock and cereal crops of Europe and Asia. Hence, by Old World standards, the red men were backward when Columbus reached the West Indies. They were, in fact, still in the Stone Age. But they had learned to supplement (and in some areas even to replace) hunting and fishing with agriculture. They had taught themselves how to weave, make pottery, and work with certain metals. They had moved ahead in architecture, government, and religion.

3

Contrasting conditions caused the various tribes to develop along different lines. Indians in northern Canada and the Amazon Valley were culturally retarded, for they were forced by environmental difficulties to devote all their energy to making a living. On the other end of the scale were the Incas of Peru, the Mayas and Aztecs of Central America and Mexico. These remarkable peoples based their economy on intensive agriculture, made efficient by irrigation, dry farming, rotation of crops, and fertilizer. Skillful farming enabled them to support large populations. These advanced Indians did outstanding work with pottery and textiles, with sculpture, architecture, and painting. Equally impressive were their complex governmental and religious structures. Maya priests learned much about astronomy and mathematics, and worked out an accurate calendar and a system of writing.

The Indians who lived in the present United States were not nearly so advanced. The present strength of the United States rests in part on favorable location, facing Europe and the Orient. That meant nothing to the Indian, who had no contact with the Old World. In addition, the United States has forged ahead by exploiting such natural resources as coal and iron ore, petroleum and copper. These minerals were not used extensively by the Indians. Nor did the Indians have wheat, a crop which helps explain the development of our western plains.

When Columbus came to the New World, there were about a million Indians in what is now the United States. Yet the Indians occupied and used the whole of the present territory of the United States. Only in the Southwest was their economy based on intensive agriculture. Elsewhere Indians combined hunting and fishing with extensive agriculture. Such an economy requires a good deal of land—in this case, more than three square miles per individual.

In 1492 the United States was divided into five well-defined economic areas. Two-thirds of the red men lived in two of these regions—the eastern maize area, a wooded section stretching from the Atlantic coast to the Mississippi Valley; and the bison area, covering the plains from Canada to Texas. The tribes in the eastern maize area relied in good part on agriculture, notably on Indian corn. While the women took care of the crops, the men went into the forests for fish and game. Indians in the bison area did some farming but depended chiefly on the buffalo, eating the flesh and using the bones for weapons and the skin for clothing and shelter.

In the salmon area of the Pacific Northwest, the economy centered around the fish which, then as now, came to spawn in the Columbia River. To the south, along the California coast and inland, was a wild seed area, where tribes eked out a poor living from nuts, berries, edible roots, and such small game as was available. Quite in contrast were the Indians of the intensive agriculture area, now Arizona and New Mexico. These red men were influenced by the progress of their Mexican neighbors. Both men and women worked the soil, and worked it well, employing irrigation and careful tillage. These Pueblo Indians of the Southwest also made substantial cultural progress.

Differing in economic patterns, the Indians were even more divided in government and language. Linguists count over 500 Indian languages within the present United States; and there were more tribes than dialects. Some tribes had a considerable population—the Cherokees, for instance. In addition, separate tribes sometimes worked together, as in the Iroquois confederacy in New York. Even so, the general Indian picture was one of hopeless division, enabling whites to defeat the tribes one by one or use one tribe against another.

Meeting the White Man

Division was only one of several handicaps under which the Indians labored after 1492. The Indian culture, though admirable in many ways, was inferior to the European in the arts of war. The red man was an experienced warrior; but he fought with bow and arrow. The Europeans had horses, iron, and gunpowder. These, plus the crusading spirit, gave the white man victory.

Disease was also in the picture. Indians had no immunity to the common European infections. When the white men reached America, Indians who escaped military damage were struck down by such diseases as smallpox. Entire tribes were wiped out in a short time. Some Europeans were distressed at this appalling toll. Others were pleased. Here, they said, was a sign of God's providence, clearing the way for His people!

In most of the present United States the Indians relied heavily on hunting and fishing. White men, on the other hand, were primarily interested in farming. As they cleared the forests, they cut into tribal hunting grounds. The Indians then had a choice—depart, or fight for their game preserves. Actually, there was no choice, for Indian wars ended in defeat and removal of the red man.

From the start, the races failed to understand each other. Indians had no concept of absolute, private ownership of land. Areas were owned by the tribe. Europeans thought in terms of private property. When they bought a plot from the Indians, they distributed it to private owners. But the natives thought they had sold only hunting rights, perhaps to be shared between themselves and the purchasers. When the white men cleared farms, destroying forests and game, the Indians felt cheated and said so.

White settlers in turn talked bitterly of "Indian givers." The tribes would then attack outlying white settlements. The whites would retaliate, and an Indian war would ensue.

North of the Rio Grande, Indian political organization was loose and informal. The chiefs were elder statesmen whose influence came from personal qualifications or from experience. There were no kings in the European sense, and important decisions were made by tribal councils. But when white negotiators persuaded some chief to sign a treaty, the Europeans assumed that this was as binding as if approved by a king or governor. If the tribe repudiated the document, the whites felt deceived, and trouble was at hand.

Some white men tried to get along with the natives. The French, who entered the Mississippi Valley primarily as fur traders, tried to befriend the Indians. Also friendly were the Jesuit missionaries who accompanied the French traders. Among English settlers, William Penn and Roger Williams dealt fairly with the tribes. But even the more generous Europeans felt superior to the Indians. Everywhere, the whites considered themselves, and not the Indians, the discoverers of the New World.

Many whites did not even attempt to be fair. If they could cheat the Indians out of their land by a show of legality, well and good. If not, the lands would be taken anyway. Time after time it was the same story—early purchase of Indian lands, friction, war, then removal of the tribes to the West or to local reservations. The pattern held for two and a half centuries, from the day of the first settlements until after the Civil War.

The Indian and American Culture

Although he called the Indian inferior, the white settler learned much from the red man. Tribesmen taught whites how to plant maize and other native crops. Some say that our agriculture is a third Indian. Certainly the wild and domesticated plants of the Americas constituted a major addition to the world's resources. New World contributions include rubber and tobacco, chocolate and quinine, peanuts and pineapple, potatoes, squash, pumpkins, and many kinds of beans.

So, too, with forest lore. White explorers, fur traders, and frontier farmers took over such Indian devices as deerskin clothing and canoes. In religious doctrine and social customs there was less exchange. Europeans were scornful of native religions, and many Indians distrusted Christianity as something the whites preached but rarely practiced. Social customs also remained distinct, although the white men took up smoking and the natives acquired a taste for "firewater."

In warfare, too, the natives influenced the newcomers. If scalping was originally an Indian custom, it was soon copied by Europeans. The English colonists learned to move in Indian file, and to fight in open formation for greater safety. When Braddock's army was attacked during the French and Indian War, the colonial contingent under George Washington saved itself by this method, while the British, fighting in traditional European close order, were cut to pieces. Fear of the Indians also determined the militia system of the American colonies. Under this, all able-bodied men were enrolled and required to report at least one day a year for muster and training. Although this often became a mere form, and training day a village holiday, the system did provide the germ of a military organization. Carried over into the republican period, the militia structure ultimately developed into the present National Guard.

In the last analysis, the white settlers regarded the natives as a part of the American environment. Like the physical features, the Indians were in some ways helpful, in many ways an obstacle and menace. The situation was reversed in the eyes of the red man. To him, the coming of the whites spelled calamity unlimited—a violent change in the environment, a challenge to Indian culture, an end to the Indian way of life. As day dawned for the white man in America, the sun was setting for the Indian.

Europe and America

The Indians came to what is now the United States from the northwest. One group of white men later followed this route—the Russians, having conquered Siberia, established themselves in Alaska in the eighteenth century and operated a trading post in California from 1816 to 1841. The Russians, however, were late in reaching the present United States. The Norsemen, the Spanish, the English, the Dutch, the Swedes, and the French all came earlier; and each approached America from the Atlantic side.

Having pushed out across the North Atlantic to Iceland and Greenland, Scandinavian seamen (otherwise known as Norsemen or Vikings) were eventually blown by storms clear to the North American coast. Here, somewhere between Labrador and New England, they spent several seasons, in what they called Vinland (about A.D. 1000).

The exploits of these adventurous Europeans were celebrated in heroic poems, or sagas. These records tell of several expeditions sent out from Greenland under Leif Ericson and others. The Norsemen transported cattle to Vinland. But they soon gave up all attempts to colonize the North American coast. After several centuries, the Greenland settlement also disappeared, perhaps because of disease or conflicts with the native Eskimos. Only in Iceland, nearer to Europe, did the Norse hold on.

THE INDIANS
IN THE UNITED STATES

INDIAN CULTURE AREAS
IN 1492

EASTERN MAIZE AREA

BISON AREA

SALMON AREA

WILD SEED AREA

INTENSIVE AGRICULTURE AREA

Before Columbus, the Indians used the whole of the present United States.

INDIAN RESERVATIONS IN 1875

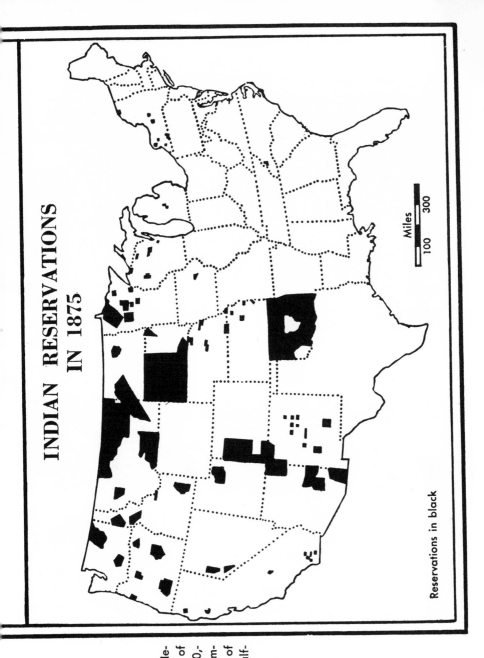

Miles

100
300

Reservations in black

By 1875 they had been deprived of all but a twelfth of the nation's area—166,000,-000 acres, much of it unimproved. And three-fourths of this would be lost in the half-century that followed.

The Norse adventure was more than dramatic; it has definite significance. Unlike the English who came over six centuries later, the Norse apparently had little trouble getting food. This is the more remarkable in that their colony was far to the north, and the settlers received no aid from the Indians. Evidently the Vinland settlers, having pioneered in Greenland, could take care of themselves in the wilderness.

Why, then, was Vinland abandoned? The military situation provides one clue. It must be remembered that these Europeans of 1000 had no firearms. Hence they had little of the military advantage over the Indians which would so aid Spain and England later. Besides, Norse ships were small and open to the elements. Anyone who has seen a storm on the Atlantic will wonder how such vessels survived at all. The Norse, moreover, had little scientific knowledge and few technical aids to navigation. Distance was thus a tremendous handicap, and Vinland settlers were in danger of losing all contact with home. This was important because of trade, and for psychological reasons.

The venture might have succeeded had there been groups at home with motives and means for assisting distant colonies. But Greenland, Iceland, Norway, and Denmark then had no national governments or churches with desire or power to aid colonists. Nor were there capitalist merchants prepared to support colonies on a commercial basis. Thus the Norse failed, not from inability to reach America, but because of the nature of their civilization at that time. Five more centuries were required before Europe would be ready for the job.

Europe in the Middle Ages

American history, then, turns on European history. Europeans in 1000 were little more advanced than certain Indian groups. But when the races met again in the sixteenth century, the Europeans had key advantages.

During the early Middle Ages (fifth to tenth centuries, A.D.) western European civilization lacked much of the complexity of the earlier Roman culture. Roman institutions had crumbled under the impact of internal disorders and invasions; and western Europe had become a region of agricultural villages with crude crafts and little trade. Each rural area was ruled by a local lord who owed allegiance to an overlord from whom he had received his lands. The local lord lived in a fortified manor house or castle and maintained soldiers to protect his estate. Farm labor was done by serfs living in a neighboring village. In return for protection and for strips of land which they worked for themselves, the serfs had to labor certain days on the lord's lands. Serfs were bound to the soil; they could not leave it, nor could they be sold away in slavery. Otherwise they were completely under the control of the lord.

A chief feature of this feudal order was the sharp distinction between classes. Members of the nobility disdained all who worked with their hands. Serfs could not hope to acquire lands of their own or in any way to improve their status. Things were even worse for the women, who on all social levels were controlled by their fathers or husbands. Marriage, which came early, was virtually the one occupation open to women, unless they entered a religious order. Hence most women were bound to household drudgery as most men were bound to the soil. The birth rate was high, but so was the death rate, especially among children, living as they did in crude, unsanitary surroundings.

The population of medieval England was less than a fifth that of England today. Yet it was hard to secure enough food for this small number. Farming methods were primitive. Little was known about the care and breeding of livestock, cattle and swine being barely half their present size. As a result, the daily diet was heavy and monotonous. Cereals, used for both food and drink, were the mainstay of the masses, particularly in northern countries where fruits were scarce most of the year.

The merchants and skilled craftsmen of the cities were neither lords nor serfs. They lacked the leisure and prestige of the nobility; but, being free and able to acquire wealth, they had a social status above the serfs. Therefore, they were known in England as the middle classes. Elsewhere they were called "burghers" or "bourgeoisie," because they lived in the burgs or cities. They organized guilds to regulate business; and, by purchase or otherwise, they obtained from local lords rights of self-government for their towns.

The middle classes did not fit into the static, feudal scheme of things. They were thrifty and self-disciplined and would in time desire to reorganize society. At first, the nobles sneered at the middle classes as mere tradesmen and moneymakers. Later, the lords came to fear the growing power of the merchants, and saw the towns as a threat to feudal institutions.

Paralleling the feudal economic and political orders was the religious system. Christianity had been accepted by German invaders of the Roman Empire as well as by the Roman authorities; so, although the invaders destroyed the empire's political institutions, they preserved its religious organization. The church was both Roman and Catholic, for authority centered in the Pope or Bishop of Rome, and extended to all peoples of western Europe. The church was "established" in all political units, and was protected by the military might of the local lords. All persons, excepting small numbers of Jews and Moslems, were expected to become members of the church. This enabled the church to exert a unifying influence, at a time when economic and political institutions emphasized local loyalties.

Religious authority, centering in the Pope and church councils, operated through archbishops. Under them were bishops in charge of dioceses. The final units were priests in local parishes. In addition, there were monastic orders living under special discipline. Since they had no ordinary parish duties, the orders could give their time to such special tasks as the founding of schools and the preservation of classical knowledge. Church courts were maintained in larger centers. Since the church was the one international authority, the concept of the bounds of religion and morals was much broader than it is in our relatively secular and "worldly" age of today. Thus, cases relating to family law, even those concerning the inheritance of property, were heard in ecclesiastical rather than civil or manor courts.

Latin continued to serve as the basic medium of learning. Religious services were held in Latin, and all priests were required to learn the language. This made the clergy, for a time, the one educated class. For several centuries, church officials were the only western Europeans with any significant knowledge of classical law and literature, medicine and science. Later, when laymen in the cities desired education, they had to begin by securing training in Latin. It was a real advantage that all educated men knew this international language. At the same time, the absence of literature in the vernacular languages—those actually spoken by the people— was a barrier to the education of the masses.

Changing Patterns

Such was the character of European culture when the Norsemen came to the New World. Between then and 1492, great changes occurred. These changes resulted from developments inside western Europe, and from contacts with the cultures of the Greek (Byzantine) and Moslem worlds. The crusades against the Mohammedans of the Near East and Spain educated western Europeans in the superior arts and sciences of the Arabic peoples. These crusades also increased European trade with Eastern lands.

With trade expansion came the substitution of money for barter, the improvement of handicrafts, and the growth of towns. Merchants became rich, guilds grew in influence. At first merchants were handicapped by a lack of banking facilities. The church condemned interest on loans as "usury"; hence Jews, who did not have to respect Christian doctrines, were long the chief moneylenders. But in time the church's objections were overcome, and primitive banks were established. Business was further aided by new bookkeeping systems, the development of commercial law, and the use of Arabic numerals in place of clumsy Roman numerals.

Merchants who sought trade in distant lands found it advantageous to pool their resources and share risks and profits. Thus was created the joint-stock company, ancestor of the corporation. The investors or stockholders entrusted the management of the company to a governor (president), or a general court (board of directors), and shared in profits through dividends. Joint-stock companies flourished especially in England and Holland. They were to play an important part in the settlement of America.

Political changes centered around the growth of national states. Through wars and intermarriage, certain nobles acquired large estates and military power. Sooner or later these men aspired to rule over areas corresponding to modern countries. The process began earlier in some regions than in others. Germany and Italy were not unified until 1870. But Portugal, Spain, England, and France each was unified under one government by 1492.

In these cases kings emerged victorious over rival nobles. While fighting the nobles, the kings were usually supported by the urban middle classes. Merchants disliked the arrogance and prestige of the noblemen and wished to see them humbled. Moreover, the commercial classes stood to gain when small political units gave way to national organization. The change eliminated the twin enemies of trade, local warfare and local tariff barriers.

The kings, in turn, encouraged business. Business groups were given subsidies; joint-stock companies were granted monopolies, rights of self-government, and other special privileges. These companies took an active part in building English, French, and Dutch colonies. Spain, however, followed a different pattern. There was no strong middle class in Spain, for the Jews and Moslems (who had held the lead in business) were expelled in religious persecutions. Spanish colonies, therefore, were under the Crown from the start.

Effective unification of the national monarchies involved more than setting up a central government. If such a government was to prosper, there was need for a common language as well as a common law. In the Middle Ages distinct dialects, even different languages, had been used in neighboring provinces. This had strengthened separatist tendencies. National-minded monarchs therefore encouraged all subjects to speak and write the language of the court and capital. Thus the language of the London area became standard "English," favored over the dialects of Yorkshire and Scotland. The language of Paris became "French," that of Ma-

drid "Spanish." Men began to write in the vernacular rather than in Latin.
Chaucer wrote in English, Dante in Italian, and the national literatures
were born.

Tied together by a common language, the people of each country came
to think of themselves as members of one nation, with common characteristics, common background, common interests and purposes. This feeling of belonging together and the sense of pride connected with the association we call nationalism. The closely related emotion of loyalty to one's
national government is patriotism.

At first, the symbol of each nation was the king, to whom all subjects
owed a personal loyalty. It was easy to promote this sentiment, for it closely
resembled the older loyalty of peasant for manor lord and of lord for overlord. Later there would be devotion to the more abstract concept of the
nation, with perhaps only a flag as its formal symbol.

Barely in existence in 1000, nationalism and patriotism were potent
forces by 1492. They had their dangers, for they often produced jingoism
and caused needless wars. But the new loyalties provided a morale that
aided in the exploration and settlement of America. Monarchs and trading
companies rallied support for their colonial ventures by announcing that
they were adding to the nation's glory. Sometimes these appeals were
sincere. But what made for national glory also made for royal power and
commercial profits. Unscrupulous kings and merchants therefore had every
reason for wrapping the flag around their own interests.

The Cultural Awakening

With political and economic changes came
improvements in the arts and sciences and in the field of learning generally.
Technology slowly improved after 1200. Some of the more important
techniques were imported through the Oriental trade, by way of the Near
East. Better steelmaking was learned from Moslem Damascus, better textile weaving from various Oriental lands. The introduction of gunpowder
from China made possible firearms which kings used to destroy troublesome nobles, and which colonists later employed against the American
Indians. Even more important was printing, which also originated in
China. Gutenberg led the way in Europe when he devised a practical
printing press in Germany about 1450. Soon printing had made books
relatively cheap, thus facilitating the rapid spread of ideas.

As increasing wealth made for leisure in the cities, laymen as well as the
clergy acquired learning. Church authorities set up educational centers
where men could study law and medicine as well as literature, theology,
and philosophy. Scholars gave increasing attention to Greek literature,

which revealed a rich art and learning that had been largely lost. It revealed, moreover, a different outlook on life, one in which the thinker or artist was expected to develop his own individuality. Even more distinctive was the secular outlook of the Greeks, who had focused their attention on man and this world, rather than on God and the hereafter. Such an outlook appealed to the merchants and princes of the later Middle Ages. It is not surprising, therefore, that in the Renaissance, or rebirth of classical learning, both art and literature turned gradually from religious to human themes.

From thirteenth-century beginnings the process flowered in the Italian Renaissance between 1400 and 1600. Spreading to northern Europe, the movement everywhere influenced society by its encouragement of secular interests. At times it tended to weaken the church, as in spreading "pagan" ideas and indifference to religion among the Italian upper classes. But the chief effect was in the fine arts, realistic painting replacing the religious "primitives" and Renaissance architecture taking the place of medieval Gothic.

Profoundly important for European culture was the new interest in classical science. The Greek idea that the world was a sphere, and Greek knowledge of geography and map making were clearly useful to Renaissance navigators. These concepts inspired Columbus' view that a short cut to India or China could be found by sailing west from Europe around the globe.

Further scientific progress called for a new and practical approach. The middle classes desired improvements in navigation; monarchs sought more effective military weapons. These needs had been partly met by master workmen in the guilds, as when metalworkers evolved the armor worn by medieval knights. But the craftsmen improved their arts slowly, by trial and error, without any knowledge of scientific principles which might have speeded up improvements in technology. Often, too, guilds kept their methods secret to enjoy monopolies, thus retarding the development of better techniques. Meantime, university men who knew something of scientific principles considered themselves a superior class and would not work with their hands.

Finally, in the sixteenth century, scientists began to take the practical arts seriously. Galileo, though a learned man, studied the work of artillerymen at the Venice arsenal. To observations made there he applied his knowledge of classical geometry and began to learn about the laws of moving bodies. Here was the basis of a new branch of mathematics, dynamics. This opened the way for research in modern physics. It also led to useful inventions, such as the pendulum clock.

Basic to Galileo's work was the process of *experimentation*. Galileo measured the motion of bodies deliberately dropped under controlled conditions, without waiting to see them fall naturally. This revealed much that could not be discovered merely by observing nature. Without the experimental method, the achievements of modern science would have been impossible.

From what source did scientists derive this method? In part from craftsmen, who had long experimented by slow trial and error. Partly, also, from alchemists. These men, popularly viewed as magicians, performed crude experiments with chemical substances. They worked blindly, seeking formulas that would yield gold or youth or wisdom. But their method, experimentation, became effective when put to sensible uses.

The new science did not catch on overnight. Alchemists were respected, not for their experimental method, but for their presumed knowledge of magic. Astrologers prospered, not because they studied astronomical phenomena, but because they claimed powers of prophecy. But science made headway. The rising universities helped, as did interested businessmen and rulers. Results were impressive as early as 1492. It was no accident that Christopher Columbus commanded relatively seaworthy ships, steered with the aid of a compass, and plotted his course mathematically on a geographical chart. Without this equipment he would probably not have embarked, or, had he started, would never have returned to tell his tale.

Religious Controversy

Statements of scientists not infrequently ran counter to religious teachings. The rising nationalism, however, was a more serious threat to the church. National monarchs were bound to resent international authority. What was more, religious leaders had great influence over the common people; and the kings desired that influence. Rulers also looked with envy on church wealth and taxes. On this, as on the question of the nobles, the middle classes lined up with the Crown. Businessmen disliked ecclesiastical as well as lay lords. They resented church taxes and religious restrictions on trade.

The church was also threatened from within. Scholars revived the original Hebrew and Greek Scriptures. The resulting knowledge led some to conclude that in doctrine, practices, and organization the church had departed from original Christianity. Some clergymen, especially in the northern countries, were shocked by what they considered the immorality or worldliness of the church in Italy, where some high religious officials lived much as did the merchants and princes of the pleasure-loving Renaissance world.

All these circumstances converged in the sixteenth century in the Protestant Reformation. The key figure was the German monk, Martin Luther, who objected to certain church methods of raising funds. His protest broadened into a general condemnation of the church as then organized. Luther and others who took up the cry appealed to the Bible as a better authority than the Pope or church councils and, on the basis of their interpretations of the Scriptures, demanded various changes in doctrine, ritual, and organization. Luther won the backing of princes and merchants who desired to break the international power of the church. All over northern Europe monarchs broke the tie with Rome. Each king then set up a national church. These state churches were headed, not by the Pope, but by the local rulers.

In some German states and Scandinavia the state church was that of the Lutherans, or followers of Luther. In England, the organization was known simply as the Church of England. In general, these first Protestant churches closely resembled the Catholic Church. All citizens were expected to belong to the national church as they had formerly to the Catholic; that is, there was no toleration of other religious groups. Much of the old ritual was retained, though the services and Bible were translated into the spoken languages. The Protestants reduced the number of sacraments and modified their meaning but retained the Catholic view that the individual should approach God through sacraments ordinarily performed only by church officials.

But there could be other interpretations besides those of Lutherans and Anglicans. The French-Swiss theologian, John Calvin, evolved a third major Protestant movement which in time became the state church in Scotland, Holland, and parts of Germany and Switzerland. His followers acquired such names as Dutch Reformed, German Reformed, Huguenots (France), and Presbyterians (Scotland and England). Calvinists insisted on a state church to which all must belong; and, like the Anglicans and Lutherans, they retained a dignified and educated clergy. But they carried their "reform" further. They substituted presbyterian control (government by assemblies) for that of bishops (the episcopal system). They rejected or simplified old rituals and doctrine, and criticized other Protestants for retaining "popish" practices.

Still other Protestant sects sprang up in England and on the Continent. Many of these sects objected to any connection between church and state and insisted on complete religious toleration. They abandoned almost all of the old forms, gave up vestments and even Gothic architecture, dropped most or all of the sacraments, and viewed their clergy (if any) as moral advisers rather than persons in authority. The Baptists were the most nu-

merous, but the logical extreme of the trend was seen in the simple, severe Mennonites of Germany and the Friends (Quakers) of England. With the latter there was no service, no clergy, almost no church organization. Each man interpreted the Bible for himself and communed directly with God. Such sects appealed, at first, chiefly to humble men who had little place in the state or the powerful state churches. In their new faith these ordinary people felt an individual dignity previously denied them. The appearance of these denominations consequently had democratic as well as religious significance; and their challenge to political authority would have importance for the New World.

The early years of the Reformation saw little violence and several attempts at reconciliation. But as gaps widened, agreement became impossible. Rulers were urged to use force to suppress or defend the new churches, and wars followed. There was much bloodshed in areas such as Germany, where the people were divided between the new and old faiths. Nor was idealism always preserved, for the selfish interests of princes on both sides became intertwined with the religious interests of their followers. This atmosphere of religious struggle existed throughout the sixteenth and seventeenth centuries, just when the New World was being colonized. Reflections of the conflict were inevitably cast upon the American scene.

Europe Looks Outward

Direct contacts between the Orient and Occident were infrequent before 1500. But there was some trade, especially after European Crusaders became aware of the excellence of Oriental goods. Products came from the Near and Middle East, from China and Japan, from India and the islands south and southeast of Asia. The goods were taken by land and water routes to the Moslem-dominated eastern Mediterranean. There they were picked up by Italian shippers, who carried them to western Europe. Many profited from this trade—businessmen of the Far East, those in charge of Arab caravans, rulers who collected transit duties, Italian merchants. All these middlemen, however, added to the cost. Western Europeans wanted the silks of China, the rugs of Persia, the spices which added variety to a monotonous diet. But how to pay for these items? Europe's goods were little wanted in the Orient, and even after reopening old mines Europeans were short of gold and silver. Plainly, it was necessary to cut the cost of Oriental products or find more gold and silver.

One way to slash costs was to find an all-water route to the Far East. Such a route would eliminate the heavy expense of breaking cargo, shifting goods from ship to caravan, then to ship again. An all-water route

would also mean the end of the burdensome transit duties charged on the overland trips; and it would enable west European traders to break the monopoly of Italian shipowners, who had grown rich because of their domination of the Mediterranean.

An obvious alternate route was around Africa. Closest to this line was Portugal. Ambitious rulers and daring seamen made this kingdom the pioneer in European expansion overseas. Location helped, as did the work of Prince Henry the Navigator. Henry had a crusading desire to spread Christianity. He also wanted to add glory to Portugal; and, being interested in science, he did much to improve the art of navigation. In Henry's day and later (he died in 1460), Portuguese sailors reached the Azores, the Madeiras, and tropical Africa. Here they found ivory and gold; here they organized a traffic in Negro slaves. Encouraged by success, the Portuguese kept going. In 1486, Bartholomeu Dias rounded the Cape of Good Hope and entered the Indian Ocean. A decade later Vasco da Gama used the same route to reach India.

Portugal, then, had opened an all-water route to the Orient. Others attempted to find a better one, Columbus by sailing west, Magellan by going southwest, others by heading northwest or northeast. But the passage around Africa was the best. Portugal followed through by founding trading posts around Africa and from India to China and Japan. Later, many of these stations were captured by the Dutch; and Portugal's epic of expansion is largely forgotten.

Portugal also figured in the story of Columbus. This Italian-born seaman settled in Portugal. The location influenced him, for Lisbon buzzed with talk of expeditions. But when Columbus talked of sailing west to the Orient, he won no backing from Portuguese officials. Like Columbus, many Lisbon scientists accepted the Greek concept of the world as a globe. But Portugal was seeking a southeast passage; and this did yield the best route to India.

Failing in Portugal, Columbus sought backing elsewhere. He obtained it in Spain, then ruled by Ferdinand of Aragon and Isabella of Castile. Aragon, being to the east, took the lead in handling Spain's Mediterranean problems; Castile, on the west, took care of the Atlantic. Thus Isabella, rather than Ferdinand, financed Columbus.

Columbus underestimated by two-thirds the circumference of the earth. This mistake caused him to feel that he had reached the Far East when he discovered the West Indies in October, 1492. In a natural confusion, he called the natives Indians. Within a few years, evidence accumulated that Columbus had not reached the East Indies but had encountered a land barrier between Europe and Asia. Disillusionment quickly yielded to the lure of what was actually a new world. What wealth, what wonders might it hold?

Spain followed up Columbus' voyages with enthusiasm. Expeditions were sent to the West Indies and the American mainland; Cortez conquered Mexico, Pizarro Peru. In both areas the Spaniards found gold and silver, and populations accustomed to autocratic political control. Once conquered, these Aztecs and Incas were exploited for the benefit of their white masters; and soon treasure ships were carrying precious metals back to Spain. This treasure enabled Spain to play a dominant role in Europe through the sixteenth century. Indirectly, the new-found wealth influenced all western Europe. American gold and silver reached all nations through trade, making possible increased purchases from the Orient. The larger store of precious metals also inflated currencies, raising prices and stimulating handicraft manufacturing as well as commerce. Besides, American plants proved valuable and the discovery of America added to knowledge and excited scientific curiosity.

Spain's American empire extended from Argentina to Georgia and California. Through this area the Spanish adjusted their economic interests to the environment. In the tropical West Indies they raised such money crops as sugar. So great was the return that Europe long considered the West Indies as more valuable than the temperate mainland regions to the north. Spain, however, had another source of wealth—the mines of Mexico and the Andes. Spaniards also brought cattle and horses from Europe and tried stock raising in sparsely settled parts of the New World.

Spain's success naturally aroused envy. Rivalry with Portugal was settled by a papal decision and a treaty dividing the non-European world between these two Catholic powers (1493–94). The line of demarcation gave Brazil to Portugal, the rest of America to Spain. Other monarchies, however, would not recognize this division. John Cabot challenged Spain's monopoly by establishing an English claim to Newfoundland in 1497; and four decades later, Jacques Cartier hoisted the banner of France in the St. Lawrence Valley.

England Gets Ready to Expand

In Columbus' day England lagged behind Spain in trade, culture, and military power. Nevertheless, there were elements of strength in England. Although working with Parliament, the able Tudor monarchs concentrated national authority in the Crown. Instead of abusing the middle classes (as Spanish rulers did), English kings encouraged businessmen. Traders spread English influence abroad. The navy provided protection, and Englishmen built fast ships for trade and war. Soon England's vessels could sail rings around the clumsy galleons of Spain. They did just that in 1588, wiping out the Spanish Armada.

Class lines were not as sharply drawn in England as on the Continent. Serfdom disappeared earlier in England than in France and Germany. By practicing thrift and other "middle-class virtues," English apprentices could become master workmen, shopkeepers could become rich merchants. Likewise, yeomen could make themselves substantial farmers, and the latter could aspire to be country gentlemen. There was a tendency to state that even humble Englishmen had rights. A man could be arrested at home only on a legal warrant; then he had to be tried promptly in a proper court employing fair procedure. The "rights of Englishmen" also included freedom of speech, petition, and assembly.

In England as on the Continent the sixteenth century saw much religious turmoil. Under Henry VIII the Church of England remained Catholic in spirit. Queen Elizabeth introduced changes in the late 1500's, but the church retained much ritual and was still controlled by bishops. This drew the fire of those influenced by Calvin's teachings. Some wished to replace the bishops with presbyteries, or representative assemblies. Others insisted that each parish or congregation manage its own affairs. Both groups—presbyterians and congregationalists alike—wanted to "purify" the Anglican Church by eliminating surviving elements of Catholic doctrine and ritual. Hence both groups came to be known as Puritans. Besides opposing "popery," Puritans favored a strict moral code, which included a ban on gambling, dancing, and the theater.

Hoping to reform the Church of England, the Puritans remained inside the official church. Others (mostly members of the lower middle class) felt that it would be better to withdraw from the Anglican organization. These Separatists were divided into Baptists, Quakers, and other groups. On morals, they tended to agree with the Puritans; but their chief demand was for religious toleration.

Though paternalistic, the English government did not curb business initiative. The Crown was glad to see merchants open commercial routes, found trading posts, send colonists to distant shores. These operations meant more trade, with the merchants securing needed raw materials and building markets for English goods. The government was especially interested in ventures likely to increase exports, or to lead to the discovery of gold and silver. This was natural, for in those days a country's wealth was measured by its store of precious metals. These could be obtained by direct discovery (as in Portuguese Africa and in Spain's American possessions) or by a so-called favorable balance of trade, exporting more than one imported and getting the balance of payment in cash.

Given this situation, English traders inevitably became interested in Africa and America. In 1562 an English captain, John Hawkins, loaded slaves in Sierra Leone, crossed the Atlantic to sell them to Spanish West Indian planters, then returned home with sugar and other products. This was an illegal expedition; foreigners were not supposed to trade with Spain's colonies. But Queen Elizabeth secretly encouraged further expeditions; and such commanders as Francis Drake seized treasure ships and looted Spanish colonial seaports.

England found it easy to defend these operations. They were profitable. In addition, they appealed to English nationalism. Patriotic leaders denounced Spain as the natural enemy of England's maritime interests. The religious-minded saw Spanish Catholicism as a threat to English Protestantism. And so came war and English victory (1588). Plainly, England was ready for colonial expansion.

Settling the New World

Spain, not England, founded the first permanent white settlements in the present United States—St. Augustine, Florida, in 1565; Santa Fe, New Mexico, about 1600. These settlements, however, were mere outposts, trading stations and military garrisons designed to protect Spain's sugar-and-gold colonies in the West Indies and Mexico. As a result, the development of the United States is associated less with the Spanish settlements than with the English colonies, which stretched along the Atlantic seaboard from Newfoundland to the borders of Spanish Florida.

The Atlantic Coastal Plain

What did this region offer to the English? Accessibility, for one thing; it was the section of America closest to the island home. Eastern North America also appealed for reasons of climate. Colonizing people tend to seek regions possessing weather like that of the homeland. Eastern North America satisfied that requirement. Temperature and rainfall were fairly well adapted to crops with which the English were familiar; and temperature and humidity were conducive to a high degree of human activity.

True, climatic extremes were greater than in England. New England winters were hard for Englishmen, as were the long, hot summers of the Virginia and Carolina lowlands. Hard winters were associated with respiratory infections. Heat and moisture along the southern seaboard encouraged flies and mosquitoes and so promoted the diseases carried by these insects (typhoid, malaria, yellow fever). But for continued immigration, disease probably would have wiped out the first Virginia settlement, at Jamestown, 1607. Ten years after the founding of the colony, less than a quarter of the 1600 who had come over were still living. But victory over disease was assured by 1650, because of continued immigration and a seasoning process. Persons born and bred in Virginia were less susceptible to the fevers than were newcomers, perhaps to some extent because of a gradually acquired immunity.

Topography also encouraged the English. From the St. Lawrence to Virginia, the Atlantic coastline is highly indented, affording many deepwater harbors. A glance at a map will show how less favored in this respect would have been an approach via the Pacific. The early settlers were further aided by the existence of a low coastal plain. Narrow in New England, this plain broadens out to the south, being sixty miles wide in New Jersey, more than 150 in the Carolinas. Access to the interior was facilitated by long, navigable rivers. Settlement naturally began on or near the coast, as at Jamestown in Virginia. Then, in the absence of roads, colonists moved inland by the rivers, settling along these waterways.

Soils in New England were chemically adequate, but the rocky debris of the glacial ages made farming difficult. From New Jersey south, the coastal plain was sandy and lacking in phosphates and other minerals needed for agriculture. The whole area was forested, and the thin accumulation of forest humus did make possible excellent crops for a few years. Early settlers were thus deceived into thinking that the soils were rich. But when the forest humus was used up, the real "topsoil" was inadequate. There followed the so-called exhaustion of soils on the southern coastal plain. Only fertilizers could make this area productive; and in colonial times these were not used extensively.

The first white colonists, in fact, cultivated their land carelessly. Accustomed to scarcities in the Old World, they were dazzled by the vastness of the natural resources of the new continent. Why save trees when there seemed no end of forests? Why bother about careful cultivation when there was so much cheap land? Standard practice was to destroy forests to make room for farms. Some colonists, however, tapped the wealth of the woodlands. American lumber and naval stores were greatly needed in deforested England. There was a big demand for furs in England, and the Indians who secured the pelts at first had little knowledge of prices across the Atlantic. Fur traders were therefore much in evidence in the northern colonies, and were in the van when the white people pushed westward.

The Piedmont Area

As the traders and farmers moved inland, they found that the flat coastal plain was succeeded by higher, rolling country. Like the coastal plain, this Piedmont area was a wooded region, narrow in New England and wider in the South. But in the South, the Piedmont's red clay soils were chemically more adequate than the soils of the tidewater region to the east.

The rivers drop from the Piedmont area to the coastal plain in a series of falls and rapids. Hence the line of division between the two regions is called the fall line. Since they could take their boats no further upstream, colonial traders tended to establish trading posts along this line: Hartford on the Connecticut, Albany on the Hudson, Richmond on the James. Later, settlers used the water power furnished by the falls for mills. And from these fall-line towns, colonists spread out to occupy the Piedmont lands. This occurred in the second century of English colonial settlement (from 1700 on).

Going further west, the colonists encountered a line of hills running from northeast to southwest, paralleling the coastal plain and the Piedmont. Beyond this Blue Ridge lies a high, fertile valley, known in Virginia as the Shenandoah. It has a cooler climate than the lowlands to the east and possesses limestone soils which are the richest in eastern North America. The region is adapted to diversified farming (cereals, fruits, vegetables) rather than to tobacco and the other staple crops which flourish in the lowlands. Thus the Shenandoah Valley never developed the plantation-slave economy of the Virginia coastal plain. In general, the western portion of the southern colonies remained a region of white farmers, distinct from the slaveholding tidewater planters.

Eastern Virginians could not easily cross the Blue Ridge. The better approach was from the north; so the Shenandoah Valley was settled after 1750 by Pennsylvanians who moved south and west into Maryland, Virginia, and North Carolina. Most of these settlers were Germans and Scots-Irish who could not see eye to eye with the English of the tidewater South.

The Appalachian Mountains

Beyond the inland valley lie the great Appalachian Mountains, which run from New England southwest to northern Alabama. These mountains checked the westward movement until the American Revolution. Then the dammed-up population broke through the few natural passes and flowed out into the Mississippi Valley.

One important pass was the Cumberland Gap, located where Virginia meets Kentucky and Tennessee. New York's Mohawk Valley would enable commerce to follow a water-level route from New York City up the Hudson to Albany, then west along the Mohawk to Buffalo. There the route connected with the Great Lakes. Operating along this line, New York City would have a trading advantage over Boston, Philadelphia, Baltimore, and Charleston, which had to use more difficult routes across the mountains. This helps explain why New York became the largest city in America.

The Appalachian Mountains offered little in agricultural resources. Eventually, poor farmers who found no cheap lands left in the East did settle hillside clearings. Here some remained, isolated while the main streams of American history passed them by. The wealth of the mountains was in timber, furs, and minerals. In Pennsylvania and Virginia, iron, coal, and oil awaited later technologies. The colonists, however, extracted only small quantities of iron ore, at first from mud flats along the shore. And, having cheap firewood, they did not use coal and oil at all.

To early Americans, then, the Appalachians were largely an obstacle. Yet the mountains were a blessing in disguise. They protected the English against Indian and French attacks from the west. They hemmed in the English settlers, forcing them to consolidate their position along the Atlantic. The concentration of strength would prove a great advantage when England fought rival Europeans in the colonial wars.

The Mississippi Valley

There were no Appalachians to hold back the French when they moved up the St. Lawrence to the Great Lakes. French missionaries and fur traders then found portages which linked the lakes to the Mississippi River system, a vast network of water communication stretching from the Appalachians to the Rocky Mountains, and from the Great Lakes to the Gulf of Mexico.

Nowhere else in the world would the expanding European peoples find a region as large, as rich, as little exploited as the Mississippi Valley. The eastern half of the valley was forested, providing timber and furs as well as farmlands. West of the Mississippi extended treeless plains. The lack of forests and (in some places) the shortage of rainfall affected the pattern of living of the plains Indians and later white settlers. But here, as in the wooded regions to the east, men could make a living from the soil. And the Mississippi Valley contains rich mineral resources. Notable are the greatest iron deposits in the world, along the southern shore of Lake Superior in the Duluth area. Once technology was equipped to exploit these deposits, the Great Lakes afforded an easy route for transporting the heavy ore to the East, which had the coal resources needed for refinement and manufacture.

The French had barely begun to tap the resources of the area when they were driven out by the British (1763). They left many place names behind them, from Detroit and St. Louis to New Orleans. But the settlement of the valley was for the most part the work of the English-speaking people from the Atlantic seaboard.

West to the Pacific

To the west of the Mississippi Valley lie the Rocky Mountains. Being more rugged than the Appalachians, the Rockies were a major challenge to settlers. To make things worse, the territory between the Mississippi and the Pacific contains large patches of desert land. But, though less useful than the Mississippi Valley, this gigantic region did have great economic value. Its furs and forests have yielded wealth. It had great stores of minerals, including copper, lead, gold, and silver. It contains good wheat and grazing areas; and some of its arid lands are highly productive when irrigated.

Pushing westward, the descendants of the settlers of the eastern seaboard would come at last to the Pacific coastal plain. They were not the first white people to settle in the Far West. In California, as in Florida, Texas, and New Mexico, they were preceded by the Spaniards. Taking over in the nineteenth century, the English-speaking settlers carried on, introducing the techniques they had developed on the Atlantic and in the Mississippi Valley.

It was no easy job, for there were geographical handicaps. The Pacific coastal area was far from markets and sources of supply. It had rugged mountains and areas of insufficient rainfall. It did not compare with the Atlantic coastal plain in harbors or navigable rivers. But California had gold, which drew men like a magnet. Traders were attracted by the fur resources of Oregon; lumbermen came in to work the magnificent forests of the Northwest. Soil and climate were right for agriculture in many sectors, and irrigation helped where rainfall was slight.

2

The Thirteen Colonies

Economic Motives and Activities

Many were the motives which sent Englishmen to the New World in the seventeenth and eighteenth centuries. Some sought adventure. Some were fleeing from political or religious persecution. Strongest of all was the economic motive. Businessmen financed colonizing schemes in hopes of making profits. Rulers lent encouragement in the thought that overseas expansion would enrich the realm. Those who migrated to America did so, generally, to improve their economic status.

In the Spanish empire, the government itself set up and ran the colonies. English rulers preferred to let individuals or groups of individuals take the financial risk. If a colonizing venture failed, the Crown had saved some money. When a project succeeded, its success meant prestige for England as well as profit for the backers of the enterprise; and, if it chose, the English government could then move in and declare the settlement a royal colony.

Joint-stock companies chartered by James I led the way. The London Company settled Virginia by sending a hundred colonists to Jamestown in 1607. A less successful Plymouth Company was later reorganized as the Council for New England. The Pilgrims who founded Plymouth on the Massachusetts coast in 1620 secured a land patent from this Council. So did the more important Massachusetts Bay Company, which improved its situation by obtaining an additional charter direct from the Crown, and colonized what is now Massachusetts in the late 1620's and 1630's.

Those who put money in the London and Plymouth companies hoped for substantial profits. But the Plymouth Company never could get started at all; and the London Company's Jamestown colony proved a financial disappointment. It was, in part, bad management. The London Company failed to provide the settlers with needed goods, equipment, or advice. And the settlers were townspeople who knew little of farming and could not take care of themselves in a wilderness. Malnutrition and fevers lowered their working capacity, and finally there was starvation and even cannibalism. Of Jamestown's first 500 settlers, only sixty were alive in 1610. Prospects remained poor until the farmers turned to tobacco as a staple crop. Then, just as the financial outlook began to brighten, King James revoked the charter and turned Virginia into a royal province (1624).

The backers of the London Company remained in England. It was expected that the Puritan businessmen who controlled the Massachusetts Bay Company would operate in the same fashion. Instead, these stockholders crossed the ocean to help organize the new settlement of Boston. Though they wanted profits, these investors also had religious aims in mind. Working on the ground, they were more successful than the London Company. But here too the Crown eventually interfered, revoking the charter and turning Massachusetts into a royal colony in 1684.

In Massachusetts and Virginia, the English government chartered joint-stock companies and gave those companies grants of land.[1] More commonly, England's rulers favored proprietors like Lord Baltimore, who was given Maryland in 1632, or William Penn, who obtained Pennsylvania in 1681, Delaware being added the next year. Descendants of the original proprietors held these colonies at the outbreak of the American Revolution. There were proprietors in New Hampshire, New York, New Jersey, North and South Carolina, and Georgia; but each of these became a royal colony before the Revolution.

The proprietors had various aims. All, however, were to some extent profit-minded. Economic motives were still more evident among ordinary settlers. These people had no capital except their own lives. These they risked to seek a better life in the New World. They were poor tenant farmers who had been driven from the land. They were unemployed laborers, petty artisans, and minor tradesmen who wanted a chance to build their fortunes. Politics meant little to these men, and they were less stirred by religious motives than were many of their leaders, but almost to a man they wanted economic opportunity.

Did they get the chance they wanted in America? Some died on the way, or perished of disease soon after their arrival. The rest found much to block their progress in America. Land was often under monopoly control. In Jamestown's early days, the London Company required the colonists to farm in common. Immigrants who settled in New York found much of the best land held by large landowners; and in the Carolinas and Maryland, the proprietors tried to rule in feudal fashion as the king's vassals. Lord

---

[1] Two other colonies, Rhode Island and Connecticut, also operated under charters, obtained in 1644 and 1662. But these charters, which lasted until the American Revolution, were granted, not to joint-stock companies, but to settlers already on the ground.

Baltimore distributed Maryland land but retained ownership and required farmers to pay quitrents indefinitely.

Here, then, were efforts to reproduce in the New World the conditions of the old. But in Europe land was scarce. It was plentiful in America. That fact gave the common man his opportunity. The Jamestown settlers refused to exert themselves when laboring on company land. Repression failing, the London Company allowed colonists to work on land of their own. Elsewhere, proprietors found it impossible to enforce feudal rules. Tenancy evolved into ownership; quitrents went uncollected.

European farmers lived in agricultural villages and went out to the fields each day. Colonial authorities would have liked such concentration, especially in view of the problem of defense against the Indians. But the lure of cheap land caused the settlers of Virginia and other southern colonies to spread out and locate on isolated clearings. In New England (Massachusetts, New Hampshire, Rhode Island, Connecticut) the settlers did manage to hold together in towns which resembled the agricultural villages of the Old World. The first Massachusetts towns were located on the deep-water harbors along the rocky coast. As more Puritans arrived, they pushed into the interior. Prospective settlers began by getting a grant of a town site from the government in Boston. Then the new town's elders distributed the land. Each man received a home lot and certain fields; but the elders reserved for common use grazing lands and a park or green in the center of town.

The pattern of settlement in the middle colonies (New York, New Jersey, Pennsylvania, Delaware) combined elements found in New England and Virginia. Some agricultural villages were established, as in the sections of Pennsylvania which were settled by immigrants from Germany. But no middle colony preserved the village tradition as systematically as did the New Englanders.

The Search for Staples

The first settlers found it necessary to engage in subsistence farming. That is, they had to devote their energy to clearing the forest, erecting some sort of buildings, and feeding their families. It was necessary also to adjust to the climate and deal with the Indians. Consequently, there was little time to create a surplus for markets abroad.

There was no way out of this. Urged on by the profit-greedy London Company, the Jamestown settlers neglected the soil to hunt for gold and to prepare forest products for shipment to England. The result was near-disaster for the colony. The founders of Plymouth also suffered because of the necessity of accumulating a surplus to pay off their financial backers in the Old World.

In time the coastal colony was able to shift to a commercial economy. Meanwhile, as lands along the coast were taken up, the sons of established colonists moved to the interior. Newly arrived immigrants from Europe joined this westward movement, and farms were cleared along the frontier. In new areas subsistence farming was the rule during the first harsh period of adjustment. Those who survived could eventually produce for profit, if their farms were rich enough and if they could get their goods to market. By then, other settlers had gone further west and were practicing subsistence farming along a new frontier.

Production for profit called for a staple product that could find an easy market overseas. The staple could be a crop, or gold, fish, livestock, furs, or lumber. Virginia found her staple in tobacco. In 1612, John Rolfe (he who later married Pocahontas) tried growing a species of tobacco that had done well in Spanish Venezuela. This, and a method of curing worked out later, yielded a product that suited English tastes. Virginia had her staple crop, the basis of her export trade.

One other southern colony, Maryland, also specialized in tobacco; and some was grown in North Carolina. Further south, in South Carolina and Georgia, the low wet lands along the shore could produce other staples: rice, introduced from Madagascar just before 1700; and indigo, domesticated a half-century later. The development of indigo, used for dyes, was largely the work of Eliza Lucas Pinckney. The southern colonies also raised livestock and produced naval stores—pitch, tar, turpentine, and other forest products needed by England's navy and merchant marine. The English government encouraged the suppliers of naval stores, and the growers of indigo, by paying bounties for these items.

Furs played an important part in the development of the middle colonies, for it was the fur trade which attracted the Dutch West India Company to the Hudson River area. But the settlers from the Netherlands did not neglect agriculture. Better farmers than the English, they made wheat a paying product in New Netherland before England took over that colony and renamed it New York. The English carried on, and wheat became the staple crop of New York, New Jersey, and Pennsylvania. Large quantities were sold to the southern colonies; and, next to tobacco, wheat and flour became the most important unit in the list of colonial exports.

New England produced no comparable crop. New Englanders generally confined themselves to subsistence agriculture and found their "money

crop" in the forests or offshore. The cod fisheries were especially important.

Without staples, the colonists could not have bought the manufactured articles they needed—tools, weapons, books, textiles, household
utensils, and Indian trading goods imported from England. These goods
were paid for with tobacco, furs, rice, indigo, and naval stores shipped to
England, also with gold obtained by selling fish, flour, and livestock to the
West Indies.

Like most new areas, the colonies bought more than they sold. Inevitably, then, the colonists were always short of cash—when they did get
gold or silver by selling goods to Spanish America, the specie flowed to
London to pay for needed manufactured products. In an effort to meet
this situation, the colonial legislatures specified that local commodities
could be used for money: tobacco in the South, wheat in the middle colonies, fish and lumber in New England. Hence the staples were both trading goods and cash.

Labor

In the production of staples, the great need
was for labor. But where to get it? In the Old World, land was scarce and
costly, labor cheap and easy to obtain. In the colonies, land was cheap and
plentiful, labor hard to get and therefore expensive. This situation did
much to help the common man in America; but it also caused colonial
farmers to tap sources of non-free labor.

There were many efforts to persuade free persons to emigrate to the colonies. The joint-stock companies and proprietors described the Western
Hemisphere in glowing terms and offered land to those who would cross
the ocean. Through most of the seventeenth century, these propagandists
concentrated in England, where there was much economic distress. When
economic conditions improved in England (after 1650) the colonizers had
to look elsewhere for recruits. Organizing the settlement of Pennsylvania
in the 1680's, William Penn attracted many Scots-Irish, these being Presbyterians who had earlier migrated from Scotland to Ireland. Penn also
searched for prospective settlers in such economically distressed regions as
the Rhineland.

Many who desired to migrate to the New World could not pay for passage. These persons still could make the trip if they were willing to sign
away their freedom for a time and become indentured servants. Then,
when they had worked out their passage, they could be their own masters.
In the middle colonies and in the upper South indentured servants consti-

tuted a substantial part of the labor force. The indenture system did give thousands of poor people their only chance of reaching America. On becoming free they received land, farm equipment, or cash. Thus many were able to develop farms of their own. Others set up as independent artisans. Either way, they were better off than they would have been in the old country.

Yet the system had faults. Many indentured servants died en route to the colonies. Others went down under the strain of overwork; for, since indentures ran out in a short time, the tendency was to drive the servants hard. Finally, the program had unfortunate results in accustoming Americans to non-free labor.

The Introduction of Slavery

American colonists also experimented with slavery. Efforts to enslave local Indians failed, for the red men resisted, ran away, or died when placed in bondage. Negro slaves brought in from Africa proved more efficient. Dutch slave traders delivered a score of these to Jamestown as early as 1619. Slavery, though, did not catch on immediately. For one thing, the supply was uncertain. On top of that, Negro slaves were expensive, and slavers wanted to be paid in specie, of which the English colonists had little.

The picture changed after 1690. By then the supply of indentured servants was drying up, what with improved employment in England. Simultaneously, international developments were making Negro slaves increasingly available, England's naval forces having broken the Spanish-Portuguese monopoly of the slave trade.

By the early eighteenth century, slavery was firmly established in both South and North Carolina. The philanthropists who settled Georgia in the 1730's tried in vain to bar the introduction of the institution in that colony. Meanwhile, Virginia and Maryland were shifting from a white-servant to a Negro-slave labor force. Slaves were little used in northern agriculture. This was not because of moral objections to slavery. It was simply that there was little need for extra labor on the small, diversified farms of the northern colonies. Slaves were expensive, and it did not pay the farmers of this region to buy them. Pennsylvania farmers, who, like the Virginians, started by using white indentured servants, never followed the Virginians in shifting to slave labor.

At first, Negro slavery seemed to help the English colonies. New Englanders profited by adding the slave traffic to their other commerce. Southern agriculturalists could now exploit large holdings, employing gang labor to produce money crops for export. Certainly the planter of the late colonial period was far ahead of his ancestors in material possessions, in cultural attainments, in graciousness of living. Without Negro slavery there would have been no such rapid advance.

Yet the long-run implications of the plantation economy were not promising. Emphasis upon a single money crop was risky. When tobacco prices fell after 1750, Virginians suffered seriously. In such periods of low prices, planters went deeply in debt to their English agents. Few were able to pull out again; and the debts became permanent, passing from father to son. Moreover, constant planting of tobacco hurried the exhaustion of the soil.

Slavery had other disadvantages. Slaves lacked the incentives of free workers. Furthermore, capital invested in slaves was not available for improvements in equipment. And this capital faced peculiar risks. The death of a field hand meant a total loss in investment. It was necessary to support some slaves who made no return—the very young, the ill, the aged. Although losses might be offset by the birth of slave children, the high death rate among these youngsters made them an uncertain source of capital gains.

The European conquerors of the New World did not try to understand the Indians; and they had even less appreciation of the African cultural background of the Negro slaves. To Europeans, Negroes were primitives, and therefore inferior. Since only Negroes were slaves, the stigma of bondage as well as barbarism was associated with color. Hence a social line was drawn between whites and Negroes. This line could not be crossed even by free Negroes, who had been emancipated by their owners. Latent in this situation were all the elements of the American race problem of a later day.

Trade and Manufacturing

Today, the United States is primarily a manufacturing nation, and the factory is the central unit in our economy. In the colonial era, the economy centered around the farm, forest, and fisheries. Trade and manufacturing were secondary. Moreover, both were linked to the basic part of the economy. Thus, the most important manufacturing pursuit was flour milling—preparing a farm product for market. And traders spent much of their time marketing staple crops or carrying European goods to the agricultural population of the colonies.

Hoping to reduce dependence on English suppliers, colonial legislatures encouraged household manufacturing and offered to subsidize individuals who would set up factories. In some respects, the results were impressive. Household manufactures prospered, as did mills for sawing lumber and making flour. Hatmakers, tanners, shoemakers found work in all the colonies. New England's forests enabled her to develop an important ship-building industry. By the eighteenth century the middle colonies had a growing iron industry; and textile manufacturing was also on the rise.

Even so, manufacturing lagged. This was due to conditions common in newly opened areas: lack of capital, lack of labor, lack of transportation, lack of a large home market. In addition, the English government tried to discourage manufacturing in the colonies. As mercantilists, the English felt that colonies should supply the mother country with raw materials and furnish markets for English manufactured goods. Colonial manufacturing would divert attention from the production of raw materials, and in time American factories would compete with English establishments. Parliament therefore prohibited the colonies from exporting woolen products (Wool Act, 1699) and hats (Hat Act, 1732) and from manufacturing finished iron and steel products (Iron Act, 1750). England made little effort to enforce these laws. But the statutes did cause friction between mother country and colonies; and the colonists developed the habit of disregarding English legislation. This caused trouble when, after 1763, Britain decided to enforce her laws in the New World.

England also tried to regulate colonial trade. The Navigation Acts, passed by Parliament from 1650 on, excluded foreigners from the commerce between England and her colonies and limited the right of colonial merchants to trade directly with foreign countries. In addition, import and export duties were imposed on trade within the British Empire.

In certain ways, the Navigation Acts helped the colonies. Colonial merchants and shipbuilders shared in the profitable monopoly of trade within the British Empire; and their ships were protected by His Majesty's naval forces. Colonial producers of indigo and naval stores were paid bounties by the London government, and products from the colonies were given tariff favors not extended to competing foreign articles. But colonial merchants disliked the rules about enumerated articles—tobacco, rice, indigo had to be shipped to London, hence could not be sold direct to continental Europe. American traders also disapproved of the Molasses Act of 1733, which imposed prohibitively high duties on the sugar and molasses bought from the French and Spanish West Indies. This was important, for New England made rum from the molasses, traded this rum in Africa for Negro slaves, and sold the slaves in the West Indies for specie and more molasses.

Until the Navigation Acts were passed, Parliament had left colonial matters to the Crown. The colonial merchants could therefore have raised objections to the laws on the ground that Parliament had no right to rule England's overseas possessions. But the colonists were less concerned about the principle than about the practical effect of the new acts. Their answer was evasion, which involved smuggling and the bribery of customs officers. This developed the spirit of colonial independence and the habit of ignoring English wishes, and set the stage for a sharp conflict when, after 1763, the English government decided to enforce its trade legislation.

The Religious Motive

Although economic factors loom large in the history of the English colonies, they do not stand alone. James Oglethorpe, founder of Georgia, planned the colony as an asylum for debtors; and the English government supported Oglethorpe in order to establish a buffer colony betwen the Carolinas and Spanish Florida. In other cases, men came to the New World to escape political persecution back home. Far more important, however, was religion, which ranks next to the economic motive in explaining the settlement of the thirteen colonies.

In the 1620's and 1630's, when James I and his successor Charles I were pursuing high-church policies, thousands of Puritans and Separatists migrated to America, locating in New England. In the 1640's, when Oliver Cromwell's Puritans secured control of the English government and executed Charles, many of the king's Anglican supporters fled to Virginia. Meanwhile, a few of England's Roman Catholics also sought haven in a new environment, under the leadership of the proprietor of Maryland, Lord Baltimore. Later, the founding of Pennsylvania provided new opportunities for Quakers and other dissenters.

These migrations of religious groups have been ascribed to religious persecution. Yet one could also find here evidence of toleration on the part of the British government. Those who disagreed with the government were allowed to migrate to English colonies, where they could, in many cases, worship God in their own way. Before terming this persecution, one should recall that in those days Spain tolerated no religious dissent, and permitted no heretics to enter the Spanish colonies.

Pilgrims and Puritans

The religious factor was of particular importance in New England. First came the Pilgrims, a small group of Separatists who had left England to live in the more tolerant atmosphere of Holland. There their religious aspirations were fulfilled, but their nationalistic loyalties were endangered. The American colonies provided the solution. In the New World one could have the English flag but be free from the bishops.

Lacking funds, the Pilgrims borrowed from London merchants (note how religious and economic trends were interwoven). A part of the Pilgrim band then crossed the Atlantic on the Mayflower (1620). The intention was to settle in Virginia, but delays and bad weather caused the party to disembark in eastern Massachusetts. There they founded the Plymouth colony.

To many Americans, Plymouth symbolizes the quest for religious freedom. Actually, however, the Pilgrims exerted little influence on colonial history. Almost from the start, their tiny settlement was overshadowed by the neighboring colony of Massachusetts Bay, which absorbed Plymouth in 1691.

Massachusetts Bay was colonized by Puritans—not Separatists, but low-church Anglicans who desired to purge the Church of England of "popish" influences. Like the Pilgrims they were devoted to religious principle. But, unlike the humble Separatists who founded Plymouth, the Puritan leaders were wealthy, well-educated gentlemen. They brought considerable capital to the Massachusetts Bay colony, and encouraged its further settlement by middle-class folk who could pay their own way. At the same time they opposed the importation of servant labor.

As Puritans, the founders of Massachusetts still claimed to belong to the Church of England. They therefore expected each town to form a single parish, with its attendant priest or minister. They further insisted on "low-church" practices. Services were simple, with no music permitted other than a somewhat dubious singing of psalms. The sermons were in the Calvinist tradition, long, crammed with logic, and stressing the authority of the Scriptures.

From the Old Testament and from medieval tradition came the view that clergymen should lead the people. Their guidance was sought in town meetings, they were likely to serve as the first schoolmasters, even as physicians. In Boston leading churchmen had great influence on the government. The Massachusetts colony has for this reason been called a theocracy, though in fact the clergy dominated the regime without operating it.

Only a minority of settlers had the privilege of church membership, this being reserved for those who had expressed repentance and had been formally accepted by their local congregations. Yet all residents were required to conform to the faith. The Puritan leaders were too zealous to permit religious dissent. They had not fled to America to provide religious toleration, but rather to establish what they considered the one true church. In their opinion, dissent would endanger souls. Exclusion, execution, and banishment of heretics was the logical result, four Quakers being hanged in Boston.

Calvinist orthodoxy in Massachusetts was in harmony with English religious trends during the Cromwell period. But Puritan influence declined in England after the Stuart Restoration of 1660. The Church of England began criticizing the intolerance of Boston Puritans and demanded that "high-church" Anglicans be allowed to enter Massachusetts and set up their own congregations. Instead of giving way, the Massachusetts Puritans cut such ties as still bound them to the Anglican Church, and became known as Congregationalists.

Congregational church government involved no such episcopal control (rule of bishops) as was found in the Church of England. Nor was there presbyterian government (rule by assemblies), as in the Church of Scotland. The members of each congregation managed their own religious affairs. Despite decentralization, the Congregational clergymen were generally agreed on theology. Nearly all stressed the Calvinist doctrine of predestination. This belief that most men were predestined to damnation might conceivably have paralyzed all effort. What was the use, if the grim outcome could not be prevented? Yet the Puritans were energetic, and Calvinism proved a real driving force in American life. Apparently Puritan leaders assumed that their piety was in itself evidence of their election to salvation.

Once convinced of their own salvation, such men felt a tremendous exaltation. Next came a feeling of duty to force God's will on the rest of mankind. Hence the laws of Puritan colonies called for compulsory attendance at meeting, strict observance of the Sabbath, the prohibition of worldly amusements, and the severe condemnation of any sex relationships outside of monogamous marriage.

Established in Massachusetts in the 1630's, the Puritans began pushing outward. In that same decade they located in the Connecticut Valley. Meantime, another group of English Puritans settled New Haven. Combination was effected after 1662, when Charles II gave Connecticut a royal charter. Massachusetts Puritans also looked northward. Maine and New Hampshire had originally been controlled by Anglican proprietors, who, however, had lost their influence when Cromwell had come to power in England. Seizing the opportunity, Massachusetts incorporated the two regions in her own domains. Eventually (1677) the English courts ruled that New Hampshire was a separate entity, and the colony was then provided with a royal government. In the religious field, however, both New Hampshire and Maine remained under Puritan influence.

The Trend Toward Toleration

The Puritan cause did not go unchallenged in New England. From the beginning, some residents of Massachusetts questioned the authority of the Congregational clergy. Chief among the religious rebels were Roger Williams, whose principles were those of the

Baptists, and Mrs. Anne Hutchinson, who was doubly disliked for her religious views and because she was so unwomanly as to speak her mind in a man's world. Driven into exile, Williams, Mrs. Hutchinson, and their followers fled south to the Rhode Island region. There, in the late 1630's, they founded Providence and Newport, presently combined under a charter which Roger Williams obtained from the Puritan government of England (1644).

Rhode Island had no established church, and all Protestant denominations were given equal status. The colony became a haven for Separatists, notably Baptists and Quakers; and the Puritan colonies long regarded Rhode Island as a nest of dangerous radicals. Today, most Americans consider Roger Williams a pioneer in establishing the principles of religious liberty.

Somewhat less successful was the Maryland experiment, launched in 1632, when Charles I issued a charter to a Roman Catholic—Cecilius Calvert, the second Lord Baltimore. As proprietor, Calvert wanted to found a colony open to members of his faith. But he also planned to admit Protestants. This would swell the number of settlers and help make the venture profitable. In any case, the English government would have objected to an exclusively Catholic colony. The charter, therefore, excluded neither Protestants nor Catholics.

Despite this promising beginning, the early history of Maryland was stormy. Most Englishmen who went to the colony were Protestants. With the intolerance typical of the era they resented the presence of Roman Catholics. They resented, too, the efforts of Jesuit missionaries to convert Indians and Protestants to Catholicism. Class feeling intensified the bitterness, for the land and best offices were controlled by Catholics.

A crisis came after the passage of the famous Toleration Act of 1649. Toleration was not extended to Jews and other non-Christians; but all who believed in the divinity of Jesus Christ could worship as they pleased. This was in line with the wishes of the proprietor. It did not, however, please all Protestant settlers. Encouraged by the Puritan Revolution in England, these Protestants wrested control from Lord Baltimore (1654). They then emasculated the Toleration Act and suppressed Catholicism. Oddly enough, the rebels were not supported by Oliver Cromwell. This fact enabled the Calverts to regain control of Maryland in 1657 and to restore the Toleration Act.

Religious friction persisted and, in combination with economic discontent, produced revolts in the 1670's and 1680's. England then made Maryland a royal colony (1691) and established the Anglican Church as the state church of the colony. The Calverts regained their proprietary rights in 1715, when the fifth Lord Baltimore abandoned Catholicism and became an Anglican.

Half a century after Charles I gave Maryland to a Catholic proprietor, that monarch's son granted Pennsylvania to a Quaker, William Penn. The Quakers (Society of Friends) were separatists whose opposition to war and to ecclesiastical authority caused them to be distrusted by both church and state. Penn therefore determined to find a refuge for his coreligionists in the colonies. Charles II coöperated, the price being cancellation of a royal debt to the Penn family.

Quaker principles dominated Pennsylvania. Arriving in 1682, Penn laid out plans for a city of brotherly love (Philadelphia), where all faiths were to be given equal status. Penn also proposed to avoid difficulties with the Indians. "Let them have justice," said Penn, "and you win them."

Located in a region of rich soils, with deep-water access to oceanic trade, Philadelphia prospered from the start. Friends occupied farmlands near the city. But Pennsylvania also attracted many other sects. The Germans who came in in large numbers were Lutherans (comparable to the Anglicans), and German Reformed (Calvinists, like the Presbyterians), and Pietists (the Mennonites, for instance, not unlike the Quakers). Penn's colony also received Scots-Irish Presbyterians, many of whom occupied farms on the frontier. Catholics came in from Maryland. Religious diversity made for toleration. But it also brought friction, as when the Scots-Irish became involved in Indian wars and the Quakers refused on religious principle to provide aid.

Quaker influence was strong in New Jersey and Delaware; and these colonies, like Pennsylvania and Rhode Island, had no official religion. In other colonies the state-church system was the rule. Congregationalists were dominant in New Hampshire, Massachusetts, and Connecticut, theirs being the official church of those New England colonies. Elsewhere —in New York and in the southern colonies—the established church was the Anglican, as in the mother country.

Save for a general desire to spread Christianity, there was no religious motivation in the settlement of most Anglican colonies. Still, the settlers took religion more seriously than has sometimes been assumed. In the Cromwellian era Virginia's assembly and governor (Sir William Berkeley) forbade Puritan preaching and ordered the expulsion of "dissenters." When Cromwell demanded submission, the colonial assembly named a Puritan as governor (1652). The end of Puritan rule in England eight years later brought the reinstatement of Sir William Berkeley, who reaffirmed his old religious views.

Despite such demands for uniformity, the Virginia Anglicans planned no campaigns of persecution. Puritans and Catholics could remain, provided they paid taxes to the established Church of England and were discreet in their public utterances. Virginia wanted settlers more than she did religious uniformity.

It was much the same in the other Anglican colonies. Although the Church of England occupied a privileged position and received a small government subsidy, Protestants were generally free to worship as they pleased. It could hardly have been otherwise, for the Anglicans were outnumbered in every colony. Of great importance in New York was the continued presence of the tolerant Dutch, who stayed on after England took control of the colony away from its Dutch founders. As proprietor of Georgia, James Oglethorpe welcomed all oppressed Protestants; and in all southern colonies the Anglicans found it difficult to control the Scots-Irish and other independent-minded settlers of back-country districts.

Religion and Democracy

As the years went by, there was increasing opposition to established churches, both Anglican and Congregational. Often this opposition was based on democratic objections to aristocratic control. The clergy and leading laymen of New England's established Congregational churches were generally drawn from the upper classes. In the Anglican colonies many ordinary farmers felt that the Church of England was dominated by the wealthy planters.

Dissatisfied with the state churches, some turned to dissenting sects. New immigrants added to the diversity of religious beliefs, and in the eighteenth century the typical colony became a land of many faiths. This alarmed some observers; but the very number of denominations made anything but toleration impractical. What was more, most of the new sects were composed of plain people who resented paying taxes to support the established churches. Thus men began to talk about the separation of church and state, to demand a complete religious freedom.

Similar impulses were present in the Great Awakening, a striking upsurge of religious activity in the 1730's and 1740's. One leader of this movement, a Congregational minister named Jonathan Edwards, suddenly experienced a sweet and mystical pleasure in the complete acceptance of God's will. This was like the Quaker inner light; but Edwards chose to work within the Calvinist framework. Shocked by the indifference of his Northampton, Massachusetts, congregation, Edwards preached a series of sermons about God's justice and the imminent danger of damnation (1735). Profoundly moved, his hearers expressed their feelings with "outcries, faintings, and the like." Edwards saw this as an indication of divine inspiration. His account of the experience was widely read both in America and in Europe.

At the same time other Calvinist preachers—Dutch Reformed and Presbyterian—aroused like reactions with similar appeals in the middle colonies. Then a great English evangelist, George Whitefield, traveled through the colonies, preaching to great crowds in simple, fervid language. With his Church of England background, Whitefield put less emphasis on predestination than did the Calvinists. This encouraged a feeling that one could win salvation by God's grace through an experience of spiritual rebirth, such as conversion at a revival meeting. This hopeful free-will view was stressed by the followers of another Anglican evangelist, John Wesley. Although they did not completely break with the Church of England during the colonial era, Wesley's supporters were becoming a distinct group, the Methodists, by the time of the American Revolution.

The clear, informal language and the emotional fervor of the revival meeting gave the average man something which had been missing in the established churches. Plain people could participate in revival excitement, instead of sitting passively in their pews. They could also attain a sense of their own worth and dignity as discoverers of the highest truth. Then, too, some revivalists expressed concern for the welfare of the commoner. So the Great Awakening was, in a way, a revolt against upper-class control of religious life.

Logically enough, the state churches tended to oppose revivalism. The methods employed by revivalists disturbed the dignity of the Anglican and Congregational services. Was it right, asked conservatives, to have God's house outraged by "beastly braying"? Besides, the gentry who controlled the established churches disliked the leveling tendencies of the Great Awakening.

When Congregational leaders spurned revivalism, many Congregational churches in the interior of New England turned to the Baptists, who were close to the pietism of the plain people. Many lukewarm Anglicans became enthusiastic Methodists. The Presbyterians were divided into Old Lights, or conservatives, and New Lights, who embraced revivalism. Splits tended to follow social groupings; and the Baptists and Methodists, who appealed effectively to the lower classes, gained the most from the Great Awakening.

Political Problems: Self-Government

Two decades before the settlement of Jamestown, Queen Elizabeth gave Sir Walter Raleigh a charter as proprietor of any settlements he might make along the eastern seaboard of North Amer-

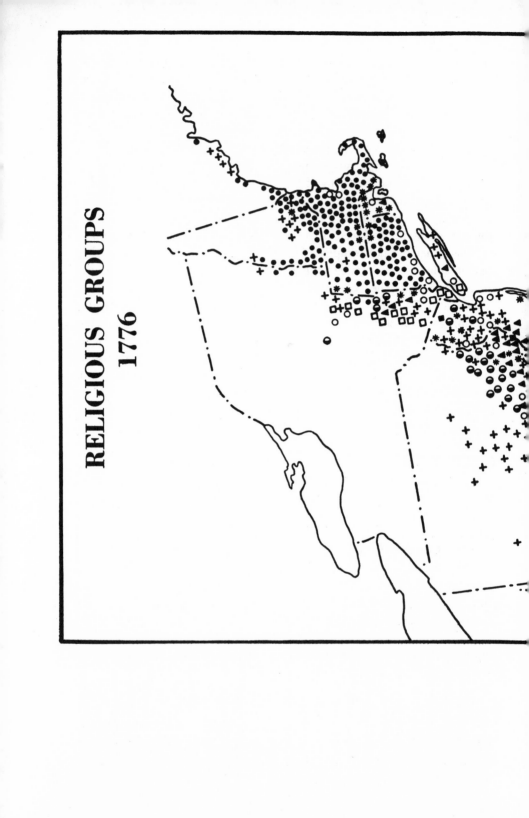

RELIGIOUS GROUPS
1776

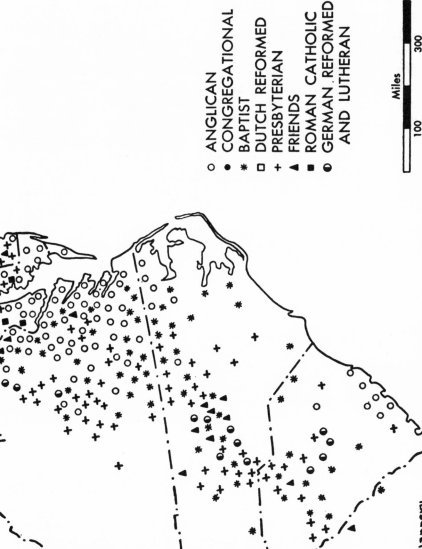

○ ANGLICAN
● CONGREGATIONAL
✳ BAPTIST
□ DUTCH REFORMED
+ PRESBYTERIAN
▲ FRIENDS
■ ROMAN CATHOLIC
◓ GERMAN REFORMED
   AND LUTHERAN

Miles
100   300

Flannery

Each symbol represents approximately five congregations. Note preponderance of Congregationalists in New England, where their church was established. The Anglicans had no comparable hold in areas where theirs was the official church (New York and the South). Quakers, Dutch and German Reformed, and Lutherans were found chiefly in the middle states. Catholics were concentrated in Maryland and around Philadelphia. Baptists, strong in Rhode Island, could also be found in the southern back-country. Presbyterians were numerous in frontier districts from Pennsylvania to Georgia. The Methodists, not having completed their break from the Anglicans, are not here indicated as a separate group.

ica. Although Sir Walter established no permanent colony,[2] the charter is significant, for it guaranteed settlers the "privileges of persons . . . native to England." These included protection against arbitrary action by officials, and the right of the citizen to share in the task of government.

During the colonization of the New World, there were various attempts to deprive English settlers of these "rights of Englishmen." In the first dozen years after the founding of Jamestown in 1607 the London Company tried to rule by arbitrary means. Maryland's charter, liberal in religious matters, was illiberal in political affairs; and the Calverts were indisposed to favor popular rule. Also undemocratic were the Fundamental Constitutions of Carolina, a proposed government which the English philosopher John Locke drew up for the Carolina proprietors.

These efforts to set up autocratic governments were not successful. Heritage and environment worked on the other side. Englishmen who came to America insisted on the rights they had enjoyed at home. The availability of land in the New World also encouraged resistance to authority. By 1619 the London Company found it expedient to instruct its governor to ask representatives of the Jamestown settlers for advice. Opposition to aristocratic rule prevented the proprietors from using Locke's Fundamental Constitutions and speeded the transition from proprietary control to royal government (in which the colonists had some voice). The Maryland proprietors held on until the Revolution, but they were forced to yield powers to the colonial legislature.

Colonial self-rule is best seen in New England. There the citizens of each community decided local questions in town meetings. Between sessions, authority was vested in leaders selected by the meeting (selectmen). Outside of New England, the scattered character of agricultural settlement made the town-meeting system impracticable. Throughout the South, the important local unit was the county; and county officers were chosen by the colonial governor rather than by the voters. But representative government did develop in some cities.

On the colony level, government functions were divided among a governor, a legislature, and a court system. The judges were appointed by the governor, who, in turn, was picked by the Crown (in royal colonies), the proprietor (in proprietary colonies), or the people (in chartered colonies).[3]

---

[2] In 1587 Sir Walter Raleigh did found a settlement on what is now Roanoke Island, North Carolina. Here was born Virginia Dare, the first English child native to America. Unfortunately, the advance of the Spanish Armada kept English ships at home during a critical period. When vessels did reach Roanoke Island, they found no trace of the settlers; and the fate of this "lost colony" remains a mystery to this day.

[3] At the end of the colonial era, there were two chartered colonies, Rhode Island and

Most colonial legislatures consisted of a council named by the governor or king and an assembly elected by qualified voters.

The organization was far from democratic in the modern sense. Voting and officeholding were restricted to property holders. Some colonies excluded all except large landowners, and apportionment of seats in the legislature favored tidewater interests against frontier farmers. Moreover, the popularly elected assembly could be checked by the appointed council, or by the absolute veto power of a governor who might be out of sympathy with local needs.

On a few occasions, dissatisfied citizens rose in arms. In 1676, Nathaniel Bacon and other Virginia frontiersmen came into open conflict with the governor (Sir William Berkeley), who had failed to take hold of the Indian problem. In that same year, and in 1689, citizens of Maryland rose against proprietary rule, as did South Carolinians in 1681 and 1719. Frontiersmen called the Paxton Boys marched on the capitol of Pennsylvania in 1764. In 1771, back-country Regulators fought a pitched battle with the governor of North Carolina, who was supported by upper-class colonists and the Crown.

More commonly, colonists expressed their grievances by measures short of rebellion. They failed to pay quitrents. They petitioned against oppressive policies. They worked through their colony's assembly. The assemblies had one great power—control of the purse. By using it, they could often dominate the royal and proprietary governors. This could be done by raising or cutting the governor's salary, or by voting the salary annually, so as to suggest the possibility of no renewal. Assemblies sometimes used their power over appropriations to force governors to sign bills to which the English authorities objected. Again, they refused to pass measures which the London government demanded. They also used their financial power to cut into the governor's executive authority, as in setting up their own committees to supervise the spending of funds. Although military forces were commanded by the governor, the assembly could and did provide expenses on condition that the militia be used only as the legislators directed. Control of money also enabled the assemblies to direct the setting up of local courts. This was important, for judges indebted to the assembly were apt to be lenient in cases involving colonial violations of British laws.

Connecticut, and three proprietary colonies, Maryland, Pennsylvania, and Delaware. The rest (New Hampshire, Massachusetts, New York, New Jersey, Virginia, North Carolina, South Carolina, Georgia) were royal colonies. Six of these had been under proprietors at one time, and Virginia and Massachusetts had started out as chartered colonies, under joint-stock company control.

The Dominion of New England

Busy at home, the English government did little to curb the colonists during the greater part of the seventeenth century. The tendency was to rely on proprietors and chartered groups; and for much of the century Virginia was the only mainland colony under direct royal control. Then the situation changed abruptly. New Hampshire was made a royal province in 1679. Five years later, the English courts declared the Massachusetts charter forfeited, and Massachusetts became a royal colony. Rhode Island and Connecticut were treated in like fashion. New York became a royal colony in 1685, when James II became king; for James (as Duke of York) had been proprietor of New York for twenty-one years before his accession to the throne. As Duke of York, he had also controlled the Jersey country. He had granted this region to his friends as proprietors; but in 1688 it too was brought under Crown control.

These changes were associated with royal fears that the northern colonies were getting out of hand. Charles II, for example, was disturbed at the way in which New England merchants evaded the Navigation Acts. There was further friction between the Church of England and the established Congregational churches of New England. Finally, James II believed in strong royal rule.

To bring the colonies under effective control, King James set up the Dominion of New England in 1686. This Dominion was to swallow all of New England, plus New York and New Jersey. The entire area was put under the administration of an able and experienced royal governor, Sir Edmund Andros.

Union was not altogether novel in the colonies. The Puritan colonies had earlier formed their own defense combination, the New England Confederation (1643). But there were differences between the Confederation and the Dominion. The Confederation had been created by the colonies themselves, and was under their control. The Dominion was imposed from without, and would be controlled from London. For in creating the Dominion of New England, the English government made no provision for an elected assembly.

Accustomed to self-government, the colonists were not disposed to accept the new royal control. The opportunity came when James II was deposed by Parliament in the bloodless uprising of 1688. When news of this Glorious Revolution reached Boston and New York, the colonists rose against the Andros regime. The rebels won the day, and the Dominion of New England was dissolved.

In the reorganization that followed, New York and New Hampshire became separate royal colonies, as they had been before the organization of the Dominion of New England. New Jersey was returned to its proprietors, though it was later made into a royal colony (1702). Connecticut and Rhode Island resumed self-government under their charters, which they managed to retain until the American Revolution. Massachusetts did almost as well. A new charter recognized her claims to Plymouth and Maine, but specified that the governor of Massachusetts should be appointed by the Crown.

The breakup of the Dominion of New England did not mean English surrender to the colonial desire for self-rule. In the years between the Glorious Revolution and 1763 four areas originally controlled by proprietors were converted into royal colonies—New Jersey (1702), South Carolina (1719), North Carolina (1729), Georgia (1751). Pennsylvania and Delaware were run as royal colonies for a brief time (1692–94), Maryland for a longer period (1691–1715).

Conflict with the Mother Country

While taking over certain colonies, the English government made some effort to bring the American possessions into line with imperial policy. Economic matters were stressed after 1688, for religious issues were declining in importance, and businessmen (the upper middle classes) were increasing their influence in Britain. In Parliament the landed nobility continued to control the House of Lords but had to work with the merchants and manufacturers who were gaining strength in the more powerful House of Commons. And Parliament was the final authority in government—the Glorious Revolution of 1688 had decided that.

Executive authority gradually fell into the hands of the legislative leaders. Until this time, those who headed the Treasury, Navy, and other executive departments had been chosen by the king. These officials had served together as a Privy Council, a sort of cabinet directed by the Crown. After 1688, parliamentary chieftains took over control of the executive departments. Department heads then formed a new type of cabinet, a ministry responsible to Parliament. In Parliament there were two major parties, the Tories, who represented mainly the landed gentry, and the Whigs, who generally spoke for business. It became customary to let the stronger party select the ministers. If a party lost control of Parliament in an election, its ministers resigned and the opposition took over direction of the administration. Nominally the king appointed the department heads. Actually, he named those suggested by the dominant party.

The colonies were affected by these changes. Until 1688, the king had possessed full authority in the colonial field, as in granting charters and appointing governors. In practice, the Crown had followed the advice of appointed advisers known as the Lords of Trade. English merchants never liked the aristocratic Lords of Trade. Gaining influence after the Glorious Revolution, the businessmen demanded a body more representative of their interests. Impressed, King William substituted for the Lords a Board of Trade. This was made up largely of businessmen, who watched colonial affairs carefully in the interest of British trade and manufactures. When George I abandoned much royal authority after 1715, Parliament assumed control over colonies. Thereafter the Board of Trade advised the parliamentary ministers. Had the Board possessed executive power, it might have kept the colonies under control. But it could only advise the ministers, on whom rested the real authority.

The cabinet member or minister who assumed chief responsibility for colonial affairs was the Secretary of State for the Southern Department This official directed European wars which involved the colonies. Acting on the advice of the Board of Trade, he appointed and instructed colonial governors. Unfortunately, the secretaryship of state changed hands frequently, and short-term incumbents were too busy to learn much of what went on in the distant American provinces. Besides, there was confusion of authority. Ministers in charge of the Treasury (Exchequer) and Navy (Admiralty) had ill-defined powers in colonial affairs. Departments often failed to coöperate with each other, and thus weakened imperial administration. This would not have mattered much if British and colonial interests had been identical. But, since they were not, the confusion of authority played into the hands of colonial leaders anxious to frustrate British plans.

It was inevitable that colonial interests would diverge from those of Britain. Americans naturally sought their own economic advantage, whereas the British just as logically wished to make the colonies a source of profit to the mother country. Thus colonists wanted to trade the world over, but Parliament attempted to restrict their trade largely to the empire. English officials desired to collect quitrents and customs fees; the colonists tried to avoid paying both. Southern colonies, fearful lest too many Negroes come into their borders, moved to stop their importation. The British ministry, reflecting the interest of slave traders, opposed such prohibitions. Colonial legislatures sometimes decided to issue paper money to raise prices and make payments easier for debtors. This too the British tried to block, fearing it would hurt British trade and British creditors.

Who would win these controversies? In theory, Britain held the whip hand. If the assembly of a royal colony was disposed to pass a paper money bill, the Board of Trade could instruct the governor to oppose it. This he could do by influencing his appointees in the council. But these men were colonial citizens and might vote for the measure. If that happened, the governor could use his veto power or suspend the bill pending action by the government in London. Even if the governor affixed his signature, an appeal could still be carried to the Privy Council in England, which could declare the act unconstitutional. A royal veto was also possible, the king, of course, acting under the direction of parliamentary leaders.

Nevertheless, the colonists usually had their way. Their assemblies dominated the colonial governors and judges. This made it possible to ignore laws passed by Parliament and instructions issued by the Board of Trade. When colonial legislation was disallowed, colonial assemblies passed new laws like the old. It would take a year or more for the new statute to be disallowed. Meantime, the colonists would have the situation they desired. Nor was the English government likely to crack down on disobedience. From 1688 to 1763, colonial aid was needed in Britain's international wars.

Colonial Wars: Fighting the Dutch

When Britain embarked on her career of colonial expansion, she found Spain already in the field and claiming a monopoly of North America. England took care of that when she defeated the Spanish Armada in 1588. Then there were other rivals, first the Dutch and then the French.

While winning independence from Spain in the late sixteenth century the citizens of Holland (or the Dutch Netherlands) developed maritime interests similar to those of Elizabethan England. In spite of their small population the Dutch built great trading companies and successfully entered the race for empire. Their most spectacular showing was in the Orient, where they snapped up Portuguese colonies; but Holland's empire builders did not overlook North America. As early as 1609 Henry Hudson, an Englishman, explored the eastern coast of the continent for the Dutch East India Company. Hudson was seeking a northwest passage to India. This he did not find; but on the basis of his voyage, Holland claimed the seaboard from Delaware Bay to New England.

Soon thereafter Dutch fur traders became active on Manhattan Island and along the Hudson River. Colonization became brisk after 1621, when the Dutch West India Company was given a governmental monopoly of American trade. This company resembled but was more efficient than the London Company which founded Jamestown. Under company direction Dutch merchants established friendly relations with the powerful Iroquois tribes, who welcomed the Dutch as potential allies against the French occupying the St. Lawrence Valley. The Dutch West India Company

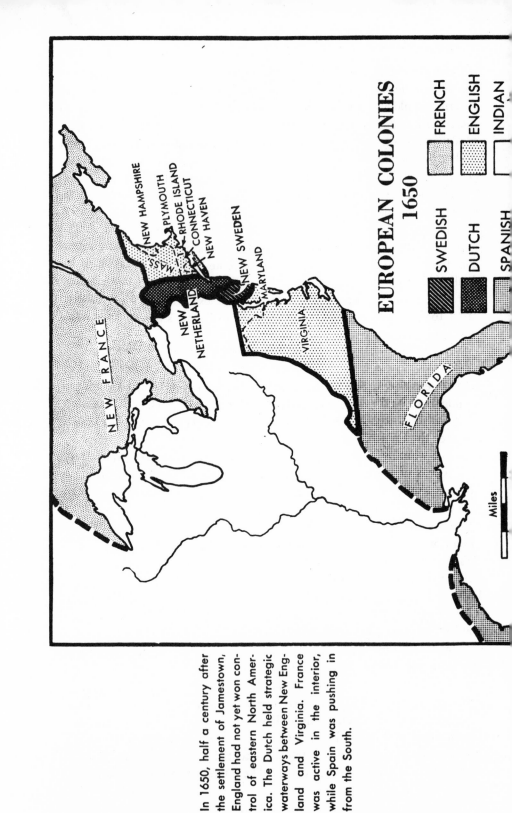

EUROPEAN COLONIES
1650

SWEDISH
DUTCH
SPANISH
FRENCH
ENGLISH
INDIAN

NEW FRANCE

NEW HAMPSHIRE
PLYMOUTH
RHODE ISLAND
CONNECTICUT
NEW HAVEN
MASS.

NEW SWEDEN

NEW NETHERLAND

MARYLAND

VIRGINIA

FLORIDA

Miles

In 1650, half a century after the settlement of Jamestown, England had not yet won control of eastern North America. The Dutch held strategic waterways between New England and Virginia. France was active in the interior, while Spain was pushing in from the South.

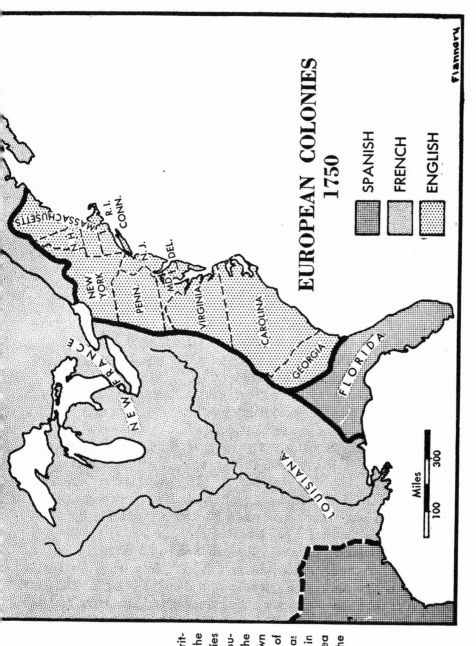

EUROPEAN COLONIES 1750

SPANISH

FRENCH

ENGLISH

NEW FRANCE

LOUISIANA

NEW YORK
PENN.
MD.
DEL.
N.J.
CONN.
R.I.
N.H.
MASSACHUSETTS

VIRGINIA

CAROLINA

GEORGIA

FLORIDA

Miles

100   300

Flannery

During the next century British sea power eliminated the Dutch. The English colonies gained in wealth and population. So, however, did the French, bringing a showdown fight. In the final stages of this contest, France was helped by Spain; but, as in the Anglo-Dutch wars, sea power brought victory to the British (1763).

maintained trading posts as far up the Hudson as Fort Orange (Albany). It planted settlers on Long Island, located on the Delaware River, established an outpost on the Connecticut River. Thus the Dutch secured control of three of the best valleys along the Atlantic seaboard before the English founded Boston in 1630.

Like the French, the Dutch had great success with the fur trade. Then as now furs commanded high prices, and at first the Indians sold their pelts cheaply. In the long run, preoccupation with furs retarded real colonization, for the fur trade required preservation of the forests and the native tribes. This, however, suited the Dutch. The Netherlands had few unemployed in the early 1600's, so there was no great pressure for the poor to emigrate. Unlike England, Holland provided almost complete religious toleration, as in furnishing asylum to the Pilgrims. Hence there were no sects anxious to flee the country for haven in the colonies. The Dutch colonies therefore were not as well populated as the English settlements on either side. This gave the English the advantage in areas of conflict. Before the end of the 1630's it was demonstrated in the Connecticut Valley that trading posts could not stand against the pressure of an expanding farm population. The Dutch were first to reach this region; but as the English moved in, the Dutch were forced to withdraw.

Meantime, another power was emerging in Europe: Sweden, then extending control over the whole Baltic area. With expansion came imperial ambitions and a desire to secure colonial profits. Sweden was ill prepared to enter the competition, for, though strong on land, she lacked sea power. Nevertheless, in 1638 a Swedish trading company set up posts along the Delaware River, in what is now the state of Delaware, and as far north as the present site of Philadelphia, Pennsylvania. These settlements were in the southern part of the region which the Dutch regarded as their own; and in 1655 the Dutch took over New Sweden.

Presently, however, the Dutch themselves met with defeat. In 1664, in the second of three Anglo-Dutch wars, English fleets seized the Dutch colonies at New Amsterdam (New York) and up the Delaware. The population of these settlements was too small for effective resistance, and the decision turned on sea power. Nine years later, in the final conflict between England and the Netherlands, a Dutch fleet recaptured New York; but the region was returned to England when peace was made the following year (1674).

Fighting the French

With the elimination of the Swedes and Dutch, the French became the major rivals of the English in North America. Fishing operations led to the settlement of Port Royal in Acadia (Nova

Scotia) as early as 1605, two years before the English landed at Jamestown. In 1608 Champlain founded a fur trading post at Quebec, far up the St. Lawrence. Later, French explorers, traders, and missionaries covered the Great Lakes and, by 1700, pushed down the Mississippi to its mouth on the Gulf of Mexico.

Lured into the interior by the waterways, the French covered great distances but achieved marked success only in the lucrative fur trade. Efforts to establish agricultural settlements in Acadia, along the St. Lawrence, and in the Mississippi Valley had only slight success. Why? For one thing, French businessmen were not as well organized for overseas ventures as were the English. For another, the enclosure movement gave England's colonizers a great pool of unemployed townspeople from which to draw recruits. Although French peasants were miserably poor, they were not forced off the land and were not easily persuaded to change their lives by emigration. Then, too, some prospective colonists were eliminated by the rule that only Catholics could settle in French colonies. Besides, the Kings of France were always deep in European problems and tended to neglect their overseas possessions. And when they did notice the colonies, they were inclined to give less attention to their mainland holdings than to their rich sugar islands in the West Indies.

Toward the end of the seventeeth century Louis XIV of France decided to expand his colonial empire. The result was the establishment of new trading posts along the St. Lawrence, on the Great Lakes, and down the Mississippi. The French then diverted from the English colonists much of their fur trade. French fishing bases in Newfoundland and Acadia competed with the fishermen of old and New England. France also seized from Spain several West Indian sugar islands. The French planned to supply these islands with food and lumber from the St. Lawrence area. But it proved difficult to persuade Frenchmen to settle around Quebec and Montreal; and those who did chose the fur trade rather than agriculture and lumbering. Thereupon the French officials dreamed of a conquest of New York and New England, so that these colonies could become bases for supplying the French West Indies. At the same time, England and English colonists hoped to drive French competitors out of the fur trade, fisheries, and rich lands of the interior. Religious feeling was involved, since French Catholicism and New England Puritanism were mutually distrustful.

In the wars that followed, there were two main theaters of action. One was the North Atlantic coast—both sides were vulnerable to attack from the sea. Fighting also raged in the forested area from New England to western Pennsylvania. Most of the Indian tribes favored the French, for economic reasons and because of hatred for New Englanders inherited from earlier conflicts.[4] An exception was the powerful Iroquois confederacy of New York. This group of tribes was economically tied to New York and competed with the pro-French Indians for control of the Great Lakes fur trade. Consequently, the Iroquois supported the English.

During the 1680's, Louis XIV attacked the Dutch Netherlands. When the Glorious Revolution of 1688 brought a Dutch prince to the English throne, England became involved in the fighting. In the course of this conflict (King William's War, 1689–97) French plans to conquer New England were broken up by Iroquois raids on Quebec. A New England naval attack did capture Port Royal; but English diplomats returned this Nova Scotian post to France when peace was made in 1697.

Five years later a new war was launched by French attempts to secure control of Spain and the Spanish colonies. Called Queen Anne's War by the English colonists, this struggle saw Great Britain lined up against both France and Spain (1702–13). In North America, the French again tried to invade New England, and the English planned to take Quebec. Neither succeeded. British and colonial fleets did, however, recapture Port Royal; and at the end of the war France gave up all claims to Nova Scotia and Newfoundland. Meanwhile, the English attacked St. Augustine in Spanish Florida, and a Spanish fleet raided Charleston, South Carolina. When peace was made in 1713 there was no change in the Anglo-Spanish boundaries, but Britain did gain commercial concessions in the slave trade with the Spanish colonies.

Having yielded Nova Scotia, the French established a stronger base at Louisburg on Cape Breton Island, nearer the mouth of the St. Lawrence. They also extended their posts on the Great Lakes and in the Mississippi Valley. This brought increased competition in the Atlantic fisheries and the interior fur trade. It was friction in the West Indies, however, which was the immediate cause for the next outbreak, King George's War (1739–48). The Spanish, still unreconciled to Britain's commercial invasion of the Caribbean, seized certain English ships. Great Britain thereupon declared war on Spain (1739). France entered the war as Spain's ally; and the Canadian-American frontier was again the scene of border raids. A New England-British expedition captured Louisburg after a siege; but the peace treaty returned this base to France in 1748.

In anticipation of a new conflict, Britain's Board of Trade assembled

---

[4] When the English settled in the Connecticut Valley, the Pequot Indians precipitated a war, only to be beaten by the better-armed whites (Pequot War, 1637). Later, "King Philip," a Massachusetts chieftain, formed a confederation of tribes from Maine to Connecticut. He descended on white settlements in 1675, inflicting heavy damage before the New England Confederation crushed the Indian forces (King Philip's War, 1675–76).

a congress at Albany, New York, in 1754. Attended by representatives from New York, Pennsylvania, Maryland, and the New England colonies, this assemblage discussed defense problems. Most interesting of all proposals was the Albany Plan of Union. Benjamin Franklin, a delegate from Pennsylvania, insisted that the colonists could oppose France most effectively if they created an intercolonial government. This would have a single-house legislature made up of delegates from each colony, elected in proportion to population. The legislature would pass laws relating to the colonies as a whole and would work with a governor general appointed by the British government. Since most of the delegates at Albany were not ready for such a super-government, no action was taken. But the plan did show that some colonists were already considering union—union, of course, *within* the British Empire. And the plan proposed was not unlike that later adopted for the Dominion of Canada.

In this same year, 1754, war again broke out between France and Britain. English merchants had cut into France's Ohio Valley fur trade by offering better prices to the Indians. To overawe the tribes and warn off the British colonials, the French had built new forts on Lake Erie and along the Allegheny River in Pennsylvania. They had also destroyed certain English trading posts. Fearing the loss of Virginia's claims to the region, Governor Dinwiddie decided to halt the French by sending a small force to the junction of the Allegheny and Monongahela rivers (now Pittsburgh). The troops were commanded by George Washington, a young planter who held a commission in the Virginia militia. After winning one skirmish, Washington was beaten and captured by the enemy. Thus began the French and Indian War (1754-63). The European phase of the conflict began two years later. Known as the Seven Years' War, it saw the Prussia of Frederick the Great lining up with England, whereas France obtained the backing of the rival German state of Austria, and later the support of Spain.

On learning of Washington's defeat, the British government sent over two regiments of regulars under the command of General Braddock. After a trying march over the Pennsylvania mountains, Braddock was defeated by the French and their Indian allies (1755). Braddock was accustomed to conventional European warfare, in which men wore bright uniforms, fought in solid ranks, and fired in volleys without aiming at individual opponents. But the French and Indians deployed in the woods and almost wiped out the British, who presented perfect targets. Following this victory, the French raided Pennsylvania settlements, captured British forts in upper New York, and blocked a sea attack on Louisburg.

The emergency brought forth an able English leader—William Pitt, who became Secretary of State for the Southern Department. While

Frederick the Great kept France busy in Europe, Pitt concentrated on America. Turning the tide in 1759, British and colonial forces drove the French from the Ohio Valley, destroyed French forts on the Great Lakes, and captured Louisburg. Land invasions of Canada failed, but the British Navy shattered the French fleet, opening the way for an attack by sea. In 1760 General Wolfe was able to sail up the St. Lawrence and encamp before Quebec. Scaling the heights above the river, his troops routed the French under Montcalm. Montreal fell soon thereafter, and all Canada was under British control.

In the next three years, the British Navy seized the French West Indian sugar islands of Guadeloupe and Martinique; also Cuba and the Philippines, which belonged to France's ally, Spain. But by this time a new king, George III, had come to the throne in Britain. Anxious to reassert the royal authority which his grandfather and great-grandfather had lost, George was jealous of William Pitt and of the Whig party which dominated Parliament. He therefore blocked Pitt's further war plans and sought a peace settlement in 1763.

During the negotiations there was serious debate in England as to whether to demand of France the sugar islands or Canada. (It was understood that France would continue the war rather than cede both.) To balance all of Canada against two small West Indian colonies now seems incomprehensible, but at the time the islands boasted forty times as much value in trade as did Canada. Some Britishers also pointed out that the return of Canada to France would keep England's thirteen mainland colonies dependent on Britain for protection. With the French nearby, they would not dare strike for independence from Great Britain.

But there was another side. Many Britishers felt that the American colonies would not revolt against Britain anyway, and that it would be unfair to expose them again to French invasions. Besides, Canada was worth taking for its size—a prestige factor—and for potential trade. Hence Britain gave up the sugar islands, taking over Canada and all French claims to the eastern half of the Mississippi Valley.

Settling with Spain, Britain withdrew from Cuba and the Philippines and in return was given Spanish Florida, which then extended west to the present state of Louisiana. At the same time, France gave to Spain all of Louisiana—New Orleans and the whole western half of the Mississippi Valley. Thus 1763 marked the withdrawal of France from North America.

The Coming Conflict

The year 1763 was a turning point in more ways than one. The narrow margin of victory had alarmed British leaders. Determined to strengthen imperial defenses, they prepared to tighten up on colonial administration. They also felt that the colonies, having bene-fited from the French and Indian War, should aid in paying the public debt which Britain had acquired during that conflict. They therefore launched a program of legislation designed to give the London government greater control of colonial areas.

Such a program was bound to encounter opposition in the colonies. For two generations Americans had been managing their own affairs. People accustomed to self-rule do not easily relinquish it. Furthermore, the re-moval of the French menace in Canada relieved the colonists of the need for protection. British ministers who ignored these realities would find trouble brewing in the apparently triumphant empire.

3

Emergence of an
American Civilization

A Changing Culture

In the century before 1763, those who lived in England's American colonies made economic progress and learned to govern themselves. And, without fully realizing it themselves, they began to build a new, American civilization. Our basic institutions have their roots in colonial soil.

During the first half-century of settlement, colonial life varied little from that of England, save in so far as the new environment forced immediate changes in ways of making a living. The original settlers were Europeans with Old World habits of mind, and the first generation born in the colonies tended to follow the parental pattern. The second native generation, however, felt wholly identified with the new environment. Meanwhile, changes in England reached overseas and mingled their influence with that of the American scene. The result was a gradual transformation of colonial life, and the emergence of new cultural patterns.

The Population of the Colonies

Population growth is related to the birth rate, the death rate, and migration. The first was high throughout the colonial years. Children were an economic asset on farms, rather than an economic burden as they often are to urban parents. Large families were therefore the rule, and the population would have increased in geometrical progression had it not been checked by mortality. But living conditions and ignorance in medical matters made the death rate very high. Losses were especially heavy among mothers and small children. Even so, the death rate was not as high as the birth rate; and natural increase was continuous after 1620.

Immigration supplemented the natural increase. Sometimes immigrants came in waves, as when 20,000 Puritans poured into New England between 1630 and 1650; or when, a century later, Scots-Irish and Germans moved into Pennsylvania. After 1660 there was a continuous though less spectacular immigration from the British Isles. This immigration, combined with the high birth rate, doubled colonial population each generation. The population was 80,000 by 1660, and 1,500,000 a century later, a fifth being Negroes.

Similarities were more striking than differences among the white inhabitants of the colonies. Nearly all were northern Europeans. The Germans and French Huguenots, though foreign in speech, were Protestants. The Huguenots were well-educated people who merged easily with the upper-class colonials. The same was true of the Spanish and Portuguese Jews, who, like the Huguenots, fled religious persecution abroad. Although the Jews seemed distinct as the only non-Christian element, they met with little of what would now be termed anti-Semitism. And Irish immigrants, even if viewed askance as Catholics, had the advantage of speaking English.

As population grew, it spread out in search of land. By 1700 the coastal plain was thinly occupied, and people were moving up the rivers into the Piedmont country. By 1760 the Piedmont was generally though unevenly occupied. Meantime, the southern back country was filling up with newcomers from Pennsylvania. In that area, migration flowed southwestward, while in New England the frontier pushed northward into Maine and New Hampshire.

In New England the pattern of settlement by organized towns was maintained. From Pennsylvania south movement was by family groups, creating a frontier of cabins and isolated clearings. Preceded only by fur traders, the first settlers lived a hard life and employed farm methods as crude as their cabins. Many were squatters who sold their improvements to later settlers, then moved on to repeat this cycle, forming the front line of settlement as it penetrated the interior.

City and Country

Although less than a tenth of the population lived in urban areas, the towns were important as centers of trade and handicrafts, and political and social life. The major cities were seaports which began as collections of thatch-covered huts built along winding lanes. Slowly they grew into well-built communities, whose brick and wooden frame buildings were placed close to the street in the European manner.

No city dominated colonial life as London did that of England. Boston was long the largest city because of its overseas trade and access to the thickly settled Massachusetts Bay region. By 1740 its population had reached 16,000. Philadelphia then had 13,000, New York 11,000, Charleston 6500. New York was handicapped by the Iroquois occupancy of most of its hinterland. Philadelphia, less accessible to the sea, had no such Indian problem and tapped a rich farming section. By the 1770's, therefore, it had become the metropolis of the colonies, with a population of almost 30,000.

With rising population came new problems. Traffic problems early appeared, as when reckless "gallopers" were fined in Boston in 1655. Streets were unpaved, refuse was not collected, and hogs which roamed as scavengers caused "great grief." There were no sewers, and water was obtained from open wells. This situation was a menace to health and a fire hazard. Neighbors fought ordinary fires with bucket brigades. But if the flames spread, houses had to be torn down to prevent the destruction of the entire city. In 1679 Boston pointed the way to a better future by importing a hand-pumped fire engine from England.

No town had a regular police force. Citizens were drafted for daytime service, and a military watch made rounds by night. In the town jails, juvenile delinquents and hardened criminals, debtors and murderers were all thrown together without segregation. But imprisonment, being costly, was less used than were fines and physical punishments. Much store was set by public whippings and hangings, since these spectacles were supposed to warn others while they dealt with the criminal. Though brutal, sentences tended to be less severe than those then handed out in England.

All towns had to care for the poor, for most Protestant sects had abandoned this function to the state. Poor people from out of town were encouraged to move on, as tramps are nowadays. Unfortunate natives were at first given financial aid (indoor relief), or were boarded out to the lowest bidders. But as early as 1685 Boston found it more economical to concentrate paupers in a workhouse.

In colonial almshouses the sick received only custodial, not real medical, care. There were also town pesthouses, the prototypes of later isolation hospitals. Here victims of smallpox and other contagious diseases could be kept from infecting the rest of the community. Fear of contagion was very great in those days, an entirely understandable attitude. In periods of epidemic, towns sometimes shut themselves off from contact with neighboring communities. And on occasion colonial assemblies maintained port quarantines so rigid that they hampered trade.

Not until 1752, when the Pennsylvania Hospital was opened in Philadelphia, was there a hospital in the modern sense in the thirteen colonies. Like English hospitals of the period, this was a voluntary nonsectarian institution, supported chiefly by private benevolence. Unlike the English models, however, it provided private care for those who could pay as well as free service for the poor. Separate hospitals for the upper classes (nursing homes in the English sense) did not appear in America.

As towns grew, they aspired to more autonomy. In New England they possessed town meetings, as did any village; and in the southern colonies they were managed by county courts, as was any rural community. Since these courts were appointed by the governors, there was almost no self-government in local affairs. The New England system was more democratic; but town meetings could be overruled by the county courts, which were important even in New England. And in all colonies local governments were subject to the colonial assemblies. In time, however, the colonial cities did get charters which permitted them to exercise greater control over their own affairs.

When municipal officials had power, they tended to supervise the economic life of their communities, just as higher officials did for an entire colony. The city fathers (usually leading merchants) often set prices and wages and enforced standards in weights, measures, and quality of goods. Such regulation followed the pattern of Elizabethan England. The rules, though, met with increasing opposition as the years went by.

Law enforcement in rural areas was handled by town constables in New England, by county sheriffs elsewhere. Where frontier conditions obtained, settlers formed the habit of taking the law into their own hands. However natural, this had unfortunate long-range results and helps explain why American crime rates remain high.

At first, transportation was largely by water along the coast and up the rivers. By 1720 a few so-called roads had been built along the coast from Baltimore to Boston. Postriders carried mail from Boston to New York as early as 1672, and in the middle of the next century the British government set up a general postal system. This carried newspapers and magazines as well as letters, but the high cost of postage held down the volume of mail.

Passenger coach service was available by the end of the colonial period. In the 1770's a special "flying machine" coach relay made the ninety miles between New York and Philadelphia in a single day! Off the main roads travel was infinitely slower, necessitating stopovers at wretched taverns. Sea travel, as from Charleston to New York, was equally uncomfortable. As a consequence, Americans traveled only when necessary. Many lived and died on one farm. Others moved inland to take up lands; but, once established in the new location, they tended to stay there. The result was widespread provincialism.

Loyalties and Conflicts

Isolated from each other, the colonies at first felt little sense of common purpose. A citizen was loyal to his own colony and to the motherland. He was a Virginian and Englishman; hardly an American. Nor did the first colonists develop strong sectional attachments.

There was some sense of sectional unity in New England, but little in the South, none in the middle colonies.

What was more, there were differences *within* several of the colonies. Usually these were East-West conflicts, with newly settled Piedmont regions opposing the older settlements of the coastal plain. The struggle was economic, social, and political. Back-country farmers had bought land and goods on credit and were in debt to merchants or planters of coastal districts. Those who moved inland were generally plain people who distrusted the wealthier Easterners as aristocrats, and tidewater residents regarded upcountry settlers as inferior. The coast communities, being first established, controlled the colonial assemblies and never granted the new communities fair representation. This enabled the eastern leaders to direct land and taxation policy in their own interest.

Indian relations were a fruitful source of trouble. Frontier farmers, who were encroaching on tribal lands, favored a stern policy toward the red men. Eastern people, remote from border raids, sought to maintain peace, with one eye on the fur trade, the other on the cost of frontier conflict. Bacon's Rebellion of 1676 was caused largely by back-country feeling that the tidewater-dominated Virginia government gave no protection against the "savages." In the following century Scots-Irish Pennsylvania frontiersmen raised the same complaints against the Philadelphia Quakers.

The closest approach to civil war came in North Carolina, just before the Revolution. Aroused by heavy taxes, gouging officials, and a currency contraction which was hard on debtors, back-country farmers formed resistance associations. In 1771 members of these associations (Regulators) engaged in a pitched battle with militia from North Carolina's eastern counties. This engagement, lost by the Regulators, caused bitterness which flared up again during the Revolution.

Class Distinctions

The upper class in colonial society was composed of wealthy merchants and planters, leading members of the clergy, and other professional men. Small businessmen, prosperous farmers, and skilled artisans made up the middle social group, and the lower classes included poor farmers, laborers, sailors, and indentured servants.

Beneath all were the Negroes. Although house servants and other favored slaves enjoyed a better living than the poorer whites, they were considered socially inferior. Nor did emancipation change the picture, for free Negroes also met with discrimination. In other words, there was a stigma attached to color. Southern colonies passed laws which prohibited intermarriage between whites and Negroes. Mulatto children, who were half-white, were called "Negroes," as, indeed, were those who were three-fourths or even seven-eighths white. All "people of color" were put into a group segregated from the whites. Free Negroes who acquired property and education could not move up through the general social strata; they could only ascend through levels within their own color caste.

Though segregation was most marked in race distinctions, class lines were sharply drawn within the white population. Different classes were addressed by different names and wore distinctive costumes (knee breeches for the gentry, pantaloons for common men). Members of the middle and lower classes were sometimes haled into court for wearing clothes unbecoming to their station. Upper-class people cultivated manners carefully and prized formal education as further evidence of status. Property qualifications for voting and officeholding helped make these "better people" dominant in political activities. They made, interpreted, and enforced the laws, and, being human, tended to use their power in their own interest.

Still, class lines were by no means as important in the colonies as in the Old World. For one thing, the English landed gentry seldom came to America. Dukes do not emigrate. In the second place, many wealthy Americans were self-made men who retained contacts with associates of their more humble days. Plain people, moreover, had a feeling of independence in a land where they owned their own farms. They showed less deference for "their betters" than did the common folk of Europe. Indeed, this phrase, "their betters," was rarely employed in the colonies after 1700. Nor were American farmers, however poor, referred to as peasants. Jefferson recognized this equalitarian trend in the Declaration of Independence, when he set down the famous phrase: "all men are created equal."

The Colonial Family

Colonial activities centered in the family to a degree now difficult to realize. The farm family was an economic unit, in which only the smallest children were free of routine tasks. Great fireplaces and spinning wheels which now seem picturesque were centers of endless drudgery. The home was important for religious observances and education. It was, in fact, almost impossible to live outside a domestic circle. Widows and widowers remarried hastily, and unmarried adults made their homes with near relatives.

Among the first settlers, courtship was controlled, as in Europe, by the parents. But young people in the colonies gradually obtained more freedom in their choice of mates. Spontaneous love affairs led to early marriages, which were encouraged in a land where it was easy for couples to get a start and where a high birth rate was plainly needed.

Most Protestants in the colonies viewed marriage as a civil contract rather than a sacrament. The wedding ceremony could be performed by magistrates; and it was the sanction of the state which made a marriage legal. Those whom the state had joined together the state could put asunder. But since the family was held in high esteem, divorces were extremely rare.

Under the common law of England and the colonies, the wife's legal personality was largely merged in that of her husband. Her relationship to him was similar to the present relationship of young children to their parents. The colonial husband could command obedience, enforce punishments, and take over his wife's earnings. Not that the wife was likely to have any earnings, for marriage was almost the only vocation open to women.

But there were limits to the husband's authority. If a wife's family had given her a dowry, the principal could not be taken without her consent. This reserve served as insurance, in case of the husband's death. American courts gave women other rights ordinarily denied in common law; and travelers of the later colonial period noted that women were more highly regarded in the New World than in the Old. One factor in this situation was the relative scarcity of women in the colonies.

Childhood was thought of as a necessary evil during the early colonial era, for life was hard and the young could not carry a full share of the burdens. Discipline was strict in an effort to make children conform to adult patterns. But as time went on, a growing consideration for children became apparent. The trend is illustrated by juvenile literature. Children's books were grim affairs in the early colonial years; they bore such titles as *The Corruption and Vanity of Youth*. As theological zeal declined, religious indoctrination gave way to moral admonition, as in the later story of Washington and the cherry tree. But by the 1750's Americans were importing books designed to *entertain* the young. Life was not so hard for Americans in 1750 as it had been a century before. That in itself made parents of the eighteenth century more indulgent than their ancestors.

Recreation

Protestant clergymen frowned on recreation on Sunday, the one day when most Christians did not toil. In any case, the colonial people prized work and thought play a waste of time. Farmers had to labor constantly to make a decent living, merchants to get ahead. Peasants and tradesmen worked hard in Europe, too, but there the landed gentry gave prestige to leisure. The absence of titled aristocrats enabled the middle classes to set standards in the New World. As a consequence, Americans were suspicious of nonproductive activities such as art for art's sake.

There were exceptions. In the South and other Anglican centers the well-to-do imitated English aristocrats in recreation as in other matters. They followed the hounds, organized horse races, played cards, and staged balls. The less wealthy found recreation at town fairs and on the muster days of the local militia. Church holidays, Christmas in particular, were celebrated by Anglicans and Germans. The "Christ-mass" was too "popish" for New Englanders, but they enjoyed their own Thanksgiving. In between these occasional holidays, farm women had their quilting bees, the menfolk their house-raisings.

Even the slaves had their diversions, especially in winter. The more benevolent masters made much of Christmas in the slave quarters. Generally, however, the Negroes were left to themselves. Lacking formal entertainment, they made the most of religious ceremonies. Since they had lost most of their own culture, they took over that of the whites, introducing subtle changes suggestive of African backgrounds. Revival melodies took new form as spirituals. Work songs were infused with rhythms reminiscent of the Guinea coast. In their singing the Negroes evolved a folk art which would provide the first novel elements in American music.

Education

Many colonial farmers and townspeople were illiterate and felt little need for book learning. They were satisfied if their children had vocational training. On the farm this training was given with the chores; in the city, by putting boys out as apprentices. In commercial areas, however, there was a vocational need for literacy and for the ability to "cipher." Protestant leaders also felt that each man should read the Scriptures for himself. Trade and religion therefore combined to create a demand for elementary education.

Town schools were early provided in New England. Since these schools were apt to be run by clergymen and aided by town funds, it is difficult to say whether they were public or parochial institutions in the modern sense. Tuition was charged to those who could pay. In the middle and southern colonies, farmers sometimes combined to hire a schoolmaster for their children, as in the old field schools. In the towns, elementary schools were normally run by the churches. Most of these were private schools which charged tuition; but there were also "charity schools." The early elementary schools were for boys only. Girls were admitted in the eighteenth century.

Americans planning to enter the ministry or other professions needed more advanced instruction. Planters and merchants came to feel that their children should have greater educational advantages. So secondary schools were founded, offering mathematics and classical studies. The more prosperous families, North and South, hired private tutors to cover this same work.

Here the emphasis was on preparation for college. Eighteenth-century students who did not plan to go to college could attend small private schools which taught bookkeeping, shorthand, and other useful subjects. The latter part of the colonial period also saw the establishment of special schools for girls.

Colleges were originally provided to train young men for the ministry. This was the case with Harvard, established in 1634 by the Congregationalists, with William and Mary, founded by the Anglicans in 1693, and generally with those that followed. Of the nine colonial colleges, only one was nonsectarian—the College of Philadelphia, which became the University of Pennsylvania. Harvard, Yale, and Dartmouth were Congregational; William and Mary and King's (Columbia) were Anglican. Princeton was Presbyterian, Brown was Baptist, Queen's (Rutgers) was Dutch Reformed.

Enrollment was small, and college buildings were simple affairs, housing students little older than those who now attend high school. The curriculum was largely confined to logic and mathematics, theology and rhetoric, and the classics. But by 1720 the colleges were reacting to the secular interests of the time. Natural philosophy (science) was admitted to the curriculum. As an increasing percentage of students looked to other careers than the ministry, there were even suggestions that modern languages replace the classics. Toward the end of the colonial era, medical schools were founded at the College of Philadelphia and at King's College.

The medical colleges reflected a real need. The better-type English physicians of the seventeenth and eighteenth centuries had attended universities where they had read in medicine but secured no practical training. A few of these men came to the colonies. But their number was inadequate. Hence boys were apprenticed to them and in due time became practitioners on their own. Others just sensed a knack for doctoring and set themselves up as physicians.

Medical science was making progress in the Old World, and the fame of such schools as Leyden and Edinburgh reached the colonies. After 1720 prosperous American students proceeded to these centers and returned after a year or two with the M.D. degree. These men raised the tone of medical practice in the larger cities; a group of them, led by Dr. John Morgan, founded the first medical school in the colonies.

During the seventeenth century, lawyers were generally distrusted in the colonies. This view was modified after 1700 as the growing complexity of land titles and urban business indicated a need for legal knowledge. This in turn called for special education. Men of means began going to the Inns of Court in London for formal training. Returning, they introduced into colonial courts their knowledge of common law. Less prosperous youths read law in the offices of professional sponsors. The next step in professional progress (after the Revolution) was to set up American law schools.

The Fine Arts

European influence was stronger still in the fine arts. As an example, English architecture shifted from medieval to Renaissance forms during the 1600's. This change in style was reflected in the colonies early in the next century.

Domestic architecture in the early colonies was essentially medieval, with the better houses using steep roofs, dormers, and gables. Even the overhang of upper stories, needed in crowded European towns, was reproduced in American settlements which had more room than they needed. Windows were small, for glass was expensive. Furniture was hard, heavy, and rectangular, but often painted in bright designs. Inside and out, the buildings now suggest the crudity of a pioneer region. But when new, these structures must have seemed luxurious in comparison with the thatched huts used in the very first years of settlement.

The Renaissance-type Georgian style used after 1700 exhibited a pleasing harmony of proportion and classical details. The roof slope was lowered and extra gables disappeared. Windows were enlarged and fitted with square panes instead of diamond casements. Interiors became more graceful, with carved staircases, white woodwork, scenic wallpaper.

Also Georgian were the new Christopher Wren churches, modeled after those of London, in which the medieval spire was transformed by classical detail. In New England these churches, like the homes, were built of wood and covered with clapboards to keep out the cold. Painted white, they presented a pleasing contrast to the greens on which they fronted. In the other colonies, churches and homes were often constructed of brick or stone. Independence Hall in Philadelphia illustrates the effective use of Georgian forms for public buildings.

Renaissance feeling also influenced other arts. What is now called colonial furniture came in through imitation of such English masters as Chippendale. Colonial silversmiths, like Paul Revere, stressed graceful simplicity. And costume improved in the eighteenth century, when Puritan severity gave way to gay Georgian fashions.

Architecture and related arts flourished because they were relatively utilitarian. Music and painting, the dance and the theater were not so necessary to everyday affairs. In the colonies the best original music was the hymnology of the Pennsylvania Moravians, who had the advantage of a German tradition. But merchants and planters came to enjoy string quartets, and concerts were given with increasing frequency after 1740. Musical societies appeared in Charleston and Philadelphia; and even in New England the decline of Puritan zeal permitted an improvement in church music. Dancing became popular in the late colonial decades, varying from the stately minuets of the gentry to the jigs of ordinary folk.

It took time for the drama to invade the colonies. New England Puritans long called the theater the house of Satan. There was less opposition in the South, where amateur performances were given before 1700. A British Shakespeare company toured the colonies for two decades in the middle of the eighteenth century. The first permanent theater was erected in Philadelphia in 1766; and there, in the next year, Thomas Godfrey presented *The Prince of Parthia*, the first American play.

Colonial artists produced all types of paintings. Native artists were self-trained, and their work has something of the quality of later American primitives. It is more appreciated now than it was a century ago. Modern approval has also revived interest in the folk arts of the Pennsylvania Germans. The best portrait work was done in Boston, where Renaissance feeling for realism and perspective began to express itself by the middle of the eighteenth century. There John Singleton Copley emerged as an artist whose work was highly praised abroad. The other outstanding colonial artist, Benjamin West of Pennsylvania, moved to London, where he became president of the Royal Academy and launched a European vogue for heroic paintings of historic scenes.

Literary Trends

Meantime, secular interests were influencing literary trends. The first printing press in the colonies (Boston, 1638) turned out chiefly government documents and religious tracts. Three generations later, there were only eight presses in the colonies, and religious publications still made up a large part of their output. But a change was on the way, with the coming of the newspaper. The first in the colonies, the *Boston News Letter*, commenced publication in 1704; in the next four decades two dozen were started. They were two- or four-page affairs which included local items, political developments, literary and scientific essays, foreign news letters, and considerable advertising. There were cartoons as early as 1754. The papers printed few copies, but each was read by many persons. These little publications may therefore be described as a real medium of mass communication. And by reprinting from each other, they aroused a sense of common interest among the colonies.

At first the papers were directly or indirectly censored by governors and clergymen. Young Benjamin Franklin and his brother found themselves in trouble in the 1720's, when their *New England Courant* attacked Puritan orthodoxy. But in the famous Zenger trial of 1735 a New York jury decided that attacks on royal governors were not libelous if true. This case did much to establish the freedom of the press, a privilege which newspapers used after 1763 in encouraging opposition to Britain.

While townspeople read the papers, eighteenth-century farmers pored over almanacs. The almanacs contained miscellaneous data and bits of worldly wisdom. Sayings from Franklin's *Poor Richard's Almanac* are still recalled. Less popular, though more significant, was Franklin's *General Magazine*, launched in 1740 in imitation of London journals. In this and similar magazines, space was given to both verse and prose, especially to serious essays.

Books were scarce in the colonies, although they did become more numerous after 1740. During the 1750's, well-established townspeople combined to buy books which circulated among those contributing to the project. These subscription societies were the forerunners of later public libraries.

Because of distance, the scarcity of English books, and the presence of non-English elements, the language used in the colonies gradually came to differ from that evolving in Great Britain. Accents changed, and the colonial people picked up new words. *Hominy* and *succotash* came from Indian terms, *prairie* from the French, *snoop* and *boss* from the Dutch. Here were the beginnings of an American language.

The secular character of eighteenth-century thought was apparent in literary output. Early New England had favored religious writings, such as those of Cotton Mather. By 1750 this type of book was giving way to writings which stressed natural phenomena and everyday affairs. Thomas Jefferson's *Notes on Virginia* and the *Autobiography of Benjamin Franklin* illustrate the new trend.

Scientific Progress

Behind the secular outlook of 1750 lay a revolution in the intellectual outlook of the Western world. The roots of this reached far back into the Renaissance, but the immediate, dynamic influence came from the impact of modern science. After 1700 most scientists abandoned attempts at final, philosophic explanations of nature, and settled down to descriptive studies summed up in the formulation of natural laws. The results were both intellectually impressive and of practical value. Thus the new astronomy—combined with trigonometry and the calculus—made possible more exact measurements of latitude and longitude, thereby improving navigation and surveying. Disputed boundaries, such as the famous Mason and Dixon line between Pennsylvania and Maryland, were finally run with precision by men skilled in mathematics and astronomy.

Except for a few college professors teaching natural philosophy, there were no professional scientists in the colonies. But various amateurs—merchants, planters, professional men—read and experimented in their spare time. They were often motivated by a desire to apply science to technology, as when Jefferson developed an improved plow based on mathematical principles. This emphasis on useful knowledge was characteristic of European as well as colonial science in the eighteenth century.

Outstanding in the physical sciences was Franklin's work on electricity. European physicists had developed the Leyden Jar as a means of observing static charges. Franklin was the first to distinguish positive and negative charges on the two sides of the jar; and in his later kite experiment he demonstrated the identity of lightning and electricity. Since Franklin promptly applied his discovery to the invention of the lightning rod, his work illustrates the practical nature of American science. But Franklin started his investigations with no thought of their usefulness. Once having established general principles, however, he looked around for practical applications.

Sometimes the method was reversed. Scientists who were trying to solve a practical problem might find themselves involved in abstract investigations. Take Benjamin Rush, a member of the first medical faculty at Philadelphia. Seeking a cure for yellow fever, Dr. Rush was led finally to theorizing about the nature of disease in general.

Recognizing few specific diseases and following the classical-medieval tradition, colonial physicians ascribed most illness to impurities in the blood and other body fluids. Their tendency was to treat all conditions by bleeding and purging in order to relieve the body of its impurities. Or they worked at random, prescribing all sorts of drugs in the hope that one might prove effective.

Around 1720, word came from England that if one were inoculated with smallpox the case would be mild and the subject would be protected thereafter from a more virulent, "natural" attack. Despite violent opposition—

for some patients died from artificial inoculation—the practice gradually spread and doubtless reduced mortality.

Despite upper-class interest in science, there was little specific aid for scientists. The Pennsylvania Assembly did help David Rittenhouse, the astronomer; but little else was done. A private organization, the American Philosophical Society (founded in 1744), offered some research prizes. But most research was done by citizens at their own expense.

The Revolution in Men's Minds

Until the eighteenth century even the educated believed that witches were all about, casting Satan's evil spells (black magic), which could be overcome only by Christian symbols (white magic). The Salem trials of 1692, during which twenty persons were hanged for witchcraft, furnished the most spectacular colonial expression of these beliefs. But as educated men became familiar with the methods of science, there arose a demand for the weighing of evidence. True, old women sometimes admitted they were witches; but perhaps they were mentally unbalanced. Where was the scientific proof of witchcraft? Proof of course was not forthcoming; and educated men were relieved of many fears.

If the solar system ran like an unchanging mechanism, as described in Newtonian astronomy, perhaps all nature operated in this manner. If so, comets and epidemics were not portents of God's wrath but simply natural phenomena. The fear of an angry God therefore declined. Liberal clergymen began to wonder whether, in any case, a kind God would predestine His creatures to torment. Boston ministers began to speak more of God's mercy than of His wrath; and they talked of man's opportunity to be saved by grace and free will. This transformed Protestantism slowly from a religion of fear to one of hope.

If the universe ran like a mechanism, would God interfere with natural laws? Such questions led radical thinkers to question miracles. These men accepted a philosophy known as deism. They believed that when God had set the universe in motion He then permitted it to run like clockwork. Others stopped short of these conclusions, denying miracles and the divinity of Christ but still believing in a personal God. These unitarians opposed the majority, who were trinitarians believing in a divine Trinity. Though few, deists and unitarians were educated men, influential out of proportion to their numbers. Franklin and Jefferson were influenced by deism, and some of the ablest New England clergy approached unitarian views.

Significant for colonial thought were certain philosophic theories of knowledge—theories about how man came to think as he does. Rational-ists held that the human mind possesses certain innate ideas (for example, of space and time), by which it interprets all phenomena. The empiricists, notably the Englishman John Locke, denied that there was any such original mental equipment and declared that men simply learned everything through their senses. They held that the mind was at first like a receptive, blank page, on which the senses stamped whatever came their way.

This was optimistic doctrine, in sharp contrast with the old theology. No longer need man be viewed as inheriting a corrupt nature. Rather he was born untouched by good and evil, but receptive to either as it came his way. If bad conditions in society could be replaced by good, man could approach perfection. Hope for this world came to replace faith in the next. This attitude had its origins, in part, in scientific attitudes; and it depended on science to realize its goals. "The rapid progress *true* science now makes occasions my regretting that I was born so soon," said Benjamin Franklin, "It is impossible to imagine the height to which may be carried, in a thousand years, the power of man over matter. . . . All diseases may be prevented or cured, not excepting even that of old age."

Franklin here speaks of progress. The word came to imply advances in science which would make men more comfortable, and improvements in social conditions which would enable all to enjoy these advantages. Medieval thinkers had envisaged no such possibilities, whereas, after Franklin's day, there was a tendency to go to the other extreme in assuming that the advance of civilization would be continuous. In past ages, man had put his confidence in faith. Now it seemed that all problems could be solved by reason. The people must be enlightened about every social evil and the rational means at hand for its eradication. No wonder the eighteenth century has been termed the age of reason, the era of the Enlightenment.

Having little awe for tradition, philosophers of the Enlightenment asked questions about political institutions. Rejecting the divine right of kings as contrary to reason, Locke and his followers evolved a theory to explain how government began. As they saw it, men had originally lived in a state of nature, without laws but with certain natural rights to life, liberty, and the pursuit of happiness. Finding these rights infringed upon by ruthless persons, they had voluntarily contracted with leaders to set up and run governments for the general protection of the people. If the leaders violated their contract, by denying rights they were pledged to protect, the people were entitled to dissolve the government and establish one which would fulfill its obligations.

These concepts of natural rights and contracts had a long history before Locke used the terms as he did; and there was little evidence that human events had followed the course he described. Locke's theory, however, seemed rational and scientific to thinkers who were trying to get away from supernatural interpretations. The theory, it will be noted, justified revolution in certain circumstances. Locke employed it to defend England's Glorious Revolution; and his arguments were ready-made for the thirteen colonies, any time their opposition to British policies reached a revolutionary stage.

Toward a National Culture

Without fully realizing it, the thirteen colonies were approaching national status in 1763. Population and wealth had grown wondrously. Increasing leisure had enabled the upper classes to cultivate the arts and sciences and to absorb a philosophy of progress which led them to look forward to a promising future.

Although each colony thought of itself as a distinct entity, there was also a growing sense of intercolonial unity. This sense was encouraged by much which the colonies had in common, and by much which distinguished them from Great Britain. Those who lived in the colonies were no longer merely Englishmen living overseas. They were becoming Americans.

Many of the characteristics later ascribed to Americans were apparent by 1763. Americans generally believed in equal opportunities and were less class-conscious than Europeans. Heterogeneous in race and religion, they were beginning to oppose special privileges for any creed. Always busy, they were practical folk who revered the middle-class Puritan virtues which aided them in getting ahead. Prosperity made them proud of their country and its growth; and they were self-reliant, certain that they were in a better position to realize their goals than were European peoples handicapped by poverty, class distinctions, and outworn institutions.

Old World critics, however, found Americans pushing and vulgar, and claimed their pride was mere boastfulness. Worshiping material success as the one mark of distinction, Americans were said to have neglected the "finer things in life." Certainly they were wasteful, squandering resources which Europeans would have conserved. And the extreme individualism of Americans sometimes showed itself in lawlessness.

For better or worse, Americans were becoming a distinct people. Colonial ways, though taking their main forms from the culture of Great Britain, had also responded to the New World environment, to selective immigration, and to the influence of non-English cultures. One could see the signs of an emerging American civilization.

Part II

From Colony to Republic
(1763-1815)

 *By 1763, Americans were becoming convinced that they were different from Europeans and that their future would be distinctively American. But the thirteen colonies were still bound to Great Britain by many ties.*

In the half-century that followed, the political tie was severed, and the thirteen colonies became the United States of America. Nor was that all. Having strengthened its central government, the new republic enormously increased its territorial holdings in the decades after the Revolution. Political independence and territorial growth developed national consciousness and made citizens of the United States desire a truly American economy and culture. Although not yet successful in 1815, they had made substantial progress toward their goal.

4

The American

Revolution

The Problem of Control

The end of the French and Indian War in 1763 set the stage for trouble. On one hand, the peace settlement gave the thirteen colonies security through removal of French power from the North American continent. On the other, the war had convinced the British that the old colonial system was too easygoing and needed remodeling. So at the very moment when the colonists felt stronger and more self-reliant than ever, Britain undertook to reorganize the imperial structure and introduce effective control and efficient taxation.

Successful revolutions are the products of many forces which have combined into patterns of antagonism and revolt. In the colonies the bid for independence came after able leaders had brought together persons who opposed the British because of their class feeling, their local pride, or their attitude on a variety of disputes over land and commerce.

Class Conflict

The Old World class system, transported to America by the wealthier settlers, clashed with the social habits formed in the pioneer environment of the new continent. Friction increased as the colonies grew in wealth and population. One continuing point of conflict was the system of representation. Apportionment made in the early years gave control of the colonial assemblies to the aristocratic coastal areas. These regions killed reapportionment schemes which would have given adequate representation to new, more democratic interior districts.

Every colony had this situation. It was most troublesome, however, in Pennsylvania, Virginia, and the Carolinas, all of which had vast and thickly settled back-country areas. Naturally, complaints were numerous. But protest movements failed. When the Paxton Boys marched to Philadelphia to demand reforms, their pleas fell on deaf ears (1764). When back-country

Regulators rose in North Carolina in the next decade, they were put down by force.

Although issues varied, inland districts most commonly complained about taxation without proper representation or benefits. Feeling against the eastern counties was also associated with feeling against the British government, which supplied the colonial governors. Hence back-country leaders like Patrick Henry came to feel that an overturn of the institutions of the empire would bring changes that would aid Virginia's western counties.

Nor was there complete harmony in the coastal districts. The cities were usually controlled by the well-to-do, rather than by small traders, artisans, and ordinary laborers. Property qualifications kept some from voting or holding office, and royal agents seemed to favor the gentry rather than the plain people. Skillful agitators—notably Samuel Adams of Boston—easily led these underprivileged persons into joining a movement against the British government as the source of aristocratic authority. The Sons of Liberty, an anti-British society of Boston, New York, and other cities, drew in large part from the ranks of workingmen.

The Commercial Dispute

To this extent, the American Revolution was an uprising of the lower classes. But it was not wholly that. Many rebels came from the middle and upper classes. Their opposition to Britain was based on commercial restrictions rather than on class distinctions.

The conclusion of hostilities in 1763 left Britain with what was then considered a staggering national debt. Budget balancing called for an increase in tax revenues; and for part of this increase Britain turned to her overseas possessions. After all, the colonies had benefited from the war and the resulting ascendancy of the British Empire. Colonists should, therefore, pay part of the war debt and the mounting imperial expenses.

The old Navigation Acts had not been designed primarily to produce revenue. The Molasses Act of 1733, for instance, had set duties prohibitively high as a means of keeping foreign goods out of the colonies. The products had come in anyway, but without payment of duties. Colonial merchants had simply smuggled their cargoes past the customs. After 1763, revenue-conscious British officials decided to reduce duties to a reasonable level, then make sure they were collected. During the ministry of George Grenville, Parliament passed the Sugar Act of 1764, which lowered the rates of the Molasses Act of 1733. At the same time, the British customs service in the colonies was overhauled, and Parliament reasserted its power to issue writs of assistance (general search warrants) in order to stamp out smuggling. New England and middle-colony merchants, of course, were profoundly disturbed by this threat to their profitable smuggling trade.

In the same year, 1764, Parliament passed the Paper Money Act, prohibiting the colonies from issuing paper currency as legal tender for debts. The Grenville ministry hoped to help merchant creditors of London and the colonies. The law, however, resulted in contraction of the currency during postwar depression. This aggravated economic difficulties and made many grumble about the failure of Britain to appreciate colonial problems.

Britain's new world power called for a larger standing army, a part of which might conveniently be kept in the colonies. Here again there was a money problem, for Great Britain expected the colonial assemblies to provide food and quarters for the redcoats. Americans were by no means pleased. When they had needed British troops to fight the Indians and French, there were few to be had. Now that danger had decreased, the military was to stay, and at the colonies' expense. Worse still, British troops were likely to enforce the new imperial legislation.

Another of Grenville's revenue-producing measures, the Stamp Act of 1765, met with even greater opposition. This law placed stamp taxes on newspapers and legal documents. Englishmen thought the sums so small that the colonists would pay readily. But the Stamp Act came when the colonies were agitated over the army, sugar, and paper money. Besides, the new law affected two highly vocal groups—journalists and lawyers.

A wave of protest swept across the colonies. Newspapers were published, court cases decided without purchase of required stamps. Mobs intimidated would-be stamp purchasers and smashed stamp offices. In Virginia, Patrick Henry warned George III that unjust rulers had been overthrown. And before the year was out, representatives from nine colonies met in New York, in a Stamp Act Congress. The delegates were lawyers and merchants who disliked the new taxes and also feared the rising popular excitement. For, once aroused, the people might turn from stamps to demand that the right to vote and hold office be extended to those who owned no property.

In denouncing the Stamp Act the Congress argued that there could be no taxation without representation. The people of the thirteen colonies were not represented in Parliament, so no taxes could properly be imposed on them save by their own colonial legislatures. At the same time, the delegates threatened a boycott.

London was unimpressed by the constitutional arguments; but boycott did mean something. English merchants, alarmed at the loss of American sales, denounced the Stamp Act. Parliament, bowing to pressure, voted repeal in 1766.

In scrapping the Stamp Act, Parliament took care to state that it retained the right to tax the colonies. In their delight over repeal, Americans generally overlooked this declaratory clause. It came to their attention the next year, when Parliament decided that the colonists should pay import duties on various articles, including tea, glass, painters' colors, lead, and paper (Townshend Act, 1767).

During the Stamp Act controversy, colonial leaders attacked Parliament's new use of internal taxation in the colonies. In consequence, the backers of the Townshend Act employed external taxation, which had often been used in the past, as in the Molasses Act of 1733. But again the colonies objected; Americans insisted that each colonial assembly was a government within the empire, bearing the same relation to the Crown as the British Parliament. Certain imperial matters, such as trade regulation, might be conceded to Parliament; but the colonial assemblies retained the sole right to lay taxes for the purpose of producing revenue. The old Navigation Laws, including the Molasses Act, had been primarily trade regulation statutes. The Townshend duties, however, were designed to raise revenue; hence they were constitutionally unsound.

One could argue this point either way. Actually, neither side was as concerned about theory as about fact. Since the power of the colonial assemblies rested on their control of finances, Americans could not afford to give way on tax questions. And the British, having yielded on the Stamp Act, felt they must assert control over the colonies.

As in Stamp Act days, the colonists tried nonimportation agreements. These cut imports from Britain by one-half. Times being better, British merchants offset these losses by increases elsewhere. But Britain found that the Townshend duties yielded little more than the cost of collection—less, if one counted the cost of sending extra troops to the colonies. Moreover, the presence of troops led to further difficulties. In 1770, a Boston mob attacked a patrol of British soldiers, who, firing into the crowd, killed seven persons. This incident increased anti-British feeling throughout the colonies.

By this time Britain had decided to yield again. In 1770 a new Tory ministry headed by Lord North declared the Townshend duties a failure and had them repealed by Parliament. Only the tax on tea was retained, as a matter of principle. Once more Americans could celebrate a triumph; and some thought that the dispute was over. But none of the underlying differences had been adjusted, and any innovation in colonial policy might bring a renewal of the conflict.

Tea Brings a Crisis

Trouble flared up again as a result of the Tea Act of 1773. The British East India Company, partly owned by the British government, was in financial difficulties. The company had a good deal of tea stored in England. To move this product, Parliament voted to allow the company to export tea to the colonies without payment of the normal revenue tax of twelvepence a pound. The company would still have to pay a colonial import tax of threepence (the one remaining Townshend duty). Even so, Americans would be able to buy tea at an exceptionally low price, through East India Company agents in the colonies.

Consumers, then, stood to profit from the Tea Act. But, since the East India Company would sell through its own outlets, established American merchants would lose their tea business. A Townshend duty being involved, the case also raised the taxation principle. Radical leaders therefore seized the occasion to rekindle feeling against Great Britain. The Sons of Liberty in New York and Philadelphia persuaded company agents of the "impracticality" of trying to land tea, and the vessels sent to those ports returned to London. Though tea was brought ashore in Charleston, South Carolina, the excitement was sufficient to keep it locked in a warehouse. A tea ship and its cargo were burned in Annapolis, Maryland. The masters of the tea ships which reached Boston would have been glad to take their tea back to England. Governor Thomas Hutchinson, however, would not permit this, for he was determined to see that tea was legally protected in its distribution. To thwart his plans, Bostonians dressed as Indians boarded the vessels at night and threw $75,000 worth of tea into the harbor (1773).

Hearing of the Boston Tea Party, Parliament passed the so-called Intolerable Acts (1774). One closed the port of Boston; another altered the government of Massachusetts so as virtually to end self-rule. A third specified that British officials accused of capital offenses in Massachusetts should be transferred to England for trial. A fourth authorized the governor of any American colony to requisition barns and vacant houses for the quartering of soldiers sent to the colonies.

Alienation of American Landholders

The Intolerable Acts explain why Massachusetts and other commercial colonies were ready to use force against Britain by 1775. British land policies help explain the like feeling of agricultural colonies.

The elimination of French power along the Ohio opened great possibilities for the British Empire. Unfortunately, Englishmen and Americans saw the western frontier from different points of view. To the Virginian and Pennsylvanian the West was a vast area offering land for settlement and speculation. The Indians, being in the way, should be pushed westward. British officials, on the other hand, had found white frontiersmen hard to tax and govern. As a consequence, they felt that westward migra-

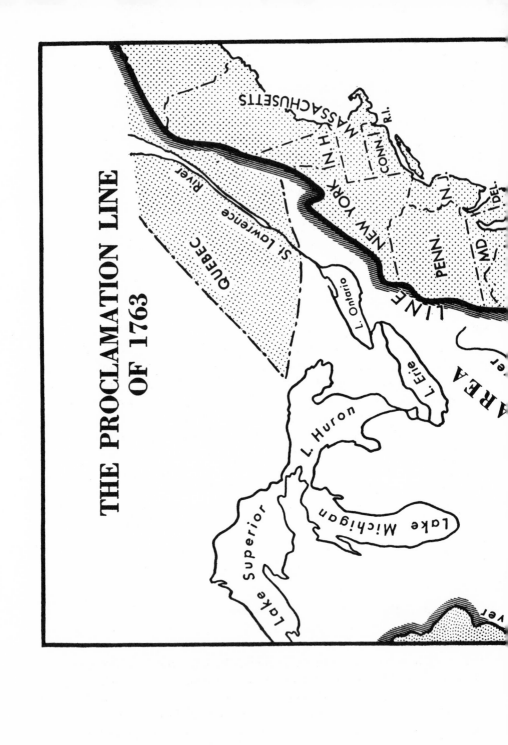

THE PROCLAMATION LINE
OF 1763

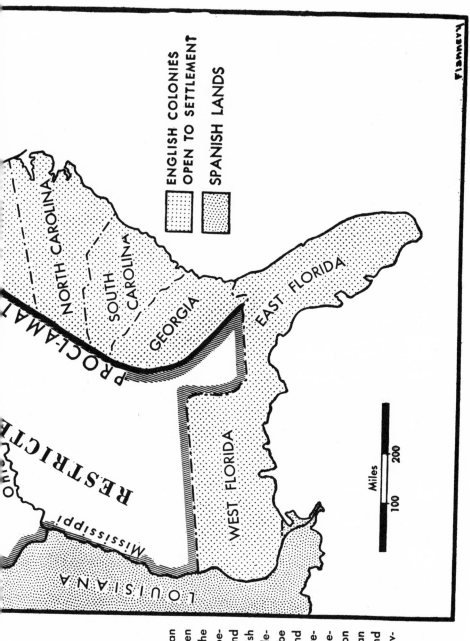

ENGLISH COLONIES
OPEN TO SETTLEMENT

SPANISH LANDS

Flannery

NORTH CAROLINA

SOUTH CAROLINA

GEORGIA

EAST FLORIDA

PROCLAMAT

RESTRICTE

Ohio

Mississippi

WEST FLORIDA

LOUISIANA

Miles

100 200

After the French and Indian War, citizens of the Thirteen Colonies planned to settle the newly acquired lands between the Appalachians and the Mississippi. The British government, however, decided that this area should be reserved for the Indians and the fur trade. Britain therefore prohibited white settlement beyond a Proclamation Line. This alienated American farmers and businessmen and helped pave the way for revolution.

tion should be stopped, at least until all eastern lands were occupied. Nor did the British wish to oust the Indian, who gathered furs for white traders.

After Pontiac's uprising, a bloody Indian war of 1763, the British view prevailed. In a royal proclamation, George III prohibited the sale of land beyond the headwaters of rivers flowing into the Atlantic—that is, beyond the crest of the Appalachians. Indian and white areas would then be clearly defined. This, Britain hoped, would guarantee peace and a continuation of the fur trade.

The Proclamation Line of 1763 was(west of any existing English settlement.) In other words, actual western settlers were not immediately menaced. But large investors were; they had planned to buy lands beyond the line and hold them for a future rise in value. Virginians were especially disturbed, for their colony claimed much western land under the charter of 1609.

For a decade, Virginians consoled themselves with the theory that the line would not interfere with their ultimate rights. As soon as population movement warranted, they said, lands beyond the line would be thrown open for settlement. By the 1770's, however, it became apparent that even if white settlers were allowed to locate beyond the mountains, the mother country might permanently reject Virginia's western land claims. Philadelphia speculators represented in London by Benjamin Franklin were prevailing on the British government to set up a new colony known as Vandalia squarely athwart Virginia's road to the West.

In 1774, when the Intolerable Acts were driving Massachusetts to rebellion, Britain announced new policies which confirmed the worst fears of Virginians. First came a royal proclamation raising the price of government lands east of the Proclamation Line, doubling quitrents on land sold, and reaffirming the line as a restriction on the colonies along the Atlantic coast. The doubled quitrent was not high enough to hurt a farmer who was actually cultivating his holdings, but it did increase the difficulties of planter-speculators who bought thousands of acres for future sale. So planters as well as merchants had a tax quarrel with London.

During the same year, 1774, Parliament extended the southern boundary of the province of Quebec to the Ohio River and provided that the fur trade of that area should be administered from Canada. Virginia's claim to land north and west of the Ohio was thereby nullified, and the movement of individual Virginians into the region was likely to be checked by an unfriendly administration. Pennsylvania fur traders also had cause to complain. Then, too, the Quebec Act allowed French Catholics to maintain their church by taxes and use their language in the schools. This policy was denounced in the thirteen colonies, where anti-Catholic sentiment was strong. Some thought they detected a British effort to align Canada against the rest of the colonies in case of trouble; and "No Popery" would be a slogan of the Revolution in Massachusetts.

Meanwhile, it appeared likely that the Pennsylvania-dominated Vandalia Company would get a land grant west of Virginia. Unwilling to yield their claims, Virginians used border quarrels with the Indians as an excuse for moving across the Proclamation Line. They then forced the Shawnees to sign a treaty giving Virginia title to all their lands east and south of the Ohio. The Vandalia group retained its backing in London, but the outbreak of the Revolution reduced the value of that support.

Land policy was not the only force driving Virginia toward rebellion. Her planters were also concerned about their large debts to British merchants. Thomas Jefferson lamented that debts had become "hereditary . . . for many generations, so that the planters were a species of property annexed to certain mercantile houses in London." Taking this factor with the others, it is not surprising that Virginia legislators openly expressed their sympathy for Massachusetts. The governor then dissolved the Assembly, whereupon the delegates issued a call for a Continental Congress.

The Road to Revolution

Both conservatives and radicals were represented in the Continental Congress when it met in Philadelphia in September, 1774. The radicals demanded immediate boycott against Britain. Supporting this strategy were letters from Franklin, who wrote from London that the English government would yield if the Continental Congress took a firm stand. Colonial conservatives, however, preferred negotiation. Consequently, the delegates pleaded their cause in humble petitions. But at the same time, they drew up a ringing Declaration of Rights and Grievances, and formed a Continental Association for the enforcement of nonintercourse.

Previous nonimportation agreements had been informally arranged and had not covered exports. The Continental Association, however, was a formal document to be signed by each individual merchant. The intention was to bar entry of British goods; but ultimately there would also be a ban on exports to the British Isles and West Indies, and on participation in the African slave trade. The Continental Association divided fence sitters into colonial patriots and British loyalists. Men who refused to sign and abide by the agreement were branded as supporters of the enemy and attacked by methods ranging from ostracism to tar and feathers. In most large ports British trade virtually ceased, and imperial government gave way to revolutionary committees or assemblies. The crisis deepened in

1775, as the British government offered no acceptable compromise. Delegates to a second Continental Congress were elected in direct defiance of the orders of the royal governors, and colonial militia units of Minute Men collected arms and ammunition.

Then came open conflict. British General Thomas Gage, then governor of Massachusetts, sent a thousand soldiers to seize a rebel arsenal at Concord. When the redcoats reached Lexington (April 19, 1775), they were met on the village green by defiant Minute Men. A skirmish ensued, and the Revolutionary War had begun.

The second Continental Congress met in May, 1775, as the central government of a nation at war. It appointed George Washington Commander in Chief. It raised troops and created a navy. It commissioned merchant vessels as privateers, authorizing them to attack British commerce. It established a postal system and a Treasury. It decided to issue paper money and float loans. It negotiated alliances with Indian tribes; it defended frontiers and took steps to obtain help from Britain's European rivals.

Clearly, Congress was exercising the powers of sovereignty. The delegates, however, hesitated to cut loose from the British Empire. Rather they maintained that they were upholding their rights as Englishmen against an unjust Parliament and a tyrannical king. But as late as January, 1776, nine months after Lexington, there was little open talk of independence. The legislatures of North Carolina and Maryland, New Jersey, Pennsylvania, and New York had only recently instructed their delegates in Congress to stand firm against any move for separation. General Washington's officers still toasted the king's health, and conservative patriots continued to insist that compromise was possible.

Gradually, however, Americans came to feel that the quarrel had gone beyond the patching stage. It was clear that France would not supply much aid unless the colonies formally set up housekeeping for themselves. It was evident, too, that nonintercourse had not brought Great Britain to terms. Radicals like Sam Adams began saying that the patriots must go further. The conservatives then faced a difficult decision. If they stood out against independence and lost, they might lose their influence and property. If they agreed to independence, they might be swept away by the growing democratic current, or they might be able to guide and control the current. Confronted with that choice, many reluctantly cast their lot for independence.

In the weeks of indecision, many Americans were won over by Thomas Paine's pamphlet, *Common Sense*, which appeared in January, 1776. Paine, of Quaker background, had just come to Philadelphia from England.

An ardent republican and champion of the natural-rights philosophy, he lent his pen to the cause of independence. In clear, crisp sentences he urged Americans to throw off the chains that bound them to Britain. The colonies, he said, had always been exploited. Once free, they could wax fat on trade in the markets of the world. They could also avoid involvement in Europe's bloody wars. Furthermore, monarchy was an outworn institution, offensive to reason and common sense; and the British constitution was a tangle of inconsistent anarchronisms.

Common Sense caught on partly because Paine reflected the rising self-consciousness of Americans. This self-consciousness, the cornerstone of American nationalism, was reinforced by the creation of a working union among the thirteen colonies. Though weak, the Continental Congress and the army under Washington did tend to draw the colonists together. Local loyalties persisted; but there was a decided shift. The old attachment was to one's colony and Britain. The new loyalty was to one's colony (now state) and to America. The people were ready for the final, formal break with the British Empire.

The Declaration of Independence

On July 2, 1776, the Continental Congress gave unanimous consent to a resolution for independence, introduced some weeks earlier by Richard Henry Lee of Virginia. Two days later a committee which had been working on the problem presented a Declaration of Independence. The Declaration was largely the work of Thomas Jefferson. Yet Jefferson did not claim originality. He drew on the body of thought developed in England by John Locke and others to justify the struggle against absolute monarchy. Jefferson also expressed ideas familiar to the American people.

The Declaration assumed that all men are endowed by nature with inalienable rights to life, liberty, and the pursuit of happiness. It further stated that governments rested on the consent of the governed. The people had created political institutions to guarantee their natural rights. When the government failed to secure these natural rights to men, the government could properly be overthrown.

Jefferson held that Parliament had no legal control over the colonies, their only connection with the mother country being through the Crown. And that connection was now severed, said the Declaration, since George III had by acts of injustice violated the natural rights of Americans. Most of the grievances listed could more properly have been laid at the door of Parliament. But the indictment was admirably phrased and well calculated to stir up enthusiasm for the Revolution at home and abroad.

The Declaration would long remain a dynamic force. Although Jefferson had not meant to apply the natural-rights philosophy to slaves and women, the abolitionists and the advocates of women's rights would appeal to the Declaration as a justification for their programs. So would labor groups and democratic leaders overseas.

The Military Problem

When the Declaration of Independence was adopted, a full-scale war was already under way. On the surface, the mother country seemed to have the military advantages. The population of Britain was much greater than that of the colonies. George III could count on the bulk of the American Indians, and on many white Loyalists. Britain had a centralized administration with great political and financial power, whereas the colonies possessed no banks, no American currency, and only a feeble central government. The rebels went into the conflict without a navy, and with no land force save that of thirteen state-controlled militia organizations, alike only in inefficiency and shortage of equipment. The British Empire, by contrast, had a large porfessional army and the world's best navy. To back up these fighting units, England possessed the facilities for turning out matériel of war. The agrarian United States, on the other hand, had neither the accumulated stores nor the manufacturing establishments needed by a military nation. Finally, in Canada and Florida, Great Britain held both flanks of the colonial position.

But the picture had another side. Some Britishers opposed the war. Many more were indifferent. Those who did fight found that distance lessened England's striking power. The redcoats had to operate on the offensive—a handicap in eighteenth-century warfare, especially in the forests of America. To make matters worse for Britain, the Patriots had interior lines, could count on aid from England's enemy, France, and were spurred on by the thought that theirs was a fight for liberty and their own homes. Nor did the rebels need to beat the British to come out on top. They could and did win the war while losing most of the battles and many of the campaigns. It was enough if the Americans could keep on fighting, maintaining resistance until the mother country tired of the cost of war.

The concept of the nation in arms, with conscription and all-out warfare, had not yet been developed. In consequence, both sides had trouble raising troops and keeping forces in the field. British regulars gave Britain a head start, but she made little progress with new recruiting. Many Englishmen thought there had been enough of fighting, with the Seven Years' War not a generation gone. In any case, who cared to fight three thousand miles from home, in the wilderness of the New World? Britain was forced to resort to the then-current practice of hiring foreign soldiers. These Germans (mostly Hessians) made up a third of King George's force in America; but they were less useful than their numbers indicated. Being outsiders, they had little interest in the war; and, trained on European principles, their units lacked the flexibility needed in forest warfare.

The patriotic impulse made recruiting better in America. But although Congress authorized a Continental Army of 75,000, not half that number was obtained. Enlistment bounties tempted some, but Washington normally had fewer men than there are in a present-day division. Few Americans desired to sign up for the duration; and many who did tired of service and deserted. Hence in each crisis it was necessary to supplement the national army with the enthusiastic but poorly equipped, ill-trained, and unreliable state militia.

The British and Americans both had problems of command. Britain was well supplied with veteran officers and professional drill-master sergeants; but some of her best officers (for example the Howe brothers) were not keen about the war. Others had trouble handling armies which combined British regulars, Hessian mercenaries, Tory colonists, and Indians. And, though they had learned much since the days of Braddock, the redcoats were still inclined to overstress fixed lines and to load their columns with nonessential supplies.

American officers, on the other hand, underrated cohesion and military discipline. This was owing partly to inexperience, partly to the practice of letting soldiers choose their own officers. The Patriots also gave commissions to men who gathered recruits; and the Continental Congress played politics with high commands. Under the circumstances, the Revolutionary forces were bound to behave erratically on occasion. Generally, however, they did fairly well, developing such able officers as Nathanael Greene, Benedict Arnold, Anthony Wayne—and George Washington.

Appointed Commander in Chief one day before the battle of Bunker Hill, Washington assumed command of the Continental Army in July, 1775. Congress picked him for his experience and known ability, and because the appointment of a Virginian would increase southern interest in the war. Washington was not a topnotch tactician or strategist, and many soldiers found him cold and aristocratic. Yet this Virginian did have qualities of greatness. He had drive, determination, perseverance. He could be discouraged, but he would not give up. He could be beaten, but he would not surrender. Thus Washington became a symbol of national resistance, gave his country confidence in the long months of adversity.

Having served with British regulars, Washington was distressed to find his command little more than an armed mob. The General worked on this all through the war. His greatest help came from the German Baron von Steuben, who had been aide-de-camp to Frederick the Great of Prussia. Washington disliked most of the European officers who came flocking to his camp in search of cash, glory and adventure; all too often these soldiers of fortune understood neither the language nor the customs of America. But a few were useful—the Pole Kosciusko, with his knowledge of military engineering; the Frenchman Lafayette, whose noble rank had propaganda value for the rebel cause; and Steuben, who taught discipline to the Patriot soldiers, barking his commands in a mixture of English, French, and German. The aim was to show the Americans how to work together without sacrificing the speed and flexibility of New World warfare. The result was an increase in efficiency; and Steuben's system of instruction, as well as his organizational ideas, influenced the United States Army on into the twentieth century.

Both sides were plagued with problems of supply. Failures on that score caused the British evacuation of Boston, the British surrender at Saratoga, American suffering at Valley Forge. Systematic crop destruction, lack of transportation, and sparse settlement caused food shortages for Americans and Britishers alike. Nor was the diet varied; by Washington's own testimony, the concentration on meat and bread led to "many putrid diseases."

British control of the sea lanes guaranteed King George's soldiers a steady flow of camp and combat equipment. Thus the redcoat was well clad and carried sixty rounds of ammunition for his muzzleloading musket. Washington rarely let his men have half that many rounds, for he was faced with a critical shortage of gunpowder. Patriot soldiers often supplied their own weapons, but many of these guns broke under steady use and could not be replaced. There was never enough clothing, tents, or blankets; the United States had not yet turned to textile manufacturing.

Congress and the military tried desperately to plug the holes. They made some progress, especially after 1777, when the capable Nathanael Greene became Quartermaster General. Clothing, powder, infantry and artillery weapons were brought in from Europe, chiefly via the West Indies. Revolutionary troops seized British stores, as when Ethan Allen took Ticonderoga (1775). Patriotic impulse and legislative subsidies increased American production. Although most of this was of poor quality, rebel gunsmiths did turn out a few good rifles. Americans were among the first to make combat use of these weapons of the future, which had been brought into the colonies by Swiss and German settlers. Being muzzleloaders, eighteenth-century rifles were hard to load; but they were accurate at two hundred yards, and muskets could not be counted on at half that distance.

While Greene rounded up supplies, Treasurer Robert Morris wrestled with the problems of finance. Morris, a Philadelphia merchant-politician, had no easy task. The Continental Congress had neither the inclination nor the power to levy taxes. That was for the states to do; and anyway, was this not a war against taxation? Congress therefore relied on gifts from France and the state legislatures, on borrowing and on the issuance of paper money.

The borrowing created both foreign and domestic debts. The former debt was owed to the French government and the Dutch bankers, the latter mainly to speculators and well-to-do Patriots. Here Morris was helpful, pledging his personal credit to raise needed funds. Both Congress and the states printed enormous quantities of paper money. Unbacked by specie, the paper lost its value quickly. A series of state price-fixing acts produced black markets for specie sales, and there was uncontrolled inflation in the last years of the war. This led to serious social repercussions in the postwar period. But the Revolution could not have been financed without paper money.

Britain's strategy was to take and hold the larger towns. That she accomplished; but the technique did not bring victory. As agrarians, the rebels had a decentralized economy and could get along fairly well without their major cities.

Winning the War

In its first phase, the Revolution centered around Boston (1775–76). After the skirmishes at Lexington and Concord, Americans swarmed in to besiege the redcoats inside Boston. The Patriots persisted even after the British had demonstrated tactical superiority at Bunker Hill. Through the rest of 1775, the English troops were supplied by sea; but their communications were threatened the next year, when Washington brought artillery to bear on Boston Harbor. The British then sailed for Halifax (March, 1776). In taking Boston, the Revolutionary army gained no battle triumph, and secured a town of little military value. But, by forcing out the British, the Patriots won prestige.

The scene then shifted to the middle states (1776–78). After evacuating Boston, Sir William Howe took New York City, decisively defeating Washington in the battle of Long Island (August, 1776). Britain also had control of Canada, having beaten off an American invasion force the preceding winter. The British high command consequently decided to have Howe hold the mouth of the Hudson, while Sir John Burgoyne pressed south from Canada. The English could thus establish a new line of communication and cut the colonies in two, separating New England from the regions south and west.

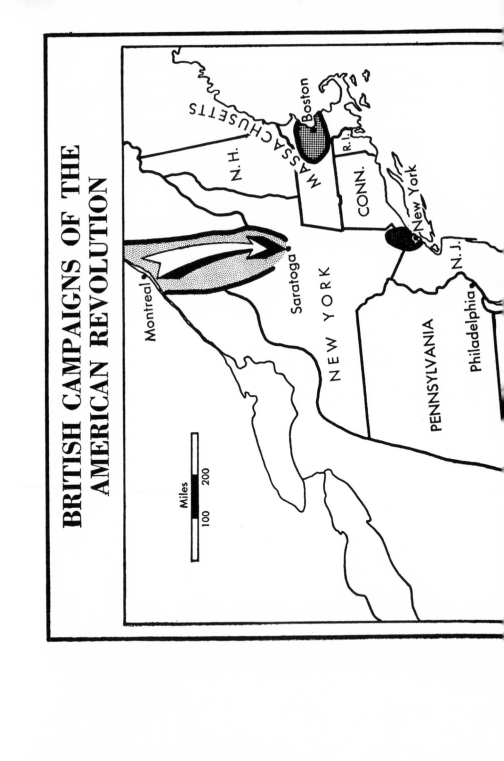

BRITISH CAMPAIGNS OF THE AMERICAN REVOLUTION

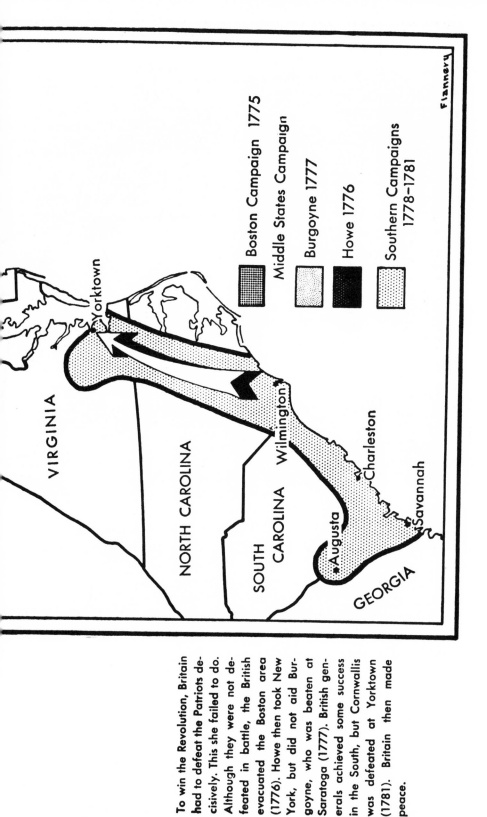

Flannery

Boston Campaign 1775

Middle States Campaign

Burgoyne 1777

Howe 1776

Southern Campaigns 1778-1781

VIRGINIA

Yorktown

NORTH CAROLINA

Wilmington

SOUTH CAROLINA

Augusta

Charleston

GEORGIA

Savannah

To win the Revolution, Britain had to defeat the Patriots decisively. This she failed to do. Although they were not defeated in battle, the British evacuated the Boston area (1776). Howe then took New York, but did not aid Burgoyne, who was beaten at Saratoga (1777). British generals achieved some success in the South, but Cornwallis was defeated at Yorktown (1781). Britain then made peace.

The British had the strength to make this plan succeed. Howe could have moved north up the Hudson to meet Burgoyne, thus assuring success for British arms. But the British underestimated Patriot strength. Instead of helping Burgoyne, Howe went south to capture Philadelphia. This left Burgoyne unaided as he stumbled south through the New York forests. Outnumbered, and short of supplies, he surrendered at Saratoga in October, 1777.

Britain's final effort was in the South (1778–81), where the British counted heavily on aid from local Loyalists. Savannah fell to Britain at the end of 1778, and in 1780 Charleston surrendered after a siege. Lord Cornwallis then drove through stiff resistance into Virginia. In most battles he defeated the Patriots; but when the redcoated regiments marched on, the countryside went back into rebellion. Then, in Virginia, the British Army was caught by Washington and by the French, Cornwallis being bottled up in Yorktown and forced to surrender (October, 1781).

There was also fighting in the West. Indians allied with Britain swooped down on American frontiersmen, forcing Washington to send General John Sullivan on a punitive expedition through Pennsylvania and New York in 1779. In that and the preceding year, George Rogers Clark of the Virginia militia operated further west. Himself a speculator, Clark knew the value of the lands north of the Ohio; and, despite obstacles, he drove the British from what is now southern Illinois and Indiana. While Clark could not take Britain's base at Detroit, his campaigns helped establish American claims beyond the Appalachians.

The colonists did little on the sea. Such commanders as John Paul Jones won individual combats with British vessels. But the largest American ships were frigates, mounting less than fifty guns. These were no match for the capital ships of the eighteenth century, ships of the line, mounting seventy-six guns. British strength in that category made it possible for the Royal Navy to control the American coastline for most of the war. Patriot vessels—public ships and privateers alike—were forced to concentrate on commerce raiding. This was less dramatic than fleet action but did have some effect. By hurting London merchants and driving up insurance rates it caused some Englishmen to feel that the war should be ended at any cost.

France Aids the Colonies

Although they fought valiantly, the Patriots could not have won without foreign aid. Fortunately, such aid came. France espoused the American cause and turned the tide of battle by providing assistance in money, supplies, and combat strength.

It was no love of liberty which led the French to help. Nor did democracy and revolution attract the aristocrats who ruled France with a heavy hand. Liberty would end their despotism, democracy would strip them of their privileges; and revolution, when it came, would mean the guillotine or exile. Yet there were reasons for supporting the Americans. With the decline of Spain a century before, France had taken over leadership of European affairs. Be it clothing, philosophy, music, or war, the dazzling court of Versailles had set styles for the Continent. Then French ascendancy had met a challenge from the rising British Empire; and, after a long series of conflicts, Britain had emerged triumphant in the Seven Years', or French and Indian, War. Smarting under defeat, the proud French Bourbon courtiers set out to get revenge. How better than by working for disruption of the British Empire? The might of England rested on sea power, which in turn depended on trade with the colonies. Strike Britain there, and she would suffer what might be a mortal blow.

When the war for American independence started, France took immediate advantage of the chance to humble her great foe. The astute Count of Vergennes, as French Minister of Foreign Affairs, established contact with the Continental Congress; and soon French military goods were on their way to General Washington. The work of British spies and naval officers prevented some shipments from reaching their destination. Enough got through, however, to help make possible the American victory over Burgoyne at Saratoga (1777). Since Vergennes hesitated to give open aid to untried rebels, the first supplies were furnished indirectly, as a secret gift to the Americans. But when the battle of Saratoga had shown the vitality of the rebel cause, the French were ready to take a more active role. Early in 1778 France bade defiance to Britain by recognizing the independence of the colonies. France then concluded a commercial treaty with the United States, and a treaty of alliance. These steps, of course, took France into the war.

After that, Vergennes stepped up his aid. Besides the subsidies (which were continued), the United States was allowed to borrow from the French Treasury. Altogether, the gifts and loans amounted to about $8,000,000, a substantial sum for eighteenth-century warfare. In addition, the Versailles court established American credit in the Netherlands, then Europe's chief financial center. That is, France guaranteed principal and interest on the first loan which the Americans obtained from private Dutch bankers. The hard-headed financiers who extended these credits did so for profit, not for diplomatic or ideological reasons. Investing in revolution was risky; but it was not so bad if France stood sponsor.

French fighting forces also went into the balance. Potentially, that meant a great deal, for France was the most populous of European nations and maintained a vast military establishment. But, being a continental power, she concentrated on land armament, which in the American Revolution was less useful than Britain's strength on the sea. Still, the very fact that France was in the fight kept the British from concentrating on campaigns in America. Moreover, Britain did not yet have the naval supremacy which would come in the days of Lord Nelson. French fleets operated along the Atlantic coast each year after 1778, and French sea power counted heavily against the British in the Yorktown campaign of 1781.

To be effective, allies must coöperate. Yet the French and Americans were separated by distance, language, and tradition. As a powerful monarchy, France was disinclined to treat the struggling American republic as an equal; and Americans, in turn, did not like to be regarded as inferiors. It is small wonder that there was bungling in the first joint operations—an attack on Newport, Rhode Island, in 1778, and the siege of Savannah, Georgia, the next year. Rather more surprising is the fact that coöperation was finally achieved. In the last important action of the war, at Yorktown in 1781, British General Cornwallis was defeated by a combination of three opposing units. One was the French fleet of de Grasse, another Rochambeau's French army, the third an American force under Washington.

France also persuaded Spain to come into the war. Like their French relatives, the Spanish Bourbons cared little for the ideas of the American insurrectionists. Indeed, the Spanish court shuddered to think of an independent United States, a living illustration of democratic and revolutionary principles. Such a republic might provide a model for Spain's American possessions, where the Bourbons had noted restlessness. But Spain, too, wished to humble England; and she had hopes of recapturing from the British that key to the Mediterranean, the Rock of Gibraltar. In consequence, Spain joined France against Great Britain during 1779. This meant taking sides with the United States. The Spanish, however, refused to recognize the Americans as full-fledged allies.

One other nation was drawn into the war. Dutch traders had sold supplies to the United States, via the Dutch West Indies. As long as the Netherlands stayed neutral, it was difficult for the English Navy to stamp out this traffic. Britain therefore chose to force the Dutch into the war (1780), after which she clamped down on Netherlands-American commerce.

Revolutionary Diplomacy

As the conflict broadened, European viewed it as an Old World rather than an American war. To Vergennes, the whole thing was a phase of the century-old struggle for power, France against

Great Britain, as it had been in the days of Louis XIV, as it would be on into the age of the French Revolution and Napoleon. The rebels in America were pawns in the contest.

Americans weighed the conflict on a different scale. Their concern was with the Western Hemisphere; their aims were those set forth by Paine and Jefferson. They fought for political and economic independence, for human dignity and human rights, for liberty, self-government, and the opportunity to fashion their own futures.

Had they been strong enough, the Patriots might have desired to fight without outside help. Certainly they neither loved nor understood their Bourbon allies. Through the years there had been little cultural or commercial intercourse between the thirteen colonies and France or Spain. Americans had disliked and feared these monarchies as England's foes, as their own opponents in fights for fisheries, the fur trade, and lands of the interior. To Protestant Americans, Catholic France and Spain constituted a religious menace; and to many colonists, the Bourbon courts stood for all that was immoral, frivolous, and cruel. One cause for distrust had been removed in 1763, when France had withdrawn from the North American mainland. But doubts remained; and only the necessities of war could drive the colonies to line up with France and Spain. It was a marriage of convenience which the Continental Congress sought in 1776, when it set up a Committee on Secret Correspondence and dispatched its first diplomatic agents to the European continent.

Normally a country designates one envoy for each foreign capital. Congress, however, sent a commission of three to Paris: Silas Deane, a Connecticut merchant-politician; the celebrated Pennsylvanian, Benjamin Franklin; and Arthur Lee, a member of one of Virginia's distinguished families. Better three, the Congressmen decided; what with Franklin's age and the uncertainties of wartime travel, one or two might not reach France. And, since Americans were not yet well united, one was taken from New England, another from the middle states, a third from the South.

Despite quarrels among themselves, the commissioners accomplished a good deal. Deane, first on the ground, made the basic arrangements for French secret aid. Lee worked hard and faithfully; and Franklin, now past seventy, was exceedingly effective, turning the French court's interest in America into enthusiasm. Part of the secret was in Franklin's wit and charm. Besides that, the French courtiers liked celebrities, and Franklin was the best-known American of his day. He had a reputation in science and philosophy, two fields popular in eighteenth-century Versailles. It was important, too, that Franklin's was a homespun philosophy, that he came from the home of simplicity-loving Quakers and was a native of America, which Frenchmen classified as a wilderness. Although Bourbon society was artificial, French aristocrats were excited over the noble-savage concept, the idea that civilization was corrupting while nature and simplicity were good. Franklin fitted into that framework; and to drive home the point, he sometimes wore the fur cap of the frontiersman. Out of that would come the legend that Benjamin Franklin was a diplomat in rags. Actually, he lived so well in Paris as to shock plain John Adams. The affectation of simplicity was to impress the French. Franklin used his popularity to spread American ideas. He wrote, printed, and circulated propaganda articles, even invented atrocity tales to discredit the British. France he covered personally, and, through such friends as C. W. F. Dumas, he also spread the word in the Low Countries and Germany.

Most Americans approved of Franklin's work and of the treaties he and his colleagues signed in 1778. News of these treaties reached the United States as the Patriots were emerging from a winter of hardships—the winter in which Washington had camped at Valley Forge. In the light of that experience, Americans were overjoyed to learn that they need no longer stand alone. The Continental Congress, after giving unanimous approval to the French treaties, spurned British compromise proposals. Gifts of terrapin and liquor sent to Congress by an English peace commission were served to Conrad Alexandre Gérard, the first French minister to the United States.

Even so, Americans were not altogether pleased. The treaties of 1778 created an "entangling alliance." In return for French aid, the United States agreed to help defend the French West Indies, and not to make a separate peace with Britain. Might this mean that the colonies had left their mother country only to be tied to France? Was it not likely that France would sacrifice the interests of the United States for the benefit of her other ally, Spain?

Making Peace with Britain

Fears such as these led the Americans to violate their agreement with the French and negotiate a separate peace with Britain. After Yorktown, the ministers of George III were ready to grant independence to their former colonies. They preferred, however, to deal with the United States directly, rather than through France. To this the American peace commission agreed.

The American commissioners had been named in 1781. In choosing them, Congress had again taken note of sectional interests. The New England appointee was John Adams, who had handled negotiations with the Dutch bankers. Franklin was picked from the middle states, as was John Jay, a New Yorker who had represented the United States in Spain. Two

Southerners were added, a Virginian, Jefferson, and Henry Laurens of South Carolina. As it turned out, the South was not well represented, for Jefferson refused to serve, and Laurens was captured by the British and imprisoned in the Tower of London. This left Franklin, Jay, and Adams, all of whom were told to work with France. Franklin was inclined to do just that, but was overruled by his younger colleagues. Jay had been snubbed in Spain and distrusted all Bourbon agents; Adams, suspicious by nature, also questioned French motives. Hence the American commissioners, ignoring instructions, reached a separate agreement with British agents in Paris during the fall of 1782. This became a formal treaty the next year, when Britain liquidated her contests with France, Spain, and the Netherlands.

In the peace treaty, England recognized her former colonies as "free Sovereign and independent." The boundaries of the new republic would extend from the Atlantic to the Mississippi, from the Great Lakes to the northern boundary of Florida (which England now returned to Spain). The United States was conceded certain privileges in the North Atlantic fisheries, and British subjects were to share with Americans the right to navigate the Mississippi. In evacuating areas still occupied, the English armies would restore captured property; and the Americans agreed not to repudiate private obligations, such as the old debts owed to London merchants. The settlement all but ignored the claims of Britain's Indian allies and white Loyalists, although it was agreed that Congess would "earnestly recommend" that state legislatures treat the Tories fairly.

While deploring the independent spirit of her New World ally, France was moderately satisfied. The government of Louis XVI had gained prestige at the expense of Britain. In the process, it had strained Bourbon credit, paving the way for the French Revolution; but few anticipated that in 1783. In Great Britain the peace settlement was so unpopular as to cause a ministry to fall. Yet the English had done rather well. To be sure, they had lost thirteen colonies; but they had retained Gibraltar and escaped a general catastrophe. Moreover, with fighting over, London businessmen could bid for their old trade with the former British colonies.

But the United States had gained the most. In less than a decade the Americans had humbled the mighty British Empire and had won the right to rule themselves. And, though they had needed foreign aid, they had managed to throw off the British yoke without yielding to French control.

The Internal Revolution

The American Revolution was a revolt against Great Britain. It was also a struggle within the colonies. Sailors, shopkeepers, artisans, small farmers, and frontiersmen had complaints against the lordly merchants and the great mansion people. Since many of these aristocrats opposed independence, the upstart patriots could pay off old scores.

The privileges which the aristocracy enjoyed were bitterly condemned by the rank and file. Titles were especially unpopular. Demanding religious liberty, the plain people of the South attacked the established Anglican Church, which they were forced to support and which was largely identified with the aristocracy. There and elsewhere there was grumbling about property qualifications for voting and officeholding, and about the under-representation of western districts. But above all, ordinary citizens wanted the desirable lands so often monopolized by the gentry, by absentee speculators, or by the Crown.

The Patriots or Whigs included many men of wealth, notably merchants and planters hostile to British trade and land policies. But many rich Americans chose the other side. The Loyalists or Tories claimed thousands of royal officials, substantial merchants, landed men, and professional leaders. These persons felt deep and genuine loyalty for the Crown and the empire. They also felt that they, as American aristocrats, should rule in the New World. They expressed horror at the leveling tendencies of the Patriot leaders. Peggy Hutchinson, daughter of the Loyalist governor of Massachusetts, spoke bitterly of the "dirty mob" about her as she rode in the family carriage through Boston. Jonathan Boucher of Maryland, an Anglican clergyman, fortified his pulpit with pistols as he preached the divine duty of submission to royal authority and knocked down a commoner who was about to lay hands on him.

Nothing daunted, the Patriots defined a Loyalist as "a thing whose head is in England, whose body is in America, and [whose] neck ought to be stretched." In regions where Patriot authority replaced British rule, Loyalists saw their estates confiscated, the right to practice their professions gone, their lives made miserable. Sometimes Tories were tarred and feathered and otherwise manhandled. Often they were driven into exile, to the West Indies, to England, to Canada—"to hell, Hull, or Halifax," as the Patriots put it. Nearly a hundred thousand Loyalists fled.

The exodus deprived America of gifted men as well as stiff-necked officials and arrogant aristocrats. Yet the loss of the Loyalists was a gain for American democracy. After the departure of the Tories it was harder for those who set stock in birth and inherited position to have things their own way. Attainments, success, accumulated wealth figured more prominently in the new scale of values. The middle and even the lower classes were free to create a civilization patterned after their own standards. Assertiveness and self-reliance would replace decorum and *noblesse oblige* in the new order launched by the Revolution.

Democratic Gains

In drawing up new state constitutions, or (in Connecticut and Rhode Island) in revamping the old colonial charters, Americans stuck close to the model of government familiar to them. Even so, the democratic impulse was apparent, especially in constitutions written in the first phases of the Revolution. Several of these documents specified the rights of man which state governments were forbidden to violate. Virtually all provided for amendments, so that the constitutions might keep pace with the changing views of the people. The first constitutions were drawn up by the regular provincial assemblies, but Delaware broke new ground in 1776 by having the voters elect a special constitutional convention. Four years later Massachusetts moved further in the direction of popular sovereignty by submitting her constitution to the voters for approval or rejection.

Experience with royal governors had made Americans suspicious of executive power. As a consequence, the state constitution makers vested chief power in the legislative assemblies. Under many early constitutions, the governor was chosen by the legislators. Later, Massachusetts, New York, and then others had the governor elected by the people. Popular selection, however, did not end distrust of the executive. His powers remained limited and he was elected for a short term, often a single year. Also designed to protect the people were checks and balances, by which one branch of the government could curb undue exercise of power by another.

Democratic aims in officeholding and suffrage were not realized. In three states (the Carolinas and New Jersey) only Protestants could be elected to the legislature. Delaware, Pennsylvania, Massachusetts, and Maryland also continued religious disqualifications for officeholding. Four states restricted voting to landowners. The other nine had property qualifications, too, but counted personal as well as real property. Thus the bottom level of society was still denied the franchise. In some states, however, the amount of property needed for voting was scaled down. Most important of all, thousands for the first time in their lives took an active part in political discussions, voting if they could and demanding the right to vote if that was still denied them.

Meanwhile, democratic forces were at work on the land question. The feudal customs of bequeathing land only to the eldest son (primogeniture) and of preventing the alienation of estates from the family (entail) never took root in New England, and made only limited headway elsewhere in the colonies. In the eighteenth century, however, the growing family pride of the Virginia and Carolina gentry threatened to give these undemocratic devices a new lease on life. But Thomas Jefferson and other Revolutionary leaders refused to budge from their conviction that primogeniture and entail did not square with the natural rights of man. Against brisk opposition, Jefferson carried through the Virginia legislature an act abolishing entail (1776); and he prepared the ground for sweeping away primogeniture in 1785.

Within a decade and a half after the Declaration of Independence, primogeniture and entail had been eliminated everywhere in the United States. The democratic forces which effected these reforms also laid to rest the quitrent system. Though small (an English penny or less per acre), quitrents had always been resented and had often been dodged. Still, the Crown and the proprietors were collecting almost $100,000 a year in quitrents on the eve of the American Revolution. The new state constitutions ended that, removing another feudal practice.

At the same time, lands were opened. The king's forests—reserved for the Royal Navy—and other Crown holdings were taken over by the states. In Maryland and Pennsylvania, the Patriot governments obtained title to the vast possessions of the proprietors. The Revolution also removed the checks imposed by the Proclamation Line of 1763 and the Quebec Act, thus opening the lands beyond the Appalachians to speculators and settlers. Simultaneously, the states were confiscating Tory estates, from Loyalist properties in Georgia to Sir William Pepperell's immense preserves in Maine.

It would be easy to overestimate the equalitarian effects of these changes. Some New York manors continued to operate for decades on the basis of timeworn feudal tenure. Large landowners and speculators who chose the Patriot side retained their holdings and supplemented them by buying confiscated land. Nevertheless, humble Americans made real gains. Lands taken from the Loyalist James De Lancey, for instance, went to 275 persons. The significance of this is the more apparent when it is recalled that suffrage was tied to landownership. Economic and political democracy, in short, went forward hand in hand.

Separation of Church and State

Except in Virginia (where they numbered perhaps half the population) the Anglicans were in a definite minority throughout the colonies. Yet in four counties of New York, and in all the southern colonies, the Church of England was established as the official faith. This meant inconvenience and injustice for dissenters, who were taxed for the support of Anglican clergymen and churches. Dissenters also had to pay marriage fees to the established ministry, even when parsons of their own faith performed the ceremony. The pill was the more bitter because of the aristocratic airs of many Anglican clergymen, and their apparent lack of religious zeal.

The Revolution introduced one more factor, a decisive one. In the Tory-Patriot line-up, most Anglican clergymen chose the king's side; and, save in North Carolina, most Loyalists were Anglicans. Dissenters were quick to take advantage of this opportunity, and to demand that the states strip the Church of England of its privileges. As early as October, 1776, Presbyterians from the uplands of Virginia were petitioning for the end of "religious as well as civil bondage."

These Virginia dissenters had the support of Thomas Jefferson, James Madison, and other Revolutionary leaders who were nominally Anglican, but who had been influenced by deism and the related doctrine that religion was an affair of private conscience and no concern of the state. The principle of religious liberty was announced in Virginia's Declaration of Rights of 1776. Three years later the Anglicans (now called Episcopalians) lost their privileged position in the state.

Some Virginians now felt that all denominations should receive state aid. Others, including Jefferson, maintained that the government should support no church at all. In the end, his view prevailed. In 1786, when Jefferson was in Europe, Madison and others pushed the Statute of Religious Liberty through the Virginia legislature. The purpose of this law was clearly stated:

"No man shall be compelled to frequent or support any religious worship, place or ministry whatsoever, nor shall he be enforced, restrained, molested, or . . . otherwise suffer on account of his religious opinions or belief."

Outside of Virginia, the Church of England had real strength only in South Carolina. It was easy, therefore, for Patriots to take away Anglican privileges. Before the end of the Revolution the United States had no established church except in New England. The Anglican Church (renamed Protestant Episcopal in the United States) continued to function, but without government support.

The divorce of church from state was not achieved so quickly in Massachusetts, Connecticut and New Hampshire. There the established church was the Congregational, which had wide popular support and which, in general, lined up with the Revolutionary cause. Separation was not effected until 1817 (New Hampshire), 1818 (Connecticut), and 1833 (Massachusetts). Dissenting groups, however, won substantial concessions during the Revolutionary era.

Complete separation of church and state, inaugurated in colonial Rhode

Island and Pennsylvania, and generally realized in the Revolution, ranks as one of the notable American contributions to the modern world. Separation might have come in the late eighteenth century without the Revolution. This, however, is by no means certain; and, in any case, the war for American independence speeded up the process.

The Slavery Question

Among the inconsistencies between the Revolutionary philosophy of the rights of man and the actualities of American life, none was more striking than the existence of slavery. Many of the more democratic Patriot leaders called attention to this fact; and not a few slaveowners freed their Negroes, saying that slavery violated the natural rights of man.

Denunciations came from every section. In 1773 Patrick Henry of Virginia called human bondage "as repugnant to humanity as it is inconsistent with the Bible and destructive to liberty." The following year the town meeting of Providence, Rhode Island, resolved that American doctrines of natural rights and personal liberty pointed to emancipation. Georgians declared that continuing slavery would set "that liberty we contend for upon a very wrong foundation." And in 1775, five days before the battle of Lexington, Philadelphia Quakers organized the first antislavery society in the world, announcing that emancipation was a duty incumbent on all Christians, especially at a time when Americans were concerned about liberty and justice.

During the Revolution state legislatures (and, for a time, the Continental Congress) prohibited importation of slaves. In doing so, Patriots announced that Britain, not America, was the protector of the slave trade. Then a Pennsylvania law of 1780 provided that children of slaves born thereafter could not be held in bondage after their twenty-eighth year. Connecticut, Rhode Island, and other states also adopted gradual emancipation schemes, and Virginia made voluntary emancipation easier than before. Slavery was wiped out altogether in Massachusetts when the Superior Court held that the institution had been invalidated by the state constitution of 1780, which said that "all men are born free and equal."

Prison Reform

Though severe, the criminal codes of the colonies had always been less harsh than those of England. On the eve of the American Revolution, England punished two hundred crimes with death, while in no colony did the number exceed twenty. There were further advances during the Revolution. The Pennsylvania constitution of

1776 instructed the legislature to humanize the criminal code, and this state soon limited capital punishment to those convicted of murder. In Virginia, where Jefferson led a movement for penal reform, murder and treason were the only crimes punishable by death. Meantime, four states modified the laws which put poor debtors into prison.

Varied forces made possible these reforms. In the colonial era, executions were few because of the shortage of man power and the conviction that the New World was an asylum for the unfortunate. Later, Americans like Jefferson and Dr. Benjamin Rush were influenced by the writings of Montesquieu and Beccaria, Europeans who argued that punishment should be graded in relation to the crime. The activities of John Howard, the English reformer, also made an impression. So did the Revolution itself. There was no longer the feeling that American law must be patterned after that of Britain. Instead, there was a conviction that one could go one's own way, following the philosophy of natural rights and the dignity of man.

In America as in Europe conditions within prisons remained extremely bad. Filth, degradation, flogging, brutality, and near-starvation prevailed. In 1787, a Philadelphia Society for Alleviating the Miseries of Public Prisons inaugurated a movement for prison reform. Legislation of 1790 provided for the segregation of the sexes and the separation of the worst offenders from those confined for minor crimes. This was a bare beginning, and outside Philadelphia even less was accomplished. But the beginning promised ultimately to remove some of the most flagrant contradictions of the principle of the dignity of human life.

The Revolution in Retrospect

In later years, Americans would recall the victories and forget the defeats of the Revolution, as they wove the conflict into the fabric of American nationalism. Fourth of July orators would minimize or ignore the value of the foreign aid received by their Revolutionary ancestors. Song and story, folklore and history books would present the war as a triumph of patriots who were as near infallibility as mortal men can be. The historian of today must note factors overlooked or distorted by the legend makers. Yet, with the myths discarded, the American Revolution remains an impressive achievement.

The Problem
of Government

The Articles of Confederation

By 1776, American Patriots were agreed that they could never again be a part of the British Empire. At the same time, it was obvious that the thirteen states needed some sort of central government to carry the mails, wage war, handle negotiations with European countries and Indian tribes. The problem was: What sort of government? Weak or strong? Should power be left largely with the states, or should the central government have real authority?

At first, the Continental Congress took charge informally. The necessities of war gave Congressional decisions popular support, and the state governments generally acted as though bound by what Congress had done. But Americans, who were accustomed to written charters, would in time want a definite statement of the powers of the central government. Realizing this, the Continental Congress, in June, 1776, set up a committee to draft articles for a central government.

This committee, headed by John Dickinson, reported the next month. Then Congress debated the matter for more than a year, taking it up whenever there was time to spare from the work of prosecuting the war. The discussions revealed a sharp division between radicals and conservatives. Many conservatives were men of property—leading merchants and large landowners. These people desired a strong central government, one that could maintain order and protect property. Radicals were inclined to oppose a strong central government. Although some of them were men of wealth, the radicals often spoke for the artisans and small farmers, who distrusted any central government, be it British or American. They figured that they might be able to control state legislatures, which were near home. Since they would have less influence at a distance, a central government would probably be controlled by the well-to-do; and it might, therefore, become an agency of tyranny.

106

John Dickinson being a conservative, his draft of July, 1776, leaned toward the strong-central-government view. But the radicals prevailed, and in September, 1777, Congress approved the Articles of Confederation, which called for a weak central government. Accepted by all the states, the Articles went into effect in March, 1781. By then, however, the advocates of a strong central government were gaining ground. Failing in efforts to amend the Articles of Confederation, these conservatives brought about the Philadelphia convention of 1787, and in 1789 the Articles gave way to the new Constitution. Adoption of the Constitution was a substantial defeat for the states'-rights people; but they fought on within the framework of the Constitution.

The western land question, which involved the Proclamation Line of 1763, had helped produce the Revolution; and after independence, it plagued the new republic. Disputes over land delayed the adoption of the Articles of Confederation, which were approved by Congress late in 1777 but did not go into effect until more than three years later.

By the peace treaty with Britain, the United States controlled territory west to the Mississippi River. There were few white settlers beyond the Appalachians, the American people being concentrated along the Atlantic coast. Yet each part of the West was claimed by one or more of the states. Claims rested chiefly on colonial charters, which were vague and contradictory. In consequence, there were many overlapping claims. Besides this source of irritation, there was bad feeling between the seven states which claimed western areas (Massachusetts, Connecticut, New York, Virginia, the Carolinas, and Georgia) and the six with no such claims.

Being at a disadvantage, the "landless" states wanted to wipe out all claims and have western lands controlled by Congress. The more favored states objected. Virginia, which had the largest claims of all, led the resistance. Maryland presented the opposition view with vigor and refused to ratify the Articles of Confederation until she had satisfaction. Since acceptance of the Articles depended on approval of all the states, this stand could not be ignored. Eventually, Maryland won her point. New York broke the deadlock by offering to give up her western claims, which were weak anyway. States with stronger claims followed suit, and Maryland allowed the Articles to go into effect in 1781.

It took two decades to carry out the land-cession policy. Many western claims were ceded to Congress in the 1780's. But North Carolina held Tennessee until 1790. Virginia early surrendered her claims north of the Ohio but retained Kentucky down to 1792. Connecticut clung to one Ohio district, the Western Reserve, until 1800, and Georgia held out even longer, yielding her western claims in 1802.

Government Under the Articles (1781–89)

By satisfying Maryland, the land-cession policy saved the Articles of Confederation. It also contributed substantially to the centralization of political power; for the United States now controlled more land than any state. The cessions thus made it possible to consider the problems of the West on a broad basis, and to apply a single set of policies to the whole frontier. This became apparent during the years when the Articles of Confederation were in effect (1781–89), notably in the passage of the Survey Bill of 1785 and the Northwest Ordinance of 1787.

The Articles created a league of states rather than a true national government. Except in admiralty cases arising on the high seas, the central government had no direct contact with the citizen; contact was indirect, through the state governments. There was no national judicial system, save for special commissions which could be set up when states desired to settle a dispute between themselves. The so-called President of the United States in Congress Assembled was a figurehead without powers, while limited executive functions were divided among four departmental secretaries responsible to Congress. As for Congress, it represented the states, not the people, and lacked the power to levy taxes or fix tariff duties. The government of the United States depended largely on the state legislatures for funds; and the Articles specifically endorsed the theory of states' rights: "Each state retains its sovereignty, freedom, and independence, and every power, jurisdiction, and right, which is not by this Confederation expressly delegated to the United States, in Congress assembled."

The central government, though, was far from powerless. Congress had the right to raise an army and navy, make treaties and wage war, strike coins, borrow, issue paper money, run the posts, regulate weights and measures, and govern territories.

During the Confederation era the United States made commercial treaties with several European countries. More important, however, was Congressional control of the territories. Here, in the sale of land, was a source of revenue, the more important because Congress could not raise money by taxation or tariff legislation. Here also was an opportunity to shape the destinies of later generations.

Among other things, Congress transferred millions of acres of Ohio land to companies planning large-scale development of the West. But these special acts had less importance than two laws which set a general pattern for the future. One of these, the Survey Bill or Land Ordinance of 1785, set up a rectangular survey system which would eventually cover most of the

United States. Operating from key North-South (principal meridian) and East-West (base) lines, surveyors were to divide western lands into townships thirty-six square miles in size. The township was then to be split into sections, each one mile square, containing 640 acres. The act also stated conditions for the sale of public lands; and it provided that Section 16 of each township should be "reserved . . . for the maintenance of the public schools."

Two years later Congress adopted the Northwest Ordinance, which was based in part on an earlier ordinance prepared by Thomas Jefferson. Though hurriedly passed by a handful of delegates, the Northwest Ordinance was no stopgap measure. It was a law designed by practical men who understood the governmental needs of a pioneer community. The ordinance applied to the Old Northwest—the American territory north of the Ohio River, comprising the present states of Ohio, Indiana, Illinois, Michigan, Wisconsin, and part of Minnesota. It worked so well that many of its features were incorporated in later territorial legislation.

The Northwest Ordinance carried over the colonial concept of the "rights of Englishmen," as modified by the reforms of the Revolution. It thus anticipated the Bill of Rights, later incorporated in the Constitution. Specifically, the Northwest Ordinance guaranteed freedom of religion, did away with primogeniture, and defined the individual's rights in court. The act further stated that Indians should be treated fairly and that education should be encouraged and slavery barred from the territory.

The ordinance also provided two stages of territorial government. In the first or pioneer stage, all governmental functions were to be exercised by a governor and three judges selected by and responsible to Congress. When the adult male population reached 5000, this outside rule would give way to limited democracy. During this second stage of territorial government male landowners resident in the territory would elect the lower house of a territorial legislature. This assembly in turn would prepare a list of ten names, from which Congress would choose five for a combined governor's council and upper house. The lower house had the traditional power to initiate revenue legislation, but all laws were subject to veto by the governor (a Congressional appointee), or by Congress itself.

The second stage of territorial government closely approximated the British colonial system as it had functioned in the North American colonies. In both cases the effort was to keep strict imperial control over colonial areas while allowing the colonial people limited self-government. In Britain's case the plan had failed. On the American scene it worked, largely because the Northwest Ordinance provided that territories could in time throw off colonial status and become states of the Union "on an equal footing with the original States in all respects." The transition to statehood could come when the population of a territorial region reached 60,000, and when the people of the territory drew up a constitution acceptable to Congress.

The Strong-Government Campaign

The partial repudiation of Continental and state paper currency caused a sharp drop in price levels after the Revolution. As a result, many farmers found themselves holding mortgages contracted at high valuations. Merchants suffered because they had stocked their shelves at high prices, and rising industrialists were ruined by the competition of lower-priced English goods. Excluded from trade with British North America and the British West Indies, American shipowners found themselves further handicapped because their vessels were no longer protected by the British Navy.

Such maladjustment could only temporarily depress an expanding agricultural economy like that of the United States; and by 1786 the commercial situation was improving. But by then difficulties connected with the depression had produced a strong conservative movement against the inadequacies of the powers of the central government under the Articles of Confederation.

From the Revolutionary years on, conservative property holders consistently deplored the combination of relatively democratic state constitutions and a weak central government lacking authority over the individual. Edmund Randolph said that no state constitution "provided sufficient checks against the democracy." George Washington added that the central government should be strengthened. "Men will not adopt and carry into execution measures the best calculated for their own good," said the General, "without the intervention of a coercive power."

In their desire for a stronger central government, the conservative landowners were joined by the holders of public securities, who wanted a national administration strong enough to raise money for repayment of the national debt. There were also patriotic nationalists who wished to see the United States strong enough to play a larger role in international affairs. Many leaders in the movement for a stronger central government combined all three of these interests.

Those who wanted to increase the power of the central government at first concentrated on proposals to empower Congress to collect 5 percent duties on imports, or to regulate trade in general. Under the amending clause of the Articles of Confederation, such measures required approval by the legislatures of all thirteen states; and unanimous consent could not be obtained. Bondholders, importers, and exporters wanted these amendments. The farmers, who made up three-quarters of the population, were indifferent or hostile. The agrarian who lived largely within the circle of his local community remained suspicious of a centralization of government authority. It was evident, too, that a national tariff would cut into state tariff revenues. In commercial states like Massachusetts, Rhode Island, and New York, these local tariffs yielded much of the income of the state governments. Reduction of that income would mean an increase in the property tax, which would directly affect the farmer.

When it became apparent that the proposed amendments had little chance, advocates of a strong central government called a special congress —thus following the strategy used by the Americans who brought about the Revolution. James Madison and others set things in motion by persuading the Virginia legislature to invite the states to send delegates to a tariff convention at Annapolis, Maryland, in September, 1786. The meeting provided no solution, for delegates appeared from only five states. But Alexander Hamilton of New York persuaded his fellow delegates to call a new convention. This was to meet in Philadelphia in May, 1787, to consider the current emergency and render the Articles of Confederation "adequate to the exigencies of the Union."

The demand for a stronger central government grew in the months between the Annapolis and the Philadelphia conventions. Massachusetts debtor farmers rose in rebellion; and their forces, under Revolutionary veteran Daniel Shays, had to be dispersed by the state militia. Congressional finances went from bad to worse. The United States lacked specie even to pay interest on its foreign and domestic debt. "We . . . have reached almost the last stage of national humiliation . . . ," said Alexander Hamilton. "The frail and tottering edifice seems ready to fall upon our heads and crush us beneath its ruins." Such was the mood of conservatives when the Philadelphia convention met and prepared a Constitution to replace the Articles of Confederation.

The Constitutional Convention (1787)

Assembling in spring, the Constitutional Convention ran through the summer of 1787. It was a noteworthy gathering. From the lower South came two Pinckneys. Virginia sent George Washington and James Madison. Venerable Benjamin Franklin represented Pennsylvania, as did James Wilson and Robert and Gouverneur Morris. New York sent Alexander Hamilton; the New England delegation included Roger Sherman and Elbridge Gerry.

Debates were often heated. Yet agreements were more basic than disgreements. Most of those present were college educated; nearly all were members of the upper classes. The artisans and poor farmers, debtors and the common people generally were represented only by the able and erratic Luther Martin of Maryland. There were many wealthy planters, many representatives of mercantile and speculating interests. These groups did not always work together; but they were on common ground in believing that a stronger central government was needed to protect the things they held most dear. They were further agreed that in such a government, control should be lodged with the upper classes. Though they had fought the British to gain freedom, they now put more stress on order than on liberty. Seeing danger in an "excess of democracy," they favored restricting the "turbulent" masses in the interests of property. Otherwise, they felt, there would be a rule of anarchy which might spell doom for the republic.

It was expected that the Philadelphia convention would suggest amendments to the Articles of Confederation. The delegates, however, decided to wipe the slate clean and prepare a new constitution. In making this decision, the members went beyond their instructions. But they felt this action necessary. Efforts to amend the Articles had failed because changes required the assent of all thirteen state legislatures. The Constitution, by contrast, was to become effective when ratifying conventions in nine states had indicated their approval.

A National Government

The new Constitution gave the government of the United States all the authority it had possessed under the Articles of Confederation. In addition, the central government was to have commercial and taxation powers. Neither grant was unrestricted. Congress was denied jurisdiction over trade inside a state (intrastate commerce), and was prohibited from interfering with the importation of slaves for twenty years. Taxes on exports were forbidden, and other taxes had to be uniform throughout the country. But even with these limitations, the United States government could now regulate interstate and foreign commerce and, having good sources of revenue, need no longer beg money from state treasuries. Nor did it stop with that. The delegates at Philadelphia also authorized Congress to "provide for the . . . general Welfare." Through the years, this clause would make possible many extensions of the power of the federal government.

Further to increase national power, the Constitution imposed restrictions on the states. Under the Articles of Confederation, the states had not been allowed to make treaties. They were now also denied the right to regulate interstate and foreign commerce and were prohibited from issuing paper money and impairing obligations of contract.

During the Confederation era all functions of the national government had been controlled by Congress, in which the members represented states. Under the Constitution, Congress retained legislative authority but was stripped of executive and judicial powers. The President and other executive officers represented not one, but all the states; and the judges of the Supreme Court and other federal tribunals spoke for the nation rather than for any section or locality. Moreover, these enforcement agencies could carry the will of the national government into any local area. All state officials were required to swear to uphold the Constitution, which, with the nation's laws and treaties, became the "Supreme Law of the land." United States courts could thus review the acts of state courts and legislatures, and declare invalid laws and decisions which were out of line. And behind the judges was the President, who could assert national authority by using the army and navy and, if necessary, by calling out the state militia.

The upper classes stood to gain by this strengthening of the central government. Many of the well-to-do held United States securities, items worth little when the national treasury was empty, but worth a good deal if the United States had an adequate income. The wealthier groups included speculators in western lands, which would appreciate in value if the national government was strong enough to control Indians. Businessmen were glad to see a uniform tariff and a national currency replacing the confusing and conflicting state systems; and the "better people" were also comforted to think that national authority could aid in putting down slave insurrections and such debtor uprisings as that of Daniel Shays. Besides, a stronger national administration would have prestige abroad, which would mean less danger and more commerce.

A Conservative Government

While strengthening the national government, the delegates at Philadelphia also gave attention to the question of control. The Constitution withdrew paper money powers from the states, to prevent debtor-dominated legislatures from creating inflation. But to make the creditor policy effective, it was necessary to make sure that the United States government would not be controlled by inflationists and other "popular" groups. The Philadelphia convention therefore adopted devices calculated to insure upper-class control of Congress, the presidency, and federal courts.

The members of one body of Congress, the House of Representatives, were to be popularly elected, for a relatively short (two-year) term. But the other chamber, the Senate, was set up for conservative control. Being chosen by state legislatures, the Senators were one step removed from popular election. They served long terms, six years, and, since terms were staggered, there could be only a one-third turnover at any time. On the theory that men grew conservative with age, membership in the Senate was restricted to those over thirty (five years above the House requirement). Here, then, was a legislative body in which the upper classes could have confidence. And it will be noted that the Constitution gave the Senate important powers not shared by the House of Representatives—the right to pass on treaties and executive appointments, and to try impeachment cases.

An age rule was also used for the presidency, the Constitution stipulating that no person less than thirty-five years old could become Chief Executive. As a further guarantee that a "safe" man would be chosen, the office was limited to the native-born and those who were citizens at the time of the adoption of the Constitution. Nor were the people allowed to pick the President. Ordinary voters cast their ballots for electors, who in turn chose the Chief Executive. If no candidate had a majority in the electoral college, the House of Representatives, voting by states, would select a winner from the three leading candidates.

The constitution makers felt they could rely on an official so elected. They therefore gave the President what was then considered a long term. In those days, most states had annual elections for governor, but the presidential term was four years, and there was no rule against reëlection. Then, too, the powers of the President were broad. His was the administrative authority, large in normal times, larger during emergencies. Subject to Senate approval, he could make treaties and appoint executive and judicial officers. He was expected to recommend legislative programs to Congress and could veto bills passed by the two chambers, a two-thirds vote in each house being required to override a veto.

The Philadelphia convention of 1787 planned to have the average voter figure only indirectly in the selection of the President and United States Senators. Even this measure of popular participation was eliminated for the judiciary. Supreme Court justices were named by the President, and when the Senate had approved of the appointment, the judge was in for life. Thus fixed, he need not yield to popular pressures; and it was expected that the national judiciary would join the upper classes in opposing forces dangerous to property and order.

Being in favor of a strong judiciary, those who prepared the Constitution naturally approved of judicial review. According to this doctrine the Supreme Court could weigh the constitutionality of state and national laws and could render inoperative laws it held to be in conflict with the Constitution. No such right was specifically assigned to the justices in the Constitution of 1787; but the definition of judicial powers was sufficiently broad to enable the Supreme Court to use the doctrine of judicial review later.

The members of the Philadelphia convention seem to have felt that the Supreme Court, the President, and Congress would look after the interests of the propertied classes. But, lest there be doubt, they included in the Constitution specific points designed to protect the property and rights of established citizens. National debts contracted before the adoption of the new Constitution were stated to be valid. Ex post facto laws were forbidden. The states were not allowed to disturb the sanctity of contracts, nor could they declare anything other than gold and silver to be legal tender. The United States was pledged to see that each state had and retained a republican form of government, and was pledged further to protect the states against "domestic violence." The delegates had this point of internal rebellion so much in mind that they offered national aid when a legislature asked for assistance, or (if the legislature could not be convened) on the call of the state governor.

Some constitution makers wanted to go further still in creating a national government for the benefit of the upper classes. Alexander Hamilton wanted life terms for Senators as well as for federal judges. Gouverneur Morris maintained that established seaboard interests would be better protected if western regions were forever denied statehood. These views, however, were rejected by the delegates.

Compromises of the Constitution

Agreed on the basic issue of strengthening the central government, the members of the Philadelphia convention disagreed on lesser issues. One controversy saw delegates from the centers of population lined up against representatives from less well-populated areas. The latter favored a Paterson or New Jersey plan, which followed the Articles of Confederation, giving each state an equal voice in the national government. Larger states preferred the Randolph or Virginia plan, which based representation on population and thus gave the chief influence to heavily peopled regions. A compromise set up the Senate on the small state model (two Senators from each state), whereas representation for the House would follow population trends.

More significant than the large state–small state split was the sectional division between North and South. In 1787 differences were not as sharp as they would be in days to come, for slavery still existed in most northern states, and cotton did not yet dominate the southern economy. But there were many more slaves in the South than in the North. Southerners, therefore, desired to have the slaves counted as full persons in calculating the number of Congressmen the South would have in the national House of Representatives. Yet when it came to taxes assessed according to population, the South wanted the slaves disregarded. Northern members of the convention took the other side both times. Eventually an illogical but mutually satisfactory compromise was reached, under which each slave was counted as three-fifths of a free man for both tax and representation purposes.

There was another compromise on the foreign slave trade. Here Southerners were divided among themselves. New plantation areas, like Georgia, wanted the right to import Negroes from abroad. Virginia and other regions already developed did not need the outside supply. In fact, they had a surplus of slaves each generation, which surplus was sold to newly opened plantation districts. And, clearly, this surplus would bring a higher price if no Negroes were brought in from overseas. The result was a provision that Congress could not bar the foreign slave trade until twenty years after the adoption of the Constitution.

If slaves were counted, the southern states had a population about equal to that of the North. But, under the three-fifths rule, the South would have less voice in the House of Representatives than the northern states—thirty votes at the beginning, in a total of sixty-five. The Senate, too, would have a northern majority, for of the thirteen states only six were below the Mason and Dixon line. Which meant that the North possessed the balance in the Union, and if unchecked might pass laws unfavorable to southern interests. Seeing this, the southern delegates at Philadelphia insisted on safeguards. Southern wealth came from the export of rice, sugar, and tobacco; consequently, on the insistence of Southerners, the Constitution prohibited Congress from placing taxes on exports. Nor could a northern President and a northern-dominated Senate sneak through a treaty which would hurt the South. Again on southern demand, treaties could not be ratified until they were approved by a two-thirds vote in the Senate. The South had, and seemed likely to retain, more than a third of the senatorial seats.

The Strength of British Precedent

As might have been expected, the Constitution rested on English precedents. The separation of powers (legislative, executive, judicial) could be justified by quoting from the French philosopher, Montesquieu. But it could also be supported by referring to British colonial practice. Not the practice of the home government, for separation of powers had tended to disappear in London. In the colonies, however, political functions had been divided, providing a pattern familiar to the Americans who constructed a new frame of government in 1787.

In setting up a Congress, the members of the Philadelphia convention drew on their knowledge of the colonial legislature—a bicameral body, with a popularly elected lower house and an upper house somewhat removed from the electorate. The President provided for in the new Constitution closely resembled the colonial governor. Since many governors were unpopular, the Articles of Confederation and the state constitutions of the Revolutionary era allowed the legislative branch to dominate. The members of the Philadelphia convention felt that this had worked out none too well. They therefore proposed reviving the strong executive. (Later, the states would move in this same direction.) Colonial practice was also reflected in the creation of an appointive judiciary, in the executive veto of legislative acts, in the provision that revenue bills must originate in the lower house. Moreover, colonial charters contributed the very idea of a written constitution, a device little used in Europe.

Finally, the Constitution prepared at Philadelphia marked a return to the British imperial pattern of control. Britain had allowed her colonies a measure of self-government. At the same time, she had maintained that the colonies should not have final authority, and that many problems called for an overall approach and centralized control. Reacting against this attitude, Americans had adopted the Articles of Confederation, which recognized the sovereignty and independence of each of the thirteen states. The Constitution of 1787 turned back to the earlier, British scheme. Under the Constitution, the states were to have important powers. Much of their authority, however, was transferred to the central government, which was empowered to act for the general welfare of the whole United States. Thus, as in colonial days, the local government shared responsibilities with a government of wider jurisdiction.

In copying certain British institutions, the members of the Philadelphia convention took care not to adopt all features of the British Empire. Britain was a monarchy, the United States a republic. The thirteen colonies had not been allowed to participate in the central government of the empire, whereas all thirteen states were represented in the central government of the United States. Important, too, was the fact that the colonial government had been headed up in the Old World, whereas the Constitution of 1787 established a government that was distinctly American Those who wrote the Constitution could therefore state that they had sought the order and efficiency of the British system without sacrificing the principles of nationalism, republicanism, and self-rule.

The Ratification Controversy

The friends of the Constitution could not rest when the Philadelphia convention adjourned (September, 1787). Their work still had to be reviewed by ratifying conventions in each of the thirteen states. There the opposition was certain to be serious. For, plainly, most Americans were not enthusiastic about the new Constitution. The debtor farmer, the ordinary artisan, the common folk in general could see little merit in a government that curbed inflation and gave great power to the upper classes. The centralization of authority, the creation of a strong executive suggested the British Empire and the hated George III. This was reaction, thought many average people; this was counterrevolution. So the forces gathered to oppose the work done in Philadelphia. Luther Martin gave the foes of ratification able leadership in Maryland, and in Virginia the Constitution was fought by Patrick Henry, James Monroe, Richard Henry Lee. Others in the opposition (Anti-federalists) were George Clinton of New York, Samuel Adams of Massachusetts, and Willie Jones of North Carolina.

But those who backed the Constitution won the day. They were favored by the state suffrage laws, which disenfranchised such natural opponents of the Constitution as the tenant farmers, indentured servants, and landless laborers. Another advantage was the fact that some members of the lower classes wanted a strong central government—notably, frontiersmen who needed protection against the Indians. No less important was the choice of the convention method for ratification, since delegates elected to the ratifying conventions were likely to be more prominent and wealthier (hence more conservative and favorable to the Constitution) than average voters. Astute political maneuvers enabled the advocates of the Constitution to stretch their strength still further, as when they rushed through the Pennsylvania voting before their opponents could organize. Propaganda also played a role, voters being bombarded with pamphlet and newspaper arguments in favor of the Constitution. Of this special pleading, the *Federalist* papers of Alexander Hamilton, James Madison, and John Jay are the best remembered. The words "federal" and "federalist" have reference to a government in which states' rights play an important part. Many backers of the Constitution aimed rather at a unitarian rule or a strongly centralized national government; but it was good politics to hold out hopes for those who prized local autonomy.

Even so, the Federalists could not have won without compromise. To swing such important states as Massachusetts, they agreed to add to the Constitution provisions which would benefit both states and individuals. This brought in what became the first ten amendments to the Constitution, a Bill of Rights voted by Congress immediately after the adoption of the Constitution and put into effect in 1791, after approval by the required three-quarters of the states.

The last of these ten amendments reserved to the states all powers not specifically granted to the United States. The other nine protected individuals against arbitrary action by the central government. Congress could not disturb freedom of religion, speech or press, assembly or petition. No person could be denied a fair trial or deprived of life, liberty or property without due process of law. Security of domicile and the right to bear arms were also guaranteed, and it was made clear that the enumeration of certain rights did not "deny or disparage others retained by the people."

In other words, the Antifederalists did not altogether fail. Though unable to block adoption, they changed the Constitution in the public interest. The civil liberties, protected by the Bill of Rights, are among the most important assets of Americans today. Furthermore, the Antifederalists demonstrated that the amending process could be used for democratic ends. In drawing up the Constitution, the founding fathers had carefully guarded against an "excess of democracy." Later, officials less fearful of popular rule could amend and reinterpret the Constitution so as to make the national government more democratic. The work is not yet completed, for the United States retains the clumsy electoral college and the undemocratic senatorial representation scheme (Nevada having as many Senators as New York). But much has been accomplished in the years since the Philadelphia convention. And the key accomplishment of the conservatives of 1787—the centralization of political power—has in the long run made possible the adoption of social legislation to benefit the great mass of the people.

Three states ratified the Constitution before the end of 1787, one of them being Pennsylvania, the second most populous state. Five others gave approval in as many months of the next year. Only one more was required to put the Constitution into effect; and on June 21, 1788, New Hampshire chose to ratify. Four days later a close vote brought in indispensable Virginia, which had a population almost double that of any other state. New York trailed in the next month. By then the Confederation Congress had decided to give up the ghost, and agreed that the Articles of Confederation would be replaced by the new Constitution early the next year.

When George Washington was inaugurated as President of the United

States in 1789, only eleven states had approved of the Constitution, and several of these had done so with reservations. But the new government was to endure. One holdout state, North Carolina, ratified in 1789, and the threat of commercial pressure brought in Rhode Island the year following. With that, all thirteen of the original states had accepted the Constitution. Moreover, the Union was about to expand; in 1791, Vermont became the fourteenth state.

The adoption of the Constitution was an important landmark in the march toward national power. Yet in that march it was neither the beginning nor the end. The central government had been building since the organization of the Continental Congress during the Revolution. The state land cessions of the Confederation era had added to the strength of the national government. Ratification of the Constitution meant further progress in the same direction but did not complete the job of centralizing political power. Much depended on the attitudes of those who controlled the new political machinery.

Controlling the New Government: The Federalist Era (1789–1801)

The men who had written the Constitution were aware of this situation. Hence, after winning their fight for ratification, these Federalists set out to capture and retain control of the national offices. They were successful at the start, and ran the United States government for a dozen years. The Federalist period covered George Washington's two terms as President (1789–97) and the single term of John Adams (1797–1801). In these twelve years, the Federalists increased the strength and efficiency of the national government, and aided certain economic groups.

Federalist success was due to a variety of factors. The Antifederalists were discouraged and disorganized after their failure to prevent adoption of the Constitution. The Federalists, by contrast, were encouraged by their victory. They were further favored by continuing support from powerful merchants and planters. They also had the enormous advantage of having Washington as their titular leader. As the most admired American, Washington attracted support from citizens unsympathetic to the Federalist point of view.

On the administrative side, the Federalists did not have to start from scratch. During the Revolution and the Confederation era Congress had set up executive offices for civil and military purposes. Employees and office routines carried over to the new government in 1789; and the Federalists built on that foundation. In building, they stressed the executive.

Until 1789, the administrative offices had been run by Congress. Under the new Constitution, power shifted to the President. This meant that the Chief Executive had control of the patronage—the jobs on the public pay roll. President Washington and his successors used their power to secure the service of men capable of administering the laws. They also used the patronage to reward political friends. Thus Washington, though he disliked party labels, preferred to give appointments to "friends of the Constitution," that is, to Federalists.

To aid the President, the Federalist Congress of 1789 provided for assistants: a Secretary for Foreign Affairs (renamed Secretary of State that same year), a Secretary of War, a Secretary of the Treasury, an Attorney General, a Postmaster General. President Washington made the first four into a board of advisers, thus inaugurating the cabinet system, now an important part of the American governmental structure.

According to the Constitution, the President and his subordinates are required to administer the laws. From the start, however, the Presidents have done much more than this. They have been national and party leaders who have formulated foreign and domestic policies. Personally and through advisers, they have outlined programs for Congressional consideration and have used their influence to secure the adoption of their ideas.

Hamilton's Financial Measures

The key proposals of the Washington administration were the financial measures of the Secretary of the Treasury, Alexander Hamilton. At thirty-two, Hamilton was the youngest member of the cabinet; he was little more than half as old as Washington. The President, however, had great confidence in his Secretary of the Treasury, and the two made an effective political team. Washington provided reputation, prestige, and personal influence, also a steadiness lacking in the impulsive Hamilton. The cabinet officer, on the other hand, could offer a brilliant style, ideas, and political resourcefulness.

Born in the West Indies, Alexander Hamilton was educated in New York. Marrying into the wealthy Schuyler family, he became closely connected with New York's merchant aristocracy. As an in-law of the Schuylers, he moved in the best society. As a successful lawyer, he obtained important businessmen as clients. In politics, his views coincided with those of the moneyed classes. Hamilton deeply distrusted the common people, and felt that the interests of the nation could more safely be entrusted to creditors than debtors.

A basic part of Hamilton's financial program was his recommendation for the funding of the national debt at par, or face value. By 1790 this debt exceeded $50,000,000. Nearly a quarter of the total was a foreign debt, owed to the French government and the Dutch bankers. All Americans recognized that this had to be paid in full. The domestic debt was another matter. These bonds had depreciated a great deal and by 1790 were in the hands of speculators who had bought them for far less than their face value. Nonetheless, Hamilton favored repayment at par. This was necessary, he said, to establish the credit of the national government. James Madison and others objected, pointing out that paying at face value would not aid the average citizen. Instead, it would burden the government for the benefit of speculators, many of whom were Hamilton's business friends. But the Hamilton scheme prevailed.

Coupled with the plan to refund at par was Hamilton's proposal that the national government take over the state debts, which ran a little over $20,000,000. The Secretary argued that it would be logical to lump these obligations, since the state debts had been incurred in a common cause, the Revolution. Assumption would aid businessmen who held the bonds of states which were reluctant to pay on their obligations. And the transfer of the debt from the states to the United States would increase the influence and prestige of the national government.

There was strong opposition, especially in the South. Some states had begun to pay off their debts; others had made little effort to attack the problem. Under the assumption plan, the states which had done nothing fared better than the others. What was more, some citizens considered the assumption program as an effort to aid speculators. Others labeled it a plot to destroy the remaining rights of states. But once more Hamilton came out on top. He won the votes he needed by a political trade not unlike what is called "logrolling" today. Hamilton and his friends in Congress agreed to vote to shift the national Capitol temporarily from New York to Philadelphia, then to move it south, to the banks of the Potomac. In return, certain southern Congressmen withdrew their opposition to assumption, and that program was carried.

With a debt of $75,000,000, the national government needed a substantial income to meet payments. Congress had voted a tariff bill in 1789, fixing moderate duties on imports. The United States also had a small return from the sale of public lands. Hamilton desired to supplement these sources of income with an internal revenue or excise tax on distilled liquors. Such a measure would yield cash and would add to the power of the national administration by taking the authority of the central government to every corner of the land.

The funding and assumption measures had caused some grumbling. The excise tax, adopted in 1791, brought a more serious reaction—open revolt along the Pennsylvania frontier. Transportation was wretchedly bad in that region, and it did not pay to move corn to market. Instead, the frontiersman turned part of his crop into whiskey. Having greater value per pound, liquor could stand the cost of transportation and yield a small profit. Hamilton's tax hit these frontiersmen hard, and they expressed their sentiments in the Whiskey Rebellion of 1794.

Back in stamp tax days, the British had yielded to this type of pressure. The Federalists did not. Rather they used the episode to demonstrate the strength of the government. Here was the first test of the power of the United States to operate directly against individuals in the states; here was a chance to provide an example for future agitators. Using his power under the Constitution, President Washington called out state militiamen to put down the insurrection. Hamilton led these 15,000 troops in person. All signs of opposition vanished as this force moved toward the scene of trouble. Two rebel leaders were arrested, convicted, then pardoned by the President; and the incident was closed. The central government had shown ability to enforce its laws.

Hamilton made one other tax proposal. He suggested that certain tariff duties be adjusted upward, so as to encourage the growth of manufacturing. Industrial development, he felt, would strengthen the nation. Hamilton's arguments, embodied in his Report on Manufactures (1791), resulted in some increases in duties the next year. On the whole, however, Congress chose to retain the moderate duties of the Tariff of 1789. Farmers claimed that a protective tariff would increase the price of the goods they bought, but not of the goods they sold. Hamilton's merchant allies were also doubtful, for higher duties might hurt their profitable import trade.

Defeated here, Washington's Secretary of the Treasury was otherwise successful. In addition to his debt and excise measures, Hamilton had Congress improve the coinage system and establish a United States Mint (1792). One year earlier, Hamilton had obtained from Congress a twenty-year charter for a Bank of the United States (1791–1811). This institution, set up in Philadelphia, had the right to establish branches throughout the United States. The Bank was a fiscal agent of the national government, and a depository for public funds. It was, however, a private corporation, the government holding only one-fifth of the stock.

In sponsoring the first Bank of the United States, Hamilton desired the efficient handling of government funds. He also felt that a national bank would aid business and be a centralizing force in the young American republic. The very act of chartering the institution was a step toward broadening the functions of the national government. Secretary of State Thomas Jefferson, who opposed the charter, said that the Constitution gave Congress no authority to create a Bank of the United States. Opposing this "strict construction," Hamilton admitted that the Constitution contained no specific mention of a bank. He argued, however, for "loose construction" of the Constitution, saying that Congress could do many things under such powers as that to legislate for the "general welfare." The President and Congress took Hamilton's side; and the first Bank of the United States began its career.

Centralizing influences were not confined to Hamilton's proposals. The Federalist years also saw the creation of a network of United States courts, which carried the influence of the central government into nearly every part of every state. Much of this was accomplished in the Judiciary Act of 1789. The court network was further extended in 1801, at the end of Adams' presidency.

Nor was this all. When "Mad Anthony" Wayne crushed the Indians of the Ohio country in the battle of Fallen Timbers (1794), the United States showed that it had real striking power. Wayne's triumph made possible the opening of many areas west of the Appalachian Mountains—areas which until statehood were under the control of the national government. Increased diplomatic activity was another indication of the growing importance of the nation, as was the upsurge of national patriotic feeling.

The Federalists Encounter Opposition

The trend toward national power was not approved by all. By the middle of the 1790's opposition led to formation of an antiadministration party. This organization, generally called Republican, gained strength rapidly. The Federalists managed to come out on top in the presidential campaign of 1796, but they were beaten four years later and never again won a national election.

Why so? The Federalists were forceful and efficient. They set up a new government and made it work. They whipped the frontier Indians, they improved the credit and increased the power and prestige of the United States at home and abroad. The Federalists, however, wanted an ever-stronger central government. In this, they represented a trend of the future. But in Washington's day, tradition and the deficiencies of transportation put the accent on state and local loyalties. To many, the American Revolution had been a fight for local rights against centralized authority. Those who held this view did not approve of Hamilton's tendency to interpret the Constitution loosely, so as to give maximum powers to the national government. Their preference was for powerful state governments; and the state governments did in fact continue to be strong throughout the Federalist era. When the Federalists were at peak strength, pressure from the states forced the adoption of the Eleventh Amendment to the Constitution (1798). This was a states'-rights amendment, providing that states could not be sued in United States courts by citizens of other states.

Those who opposed the Federalists did not do so solely because of the states'-rights issue. They also disapproved of the ways in which the Federalists were using the power of the national government. Hamilton, they said, favored city over country though most Americans were farmers. Federalist legislation aided merchants, speculators, financiers, shipowners, and other men of wealth, but did little for ordinary citizens. Creditors were favored by debt funding and the establishment of the Bank of the United States, but debtors found their lot as hard as ever. There was no cheap money to pay off debts, no easy credit to afford relief. Instead, the hard-pressed farmer had to pay a hated excise tax.

Then, too, it was apparent that many Federalists believed in rule by the "better people." Alexander Hamilton, for one, had little faith in democratic processes. The average voter found John Adams cold and haughty, aristocratic and aloof. Even Washington reflected the Federalist attitude; his public appearances as President were characterized by pomp and ceremony rather than simplicity. Such matters disturbed many democratic-minded Americans, especially those who feared that the Federalists planned to overthrow republican government and bring back monarchy.

Old Antifederalists—those who had opposed the adoption of the Constitution—made up much of the rank and file of the new Republican party. Leadership, however, was provided by two Virginia planters who had for a time worked closely with the Federalists. One of these, James Madison, had been a key figure in the Philadelphia convention of 1787 and had helped Hamilton write the *Federalist* papers. The other, Thomas Jefferson, had served as Secretary of State in the cabinet of the Federalist President, George Washington. But Jefferson and Madison had come to distrust Hamilton, and to feel that the Federalist party was too aristocratic and was doing too little for the South and for agrarian interests everywhere.

Of the two, Jefferson was the leader, and soon emerged as the chief foe of the Federalists. Jefferson was not much of a mixer or public speaker; nor was he as quick and dashing as his young rival Hamilton. But Jefferson was an able lawyer, a recognized philosopher, a distinguished man of letters. A farmer and a scientist, he invented a new plow and pioneered in several fields of science. He was interested in religion and in education and made a lasting impression on American architecture. Yet Jefferson found time for public service, as author of the Declaration of Independence, as wartime governor of Virginia, minister to France, Secretary of State, Vice-President and President of the United States.

Through all of Jefferson's career runs a devotion to democracy and to the soil. This Virginian felt that the secret of the democratic greatness of America was in the land. Thomas Jefferson had a deep distrust for cities. He viewed the commercial classes with disfavor and, despite his democratic views, had doubts about urban workers. It was better, he believed, to put faith in farmers. But, in town or country, the real task was to fight special privilege. As a Virginian, Jefferson fought for the abolition of primogeniture and entail, for the disestablishment of the Anglican Church. On the national scene, he opposed a strong judiciary, disliked the Bank of the United States, and had bitter words for the "stock-jobbing herd" which profited from Hamilton's financial measures.

Resigning from the cabinet at the end of 1793, Jefferson turned his attention to the organization of the new Republican party. Working with Madison and others, he lined up northern artisans, western frontiersmen, southern ·planters, and small farmers everywhere. The most significant alignment was with Aaron Burr and the Clintons in Hamilton's state, New York. The importance of this connection can be seen in the fact that in six of the seven presidential campaigns from 1796 to 1820 the Republican ticket consisted of a Virginian and a New Yorker.

Overthrowing the Federalists

As the Jeffersonians gained strength, the Federalists should have tightened their own lines. Instead, they squabbled among themselves. When Washington refused to run for a third term in 1796, the Federalists put up John Adams of Massachusetts. Alexander Hamilton, however, tried to manipulate votes so as to secure the presidency for Adams' running mate, Thomas Pinckney of South Carolina. He failed, and Adams was elected President; but the maneuver resulted in the election of the Republican presidential candidate, Thomas Jefferson, to the vice-presidency.[1] Even after that, the Federalists failed to stand together; and their divisions played into the hands of the Jeffersonians.

Irritated at Republican gains, the Federalists tried to solve the problem by legislation. In 1798, during the administration of John Adams, they passed the Alien and Sedition Acts. The Alien Act empowered the President to expel or imprison foreigners deemed dangerous to the republic.

---

[1] In the first four presidential elections, each elector voted for two men, the man polling the most votes being chosen President if he had the support of a majority of the electors. The runner-up became Vice-President. In 1800 the Republican candidates, Jefferson and Burr, were tied for the lead. This threw the election into the House of Representatives, which after a long contest named Jefferson President, Burr Vice-President. To avoid a repetition of this situation, the Constitution was changed (Twelfth Amendment, 1804), and electors now vote separately for President and Vice-President.

The Sedition Act prescribed punishment for persons who attacked or challenged the authority of the government, officers, or laws of the United States. The laws were aimed at and were used against Republican politicians and editors; but the effort reacted against the already slipping Federalists. Citizens everywhere saw grave danger in the curbing of civil liberties. Republicans jailed or fined by Federalist judges became public heroes, and the Federalists were jeered as tyrants.

In two states, Republicans did more than jeer. In the Kentucky and Virginia Resolutions, they set state power against national authority. Both sets denounced the hated statutes and asserted states'-rights doctrines. The Kentucky resolves went further, boldly announcing that states had the right to pass on the constitutionality of Congressional legislation and to resist or nullify laws considered unconstitutional.

As it turned out, there was no showdown on the nullification issue at this time. But the Federalists were finished. President Adams, running for reëlection in 1800, lost some of the states he had carried four years earlier and went down to defeat. Jefferson was chosen President, and when he was inaugurated in 1801, in the new capital city of Washington, the Federalist era was at an end.

While they controlled the offices, the Federalists had seemed strong indeed. Actually, the party had been weak from the beginning. Although the United States was primarily agrarian, the Federalists had won support from few farmers. Although democratic feeling was rising, the Federalists had made no real effort to befriend the average citizen. Although the West was growing (Kentucky, Tennessee, and Ohio became states in 1792, 1796, and 1803), Federalists were weak along the frontier. So the Federalists, defeated in 1800, failed to stage a comeback in the years that followed.

The Jeffersonians in Power (1801–25)

The Republican organization, by contrast, rested on a strong foundation. Though distrusted in business circles, the party had popular support in all sections. Small landowners, city workers, backwoodsmen were attracted by the democratic views of Republican leaders. Farmers everywhere approved of Jefferson's agrarian philosophy. Finally, the party's championship of states' rights appealed to the local loyalties of average citizens, who continued to distrust centralized authority and remained suspicious of national courts, banks, and excise taxes.

As a result, the Republicans stayed on top for a generation, controlling most state and local governments as well as the national offices. The party's strength is indicated in the history of the presidency under the Virginia dynasty (1801–25). Easily reëlected, Jefferson occupied the White House from 1801 to 1809. Not desiring a third term, he chose as his successor his Secretary of State, James Madison. After Madison's two terms (1809–17), the job passed without difficulty to another Virginia Republican, James Monroe, who won two overwhelming victories and served as President from 1817 to 1825.

The Republican victories owed much to party organization. By present standards, the Jeffersonian machine was tied together very loosely. Still, party leaders held their followers in line through a party press, a Congressional caucus, and the patronage. Federalists filled the appointive posts at the time of Jefferson's inauguration. Some resigned; others were dismissed to make way for deserving Republicans.

It is sometimes said that the Republicans in power tossed aside the states'-rights principles they had advanced while their party was in opposition, and adopted the nationalist view of the Federalists. To a degree, this interpretation is correct. Republicans who had feared a national government run by Hamilton trusted that same government when Jefferson was in control. And Federalists who had been confirmed nationalists in Hamilton's day talked states' rights when they disapproved of Jefferson's use of presidential power.

The reversal, though, was incomplete. In their first years in office, the Republicans used the power of the national government much more cautiously than had the Federalists. They repealed the Alien and Sedition Acts, scrapped Hamilton's excise taxes, and did their best to curb the influence of the national executive and the national judiciary.

The Federalist Presidents had emphasized executive authority and had given the presidential office prestige and dignity. Jefferson, as President, chose to deëmphasize the executive. He sent his messages to Congress by a clerk instead of delivering them in person. He stayed away from the capital city a good deal of the time; and when he was in Washington, formality went by the board. The idea was to have the presidency represent democratic simplicity rather than the weight of national power.

Jefferson's Secretary of the Treasury, Albert Gallatin, made another contribution along the same line. The Federalists had asked Congress for general appropriations—lump sums, permitting the executive departments to decide on details of expenditure. Gallatin shifted to the basis now used— specific appropriations and strict accountability. That is, Congress broke down totals, set aside a sum for each specific project. This system had defects, for it led to logrolling and pork-barrel legislation, with each Congressman getting something for his district by swapping votes with other members. The method did, however, limit the executive authority.

The Question of the Courts

The Republicans were especially interested in holding down the federal judiciary. United States judges had enforced the hated Sedition Act; and, despite Federalist defeats at the polls, the national courts were staffed with Federalist judges on life appointment. Some of these "midnight judges" had been appointed in the dying days of the Adams administration, after Jefferson's election but before his inauguration.

To get rid of these hostile judges, the Republicans wiped some courts out of existence. They also tried out the impeachment process outlined in the Constitution. For a test case they chose a choleric Federalist Supreme Court justice, Samuel Chase. Chase was intemperate and unfair, and probably insane. But, though the House voted articles of impeachment, the Republicans could not muster enough Senate votes to have Chase removed from office. It was useless, therefore, to start impeachment proceedings in other cases. The Republicans could only hope that the Federalist judges would die soon.

Some did. Others, such as John Marshall, lived long lives. A leading Virginia Federalist, Marshall was named Chief Justice of the Supreme Court in 1801, at the very end of the Federalist era. He held on until his death thirty-four years later, the last representative of a long-dead party. Through those years, Marshall dominated the court, even winning over judges appointed by his political opponents, the Jeffersonians.

As Chief Justice, Marshall did everything he could to defeat Jefferson's attempts to limit the influence of the judiciary. Indeed, Marshall organized a counterattack which increased the importance of the courts. In the case of Marbury vs. Madison (1803), he asserted that the Supreme Court had the right to pass on the constitutionality of Congressional legislation, and to declare null and void any law which the Court considered unconstitutional. The decision was denounced by many Republicans, but in the end this doctrine of judicial review was to prevail.

Marshall also attacked the whole Republican doctrine of states' rights. It was understood, of course, that the governors, legislatures, and state courts would take no action contrary to the Constitution of the United States. But who was to pass judgment as to constitutionality? The states themselves, said the advocates of local rights. No, said Marshall, the final interpretation would come from the Supreme Court of the United States. In case after case he held his ground, maintaining the supremacy of the national government over the states. He overruled state courts when in his opinion those courts rendered decisions in conflict with the Constitution of the United States (as, for example, Martin vs. Hunter's Lessee, 1816). In Fletcher vs. Peck (1810) and the Dartmouth College case (1819) Marshall invalidated state laws which he felt infringed the Constitution's guarantee of the inviolability of contracts. Gibbons vs. Ogden (1824) gave him an opportunity to throw out state legislation in a field reserved for the national government—interstate commerce. He was less inclined to limit the powers of the national government, even when the Constitution contained no clear statement of authority. Thus, in McCulloch vs. Maryland (1819) he defended the right of Congress to charter a national bank, basing his argument on the "implied powers" of the government.

The Republicans were never fully reconciled to Marshall. Among other things, they grouped him with Hamilton as a defender of vested interests, a Federalist who put property rights ahead of the public interest. They noted that in the Dartmouth College case Marshall upheld a charter as sacred when the New Hampshire legislature was attempting to change the charter in the interest of the public. Fletcher vs. Peck was even more in point. Georgia legislators influenced by bribery granted title to certain Yazoo lands. The fraud was revealed, and a reform legislature revoked the grants, only to be told by Marshall that a contract could not be impaired and that the fraudulent grants must stand.

Marshall's arguments for national supremacy met with less opposition. In principle, the Jeffersonians remained devoted to states' rights and to strict construction of the Constitution. In fact, they moved in Marshall's direction as it became apparent that loose construction and a strong national government could assist the groups behind the Republican organization. The Republicans were strong in the growing West. In consequence, the party favored the purchase of Louisiana (1803), although the Constitution did not specifically authorize annexation of territory. At this same time it became evident that the Republicans would profit by the building of a national highway across the Appalachian Mountains. Constitutional objections were brushed aside, and the Cumberland, or National, Road was started. Much stronger national impulses were to come after the War of 1812.

6

Toward a National Economy and Culture

The Westward Movement

In the half-century of revolution and readjustment between the 1760's and the War of 1812 the American people crossed the mountains which had hemmed them in during colonial decades and settled the eastern Mississippi Valley. Population pressure was one factor in this movement to the West. Unchecked by European limitations on subsistence, American farm families grew prodigiously. But five sons could not be employed on the family homestead. Ambitious younger men therefore went west. So did adventurous landowners, who saw a chance to profit by selling eastern holdings and buying larger farms for less money in the West. In addition, the frontier attracted persons anxious to escape from unpleasant lives or pressing debts. Because of Old World wars and restrictions on emigration, relatively few Europeans entered the United States in these years. But some came each year, and a fair proportion of them headed for the cheaper lands of the interior.

Few western settlers changed occupations. They were farmers, and farmers they remained. Those who had raised wheat, corn, and hay in New England took these crops into Ohio. Settlers who had grown tobacco and corn in Virginia carried their products and practices over the mountains to Kentucky.

The West of the early post-Revolutionary years was not far distant from the coastal settlements. Western New York, western Pennsylvania, Kentucky, and Tennessee were the "promised lands." Few moved into the Northwest Territory until Wayne humbled the Indians at Fallen Timbers (1794). White settlers were not safe in Alabama and Mississippi until Andrew Jackson defeated the Creeks at Horseshoe Bend in 1814.

Although the trip west was short in miles, the journey often involved great hardships. The rigors of the passage westward were, however, just an introduction to the hardships of a frontier farm. The cost of such a farm was small compared with the expense of moving, building, clearing, seed-ing, fencing, and sustaining life until crops could be harvested. Owners seeking to develop extensive tracts were often willing to lease land rent-free for several years to get it cleared. Three-year leases in return for fencing alone were made in Ohio in 1796. Nor could those able to buy use all they purchased. Hand methods limited the space that a single adult could clear and care for, even in the case of wheat, to twenty-five acres. Often not more than ten acres would be cleared in a half-dozen years. The farmer who bought a hundred acres of "wild" land was investing only part of his money in immediate production, the rest in unused real estate.

New Englanders went west in small groups and raised frame houses. Southerners more commonly built log cabins in isolated clearings. But, whatever the area of origin, frontier farmers had to rely on subsistence agriculture at the start. Living conditions were primitive, and the women and children worked in the fields. Soap, candles, clothing, and furniture were manufactured in the home.

By working hard, the frontier farmer could eventually construct his buildings and clear enough land to try commercial agriculture. Here he was aided by nature, for the virgin soil of the Ohio and Mississippi valleys would grow splendid crops. Although frontier farmers used no fertilizer, many obtained forty-five bushels of corn or forty bushels of wheat per acre —double the yield of later, more scientific agriculturalists. But even then the frontier farmer might fare poorly if his location made it difficult to get his goods to market.

Some frontier farmers cared little about reaching the commercial stage. These individuals opened up new land and, after a few years, sold out to newcomers from the East. They then staked out a new clearing further west and repeated the process. Most of these drifters were squatters who made no effort to acquire title. They simply "squatted" on a piece of property, and made crude improvements. If the lawful owners came along, the squatters simply sold their improvements and moved on west.

The more permanent settlers were, of course, concerned about land titles. Some bought their farms at the outset, paying in a lump sum or in installments. Others, lacking cash or credit, became squatters but hoped to buy at a later date. Both groups, therefore, were keenly interested in government land policy.

Government Land Policy

Much of the land settled between the Revolution and the War of 1812 belonged to the states. The western counties of New York and Pennsylvania were still thinly populated, and all the states from Virginia south owned a great deal of virgin land. Though distribution programs varied, all states encouraged the westward movement. They passed out land to veterans, sold it to farmers and to speculators.

In these decades Congress was working out a land policy for areas under national control. The state land cessions of 1782–1802 gave the central government an enormous region beyond the mountains. The purchase of Louisiana from France in 1803 added an even larger tract, the whole western Mississippi Valley. Since Americans favored private enterprise, it was clear that the government would not itself develop these holdings. The problem was how to transfer them to private ownership—at what price and in what size units.

In deciding these questions, Congress was guided by the desire to raise money and the desire to aid businessmen interested in land development. Generally, Congress chose to sell land for as high a price as large investors were willing to pay. The policy, in other words, was not to sell directly to small farmers. If the United States sold small farms, it would be competing with private and state land-selling interests. Moreover, many Congressmen were substantial men of property, who feared the "radicalism" of small back-country farmers. A number of these lawmakers wanted to promote conservatism by having western settlement channeled through a landlord system. In addition, eastern business interests feared that easy access to western lands would diminish their labor supply and drain capital westward.

The policy of putting United States land beyond the reach of the average settler was opposed to the traditional practices of most British colonies, hence to the expectation of the people. Township grants had been made freely in New England, and settlers in the western part of the southern colonies had generally been rewarded with donations of fifty or more acres of free land. The national government departed from this pattern even before adoption of the Constitution. During the Confederation era, Congress passed the Survey Bill, or Land Ordinance of 1785. As we have seen, this established the township-section method of designating national lands. It also provided that these public holdings were to be sold at auction at the "seat of Congress." The minimum unit for sale was one section (a square mile, 640 acres); the minimum price, a dollar per acre. This ruled out ordinary settlers, who could not travel to the Capitol and could not afford to pay $640 for a farm.

During the Confederation period land speculators received special consideration. In 1787, Congress sold 5,000,000 acres to land companies at the specie equivalent of a few cents an acre. The companies, if they chose, could then sell small farms to settlers at low cost. But this policy of selling

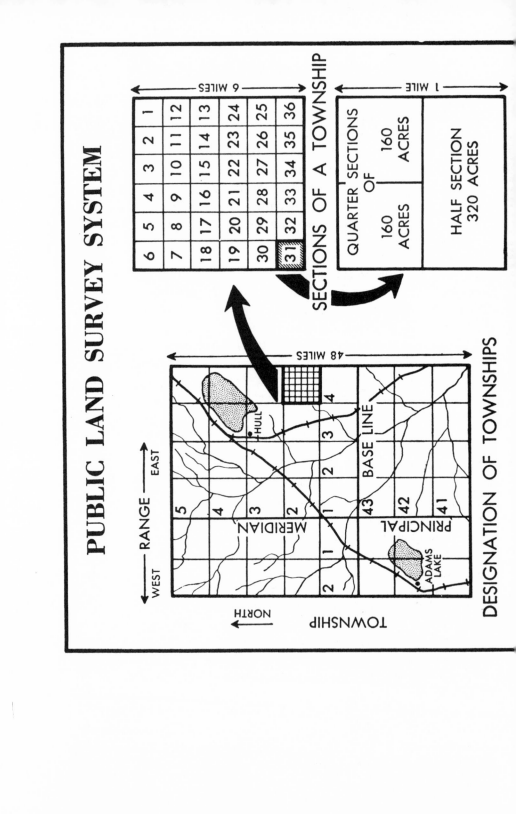

PUBLIC LAND SURVEY SYSTEM

SECTIONS OF A TOWNSHIP

6	5	4	3	2	1
7	8	9	10	11	12
18	17	16	15	14	13
19	20	21	22	23	24
30	29	28	27	26	25
31	32	33	34	35	36

6 MILES

1 MILE

QUARTER SECTIONS OF 160 ACRES

160 ACRES | 160 ACRES

HALF SECTION 320 ACRES

DESIGNATION OF TOWNSHIPS

48 MILES

RANGE — EAST

WEST — RANGE

MERIDIAN

PRINCIPAL

BASE LINE

HULL

ADAMS LAKE

TOWNSHIP

NORTH

5 4 3 2 1

1 2

4 3 2 1 43 42 41

~~ATLAS COVERED BY THE~~
PUBLIC LAND SURVEY SYSTEM

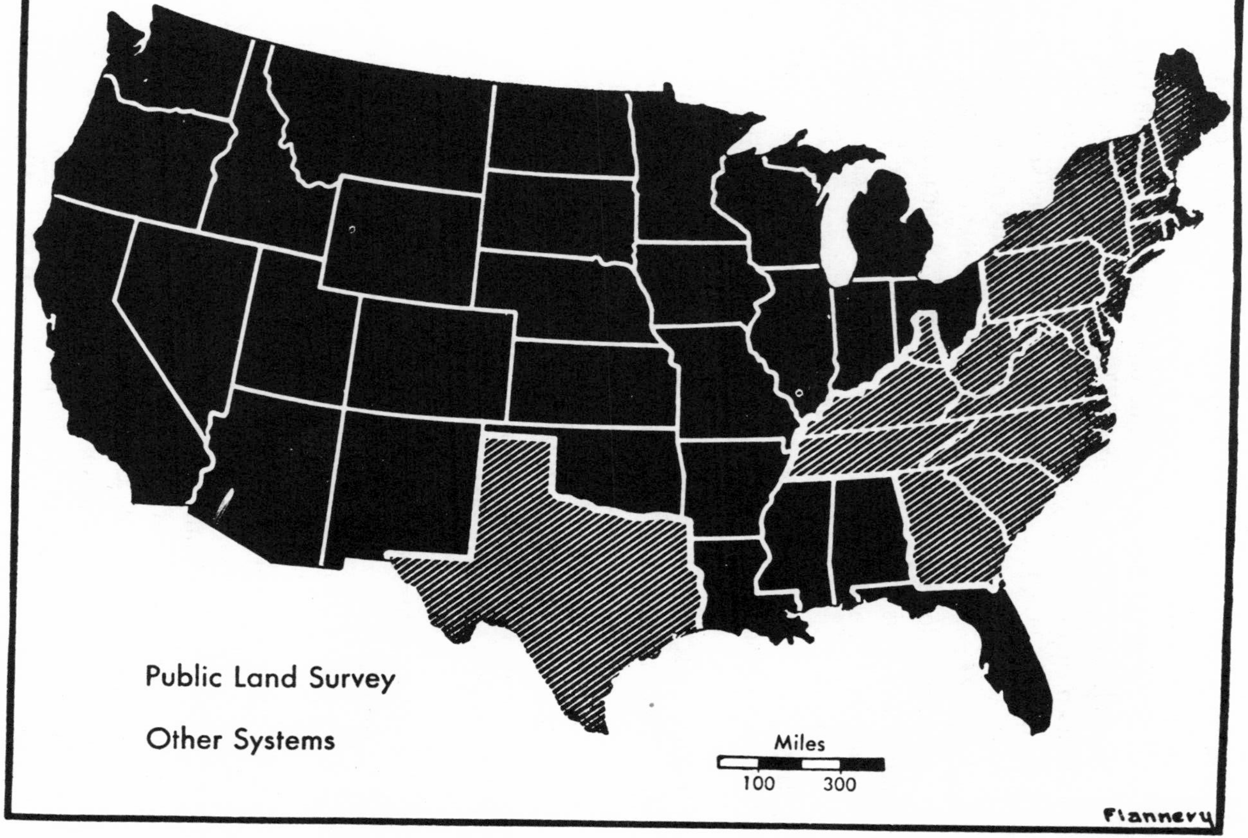

Planney

Miles

100   300

Public Land Survey

Other Systems

In the Survey Bill of 1785, Congress created a survey system for the national government's recently acquired western lands. This system is still used for nearly all the area from the Appalachians to the Pacific coast.

large tracts at special prices was disappointing as a source of revenue. The land companies defaulted on some of the contracts, and ultimately only 1,100,000 acres were transferred. The basic difficulty was that though businessmen wanted to invest in land, few had much cash. The largest purchase, 3,500,000 acres (more than an eighth of the present state of Ohio), was forfeited because the promoters could not raise $500,000 in any kind of government certificates to meet their second payment.

With the adoption of the Constitution in 1789, the national government acquired powers of taxation. This lessened the pressure for revenue from land sales and ended the wholesale grants, save for a sale of 200,000 acres fronting on Lake Erie to the state of Pennsylvania in 1792. When the large-sale policy was dropped, some felt that national land should be sold to actual settlers in small parcels. But this was vigorously resisted by private citizens who had western lands for sale—speculators who had acquired bounty lands, land companies that had bought land from Congress, others who had shadowy titles based on purchase from the Indians or on British or other special grants. All these persons were anxious to keep government lands off the market until they could dispose of their holdings. The Land Law of 1796 played into their hands. Under this statute, as under the Survey Bill of 1785, the section was the minimum unit of sale; but the minimum price was raised to two dollars an acre. No ordinary farmer could hope to have $1280 in cash. Speculators also hesitated to buy at that price; so less than eighty sections were sold in four years.

Meantime, the Ohio Territory had chosen William Henry Harrison as its first representative in Congress. Some of the territorial legislators who had elected Harrison expected him to fight for land laws favoring the small settler. But Harrison was also linked to speculators—he was the son-in-law of Judge John Cleves Symmes, one of the largest real-estate operators in Ohio. Harrison and others worked out the Land Law of 1800. On the surface, this law helped the common man; actually, it left the average settler about as badly off as before. Four land offices were set up in the West, the minimum unit was reduced to 320 acres (a half-section), and purchasers were given four years to pay. The price, though, was kept at two dollars an acre; and a half-section was more than a settler could use. Nor was a man lacking $640 in cash likely to amass it during the first four years on a frontier farm. "Relief" laws extended the time for payment, but as the laws were neither continuous nor all-inclusive, there were numerous forfeitures of land.

In 1804, Secretary of the Treasury Albert Gallatin and other friends of the small settler won a few concessions. The minimum purchase was cut to a quarter-section, 160 acres. Although time payments were still permitted, a discount was allowed for cash. This took the minimum cash cost of a farm below $275. But that was still a high price compared to land that could be bought on credit from private interests.

The Transportation Problem

Although western farmers made most of what they needed, they had to buy salt, farm implements, household utensils, hardware, firearms, ammunition. To pay for these items, the farmer had to move part of his crop to market. But how? In the eighteenth century waterways alone provided transportation cheap enough to move farm products long distances. There were navigable streams beyond the mountains; but they flowed away from, not toward the eastern cities.

One possibility was shipping through New Orleans. Here there were diplomatic problems, for the United States did not acquire that city until 1803. Spain, however, made concessions in the Pinckney treaty of 1796. Meat and grain then moved down the Ohio and Mississippi rivers to New Orleans, and on by sea to New York. This was cheaper than sending goods overland across Pennsylvania. Still, the New Orleans route was long, costly, and dangerous, and profits were small.

Conditions improved when the steamboat came to western waters. The steam engine, an ancient device, had been revived in Europe about 1650. The Scotsman James Watt patented an improved engine in 1769. Many persons then tried to use the machine in land or water vehicles. John Fitch ran a steamboat on the Delaware in the 1790's, and in Philadelphia Oliver Evans operated a clumsy amphibian (a primitive steam automobile and ship combined). In 1807 Robert Fulton began running his *Clermont* up the Hudson with an engine built by Watts' firm in Britain—an event known in America, curiously, as the "invention" of the steamboat. Four years later the *New Orleans*, a side-wheeler, was launched at Pittsburgh; and within a decade sixty steamboats were operating on western rivers. Traffic could now move up as well as down the Mississippi. Trade totals increased, freight costs fell. And, as New Orleans prospered, Atlantic coastal cities began agitating for roads and canals to divert trade to the East.

Many Westerners lived too far from navigable rivers to use them to advantage. Some of these farmers grew corn, fed the corn to hogs, then drove the swine to market on the hoof. There were difficulties, notably the feeding problem and the hog's loss of weight on the trip. Nevertheless, enormous herds were driven from farms in western Pennsylvania, Kentucky, and Ohio to markets in Philadelphia and Baltimore. Some farmers handled their own drives; others handed the job over to professional drovers.

Inevitably, the marketing problem created a demand for road improvement. This affected the East and South as well as the West. Whatever the section, farmers located off the waterways suffered. The dirt-surfaced roads of the Revolutionary era, even when kept in repair (which they seldom were), were inadequate for the transportation of bulky farm products. On such routes no horse could pull as much as a half-ton; and it cost almost a cent a mile to haul a bushel of wheat.

The post-Revolutionary drive for better roads featured introduction of the McAdam type of road, made of successive layers of broken stone. Connections with the West were stressed. Coastwise schooners still offered the best means of transportation between the seaports, and these small ships could penetrate far inland on rivers like the Connecticut, Hudson, Delaware, and Potomac. The new highways, in consequence, generally headed away from the coast. From Maryland south, where capital was tied up in land and slaves, road building was generally left to state enterprise. In the northern states private turnpike companies laid down improved roads, deriving their profit from tolls collected at gates placed strategically along the route. By 1800 there were seventy-two such corporations; a decade later there were more than a thousand.

Private bridge companies also appeared. These, like the turnpike companies, sought franchises to protect them from the competition of parallel routes. The practicality of the wooden truss type of bridge was demonstrated in Vermont in the 1790's. But ferries or fords remained the usual means for crossing streams.

In their desire to get good roads, government officials tried many schemes. The Northwest Territory made all males over sixteen liable for ten days' work on the roads each year. There was, however, no adequate enforcement. Congress was more successful when it granted Ebenezer Zane three sections of land, plus inn and ferry rights, for constructing 298 miles of road from the Ohio River opposite Wheeling to Limestone, Ohio (1796). This became the main artery of the Northwest, but its character is indicated by its name: Zane's Trace.

Neither private nor state enterprise could finance hard-surface roads across the mountains. Despite state efforts to improve it, the road from Harrisburg to Pittsburgh was almost impassable. Equally bad was the route from eastern Maryland to Wheeling. Worse, if possible, were roads further south—for example, those that led to the Cumberland Gap, the pass connecting Virginia and North Carolina with Kentucky and Tennessee. Westerners therefore urged the United States to do the job. Having lands to sell, the central government had a direct stake in the development of the West; and it wanted good roads for military and postal purposes, and for the general benefit of the nation.

As early as 1803 Congress agreed to devote to road building 5 percent of the proceeds of public land sales in Ohio. Part of this sum was reserved for a hard-surface road across the mountains. In 1810 Congress formally authorized construction, and in seven years the National Road had been completed to Wheeling on the Ohio River. The eastern terminus of the National Road was Cumberland, Maryland, where the route connected with the privately owned Baltimore Pike.

Since a horse could pull a ton on the improved roads, the cost of transportation was cut in half. This gave more eastern farmers access to urban markets. But costs were still too high to permit the shipment of grain across the mountains. The National Road speeded the movement of immigrants and equipment and reduced the price of manufactured goods shipped from the East to the frontier. The key question of finding a satisfactory outlet for western crops, however, carried over to the future.

Farming in the East

The westward movement had an important influence on farming in the older, eastern states. For one thing, the settlement of western areas drained population from seaboard regions. More serious was the fact that rocky New England farms could not easily compete with those of western New York and Ohio. Southern New England eventually solved this problem by turning to manufacturing and by an expansion of maritime interests. Farming was continued only in terms of local needs. Some young people moved west; others went to nearby towns.

Pennsylvania suffered little by agricultural competition with the West. Parts of this state were in or west of the mountains, so they took part in the western movement. At the same time, good soils and the superior methods of Pennsylvania German farmers made the southeastern part of the state one of the richest grain and livestock areas in the country.

The Pennsylvania Germans were not the only Easterners interested in good techniques. Many educated men echoed English talk about agricultural reforms. Gentlemen-farmers corresponded with one another and maintained contact through a few pioneer agricultural societies. They discussed new plants and fertilizers. They favored rotation and diversification of crops. All this was based on empirical (practical) knowledge, rather than on scientific theory, for little was yet known about plant biology and soil chemistry.

Practical though it was, the talk about better methods made little impression on the average tiller of the soil. Like their grandparents, American farmers of 1800 were interested in making cash profits as soon as possible. As long as land was cheap, the quickest way to wealth was to use virgin soils until they were half-exhausted, then move on to new fields. The man who farmed intensively, plowing carefully, rotating crops, using fertilizers, would preserve the soil for his grandchildren. But he might not make money as fast as his neighbors.

Agricultural reformers could point to a few gains. Improved iron plows were developed in the late 1700's. These were drawn by horses, mules, and oxen, the latter being the most powerful, but hardest to guide. In the North, where barns provided winter protection for animals, there was some effort to use manures as fertilizer.

Farming in the South

South of the Mason-Dixon line, agriculture faced hard times after the Revolution. Soils along the coastal plain were becoming exhausted. Yields had also declined in the Virginia Piedmont. There had been a decline in world demand for American tobacco. European development of artificial dyes had spelled the doom of the indigo culture of Georgia and the Carolinas; and rice planting yielded only modest profits.

Although income was down, southern planters could not easily slash costs. Unlike free workers, slaves could not be discharged. Nor could they be sold with profit, since slave prices declined along with those for staple crops. Hence, in the late eighteenth century, many a planter complained that his Negroes were a burden to him.

To be sure, slaves could be freed; and many Virginia masters did emancipate their bondsmen. Such action resulted partly from humanitarian feeling, at a time when the Revolution was pointing the way toward social reform. Also, manumission was made easier by the low value of the property rights which the owners relinquished. Yet many masters doubted the wisdom of emancipation. What would become of freed Negroes? Must the owner give them land as well as liberty? How would free Negroes get along with neighbors attached to the doctrine of white supremacy? Puzzled, some planters backed an American Colonization Society. Founded in 1816, this organization in 1822 helped found a settlement on the west coast of Africa, in what is now the republic of Liberia. At this time more than a thousand freed Negroes were shipped to the area. But Africa proved a hard land for American Negroes; and the project was expensive. It soon became apparent that the American Colonization Society would never be able to transport a significant portion of the slave population. Slave or free, the Negro was destined to remain in the United States.

Realizing this, many southern whites who were critical of slavery decided not to wreck the system. Better keep it, they said, than have large numbers of free Negroes in their home communities. Such reasoning helped kill the emancipation movement in the upper South (Maryland, Delaware, Virginia, North Carolina, Kentucky). More important was the spectacular revival of slavery as a profitable institution. The key was the cotton gin, the first striking example of the impact of technology on American agriculture.

Cotton had been grown in small quantities before the Revolution, from New Jersey to Georgia. The demand increased with the British boom in textile manufacturing. But the hand process of separating fibers from seeds was so slow that there was no way of supplying this demand. As late as 1791 total cotton production for the United States was only 400 bales.

In 1793 Eli Whitney of Connecticut was visiting a plantation near Savannah. He there became interested in the seed-and-fiber problem, for he realized that its solution would make cotton pay. No real scientific knowledge was involved; it was simply a matter of mechanics. Whitney had a genius for this sort of thing and soon contrived a gin that made cleaning of fibers quick and easy. Production increased to 175,000 bales by 1810 and to twenty times that amount in 1860.

In much of the upper South the summers were too short for cotton culture. But cotton planting replaced subsistence farming in the Piedmont or upstate areas of the Carolinas. In Georgia, where little more than the coastal region was occupied in 1800, cotton speeded the settlement of the central part of the state. Then southern farmers looked to the virgin lands of Alabama, Mississippi, and Louisiana. The needs of English mills were enormous, for Britain was supplying a large part of the world with textiles. Great areas of virgin soil would give splendid yields, and Negroes were available for large-scale labor. The new steamboats could load directly at plantation levees and carry cotton to coastal ports for transshipment overseas.[1]

As the cotton kingdom moved inland, many made fortunes from the product. Trading towns of the interior—Columbia, Augusta, Macon—grew in size and importance. Even Virginians, who were too far north to raise the new crop, benefited by selling surplus slaves to planters of the

---

[1] Optimism in the lower South was further encouraged when, in 1795, a Louisiana Creole demonstrated that sugar could be grown profitably in the Mississippi delta country. By 1802, just before Louisiana was incorporated into the United States, there were eighty-one sugar plantations in that area. The number grew to 700 by the 1830's. But sugar never rivaled cotton in importance.

lower South. Tobacco planters who could not break even on their crops could realize a profit in this fashion—and were thus tied to cotton.

Being short of workers, some cotton planters wanted to reopen the African slave trade. All southern states had stopped this prior to 1800, partly for humanitarian reasons, partly because of the feeling that slavery was dying out. New needs caused South Carolina to reopen foreign commerce in slaves in 1803. Federal legislation outlawed the trade entirely in 1808, but considerable smuggling ensued.

Since cotton brought quick profits, few Southerners considered the long-range consequences of the introduction of the new staple. These were not all for the good. The spread of cotton culture fastened on the South institutions that had seemed decadent before 1800: the plantation system, a single money-crop economy, Negro slave labor.

Business in the Merchant Era

Although a business cycle can be traced back into the colonial era, up to 1815 the cycle was more the result of conditions in Europe than in America. Bad European harvests and good ones here spelled prosperity for the United States. War in Europe with relative freedom for neutral commerce increased American exports and helped American shipping. But periods of restricted trade—the undeclared war with France (1798–1800), the Jeffersonian Embargo of 1808—turned prosperity into depression.

Foreign trade, the "big business" of those days, was distinct from the small business of retailing. A man needed considerable capital to engage in overseas ventures, and the title of "merchant" was generally reserved for international traders. Local businessmen were called storekeepers or shopkeepers. The typical retailer ran a general store in a small town with no competition save from traveling peddlers. His monopolistic position forced him to become a supplier of many services. Exchanging farm products for store goods, he was a produce middleman. Having contact with outside capital, he became a promoter of new enterprises. Extending credit, he could be called a banker. Selling books and periodicals, he was the purveyor of news and "culture." And, since he traveled once or twice a year to a metropolitan market to buy his wares, he was considered an authority on new styles.

The large merchant of the seaports enjoyed none of the security of the small-town storekeeper. In exchanging American farm products for the manufactures of Europe and the Orient, the great merchant was in competition with traders from all the principal commercial countries. The profit he made depended on how many other merchants brought similar cargoes to his home port at about the same time.

Yet, like country storekeepers, leading merchants had to perform a variety of functions. They owned ships and carried other people's goods as well as their own. They bought and sold on commission and extended credit. They owned warehouses and rented space to small traders. They bought and sold foreign exchange, took deposits at interest, purchased securities for a fee, and performed all the functions of private bankers. The credit the city merchant allowed the country storekeeper on his annual purchase of goods might be extended by the latter in turn as a store credit to men who wished to build a tannery or a flour mill. Thus the merchant became a financier supplying capital to underwrite new ventures. Or a small manufacturer might get his start by going directly to the big merchant for an advance of cash or credit in return for a consignment of future goods.

Although French and Dutch merchants hoped to supply the United States market after the American Revolution, old habits and lines of credit led instead to a resumption of American relations with Liverpool and London firms. American merchants also found markets in Spain, Latin America, Hawaii, and the Far East. The China trade offered great opportunities. But a China voyage could be attempted only by rich merchants, for it involved tying up capital for two years and running the risks of piracy and shipwreck.

The sea offered other opportunities. Subsidized by the federal government after 1789, American codfishing fleets continued to compete with those of France and England. Coastwise vessels carried goods between American seaports. American shipbuilders sold vessels to Europeans. And by the 1790's marine insurance was becoming a substantial business.

The Dawn of Industrialism

In colonial days a large fraction of the finished products used by Americans were produced in the home. Local grain milling and the manufacture of wood, iron, pottery, chemicals, leather, and textiles were carried on in small buildings by a few men with little machinery beyond a mill wheel. New enterprises of this type throve when British supplies were cut off during the Revolution; but many died in the face of postwar competition from abroad. The young United States still lacked the labor and management, the capital and markets necessary for adapting the new British inventions such as the steam engine, spinning jenny, and power loom to a successful factory system.

After the Revolution Americans continued to lag in manufacturing. A

Society for Useful Manufactures, promoted by Hamilton and some of the nation's richest men, failed. Among the few who did succeed were Almy and Brown, of Providence, Rhode Island. Working with Samuel Slater, a highly competent English mechanic, this firm started spinning mills at the end of the eighteenth century. Also successful was Eli Whitney of cotton-gin fame. Whitney built a gun and hardware factory in Connecticut, introducing the important principle of interchangeable parts.

After 1800 the Napoleonic Wars all but eliminated United States contacts with much of continental Europe; and by 1807, commercial quarrels reduced Anglo-American trade. This hurt American shipowners but helped American manufacturers, by protecting them from foreign competition. As shipping profits dwindled, merchants invested capital in industrial ventures. During the War of 1812 a group of Boston merchants led by Francis Lowell and Nathan Appleton set up the first complete American cotton textile factory, in Waltham, Massachusetts. For these businessmen, the second war with Britain was a blessing in disguise. But it remained to be seen whether industrialism nurtured by war could survive the competitive rigors of peace.

Business and the Government

Merchants financed and led the movement for the Constitution in the North. They influenced the urban press, controlled several state political machines, and were the strongest element in the Federalist party, which controlled the national offices from 1789 to 1801. It is not surprising, therefore, that the merchants got what they wanted from the new central government. The coastwise trade was reserved for American shipowners. In foreign trade differential tonnage duties favored American vessels. Federal bounties aided New England fishing interests. Relatively low tariff duties helped importers, and a new navy protected American traders in distant areas.

In general, merchants favored the financial measures of Alexander Hamilton. As bondholders and businessmen interested in economic stability, the merchants stood to gain by the refunding of the national debt, the assumption of state debts, the establishment of a mint and national bank. Most merchants also favored Hamilton's excise taxes; but they did not like his *Report on Manufactures* (1791), which called for a protective tariff. And this was the one Hamiltonian proposal which was not adopted.

When the Federalists went out of office in 1801, the merchants lost some of their influence. The Jeffersonian party, which ruled the roost for a generation, was dominated by agrarians. Still, commercial interests were not totally neglected. Jefferson retained the fishing subsidies and differential tonnage duties, and protected American trade in the Mediterranean by fighting the Barbary pirates. But in real crises, the merchants were apt to be ignored, as when the Jeffersonians voted for the Embargo of 1808 and war with Britain in 1812.

Capital and Credit

The ultimate greatness of the United States depended on development of the vast resources of the interior. This in turn called for the accumulation of capital. Successful foreign trade was one source of capital accumulation. During the Revolution state and continental currency, bonds and certificates offered speculators new ways to amass fortunes. Confiscated Tory properties, sold at auction, and western lands provided additional opportunities. When speculators simply bought and sold land, they did little to further the country's growth. But when they used money to attract immigrants, to provide inns, mills, and road improvements, they developed the productive power of the nation.

Capital could also be obtained from abroad. A British investment in American securities made money available for American purchases in the British market. Thus the credit would ultimately cross the ocean in the form of English products which could help develop the American economy. After 1789 American government bonds and the stock of the first Bank of the United States found a ready sale in the Netherlands. State bonds and the stock of small corporations were less attractive. By 1793 the London and Continental money markets were burdened with war finance. As a result, little foreign capital came to the United States until after 1815.

Selling American securities at home was almost as difficult as marketing them abroad. The average citizen was disinclined to trust his meager savings to sellers of paper certificates. Experience with state and national bonds during the Revolution made him doubly suspicious. Only the well-to-do felt at home in the security markets; and there were few rich men in the young republic. Moreover, some of the wealthiest had no cash—planters, for example, had their capital tied up in land and slaves, and could not invest in securities.

Unable to raise much by selling securities, American businessmen anticipated future earnings in another way, by creating bank credit. Back in the colonial decades, London merchants allowed "book credit." When the Revolution severed these credit lines, Robert Morris, Thomas Willing, and other enterprising Americans decided to build a new credit structure in the United States. Their Bank of North America, chartered by Congress in 1781, and by Pennsylvania a year later, was the first true commercial bank in America. It was also the third government-incorporated commercial bank in the world. Similar institutions were set up in New York and Boston in 1784, providing Americans with credit needed for the expansion of economic operations.

After the adoption of the Constitution, Secretary of the Treasury Alexander Hamilton asked for a central bank. Despite opposition based on constitutional scruples and fear of banks, Congress chartered the first Bank of the United States for twenty years (1791–1811). This institution, empowered to create branches, had $10,000,000 in capital, 20 percent of which was subscribed by the government.

Hamilton had high hopes for this bank. It would, of course, handle government financial transactions. In addition, it could supply urgently needed private credit. There was also the distinct possibility that it, like the Bank of England, might enforce "sound" banking practices through its domination of the national money market. But that was not to be. Eager for credit, merchants and farmers demanded more banks, so that any citizen could obtain cash by signing a promissory note at his local institution. Existing banks lobbied to prevent the chartering of competitors; and some farmers opposed all bank charters, on the ground that bankers obtained a monopoly control of money. But eventually state legislatures bowed to the demand. While the Bank of the United States established eight branches, the states chartered eighty-eight banks.

The Bank of the United States issued paper money and made loans; but its managers were careful not to extend credit freely to persons who lacked liquid assets. Most state-chartered banks were more generous. Many printed bank notes in quantity and made loans to anyone who wanted credit. Unchartered private banks, brokers, and merchants also entered the lending business, issuing "bills" which passed for currency in local communities. In other words, small-town bankers and moneylenders pursued an easy credit policy. On the whole, this pleased the American people, who needed money for productive enterprises. Easy credit meant inflation, but that alarmed few citizens. Indeed, inflation helped the debtor farmer by making it easier for him to pay off his mortgage and bills at the store. And by increasing the money in circulation, the wholesale issuance of state bank notes enabled American businessmen to expand, and build up the national economy.

Determined to curb inflation, the Bank of the United States collected notes of state banks, then presented them, demanding payment in specie. Since specie was hard to obtain (the United States having an "unfavorable" balance of trade), this practice tended to make small financial institutions limit their note issue. But the practice also irritated local bankers and other advocates of easy credit. When the charter of the Bank of the United States expired (1811), Congress refused to grant a recharter, and allowed the national bank to die. After that, the lid was off. Banks multiplied all over the country. With the Bank of the United States out of the way, there was no effective check on note issue. Instead, partly because of the financial operations connected with the War of 1812, there was a tendency to print more and more paper money. Bank notes depreciated sharply; and by 1815 the situation was so chaotic that merchants were having difficulty in conducting interstate commerce.

Population Growth

At the beginning of the Revolution, the population of the colonies was about 2,500,000. When the first census was taken in 1790, the number had increased to 4,000,000. By 1810 it was nearly 8,000,000, four times what it had been fifty years before.

This growth seems the more remarkable because immigration slackened after 1776, averaging only 4000 a year from then to 1800. The Revolution discouraged Europeans from coming over; and after 1789, the French Revolution and Napoleonic Wars had the same effect. Growth was therefore largely the result of natural increase. The birth rate continued high; and the death rate was beginning to decline.

Improved living conditions—for example, better food—increased resistance to disease, thus reducing the death rate. Also significant was the new interest in hygiene and public health. During 1793 the nation's capital, Philadelphia, suffered an epidemic of yellow fever. President Washington and thousands of others fled; yet 10 percent of the population succumbed. Many blamed the epidemic on foul airs which arose from filth, and demanded sanitary improvements. The city began cleaning its streets. It also introduced the first municipal water supply in the United States (1802), the water being pumped by steam engines to all parts of the town. Here were the beginnings of a public health movement which would substantially cut the death rate.

Physicians played a leading part in the hygiene and public health movements. Thus Dr. Benjamin Rush published one of the first American manuals of health, and urged sanitary reforms in Philadelphia. He was mistaken, however, in considering bleeding and purging a cure for yellow fever. Since he advocated removing as much as three-fourths of the blood in the body, patients who recovered must have done so in spite of, rather than because of, his treatments. Indeed, medicine still had few cures to offer other than the ameliorative effects of mercury against syphilis and cinchona bark against malaria.

At the turn of the century, word reached America that the English physician, Jenner, had proved that inoculation with cowpox would protect humans against smallpox. Since cowpox usually produced only a local sore at the point of vaccination, this was a safer means of protection than was the colonial practice of inoculation with smallpox itself. Vaccination was rapidly introduced in the towns. Results were excellent, and preventive medicine had scored a great victory.

Rural America

In these years Philadelphia grew from 40,000 in 1790 to 110,000 in 1820. New York jumped from 30,000 to 120,000 and became the largest American city. Meantime, there was steady growth in Boston, Baltimore, and New Orleans. Urban expansion everywhere was linked to commerce, handicraft manufactures, and associated activity in fishing and shipbuilding. But, although the cities were social, cultural, and business centers, they did not yet dominate American life. Nearly nine-tenths of the people remained farmers. Rural interests wielded major political control, as in bringing the Jeffersonians to power in 1800. They also exercised great influence on the customs and outlook of the people as a whole. In religious affairs, for instance, it was the rural folk who responded most heartily to the revivals which swept the country after 1790 and left the stamp of evangelical enthusiasm on the nation.

Even city folk remained partly within the rural orbit. Agriculture was the chief occupation, and townspeople were conscious of dependence on it. Many city dwellers had had personal contact with farm life. Rural institutions and customs, such as the patriarchal family and early hours for rising and retiring, persisted in the towns although they were not so well adapted to urban conditions. Habit rather than good sense led city clerks to go on eating as if they were still doing heavy labor in the fields.

There were sectional differences. Town life was more the rule in southern New England than in other areas. Economic power was concentrated in the urban merchant class around New York and Philadelphia, too. But in the South planters dominated economic and cultural life. Such towns as Williamsburg and Charleston were primarily centers for plantation business and society.

Not content with leadership in the South, planters advocated the rural way of life as ideal for the whole country. To planters, cities seemed crowded and filthy. Poor workers were demoralized by poverty and a slum environment; prosperous merchants were corrupted by the search for profits. In the free air of the country, even small farmers could raise their families under decent circumstances, and the gentry lived a gracious life uncorrupted by a scramble for money. A society composed of honest farmers and country gentlemen would be sound and stable, whereas urban societies would be undermined by avarice and disorder.

Jeffersonian Democracy

Foremost in advocating this philosophy was Thomas Jefferson. Never having seen a town until he approached manhood, Jefferson always preferred the country. He received very unfavorable impressions of the city proletariat while serving as American minister in Paris on the eve of the French Revolution. Hence when he spoke of the American people, he meant American farmers. And he observed that "those who labor in the earth are the chosen people of God."

In other words, Jefferson had confidence in the common man *if* that common man was a farmer and property holder. Jefferson's plan for a Virginia state constitution did not provide for manhood suffrage; there was to be a small property qualification. At the same time, Jefferson urged the state to grant each man enough land to meet the requirement. Political opportunities were to be based on a stabilizing interest in property. Jefferson was not opposed to private property and capitalism as such. Rather he feared that merchants and bankers would use wealth and power at the expense of the farmers. He was a defender of small (farmer) capitalists against the big urban capitalists, which identifies him with later agrarian reformers down to William Jennings Bryan.

Jefferson wanted elementary education to be available to all boys and favored a state system of public schools for this purpose. For those sufficiently intelligent, public secondary schools and universities should be provided. Yet Jefferson failed to secure this system even in Virginia, and the university he established there came in time to serve chiefly the more prosperous.

Here was a contradiction. The equal opportunities which Jeffersonians urged did not exist when boys were denied education because of poverty. The contradiction is explained, however, by another aspect of Jeffersonianism. Reacting against Hamilton's financial measures, Jefferson's backers insisted that the government should interfere with men's affairs as little as possible. This was in line with rural thinking anyway. Farm families were still self-sufficient in most respects, and felt that the government should limit itself largely to keeping the peace—any more was likely to be interference with free enterprise. Ironically, this position was taken over by businessmen a century later, when the government began to regulate rather than simply to aid business interests. Most free enterprise arguments now advanced by conservative industrialists could be taken right from the views once set forth by Jefferson in defense of farmers.

Rural citizens of 1800 were especially anxious to avoid increase in taxation (the most objectionable government "interference"). Establishing public schools meant tax increases. In most parts of the United States education had traditionally been a private matter. Families taught their children, or paid their expenses in private schools. Why should the man who had saved enough to provide for his children be forced to support schools for children of the improvident? Nor were farmers altogether convinced of the necessity of formal schooling. Did not farm chores provide the training that was most essential? Such reasoning kept some rural states from providing real public school systems until after the Civil War. Urban areas did somewhat better. This was logical, for the poor were concentrated in the towns, and formal schooling was required for many urban occupations.

In class feeling, too, the Jeffersonians fell short of later democratic standards. The Federalists, of course, openly expressed disdain for common folk. But even among Jeffersonians the assumption persisted that gentlemen should direct social institutions. Jefferson himself shared these sentiments. Reared among Virginia planters, he never forgot that he was a gentleman. He sympathized with the plain people but was not one of them. In this sense, he stood halfway between the aristocratic Hamilton and Andrew Jackson, the equalitarian leader of a later generation.

The Family

Americans were inclined to be suspicious of the English common law. Nevertheless, that body of customs still governed the place of the family in the American community and the relationship of members of the family to each other. In good patriarchal tradition, the father was the master of the house, with authority over his wife and children. The federal census recognized this when it listed population by heads of families. The courts followed suit. American judges granted that women had rights not enjoyed under English common law; but they allowed the husband almost complete control in cases involving property. Nor did mothers have the legal right to interfere with the decisions of the father with reference to the discipline, education, and marriage of their children.

In these years from the Revolution to the War of 1812, Americans were moving toward a philosophy of democracy and individualism. Patriarchal control curbed rather than encouraged individualism; and the father's rule left little room for the shared decisions and compromises characteristic of democracy. Yet, being set, the family pattern changed only very slowly. There were, however, a few indications of change. Some of the more straitlaced claimed that the Revolution had ruined the younger generation. Perhaps it was the absence of fathers, who were away fighting the British.

Perhaps it was the generally disrupting effect of war on morals and manners. Anyway, mourned these pious critics, boys and girls no longer seemed to know their place; they were becoming frivolous, profane, and worldly.

Here and there a voice was raised on behalf of women. *The Vindication of the Rights of Women*, by the English feminist Mary Wollstonecraft, was republished in Philadelphia in 1794. This tract insisted that women were intellectually equal to men. It scolded the women for accepting a position of subordination and denounced men for lording it over their wives and daughters and denying them education. Among American supporters of women's rights was Charles Brockden Brown, a novelist whose *Alcuyn: A Dialogue on the Rights of Women* (1797) was a defense of feminism. The cause was further aided by the success of such women as Mercy Otis Warren, poet, playwright, and historian of the American Revolution, and Hannah Webster Foster, whose sentimental novels passed through many editions.

Feminism was a minor movement. Family patterns were affected more seriously by the westward movement. The frontier gave young men a chance to free themselves from parental control. Many went alone, thereby weakening family ties. Others were married just before they started west, and took their brides with them. These men often came to regard their wives more as partners than as servants; that is, the courage and accomplishments of frontier women tended to improve their status. The high ratio of men to women in the western country added further to the prestige of women.

The traditional family pattern was also challenged by economic trends in the Northeast. Even before 1815 that area was shifting from a household, handicraft economy to the factory system. Hamilton and others who favored industrial development argued that the women and children of the lower classes could increase their usefulness by laboring in factories. In Samuel Slater's first Rhode Island cotton textile mill, the workers were chiefly women and children, some of the latter being as young as seven years of age. Equally deplorable conditions existed in other manufacturing establishments.

Although their wages were controlled by their menfolk, the women employed in factories were taking a step toward economic independence. In working away from home, they of necessity neglected the household crafts which had long provided an economic base for the close-knit family. Children employed in industry also ceased to work with the family unit. Kept at the factories from sunup to sundown, they were removed from parental control for most of their waking hours. Thus the industrial revolution would help force a modification of the old system of patriarchal control.

Old World Influence on American Culture

Although colonial Americans had never been entirely isolated from the thought of continental Europe, they had in general looked to England for intellectual leadership. After the Revolution, Americans continued to derive much of their cultural stimulus from Britain. But these years brought other impulses, too. The Revolution made Americans anxious to break with their English past. The tendency was strengthened by anti-British propaganda during the Revolution and the War of 1812. Britishers also contributed to Anglophobia by belittling the republican experiment.

Other developments also served to open the doors to cultural relations with the non-English world. The foreign legations in the successive capitals (New York, Philadelphia, and Washington) acquainted Americans with Europeans of culture and distinction. Americans who went abroad on diplomatic missions also helped bring their fellow countrymen into the main stream of European life. The impact of the Orient was less notable but in growing evidence. Seeking markets to compensate for the loss of trade with British possessions, New England merchantmen began to visit China in the 1780's. These seamen brought back tea, silks, and porcelain—and some notion of a rich culture. Then, in 1812, the first American missionaries set out for India. As their numbers multiplied, the missionaries helped all Americans to become acquainted with the Orient.

Of the countries providing cultural inspiration to the United States, France led the rest. This was logical in view of the Franco-American alliance of 1778, and the desire of France to make the United States a French satellite. Louis XVI sent books to American libraries. France assigned able diplomats to the United States and paid attention to Americans traveling in Europe. French officers serving in the United States during the War of Independence spread knowledge of French culture. Some stayed on after the war; one, Major L'Enfant, drew the plans for the new federal capital on the banks of the Potomac. Chastellux and other French intellectuals toured the United States and wrote enthusiastic accounts of the republic's condition and prospects. (By contrast, English visitors specialized in hostile comments.) And French influence grew in the era of the French Revolution and Napoleon (1789–1815), when distinguished refugees sought American shores.

As interest in France increased, well-to-do Americans studied the French language, read French books, experimented with French cooking, followed Parisian fashions in dress, household furnishings, and the fine arts. The founders of a Boston institute to promote scientific studies announced that they wanted to import "the air of France rather than that of England." When the French Revolution broke out in 1789, most Americans were enthusiastic. France, it seemed, was following the path of the United States, accepting principles of the Declaration of Independence and the Virginia Statute of Religious Liberty. When violence increased, American conservatives condemned the French Revolution as an attack on property, religion, and civil authority. But many plain people still considered the French Revolution part of a world struggle for liberty. Throughout the United States enthusiasts sang French revolutionary songs, wore liberty caps, and set up Democratic-Republican clubs, modeled on those of France. These clubs added to the political influence of Thomas Jefferson, and helped those Americans who were fighting the forces of privilege within the United States.

Two movements of thought closely associated with the French Revolution were to have special importance in the United States. One was the idea of progress—formulated earlier, but brought into new prominence by its popularity in revolutionary France. The other was deism, which also broadened its appeal after 1789.

Those who advanced the idea of progress claimed that the golden age lay, not in a shadowy past, but in a future which man might shape by his intelligence. The best way to assure progress was to promote rationalism and natural science; armed with reason and scientific method, man could reform society and realize his full potentialities. This concept was especially attractive in America. Here the stage was little cluttered with feudal vestiges. Here the newness of the land provided an invitation to the full realization of a golden future. So thought Benjamin Franklin, Philip Freneau, Joel Barlow, Dr. Benjamin Rush, and Thomas Jefferson.

Deism had emerged in seventeenth-century England and had become known to colonial Americans through English writings. The deists rejected most of the traditional Christian creed. They doubted the Biblical account of the creation of man and the universe. They questioned the miracles, the sacraments, the doctrine of salvation by grace, the idea of a personal God daily intervening in human affairs. Instead, they saw God as the architect of the universe, the crystallization of the laws of nature.

Even before 1789, deism had sharpened the cleavage between religious conservatives and liberals in New England, paving the way for Unitarianism, a rationalistic movement well defined by 1800. The French Revolution added to the flames of controversy. When French books were popular, Americans read Voltaire and other French exponents of deism. Moreover, in the minds of many the French Revolution identified orthodox religion with reaction, deism with liberty, equality, and fraternity. The most popular treatment of deism was Thomas Paine's *Age of Reason*, written while its author was championing the revolutionary upheaval in France. The book was sure of a good reception in the United States, for Americans remembered *Common Sense*, the pamphlet Paine had produced to support the Patriot cause in the American Revolution. *The Age of Reason*, therefore, was read by humble citizens as well as intellectuals. Its influence persisted even when, at the turn of the century, an evangelical movement won back to the fold thousands of Americans who had become indifferent to orthodox Christianity.

By 1800 the tendency to revere French cultural leadership was on the decline. For one thing, the United States and France had come to blows, in an undeclared war of 1798–1800. Then, too, the much admired French Revolution gave way in 1799 to Napoleonic dictatorship. But France had permanently contributed to the broadening of mental horizons in the United States.

Science and Technology

Concentrating on economic and political tasks, the American republic continued to lean heavily on the Old World for knowledge of the scientific developments that were beginning to revolutionize intellectual i.ie and lay the foundations for modern industrial society. Many of the scientists active in the United States during this period were immigrants. Dr. Joseph Priestley, discoverer of oxygen, came to the United States in the 1790's, a refugee from the reaction that swept over England when the French Revolution challenged the existing order in Europe. So did Dr. Thomas Cooper, who indicated ways in which geological findings contradicted the Biblical account of creation. William Maclure, a wealthy Scotsman, carried on pioneer geological studies in the trans-Appalachian area and familiarized Americans with the cataclysmic and quasi-evolutionary theories of the earth's origin. Other immigrants, including John James Audubon and Constantine Rafinesque, collected specimens of American birds and flowers, classified these according to prevailing European systems, and thus enlarged knowledge of the New World scene.

As in the past, American-born scientists also leaned heavily on European learning. Many went abroad for training in the sciences or medicine. Others adapted (and sometimes improved) European scientific treatises. Nathaniel Bowditch aided countless seamen by publishing his *New American Practical Navigator* (1802), a useful modification of an English manual. He next prepared a translation of and commentary on Laplace's classic work on astronomy, *La mécanique céleste*. Meantime, Professors Benjamin Silliman of Yale, John Maclean of Princeton, and Robert Hare of Pennsylvania were teaching students Lavoisier's new quantitative chemistry, and its implications for medicine, industry, and the fine arts.

The United States also owed much to the Old World in the field of mechanical invention. Anxious to protect her rising textile industry, Britain prohibited export of new types of machinery. But Samuel Slater became so thoroughly familiar with British machines that he could reproduce them from memory. He did just that when he migrated to America and helped set up New England's cotton textile industry (1790). Another Englishman who brought knowledge with him to the United States was Benjamin Henry Latrobe. A noted architect, Latrobe also pioneered in a new field when he built a municipal water-supply system for Philadelphia. Robert Fulton, who built the first commercially successful American steamboat, used an English (Boulton and Watts) steam engine.

Americans, however, did more than borrow. James Rumsey, John Fitch, John Stevens, and Fulton all did important work on the steamship. Rumsey experimented with the jet-propulsion principle. Stevens developed a multitubular boiler; and he and others used the screw propeller, which would in time replace the paddle wheel of Fulton's *Clermont*. Besides working on steamships, Fulton experimented with submarines and torpedoes. Another American, Oliver Evans, devised new mill machinery—important in a country short of labor—and built good stationary engines.

Most important of all was Eli Whitney. While sojourning in Georgia, this New Englander invented the cotton gin, a machine which separated the seeds from cotton fiber. By making cotton culture profitable, the gin changed the southern economy and fastened slavery on that region. Copied without authorization, the cotton gin brought Whitney more fame than fortune. But he did make money later, manufacturing small arms. Here again he hit on a vital principle. He took care to standardize his product. His guns could be repaired easily, with standard spare parts. Manufacturers of other products followed Whitney's example; and the ultimate superiority of American technology was to depend in good measure on this interchangeability of machine parts.

American originality was likewise evident in the dissemination of scientific knowledge among the people. Scientific farmers of the United States were deeply indebted to Arthur Young and other English agricultural reformers. But the Americans also struck out on their own—in establishing agricultural societies, fairs, and journals designed to promote efficiency and profit among the rank and file of farmers.

The Fine Arts

Apart from Indian influences, Americans had no art traditions of their own during the colonial period. Long thereafter, the vast majority of the people were intent on making a living and possessed neither the ability nor the inclination to patronize the arts. The Puritan tradition also held back the arts, especially the theater. John Adams, though a cultivated scholar, maintained that the arts, having sprung from luxury and despotism, should be avoided in America as tending to prostitute the simple virtues of republicanism.

In view of such handicaps, it was natural for writers, architects, artists, and musicians to lean heavily on European models, and on the patronage of a few upper-class Americans. The influential Benjamin West, an aristocratic American painter who chose to live in London, encouraged younger artists to work in the formal and classical traditions then in vogue in the Old World. Thus Gilbert Stuart, who returned to America after apprenticeship with West in London, painted in a stilted manner that had little meaning save for the wealthy Americans who sat for their likenesses; and John Singleton Copley did his best work in New England, before he moved to London. English influence was supplemented by the impact of the French school.

The classical taste then current in Europe predominated in many other fields. Jefferson, having mastered the classical style of architecture, applied it with distinction in designing his estate at Monticello, houses for his friends, and the University of Virginia. Sculpture had no roots in America, save as a folk art (ship figureheads and the like). Hence Virginians, desiring a likeness of Washington, turned to the French sculptor, Houdon. In music, the prevailing English ballad-opera and the classical compositions of Handel and Haydn dominated the American scene.

European influence was equally strong in literature. American periodicals followed the pattern of English reviews. Hugh H. Brackenridge's novel, *Modern Chivalry*, though American in materials, was inspired by Cervantes' *Don Quixote*. The verse of the Hartford Wits, and that of Francis Hopkinson and Philip Freneau, suggested Alexander Pope on the one hand, or the rising romanticists on the other. American drama, too, showed a dependence on England, or (as with William Dunlap, "father of American drama") on the romantic schools of France and Germany.

Yet native impulses were also important. America provided an abundance of themes: natural beauty, Indian warfare, the Revolution, contests between Jeffersonians and Federalists. And, being politically independent, Americans felt a new sense of cultural responsibility.

The Revolution naturally engaged the pens of patriots. During and after the struggle the American cause was defended by poets, playwrights, novelists, composers, and painters. The fight for freedom brought forth the moving lyrics of Philip Freneau, and Joel Barlow's ambitious epic poem, *The Vision of Columbus*. Plays included Mercy Otis Warren's *The Group*, a Revolutionary propaganda piece, and *André*, written and produced by William Dunlap. The Revolution popularized the folk song "Yankee Doodle," and William Billings, a Boston tanner and self-trained composer, turned out patriotic songs. The post-Revolutionary period brought forth other efforts: Joseph Hopkinson's "Hail Columbia" and Francis Scott Key's "Star-Spangled Banner," now the official national anthem. (Here, however, one may note Old World influence. Key wrote the words for "The Star-Spangled Banner," but the tune was an English air, "To Anacreon in Heaven.")

American painters also tried to capture the spirit of the Revolution. After fighting in the war, John Trumbull depicted on canvas the "Battle of Bunker Hill," the "Signing of the Declaration of Independence," and the "Surrender of Cornwallis." Though formal and idealized, Trumbull's paintings evoked a mood of patriotism. Also popular were representations of Patriot leaders. Gilbert Stuart's stylized portraits of Washington reflected the artist's aristocratic preferences. Those by Charles Willson Peale came closer to the actual Washington.

Peale, incidentally, disliked the aristocratic conception of patron-fostered art. Approving of the rising democratic spirit, he tried to familiarize the public with art by opening a popular museum in Independence Hall, Philadelphia, in 1782. The democratic movement also influenced music. Concerts, long the privilege of the few, multiplied; Boston's artisan-composer William Billings organized singing societies.

Literature was much affected by political trends. Philip Freneau vigorously belabored the Federalists. Joseph Dennie, the leading magazine editor, was equally scurrilous in denouncing the Republicans. The Federalist-minded Hartford Wits satirized democracy and agrarianism in "The Anarchiad" and other poems, while Charles Brockden Brown's novels praised the rationalism and democratic sentiments of the Jeffersonians. Brackenridge's *Modern Chivalry* was a Jeffersonian treatment of the shortcomings of the republic.

Educational Progress

In many respects American education of 1815 resembled colonial education. Most common (elementary) schools were housed in cramped quarters and run by untrained men. In some respects the New England schools seem to have slipped backward, for, as population spread into the interior, lawmakers relaxed the traditional requirement that towns maintain schools. In the middle states elementary education was still largely in the hands of the churches, and southern educational opportunities were even more meager so far as the plain people were concerned. Colleges served a very small part of the population, and the traditional curriculum of ancient languages, metaphysics, and mathematics prevailed. As before, most doctors and lawyers acquired their training through apprenticeship. That is, a young man read law in the office of a practitioner, or studied a few medical books and assisted a physician for a time.

Yet much happened to improve the situation after 1763. The shortage of teachers was in part relieved by the introduction of the Lancasterian or monitorial system. This called for huge classrooms, with the more clever students passing on to other pupils the rudiments of reading, writing, and figuring, which they had learned by the rote method from the teacher. Inadequate though this was, it provided mass education of a sort at a time when taxpayers were reluctant to do much to support the schools.

Another importation from England was the Sunday School. This supplied weekly instruction in reading and church catechism for children unable to attend any other type of school. The first Sunday School Society, organized in 1791 in Philadelphia to promote instruction among the poor, led to the establishment of many schools. Although soon transformed from agencies of secular instruction into sectarian institutions, the Sunday Schools broadened educational opportunities.

New textbooks were superior to the traditional *New England Primer* and imported English manuals. Noah Webster, a lawyer-teacher-philologist, decided to improve instruction and promote American patriotism through improved schoolbooks. His *Elementary Spelling Book* (1783), a reader-speller, achieved amazing popularity (50,000,000 copies) because of its simplicity, human interest, and combination of moral and religious with secular and patriotic sentiments.

Another New Englander, Jedidiah Morse (father of the inventor of the telegraph), published in 1784 the first of his geography textbooks. Like Webster, Morse was anxious to improve teaching and at the same time to promote patriotism. In contrast with Old World geographers, Morse centered his description of the earth around America rather than Europe. Textbooks in arithmetic followed the same practice when they adopted the American monetary system.

Although the high school was in the future, this period saw the appearance of its predecessor, the academy. Started by church groups and enterprising schoolmasters, the academies spread rapidly. Unlike the colonial Latin grammar schools, the academies taught English, French, history, geography, and the natural sciences, as well as Greek and Latin. The years before and after 1815 also saw the establishment of a number of secondary schools specially designed for girls.

Many new colleges were founded in the post-Revolutionary era, and opportunities for acquiring higher education more than kept pace with the growth of population. Most of the new institutions were started by church organizations; but by 1815 Vermont, North Carolina, Maryland, Virginia, and Pennsylvania had set up state universities or taken steps in that direction. Jefferson persuaded William and Mary College to liberalize its curriculum by adding modern languages, history, political economy, natural science. Other colleges, including Williams and Union, allowed students to substitute French for Greek. Yale took a long step forward in appointing Benjamin Silliman professor of the natural sciences, for Silliman then promoted scientific study through the whole country. Several colleges offered work in law or medicine, and, as colleges became secularized, special theological schools were founded. Judge Tapping Reeve founded the first professional law school at Litchfield, Connecticut, just after the Revolution.

Looking ahead, the American Philosophical Society sponsored an essay contest on education. Several participants advocated federal aid to schools and the establishment of a great national university. There was sentiment for increased instruction in the natural and social sciences and greater emphasis on hygiene. These subjects, it was claimed, offered greater benefits to the republic than the classics, metaphysics, and theology. Some contestants also wanted girls educated. But this was planning, not performance. Few Americans were ready to put up the money needed for a satisfactory system of free public education. The national-university idea, though favored by George Washington, did not materialize.

Learning is by no means confined to schools and colleges. These decades saw progress in the periodical field. Joseph Dennie's *Port Folio*, launched in 1801, attracted such talent as Charles Brockden Brown, Joseph Hopkinson, and Dr. Benjamin Rush. Less conservative was the earlier *American Museum* of Mathew Carey, best remembered for his writings on economic theory. Special-interest magazines (religion, science, medicine, literature) also made their appearance. An outstanding success was the *North American Review*. Established in 1815, it set a high standard in periodical journalism and did much to promote a national culture.

At the end of the Revolution, the United States boasted forty newspapers; by 1810, there were 350. The first daily, the *Pennsylvania Packet* and *Daily Advertiser*, appeared in 1784; many others followed. News coverage was poor, for there were no cables, telegraph lines, news agencies, or special reporters. The tone was partisan, for all were party organs. Since newspapers were expensive, journalists catered to the middle and upper classes; but the appeal broadened with each passing decade.

Religious Change

The drive to separate church and state, during the Revolution, and the popularity of deism weakened traditional orthodoxy. So did the rise of Unitarianism, for the Unitarians rejected the Trinity and Calvinistic ideas of depravity of man, with predestination of a few to salvation, many to damnation. Instead, Unitarians assumed that human nature is good, salvation a matter of character. Unitarian doctrine gained ground chiefly in New England, in the Congregational churches. The outstanding interpreter of Unitarianism, William Ellery Channing, became pastor of a Boston Congregational church in 1803; and two years later, a Unitarian was named professor of divinity at Harvard. The Universalists, who resembled the Unitarians in many respects, also made headway in New England.

The growth of deism, skepticism, and Unitarianism occasioned a reaction, for most Americans still felt the need for conventional religion. A wave of revivals swept over New England in the 1790's, strengthening orthodoxy. Churchmen like Timothy Dwight, president of Yale, and Jedidiah Morse, the geographer, denounced the atheism which they attributed to the French Revolution, and urged people to return to traditional faith. Far more violent were the revivals which broke out in the middle and southern states and across the Appalachians. In 1800 a great wave of open-air camp meetings in the West won (for the moment at least) the enthusiasm of border people starved for excitement and companionship.

The revivals were especially marked among Baptists, but Presbyterians were also involved. The Methodists likewise provided leadership in the evangelical awakening. On the eve of the Revolution, Charles and John Wesley, English originators of the so-called Methodist societies within the Anglican Church, had few American followers. But Methodism grew rapidly in the United States under the leadership of Bishop Francis Asbury. Before his death in 1816, Asbury crossed the Appalachians sixty times, traveled more than 250,000 miles, and aroused the emotions of countless men and women by his colorful pictures of the horrors of hell, the delights of heaven, the compassion and love of Jesus. The Bishop's athletic type of religion appealed to the common people in particular.

In efforts to curb worldliness and vice, clerical leaders organized Bible, temperance, and tract societies, all of which distributed reading matter. Home and foreign mission work was launched, and crusading zeal also expressed itself in movements against dueling, lotteries, and slavery.

Meantime, patriotism had set a stamp on ecclesiastical organization. American Methodists wanted and obtained the right to make their own decisions, independent of the English Methodists. The Revolution made reorganization even more essential for the Anglicans. Since their church was established in England, Anglican bishops were officers of a country now considered foreign; and the Church of England was headed by the hated George III. After difficulties, American members of this church obtained bishops of their own and organized an independent Protestant Episcopal Church. The Book of Common Prayer was altered to the needs of a republic, and the lay element was given more influence than in the English establishment.

American Catholics had long been governed by the hierarchy in England. The Holy See now saw the wisdom of placing the American church directly under Rome. This decision involved the consecration of an American bishop. Father John Carroll of Baltimore was given the episcopal ring, and organized Catholic activities in a diocese that embraced the whole country.

Most of the other churches already had organizations virtually independent of the mother churches in England or elsewhere. Independence, however, further weakened ties with the Old World, as with the Dutch Reformed and Lutheran denominations. For in religion as in other fields, an American nation was beginning to emerge.

7

Building an American Foreign Policy

Development of American Nationalism

American nationalism involves belief in the superiority of the United States, and loyalty to the United States above loyalty to any other country, state, community, or social group. Today, American nationalism affects the life of every resident of the republic from birth to death. But in the days of the American Revolution, nationalist feeling was just beginning to develop. Thereafter, it grew rapidly and by 1815 was a significant force.

In September, 1776, the Continental Congress decided that "the United States" should replace "the United Colonies" on all official documents. The term, however, was confusing. "The United States" might mean a firm national union—or a mere league of states. As late as 1815, stanch patriots referred to the United States both as "them" and as "it." James Madison, John Adams, and Thomas Jefferson each called his state his country, yet also used country to refer to the United States. Certain ardent nationalists, feeling that the term "United States" suggested dual loyalty, advocated using "America," as a term that implied organic unity. The word, however, referred not only to the United States but also to the rest of the hemisphere. "Columbia" and "Fredonia" found favor in literary circles. But the people became attached to the term "United States," and the words did suggest the prevailing conception of the republic as a *federal* union, with powers divided between central and state governments.

The most important patriotic symbol is the flag. During the Revolution, Americans at first relied on British emblems. But the Patriots also made their own flags. One contained the rattlesnake design, with the caption Franklin had made famous during the Stamp Act controversy: "Don't Tread on Me." On January 1, 1776, Washington displayed a new Great Union flag. This suggested union for American rights and continued loyalty to Britain, for the British crosses were combined with thirteen red and white stripes representing the united colonies.

162

When independence was declared, Congress eliminated the British crosses (1777), adding thirteen "stars white in a blue field, representing a new constellation." For some years a stripe and a star were added as each new state was admitted to the Union. The final decision (1818) was to have thirteen stripes, plus as many stars as there were states. As poets, orators, painters, and song writers hailed the Stars and Stripes, the flag became a symbol of attachment to the nation.

Another symbol of unity was the motto: *E Pluribus Unum* (one out of many). This was accepted by the Continental Congress on the recommendation of Franklin, Jefferson, and Adams soon after the Declaration of Independence. Congress adopted the eagle as the national emblem. To Americans, the eagle seemed a noble bird, a republican incarnation of the Roman symbol of courage and authority.[1]

As the central government gained influence, the eagle became increasingly popular. It was used on coins, ballots and the mastheads of newspapers and magazines; it was featured by furniture upholsterers, manufacturers of porcelain ware, and tattoo artists.

The same years witnessed the evolution of symbols for the American people collectively. Even before the Revolution the British seem to have dubbed the New England militia "Yankee Doodle." Taking over the term, Patriots used it to symbolize the shrewdness, vigorous independence, and roughness of the American rural type. The American people were also called Brother Jonathan. In cartoons the fellow was lanky, awkward, good-natured, shrewd, and, above all, youthfully militant and cocky. In some way Yankee Doodle and Brother Jonathan were gradually metamorphosed into Uncle Sam. During the War of 1812, opponents of the contest sneeringly called the general government Uncle Sam. Patriots soon adopted the term. Tall, sinewy, wise in the ways of the world, generous in his zeal for soldiers and their widows, Uncle Sam was both the government and the American people themselves. His present form owes most to Thomas Nast, the illustrator of Civil War days.

In monarchies the king symbolizes the nation; in republics a great hero may play a comparable role. George Washington had dignity easily mistaken for aloofness; and he was criticized by those who disliked his alignment with the Federalists. Nevertheless, Washington was a national hero, generally regarded as the father of his country and the embodiment of devotion to national unity. Even before the General's death his birthday was

---

[1] With his usual wit, Franklin said that the eagle, with thirteen arrows in his left talon and olive branches in his right, looked more like a turkey than anything else. Which was all right, he added, for "the Turkey is . . . a much more respectable bird, and withal a true original native of America."

celebrated with patriotic exercises. This custom became nation-wide after he died, in 1799. Children imbibed patriotism when they read Parson Weems' popular though inaccurate biographies of the great American. By 1815 Baltimore undertook the building of a Washington monument; and in time patriotic ladies would join hands to convert Mount Vernon into a national shrine.

Observance of the Fourth of July became general by 1815. The celebration normally included the reading of the Declaration of Independence. Fourth of July orators pictured the glorious destinies of the republic and identified America with liberty. Federalist speakers often restricted the meaning of liberty to independence; Republicans included democracy. Both sides mixed patriotic sentiments with denunciation of the opposition. Along with the speeches went feasting and drinking, cannon salutes and fireworks, parades and flag displays. And as they celebrated, the participants contributed to the development of American nationalism.

Demand for Cultural Independence

The growth of patriotism directly affected cultural trends. Jefferson held that American youth should be educated, not in the aristocratic and monarchical institutions of the Old World, but in native academies designed to inculcate the principles of Americanism. To that end he bent his efforts to found the University of Virginia. In that state university (founded in 1819), boys could choose from a wide range of subjects according to their preference. They could also govern themselves without faculty surveillance and imbibe natural-rights philosophy, agrarianism, and individualism—Jefferson's conception of American principles.

Many citizens wanted to develop scientific studies along patriotic lines. This could be done by concentrating on the study of American flora, fauna, and geological formations. Jefferson's *Notes on Virginia* (1787) constituted the first comprehensive scientific description of the natural resources of an American state. The book was further notable for its refutation of an idea current among Europeans, that the American environment was responsible for the deterioration of animals introduced from the Old World.

The same nationalistic tone ran through other fields. *Reason the Only Oracle of Man* (1784), a crudely written volume by the Vermont Revolutionary, Ethan Allen, identified deism with American republicanism. Those who favored the classical revival in architecture claimed that the simple lines of Greece and Rome suited a republic better than the Gothic, Renaissance, and Georgian styles. Some Americans demanded a distinctively American art or music. Others denounced English common law as favoring property rights instead of human rights, creditors instead of debtors. As a substitute, these critics asked for a simplified, democratic, distinctly American code, which could be understood by the plain people.

Even more impressive was the patriotic effort of Noah Webster, who felt that literary distinction was impossible until the nation had a language of its own. Already, he observed, the spoken English of America was different from that of Britain. Immigration and American experience would mean new changes; and, added Webster, time would see an American English as different from the language of Britain as Swedish is from German. Webster did what he could to speed the process. In his speller and dictionaries, he sanctioned popular usages, such as "you was"; and he tried to reform spelling along simplified, phonetic lines. He favored dropping the silent u in "honour," "colour," "labour." He substituted "plow" for the English "plough." Custom defeated Webster in his more extreme proposals; and the English used in the United States is more like that of Britain than Webster anticipated. But he was right in thinking that Americans would invent many new words and expressions, and a number of his spelling proposals were accepted by his countrymen.

Noah Webster's call for cultural nationalism became a dominant note in the intellectual history of the young republic. Joel Barlow insisted that America had already achieved a distinctive art and literature. This thesis was reasserted in more modest terms by Charles Jared Ingersoll, a Jeffersonian lawyer-politician who wrote books on the side. In 1810 Ingersoll brought out *Inchiquin*, which praised American culture, particularly American eloquence and social idealism. Yet Americans continued to rely on European culture. To man the faculty of the University of Virginia, Jefferson was compelled to import British scholars. Scientists exploring the American scene used Old World equipment and systems of classification. The vogue of classicism in literature, architecture, and art likewise signified continued reliance on European leadership. So did the Lancastrian educational system. Also the Pestalozzian method, which focused attention on the growth of the whole child, working through the project method and learning by doing. This fitted in with American concepts of the free and fully developed individual; but the principle came from Europe, not America.

In short, the time had not yet come when cultural nationalists could correctly maintain that American intellectual and aesthetic life had found a characteristically American expression. But the desire for cultural independence was keenly felt, the demand for it vigorously maintained. And by 1815 Americans had made progress toward that goal.

Nationalism and Diplomacy: Expansionism

The upsurge of nationalist sentiment, which so profoundly influenced American domestic development, also affected the foreign relations of the new republic. In diplomatic matters, citizens of the United States tended to be reckless, belligerent, superpatriotic. Were they not a "chosen people," marked for greatness by the "hand of destiny"? Those in positions of responsibility might feel that the country was unprepared for war, had no army or navy worthy of the name. But Americans who had conquered the wilderness were confident that no power could match strength with the United States. When there was trouble with Great Britain, these enthusiasts cried that a regiment of American militia could conquer Canada. When the French Revolution overthrew the Bourbons, many Americans wanted the United States to help the French republicans against their royal enemies: "If kings can combine to support kings, why not republics to support republics?"

Many were the dislikes of American patriots—they were anti-foreign, anti-European, antimonarchical. But above all they hated Spain and Britain. Bitterness against the mother country carried over from the American Revolution; and it was galling not to be able to trade freely with Spanish and British colonies. Besides, Spain and Britain, with their Indian allies, prevented Americans from reaching the "natural boundaries" of the United States. The natural-boundaries concept is closely related to nationalism. American nationalists looked beyond their country's borders, toward distant rivers, seas, and mountains. Security and prosperity, they felt, depended on the absorption of intervening areas.

During the Revolution many Americans felt that the United States must include Canada. The invasion of 1775–76 proved a failure, but the authors of the Articles of Confederation still hoped that Canada could be brought into the Union. In the Paris peace negotiations of 1782, Benjamin Franklin asked the British to cede unconquered Canada to the United States. He settled for less; but Americans continued to look northward. They also yearned for areas which Spain controlled: the mouth of the Mississippi, the rest of Louisiana, the Floridas. Later, the urge would be for Texas, Oregon, New Mexico, and California.

In pushing outward, Americans were seeking security. A Canada held by others jeopardized American safety. For one thing, Britain might invade the United States from Canada. For another, the British and Canadians could easily stir up the Indians against white settlers of Ohio. In like fashion, the safety of the southern states was threatened by Indians who received encouragement from Spanish Florida.

Nor was the situation different to the west. Americans who lived beyond the Appalachians insisted that their vital trade down the Mississippi could be secure only if New Orleans were in the possession of the United States. Their fears grew when (after 1800) they heard that feeble Spain would transfer Louisiana to mighty France. Americans from every section agreed that such a threat to national security could not be endured. So said an Easterner, Gouverneur Morris, when he wrote that "no nation has the right to give another a dangerous neighbor without her consent."

The yearning for security was coupled with a quest for economic opportunity. Fur traders, land speculators, western farmers who craved new land found it convenient to associate their ambitions with a higher destiny. "The waters of the St. Lawrence and the Mississippi interlock . . . ," exclaimed an expansionist Congressman, "and the Great Dispenser of Human Events intended those two rivers should belong to the same people." Andrew Jackson of Tennessee felt that "God and Nature have destined New Orleans and Florida to belong to this great and rising empire."

For others the riches of Spanish Mexico beckoned. Some would not stop there. "Where is it written in the book of faith that the American republic should not stretch her limits from the Capes of the Chesapeake to Nootka Sound," screamed the Nashville *Clarion* in 1812, "from the Isthmus of Panama to Hudson Bay?"

In defending expansionist philosophy, American nationalists claimed that the Indians, British, French, and Spanish could not develop the rich interior. "Is one of the fairest portions of the globe to remain in a state of nature, the haunt of a few wretched savages," asked William Henry Harrison, governor of the Indiana Territory, "when it seems destined by the Creator to give support to a large population and to be the seat of civilization, of science, and of true religion?"

This argument as to "destined use of the soil" was most impressive when red men were involved. Yet patriotic Americans talked of their "superior" civilization even when Europeans were concerned. Thomas Jefferson reasoned that the shift of Louisiana from European to American hands meant "a wide spread for the blessings of freedom and equal laws." John Adams, predicting that the American republic would absorb most of the continent, said that such expansion would be a "great point gained in favor of the rights of mankind."

These prophets of conquest did not go unchallenged. Josiah Quincy and other New England Federalists wailed that territorial expansion would ruin the United States. They claimed that the nation could survive as a republic only if confined within a relatively small area. They said that expansion into the interior would bring costly wars. It would also strengthen agriculture at the expense of the commercial interests of the Northeast. That is, a movement of population westward into newly annexed areas would depress land values along the Atlantic seacoast and create a labor shortage there. The Northeast's merchant aristocracy therefore wanted the United States government to deëmphasize territorial expansion and concentrate instead on building foreign trade.

Trade Promotion or Territorial Expansion?

The Jay-Gardoqui negotiations of 1785–86 brought out the fundamental conflict between trade promoters and territorial expansionists. At that time Spain, as owner of Louisiana, controlled the mouth of the Mississippi River. This disturbed American expansionists, for the Mississippi was the natural outlet for goods produced in American-owned Kentucky and Tennessee. The expansionists therefore insisted that Spain recognize that Americans had the right to navigate the Mississippi. Without that right the United States could not build up large settlements west of the mountains.

Spain, of course, had no desire to have Americans beyond the Appalachians. Such settlements would threaten Spanish territory. In consequence, Gardoqui, Spanish minister in the United States, asked the American government to yield on the navigation question. If the United States would give way, Spain would give commercial concessions in return, and welcome American ships to Spanish ports.

Merchants from New England and the middle states were tempted. So was John Jay, a trade-conscious New Yorker who was serving under the Confederation Congress as Secretary for Foreign Affairs. Jay said that the trade agreement was worth having, and that, to get it, the United States should waive the right of navigation on the Mississippi for a decade. The commercial-minded northern states agreed; but southern Congressmen, more interested in territory than in trade, forced Jay to abandon his proposal.

Though defeated here, the shipping interests won consideration from the national government. During the Confederation years, American diplomats negotiated commercial treaties with Sweden, the Netherlands, Prussia, and Morocco, and won trade concessions in the French West Indies. Merchants fared still better after the adoption of the Constitution. Congress barred foreigners from the coastwise trade, gave American vessels special tariff and tonnage rates, encouraged fishing interests, and helped those developing trade with the Far East.

Meanwhile, the advocates of territorial expansion were not inactive. Settlers pushed west so rapidly that Kentucky and Tennessee gained statehood during Washington's administration. Pleased, expansionists were looking toward Spanish Louisiana and Spanish Florida. Acquisition of these would give the United States control of the Mississippi and other waterways. It would add good land and enable the Americans to take care of border Indians whom the Spanish used against the United States.

American settlers met with Indian resistance north of the Ohio River. The red men were to some extent supported by the British, who occupied Great Lakes trading posts on American soil. Finally, in 1794, Wayne whipped the Indians at Fallen Timbers. The resulting Treaty of Greenville opened Ohio to white settlers. As Americans poured in, there was talk of going on, so that the United States might control Canada, with its rich fur trade and the St. Lawrence outlet to the sea.

Problems of a Neutral

Before these matters came to crisis, the wars of the French Revolution and Napoleon (1792–1815) brought to a climax the age-old conflict between France and Great Britain. These wars brought opportunities to the United States. Americans were able to build a profitable neutral trade; and those interested in territorial expansion could squeeze advantage from the fact that European nations had little time to give to the New World.

When war broke out in Europe, very few Americans wanted to have the United States involved as a belligerent. War meant expense and not a little danger for a young republic. Peace meant time to build the country and to maneuver on the diplomatic chessboard. Consequently, most Americans approved when President Washington and Secretary of State Jefferson announced neutrality (1793). Congress passed neutrality legislation the next year.

Neutrality did not mean indifference. Some Americans condemned the French Revolution and hoped that England would win the European war. Others denounced the British for opposing the new French regime.

The Federalists were pro-British. They disapproved of the French Revolution much as they had disapproved of Shays' Rebellion and other movements aimed at those in power. In Britain, where upper-class influence was strong, established institutions were secure. In France, revolution had wrecked the existing order and had produced wholesale executions and mob rule. Then, too, the Federalists had strong economic ties with London; and Federalist shipowners, knowing the strength of the British Navy, were determined to avoid conflict with Britain.

The Jeffersonians, on the other hand, were anti-British and pro-French. To them, the French Revolution was a victory for democratic and republican institutions, a defeat for monarchy and repression. By opposing France, Britain became the foe of progress and reform. Also, Jeffersonian plantc rs were in debt to London merchants; and in the West Jeffersonian frontiers-men were in conflict with the British and with Britain's Spanish allies.

Both parties featured diplomatic issues in their political campaigns. The Jeffersonians were the more successful, for they were better organizers and had the popular cause, that of revolutionary France. To most Americans, the French seemed like sisters in rebellion against the power of the kings. The Jeffersonians therefore found it easy to organize Republican clubs. Members of these clubs flaunted the emblems of the Revolution and talked of liberty, equality, and fraternity. They also talked politics, and helped build a combination to defeat the Federalists. This aspect of the societies was so important that one French agent said that Jefferson and his friends cared nothing for France, but merely wished to use the diplomatic issue for domestic purposes.

Actually, it worked both ways. While American politicians were using the European war for political purposes, European diplomats were mixing in American politics. George Hammond, British minister to the United States, established a close relationship with Alexander Hamilton. This contact enabled Hammond to gather useful information and to exert influence on the Federalists, who then controlled the American government.

Even more spectacular was the work of E. C. E. Genêt, who became French minister to the United States in 1793. The American people received Genêt with open arms, and Secretary of State Jefferson was cordial. Genêt thereupon decided that he could make the United States a base for French operations against Britain and Spain. He used American ports to outfit privateers which were to operate against the British. He negotiated with George Rogers Clark, the frontier fighter, having in mind a Franco-American attack upon Spanish Louisiana. All this, he claimed, was in line with the 1778 treaty of alliance between France and the United States.

Genêt failed. Although they favored France, Jefferson and his friends felt that the French diplomat had gone too far, and if unchecked might involve the United States in war. The Federalists, being anti-French, were more severe. The treaty of 1778, they said, had been made with the French monarchy of Louis XVI. Louis had been guillotined, the monarchy abolished; hence the alliance was no longer binding. In any case, American obligations were limited to protection of the French West Indies. Having gone beyond that, Genêt had exceeded his authority. In consequence, the American government demanded and obtained the French diplomat's recall.

Such complications led President Washington to denounce permanent alliances in his Farewell Address (1796). This document, composed with Hamilton's assistance, called on Americans to avoid entanglements with European nations and to concentrate on building the United States. Given the weakness of the young republic, Washington's announcement was logical. But even in the eighteenth century, the United States could not easily remain aloof from European affairs. While the Farewell Address was being issued, Americans were becoming involved in more and more of the incidents which so often produce war.

Most of these incidents occurred on the high seas. As a neutral, the United States claimed the right to trade with both belligerents. Trading with Britain was no problem, for France lacked the sea power to make such commerce dangerous. But the British Navy could and did seize American vessels on their way to France. When Americans protested, British courts upheld the seizures. International law clearly allowed the capture of contraband articles, such as arms and ammunition. Britain, however, expanded the term to include foodstuffs. When American vessels tried to sail from the French West Indies to France, they were seized under a British Rule of 1756, which held that trade prohibited in time of peace could not be allowed in time of war. Since France normally monopolized her colonial commerce, the British Navy would not let American vessels participate in that commerce during emergencies.

To get around this Rule of 1756, American ships took goods from the French West Indies to the United States, then from the United States to France. But Britain's courts called this a continuous voyage and allowed His Majesty's Navy to seize ships involved. Meanwhile, British naval officers were resorting to impressment—taking sailors from American merchant vessels and forcing them to serve in the British Navy. In theory, impressment was confined to British subjects. In fact, mistakes were made; and there were further troubles because Britain did not recognize the right of expatriation (that is, the right of a British seaman to become a naturalized American).

Yielding to Britain: The Jay Treaty (1795)

Denouncing these practices, the anti-British Jeffersonians demanded reprisals, including an embargo on shipments from the United States. But the Federalists, who were in power, rejected these proposals. Despite British seizures, Federalist shipowners were making profits and had no desire to abandon neutral trade. Instead of an embargo, they suggested negotiating with Britain, and had President Washington send John Jay across the ocean on a special mission.

In the resulting Jay Treaty (1795), the United States obtained a few concessions. The British agreed to give up the Great Lakes fur trading posts which they had held since the Revolution, in violation of the treaty of peace. But Jay was forced to yield to the British on the definition of contraband and many other points. In consequence, the treaty was unpopular in the United States; Jay was burned in effigy. But President Washington and the Federalist Senate accepted the treaty, to keep peace with England and guarantee continuance of neutral trade.

Unpopular though it was, the Jay Treaty set the stage for many American gains in the years to follow. The trading post concession, together with Wayne's campaign against the Indians, made it easy for Americans to pour into the Great Lakes area. Further, the fact that the United States had made a treaty with Britain caused Spain to come to terms with the United States, lest the American republic form a combination with the British against Spain.

Spanish concessions were substantial. In a Pinckney Treaty of 1796, Spain agreed to a West Florida boundary settlement favorable to the United States. At the same time, she recognized the right of Americans to navigate the Mississippi River. In addition, the Spanish granted for at least three years the right of deposit in New Orleans. This was the key point. Goods floated down the Mississippi had to be unloaded at the mouth of the river for later reloading on ocean-going vessels. Without the right of deposit, the right of navigation would have meant little. With the right of deposit at New Orleans, Americans could develop Kentucky, Tennessee, and other areas drained by the Mississippi.

"War" with France (1798–1800)

By this time, Franco-American relations had become very strained. The Genêt affair, American reluctance to recognize the alliance of 1778, the signing of the Jay Treaty with France's foe all made for bad feeling. There was further friction when France interfered with American ships in European waters and when, in the presidential campaign of 1796, French Minister Adet committed the diplomatic indiscretion of asking the American people to vote the Federalists out of office. Finally, in 1798, three French agents (X, Y, Z) asked American diplomats in France to pay bribes. This X Y Z affair caused an upsurge of anti-French feeling in the United States. Diplomatic relations were broken, and for two years a state of war existed between France and the United States (1798–1800).

It was a strange war. There was no declaration of hostilities. Fighting was confined to naval action, largely to seizure of merchant vessels. Washington and Hamilton were named to head an American expeditionary force. Hamilton planned to attack Louisiana, which belonged to France's ally, Spain.[2] But he did not have the opportunity, for President John Adams chose peace, and patched things up with France. This was done in an agreement of 1800, which also canceled the Franco-American alliance of 1778. The cancellation satisfied the French, who had found the alliance nearly worthless; and it pleased Americans to have no long-range affiliations with European powers. Despite their differences, Federalists and Republicans agreed on this. Washington had denounced permanent alliances in his Farewell Address of 1796; Jefferson pursued the same line in his first inaugural address (1801).

Purchasing Louisiana

The treaty of 1800 was signed with Napoleon Bonaparte, who had just grabbed the reins of power in France. Napoleon wanted peace so that he could develop a French empire in the New World. The center was to be the French sugar colony of Saint Domingue (Haiti). A great slave insurrection had wiped out the colony's plantation system in 1791. Napoleon proposed to reintroduce slavery and get the region back into large-scale production. Desiring a mainland colony that could supply Haiti with foodstuffs, the French dictator decided that he should have Spanish Louisiana, which had belonged to France until the French and Indian War. He therefore persuaded his ally, Spain, to cede Louisiana to France (1800).

For the moment the deal was secret, and the Spanish flag continued to fly over New Orleans. But there were leaks; and the news caused grave concern in the United States. Spain had been a difficult neighbor, but she was weak. Since France was strong and bent upon expansion, Napoleon's acquisition of Louisiana would be a major threat to the security of the United States. The future could be seen in incidents which took place even before the formal transfer of the colony to France, as in 1802, when Americans were notified that their right of deposit at New Orleans would soon be withdrawn.

Dismayed, Americans dependent on the Mississippi turned to President Jefferson for aid. Jefferson had approved of the French Revolution as a democratic movement; Napoleon, however, was no democrat. Besides, France now menaced the United States. Jefferson therefore decided to act. First, he would try to buy New Orleans from the French. If negotiation

---

[2] At the outbreak of the wars of the French Revolution, Spain had been allied with Great Britain against France. Soon after the signing of the Pinckney Treaty, Spain shifted sides, turning against England and lining up with France. Such changes were not unusual in eighteenth-century diplomacy.

failed, the United States would line up with Napoleon's enemies ("marry . . . the British fleet and nation") and substitute force for diplomacy.

Fortunately, force was not necessary. By 1803 Napoleon had changed his mind about the New World. His plans for Haiti had worked out badly. Armies sent to that colony had been wiped out by yellow fever, or had been defeated by Toussaint L'Ouverture and other Negro leaders bent on retaining freedom for their people. Without Haiti, Louisiana seemed less important to Napoleon. Besides, the French dictator had decided on a new war against Britain. During such a conflict, France could neither protect nor develop Louisiana; so Napoleon decided to unload the colony on the best terms obtainable. American diplomats were surprised to find Napoleon willing to sell not only New Orleans but the whole of Louisiana, a million square miles of territory stretching from the Gulf of Mexico to Montana. Terms were quickly arranged, the United States securing this area for the bargain price of $15,000,000.

The Trend Away from Trade Promotion

The Louisiana Purchase marked a turning point in American foreign policy. From the Revolution down to 1803, the United States had concentrated on trade promotion. After 1803, commercial interests were given less attention and the tendency was to stress territorial expansion. The shift reflected the changing trend of party politics, for Federalist merchant-politicians had given way to Republican agrarians (1801). And with the acquisition of Louisiana, more and more Americans turned their attention from the Atlantic to the interior.

Not that commerce was forgotten. Though unsympathetic toward Federalist shipowners, the Republicans were interested in finding foreign markets for American farm products. In consequence, they devoted some energy to promoting the export trade. When the Barbary States interfered with shipping in the Mediterranean, President Jefferson and his successor, Madison, used naval force to punish the wrongdoers and force them to suspend their piratical activities.

Even so, the Republicans did not propose to be drawn into a major war for the protection of commerce. To their minds, the great work at hand was the settlement of inland areas of the United States. They did not want Americans to be diverted from that basic task. If incidents growing out of foreign trade threatened to involve the United States in hostilities, Jefferson was prepared to sacrifice commercial interests to keep his country out of war.

Incidents came thick and fast when, after two years of truce, Anglo-French hostilities were resumed in 1803. This was a death struggle between

Napoleon and the British, and both sides cracked down on neutral shipping. There were the old quarrels and some new ones over contraband and
continuous voyage, impressment and the Rule of 1756. Most conflicts
concerned private merchant vessels; but in 1807, a British naval vessel, the
Leopard, fired on an American man-of-war, the Chesapeake. When the
Chesapeake surrendered, the British impressed four members of the American vessel's crew. Indignant Americans cried for revenge. Instead, President Jefferson and Congress chose embargo (1807–09). American vessels
were to stay at home. The plan was to eliminate the incidents which might
lead to war, and, by depriving England of American markets, force that
belligerent to respect neutral rights. The embargo would mean loss for
the United States; but Jefferson thought peace was worth the sacrifice.

The embargo failed. There were widespread evasions of the regulations.
Ship captains sailed without permission or, obtaining papers for the coastwise trade, headed for Europe. Where there was enforcement, the embargo
hurt Americans more than it did the European belligerents. Wealthy
merchants suffered, but so did ordinary people—common seamen, fishermen, farmers who grew crops for export. Loud were the cries of anger and
despair, and in 1809, as Jefferson left the presidency, the embargo was
repealed.

Despite this setback, the Republican leaders continued to feel that foreign trade was less important than the development of the interior of the
United States. Few of them desired a war to defend neutral rights on the
high seas. But many were willing or eager to take up arms to protect or
enlarge the territory of the United States.

The Floridas and Canada

The first case in point involved West Flor-
ida (now southern Alabama, southern Mississippi, and eastern Louisiana).
In ceding Louisiana to France, Spain had retained title to Florida. But
boundaries were uncertain. American diplomats argued that West Florida
was part of Louisiana, hence belonged to the United States. When Spain
rejected this interpretation, Americans who had settled in the area staged
a revolt, declared West Florida independent, and asked for annexation to
the United States (1810). President Madison proclaimed the region under
American rule. So it remained, except for Mobile, which the Spanish
evacuated in 1813.

Having snapped up West Florida, American expansionists turned their
attention to East Florida. Here the United States had no shadow of a
claim. Still, the territory was worth getting for its rivers and land and as
a means of controlling the troublesome Seminole Indians. The result was

an armed invasion in 1811, led by an aged Georgian, George Mathews. Bad management wrecked the Mathews expedition, but the episode showed what was ahead. Mathews was no wild frontiersman. He was a shrewd land speculator, and his invasion plans had the informal approval of President Madison.

While some Americans were eying Florida, others were looking toward British Canada. There were good farmlands in Ontario, directly west of New York State, across the Niagara River. Equally tempting was the thought of owning all the Great Lakes and the route of the St. Lawrence to the sea. More urgent still was the question of the red men and their leader, Tecumseh.

After their defeat by Wayne, the Indian tribes had agreed to leave Ohio (Treaty of Greenville, 1795). In return, they had been promised permanent possession of new lands in Indiana. Presently, though, white men began to push into this reserved area. The newcomers had the strong support of William Henry Harrison, governor of the Indiana Territory. Harrison used persuasion, bribery, and whiskey to secure land cessions from the various Indian tribes. When possible, the governor dealt with official representatives of each tribe. But if he found those agents uncoöperative, Harrison was willing to make his deal with individual Indians, including renegades. With an agreement on paper, he could carry out the terms by force.

Then Tecumseh, a Shawnee chief, came into the picture. Tecumseh's tribe had left Ohio to settle along the Wabash, only to find its new location insecure. Naturally, the Indians wondered where this would end. Pondering the problem, Tecumseh saw one possible solution. Wayne had dealt with the Indians as a unit. All the tribes had agreed to leave Ohio, all had been promised land in Indiana. Harrison, on the other hand, negotiated with each tribe separately. That, said Tecumseh, was improper and illegal. Land did not belong to individual Indians, or to individual tribes. Rather it belonged to all red men, and no tribe had any right to cede land title. Harrison's agreements, therefore, were invalid, and the Wayne grant still held.

Though he argued well, the chief made little impression on Harrison and his land-hungry followers. Tecumseh then decided that he must use force. He told the Indians that they must strengthen themselves for a long, hard fight. They must stop imitating the white man, must revive Indian culture. They must give up liquor, which reduced powers of resistance. They must turn from the fur trade, which helped the white man, and concentrate on agriculture. They must forget petty squabbles and form an Indian confederation from the Great Lakes to the Gulf of Mexico.

Finally, since Americans were the great threat, the Indians must use Britain and Spain against the United States.

As Tecumseh whipped his program into shape, American frontiersmen became alarmed. Harrison checked the movement to a certain degree when he clashed with some of Tecumseh's braves at Tippecanoe (1811). But the battle was far from decisive, and Tecumseh worked on, bettering his connections with the British in Canada. More and more Americans were saying that the problem must be taken care of for all time, by breaking the power of Tecumseh and by driving the British out of Canada.

In this situation the War Hawks played the decisive role. These were young Republican politicians who gained control of Congress in 1811–12. Most War Hawks were from the frontier, which stretched in a great half-circle from Maine to Georgia. Their chief leader was Henry Clay of Kentucky. Their ranks also included John Harper of New Hampshire, Peter Porter of western New York, Felix Grundy of Tennessee, John C. Calhoun of upcountry South Carolina, and William H. Crawford of Georgia. The War Hawks wanted war with Britain and Britain's ally, Spain.[3] Such a conflict would give the United States an opportunity to invade Canada and Florida. War would also satisfy the exuberant patriotism of the War Hawks; and it would enable Americans to punish Britain for having violated neutral rights.

There was opposition to the War Hawk program. Federalists did not want a conflict that was sure to drive their shipping from the seas, and that might add more Republican frontier states to the Union. Many older Republicans felt that the United States was still too weak to take on major military tasks. But the War Hawks kept insisting, and President Madison finally gave way. In June, 1812, the United States declared war against Great Britain.

The War of 1812

Americans were better able to face war in 1812 than in 1775. Their population had trebled. There was a well-established national government, with a good credit rating. An improved industrial establishment had eliminated some of the more critical shortages of the Revolutionary era (for example, that in gunpowder). In 1812 the United States possessed at least a skeleton army and navy, plus experienced political and military leaders. And Britain, deep in the Napoleonic Wars, could not give American problems the attention they had received in 1775.

---

[3] Spain at this time had two governments. One was pro-French and was headed by Napoleon's brother, Joseph. The other, which was anti-French, helped England in the Peninsular campaigns. Florida and most other Spanish colonies supported the latter faction.

On the other hand, the military situation of the Americans was more difficult than before. The Revolutionary Patriots had fought on the defensive, using forests and distance as allies against Britain. Defense would not do in 1812; to win the war, the Americans had to carry the fight into Canada and Florida. Geography made conquest difficult, and the United States had to contend also with overconfidence, divided opinion at home, and incompetent leadership. The result was failure at the start, when the opportunities were best. Toward the end, the Americans became less inefficient; but by that time the British were able to rush in reinforcements and organize counterinvasions of the United States.

As in the War of Independence, the American republic fought Great Britain while the British Empire was in conflict with the French. This time, though, there was no coöperation between France and the United States. This meant that there was no flow of military goods from Europe to the New World republic, none of the naval aid that had helped defeat Cornwallis at Yorktown. Instead, sea power was in Britain's hands.

American naval vessels did win a few individual engagements and, with aid from privateers, damaged enemy shipping. (Captain David Porter all but cleaned British whalers out of the Pacific.) But King George's fleet ruled the Atlantic and extended its superiority even to the territorial waters of the United States. The tiny gunboats in which Jefferson had placed confidence proved worthless under war conditions; and the best units of the American Navy, fast and efficient frigates like the *Constitution*, were no match for the larger British ships of the line. It was easy for Britain to blockade the American coastline and, when she took the offensive, to land troops where she pleased.

Not expecting victory at sea, Americans placed their hopes in land campaigns. Yet there, too, were difficulties. The War Hawks had secured war by pooling the votes of those who wanted Canada with the votes of those interested in Florida. It was less simple to maintain coöperation during hostilities, with some demanding southern, some northern operations. In compromise efforts to please both factions, Madison reduced the army's striking power.

More serious was the opposition of much of the Northeast to any operations. Some New Englanders did aid the war effort; others were in determined opposition. As Federalists, they objected to a conflict brought on by Jeffersonians. As merchants little interested in the frontier, they did not care to support an expansionist conflict that placed their ships in danger. They therefore withheld assistance. They had money, but would not lend it to the government. They had men, but resisted presidential orders to turn out the militia. Some of their merchant vessels were turned into privateers—that meant profit—but other ships were set to trading with the enemy.

In defending their position, these opponents of war used states'-rights arguments. Back in Hamilton's day, most of them had been nationalist; but they had then approved of the administration. Having slipped from power, they had become more concerned for the rights of minorities. Their Hartford Convention (1814) echoed with the states'-rights spirit of the early Jeffersonians, as expressed in the Virginia and Kentucky Resolutions. And there was talk about the possible secession of the Northeast from the Union.

Even so, the War Hawks expected easy victory. Taking Canada, said ex-President Jefferson, would be a "mere matter of marching." So simple did it seem that the Madison administration did not bother to make careful plans; and Congress adjourned in 1812 without voting war taxes. The consequences soon became apparent. In peacetime, the Treasury counted chiefly on customs duties. By cutting trade, war reduced this tariff income just when the government needed money most. And the first Bank of the United States, which could have helped, had been allowed to die on expiration of its charter in 1811. Turning to the local, state-chartered banks, Madison found some uncoöperative, others too feeble to be very useful. The Treasury was thus obliged to borrow where it could, and try to fill in the gap by issuing unsupported paper money.

Military matters were in even worse condition. The Navy and War departments were so short staffed that the Secretaries could have accomplished little even if they had been competent—which they were not. The Regular Army being but a feeble fifth of its authorized strength of 35,000, President Madison called out 50,000 militiamen. Few of these state troops reported; and those that did proved as inefficient as the Revolutionary militiamen of whom Washington had frequently complained. In the Lake Champlain offensive of 1812, these soldiers broke their own advance by firing at each other. On the Niagara front that same year, American regulars were defeated at Queenstown Heights because New York militiamen refused to leave their state to carry on the fight in Canada. The regular regiments, though more willing, were often ineffective, for they were indifferently trained, poorly supplied, and commanded, often, by villainous, inept, or superannuated officers. The ablest British general, Isaac Brock, was killed in the early fighting, and on both sides the war had more of blunder and pillage than of well-executed campaigns.

Sound strategy called for the United States to drive toward the St. Lawrence, trunk of the Canadian tree. Instead, Americans nibbled at the branches, entering upper Canada near Niagara and Detroit. Shockingly mismanaged, these first invasions were hurled back by Brock, old General William Hull surrendering Detroit without a battle. Brock's death and that of his Indian ally, Tecumseh, improved the American position in 1813, as did the victory of United States Commander Oliver Hazard Perry, whose new-built ships won strategic control of Lake Erie. Thus William Henry Harrison, despite his inadequacies, was able to control the Detroit area. But, with opportunities as good as Perry's, Commodore Isaac Chauncey failed to establish American supremacy on the more important lake, Ontario. Down south, meantime, General James Wilkinson had occupied the old Spanish fort at Mobile. But he and other American commanders missed chances to capture East Florida, where Britain had moved in to give help to Spain.

By 1814, the United States had found able officers—Andrew Jackson, who demonstrated ability against the Creeks, and Winfield Scott, who fought British regulars to a standstill at Lundy's Lane. Each of these men had the resourcefulness, dash, and determination needed to supply and control troops in a frontier campaign. But that was not enough, for by 1814 Britain had dispatched Wellington veterans to the New World and was carrying the fight to the Americans. She invaded the United States at several points: from Canada, along the Atlantic coast, at the mouth of the Mississippi.

Although they had bungled their offensive operations, the Americans did fairly well on their own soil. Their most significant success came at Lake Champlain, where Commodore Thomas Macdonough's quickly constructed fleet checked the southward movement of Sir George Prevost. Prevost, who was governor general of Canada, headed one of the largest European armies yet assembled in the Western Hemisphere, over 10,000 seasoned troops.

More dramatic, though less important, was the capture of Washington. The British were attempting to create a diversion on Prevost's behalf. Finding the American capital virtually undefended, they took possession. Then, after eating a dinner which Dolly Madison had left behind, the invaders burned the public buildings. This, they felt, made up for the American destruction of York (now Toronto) the preceding year. The British then withdrew to try their luck against Baltimore. But there they were repulsed by a hastily assembled force directed and inspired by Samuel Smith, a United States Senator and a major general in the Maryland militia. At the same time, Baltimore's Fort McHenry survived a naval bombardment, inspiring Francis Scott Key to write the words for the "Star-Spangled Banner."

The final British effort was directed at New Orleans. Andrew Jackson was in charge of the defense; and Jackson, for all his lack of formal military education, was a capable commander. In the battle of New Orleans (January, 1815) he had a strong position, one flank being protected by cypress swamps, the other by the Mississippi River. Charging head-on, the British moved straight into a field of fire and were repulsed with heavy loss.

The battle thrilled the country and helped make Jackson President; but it did not affect the outcome of the war. Unbeknown to those fighting in Louisiana, British and American diplomats had signed a treaty of peace at Ghent, in the Belgian Netherlands, in December, 1814. This pact was ratified without change of terms in 1815.

Results of the War of 1812

Although negotiations had dragged on for months, the peace treaty was a simple document. It called for *status quo ante bellum*, all to be as it had been before the war. Territory captured by belligerents was to be returned, neither side was to pay an indemnity, and controversies over neutral rights were left undecided. A few special arrangements, notably those involving American participation in North Atlantic fisheries, lapsed because of the war; but new arrangements were worked out after 1815.

Technically, then, the war ended in a draw. But drawn engagements often have significant results. This one brought lasting peace between Britain and the United States. Americans remained convinced that they could thrash the British and conquer Canada. Britishers and Canadians were sure they could handle the United States. Each, however, recognized that the cost of triumph might outrun the gains. Out of such thoughts came an uneasy truce, which turned in time into a lasting peace of friendship and coöperation. There were many quarrels after 1815, and a war scare now and then; but as the years went by, a third Anglo-American conflict came to be regarded as unthinkable. Symbolizing the changed relationship was the Rush-Bagot agreement of 1817. The purpose of this pact was to save money by eliminating naval armament on the Great Lakes. Its success, however, led to land disarmament as well. The 3000-mile Canadian-American boundary line thus became the longest unfortified frontier in the world.

The War of 1812 also marked the end of Indian power in the Great Lakes country and the beginning of the end of their resistance further south. Tecumseh's passing left the tribes with no effective leader in the Old Northwest; and, after 1815, there was little aid from a British government that did not care to run the risk of war with the United States. Thus handicapped, the Indians were forced to grant that the Great Lakes country had become a white man's land. The last spark of tribal resistance in that area—the Black Hawk "war" of 1832—would merely serve to show that the day of Indian power, the day of Pontiac and Tecumseh, had long since passed away.

Nor was it very different to the south. In 1814, at the battle of Horseshoe Bend in what is now Alabama, Andrew Jackson had broken the back of the Creek confederacy. This left Americans in control of the Southwest frontier at the close of the War of 1812. Of the Five Civilized Tribes (Creeks, Cherokees, Choctaws, Chickasaws, and Seminoles), only the Seminoles remained in opposition. They were taken care of two years later, when a frontier force under Andrew Jackson pursued them into Spanish Florida (1817). The white man's rule had been established from the Atlantic to the Mississippi, from the Gulf of Mexico to the Great Lakes.

While crushing the Seminoles, Jackson sounded the death knell of the Spanish government in Florida. During the War of 1812, General James Wilkinson had occupied Mobile, thus completing the American conquest of West Florida. East Florida might have fallen, too, had Spain not been backed by Britain. When the backing was withdrawn after 1815, the fate of East Florida was sealed. The Spanish were unable to check Jackson when he came sweeping into their domains in 1817. Nor did the British move to aid the Spanish Bourbons, even when the fiery Jackson hanged two Brtishers who were working with the Seminoles. Recognizing her impotence, Spain ceded East Florida to the United States in the Transcontinental Treaty, ratified in 1821. The New World republic paid no cash for the territory. It did, however, assume certain claims of American citizens against the Spanish government, and recognized Spain's rights in Texas, New Mexico, and California.

After the War of 1812 was over, Americans tended to gloss over their errors and defeats in the conflict, and to overemphasize the brighter side. The talk was of Lake Erie and New Orleans, not of the siege of Detroit. There was much of the "Star-Spangled Banner" at Fort McHenry, little of the capture of Washington. All would remember the *Constitution* (*Old Ironsides*); many would forget that that British Navy ruled the seas all through the war. The United States, in other words, came to believe that Britain had been soundly beaten in the War of 1812.

Though incorrect, this view had great significance. For one thing, it tended to blind Americans, to prevent them from learning from the military blunders made during the conflict. In addition, the myth of overwhelming victory contributed to the development of American nationalism. Certainly the war and its traditions helped to build the concept of unity and of devotion to the nation. In retrospect, opposition to the war seemed improper or worse—a reflection which helped to keep the Federalist party in its grave. And the bursting pride of the new patriotism increased interest in national legislation, and in the further territorial expansion of the United States.

Part III

Spanning the Continent

(1815-1850)

 *Economic growth was the keynote of the four decades after the War of 1812. Americans settled the Mississippi Valley and pushed further west, to the Pacific. The cotton culture flourished in the South. Farming prospered in the North as well, and the period saw an upsurge in commercial and industrial activity.*

Along with economic expansion went a growing attachment to democratic ideals. There was a sense of social responsibility, too, and Americans took part in reform crusades. Equally significant was the rising tide of nationalist feeling. Proud of their economic and political power, pleased with their intellectual accomplishments, Americans were convinced that they had achieved cultural independence and had built a new, American civilization.

8

Economic Expansion

Moving West

By breaking the power of the Indians east of the Mississippi, the War of 1812 opened the eastern half of the Mississippi Valley for settlement. American farmers and investors and European immigrants hastened to take up these lands. By 1850 the farming frontier had reached the Mississippi and had gone one hundred or more miles beyond, from central Iowa to the Gulf of Mexico.

Not that the area was thickly settled. Much of the best land was bought by wealthy men for long-run investment. Many of these landowners allowed their holdings to lie idle. Farmers also acquired more land than they could use, holding the extra acreage for a rise in price. Hence as late as 1850, the average density of population in the settled areas of Iowa, Missouri, and Arkansas (states west of the Mississippi) was less than ten inhabitants per square mile. East of the river, in the settled parts of Michigan, Wisconsin, and Illinois, settlers averaged only about fifteen to the square mile.

It cost a good deal of money to move a family west. In 1820, a wagon fit for crossing the Appalachians cost forty dollars, a good horse more than that. A skiff down the Ohio would add six or eight dollars. In his own labor, or that of others, a log cabin would cost the new settler the equivalent of fifty dollars, a log barn double that amount. The farmer also needed food for his family until the first harvest. And money for land. The needed capital might be raised in good times by selling or mortgaging a family farm in the East, and by obtaining "store credit" in the West. If times were bad, money was harder to get. Hence men moved to the frontier in periods of prosperity, stayed put in depressions.

To what western region would a settler go? Often the decision depended on rumors and newspaper articles inspired by large owners anxious to sell land. State and territorial governments also advertised land and sent special agents to the East and even to Europe. As a result, settlers poured into areas being "pushed" in each boom period. The location of these booms

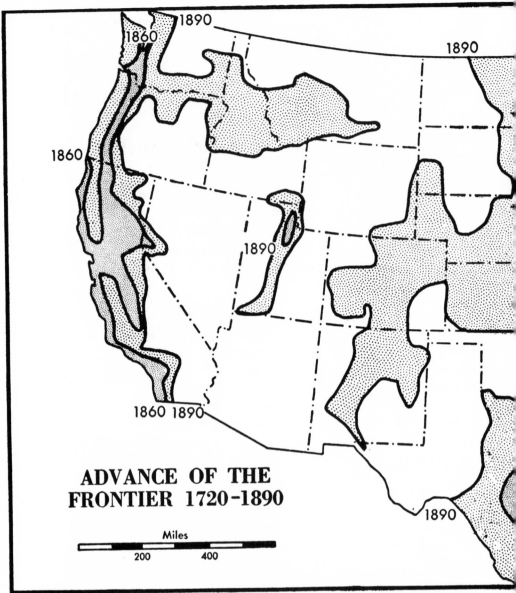

ADVANCE OF THE
FRONTIER 1720-1890

Miles

200 400

This map is designed to show the westward movement, and to indicate the settled areas for various periods of American history. The frontier line for each date is the last line of settlement, two persons per square mile being considered settled country. It will be seen that settlement still hugged the Atlantic coast in 1720, a century after the establishment of England's first colonies in the New World. Americans had reached the Appalachians by 1790, and there was an island of settlement on the Ohio River. By 1810 the frontier had gone west to the Mississippi River. It will be noted that the frontier line ran from northeast to southwest through much of the nineteenth century. That is, the Southwest was settled more rapidly than the Northwest, partly because of the cotton boom. Further-

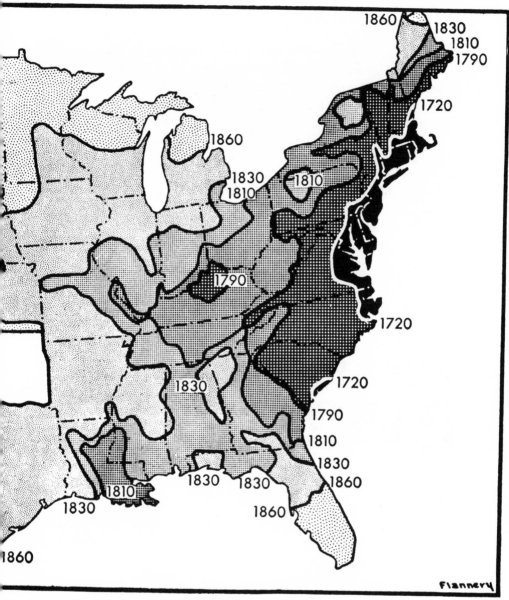

1860

1830
1810
1790

1720

1860

1830
1810

1810

1790

1720

1720

1790

1810

1830

1860

1830

1810

1830   1830

1830

1810

1860

1860

Flannery

more, the lines of settlement tended to follow water routes (see the frontier of 1830). By 1860 Americans had settled the Great Lakes country and most of the Mississippi Valley, and had established themselves along the Pacific coast. Three decades later, the Pacific coast settlements had expanded; and Americans, pushing west from the Mississippi, had conquered much of the Great Plains. Only the western plains, the mountain country, and some arid and semiarid areas remained unsettled. As the noted American historian, Frederick Jackson Turner, carefully pointed out, the frontier was passing, and the United States, which had long benefited from the westward movement, would need to look elsewhere for future opportunities.

was reflected in the admission of new states. Ohio (1803) and Louisiana (1812) became states in the decade before the War of 1812. The next boom came immediately after the war. It saw states coming in at the rate of one a year: Indiana (1816), Mississippi (1817), Illinois (1818), Alabama (1819), Maine (1820), Missouri (1821). The panic of 1819 stopped this procession, but the boom of the 1830's brought in Arkansas (1836) and Michigan (1837). Again there was depression, after the panic of 1837; but as prosperity returned, a new migration produced the states of Florida (1845), Iowa (1846), Wisconsin (1848). Texas, the other state added to the Union in this decade, had a more complex but somewhat similar origin. The boom of the thirties gave it sufficient population to enable it to win independence from Mexico, but political complications delayed its annexation to the United States until 1845.

When each boom collapsed, the areas which had been favored by speculators were left with foreclosed mortgages, broken banks, desperate farmers. Yet there were compensations. Without speculative credit and high-pressure salesmanship the country would have developed less rapidly; men would have worked less feverishly and laid less ambitious plans. The speculative system fitted in with the American dream of hard work today and wealth tomorrow. The frontier therefore remained the land of promise.

In the squatter stage the Southwest and the Northwest were essentially alike. The next stage saw differences. Commercial agriculture developed very slowly in the Old Northwest—the Great Lakes states. But in such Southwest areas as Alabama and Mississippi, purchasers counted on immediate profits from the sale of cotton as well as capital gains from the increasing value of land. Small planters from upland regions of the Southeast moved their slaves to the rich new soil of the Southwest. Great planters of the tidewater region invested their surplus capital in Mississippi Valley plantations run by overseers. In the Southwest, as in the Northwest, small, nonslaveholding farmers could make a fair living; but they had to be content with a position inferior to that of the cotton aristocracy.

Immigration

Climate, and unwillingness to compete with slave labor, kept British and German immigrants away from the Southwest. Down to 1840, however, immigrants formed only a small part of settlers moving westward in any region. Alabama, Mississippi, and Arkansas grew almost as fast as did Missouri, Iowa, and Wisconsin. From then on, immigration helped the Northwest spurt ahead. Still, even in the period of heaviest immigration, most people going west were of native origin.

Down to 1832 foreigners arriving in America never exceeded 30,000 a year—and this included travelers as well as immigrants. But the boom of the 1830's brought chances for employment on American railroad and canal projects, and in new factories. Improved transportation also promised better profits for inland farmers. At the same time (and especially after 1840) bad conditions in Ireland and Germany were driving tenant farmers and small landowners to face the hardships of migration. Better steerage accommodations on sailing packets and steamers also speeded the movement. Hence by 1850 immigrants were coming in at a rate of 300,000 a year. The Irish generally reached American ports without funds and had to take whatever jobs were available. (Many became construction hands and built the new roads, canals, and railroads.) The Germans often brought enough capital to buy western farms.

Democratization of Land Policy

Migration to the Mississippi Valley was mainly a movement into land initially owned by the United States government. Federal land policy was therefore a powerful force in shaping the new civilization. For a generation before 1812, land speculators had prevailed on Congress to refrain from selling to small farmers at bargain rates. The position of the speculators had been endorsed by northern employers who felt that a cheap land policy would exhaust eastern capital and drain the East of needed laborers, thus raising wages.

In time, though, popular pressures triumphed. The depression of 1819–21 saw the breakdown of the credit system set up in the land laws of 1800 and 1804. Salvage operations being necessary, Congress adopted a land law in 1820, providing for hundred-dollar farms—the cash sale of eighty-acre plots at a minimum price of $1.25 an acre.

From the standpoint of the potential settler, this was an improvement on the 160-acre minimum and $2.00 price of the 1804 statute. But the auction system and an understaffed land office still operated against the small purchaser. The basic difficulty, as before, was the necessity of traveling hundreds of miles to attend an auction.

Most of the men at auctions were squatters, or agents of large investors. If the squatters were few, they might have their land bid away from them, or might be forced to bid so high as to pay again for their own improvements. But if the squatters were numerous, they organized claims associations capable of intimidating other bidders. After the claims associations had secured their rights, the speculators, using various stratagems, bought the choice remaining sections at about the minimum price. Since most of their corrupt devices depended on the aid of government land agents, farmers came to regard the land office as a "den of thieves and robbers."

Even so, there was still plenty of land for all comers. Seldom was all the farming land in an area disposed of at the initial auction, and much fair to good property remained for sale at the local land office at $1.25 an acre. In 1829, after fifteen years of land sales in Illinois, six-sevenths of that fertile state remained in the hands of the federal government. The sale of land to speculators did, however, withhold from use much of the best land. This forced owner-operators to take inferior land or move further west; which led, in turn, to a dispersed population with high transportation costs. The withheld land might gradually be brought under cultivation by tenants; but Westerners considered tenant farming contrary to American ideals.

Congressional champions of the settler gradually came to see that the best cure for the evils of the auction system was automatic preëmption. By this method the settler could select land, settle on it, and have it transferred to him at the time of the auction for the minimum price. Special preëmption statutes were early and often passed, and there was growing agitation for a general preëmption law. Since preëmption would draw off choice sections in advance of public sale, and break the continuity of large tracts, speculators opposed preëmption legislation, as did eastern interests opposed to westward migration.

One way of defeating preëmption was to link it with the distribution issue. In the 1830's, some politicians were agitating for the distribution of the proceeds of public land sales to the states; others were demanding distribution of the land itself to the states. Congressmen from eastern states (which contained little national land) preferred the former, those from western states the latter. The result was an impasse; and by joining distribution with preëmption, speculators and others increased the confusion and prevented passage of a general preëmption bill.

The depression after the panic of 1837 slowed down the westward movement; but it increased popular pressure for preëmption. Finally, in 1841, Congress passed the Preëmption Act, which provided for distribution as well as preëmption. After subtracting donations already received, each western state was given half a million acres of national land. Eastern states also stood to profit, by distribution of the proceeds of federal land sales (but, under the formula adopted, such distribution never took place). The heart of the act, of course, was the preëmption rule. Bona-fide settlers on surveyed land could preëmpt from 40 to 160 acres, provided they did not already own as much as 320 acres.

The Preëmption Act of 1841 helped the small settler; but it was far from perfect. Since the land office remained corrupt and inefficient, abuses developed in the filing of preëmption claims. In addition, the half-million-acre state allotments were a new source for speculation. Also, the Preëmption Act required the settler to follow the surveyor. True frontiersmen who took up land beyond surveyed areas were not protected.

A Changing Agriculture

In 1815 most Americans were still subsistence farmers, selling few products and raising most of their supplies. But markets were expanding. Europe's new textile factories required more and more cotton and wool. Then, in the 1840's, the British Parliament repealed the old protective tariffs on grains (the corn laws). This made bread cheaper for English workers and increased the market for American crops. Similar urban needs appeared in the eastern United States. Hence a commercial spirit (as distinct from a subsistence outlook) spread even among small farmers after 1815.

Most spectacular of the agricultural changes in these years was the cotton rush to the Gulf states. Psychologically similar to a gold rush, this westward movement of cotton planters peopled such new states as Alabama and Mississippi rapidly in the 1820's. At the same time, there was a relative decline in tobacco raising in the upper South. The use of snuff was declining by 1850, and cigarettes were yet unknown. Cigars and plugs were to achieve great popularity only with the Civil War. In addition, foreign competition cut into profits; which, with soil exhaustion, made for depressed conditions in tobacco areas. Virginia farmers began shifting to grain by 1840, but not until the later rise of the cigarette industry (based on "bright leaf" tobacco, discovered about 1850) would some measure of agricultural prosperity return to North Carolina and Virginia.

Farming in the Middle Atlantic states had long centered around grain raising and animal husbandry. With the growth of cities, market gardening increased; and as cattle raising appeared in the Middle West, some eastern farmers fattened western stock for urban butchers. Better methods and easy access to markets enabled New Jersey, Pennsylvania, and New York farmers to compete with the new farms of the Middle West. They prospered while South Carolina planters found it hard to compete with Alabama producers.

New England had never secured much wealth from the soil. After 1815, many New Englanders moved west or to eastern cities. Subsistence farming survived, especially among the less ambitious. Dairying and market gardening paid near industrial towns, until improved transportation made it possible to bring in goods from New York and the Middle West. Though the old agricultural villages survived, their role as centers of activity was taken over by factory towns. Here the experience of New England resembled that of old England—the region was well named.

Agriculturally the Middle West became a colonial area for eastern cities. Basic was the raising of grains—wheat, oats, rye, barley, corn. A more balanced economy would emerge after 1850, with the rise of manufacturing around Cincinnati and Chicago and the development of lumbering. Meantime, much forest growth was cut down simply to clear the fields. This practice led to a further waste of natural resources, since deforestation allowed soil waters to drain off too rapidly and led to floods and soil erosion.

While crops moved west, so did animal husbandry. Mule breeding centered in Kentucky, then shifted west to Missouri. The sheep raisers moved from New England to Ohio. Hogs, formerly fattened on eastern swill, did better on corn; so hog raising moved west with the corn crop. Pork packing became important, centering first in Cincinnati, later in Chicago.

Scientific Farming

By 1815, the more prosperous and better-educated farmers were getting interested in scientific agriculture. The response was encouraged in the East by the increasing value of land and the competition of the new West. The first agricultural town fair was held at Pittsfield, Massachusetts, in 1807. Thereafter many of these events were staged annually. Competition for the best products and animals stimulated efforts to improve farming methods.

No less important was the agricultural press. Between 1820 and 1860, 400 farm journals were founded; and the hundred in existence in 1860 reached a quarter-million subscribers. The editors condemned the slovenly character of American farming and urged use of new crops and techniques.

Three years after the first fair was held at Pittsfield, the farmers of that area organized the Berkshire Agricultural Society (1810). Within a decade there were a hundred such societies, distributing literature, encouraging fairs and journals, and (presently) petitioning legislatures for laws favorable to farmers. A United States Agricultural Society, founded in 1852, helped secure the establishment of the federal Department of Agriculture in 1862.

The better farmers used barnyard manure and Peruvian guano as fertilizer; also—to correct soil acidity—limestone, gypsum, and marl. Crop rotation had been introduced into the middle colonies by German-speaking immigrants from Switzerland. English scientific farmers became interested in crop rotation before 1800. American reformers followed suit, pointing out that it was unnecessary to let land lie fallow in the medieval manner when a given crop like wheat had partially exhausted the soil. Instead, the farmer could restore needed nitrogen to the soil by growing turnips and clover.

As a result of crossbreeding and inbreeding, the average weight of English sheep and cattle doubled from 1750 to 1825. Nor was size the sole consideration: cattle breeders paid heed to milk production, sheep raisers bred for more and better wool. Famous breeds of cattle were developed in the Channel islands (Jerseys, Guernseys), in England proper (Herefords, Durhams), and on the Continent (Holsteins). Aware of the superiority of these breeds over their own nondescript animals, enterprising Americans imported them after 1820. They also brought in British hogs. For better sheep, Americans turned first to England, then to Spain and France (for fine-wool merinos), and after 1820 to Saxony.

When farm implements were crude and heavy, oxen were more effective than horses as draft animals. When machinery came in, horses—being more easily guided—became preferable. Oxen then became less common on American farms. Mules were widely employed after 1820, notably on southern farms. These sterile hybrids proved tougher than horses, more maneuverable than oxen. To improve their product, mule breeders imported asses from Europe to be bred with American horses. In stock raising as in planting, basic science (e.g., genetics) was of little use before 1850; gains came from empirical (trial-and-error) methods.

Farm Machinery

So it was with farm machinery. Few of the new devices depended on basic principles discovered by modern science. Inventors had some knowledge of statics (the working of levers, wheels, gears, pulleys). This they applied with a mechanical knack to the making of practical gadgets. In this era practical inventors tinkered with nearly every essential farm process. The lines of plows were improved by Jefferson. Wooden plows were replaced by cast iron (1797), then (1833) by steel implements with interchangeable parts. Like improvements were made in spades, hoes, rakes, scythes.

Much more complicated was the reaping machine, invented in the 1830's by a New Englander, Obed Hussey, and a Virginian, Cyrus McCormick. The reaper involved wheels, gears, knives, and "deviders," all set on a moving carriage to be drawn by animals. The machine cut and arranged grain in bundles. Two men operating it could cut as much as ten hand workers in a given time. Obviously this was a great boon to grain growers, especially on farms in the Middle West, where labor was scarce. McCormick therefore located in Chicago. Eventually (1902) this business evolved into the present International Harvester Company, the largest manufacturer of farm machinery in the world. These farm inventions made little or no use of power engines. Water mills were occasionally employed for threshers, but usually there was continued dependence on animal power. The steam engine was too clumsy for most farm tasks. The use of power machines on the farm would have to await the later development of the internal-combustion motor.

By the 1850's, American farm machinery was achieving a reputation in Europe. English manufacturers had long assumed that their equipment was superior to anything made elsewhere. Did not Americans depend on Britain for their early steam engines and textile machines? When McCormick's reaper was shown at the London World's Fair of 1851, the London *Times* ridiculed it. But, once demonstrated, the reaper won a prize, and the *Times* apologized. At a Paris exposition in 1855, an American reaper cut grain in a third the time taken by any European competitor. Since that time, American technology has won increasing respect abroad.

The Slave System

It is always dangerous for a large area to concentrate on a single commercial crop. This places all the eggs in one basket. The prosperity of the whole region can be destroyed by calamities befalling the key crop—falling prices, a blight, soil exhaustion resulting from continuous cultivation of a single plant. Virginia tobacco planters had been caught after the Revolution. In similar fashion, cotton producers suffered when, after the panic of 1837, cotton prices fell from twelve to four or five cents a pound and stayed down for ten years.

Under such circumstances, a cotton planter could make no profit unless he had rich soils, the best equipment, efficient labor, and good marketing facilities. These assets were denied to most southern farmers. By 1815, soils of older cotton areas in the Carolinas and Georgia were worn thin by careless planting. Energetic men tended to move west to virgin lands in Alabama, Mississippi, and Arkansas, leaving the less fortunate and less competent to struggle with exhausted fields. This, in turn, made it peculiarly difficult to restore partly deserted areas.

In the cotton kingdom, much of the labor was performed by Negro slaves. The slave system yielded profits in periods of high prices. Nevertheless, slave labor was costly. Slaves lacked the incentives of free workers. They might win the favor of a master and so improve their treatment; but they were denied the basic privileges of freedom. Hence they tended to be indifferent workers. If handled leniently, they loafed; if severely, they became resentful or ran away.

Because of the desire to keep Negroes "in their place," most slaves were denied education and remained ignorant and unskilled. This caused many planters to refrain from experimenting with crops other than corn and cotton—it was too much trouble to teach slaves new routines. Hence slavery encouraged the soil exhaustion which resulted from addiction to staples.

Besides being a system of labor, slavery was also a form of property in which money was invested. It was an investment which reproduced itself. In the late 1840's a slave baby was worth $15, a prime field hand approaching manhood $500. But production of slave children was not all profit to owners. Because of bad living conditions and ineffective medical care, mortality among slave children was high. Those who died before the age of ten represented a total loss to the owner. Moreover, all costs of caring for unproductive slaves were borne directly by the owners. In contrast, the cost of maintaining orphans, the sick and aged in the North was spread over the whole community in the form of taxes.

The slave system tied up money in laborers. That left less for farm equipment and other projects. During the 1840's, some southern leaders tried to finance textile manufacturing in their section. But many planters objected on principle, maintaining Jefferson's view that farming was the ideal life. More significant was the fact that planters could not raise the cash to build factories—their capital was tied up in land and slaves. It was difficult, in fact, for planters to remain solvent. Many fell into debt to merchants who handled their crops. In bad years the merchants advanced credit on the next year's yield. A few such advances made the debt chronic.

Besides being a labor system and form of investment, slavery was a method of race control. Race prejudice is largely a modern phenomenon, one that has increased in the last century. It was developing, however, in the colonial era. White colonists felt superior to "uncivilized" Indians. Then, since most Negroes were slaves, color came to be associated with menial status. Hence anyone who was not white came to be viewed as inferior. Negroes who became free had opportunities denied to slaves, but freedom did not eliminate social disadvantage. Negroes slave or free had to be respectful. They could mix with the master race on terms that implied servitude (as in the relation of white children to colored "mammies"), but not on terms that implied social equality. Negroes must never, therefore, use the same facilities in schools, hotels, theaters, trains. This "Jim Crow" segregation pattern was enforced by public opinion and an implied threat of violence.

Race distinctions were also written into law in the South. A slave could not defend himself against a white man, the theory being that the Negro's master would protect him. And a slave's testimony had little weight in the trial of white persons. This relatively defenseless position of Negroes brought out the less desirable qualities of the whites. On the whole, the well-to-do planters were reasonably kind to the slaves, whom they regarded as economic assets. Overseers and small farmers were more likely to be brutal. Whites at the bottom of the social scale had nothing to boast about but race. Small white farmers were jealous of Negroes, sensing their competition as workers on southern farms. This would continue after emancipation. Lynchings have generally been the work of poorer, more ignorant white citizens.

Slave women were often at the mercy of white males. Negro men resented this. But Negro women sometimes welcomed affairs with white men. If the man involved was the owner or a member of the owner's family, the slave woman might hope for special favors. When the relationship resulted in offspring, the presence of these mulatto children posed a problem. What should a white man do with slaves who were his own sons or daughters? Some owners sold the children to escape embarrassment; others set them free.

Inasmuch as light-colored women were preferred by white men and acquired prestige among slaves as well, there was a tendency to breed out the percentage of Negro blood. First mulattoes, then quadroons and octoroons appeared. Many "people of color" had some white blood. Social and legal practice, however, was to classify all these persons as Negroes. Most southern law codes defined as Negro any person having one-quarter or one-eighth of Negro blood. An octoroon might be entirely white in appearance, yet legally a Negro. Although seven-eighths white, an octoroon could not marry a white person and, even if free, had to obey curfew and segregation laws and was deprived of educational and voting privileges.

The race problem would have existed if the Negroes had come into the South as free workers. As evidence, race discrimination and race riots appeared in northern cities which contained any considerable number of free Negroes. Yet there was a connection between slavery and race prejudice. The existence of slavery in the South put a stigma on color throughout the United States. In addition, white Southerners came to view slavery as the most effective way of keeping Negroes in subordination. If freed en masse, the colored people could be expected to demand the rights of free men, including ultimately the right to vote and intermarry. Southern whites were appalled by the thought and determined to maintain the system of bondage at all costs.

Closely associated was the fear of slave insurrections. Occasionally, an owner or overseer was murdered by his slaves; and several serious uprisings occurred in which a number of whites were killed. Some southern whites denied that there was any danger of rebellion. Others recalled the successful revolt of the Haitian slaves in the 1790's, and warned that the same thing could happen in the United States. Nat Turner's insurrection of 1831, in Virginia, increased the feeling of concern.

The generation before the Civil War saw a tightening of racial controls. Southern states now prohibited emancipation. North Carolina, which had allowed free Negroes to vote, withdrew the privilege. In the black belts, slaves were forbidden to leave their plantations without passes; and a patrol of local farmers rode the highways at night to enforce this rule. Slaves caught off their places were punished as the patrol saw fit. The patrols, therefore, may be viewed as models for the later Ku Klux Klan.

Fearing trouble, southern whites were disturbed when northern abolitionists sent incendiary literature into the South. One way or another, the literature was excluded; and Southerners fought abolition agitation by developing a proslavery argument. Slavery was defended on economic, legal, moral, and religious grounds, and as necessary to preserve a "white man's country." By 1850, there was an increasing tendency to suppress criticism of the institution. Journalists and teachers had to be careful; in extreme cases, those suspected of antislavery sentiments were silenced or exiled. In this way slavery became an indirect cause of the suppression of freedom of speech, an essential freedom of the democratic tradition.

Rural Attitudes

Rural attitudes depended on the farmer's background and location. Farmers of immigrant stock differed from native Americans in language, agricultural skills, and culture generally. New Englanders who moved west set considerable store by common schools. Frontier farmers from the South were less interested. New England agriculturalists were more inclined to accept antislavery arguments than were southern-born tillers of the soil. (Some Southerners, however, moved to the region north of the Ohio in order to live on free soil.) Those who clung to the East resented the westward movement, which meant lower farm values in the East and high wages for hired hands. Besides, eastern landowners were discouraged when they heard of the high yield of rich western soils. Most eastern farmers stuck to the old ways, stressed thrift and hard work. Western farmers were more likely to be speculation-minded. Disinclined to be thrifty because there was plenty of good land, they were more mobile than Easterners, more inclined to pull up stakes and move further west.

Notwithstanding these differences, farmers of every section shared many ideas. They regarded agriculture as the fundamental employment of man: Did not all else depend on the land? Thus the farmer, without having heard of the eighteenth-century French physiocrats or the romantic writers of his own day, shared their views.

The conviction that agriculture was of prime importance, and the relative isolation of the rural population, made the farmer depend on himself. Neighbors helped each other clear the forest, "raise" houses and barns, and get in the crops. Still, the New World farmer was basically independent, individualistic, self-reliant. Unlike the European peasant, he considered himself the inferior of nobody.

Cut off from the outside world, the farmer was loath to admit that he could be much affected by remote factors such as market conditions, political events, even wars and social upheavals. Inevitably, then, the farmer was reluctant to accept new ideas. His father had planted and harvested at certain phases of the moon; so did he. Inasmuch as his chances of getting new ideas were limited, he tended to be narrowly partisan both in religion and in politics. Dependence on the weather, over which he had no control, made him indifferent toward planning, and he was, in a way, a fatalist.

Being a jack-of-all-trades, the farmer frowned on the specialist. He had little use for abstract thought, seldom reflected on anything that had no immediate practical bearing. He thought the city artificial, aristocratic, and corrupting, viewed with concern the migration of boys and girls to urban areas.

Formal education beyond the common school seemed to most farmers a waste, even a menace. Farm boys who acquired book learning abandoned their fathers to become doctors, lawyers, merchants, or ministers. The beginnings of scientific agriculture left the average cultivator cold. Here and there, however, an enterprising, open-minded farmer did try out suggestions offered in rural periodicals, thus leavening the inhospitality toward innovation.

Despite their narrow outlook, those who lived in country districts acquired knowledge not unsuited to their way of life. Children learned much about nature in connection with everyday tasks about the farm. During winter evenings the Bible was read and discussed in farm families. Some subscribed to farm magazines. Many more read almanacs, from which farmers could pick up concrete advice on rural problems; and they could obtain amusement and some familiarity with the wisdom of the ages. If the district schools offered relatively little, the village lyceums in many parts of the country gave interested farmers a chance to debate, borrow books, and listen to lectures. The annual fair likewise familiarized the farmer with new developments; and of course it provided recreation for the family.

The church helped, too, for clergymen were a step in advance of their communities. Thanks to denominational zeal, all sections were increasingly well provided with academies and colleges, to which bright farm boys might turn. And, despite suspicion of book knowledge, agricultural education slowly gained support. Farmers' schools sprang up at Gardiner, Maine, and near Cincinnati, Ohio. In 1819 New York created a board of agriculture with certain educational functions. The ground was thus prepared for federal support of agricultural schools, which would be inaugurated during the Civil War.

Revolution in Technology

While technologic improvements were transforming agriculture, they were having equal influence on manufacturing and transportation. Combined with rich natural resources and an economic system which encouraged their exploitation, these developments were responsible for the rapid increase in the wealth of the United States after 1815.

The importance of the new devices and techniques can be seen in colonial history. Soils were cultivated ineffectively; there was little mining and manufacturing; trade was hampered by the clumsy transportation. But when technology (the sum total of the practical devices and techniques known to a people) accelerated its advances, the scene changed. Came the steam engine and its application to travel by rail and water; textile machinery; new processes for making iron and steel; and farm inventions. Americans, who had taken 150 years to occupy a narrow seaboard plain, expanded in fifty years after 1815 across a valley a thousand miles wide and went beyond to the Pacific coast.

The speed-up in technologic advances, which has so transformed modern civilization, was linked to the rise of the middle or business classes, who felt more need for improved techniques than did the old landed nobility. In the United States, businessmen early became influential; and this class always encouraged technologic improvements. American businessmen, and farmers, too, were anxious to secure better techniques because of the shortage of man power. A large proportion of American inventions of 1800–50 were labor-saving devices.

As has been noted, most such inventions were of an empirical nature, made by practical men who saw a need, then used their mechanical ability to work out a solution. Unfortunately, a merely practical invention does not lead to further devices in other fields. The appearance of the cotton gin suggests only better cotton gins. On the other hand, a discovery in science which adds to a knowledge of natural phenomena may enable men to apply this knowledge to making all sorts of devices. The seventeenth-century Europeans who revived interest in the steam engine were primarily curious about the behavior of gas pressure. Once the steam engine had been made, however, it was found to be a new type of power engine. Then, when it was finally made efficient after 1770, it made possible a whole series of inventions which revolutionized transportation, heating, printing, and other fields.

Although most American inventions of 1800–50 were worked out to meet a specific need, there were exceptions, as in the electrical industry. By 1820, it was known that an electric current set up an adjacent magnetic field, which suggested that currents could do work (as magnets) at a distance. By the 1830's the American Joseph Henry had set up wires carrying currents across a yard and operating keys moved by magnetic effects at the far end. This was a primitive electrical telegraph. Some years passed before it was improved to the point of being useful; but by 1844 Samuel F. B. Morse, a painter, had produced a telegraph that proved commercially successful. Meanwhile, other inventors studied the possibilities of using a scientific knowledge of electricity to produce a new power engine which would be more efficient than a steam engine. Success would crown their efforts after the Civil War, when a knowledge of the physics of electricity would open up means for applying this science to transportation, lighting, and a host of other fields.

Recognizing the need for inventions, the American colonies had early followed English practice in granting legal patents, giving inventors exclusive use of their inventions for a term of years. In 1790 Congress passed a general patent law. Beginning as a small unit in the State Department, the Patent Office became a separate bureau of that department in 1832. As business grew, this bureau was transferred to the new Department of the Interior in 1849. Some indication of how invention was accelerating in this era is given in the number of patents issued. In 1791, only three were granted; by 1860 the annual figure approached 5000.

The Age of Iron and Steam

Few new types of machine parts were developed between 1815 and 1850. There was, however, a significant change in materials, as wooden machines gave way to iron. The boilers of early steam engines had sometimes been made of wood wrapped with iron bands—an outgrowth of the cooper's art of barrelmaking. But these boilers blew up under pressure. Iron boilers provided the solution. It was the same in many other fields, as can be seen by comparing the wooden works of an old clock with the metal parts of a modern timepiece.

The coming of the iron age was associated with the use of steam in power engines. All tools and machines are operated by some sort of power.

Simple tools like hammers employ man power. Treadmills use man or animal power; wind and water mills use the force of wind or water currents. The steam engine did not at once supersede other power engines. Textile mills, for example, were long operated by water wheels—which is why American cotton factories as well as flour mills were located along the fall line of the rivers. The cars on the earliest railroads were pulled by animals, and experiments were made with wind power. It seems strange to think of "sailing" a train, but this was actually tried in the 1830's. The steam engine, however, won out—once it was made of iron and fueled by coal. Other uses for steam engines also became apparent. During the 1840's, for example, steam presses replaced hand presses in printing establishments.

When steam power could be utilized in a technologic process, that process became cheaper because it could be handled by fewer men. A few operatives could turn out more cloth in a steam-powered mill than many more could produce in an old-fashioned water mill. This was because steam was more powerful and more dependable. Trains drawn by steam locomotives were more rapid and more economical than horse-drawn stagecoaches. And, since steam-powered processes were cheaper, their products became available to more people. Cheaper clothing improved living standards and cleanliness.

The social consequences of inventions were most apparent in transportation and communication. The steam railway increased travel. The steam press, combined with a rotary device invented by Hoe for printing on cylinders, cut printing costs and made penny newspapers available to the people. Meantime, the telegraph provided these mass circulation papers with quick news.

In textiles, inventors at first concentrated on spinning and weaving machines. Improvements in one stimulated advances in the other; when spinning was made more rapid, there was an immediate need for improved weaving machines to handle the increased amount of thread available. An advance along another line came in 1846, when the American Elias Howe patented a sewing machine. This helped hand sewing in homes and aided factories which produced ready-made clothing. Women's wear continued to be largely homemade, but the making of men's suits was rapidly taken over by factories. In consequence, women's clothing continued to be varied, while that of men became standardized. Sewing machines were also adapted to leather, as in the manufacture of saddles and shoes.

Technologic advances in iron were of great significance, for machines of every sort were now made from iron. The first process in iron manufacture is smelting—separating the metal from the rest of the rock ore in a furnace. When wood was cheap, charcoal was used in furnaces; but by 1850 charcoal was giving way to anthracite and bituminous coal. After smelting, the liquid metal was channeled into pigs or bars and hammered into shape at the forges. A rolling process was introduced from England after 1817. Castings, hammered and rolled iron were required for all types of machines; and secondary improvements were made in the processes of shaping these products for heavy machinery and small gadgets.

Technical improvements were rapid in the railroad field. The train of the 1830's had a locomotive with an upright boiler and a mere platform for the engineman; passenger cars were stagecoaches hitched on to "the engine." By the 1850's, locomotives had the present-day horizontal boiler and enclosed cab; and the industry was using long passenger cars with the present arrangement of seats (still called coaches). Couplings and brakes had been improved. All-iron "T" rails had taken the place of wooden rails with metal strips. The old roadbeds, made of gravel which was too soft or stone which was too hard, were replaced by modern foundations and crossties. Curves and grades had been reduced by civil engineers, so that even in wet weather these could be safely negotiated. Signaling and switching devices had been introduced.

Early locomotives, textile machines, milling machinery such as power lathes, and iron processes were imported from England. Americans adapted this equipment to American conditions. American locomotives and cars became heavier than those used in Britain, because of the long hauls of bulky goods required in this country. By 1850, moreover, Americans were displaying originality in producing such new inventions as the sewing machine and reaper. Thereafter, there was a continuous interchange of technologic knowledge between the United States and Europe.

By 1850, Americans were conscious that technology was transforming their civilization. Standards of living were rising; men's minds were benefiting from travel and from the supply of low-priced books and newspapers. Hence there was widespread enthusiasm for technologic advance in the interest of the people. This was true progress in a democracy, employment of "science" for the benefit of mankind.

Pure Science Is Neglected

At the same time, the United States gave little support to "pure" or theoretic science. Geologists had learned enough about rocks and ores by 1840 to lead state governments to finance geologic surveys of these natural resources. But, generally speaking, the theoretic scientist was still regarded as one living in an ivory tower, pursuing merely his own curiosity. A practical people had small use for such a person. He was tolerated in colleges largely because he served a useful purpose as a teacher.

This was short-sighted. In the long run, chemists, biologists, and physicists would discover truths about soils, animals, and electricity which would revolutionize agriculture, animal husbandry, and industry. This was apparent to few Americans in 1850. But even then, Americans were benefiting from European discoveries in basic science (as with electricity and the telegraph). Later American technology, therefore, owes a great debt to the Europeans, who supported basic research when its utility was not as apparent as it is today.

Take medicine. Since classical times, illness had been laid to impurities or lack of balance of the body fluids or "humors" (blood, bile, etc.). Curing an ill person involved relieving that person of fluids by bleeding, purging, or sweating. In the spring, children were given doses of sulfur and molasses to "purify" the system. By 1800, however, European physicians had secured a sound knowledge of normal and pathologic anatomy. They saw that they could get a better idea of what a particular disease was if they noted what damage had occurred to tissues within the body as observed in post-mortem studies. They could then correlate the damage with symptoms observed before death, so as to identify the particular disease. Instead of talking vaguely about "inflammation of the chest," they could now distinguish between such specific conditions as pneumonia, bronchitis, and pleurisy. Knowing what different diseases were, they could begin to look rationally for causes, prevention, and cure. Pasteur and others who later worked on causal factors and on means of preventing and curing infectious diseases could never have succeeded without the earlier, basic work in diagnosis.

Research in identifying diseases was thus of great significance for future medical practice. Unfortunately, there was little immediate value for medical practice. During the 1840's, for example, Americans learned the difference between typhoid and typhus fevers. But this did not help patients at the time, since physicians could not prevent or cure either disease. Such medical discoveries therefore seemed of no use to "practical" Americans. Consequently, physicians interested in research were helped neither by the government nor by philanthropists. The respected doctor was the one who had a large practice.

Americans did show enthusiasm when science promised immediate return. Thus, when chemists produced new gases which caused unconsciousness upon inhalation, the possibilities in surgery became apparent. It was then that two American dentists (Drs. Horace Wells and W. T. G. Morton) independently "discovered" anesthesia. From the 1840's on, this "applied science" was a great boon to patients undergoing operations, hence was appreciated by Americans as well as other peoples.

American neglect of theoretic science had one other aspect. In Europe an old, aristocratic tradition supported the prestige of theoretic scholarship and learning; in "democratic" America this tradition was largely lost. European governments, influenced by aristocrats, supported university research. American governments, influenced by businessmen or planters, encouraged science only when it could be "applied" quickly to the making of profits. So it was no accident that the United States of 1800–50 remained backward in basic science, at the same time that it became advanced in technology.

The Steamboat Opens the West

No other nation had as much to gain from applying steam power to river travel as did the United States; and no other nation developed the river steamboat so rapidly. Once the problem of traveling upstream could be solved, Atlantic coastal streams and the Mississippi system offered natural avenues for commerce. The steam-powered paddle wheel that met this problem was the key that opened the interior to industrial mass production. By 1850 the key had been turned and the doors to the great home market were swinging open.

Robert Fulton had shown the value of the steamboat on such calm waters as the Hudson in 1807. But Fulton's *Clermont* could not have traveled against the Mississippi current. The shallow, swiftly flowing western rivers called for higher-pressure boilers, more powerful engines, and a new type of hull. The result was the "Mississippi steamboat," developed by trial-and-error methods by 1820. Soon hundreds of shallow-draft steamers were nosing their way far up the lesser tributaries of the Mississippi. Palatial three-decked liners carried passengers at fifteen miles an hour up and down the major rivers. Steamboats of a different design operated on the Great Lakes.

There was danger in the new forms of power transportation. Side-wheel steamboats were less seaworthy than stoutly built sailing ships and were often wrecked in the sudden squalls that swept across the Great Lakes. Sand bars, submerged timber, and wild competition for speed records made the Mississippi another graveyard for steamboats. Many of the high-pressure boilers exploded, killing a number of persons instantly and starting fires which were fatal to many more. European visitors were shocked by the tragic record—a thousand river boats wrecked by 1850, with the loss of twice that many lives. But occasional disasters were of minor importance to Americans. The great fact was that the steamboat carried

freight at rates the inland farmer could afford to pay. Steam conquest of
the Mississippi system meant connection with the whole world. Manufactures from British factories came upriver from New Orleans. By return
boat the farmers' products moved to nearby towns, to the deep South and
the eastern seaboard, and to the Old World. At the height of the traffic
(in the forties and early fifties), the vessels plying the rivers had a larger
tonnage than those in any other American trade. And they represented a
steam tonnage larger than that of the British Empire.

Profiting from the Mississippi River trade and the cotton boom in the
1830's, New Orleans grew rapidly. As the chief exporting city of the United
States, it was a shipping center to be ranked with New York, Liverpool,
and London. The other leading ports of the interior waterway system also
grew prodigiously. Cincinnati, linked to both East and South, became the
largest city of the Northwest. Her water-borne commerce was surpassed in
value only by that of New York, New Orleans, and Philadelphia.

Canals Connect East and West

The steamboat was only a partial solution
to the western transportation problem. Navigable rivers were relatively far
apart. In any case, they did not connect directly with the East. The first
difficulty was imperfectly met by the turnpikes, later by railroads. But direct connection with the East was first supplied by canals.

Canals were expensive, costing up to $50,000 a mile. But, once built,
they afforded very cheap transportation. Four horses could pull a hundred
tons in barges twenty miles a day. A bushel of wheat might travel 200 miles
by canal as cheaply as one mile by wagon.

Between 1800 and 1830 canal projects were undertaken in all the eastern
states. Some promoters desired to connect two existing bodies of water.
Others wanted to extend the navigable length of a river, or to enlarge the
area shipping goods to a seaport. Merchants from Portland, Maine, to
Charleston, South Carolina, sought to increase their business by financing
canal companies with or without the aid of state governments. These local
projects did little to solve the problem of communication with the West;
but they accustomed men to thinking in terms of canals, and paved the
way for the beginning of New York State's Erie Canal in 1817.

New York City businessmen had every reason to be interested in canals.
Montreal, Philadelphia, and Baltimore were all more closely connected
with the growing West by natural waterways. New York, however, con-
trolled the one comparatively level avenue to the interior—the Hudson-
Mohawk line from New York to Albany and on to what is now Buffalo.
Elkanah Watson, who had studied European canals, declared in 1788 that

a New York canal could "divert the full trade of . . . the Great Lakes . . . to Albany and New York." Four years later Watson persuaded the legislature to appoint him to a state canal commission, which extended the navigation of the Mohawk River by locks completed in 1796. There progress halted. The federal government, Ohio, and the Indiana Territory refused to help; and when New York decided to go ahead alone, the War of 1812 forced a new delay. After the war, the project was taken up again. A political faction led by DeWitt Clinton secured authorization for a completely state-financed canal. It took eight years and $8,000,000 to complete this Erie Canal, which ran from Albany to Buffalo, connecting the Hudson River and the Great Lakes.

The canal was an immediate success. Tolls took care of maintenance, repaid the cost of construction, and yielded a substantial profit. The canal, moreover, confirmed New York's position as the greatest city on the continent. The Great Lakes and their tributary rivers were now part of the inland waterways of the Atlantic seaboard. Once canals were completed from the rivers flowing into the Great Lakes to the Mississippi system, the farmers of the whole interior basin could supply water-borne goods to the East. With the proceeds they could buy the products of eastern industry, or European goods imported by New York merchants.

Boston, Philadelphia, and Baltimore were powerless to meet the challenge of New York. Boston had to wait a generation for railroad connections, and even then could not compete with New York's water transportation. Pennsylvania and Maryland undertook expensive canal projects, and by 1850 Philadelphia and Baltimore had all-water connections with the West. But in each case the Appalachians forced the use of circuitous routes, and New York retained its advantage.

By 1850 the United States had 4000 miles of canals. Among the most important were canals connecting the Mississippi and the Great Lakes. In the late 1820's both Ohio and Indiana began construction designed to link Lake Erie and the Ohio River. First completed was the Ohio Canal, from Cleveland to Portsmouth on the Ohio. Further west the Miami Canal connected Toledo and Cincinnati. Indiana's Wabash Canal ran from this Miami Canal to Terre Haute on the Wabash River. Later, in 1855, it was completed to the Ohio. By then a fourth connection had been established, the Illinois and Michigan Canal joining Chicago and Lake Michigan with the Mississippi, by way of the Illinois River.

These long western canals were built partly by private companies, partly by the states. The United States government also aided by granting land to the states. This practice started with a turnpike land grant to Ohio in 1823, but emphasis soon shifted to canals. The federal government granted alternate sections on both sides of the right of way. The states could sell their plots or borrow against them, thus raising capital for construction. When the highway or canal was built, the United States stood to gain from the increase in value of the sections it retained. Altogether, the states and territories of the Old Northwest received nearly 5,000,000 acres for canal purposes; and Alabama, Iowa, and Wisconsin were given half that amount for river improvement.

The growth of inland water traffic profoundly affected population patterns. The Great Lakes, for example, had few good harbors. Each of these therefore attracted a large commerce and became the site of a major city. On rivers and canals, cities sprang up at the heads of navigation, and at points of transshipment from barge to river boat, or from river boat to seagoing vessel. Accentuating the dispersion of population produced by the public land system, farmers settled along the banks of canals and navigable rivers, leaving large unpopulated areas between the waterways.

Ocean Shipping

In the early part of the Napoleonic Wars American ships carried 80 percent of the foreign commerce of the United States, plus much of the trade between the warring nations and their colonies. This, however, was temporary. Jefferson's embargo and the War of 1812 hurt American shippers; and after 1815 Old World nations were back in competition. Equally discouraging was the drying up of the supply of native sailors. New England youths had long looked to the sea for a career; but interest dwindled as manufacturing and the westward movement offered other opportunities.

Refusing to give up, American shipowners hired foreign crews. By driving these crews hard, and taking risks which Europeans avoided, American captains retained the bulk of their country's overseas trade. The Black Ball Line of New York pioneered with fast liner schedules, announcing that from January, 1818, on, a fast ship would sail for Liverpool at a specified day and hour each month. Down to 1840 the British failed to duplicate such service, so smart businessmen traveled and shipped "American." Meanwhile, American ship designers met the demand for speed with many innovations. Most notable was the development in the 1840's of the clipper, a beautiful ship with fine hull lines and a great spread of sail. The clippers were the fastest sailing vessels ever constructed. With favorable winds they could cross the Atlantic westbound in two weeks and eastbound in three, as against one to two months for old-style ships.

Efficient though it was, the clipper was doomed from the start. In 1838, two English steamships arrived in New York on a single day. Seeing their practicality, the British government offered postal subsidies for the introduction of wooden side-wheelers on certain routes. Samuel Cunard secured the contract for the North Atlantic. American steamship interests, unable to obtain a subsidy until 1845, lagged behind.

The clippers could compete with these first ocean-going steamships. Moreover, American shipbuilders could match the British in turning out wooden side-wheelers. But after 1845 a more powerful competitor appeared in the iron screw-propeller steamship. The first vessels of the new type were slow. The propeller, however, made for more efficient use of power; and, by necessitating iron construction, it gave the British a great advantage. Crude iron at the water edge cost much less in England than in the United States, and Britain's iron industry was better prepared to make large shapes. Nor could American merchants buy British ships for United States registry. That was prohibited by the Navigation Act of 1819, passed by a Congress anxious to protect native shipbuilders.

The final victory of the British iron steamship came in the late 1850's. Meanwhile, American clipper ships profited from the Mexican War, the California gold rush, and the Crimean War in Europe. American shipping appeared secure and prosperous in 1850. The American merchant marine of 1,500,000 gross tons was twice as large as it had been a decade earlier, and was second only to Britain's. American ships carried two-thirds of the exports and imports of the United States. Clippers made fabulous speed records (300 miles a day), and the less spectacular tramp freighters held their own in world competition. The coming eclipse of American sea power was foreseen by few.

Most of the foreign trade of the United States continued to be with Britain. The British took raw materials—cotton in particular, that product representing half the value of American exports. In return, Britain shipped to the United States textiles, iron and steel products, pottery, and other manufactures. Next in importance was the old West Indies trade, sugar and molasses being exchanged for food and building materials. Meantime, the United States was increasing purchases of coffee from Brazil and Central America. The famous China trade declined slowly after the middle 1820's, owing partly to the declining demand for tea and the rise of silk production in Europe.

Foreign trade increased from 1815 to 1850. But, with the phenomenal growth of domestic industry, overseas commerce came to represent a smaller percentage of total national income. The change, of course, was gradual; and even in 1850 foreign trade was relatively more important than it would be later. As in colonial days, imports normally exceeded exports in value. This was natural in a nation not yet adequately supplied with factories. Ocean freights paid to American carriers helped even the balance, as did European investments in the United States.

In the colonial era, British merchants had dealt directly with American planters. As trade grew more complex, middlemen entered the picture. An English cotton importing house advanced credit to a commission merchant in the northern part of the United States. A southern representative of this commission merchant bought the cotton from a local factor. The factor (usually a merchant of New Orleans, Mobile, Savannah, or Charleston) dealt with plantation owners. Advancing credit between crops, and taking liens on future cotton as security, the factor came largely to dictate conditions of production. Planters thus lost independence of action, and groaned under a burden of brokerage fees and interest.

The increasing concentration of economic activities benefited the larger ports. Small eighteenth-century vessels had called at all the tiny ports along the Atlantic coast, and had run up coastal rivers. Larger nineteenth-century vessels confined themselves to major ports. There they could exchange whole cargoes, and they could avoid the risks of coastal storms and sand bars. By 1850 most of the foreign commerce of Portsmouth, New Haven, Norfolk, Wilmington, Charleston, and Savannah had transferred to Boston, New York, Philadelphia, and Baltimore. New York obtained the lion's share, and by 1850 nearly half of the nation's imports and exports moved through that single city.

The coastwise trade lacked the romance of the overseas merchant service but moved a larger volume of goods. Given an absolute monopoly by Congressional action, Americans did not have to fear foreign competition. The chief competition came on short hauls from barges on inland waterways paralleling the coast. Inland water shipment was quicker, but ocean sail was cheaper, and on long hauls the coastwise vessels got the freight.

Schooners of a hundred tons or less shuttled goods back and forth between the various ports from Maine to Virginia. Such vessels were economical, and could run far up the coastal rivers—to Albany, to Trenton, even to Richmond. Larger sailing ships operated mainly in the cotton triangle (New York, New Orleans, and Liverpool). Some ships sailed direct from New Orleans to Liverpool, returning by way of New York. Others took cotton from southern ports to northern cities, different vessels carrying the cargo on to England. From the 1820's on, regular liner services developed on the long coastwise trips, a few passenger steamers joining the many sailing ships. Although the vessels were seldom far from land, insurance rates show that a voyage between New Orleans and New York was more hazardous than an ocean crossing, because of the West Indian passages, the reefs and capes of the North Carolina coast, and the very nearness to shore.

Outside the few cities that used illuminating gas, whale oil supplied the best source of light. Whaling, therefore, remained a big business. Its yearly product was worth $10,000,000 by mid-century; and the tonnage of the whaling fleet was over a tenth as large as the tonnage of all American vessels employed in foreign trade. The cod and mackerel fisheries generally had an even larger tonnage. Aided by government subsidies, the New England fishing fleets managed to compete with the English and the French in the battle for the American market.

Pioneer Railroads

John Stevens, the steamboat inventor, obtained the first American railway charter in 1817, and in 1826 built a small steam railroad on his Hoboken estate. By then railroad promoters were pleading their cause before legislators and investors in every state. At the end of the decade—before a steam locomotive had operated commercially either here or abroad—the Baltimore and Ohio was laying tracks, and the Mohawk and Hudson and the Charleston and Hamburg were being surveyed.

The railroad gave cities a chance to bid for traffic. Boston's builders hoped to attract inland producers who sent their goods to market by the canal from Worcester to Providence, or down the canalized Connecticut River. The state of Pennsylvania financed a railroad from Philadelphia to Columbia to draw off the traffic going down the Susquehanna River to Baltimore. The businessmen of Baltimore in turn sought to extend their tributary area by running the state-aided Baltimore and Ohio Railroad westward. Charleston tried by means of a railroad to win inland cotton trade away from Savannah. The result was that both cities built railroads whose inland junction developed Atlanta.

Railroads also offered seaboard cities the larger opportunity of tapping the wealth of the Mississippi Valley. Here New York City took the lead. Having the Erie Canal, New York had less need for a rail connection with the West than did competing cities. But the geographical advantages which made the Canal possible also operated in favor of railroad building. In addition, the Canal had developed thriving communities which provided local traffic from tidewater to the Great Lakes. By the early 1840's, therefore, New York State was completely traversed by privately owned railroads. Stock subscriptions from the state of Massachusetts and the city of Albany aided the Western Railroad, which linked Boston to Albany, tying together the New York and New England systems.

Other areas were less fortunate. Some railroads made progress—the Baltimore and Ohio, which was aided by state and local subsidies, and the government-owned Western and Atlantic in Georgia. These lines, however, did not tap the West until after 1850. Somewhat typical was the experience of Pennsylvania. This state acquired a staggering debt by building a railroad and canal system, which could not compete with New York's railroads for speed or New York's waterways for cheapness.

In the long run, American railroads would supply the cheap transportation essential to large-scale specialized agriculture and mass production industry. But railroad rates were not yet cheap in 1850. The core of the problem was the failure to arrange for through shipments. Part of this was unavoidable, for the railroads did not yet blanket the country. Nor could the railroads afford to build strong bridges across all streams. It was necessary, therefore, to use ferries, which meant unloading, reloading, and endless delays. It was the same along land routes. Normally, each company controlled only a few miles of road, and neither equipment nor gauge of track had been standardized. In consequence, it was necessary to unload and reload at the end of one railroad and the beginning of the next. This process made the already high rates prohibitive for bulky products.

Still, the future looked bright in 1850. Passengers could go by rail and ferry from Maine to North Carolina; there were railroads from Chicago to Detroit, from Cincinnati to Cleveland. Private express companies were beginning to arrange for transfers and deliveries. The railroad was the most important customer of the telegraph, and helped by 1850 to make possible a network of wires connecting eastern ports with New Orleans, St. Louis, and Chicago.

The Business Cycle

There have always been cyclical movements in economic activity, in agricultural as well as industrial areas. The increase in manufacturing made these movements more pronounced in the United States after 1815, and they meant more, because of the close link between employment and prosperity.

The business cycle had standard features. During periods of prosperity, productive capacity was expanded too rapidly. For this purpose credit was created beyond true savings. Materials and labor were sought beyond supply, bringing a spiral of increasing costs, accompanied by a rise in land values. Then came the downward turn. Men building canals, railroads, or factories saw there was little chance for profit from works costing so much to construct. When they stopped building, they canceled contracts and threw laborers out of work. A stampede to dispose of doubtful assets caused a break on stock exchanges. There followed a general slowing down of commercial and industrial activity, with widespread unemployment.

Most severe were the depressions which followed the panics of 1819 and 1837. These were preceded by runaway booms. When the speculative bubble burst, business failures were so numerous as to prevent the resumption of normal activity for years. Society had to find new capital to reopen closed banks, new entrepreneurs to start ruined factories, new investors to inject life into stranded canal and railroad projects. The country pulled out of the panic of 1819 during the early 1820's. The damage of 1837 was not so easily repaired; not until 1843 did the republic have good times again.

Raising Capital: Foreign Loans

As they expanded their activities, Americans constantly found themselves short of capital. In consequence, all methods of raising real or fictitious capital were pursued, without much thought as to how interest was to be paid.

Much of the capital used to develop the United States came from abroad. American states sold bonds in London (nearly $20,000,000 a year by 1830), then invested the proceeds in transportation companies and banks. At the same time, American financiers pursued the old colonial method of securing capital through short-term mercantile credits. American correspondents drew on British houses which specialized in the cotton trade and owed $27,000,000 by 1837. England, in other words, was carrying the United States boom, and Americans were mortgaging their savings for years ahead. By 1836 rising production costs put crucial pressure on the boom. So did President Andrew Jackson's Specie Circular, which ordered federal land offices to stop accepting paper bank notes, and to sell only for gold and silver. The immediate cause of the panic of 1837, however, was the stoppage of further British advances on cotton, at the advice of the Bank of England. An American pool organized by the Philadelphia banker, Nicholas Biddle, sustained the price of cotton by redeeming cotton paper with short-term notes. When these fell due, they were replaced by new notes and new issues of state bonds. With these devices United States banks eased the liquidation of their southern and western loans, and American states continued to build internal improvements with English money. But in 1838 the European boom collapsed, and all forms of British lending came to an end.

The next four years of world depression checked American growth for a decade. In general, the improvements for which the money had been borrowed were incomplete. With declining tax revenues, states could not meet their obligations. Foreign bondholders were not altogether surprised when western and southwestern states defaulted on bond interest; their securities had long been regarded as speculative. But when Pennsylvania and Maryland joined the nonpaying ranks, English leaders were shocked. Maryland and Pennsylvania presently resumed payment on their obligations. Some states, however, resorted to complete repudiation, adding the final touch to the destruction of American credit abroad. Not until after the discovery of gold in California did European investors again feel optimistic about the future of American securities.

Raising Capital: Banking

Even in flush times the average American did not borrow directly from abroad. Instead, he obtained his capital by borrowing from local institutions. From the 1790's on, fire and marine insurance companies invested reserves in bonds and urban mortgages. Life insurance concerns came into the picture in the 1840's. Savings banks and building and loan associations made direct loans to businessmen, or took mortgages on assets. But down to 1850 the resources of commercial banks were more important than those of all other credit institutions put together.

The chaotic state of local banking and the breakdown of government credit during the War of 1812 led to the chartering of the second Bank of the United States in 1816. Like the first Bank of the United States (1791–1811), the new institution was chartered for twenty years and was privately controlled, with the United States government subscribing one-fifth of the shares. But, in line with the growth of the country, the second Bank had $35,000,000 in capital, three and a half times that of its predecessor.

Under Nicholas Biddle, who became its president in 1823, the second Bank did much to stabilize banking. Its bank notes provided a genuinely national paper currency. The main office and branches supplied businessmen with credit and acted as a sort of clearing house for local banks. Still, the second Bank of the United States was far from popular. Biddle, a conservative financier, wanted to prevent state-chartered banks from issuing unlimited quantities of paper money. He tried to keep "wildcat" banks in line by threatening to collect their bank notes and present them for redemption in specie. Inevitably, this aroused opposition. Small-town citizens expected their local banks to provide the credit needed to build up their communities. That meant issuing bank notes, for checks were little used in those days. And Biddle, by forcing local banks to limit note issue, was preventing the people from obtaining needed credit.

The drive against the second Bank had many aspects. There was personal animosity toward Biddle, a reactionary in a democratic age. Biddle's bank was denounced as a monopoly, an ally of the rich. In the South and West, the second Bank was attacked as an eastern institution (it had headquarters in Philadelphia). And everywhere, the national bank was assailed as a foe of local institutions. In 1832 President Andrew Jackson vetoed a bill to recharter the Bank, then won reëlection when he carried the issue to the voters. The second Bank of the United States therefore died as had the first, and from 1836 to 1913 the republic had no central banking system. (Biddle continued with a state charter, but his Pennsylvania-chartered Bank of the United States went down in the depression which followed the panic of 1837.)

After 1834 the expiring second Bank of the United States exercised little restraining influence on country banks, and the inflationary extremes of 1811–16 reappeared. By 1840 there were 900 banks in the United States, double the number that had existed seven years before. Often banks were promoted by men who paid for their stock by borrowing from the bank. In such cases the bank's capital was fictitious, and there was no adequate specie reserve to redeem bank notes issued to borrowers. Many banks took care of that by making the legal office for redemption inaccessible, placing it in some spot where wildcats were more common than men. Hence the name "wildcat currency."

The 1840's saw some improvement. Depression had eliminated the weakest banks; and many states were passing laws to prohibit or regulate banks. A number of states required that capital stock be paid for in cash, that bank notes be backed by approved securities deposited with a government official, and that specie reserves be maintained against the bank's paper currency.

Desirable though this legislation was, the ability of banks to survive hard times depended chiefly on the liquidity of the risks offered in their localities. In the Southwest, where land and slaves were the basis for credit, mortgages filled the bank portfolios. In that area state governments used their credit to provide bank capital, just as the Northwest states used theirs for internal improvements. State-supported banks in Tennessee, Alabama, Florida, Mississippi, and Arkansas all issued currency backed by boom-time mortgages. When financial crisis led depositors and noteholders to run to the banks for specie, the bankers had no liquid assets. The result was suspension of specie payments in all these states.

In Indiana and Ohio the need was for credit to move crops and merchandise. There branch banking systems in which the state was the main stockholder operated with success. Similarly, banks fared well in such trading centers as New York, Philadelphia, and New Orleans, where financiers could quickly realize on their loans to businessmen (short-term commercial paper).

Sound or unsound, bank notes helped the United States develop. Adverse trade balances kept the nation short of specie until after 1850, when California gold began coming east. Down to that time gold and silver coins and Treasury certificates were seldom seen. Business transactions were made with bank notes, and a great deal of country trading was by barter or book credit.

One great difficulty with bank notes was their local character. "Foreign" (out-of-town) money was unacceptable in most communities. This created exchange problems. Since the West generally owed balances to the East, eastern exchange commanded a premium. Western and southern banks therefore kept balances with New York banks, from which they could make eastern payments for clients. This practice was encouraged by state laws which allowed country banks to count such deposits as part of their reserves. So a substantial part of the banking reserves of the nation accumulated in a few New York City banks, making that city the republic's financial center.

The piling up of deposits in New York produced instability. Desiring to keep out-of-town deposits liquid, New York banks used them for demand loans, secured by stocks or bonds. Hence, whenever country banks drew down their deposits, the city banks called in demand loans, transferring pressure to the stock market. The job of moving a large western harvest might thus precipitate a stock market crash in New York, with repercussions all over the United States. Not until 1913 was this corrected.

For all its defects, the banking system met the needs of an expanding debtor nation. Credit was manufactured so fast in good times that full employment of all available resources was guaranteed; and, despite mismanagement, the projects financed were usually those essential to the nation's development. American banks, moreover, were designed to aid the enterpriser rather than to protect the lender. And new enterprise was what the great majority of Americans desired.

Raising Capital: The Corporation

Many businessmen needed more capital than they could raise among friends or borrow from local banks. They therefore obtained money by selling stock. At first the practice was to form a joint-stock association with freely transferable shares. Such a company could be formed by having a lawyer draw up articles of association. It could not, however, give investors the protection of limited liability.

Turnpikes, bridges, canals, and railroads needed state charters granting rights of way. These charters set up corporations with limited liability. That is, investors were not responsible for losses beyond the money paid for their stock, and creditors could not collect more than the assets of the company. This arrangement helped the sale of stock. So did the practice of attracting small investors by offering shares at low par value. Corporations were thus able to acquire substantial sums, despite the shortage of capital in the United States. Some trunk-line railroads completed in the 1850's cost $30,000,000 and had 2000 stockholders.

At first the promoters of each new company had to get a special act of incorporation through the legislature. The trouble and expense discouraged the use of limited-liability companies but also enabled shrewd incorporators to gain special privileges such as the power to condemn property or monopolize traffic. Resultant abuses caused opposition to special charters. Led by Connecticut in 1837, eastern states and Indiana passed laws prescribing standard charter provisions that could be secured by applying to a state bureau. Some states also passed "free banking" acts, setting standard conditions for bank charters. The purpose was to prevent charter provisions contrary to public interest and to focus publicity on any group applying for a special act of incorporation. The net effect, however, was to make incorporation so easy that it was used increasingly.

Investors liked corporation stock because of its salability. As early as 1792 New York traders who regularly met beneath a buttonwood tree on Wall Street drew up an agreement regulating procedure and commissions. Twenty-five years later, when bank, canal, and turnpike stocks were swelling business, these dealers organized the New York Stock and Exchange Board. Smaller exchanges grew up in other cities.

Although they provided a market for trading securities, stock exchanges had no machinery for issuing shares. This called for a special middleman, the investment banker. The earliest of these were merchants like the Brown brothers. Early in the nineteenth century the Browns began to specialize in domestic and foreign exchange. As note brokers, they dealt with moneyed men; hence they were natural salesmen for new securities. As business grew, they dropped mercantile activities and specialized in investment banking. Since Britain was a leading market for American securities, the Browns established branches there. Others followed suit; and the Rothschilds of Europe opened a New York agency under August Belmont.

As fortunes made in transportation and manufacturing were invested in corporation stocks, a group of general entrepreneurs or financiers arose. Nathan Appleton, Cornelius Vanderbilt, Erastus Corning, and others were no longer content with one company. They found that an organized minority in a company with widely distributed stock could exert control without reference to the unorganized majority. Using their capital to buy strategic blocks of shares, they ran many companies, adding to their fortunes by manipulating the security markets.

Under this system, ownership and management were separated. The financiers could not personally direct all the companies; and the managers often had little or no capital invested in the companies they directed.

Manufacturing

Americans who set up factories during the War of 1812 feared foreign competition most. But when peace came, many of the new factories stood up against British competition. American manufacturers possessed certain advantages. Most of them used cheap water power, obtained by setting a mill wheel in the main channel of a swift stream. Low transportation costs also helped, for most mills sold their small production near home. In addition, the United States provided moderate tariff protection. The tariff of 1816 was passed when the South as well as the Northeast hoped to become a textile-manufacturing area. The rates, however, failed to satisfy American producers. By 1820 eastern manufacturers were organizing for increased protection, in such bodies as the National Institution for the Promotion of Industry. In 1827 the high-tariff people held a national convention at Harrisburg, Pennsylvania. The political situation played into their hands the following year, and they obtained from Congress a general increase.[1] Rates stayed up in the Tariff of 1832, and it took John C. Calhoun's nullification movement to force a reduction the next year.

Offsetting the advantages possessed by American manufacturers were serious obstacles. Transportation was one problem. It was difficult to get raw materials to the factory, finished products to market. In the remote interior, therefore, settlers used household manufactures instead of factory products.

No less serious was the shortage of labor. The lack of trained artisans was felt acutely, for every manufacturing establishment needed a few workers who understood power machinery. Competent managers were still more scarce. Manufacturers ordered equipment too large or too small for their plants. They chose poor locations, underestimated credit needs, misjudged markets. As a consequence, many failed.

Capital was another problem. Able promoters with large sums at their command often did well—for example, Almy and Brown, who were behind Samuel Slater, and the Lowell-Appleton combination which backed the

---

[1] There had been a minor revision of the tariff in 1824. There was much political jugglery while the Tariff of 1828 was under consideration, and it became known as the "Tariff of Abominations."

Boston Manufacturing Company. But, since general investors preferred to put money in transportation, most factories were started on a shoestring. If all went well, the business could be expanded with bank loans and re-invested earnings. But cash reserves were insufficient during crises and many failed in depression years.

New England textile factories were fortunate in their location. They were built on the banks of streams that provided water power. They were near ports where cotton was received, were close to the chief consuming centers, and were in a declining agricultural area that offered a fair labor supply. Northeastern cities also afforded good credit facilities.

Since textiles are light in weight compared with value, the eastern industry could market its wares all over the country. In bulkier products such as furniture, farm equipment, and cast iron, local factories had a considerable advantage in transportation costs. As population moved inland, and as the steam engine improved in efficiency (diminishing the need for water power), these industries grew up in western cities. By 1850 Buffalo, Pittsburgh, Cleveland, Chicago, Cincinnati, Louisville, and St. Louis were manufacturing centers.

In food processing, the nation's greatest industry, western cities forged ahead. St. Louis was the western flour-milling center. Cincinnati became the meat packing metropolis, and a leather center, too. Pittsburgh also boomed. Located near iron ore, coal, and wood, and supplied with a stream of westward-moving labor, Pittsburgh grew rich from iron milling and boat-building. As yet, however, the city had not become predominant in iron. Iron ore was mined and processed all through the Middle Atlantic states and as far west as Kentucky and Tennessee. Richmond, Virginia, was an important iron center.

Though losing crude industry to other sections, New England retained the lead in manufacturing which called for careful workmanship and intricate machinery. European visitors marveled at the efficiency of mass production in Connecticut hardware and firearm factories, commenting particularly on the principle of interchangeable parts. By 1850 Aaron Dennison of Waltham, Massachusetts, was applying mass production methods to watchmaking, the province of skilled hand workers abroad. New England textile and shoe factories expanded with the national market, and barrels of New England shoes appeared in general stores beyond the Mississippi.

The Problem of Competition

The first persons to use machinery in a new field generally made high profits, for they undersold the old hand operators. But the favorable returns attracted competitors with still newer machinery, and the market soon was oversupplied. Prices then fell to unprofitable levels. Yet producers could not easily withdraw. Caught with a heavy investment in machinery that could not be converted to other uses, manufacturers and transportation companies continued to run on returns that covered neither interest nor depreciation. Stoppage, after all, would mean a permanent loss of invested capital.

Businessmen who faced cutthroat competition tried to make their products or services more attractive than those of competitors. A gun or clock might have patentable features that would make its trademark famous and command a price above the general market. In plain or bulk goods differentiation was more difficult. One could, however, use attractive packaging or build a reputation for reliability even with such standard commodities as flour and sheet brass. One could also advertise a trade name.

Another way of meeting competition was to join competitors in agreements to hold up prices. The figures set by the largest firms might be copied voluntarily by lesser competitors, who knew that price cutting would bring retaliation. Or producers might hold informal discussions and set prices for the year. Or a trade association could prepare a formal agreement. Such agreements worked in Europe. But after 1820 American state courts nullified many of them; under American interpretation of common law, price-fixing agreements were considered conspiracies in restraint of trade. Unwritten understandings ("gentlemen's agreements") could be used; but these were difficult to maintain. So, on the whole, individualism predominated in the first half of the nineteenth century.

The Working Classes

White-collar workers had not been numerous in early America. Even great merchants like John Jacob Astor, Stephen Girard, and William Derby needed only three or four clerks to keep track of their ventures. Aside from captains and supercargoes, they hired no managers or foremen. But factory, railroad, canal, insurance, and banking companies required special office and managerial forces. This was notably the case in companies where the owners (stockholders) took no active part in management.

In comparison with manual workers, managerial employees were well paid. They created a new consumer demand for newspapers, theaters, retail stores, and passenger travel. This in turn provided more jobs. As a result positions multiplied faster than the supply of men trained to fill them, and advancement was certain for able clerks. Manual laborers found the period less satisfactory. Until the panic of 1837 skilled workers benefited from a relative shortage of labor. After that came a long depression, then a decade of heavy immigration. Both factors tended to create an oversupply of workers in eastern industrial centers, holding down wages. To put it another way: there was a labor shortage between 1815 and 1850. Workers, however, were unevenly distributed. There might be a desperate labor shortage along the frontier, and at the same time an oversupply of workers in eastern factory towns. Thus, in this land of opportunity, industrial wages were often at the level of bare subsistence.

One factor was the decline in farming in the East. Factory owners could send recruiting wagons into depressed districts and obtain women and children to run their machines. Immigrants were an even more important source of supply. Europeans (Irishmen in particular) were brought in under time contracts to work with construction gangs. This system declined when the supply of free immigrants increased in the 1830's, but contract laborers were used until the United States prohibited the practice in 1884. Besides Europeans, immigrants included French Canadians.

Although most associations of employers were considered legal under the English common law, workers' organizations were viewed as criminal conspiracies. But United States courts did not rigidly adhere to these doctrines. Craft unions met with legal interference only on occasion. Local labor organizations therefore gained in strength as American cities grew. In the late 1820's the crafts of Philadelphia joined together in a Mechanics Central Union of Trade Associations, issued a newspaper, and started a political party. Similar developments took place in New York and Boston, and by the mid-1830's there were central trade organizations in a dozen cities, one as far west as Louisville, Kentucky.

In years of business uncertainty from 1827 to 1833, the unions worked chiefly for political reforms. They demanded abolition of imprisonment for debt. They asked for mechanics' lien laws to prevent seizure of craftsmen's tools, and statutes to keep distressed workers from losing their homes. They called for abolition of chartered monopolies. They demanded free public education, in the thought that educated workingmen could control a democracy. The workingmen's parties formed in New York and Philadelphia soon disappeared; but the reforms they advocated were taken up by major party politicians anxious to secure labor votes.

By increasing the demand for labor, the boom from 1834 to 1837 gave skilled workers an opportunity to stage successful strikes. Wage increases and the ten-hour day were obtained in a number of cities; and union spokesmen began to talk of national labor organization. Alarmed, employers fought back through the courts, seeking legal prosecution of pickets. They won a few decisions. But workingmen appealed to public opinion; and juries became reluctant to convict on conspiracy charges. Ultimately, employers found it cheaper and safer to fight strikes by hiring strikebreakers, or locking out the strikers.

The period of labor militancy was brief. The depression after the panic of 1837 ended national labor organizations, labor congresses, and direct action. Where unions survived at all they did so by emphasizing their old activities of collecting funds for health insurance and death benefits. Not until the boom of the 1850's did skilled workers return to militant action for better conditions.

Unskilled factory workers sometimes went on strike, but they did not organize unions. Girl operatives at Lowell, Massachusetts, fought wage cuts by peaceful demonstrations. Less gentle male workers in Paterson, New Jersey, staged a riot that was quelled by state militia. But disturbances grew less frequent as workers became resigned to industrial discipline, as unskilled labor became more plentiful, and as employers' associations developed systems to guard against hiring "troublemakers."

Except for 1834–37, labor disputes were not of much importance from 1815 to 1850. Employers set wages and hours on the basis of custom slightly modified by price movements and the immediate supply of workers in relation to demand. In these years average hours declined somewhat. Trade-union activity had little to do with the change. Liberal reformers did their bit, working on public opinion. More important was the realization that long hours made for inefficiency as the tempo of factory machines quickened. Textile operatives of 1850, working less than twelve hours, were more worn out at the day's end than operatives of 1820, who had worked longer hours.

Industry and Culture

The rise of manufacturing affected cultural patterns. It strengthened East-West ties. A new nationalism came out of the desire of eastern manufacturers to sell goods and the desire of western farmers to buy. Combining philanthropy and the profit motive, New England industrialists found a new interest in spreading their culture to the West.

The needs of industry also produced a new emphasis on education. The rising cities spearheaded the movement for abolition of school rates and were responsible for the spread of high schools and development of technical education. Hand in hand with this democratic trend in education went the enfranchisement of non-propertied urban citizens. Industrial labor helped effect this removal of restrictions on male suffrage. More important were the efforts of white-collar and managerial employees, the urban middle class.

Cheap newspapers and magazines came when improved printing presses and a growing city population made possible large circulation and higher advertising revenues. In 1833, when papers sold for about six cents, the New York *Sun* cut its price to a penny. Other papers followed, and the reading public grew by leaps and bounds. Advertisers helped pay the costs. Railroad companies, dry-goods stores, manufacturers of patent medicines poured large sums into newspaper advertising. P. T. Barnum developed the orderly "build-up" for a coming event through news releases. Public relations men like Rufus Griswold perfected techniques for using newspaper publicity to boost book sales. Manufacturers needing tariff protection subsidized papers to plead their cause. These years, in other words, ushered in the modern age of business-subsidized reading matter.

Business influences were by no means limited to trade, industry, and the daily press. As industrialists came to set the tone of business society, they naturally took over much of the patronage of religion and learning previously dispensed by landlords and foreign traders. Some reformers and agrarians complained, saying that religion and education should steer clear of any partnership with business. But most Americans were pleased to contemplate the contribution of commercial and industrial leaders to the growth of the republic.

9

Social Forces and
Social Reform

Population Growth

The economic expansion of 1815–50 was associated with a rise in population. The total during the Revolution had been 2,500,000; by 1810 it had passed 7,000,000. Between then and 1850 the number jumped to 23,000,000—a threefold increase in forty years. Though the rate of increase was not as great as in colonial times, the totals were impressive. The population was becoming comparable with that of major European countries and seemed destined to expand indefinitely.

The growth of population came largely from natural increase, for the birth rate continued to be high. The rate of natural increase declined slightly after 1810, more after 1840; but these declines were insufficient to check the general trend. Natural increase was also influenced by a declining death rate. This had little to do with improved medical care. Vaccination had cut the death rate from smallpox. Otherwise, the physician of 1850 could do little more for his patients than his predecessor of 1800. The decline in the death rate was related to a rising standard of living—well-fed, prosperous people can resist disease.

To natural increase must be added that which came by immigration. Increasing after 1835, immigration reached a peak between 1848 and 1855, when 100,000 Germans and 130,000 Irish reached the United States each year. The British were also well represented. There was little immigration from southern and eastern Europe.

Because of immigration and internal migrations, sections grew at different rates. New England and the South Atlantic states trebled population from 1790 to 1860. The Middle Atlantic states, meanwhile, grew from 1,000,000 to nearly 6,000,000. The Great Lakes states (Old Northwest) went from a few thousand to more than 4,500,000.

The percentage of foreign-born in the population increased steadily after 1835, and by 1850 represented almost 10 percent of the total. With regard to race, the percentage of whites was increasing. Immigration of Negroes largely ceased after 1808, when the foreign slave trade was outlawed; at the same time white immigration increased. In 1790, the Negro population had amounted to almost 20 percent of the total. By 1850, it constituted only 15 percent.

Rise of the Cities

In all sections urban population increased after 1815. The percentage of population living in places over 8000 went from 3.3 percent in 1790 to 12.5 percent in 1850. Baltimore went from 13,000 in 1790 to 170,000 in 1850, New York from 30,000 to half a million. Among western cities, Cincinnati showed the greatest expansion, increasing from less than a thousand in 1800 to 115,000 in 1850. New Orleans, the largest city west of the Appalachians, boasted 116,000 people at mid-century.

With growth came growing pains. Colonial interest in city planning (as in Savannah) gave way to haphazard multiplication of factories and tenements. Little effort was made to set artistic or sanitary standards. Early colonial municipalities might have done this, but by 1815 government controls had been weakened by laissez-faire feeling. Let things alone, said laissez-faire advocates, and conflicting self-interests would average out for the general good. This was a comforting thought for those who grew rich by building ugly factories and renting crowded tenements. In the slums it was not unusual for entire families to live in a single room, in buildings without running water or adequate heat. Children reared in such tenements had only the crowded streets as places for play.

Disease, drunkenness, and crime were most acute in the immigrant-occupied slums. Poverty was the basic difficulty. Poor men had limited educational opportunities. Ignorance, combined with poverty, produced conditions which made for disease; illness in turn involved loss of wages and still greater poverty. There being a temptation to turn to drink to forget troubles, drunkenness further added to the woes of the poor.

Disease and death rates increased in the cities between 1815 and 1850, when the national rate was going down. Chief among causes of death were endemic (constantly present) diseases which resulted from overcrowding, filth, and contaminated food and water. Typhoid and typhus fever, today almost unknown in American cities, flared up and declined intermittently, and tuberculosis was ever present. Epidemics such as the cholera epidemic of 1833 caused fewer deaths than did endemic illness. But epidemics caused greater fear. They thus served a social function, in that they terrorized people into taking protective measures.

After 1820 boards of health in the larger cities enforced quarantine and isolation regulations in an effort to check epidemics. Some doctors said that more epidemics were caused by impure air, water, or food than by contagion. Hence sanitary reform was more needed than quarantines. Cities must clean streets, provide pure water, replace unsanitary tenements. Such measures were costly, however, and people living uptown were reluctant to be taxed for slum improvements. Then, too, city governments were often corrupt and inefficient. Many large towns had no central water and sewerage systems until after the Civil War; and as late as 1900 their public bathing facilities were inferior to those of ancient Rome.

Drunkenness and crime were equally disturbing. In tough districts, gangs battled each other on the streets. Anti-Catholic and race riots occasionally reflected feeling against minority groups. Efficient police organizations could have reduced disorder. Many towns, however, tried to get by with the old system of constables and town watches. Eventually, crime waves and gang warfare frightened enough people to force a change; and the 1840's saw a few large cities providing uniformed policemen. This, together with the introduction of gas lighting, made streets safer by night. But fire protection was still supplied by inefficient volunteer companies.

Outside the overcrowded slums, American cities were reasonably safe and comfortable. Skilled workers, white-collar employees, business and professional men of modest means occupied large areas of solid, respectable middle-class dwellings. No sharp class lines were drawn within these groups. If a man's income increased, he simply moved from a neighborhood of small frame or brick houses to one that boasted brownstone fronts. On the top social level were families who made their fortunes in trade, industry, or real estate. This small element was divided between old families and newly rich; but the latter usually achieved acceptance in time. In this era moneyed groups lost political influence with the rise of equalitarian feeling. The Federalist tradition that gentlemen should rule was gone. As a result, the rich retreated from politics and concentrated on business and society. They built mansions on exclusive avenues, where they lived with increasing ostentation.

Urban people no longer felt, as in colonial days, that they were directly dependent on rural interests. Business, education, entertainment, arts, and sciences centered in the cities. Rural citizens became dependent on towns for styles and ideas as well as material things. Only in political activities did farmers maintain supremacy, by not granting growing cities increases in representation in the state legislatures. But by 1850 the United States was shifting from a rural-based, rural-minded nation to one dominated by city ways.

Family Life

Upper-class family patterns changed little in these years. Lower-income groups were much more affected by changing economic trends. Household crafts declined as factories turned out machine-made thread, cloth, and clothing. Farmers' daughters, less needed at home, taught in the new schools or worked in factories. The money earned could buy factory products for the farm family, or send younger brothers to college, or build a dowry for the girl herself.

In some mill towns country girls lived in company boarding houses and worked in poorly ventilated factories from sunrise to sunset. The male head of the family retained legal control over the wages earned by wife and daughters. Still, it was a broadening experience to leave the farm; and women who took jobs outside the home were moving toward economic independence. So, too, were younger sons who sought opportunities in cities and on western farms.

Lower-class urban families also experienced a weakening of the patriarchal pattern. Wives and daughters worked out as domestic servants and factory hands. This supplemented family income, a necessity in view of low prevailing wages for male workers. In the process, the household became less important than before.

Children, too, were affected. Many worked in the mills and were thus less subject to family controls. (In 1831, 7 percent of employees in cotton-textile manufacturing were under twelve.) Other lower-class city children were left by their mothers to roam the streets. Nor was home much better in slum districts.

On the frontier the surplus of males enhanced the prestige of women. Important, too, was the work done by frontier women in establishing homes, schools, and churches. Their courage and resourcefulness contributed to the emerging idea of the equality of sexes. And since young people could acquire frontier land easily, they had less need for parental aid than in regions where economic opportunities were limited. This made for marriages of choice, as against seaboard alliances arranged by parents. Hence old customs faded fast. Publication of marriage banns was dispensed with in the West; and divorce became easier. With Georgia, Mississippi, and Alabama leading, the cumbersome legislative divorce system began to give way to divorce by court decree.

Down to 1840 the American population multiplied more rapidly than that of any other Western nation. American discussions of population brought forth little support for Malthus, the English economist who held that war, famine, or abstinence from sexual relations must limit population growth to prevent it from exceeding food supplies. Thus Alexander H. Everett, of Massachusetts, declared in *New Ideas on Population* (1823) that American resources justified unlimited expansion of population. If misfortune struck a family, the community was bound to help.

A few dissented. In 1832 Charles Knowlton, a New England country doctor, published a pamphlet advocating birth control. Knowlton had struggled with poverty and had seen others making sacrifices to support large families. He therefore felt that parents were unfair to themselves, their children, and society if they produced larger families than they could comfortably support. Such views met with opposition from religious leaders and others. Nevertheless, the practice of birth control increased. The movement, however, was in its early stages. Large families continued to be regarded as desirable by most Americans.

The Recession of Religious Orthodoxy

Religion also felt the impact of the westward movement and the growth of cities. Competing secular interests were a challenge to religion; and all religious groups were influenced by rising democratic sentiment.

Deism and skepticism had been checked in the 1790's by an evangelical revival. But, despite condemnation by the clergy, Tom Paine's *Age of Reason* continued to circulate. City workers showed interest in free thought in the 1820's. They were urged on by two British critics of orthodoxy: Robert Owen and Frances Wright. The free-thought drive, however, encountered much opposition. Dr. Thomas Cooper was virtually ousted from the presidency of South Carolina College on the charge of teaching the incompatibility of geologic knowledge and the account of creation in the Bible. But in Massachusetts the orthodox failed to silence the "atheistical" Abner Kneeland.

The Unitarians made steady though unspectacular progress after 1815. New England, Massachusetts in particular, led the way. Harvard, which had swung toward Unitarianism early in the century, was the intellectual center. Two famous Unitarian spokesmen occupied Boston pulpits: William Ellery Channing and the even more radical Theodore Parker. Massachusetts courts helped, ruling (Dedham decision, 1820) that congregations deciding in favor of Unitarianism could control church property.

The Unitarians, and Universalists as well, refused to believe in the Trinity, depravity of man, and condemnation of all save the elect few to eternal damnation. This rejection of orthodox Calvinist doctrine appealed to individualists. Also attractive was the Unitarian-Universalist belief in salvation by love and character, and insistence that the universe operated according to a rational scheme.

Besides winning converts, these groups influenced many outside their ranks. Many Congregationalists who disapproved of Unitarian rejection of the Trinity accepted other Unitarian views. Reverend Horace Bushnell of Hartford tried to harmonize traditional Congregational doctrines with the rising liberalism. Though charged with heresy, Bushnell persisted in teaching that religion was less a matter of doctrine than of insight into God's love.

Other sects wrestled with the same issue. After two decades of debate, the Presbyterians split into Old School and New School groups (1837–39). Similar conflicts led to organization of the Cumberland and the United Presbyterians. Even the Quakers divided into conservative and radical factions, Elias Hicks organizing the latter as the Hicksite Friends by 1830.

Meantime, the Methodists and Baptists continued to gain. While these sects rejected Unitarian rationalism, they also spurned old-style Calvinism, with its aristocratic emphasis on salvation of the few. Baptists and Methodists set store by man's ability here and now to come close to Christ. This pleased humble people, as did the claim that repentant sinners could be redeemed. Appealing also were the simple hymns and emotionalism of Methodist and Baptist preachers.

These two sects were especially successful along the frontier. Their itinerant evangelists (of whom Peter Cartwright is best remembered) did not wait for settled communities to grow up in the West; instead, they carried the word to remote and scattered frontier farmers. These circuit riders were untutored men but full of religious zeal; and they spoke the language of the people. Relying on revival methods, they addressed great camp meetings on the horrors of hell, and said salvation was within the reach of any man.

The Protestant Episcopal Church was also affected by the times. There was a bitter contest between an evangelical, low-church party and a ritualistic, high-church group. In 1843 two priests left the church in protest against growing high-church influence. There was, however, no general split. Episcopalians continued to be associated in the American mind with wealth and social prominence. Their church differed, therefore, from the democratic, "shirt sleeves" churches of humbler folk.

Even more than Episcopalianism, Roman Catholicism held to tradition. It made no compromise with liberal thought. Still, the laity was affected by the democratic feeling which subordinated the clergy and insisted that the rank and file should have their say even in ecclesiastical matters. In defiance of canon law, several parishes demanded control over church property. St. Mary's cathedral in Philadelphia was put under the interdict for such democratic heresy. This controversy, which ended in victory for the traditional Catholic conception of clerical control, reflected the individualistic, democratic tenor of the times. Meanwhile, Catholic leaders were adjusting to the demands of the New World environment. They worked in city slums, where Irish Catholic immigrants were concentrated. They appeared on the frontier, setting up bishoprics and founding churches and schools.

Comeoutism

The democratic, individualist fervor produced such new religious movements as perfectionism. A mystical, enthusiastic expression of "heart" religion, it was the antithesis of Old School Calvinism. Its major figure, Charles G. Finney, felt that every man could coöperate with God and His Son in achieving perfection or "sanctification" on earth.

Comeoutism—the trend toward extreme individualism in religion—produced several new sects, notably the Millerites or Seventh-Day Adventists. In the mid-1830's William Miller, a New England farmer, became convinced that the second coming of Christ would take place on April 23, 1843. Moving about, Miller preached to thousands who were discouraged by hard times. By 1842 Millerites were preparing for the second coming by selling their goods and buying muslin for special ascension robes. When nothing happened to the thousands assembled on the tops of churches, barns, and houses on the appointed night, Miller announced that he had miscalculated the date. After a second disappointment the next year, Miller's followers melted away. But enough remained to keep alive a new sect.

More significant was Mormonism. Its forceful founder, Joseph Smith, was a rural New Yorker. Smith claimed that in 1827 an angel placed in his hands plates engraved with "reformed Egyptian" characters. Deciphering these with transparent stones, he obtained the Book of Mormon, which purported to be a revelation of God especially designed for America. The volume taught, among other things, that Indians were descendants of the lost tribes of Israel. As Smith moved west, he decided that the faithful should set aside for the Bishop's Storehouse all earnings not needed for their families. This fund would aid the needy and support missionary and publishing enterprises of the Church of Latter-Day Saints. From Ohio the Mormons pushed on to Missouri and, after experiencing persecutions, to

Nauvoo, Illinois. Here Smith had a vision approving polygamy. This, and local jealousy of Mormon success, led to trouble. There was internal dissension, too; and in 1844 Joseph Smith was murdered by a mob.

Under Smith's successor, Brigham Young, the Mormons again pushed west. In 1847 they reached the Great Salt Lake. There, in Mexican territory, they founded Deseret and began to reclaim the land by irrigation. Community projects flourished, and the state-church· profited by selling supplies to California-bound gold seekers. Deseret enjoyed autonomy even after it was acquired by the United States at the end of the Mexican War (1848). Recruits came from Europe, and colonies were established in Utah, Idaho, Colorado, and Arizona. In the process, Brigham Young proved himself a great builder, and the Church of Latter-Day Saints enjoyed remarkable success.

The Benevolent Empire

Evangelical Protestants made such progress after 1815 that their work was called the Benevolent Empire. The Benevolent Empire stressed missions. In 1810, the American Board of Commissioners for Foreign Missions began work. The first American missionary abroad was Adoniram Judson, who set out for Burma on the eve of the War of 1812. By 1830 the Near East, Africa, and China had come within the scope of American missionary work. Nor was the United States neglected. The Congregationalists and Presbyterians divided the home field in a Plan of Union. The American Home Missionary Society, launched in 1826, sent missionaries to Indians and frontier communities. At the same time denominational zeal led to the founding of colleges to train ministers. Hundreds of societies raised money for this work.

Christian literature was widely circulated. The American Tract Society (1825) distributed leaflets designed to encourage piety and morality. The American Bible Society (1816) worked to put a Bible in every American home and public place.

Realizing the importance of young people, the sponsors of the Benevolent Empire stressed the Sunday School. In 1825 an American Sunday School Union began collecting funds and circulating materials for the Sunday classes. Inspired by English example, the Young Men's Christian Association (Y.M.C.A.) was organized in 1851 to provide Christian influence in cities for young men living away from home.

Evangelical churchmen were generally agreed on opposition to liquor. The American Temperance Society won support from those who saw in the saloon a challenge to piety and an invitation to broken homes. Preachers helped flood the country with temperance literature and by 1850 were demanding state legislation to curb demon rum. Simultaneously, Charles G. Finney, sponsor of perfectionism, inspired his followers to attack slavery. The abolition movement was strong in areas influenced by evangelical revivals. The churches as a whole, however, were divided on slavery. Southern members of every denomination objected to official criticism of slavery. Northern antislavery sentiment, therefore, led to cleavages within the Methodist and Baptist churches after 1840 and sharpened the tension between Northerners and Southerners in most other sects.

The Anti-Catholic Crusade

Home missionary activities of Protestants were stimulated by antipathy toward Catholicism. In 1815 the population included less than 100,000 Catholics out of 8,000,000. Irish and German immigration soon swelled the number, and by 1840 over a million Catholics resided in the United States. This was over 5 percent of the population. What was more, the number grew rapidly in the 1840's, when the potato famine drove Irish peasants to the New World. The Catholic hierarchy multiplied churches, parochial schools, and seminaries. Able leaders, like Bishops John England of South Carolina and John Hughes of New York, strengthened the church. From France and Austria came funds for missionary activities, and Catholic nuns set up schools for girls.

Alarmed, the theologian Lyman Beecher turned out a *Plea for the West* in 1835. Pointing to Catholic activity on the frontier, Beecher called for Protestant effort. Catholicism, he said, was undemocratic, un-American, monarchical, aristocratic. Catholicism was led by alien priests, Beecher continued; its head was the Pope in Rome, and it put allegiance to the Holy See above loyalty to country. Even stronger views were expressed in that same year in *The Imminent Dangers to the Free Institutions of the United States Through Foreign Immigration*, by Samuel F. B. Morse, later inventor of the telegraph. Morse insisted that Jesuits were plotting to undermine American liberties, and said that immigration, the source of Catholic strength, must be checked. Rebecca Reed's *Six Months in a Convent*, also published in 1835, purported to "tell the truth" about conditions inside the Ursuline convent school which a Boston mob had burned the year before. More sensational volumes followed. Even when the most notorious, Maria Monk's *Awful Disclosures*, was proved a dishonest hoax, the credulous continued to insist on the truth of the indictments.

The growing bitterness expressed itself in the organization of anti-Catholic societies, and in actual violence. During the 1840's Bishop Hughes of New York fed the fires by demanding a portion of the Public School Fund for support of parochial schools. To many Protestants this seemed to violate the principle of separation of church and state. Antagonism increased when Catholics criticized the prevailing practice of reading the Protestant version of the Bible in public schools. Hughes carried the school fund question into politics, but without success.

Since most Catholics were immigrants, the anti-Catholic drive increased sentiment for immigration restriction and prolongation of the period required for naturalization. During the 1830's the nativists entered politics. They blamed Catholic immigrants for labor unrest, slums, municipal corruption. Nativist agitation declined when the panic of 1837 checked immigration and shifted attention to other issues. But the crusade was resumed after 1850.

Despite the growth of Catholicism and vigor of evangelical Protestantism, American life was becoming more secular in tone. The decline of Sabbath observance in the older, stricter sense was a straw in the wind.[1] Preoccupation with the westward movement and industrialization took attention away from spiritual affairs. And much of the idealism that often finds expression in religion was channeled into social reform between 1815 and 1850.

Traditional Educational Patterns

In 1850, as in 1815, much of the rural population received no formal education. This was likewise true of many city workers. Where elementary schools did exist, training consisted chiefly of reading, writing, and figuring. In cities youths might equip themselves for business careers by studying mathematics and bookkeeping in private evening schools. The urban middle class and prosperous farmers could send promising sons to private academies, which offered Latin, Greek, mathematics, and a bit of history, science, philosophy, and psychology.

Ambitious boys could attend college by working in the summer and teaching in a rural school during long winter vacation. But in 1850, higher institutions were still mainly for the few who planned to enter the ministry or who attended college as a matter of class custom. Candidates for the ministry continued studies in the theological department or at a separate divinity school. Training for law and medicine was usually obtained under the traditional apprenticeship system.

Most educators assumed that knowledge was static, to be acquired by memorization. There was little interest in the "learning by doing" theories

---

[1] A General Union for Promoting the Observance of the Christian Sabbath (1828) frowned on travel and other worldly activities on Sunday, and asked Congress to forbid the moving of mail on the Sabbath. Although John Quincy Adams and others showed interest, the movement failed.

of the Swiss reformer, Pestalozzi. The teacher was drillmaster rather than stimulator of intellectual curiosity. Corporal punishment was widely used. Most schoolhouses were overcrowded and uncomfortable; and there were no uniform, free textbooks.

New Emphases

Despite the accent on tradition, this was an age of change. Traditional methods were criticized, and free public education won more backing than before. In demanding tax support for education, reformers stressed the duty of the citizen. If the people could not weigh issues, tyranny or anarchy might result. Reformers further claimed that free public education would promote democracy by breaking down class barriers. In 1815 the well-to-do of every section tended to patronize private schools. Nor were public schools entirely democratic. In New England, for example, parents paid the rates (tuition) if they could. If they could not, the town would foot the bill. This put the pauper's label on the poor. Progressive educators therefore urged the elimination of the rate system and the substitution of free, tax-supported schools. In such institutions children of all classes would be on an equal footing, as was proper in a democracy.

Neglect of public education also meant denial of opportunities. Massachusetts led in public education. Yet as late as 1837 a third of that state's children received no schooling; and many of the rest had instruction only two months a year. How, then, could a humble youth expect to rise in the world? Labor leaders contended that knowledge enabled the rich to "grind down" the poor. Educated workingmen would be less easily abused.

Privileged groups were at first opposed to public education. Gradually, however, some upper-class leaders came to feel that public education was good insurance against revolution. An ignorant populace might attack private property. Public school teachers could take care of that by teaching youngsters to cherish established institutions and respect authority.

Much of the work was at the local level, for the American school system has always been community-centered (in contrast to Europe, where national control has been the rule). Results varied. The South, for instance, lagged behind the North and West. But there was progress there, as in North Carolina under Calvin Wiley.

Many educational reformers operated at the state level. Although state governments did not control local schools, state boards could call attention to weaknesses and opportunities. State legislatures could pass compulsory-attendance laws and, by creating normal schools, improve standards among teachers. As secretary of the Massachusetts Board of Education (established in 1837), Horace Mann pushed on all these points. He wrote reports, addressed public meetings, talked with businessmen and politicians. Teacher salaries must be raised, he said; teachers must be better trained. There must be more schoolhouses, and they must be adequately equipped. It was necessary, too, to reconsider discipline and rote-learning practices. To prepare young people for citizenship, schools should stress American history and government, and help children develop responsibility and power to think intelligently on public issues.

Bit by bit Mann won. Massachusetts schools were divided into grades. Corporal punishment was used less than before. Mann demonstrated the value of state-supported normal school training for teachers. And in 1852 Massachusetts adopted a law requiring every child to spend a certain number of months in school each year for a given period of years. Some called this compulsory-attendance statute an unwarranted encroachment of the state on the family; but it was indispensable if public education was to prevail. Other areas took interest, and soon each state had its "Horace Mann." These educators met with opposition from private schools and from citizens who objected to school taxes. Church leaders charged Horace Mann with creating a godless educational system. But, in spite of obstacles, the school reformers were winning the fight by 1850.

Reform centered on elementary education. Here and there, however, there was sentiment for government-supported secondary education. As early as the 1830's Massachusetts was planning public high schools, to take the place of the virtually defunct Latin grammar schools. Several northern cities had such high schools by 1850. More important, though, were the private academies, which provided college preparatory work at relatively low cost. Some admitted girls. Although the academy movement spread into the South, well-to-do planters continued to employ tutors for their children.

The college also felt the democratic upsurge. The feeling that higher education should be more generally available led to the founding of 200 new colleges from 1815 to 1850. Most were church-affiliated institutions of the traditional type. But there were innovations, as when democratic educators imported from Europe the pattern for the manual-labor college. Oberlin, Wabash and Knox combined classroom work with labor on a college farm, so that poor boys could earn while they learned.

More important was the rise of state universities. The Supreme Court upset New Hampshire's effort to turn Dartmouth into a public institution (Dartmouth College decision, 1819); but there was nothing to prevent legislatures from founding new government-controlled universities. This was done in many states by 1850, with the South and West leading the way. The new state universities had hard sledding at the start. Legislatures saw no need for regular appropriations. The universities were endowed with public land, but these properties were badly managed or sold prematurely at low prices to raise needed cash. There was opposition, too, from private colleges and religious leaders. Yet by mid-century the University of Michigan was on the way toward becoming a true state university. And when the State University of Iowa opened its doors to women as well as men in 1858, another milestone had been passed.

Most colleges remained loyal to the classical curriculum. The new University of Virginia, however, provided a wide choice of studies, including sciences and modern languages. The University of Vermont, Brown, Union, and other institutions made concessions to the changing times. Harvard, Yale, and Dartmouth established scientific schools; and Rensselaer Polytechnic Institute pioneered in training engineers. The laboratory method of instruction gained ground, as did field work, especially in geology.

Early in the nineteenth century a few Americans went abroad to study in German universities, then known for critical scholarship, library resources, and professional training. These students brought back an enthusiasm for research and the application of science to agriculture and industry. Professional education also owed a great deal to European models. Following Old World practice, American educators set up law, medical, and normal schools. Much remained to be done in 1850; but paths for the future had been marked out.

Adult Education

Although schools were getting better, they did not reach all Americans. Farm children who migrated to the city were unprepared for opportunities before them. Immigrants who poured in from Europe were illiterate. And the apprenticeship system was dying. Under that system, masters had been responsible for education of apprentices. Under the new factory system, employers had no such responsibility.

Faced with this problem, the English had tried adult education. Americans followed suit, founding mechanics' institutes in the cities. Sometimes the initiative was taken by workers, sometimes by employers or philanthropists. Skills were taught in evening classes at the institutes, and students could study history, economics, and literature. By 1850 there were also other evening schools, including some for young ladies.

Even more significant was the lyceum. Fathered by Josiah Holbrook of Connecticut, the lyceum was a voluntary association dedicated to pursuit of knowledge. Members collected books, held debates, prepared papers.

The next step was to bring in lecturers on science, government, literature, and morals. Politicians and reformers found the lyceum platform a good sounding board and source of income. Lyceum audiences also welcomed such European visitors as Charles Dickens. By the 1840's there were 4000 local groups, held together by a national organization, which facilitated the booking of lectures.

Meantime, the public library movement was launched. The mechanics' institutes and lyceum groups were book-conscious, and built up collections. So did apprentices, young merchants, and others, who organized subscription libraries and reading rooms. In 1833, Peterboro, New Hampshire, set up perhaps the first tax-supported library in the United States. Five years later New York State appropriated funds for school libraries. By 1850 there were 12,000 such libraries in that state alone. This was only the beginning, but European visitors were already calling the public library an American innovation of prime importance.

European Influence in Literature

As in earlier periods, Americans relied heavily on Old World literature. Translations of French and German books were popular; and English literary efforts enjoyed wide favor. American publishers ran races to seize from incoming ships the first copies of new novels by Charles Dickens and Sir Walter Scott. They then turned out editions for an eager American public. In addition, British magazines were reissued in New York and Boston. Americans therefore tended to accept standards set by London's literary critics. The prestige of English letters was so great that James Fenimore Cooper presented his first novel as the work of a British author.

This literary vassalage stemmed from the fact that the United States was a new country, preoccupied with material tasks and lacking a well-defined literary class and an independent literary tradition. Moreover, American culture was largely derived from that of Britain, and the common language made for close contacts. Also important was the lack of an international copyright system. United States publishers could reprint English books without paying royalties to authors. This "pirating" infuriated Dickens and other writers widely read in the United States. The pirating also hurt American authors. Since a national copyright law did exist, American writers had to be paid royalties. Consequently, American publishers preferred to bring out English titles. Hoping to clear up this situation, American and British writers urged their governments to negotiate an international copyright arrangement. But American publishers fought this proposal, and nothing was worked out until 1891.

Call for a Distinctively American Literature

Even so, the passing years brought an increasing demand for a distinctively American literature. Patriots felt that Americans should read chiefly about American institutions and ideals. "Let the passion for America cast out the passion for Europe," said Ralph Waldo Emerson.

Some disagreed. Edgar Allan Poe objected to praising American books merely because they were American. Poe separated beauty from politics. Writing, he maintained, must be distinguished in form, must deal with universal beauty rather than ephemeral social or political values. But the nationalist trend continued. Some 30 percent of the books issuing from American presses in 1820 were by native authors. By 1850, the figure was 70 percent.

The demand for an independent American literature was not the only factor in the situation. Significant, too, were the advances in literacy associated with school awakening; technological improvements which resulted in mass production of books and magazines at low cost; accumulation of means for purchase of books in an ever-larger number of families; growth of leisure time as machines replaced hand production. Urban life provided intellectual stimulation through libraries and lecture programs.

The output reflected every major interest in American life. *Two Years Before the Mast*, by Richard Henry Dana, and Herman Melville's *Moby Dick* portrayed life in the merchant marine and on the whaling vessels. James Fenimore Cooper wrote about frontier warfare. Washington Irving's *Astoria* dealt with the Oregon fur trade and his *Tour of the Prairies* described the nearer West. Many authors reached back into the American past. Nathaniel Hawthorne wrote critically of New England Puritans in his *Scarlet Letter* and *House of Seven Gables*. Henry Wadsworth Longfellow treated the same traditions more favorably. William Gilmore Simms of South Carolina wrote of Patriot and Tory adventures in the Revolution.

Many took up current issues. In *Swallow Barn*, John Pendleton Kennedy dealt with life on a Virginia plantation, presenting an idyllic picture in sharp contrast with Harriet Beecher Stowe's antislavery effort, *Uncle Tom's Cabin*. Other novelists lined up, North against South, on the same question. So did poets, Southerners like Paul Hamilton Hayne challenging the interpretations of such antislavery Northerners as James Greenleaf Whittier.

American democracy was an enduring theme. Longfellow and Whittier appealed to democratic tastes with subjects like the "Village Blacksmith" and the "Barefoot Boy." But the great poet of American democracy was

Walt Whitman, whose *Leaves of Grass* appeared in 1855. It did not win wide acclaim. Discriminating critics, however, saw in the unconventional rhythms and vigorous verse something truly American. Whitman wrote of the dignity of man, the equality of all people. He glorified democratic comradeship and identified democracy with Americanism, thus justifying the reputation he would eventually win as the first great poet in the American democratic tradition.

A few Americans probed the persisting problems of mankind. Oliver Wendell Holmes discussed science, superstition, and religion in his *Autocrat of the Breakfast Table*, and pictured the sudden collapse of long-outworn Calvinist theology in "The Wonderful One-Hoss Shay." Nathaniel Hawthorne showed philosophic insight as well as literary talent in his somber tales. Stressing psychological and ethical conflicts, he wrote of the pervasiveness of evil. In *Moby Dick*, Melville inquired into man's fate in his struggle with himself and the forces of nature.

Emerson and the Transcendentalists

Of the Americans who concerned themselves with man's destiny, Ralph Waldo Emerson made the most enduring contributions to literature and thought. An ordained clergyman, Emerson left his Boston pulpit because of dissatisfaction with Unitarianism. He had come under the influence of European thinkers such as Kant. Presently Emerson was also studying Greek and Oriental thought. But he responded positively to the democracy and individualism of his own republic.

In a famous Phi Beta Kappa address of 1837, Emerson deplored the tendency of American intellectuals to lean on Europe and to depend on books alone. He had already suggested in an essay, "Nature," that man must learn the lessons of the universe at first hand. The world of matter and motion, said Emerson, was only a small part of the universe. The world beyond—the transcendental world of eternal truth—was within reach if human beings used intuition as well as ordinary senses. God was all things, and man, being capable of experiencing God in the whole universe, could transcend the world of normal experience. In that way, man might achieve his true potentialities. This philosophy, in which Emerson was a principal figure, though not the originator, became known as transcendentalism.

At first Emerson chiefly inspired friends who met informally, in a Transcendental Club. From 1840 to 1844 this group edited the *Dial*. Though a financial failure, the *Dial* had influence. So did Emerson personally when he talked to lyceum audiences. Published in book form, these lectures made a further impression; and Emerson's greatness was recognized long before his death in 1882.

European Influence in the Fine Arts

Americans of today readily recognize such names as Emerson, Poe, Hawthorne, Longfellow, and Melville. But there was no like record in the fine arts. Save for the ballad writer Stephen Foster (who did his chief work after 1850), the composers of this era are forgotten. Among painters, Samuel F. B. Morse is remembered—but as an inventor, not an artist. So, too, with sculptors and architects.

Why did the fine arts fare so badly when letters fared so well? Partly because writing offered a better financial return. Partly because the fine arts remained imitative, chained to European models. Painters, sculptors, artists, and musicians made no such declaration of cultural independence as did Emerson and other writers.

American nationalism, of course, influenced the fine arts. New World themes were in evidence, as when George Catlin put American Indians on canvas. Rembrandt Peale (son of Charles W. Peale) pleased patriots with his portraits of Washington, and Robert Mills designed the Washington Monument in tribute to the first President. And there was much patriotic music. In all of this, however, there was little effort to depart from European patterns. Washington Allston, the leading artist of the period, studied in London, Rome, and Paris and so closely followed European models that he was called the "American Titian." Peale, like Allston, worked under Benjamin West in London; and Samuel F. B. Morse (an Allston pupil) also studied in Europe. Toward the end of this era, William M. Hunt, trained in France, turned attention of American painters toward Paris; but the change did not bring immediate improvement.

Classical influence was strong in sculpture and architecture. The Greek revival was in full swing after 1815. Its chief exponent was British-trained Benjamin Henry Latrobe, who had a lasting influence on American public architecture. The style was also reflected in dwelling houses. At the end of the 1830's came a Gothic revival, represented by Richard Upjohn, who designed Trinity Church in New York. Like Latrobe, Upjohn was trained in Great Britain, and applied European standards.

With the emphasis on European training, the United States did not develop adequate training centers in painting, sculpture, music, and architecture. There was, however, some attempt to stimulate interest in the arts. Important work was done by the National Academy of Design, founded in 1826 with Morse as president. And, as wealth accumulated, there was more money available to hire architects and artists.

Recreation

In 1815, recreation was subordinated to toil because of the problem of conquering the new land. Funmaking was also affected by class lines, for until the Jackson era horse racing, card playing, and theater going were largely limited to those of means. Calvinist taboos also checked leisure-time activities, as did the influence of evangelical sects.

Even so, Americans had recreations: horseshoes, ball games, hunting, fishing, swimming. Farmers gathered at crossroads stores to swap tall tales. Militia day provided opportunities for celebration, and county fairs spelled sport as well as education. Funmaking on the frontier was rough. A friendly bout might end in a battle royal, featuring knives, clubs, even gunfire. Brutality figured in many contests, as in goose-head pulls. In this "sport," a goose was greased, then hung upside down from a limb. Contestants then rode by and tried to twist off the goose's head.

Improvements in transportation brought new recreational opportunities. Steam navigation made possible the gaudy showboat, which operated on inland waterways. Meantime, the stagecoach and railroad took featured players to the interior. Shakespearian productions were popular, also comedy and melodrama. Blackface minstrel shows were received with enthusiasm. The pace setters were Christy's Minstrels, for whom Stephen Foster wrote several songs.

As cities grew, theaters multiplied. There was classic drama, serious music, a little ballet (the European dancer Fanny Elssler made a triumphal tour of the United States in the 1840's). There was also burlesque and cheap melodrama. Show business had come to stay—and to win converts. Temperance people who had condemned the theater changed their tune when *Ten Nights in a Barroom* helped their cause. So did abolitionists when *Uncle Tom's Cabin* became a smash success.

The great showman of the period was Phineas T. Barnum, who used novel advertising tricks to promote his American Museum (a side-show affair). Barnum organized an American tour for Jenny Lind, netting the Swedish Nightingale $175,000 and her sponsor half a million. Later, Barnum carried his talents into the circus field.

Spectator sports developed rapidly in the cities, both promoters and gamblers seeking the patronage of the average man. Despite hostile legislation horse racing and prize fighting gained in popularity. Cricket was played in several cities; and the organization of the National Association of Baseball Players in 1858 marked a turning point in the history of the "national game."

As spectator sports won favor, some said that Americans were getting soft. To counteract this trend, Dr. Oliver Wendell Holmes tried to popularize ice skating, a recreation neglected in settled areas. German immigrants set up gymnastic societies, and the Y.M.C.A. would soon stress indoor exercise.

Wealthy Americans had special pleasures. Opera was introduced in New York and New Orleans. The upper classes took up sea bathing at such exclusive resorts as Newport, Rhode Island. But in recreation as in other fields the tendency was away from class distinction and toward the democratization of American life.

The Reform Impulse

The second quarter of the nineteenth century was an age of reform. The period saw active efforts to improve prison conditions and end capital punishment. Humanitarians tried to uplift fallen women, help the blind, deaf, and insane. Reformers advanced the cause of public health and sought better educational and cultural opportunities for the children of the common man. There were movements against liquor, war, and slavery. A few idealists attacked capitalism and private property; and there were experiments to prove the superiority of common ownership and production for use rather than for profit. Some extremists wanted to abolish money, and a handful of philosophical anarchists called for elimination of the state.

These reforms were closely related to economic trends. The increase of population, growth of cities, rise of manufacturing, and inflow of immigrants created new problems. At the same time reform sentiment reflected the democratic impulse, which demanded that each individual realize his potentialities. That is, the United States was a social laboratory where the American dream of universal well-being and happiness was to be achieved.

Religious sentiments were involved. The Puritan tradition of community responsibility for prevention of sin lingered. Closely related was humanitarianism, rooted in the secular conviction that man's inhumanity to man was wrong. The key influence here was utilitarianism. Jeremy Bentham, British exponent of this doctrine, held that moral values and laws came into being because of their usefulness. Hence legal and moral concepts had to be revised constantly in the light of changing needs. Whatever failed to yield the greatest good for the greatest number had to be changed or eliminated.

Further, this was the age of the Romantic Movement in literature. European and American writers of this school idealized the common human element in all men. They stressed the universal spark of humanity, glorified the humble and obscure. Which, of course, pointed toward movements that would help the less fortunate. Finally, reformers accepted the doctrine of progress, which had influenced Americans since the Revolution. This doctrine assumed that human beings and institutions could become perfect. Being in accord with natural law, social progress was considered inevitable. It could be hastened, however, by science, reason, and knowledge.

Here was an impressive combination of influences—democracy, Christianity, humanitarianism, romanticism, the idea of progress. The international character of the drive made it stronger still. American prison reformers, temperance leaders, pacifists, abolitionists borrowed ideas and arguments from Europeans. So did United States citizens who wanted to improve education or help the deaf, blind, and mentally ill. International congresses, visiting lecturers, European books reprinted in America all did their bit. Some Utopian communities stemmed directly from interest in the experiments of Robert Owen at New Lanark, Scotland. Owen's New World venture, the communal settlement at New Harmony, Indiana, likewise invited imitation. Another influence was the doctrine of the French Utopian socialist, Charles Fourier, whose views were publicized in the United States by Albert Brisbane and Horace Greeley.

All the reform movements were related. Many performers worked in a number of movements at the same time. Others put their energy into a single cause. Wrapped up in their specialties, these zealots came to feel that the fate of mankind hinged on the success of their efforts.

A Variety of Reforms

One group concentrated on helping unfortunates who could not be blamed for their condition. Thus Samuel Gridley Howe of Boston established what became the Perkins Institute for the Blind. Dr. Howe sought in Europe the best methods of helping the blind to enter the world of books and live as normal human beings. Thomas H. Gallaudet established in Hartford, Connecticut, the country's first free school for the deaf. Using techniques developed in England and France, Gallaudet's school taught the deaf to read and write and to talk by manual signs.

Most nineteenth-century Americans regarded the insane as criminals rather than sick souls. On a visit to the Cambridge House of Correction, Dorothea Dix of Boston found the insane pinned up in a dreary, unheated room. Shocked, she investigated treatment of the insane in other Massachusetts jails and almshouses. She then petitioned the legislature (1843) for state support of institutions where the mentally ill might receive sympathetic care. Later, she carried her fight into many states, even to foreign lands. She persuaded Congress to vote land grants to aid state institutions. This bill was vetoed by President Franklin Pierce, in the name of states' rights. Dorothea Dix, however, won her fight in many state legislatures.

Reformers also attacked imprisonment for debt. In 1820 five-sixths of those in prison were there because of inability to pay off debts, generally for sums under twenty dollars. A concerted drive for abolition of imprisonment for debt brought victory in New York in 1831, elsewhere later. Also successful were movements to protect from seizure tools and homes of workingmen in financial difficulties.

Prison reformers found that existing types of prisons bred crime. They therefore set up model institutions which might reform, instead of merely punish, culprits. One new type, originating at Auburn, New York, confined prisoners in separate cells at night but permitted them to work silently together by day. A Pennsylvania system allowed inmates no contact at all with each other or the outside world but provided tasks in individual cells, each of which had its own outdoor court. We now regard the solitary and silent features of these systems abnormal and little designed to effect rehabilitation. But each marked an advance a century ago.

Linked to prison reform was the movement to abolish the death penalty. Reformers called capital punishment "an antique relick of barbarism," and questioned the effectiveness of capital punishment as a method of reducing crime. Did not hanging condemn the unrepentant sinner to eternal damnation? Imprisoned for life, he might discover faith. And what of the sanctity of human life?

Other earnest people, full of compassion for "fallen women," set up Magdalen houses for these unfortunates. Lurid exposures of conditions in brothels gave this reform a sensational character. But the movement fitted in with dominant ideals of the times—chastity for unmarried women, and the monogamous home.

Back in the eighteenth century Dr. Benjamin Rush had pointed out the ill effects of excessive use of alcohol. Early in the nineteenth century, Lyman Beecher and other clergymen spoke out against drinking at funerals, ordinations, and other social functions. The first effective organizations appeared in the 1820's, many of the societies pledging members to total abstinence. More than a thousand temperance societies were active by 1840, including Washington Societies, composed of reformed drunkards. Some temperance advocates favored voluntary methods. Others insisted on state legislation against manufacture and distribution of alcoholic beverages. Prominent among prohibitionists was Neal Dow, author of the Maine law of 1851, the first effective, lasting state prohibitory statute. Dow cited industrialists who stressed the inefficiency of bibulous workers. Preachers denounced alcohol as the enemy of piety. The tavern, they said, was a threat to the home. Drunkards wasted family earnings and mistreated their wives and children.

Meantime, dietary reformers were active. Among them was Sylvester Graham, who gave his name to graham bread and crackers. Graham favored simple vegetables and rough bread. Meat eating, he said, reflected animal passions; and he condemned tobacco, tea, coffee, spices, and sweets. Some Grahamites felt that dietary reform would promote social progress. Such claims caused many to laugh at the Grahamites; but city living did call for changes in diet.

Women's Rights

Graham was also interested in dress reform. He saw harm in tight, heavy clothing. Women, in particular, were the victims; and these years saw an attack on the middle-class fashion of tight lacing. After 1851, Mrs. Amelia Bloomer, who worked for temperance and women's rights, tried to popularize the costume which bears her name.

Dress reform was just one aspect of the crusade for women's rights. Law and society discriminated against women in family relations, property matters, education, and the vocations. A growing group found this intolerable. To them the subordination of their sex was an offense against Christianity, humanity, reason, natural rights, and democracy.

In the 1820's a visiting Scotswoman, Frances Wright, campaigned for slaves, laborers, and females. Most Americans were scandalized at the thought of a woman on the public platform. But, though insulted, Fanny Wright persisted. She won support from Quakers, who were accustomed to equal religious privileges. Women's rights again came to the fore when many abolitionists objected to the participation of women in the crusade against slavery. When a women's antislavery convention met in Philadelphia in 1838, the meeting place was surrounded by an angry mob. Undaunted, the women abolitionists kept on, demanding rights for women as well as for bondsmen. Leaders of this effort were the Grimké sisters, Sarah and Angelina, daughters of a South Carolina slaveholder. Freeing their slaves, they went north to work against slavery and for women's rights.

Elizabeth Cady Stanton and Lucretia Mott, excluded from the World Antislavery Convention in London because of their sex (1840), organized a women's rights convention at Seneca Falls, New York, in 1848. The delegates adopted a famous Declaration of Sentiments, which said that "men and women are created equal." In consequence, the delegates demanded equal civil rights (including the ballot) and equality in educational, professional, and cultural opportunities.

The Peace Movement

Quakers had long held that war was the greatest human evil. Others took up the cause after 1800. Appeal to the sword seemed contrary to Christianity. War likewise ran counter to reason and common sense, for it wasted resources and brought burdensome taxation and other ills. Peace advocates further contended that fighting seldom solved problems.

Peace societies were formed during the War of 1812, in New England, a section opposed to this conflict. Led by Unitarian clergymen, William Ellery Channing and Noah Worcester, the societies won Quaker and evangelical support. In 1828 local groups were combined into an American Peace Society by William Ladd, a sailor-farmer from Maine. Ladd worked with English pacifists, proposing substitutes for war (disarmament, international arbitration, world organization). His *Essay on a Congress of Nations* (1840) was reprinted during World War I.

Another peace advocate was Elihu Burritt. This Connecticut youth, known as the Learned Blacksmith, held that all war, defensive as well as offensive, was unchristian and unjustifiable. Taking the pledge idea from the temperance movement, he persuaded 20,000 Americans to promise that they would take no part in war. From 1848 on, Burritt organized peace congresses in Europe.

Opposition to Negro Slavery

No institution aroused such opposition as Negro slavery. During the Revolution many Patriots North and South felt that bondage contradicted the natural right of every human to life, liberty, and the pursuit of happiness. Subsequently, slavery declined in the North, where it had never been profitable. But the institution became fastened on the South by the cotton gin and the advance of the cotton economy into the Gulf states. Led by John C. Calhoun and Thomas R. Dew, Southerners came to defend slavery as a positive good, defensible on religious and moral as well as economic grounds. Some southerners were willing to join hands with northern philanthropists in the American Colonization Society's program of sending freedmen to Liberia in Africa. But only a handful of Negroes were in fact transported.

During the 1830's, uncompromising antislavery reformers launched a more militant crusade. The New England leader was William Lloyd Garrison of Boston. In his *Liberator*, this intense but bigoted reformer condemned slaveowners as heartless brutes and denounced Northerners who were indifferent to the "crime of the age." To the west, leadership was provided by Charles G. Finney, the Ohio evangelist, who condemned slavery with all the fire of a prophet. Theodore Weld, a Finney disciple, attracted large crowds when he denounced slavery as unchristian and undemocratic. Working with Weld were his wife (Angelina Grimké) and her sister Sarah. The Grimkés and James G. Birney, as former slaveowners, gave impressive testimony against human bondage. Even more telling were the words of former slaves, especially the eloquent Frederick Douglass, who escaped from servitude and was an outstanding antislavery editor and lecturer. Northern free Negroes were also active in the drive.

Antislavery societies were backed by a few men of wealth, notably the Tappans, New York merchants, and Gerrit Smith, a New York landowner. On the whole, however, prosperous Northerners condemned the movement. Abolitionists, violently denounced by Southerners, were little better received north of the Mason-Dixon line. Wherever they went they met with scurrilous attacks and even mob violence. Garrison in particular was labeled a troublesome agitator—did he not wish "success to all slave insurrections"?

Locofocos and Utopians

Many reformers centered attention on land and bank monopolies. George Henry Evans, a land reformer, urged the people to demand free access to the public domain. "Vote Yourself a Farm" became a popular slogan. At the same time, "Locofoco" Democrats denounced corporate monopolies, especially in the money field. This agitation wrecked the second Bank of the United States in the 1830's; and it brought much state reform legislation in the next decade.

Organized labor supported the locofoco program of free homesteads and antimonopoly. Other demands included a ten-hour day, free public schools, the abolition of compulsory militia service and of imprisonment for debt. Workers also wanted the right to organize. Most labor leaders sought justice within the capitalist system. A few extremists, however, demanded overthrow of capitalism and production for profit. These radicals advocated equal distribution of wealth, with redistribution each generation if necessary.

Also opposed to the existing system were the Utopian socialists. Some of these were convinced that Christianity required that property be held in common. Religion was the dominant note in the communal enterprises launched by the Shakers, the Amana Society, George Rapp's Harmony Society, and John Humphrey Noyes. Individual profits were outlawed in these communities, and coöperation replaced competition. European influence was strong. (Rapp and the Amana founders came from Germany; Mother

Ann Lee, the Shaker leader, was English-born.) The Shakers and the Rappites believed in celibacy; and Noyes, who founded the Oneida community in New York, favored complex or plural marriage.

Secular-minded reformers also tried to show the superiority of the communal way of life. Robert Owen's New Harmony experiment in Indiana attracted for a time distinguished scientists and educators. Equally impressive was Brook Farm, founded near Boston as a joint-stock venture and later transformed into a Fourierist society. Altogether, forty Fourierist communities (or phalanxes) were established in the United States. They reflected interest in the philosophy of the French Utopian, Charles Fourier, and the zeal of his American disciples, especially Albert Brisbane. Plain living and a pleasant, friendly atmosphere generally prevailed in the phalanxes. Each member was given his choice of jobs, and it was hoped that the talents of each would promote the welfare of the group. Bad management, competition with private enterprises. and the difficulty of holding younger members ultimately wrecked most phalanxes. The Fourierist movement, however, expressed certain American ideals and demonstrated tolerance of dissent from prevailing practices. Obviously, the elbow room in the United States invited the practical testing of much that remained theory in Europe.

Of more lasting influence was the development after 1840 of coöperatives for production and sale of certain products. Profits were divided among members. Many coöperatives failed because of bungling managers or lack of adequate capital. But the idea survived, and would mean much later.

Techniques of Reformers

Fourierists tried to demonstrate the superiority of their ideas by establishing experiments. Antislavery reformers also tried this technique. Frances Wright bought a plantation in Tennessee and set out to prove the case for emancipation and race equality. Plantation earnings were to repay the purchase price of the freedmen. But the experiment ran more to idealism than efficiency, and failed. A Quaker plantation, using northern and European workers, did a little better. On the whole, however, reformers counted on argument rather than demonstration.

The first step was to form societies. This organizing work followed a general American pattern. (Europeans were already calling America a nation of joiners.) Local associations sponsored meetings, raised money, distributed literature, circulated petitions. The more ardent members attended annual national conventions, held in Boston and New York in May so that those associated with several causes could attend one meeting after another. There were international meetings, too, notably in the peace and antislavery movements.

The lecture platform assumed great importance in reform movements. Lecturers learned to handle hecklers and to sway their audiences with appeals to reason and emotion. Reformers also relied on the printed page. Each crusade had its periodical to supply arguments for local workers. Reform tracts aimed at a wider audience, with descriptions of conditions that required reform.

In their zeal, reformers often stretched the truth. Some frankly used the fiction form. Lucius M. Sargent turned out effective *Temperance Tales*. The most successful reform novel, of course, was *Uncle Tom's Cabin*, by Harriet Beecher Stowe. Published in 1852, it quickly sold 300,000 copies. Translated into forty languages, it went through a hundred editions. Purporting to be a true picture of slavery, the novel was misleading. Yet it was a moving story which exerted a powerful influence on northern opinion.

Reformers also used the theater. One favorite play was Timothy Shay Arthur's *Ten Nights in a Barroom*. Still more popular was the stage version of *Uncle Tom's Cabin*. This ran more than 300 nights in New York City and toured the whole North and West.

Reformers did not neglect the church and family. Special materials were prepared for Sunday Schools. Clergymen used their sermons to support the crusades. Women were encouraged to indoctrinate their children and raise money for reform work by selling embroidery at bazaars.

The schools did not become major agencies for the spread of reform ideas. Foes of war and alcohol persuaded some writers of schoolbooks to use material designed to win the young. Most reformers, however, proceeded cautiously in educational matters. Conservatives were just beginning to back the cause of public education. If reforms were pushed too actively within the schools, conservatives might pull out, ending the chances for a rapid increase in educational budgets. Horace Mann was a foe of slavery. Yet he would not allow students in the Massachusetts state normal school to attend abolitionist meetings. Such attendance, he felt, might jeopardize the teacher-training experiment.

Reformers lobbied with enthusiasm. Labor and temperance leaders concentrated on state legislatures. Pacifists went to Congress and the White House. Abolitionists also looked to Washington, demanding outlawry of slavery in the District of Columbia and the territories. Lobbyists featured petitions and memorials prepared by local societies. During the 1830's abolitionists flooded Congress with memorials against slaveowning in the District of Columbia. Southerners then secured the passage of a "gag rule," which specified that such petitions be tabled without debate (1836). Ex-President John Quincy Adams, now an antislavery Congressman, cried that this violated the constitutional right of petition. He won his point in 1844, when the House rescinded the rule.

Besides presenting petitions, reform lobbyists argued with legislators. The modest, soft-spoken Dorothea Dix became a well-known figure in legislative halls as she worked for the insane. State legislators learned to respect temperance lobbyists, who controlled many votes. In Washington, the best-organized lobby was that of the abolitionists. Theodore Weld and others clipped from the southern press items designed to condemn slavery from the testimony of its supporters. Weld also wrote speeches for antislavery Congressmen.

Many reformers worked within existing political parties. Others preferred minor parties, since they could adopt uncompromising platforms and might obtain the balance of power between the major parties. Local workingmen's parties appeared in New York and Philadelphia in the 1820's, only to be swallowed by Jacksonian Democracy before a national labor party could be organized. The Anti-Masonic party, which fought secret societies, ran a presidential candidate in 1832 and carried one state, Vermont. In 1840 politically-minded antislavery leaders founded the Liberty party, which put its emphasis on restriction of slavery in the territories. Weak at first, this party grew in strength and helped create the important Free-Soil party in 1848.

Some reformers rejected all party organizations. William Lloyd Garrison, the Boston abolitionist, preferred to depend on moral suasion and the "underground railway," which aided runaway slaves en route to Canada. The Garrisonians also approved of slave insurrections, such as that which the Virginia slave Nat Turner had undertaken in 1831 with disastrous consequences.

Debits and Credits

Divided on political tactics, reformers split on other issues, quarreled so often that they weakened their crusades. Every reform movement had cleavages, purges, secessions.

Why so? Foes explained it by saying that reformers were cranks. After losing his early enthusiasm for reform, James Russell Lowell said that every reformer had a Mission (with a capital M) to reform everyone except himself. Horace Greeley, an ardent reformer, noted that personal frustration often led men and women into the ranks of reform. These eccentric extremists were unreasonably intolerant and prone to flaunt their sense of moral superiority.

What was more, reformers oversimplified. Certainly they failed to understand the deep-rooted complexity of the evils they assailed. Many neglected to measure enemy strength and to observe the opposition's tie-up with basic economic interests. Others so oversimplified their picture of society as to fail to consider the social readjustments that would follow the triumph of their reforms.

Many reform movements suffered as antislavery gained momentum. Moral energy previously devoted to many causes was channeled into this one crusade. Any number of reformers came to feel that no evil was so pressing as slavery. This must come first; when the slave was liberated, reformers could take up other causes. After 1850, therefore, many reform movements declined. The lost ground was not to be regained until after the Civil War.

The reformers reached few farmers. Many rural people were too isolated or uneducated to be aware of reform movements. The farmers, however, joined city workers in demanding free homesteads. Some country groups also joined the temperance movement. And by 1850, free-state farmers were beginning to show interest in slavery. Increasingly, they were coming to feel that the spread of slavery into the unoccupied West endangered their chance to move west if they so desired.

Urban workers backed campaigns for public education, free homesteads, labor legislation, and the abolition of imprisonment for debt. They saw little to attract them in pacifism, temperance, feminism, Sunday observance, diet and dress reform, and the attack on capital punishment. As for slavery, free laborers tended to be anti-Negro, for they feared economic competition of freedmen. In this instance, abolitionists might have stressed the argument that slavery lowered the status of free workers. Few did, for most abolitionists preferred a moral emphasis. Then, too, most reformers were middle-class men and women who found it hard to understand or to appeal to laboring people. All too many reform leaders felt no interest in the wage earner's problems of economic insecurity and unsatisfactory working conditions. Even the intellectuals who did coöperate with labor often struck the worker as impractical idealists.

Despite their limitations, the reformers accomplished a good deal. By mid-century the advocates of women's rights could claim substantial victories. Half a dozen states had enacted laws giving married women control of their property. Educational opportunities were improving. Emma Willard opened a seminary for girls at Troy, New York, in 1821; by 1860 there were more than sixty such institutions. By 1855 two Ohio colleges (Oberlin and Antioch) were experimenting with coeducation. Dr. Elizabeth

Blackwell, the first woman to receive a medical degree, opened a New York Infirmary for Women and Children. One sister-in-law, Mrs. Antoinette Brown Blackwell, became an ordained Protestant minister. Another, Lucy Stone, was a leading suffragist. (Although she married a Blackwell, she used her maiden name, as a matter of principle.) Several women, including Margaret Fuller, succeeded in journalism; others, notably Harriet Beecher Stowe, won fame as novelists.

Though set back by the depression after 1837, labor reformers made real headway. In Commonwealth vs. Hunt (1842) the Massachusetts Supreme Court rejected the old judicial claim that labor unions were illegal conspiracies in restraint of trade. Philadelphia strikers won the ten-hour day in 1835. President Andrew Jackson extended this to workers in the federal navy yards the next year; four years later President Martin Van Buren decreed a similar working day for all employees of the United States government. In 1847 New Hampshire passed a ten-hour law for factory workers. Other states followed suit, and enacted legislation to protect workers' homes and tools from court seizure. Labor reformers could also take some of the credit for the public education movement, and for state statutes ending imprisonment for debt and abolishing compulsory militia service. Labor was also learning how to present grievances, through effective leaders and fifty labor newspapers.

Other reformers improved prisons and other state institutions. Flogging was abolished in the United States Navy in 1850, partly because of the influence of Richard Henry Dana's Two Years Before the Mast. Several states abolished the death penalty; others outlawed public hangings. Foes of liquor were encouraged when a dozen states followed Maine in barring alcoholic beverages. (Most of these laws were repealed later.)

Nor were antislavery leaders discouraged in 1850. Congress had upheld the right of petition, and the underground railway had spirited thousands of fugitives to safety in Canada. Oberlin College had pioneered in admitting Negro students. Literary figures provided emotional ammunition against human bondage. Henry Wadsworth Longfellow published his Poems on Slavery in the early 1840's. Later in the decade James Russell Lowell's Biglow Papers satirized slaveowner aggressiveness. Antislavery sentiment was growing in religious circles.

Working together, reformers became less loyal to locality and more national-minded. Coöperation with European reformers fed the spring of internationalism, developing ties that knew no nation. More important, a reform tradition was emerging. In building their organizations, reformers were developing a major American pattern. They appealed to Christianity, natural law and the rights of man, humanitarianism, democracy. Doing so, they convinced Americans of the necessity of reëxamining their institutions and working for the betterment of their fellow men. Individual reforms would collapse; but the idea of reform would survive. That would mean much later, when the United States was dealing with the problems of the new industrialism.

10

Political Patterns

The growth of population, changing economic patterns, and the upsurge of new ideas had a profound effect on American political life after 1815. These years saw Americans reconsidering the relationship of government to economic life. There was a democratic advance in politics and a professionalization of political life. And out of the party struggles came new sectional alignments.

Clay's American System

Conditions were favorable for government planning after the War of 1812. There was party unity, for, with the collapse of the Federalists, the Jeffersonian or Republican party was in complete control. There were able men among the younger public figures—Henry Clay of Kentucky, John C. Calhoun of South Carolina, Daniel Webster of Massachusetts. And the American people regarded the future with confidence.

What line should the national government pursue? Of the plans proposed, none received more attention than the American system of Henry Clay. This called for a protective tariff to encourage manufacturing. It provided also for government financing of internal improvements (improving of rivers and harbors, building of roads and canals). New factories would supply American needs with manufactured goods. The improved transportation network would speed the flow of raw materials to industrial centers and the flow of manufactured products to markets. This, Clay felt, would bind together the sections and, by reducing dependence on foreign trade, would create a truly national economy. A national bank, and land laws designed to encourage settlement of the West, would contribute to the same end.

In some ways, this program resembled the measures proposed by Alexander Hamilton as Secretary of the Treasury under Washington. There was the same loose construction of the Constitution, the same attempt to use the central government to build a national economy. Clay, like Hamilton, put stress on promotion of trade and manufacturing and wanted a banking system connected with the government.

But there were differences. Hamilton had been tied to commercial interests and was contemptuous of the lower classes. Clay, too, believed in working with business people; but he also appealed to average citizens. The Hamiltonian program had offered little to the West; Hamilton was an Easterner who did not understand the frontier. Clay, himself a Westerner, bid for that section's favor with internal improvement schemes. In the West and elsewhere he also linked his American system to the new nationalism, a force much stronger than the nationalism of Hamilton's day.

Clay and those who shared his views scored victories at the start. In 1816 they pushed through Congress a twenty-year charter for a second Bank of the United States. The same year they secured the first really protective tariff in American history. Rates were raised later (1824, 1828, 1832), giving real protection to textile and iron manufacturers. Meanwhile, Congress appropriated funds to extend the Cumberland or National Road, until this highway reached out into Illinois. The West was further favored by the Land Law of 1820, which enabled a settler to buy a farm for a hundred dollars (eighty acres at $1.25 an acre).

The American System Is Rejected

Sponsors of these measures hoped to fix the legislative pattern for years to come. But they could not long control the national government. A number of internal improvement bills ran into presidential vetoes;[1] and the states, rather than the United States government, financed canal construction. The upward trend of tariff rates was reversed in the Tariff of 1833, and the second Bank of the United States was allowed to die when its charter ran out in 1836. Apparently the nation was not yet ready for the Clay program—would not be ready until the era of the Civil War.

The American system had opposition from the start. New Englanders who had disapproved of the War of 1812 had come to distrust national power and to favor states'-rights views. Their merchants made their profits out of foreign commerce, hence opposed protective tariffs designed to reduce imports. These traders looked outward, so were not enthusiastic about internal improvements to build up the interior. And, having strong state banks in their section, they felt no crying need for a national banking system.

Daniel Webster of Massachusetts, New England's leading Congressman,

---

[1] E.g., the bonus bill, vetoed by James Madison in 1817; the Cumberland tolls bill, set aside by James Monroe five years later; and the Maysville Road bill, which Andrew Jackson killed in 1830.

set forth these states'-rights, anti-tariff, anti-national-bank views in votes and speeches of 1816. Soon afterward the "Godlike Daniel" shifted ground. In the next two decades he came to favor a protective tariff and national bank, and turned into an ardent nationalist, famous for his spread-eagle oratory. Webster's switch reflected the changing trends in New England. As Francis Lowell, Nathan Appleton, and other merchant capitalists shifted investments from foreign commerce to textile manufacturing, other old-time traders interested themselves in western lands and domestic transportation. This created a new demand for tariff protection and a rising interest in the interior of the United States. New England businessmen were swinging over to a "national" point of view.

While New Englanders were abandoning states' rights and accepting nationalism, many southern leaders were moving in the opposite direction. Southern War Hawks like John C. Calhoun had been aggressive nationalists during the War of 1812; and at war's end Calhoun endorsed the ideas that became the basis of Clay's American system. Calhoun then believed that manufacturing would develop in the South, and that a protective tariff, internal improvements, and national bank would aid all sections. Other Southerners were less sure, but patriotic fervor and Calhoun's appeals turned many southern votes toward the Clay program.

Not for long. It soon became evident that the South was to be a farming, not a factory region. Most cotton was sold abroad, at the world price. A protective tariff, therefore, would not help southern producers. On the contrary, the tariff would hurt that section by raising the price of goods which the South purchased. Then, too, internal improvement bills seemed to help the North and West more than the South; and to many Southerners the second Bank of the United States became a symbol of northern financial power. Southern leaders were becoming painfully aware that theirs was a minority section. The population of the free states was increasing more rapidly than the population of the slave areas. Under the circumstances, many who resided in the South came to think it best to restrict the power of the central government—to stress states' rights and regional attachments instead of national sentiments.

Shifting with his section, Calhoun turned his back on nationalist doctrines he had espoused in 1816 and became a states'-rights leader. His reversal on the tariff was dramatic. In 1816 he favored protection. He turned against it in the 1820's and led his state of South Carolina in the Nullification fight against the Tariff of 1832. By then Calhoun, the former nationalist, was convinced that states had the constitutional right to prevent enforcement of national legislation harmful to local interests. Before his death in 1850, he took more advanced states'-rights ground, advocating secession from the Union under certain circumstances.

The views of Calhoun were rejected by many Southerners and by most agrarians elsewhere. But in all farm regions there were doubts as to the desirability of Clay's program. Clay, like Hamilton, envisioned a national economy dominated by commerce and industry. Yet the United States was still predominantly agrarian. The farmer was suspicious of merchants and manufacturers. And, despite his rising national patriotism, he was local-minded, unconvinced of the need for centralized political power.

Nor did specific issues change this view. The drive for a higher tariff appealed to manufacturers, and to some farmers, including wool growers of Ohio; but most Americans, in cities and out, failed to get excited about tariff questions. There was lively interest in internal improvements. Many felt, however, that they could obtain these from state governments. The greatest internal improvement was the Erie Canal, dug by New York State; and by the 1840's attention was focused on state-chartered railroad companies.

Opposition to national handling of economic problems was closely linked to land and bank questions. Although a man of moderate means was given some consideration in the land laws of the era, speculators figured largely in disposal of the public domain. Average citizens resented this. They also disliked the attitude of the second Bank of the United States under Nicholas Biddle. Being short of cash, ordinary people of town and country wanted easy credit. This they could not get from the Bank. Rather, Biddle cracked down on state banks which gave loans without adequate security. Resentment turned many voters against all national economic legislation.

The bank issue came to a head in 1832. Andrew Jackson, then President of the United States, ran for reelection as a foe of the Bank, which he denounced as monopolistic and antidemocratic. Jackson's opponent, Henry Clay, favored the Bank, for it fitted into his blueprint for a national economy. Jackson won. Strong as was the nationalist impulse, the appeal to democratic sentiment was stronger. Logically so, for this age saw the democratization of political life.

Democratic Advance in Politics

The democratic advance in politics rested in part on ideas set forth in the Declaration of Independence. Economic trends were still more influential. Especially notable was the amazing growth of the equalitarian West. Although some Westerners were rich, class lines were less rigid than in the older sections, and the West became known for democratic individualism, also as a region of protest. As debtors, Westerners resented control of credit by eastern financiers. As farmers, they demanded government support of canals and railroads so they could market produce. As land-hungry frontiersmen, they insisted on adequate defense measures and removal of the Indian westward beyond the line of white settlement.

In older sections the common people became increasingly interested in politics. Industrial development produced a new working class in the Northeast—and a new propertyless urban middle class. This caused a demand for manhood suffrage and better schools, and increased pressure for curbs on monopoly and the end of debt imprisonment. Wealthy Easterners were none too eager to grant these concessions. But if they gave no ground, the workers might go west. Hence, to hold the workers, those at the top yielded to democratic demands. Many southern states went through the same process, rich planters sharing control of the government with whites who owned few or no slaves.

All over the United States, new constitutions scrapped or scaled down property and other requirements for voting and officeholding. Many came to feel that any good American was qualified for any office. "Let the people choose" became the cry. Let judges be elected, not appointed by an executive. Let terms be short, so that the public could "turn the rascals out" when it chose. Rotation in office struck many as desirable. Long continuance in power, said democrats, bred arrogance and aristocracy.

The rotation principle was tied to the spoils system, which spread rapidly after 1812. Democratic-minded Americans believed that "to the victors belong the spoils." Winning an election meant a clean sweep—tossing out appointed officials of the other party and bringing in "our boys." Jackson's election as President in 1828 resulted in a spectacular application of this system. Old Hickory, however, was not the first political spoilsman. White House predecessors had often picked subordinates for partisanship rather than ability; and the spoils system was intrenched in every state.

Two changes made the election of the President more democratic. Under the Constitution, each state could pick presidential electors in its own way. At first, most states delegated the function to the legislatures. But by 1828 electors were chosen by popular vote in all states except Delaware and South Carolina. Moreover, electors voted automatically for whatever presidential candidate their party designated. The people thus had much to say about the choice of Chief Executive.

At the same time, national nominating conventions were replacing the old inside-controlled party Congressional caucus system. The Anti-Masons led the way with a national convention in 1831, and the major parties followed suit. The conventions were often controlled by professional politicians; yet they were less aristocratic than the caucus, which had been dominated by a few Congressmen.

In addition, this era saw the appearance of political newspapers which ordinary people could afford and understand. Broadsides and leaflets, many of them scurrilous, further encouraged the common man to help shape political decisions. So did barnstorming speakers, who addressed crowds at rallies and barbecues, and ward workers, who organized newly naturalized immigrants and other humble city folk into powerful machines.

The result was an increase in popular participation in elections. In some areas the change was extraordinary. The turnout of voters trebled in Pennsylvania between 1824 and 1828, although there was no important change in electoral laws. Political power had come to the people, and they were using it.

Political activity was not limited to those who had the vote. A growing number of women demanded the ballot, and the right to discuss public issues. Although generally scorned by both sexes, these pioneers won the support of Horace Greeley, Ralph Waldo Emerson, and Abraham Lincoln. Simultaneously, some antislavery people wanted to enfranchise the Negro. This was done in New England and New York. In the Northwest, settlers born in southern states defeated such proposals; the Negro, though free, could not vote. Universal adult suffrage had not yet been achieved; but Americans had taken giant strides toward that goal.

Democratic Ideology

These gains were accompanied by a growing attachment to democracy as a way of life. Spokesmen for the democratic faith praised the individual and talked of the dignity of man. They felt it safe to trust the judgment of the common man, said that, after discussion, the people could without violence work for the general welfare. European visitors commented on the turmoil of American life. Yet the democratic advance was secured by nonviolent means. Only in the Dorr Rebellion in Rhode Island (early 1840's) did the underprivileged masses use a show of force to win their aims.

In general, democratic theorists believed in the inevitability of progress and the rational nature of man. Closely related was a conviction that the world was governed by a higher law. Equipped with reason, mankind could understand this higher law and use it as a guide. Abolitionists refused to obey the Fugitive Slave Law of 1850, claiming it contradicted the higher law of God.

American democratic ideology identified democracy with the United States. Providence, it was said, had intended America to be the home of freedom and prosperity, the asylum of the oppressed. In time, the light of the American republic would inspire Europeans to cast off monarchism, clericalism, aristocracy, tyranny. Some Americans said that the United

States should give direct aid to European reformers. Most citizens, however, were content to have their country furnish an example.

Despite these gains, a few Americans rejected democracy on principle. Some said that the triumph of democracy meant the doom of culture. James Fenimore Cooper contrasted the decorum of the eighteenth-century landed gentry with the vulgarity of the nineteenth-century masses. Nathaniel Hawthorne said that elevating the common people would lower the stature of the great. Raise the valleys to the level of the hills: what then became of the hills? Critics complained that mass education neglected quality, focused on the lowest common denominator of superficial achievement. No less distressing was the spoils system, with its rejection of the expert. Democratic legislators even relaxed medical training standards, on the ground that untrained persons should have equal rights with trained physicians.

It was a southern planter who worked out the most elaborate condemnation of equalitarianism. John C. Calhoun flatly rejected the natural-rights theory, basic in democracy. He maintained that neither individuals nor races were born free or equal. He felt that vast differences in ability marked off the Negro from the white, the elite from the masses. In every society, he said, inequality of talents indicated the mission of the strong and competent to rule. He justified slavery on the ground that if freed men on top from drudgery, releasing their energies for statecraft and other higher values. The North had eliminated slavery. But, said Calhoun, the North still had class lines, dividing financier from mechanic, manufacturer from factory worker.

In Calhoun's judgment, a national program would be all right if southern slaveowners worked in collaboration with the economic masters of the North. If such teamwork was impossible, the several parts of the republic should have political autonomy, so that the "natural leaders" of each section could pursue their interests without interference. In either case, Calhoun relied, not on democracy, but on the self-interest of dominant economic groups.

Rise of the Professional Politician

The years of democratic advance also saw the rise of the professional politician. The ordinary citizen was so busy making a living that he had little time to study public issues. It was natural, therefore, that political affairs should slip into the hands of men who made politics a business. There had been such men in the United States before 1812. Their numbers increased rapidly in the next two generations.

Drawing his bread and butter from politics, the professional politician centered attention on patronage. When he gained power, he handed jobs out to his friends. The practical politician saw no merit in the civil service concept of government by trained public servants. His was the contrary doctrine of political preferment. This spoils-of-office doctrine was rooted in greed but defended on democratic principles. (There was "no need for experts"; any democratic-minded American could handle any public duty.)

When possible, the professional politician side-stepped issues. He preferred to get his votes by friendship and showmanship. Sometimes votes were bought for cash. More commonly, they were attracted by catchwords, parades, barbecues, and empty promises of political spellbinders.

Virtually all professional politicians appealed to the common people. Some were sincere. But many found it inconvenient to depend upon the poor, and lined up instead with the dominant upper-class elements of their sections. Such connections brought politicians social recognition, financial backing, and the support of newspapers owned by the well-to-do. Also the votes of controlled blocs—for instance, factory employees in the days before the secret ballot.

There were sectional contrasts. In the South, some planters ran for office as in the days of Washington and Jefferson. In the North, merchants, financiers, and upper-class leaders generally achieved their political aims indirectly, through sympathetic agents. Each section had political machines. These machines were tightly organized in older sections, notably the Northeast, more loosely held together on the frontier. In all regions, though, politicians tried to win for their organizations the long-range backing of as many citizens as possible. One result was a growing attachment to party labels. By the 1840's, few people called themselves independents. They were Whigs or Democrats.

In the twentieth century, many consider party politics a sordid calling; and most young people steer clear of this field. Such was not the case in the early nineteenth century. Journalists, historians, literary figures stressed politics, glorifying living and bygone party leaders. Politicians won notice with their long-winded oratory, their appeals to patriotic and democratic feeling. To be sure, men in public office were vilified by their foes; but politicians stood so well in the public eye that it was the ambition of young Americans to enter and succeed in politics.

Party History: Jeffersonian Domination

The War of 1812 having killed the Federalist party, the Jeffersonian Republicans were left in possession of the field. They controlled the presidency, Congress, and most state governments. James Monroe, their presidential candidate in 1816 and 1820, encountered only nominal opposition in 1816 and none whatever four years later, when he obtained all but one of the 232 votes in the electoral college.

Some were comforted to see farmers and merchants, rich and poor, tidewater and frontier, brought together in a single political organization. Not a few hoped that the alliance would end partisan controversy, "exterminate the monster called party spirit." But the monster survived. Party spirit was the natural result of ever-present personal and sectional differences. They were evident when the national-minded Congress of 1816 adopted protective tariff legislation and established the second Bank of the United States; when, in that same year, President James Madison vetoed an internal improvement measure, the bonus bill; and when, four years later, western Republicans secured passage of a land law which enabled a settler to buy a farm for a hundred dollars. By then, sectional feeling had been sharpened by the economic depression that followed the panic of 1819, and by the controversy which led to the adoption of the Missouri Compromise.

The Missouri Compromise

The Missouri controversy represented a North-South, free state-slave state split. During the War of 1812, the Union consisted of nine free, nine slave states. The balance was retained in the early postwar years, the admission of Indiana and Illinois being offset by the admission of Mississippi and Alabama. Having the edge in population, the North controlled the House; but the South had an equal voice in the Senate, where representation was by state. Then, in 1819, Missouri asked to be admitted as a slave state. Congressman Benjamin Tallmadge of New York countered by proposing a gradual emancipation program for Missouri; and the fight was on. In a sectional division, the House approved the Tallmadge amendment. But in the Senate, where the South had greater weight, the proposal failed.

The problem was resolved by the Compromise of 1820. Missouri was brought in as a slave state. Simultaneously Maine (heretofore part of Massachusetts) was admitted as a free state. This preserved the free-slave state balance in the Senate. But, while admitting Missouri as a slave state, the Compromise specified that slavery was "forever prohibited" in all other Louisiana Purchase territory north of 36°30′ (the southern boundary of Missouri). This barred slavery from four-fifths of the Louisiana Purchase area not yet admitted to statehood. Which meant that in due course the free would outnumber the slave states.

End of the Virginia Dynasty

The sectional divisions in the debates on Missouri were clearly shown in the presidential election of 1824. This contest came as Monroe was completing his second term in the White House. Like his predecessors, Jefferson (1801–09) and Madison (1809–17), Monroe (1817–25) belonged to the Virginia dynasty which had dominated presidential politics for a generation. Although this dynasty had drawn its presidential candidates from a single state, it had provided genuine party leadership on a national scale. Jefferson, Madison, and Monroe were men with established national reputations. In addition, these Virginians took care to choose northern running mates (New Yorkers, usually). They also appealed to all sections in their legislative programs and distribution of patronage.

By 1824, however, Virginia had run out of presidential timber; and candidates from other states had difficulty in attracting national support. A Congressional caucus made William H. Crawford of Georgia "official" Republican nominee for President. Crawford, however, had little support outside his section. New Englanders preferred John Quincy Adams of Massachusetts, Monroe's Secretary of State. Western party leaders supported Andrew Jackson of Tennessee and Henry Clay of Kentucky. As a result of these sectional and personal divisions, no one had a majority in the electoral college. This threw the election into the House of Representatives. In popular and electoral votes, Jackson was the leader, Adams trailing, followed by Crawford and Clay. The House had the right of choosing any of the top three contenders. Passing over Jackson, the Representatives chose Adams, partly because the Massachusetts man was backed by Clay after the Kentuckian's elimination from the race.

Becoming President (1825–29), Adams chose Clay as his Secretary of State. Embittered by defeat, the Jackson men said Clay and Adams had made a corrupt bargain. Comparing the strait-laced Adams with the pleasure-loving Clay, John Randolph of Roanoke called their partnership a union of "Puritan and blackleg." This caused a duel, but since Clay and Randolph were bad shots, no blood was shed. The duel, indeed, was as ridiculous as the corrupt-bargain charge. For, given the sectional fragmentation of the Jeffersonian party, political combinations like that of Clay and Adams were necessary and proper.

Jackson, in fact, formed combinations of his own. He had some in 1824, more in 1828, when he made his second bid for the White House. By then Jackson had won the support of the old Crawford faction. This and other accessions enabled Jackson to defeat Adams.

Viewed in one light, the election of 1828 was just another squabble within Jeffersonian ranks. Adams had won a narrow victory in 1824. As President, he was honest and conscientious, but politically inept, unable or unwilling to build political fences or to please Congress and the people. This situation produced a shift of sentiment among Republicans, causing Adams' defeat when he ran for a second term. But the 1828 contest reached deeper down than that. It marked a great increase in popular interest in presidential campaigns. This was associated with the democratic trend, the broadening of the franchise by state legislation, the popular choice of presidential electors. Over a million votes were cast in the presidential contest of 1828, more than three times as many as in 1824.

Not only that. The 1828 election also sounded the death knell of the old Republican party. The confused sectional divisions of 1824 had given way to a two-party split in 1828. The split was permanent, and the Jeffersonian party soon was replaced by two new organizations—Jackson's Democrats and Clay's Whigs. These two parties were to dominate the American political scene down to the 1850's.

Democrats Versus Whigs

The Democratic-Whig division resembled the old Jeffersonian-Federalist line-up. Like the early Jeffersonians, the Jacksonian Democrats drew support from northern workingmen and from rural interests everywhere—small planters in the South, frontier farmers, northern agriculturalists from counties where land values were low. Though far from homogeneous, these groups were drawn together by opposition to richer planters and to the urban elements which controlled the nation's trade, finance, and manufacturing. The Jacksonians, like early Jeffersonians, preached equalitarian doctrine, opposed special privilege, and used states'-rights arguments in an attempt to prevent the use of national political power for the benefit of the rich.

The Adams-Clay combination of 1824–28 and the Whig party set up in the 1830's suggested the Federalist party. There was the same appeal to business groups, the same support from the more powerful planters. Most Whig leaders, like Hamilton's Federalists, spurned states' rights and favored promotion of commercial, financial, and industrial development through the use of national political power. Among other things, this meant supporting a protective tariff and national banking system.

Comparisons should not be pushed too far. The United States had grown since Washington's day. With growth had come a new attachment to the nation. States'-rights men though they were, the Jacksonian Democrats had moved away from the states'-sovereignty concepts of the early Jeffersonians.

As a cabinet officer, Thomas Jefferson had questioned the power of Congress to charter a Bank of the United States. The Jacksonians of the 1830's agreed that a national bank was undesirable; but many felt that the United States had the *right* to legislate in that field. Back in the 1790's Jeffersonians had fought the Alien and Sedition Laws with the Kentucky and Virginia Resolutions, which maintained that states had a constitutional right to keep national laws from going into effect. But when Calhoun advanced the same doctrine in the Nullification controversy of the 1830's, President Andrew Jackson vigorously upheld national supremacy.

In backing business, the Federalists had concentrated on helping shipowners. The Whigs, however, focused their attention on internal improvement programs. This too reflected the changing times; national growth had caused many merchants to turn from foreign trade to domestic commerce and manufacturing.

The Federalists and Jeffersonians had of course drawn their leaders from seaboard states. As the center of population moved westward, so did political leadership. Jackson and Clay, the Democratic and Whig leaders of the 1830's, came from beyond the Appalachians. In addition, both were men of strong popular appeal. Such appeal had been useful but not altogether necessary in the days of Washington and Jefferson. It was absolutely indispensable when manhood suffrage became a reality, with votes to be won in the booming West and among city workers.

In analyzing Whig and Democratic strength, it must be remembered that party lines were shifting constantly, as issues and candidates changed. It must be remembered, too, that most politicians in both parties were professionals who sought patronage rather than principle, and preferred vilification to calm presentation of the issues. In consequence, American voters, then as now, were often sadly confused.

Of the two parties, the Democrats were normally the stronger. Democrats controlled most states most of the time from the 1830's through the 1850's. They also won most national contests, the Whigs winning only two presidential races, 1840 and 1848.

Democratic successes were won by a well-organized machine. To be more accurate, the Democratic organization was a grouping of state machines which varied greatly, for the Democratic politicians of each section had to appeal to local prejudices. Democrats of the rural South and West (for example, Robert J. Walker of Mississippi) were for a low tariff; but in the iron and steel state of Pennsylvania, such leading Democrats as James Buchanan favored high protective duties. In New England, party organizers wooed such minority groups as the Boston Irish. By way of contrast, Georgia Democrats denounced their state's chief minority group, the Indians—Georgians wanted to drive out the red men and take their land. In more settled areas, including New York, party leaders were more apt to concentrate on locofoco legislation to aid workingmen: mechanic lien laws, curbs on inflation and on monopolies. But this was not predictable, for in many states the Democrats were composed of several factions, with conservatives pitted against reformers, city workers against farmers.

To hold these groups together, national Democratic leaders gave their presidential tickets geographical balance, linking East with West, free state with slave state. In 1832 Jackson of Tennessee was teamed with Martin Van Buren of New York. When Van Buren ran for President (1836 and 1840), his running mate was a Kentuckian. The 1844 ticket joined James K. Polk of Tennessee with George H. Dallas of Pennsylvania. Here the balance extended beyond geography, for Polk was against and Dallas was for protective tariff legislation.

Another force for party harmony was the spoils system, the "cohesive power of the public plunder." If the Democrats divided, they would lose their chance to control elective and appointive offices. They therefore stuck together, especially before elections.

Jackson in the White House

The national Democratic party was organized during the two-term presidency of Andrew Jackson (1829–37). Jackson was a curious leader for a party that appealed to debtor farmers and city workingmen. For, legend notwithstanding, Jackson was no crude frontiersman. He was a well-to-do creditor, a hard-money man, an aristocratic cotton planter who distrusted the multitude. But Jackson's military reputation endeared him to the average voter; and as a blunt, straightforward, self-made man, Old Hickory seemed more democratic than the cold, reserved John Quincy Adams. An experienced politician, Jackson knew how to play down his wealth. His enemies coöperated when they called Jackson a vulgar frontiersman whose wife smoked a pipe. Far from hurting Jackson, these tales helped convince the common people that the general was their man.

As President, Jackson increased his popularity by expert distribution of the patronage and clever handling of the issues of the day. He was himself a competent political manager and had the aid of such astute subordinates as Secretary of State Martin Van Buren. Jackson also had the aid of unofficial advisers, a "Kitchen Cabinet" which included Amos Kendall, one of the ablest politicians of his day, and Francis P. Blair, Sr., a topnotch party editor.

When elected President in 1828, Jackson had defeated John Quincy Adams, who had competence but little personal appeal. In his campaign for reëlection in 1832, Old Hickory faced a more popular opponent, Henry Clay, nominee of the National Republican (later Whig) party. The contest was further complicated by the appearance of a third candidate, William Wirt, put up by the Anti-Masons, who were opposed to secret societies.

Jackson, however, won a decisive victory. Personality and party organization were factors in the triumph; so was the bank issue. The bank in question was the second Bank of the United States, which had been chartered in 1816 for twenty years. By the 1830's the Bank was a going institution, with many branches. Its president, Nicholas Biddle, operated on "sound principles," handled public funds efficiently, provided businessmen with needed capital. But the Bank was far from popular in debtor areas like the South and West, and among ordinary people. Average citizens desired easy credit, to buy land and for other purposes. But, being short on security, they could not borrow from the Bank of the United States. Banks chartered by the states were more willing to make loans; but Biddle's institution held down the state banks by presenting state bank notes for specie payment, thus forcing the state banks to limit their issue of paper money and check the flow of easy credit to the people. On top of that, Biddle openly expressed doubts about democracy.

Webster, Clay, and others backed the Bank, and in 1832 persuaded Congress to pass a bill extending the Bank's charter. By vetoing this bill, President Jackson took a stand that endeared him to the nation's debtors. After reëlection, the Chief Executive withdrew government funds from Biddle's institution and placed these deposits in state ("pet") banks.[2] This caused excitement, but Jackson held his ground until the charter of the Bank of the United States ran out, in 1836.

In this controversy, Jackson took the side of those who favored easy credit. Basically, however, the President was a hard-money man. He showed this at the end of his second term, when he issued the Specie Circular of 1837. This declared that paper money would no longer be accepted in payment for government land; instead, purchasers must pay in coin. This was a heavy blow to ordinary purchasers and for state banks, as heavy as any struck by Biddle. Jackson, who was retiring, retained the good will of his public; but the Specie Circular contributed to the unpopularity of his successor, Martin Van Buren.

---

[2] Later, under Presidents Van Buren and Polk, the United States arranged to handle public funds itself, through the independent-treasury system.

Nullification

While the bank controversy raged, the Nullification issue came to the fore. This was in part a personal conflict between Jackson and John C. Calhoun. Calhoun had backed Jackson in 1824 and 1828, and was Vice-President during Jackson's first term as President. But the two did not make a satisfactory team. Both were ambitious and headstrong. Calhoun considered Jackson shallow and impulsive, the President found Calhoun austere and intellectual. Van Buren and the members of the Kitchen Cabinet played on these differences for their own political profit, producing a real split in the administration. The patronage was involved, as was the succession (Calhoun backers had hoped that Jackson would serve a single term, then turn the White House over to their champion). There was also a bitter quarrel over Peggy Eaton, a gay young lady who had married one of Jackson's cabinet officials. Looking with disfavor on Peggy's past, Mrs. Calhoun and other social leaders barred the young woman from their circle. This infuriated Jackson, who liked the Eatons and remembered how his own wife had been maligned. The result was a general reshuffle of the cabinet, in which the Calhoun faction lost influence.

But the Jackson-Calhoun struggle went far beyond this. In 1832, the President signed a tariff bill which maintained the protective tariff principle established in 1816. Calhoun had favored high duties back in 1816 but by 1832 was convinced that the South could not prosper under a high-tariff system. Since Congress was not disposed to reduce rates, Calhoun proposed that the South find its remedy in states' rights. He found his precedent in the Kentucky and Virginia Resolutions, which had preached defiance of the federal government. In Calhoun's state of South Carolina, a Nullification convention of 1832 said that the states were sovereign, and had the right to declare acts of Congress void. Applying this principle, the convention called the Tariff of 1832 null and void. The United States, in other words, could not collect duties in South Carolina.

As President, Jackson had to take a stand. In many ways he agreed with the low-tariff, states'-rights view. He was no protectionist, and would have welcomed a Congressional reduction of tariff schedules. He had taken a states'-rights stand in vetoing the Maysville Road bill, an internal improvement measure (1830). He would do the same again, when Georgia prepared to take over tribal lands. (The United States Supreme Court would direct Georgia to respect the red man's rights; but Jackson, who favored the Indian removal, would allow the state to defy the national tribunal.)

Nullification, however, was different. For one thing, it was urged by Calhoun, whom Jackson rated as a foe. Then, too, Nullification was backed by just one state, not by a united South. More important, South Carolina's declaration constituted a defiance of the government which Jackson headed, a challenge to the national spirit which Old Hickory represented. It was inevitable, therefore, that the President would favor enforcement of the laws of the United States. He had said as much in a famous toast of 1830 ("The Federal Union—It Must Be Preserved"). He was no less firm in a Nullification Proclamation of 1833.

Under the circumstances, Calhoun had little chance to win. He did obtain a compromise, worked out by Henry Clay. Congress passed a Force Bill, which recognized Jackson's right to use force to administer the laws. But, to placate Calhoun, and the South in general, Congress adopted a Tariff of 1833, which provided for a gradual reduction of rates during the next decade. Calhoun could say he had won his point, that Nullification had forced down the tariff. Yet it was a meager victory. Nullification was condemned in such a way that it could not be used again. As in the Missouri Compromise, the South had been forced to accept a settlement good enough in the short run but which left the road open to later northern triumphs. The Force Bill, with its recognition of national supremacy, was a major setback for states' rights. Calhoun saw this, and presently would say that, since the rights of states were not safe within the Union, the South should consider secession.

Jackson added to his popularity in this fight. Had he desired, he could have had a third term; but, being old and ill, he chose to retire to his beloved Hermitage. As his successor he picked Martin Van Buren of New York, who had been Secretary of State for part of Jackson's first term, Vice-President in the second. With Jackson and the Democratic machine behind him, Van Buren won the election of 1836 handily, his triumph being made the easier by the failure of the Whigs to agree upon a single candidate.

Rise of the Whigs

When Van Buren was inaugurated, the Democrats seemed well entrenched in power. Some predicted a long period of Democratic rule, comparable to the generation of victories of the Virginia dynasty. But after one term as President (1837–41), Van Buren was defeated for reëlection in 1840, and the Whigs took over the national administration.

Several factors combined to bring about this sudden ending of Democratic control. To begin with, the Democrats suffered when Jackson retired

—Van Buren lacked the personal appeal of his predecessor. Besides, Jackson had been a boom-time President, his administration coinciding with a period of speculation and prosperity. Van Buren had the misfortune of encountering hard times. The speculative bubble burst in 1837, partly because of Jackson's Specie Circular. There was a panic, then a depression extending into the 1840's. The public debt, paid off in Jackson's day, reappeared. There were bankruptcies and defaults, and widespread unemployment. The flow of funds from Europe ceased. States were forced to abandon canal digging. Railroad building was checked, agriculture suffered; and for all of this Van Buren was blamed.

Meanwhile, the opposition had improved organization. As before, the Whig party was dominated by wealthier southern planters and men of substance in the free states; but, watching Jackson, the Whigs had learned how to broaden their appeal. They agreed on a single ticket for 1840, and it was a ticket built to win. The Whig presidential candidate was William Henry Harrison of Indiana, who, like Jackson, was a military hero of the War of 1812. Like Jackson, Harrison was well-to-do and owned a handsome house. But, since he had fought Tecumseh, Harrison could be presented as a frontiersman who lived in a log cabin, wore a coonskin cap, and drank hard cider. Pushing their nominee as the people's candidate, Whig spellbinders called Van Buren an eastern aristocrat who dined from plates of gold. Serious discussion of the nature of depressions was combined with use of circus tactics. There were parades, barbecues, and party songs in this Log Cabin Campaign. The favored Whig slogan was "Tippecanoe and Tyler, Too." This avoided issues to stress Harrison's most famous battle; and it called attention to the vice-presidential candidate, John Tyler of Virginia, who had been stuck on the ticket to pick up southern votes.

Party Confusion in the Forties

It worked, and the Whigs won. But, though united in the campaign, the Whig party fell apart when faced with the responsibilities of office. President Harrison, the oldest individual ever elected President of the United States, died after one month in office (1841). John Tyler, who succeeded him (1841–45), was unable to hold the party together.

The immediate problems included a fight between Tyler and Henry Clay, the Whig leader in Congress. Underlying this special dispute was the fact that the Whig party was made up of dissimilar elements with conflicting interests. Wealth linked great Whig planters of the South with Whig merchants of the free states; but the two could not agree on legislation. Nor could Whig farmers of the frontier states—interested in internal improvements—see eye to eye with subsidy-minded Whig shipowners. Whig employers failed to agree with workingmen brought into the party by the excitement of Log Cabin oratory. A great party chieftain might have tied these groups together. No such man appeared. The Whigs had able state and sectional leaders—Clay, Webster, John Quincy Adams, William H. Seward, Horace Greeley, Alexander H. Stephens, Abraham Lincoln—but in the 1840's there was no one who could do the job on a national scale.

Of the Whig leaders Clay was the most important. When Tyler broke with Clay, the President was virtually read out of the party. But, with his veto power and control of patronage, Tyler was able to check Clay. As an example, the Chief Executive prevented the establishment of a new national bank. The split also hurt the party in the next presidential campaign (1844). Clay, the Whig nominee, suffered further from his failure to make a clear-cut endorsement of territorial expansion, and the Democrats elected their presidential candidate, James K. Polk.

Polk was not a major Democratic leader. Rather, he was a dark-horse candidate, nominated when the Democratic convention of 1844 failed to agree on a more prominent man. Polk's chief asset was the fact that he was a Jackson man from Tennessee. Polk, however, was surprisingly successful in his single term as President, 1845–49. (He thought one term enough and would not run for reëlection.) He chose capable subordinates. One, Secretary of the Treasury Robert J. Walker, gave his name to the Walker Tariff of 1846, which reduced the relatively high rates of the Whig Tariff of 1842. Others helped Polk settle the Oregon question and carry the Mexican War to a successful conclusion.

Despite these accomplishments, the Democrats lost the next presidential election (1848). As in 1840, the Whigs captured the popular imagination by putting up a military hero, Zachary Taylor of Louisiana. Taylor had little background for the presidency, but he had fought with vigor against Mexico. He was thus able to defeat Lewis Cass, the better-qualified but less glamorous Democratic nominee. Another factor was the appearance of a strong third party, called Free-Soil and boasting ex-President Van Buren as its standard bearer. Like the weaker Liberty party, which had run candidates in 1840 and 1844, the Free-Soilers were chiefly interested in the slavery question.

Harrison, the first Whig President, had died in office, and his successor, Vice-President Tyler, had been unable to control the Whigs, who were divided on public questions. This pattern was repeated after the Whig victory in 1848. Zachary Taylor, the second and last Whig to be elected President, also died in office (1850). Vice-President Millard Fillmore of

New York, who then became President (1850–53), was unable to run the party in the crisis connected with the Compromise of 1850. The Whig convention trotted out another general, Winfield Scott, in the presidential election of 1852, but Scott was beaten by the Democratic candidate, Franklin Pierce of New Hampshire.

All these details of party history are hard to bear in mind, and most of them are unimportant in themselves. But they acquire significance when put together. It will be noted that from 1840 to 1852—four elections in a row—party control changed each time. From Jackson to the Civil War, no President served more than a single term, and the decade and a half from 1840 on saw seven different individuals in the White House.

Given the spoils system, this meant a clean sweep of the federal offices at least once each four years. It meant government by inexperienced officers, with frequent shifts in policy and no long-range planning. To many citizens, this did not seem to matter. The national government did not touch the individual's economic life as intimately as today. Most legislation affecting the citizen directly was handled through the states. But in those years the rapid development of the free states and the slower growth of slave areas was preparing the way for a sectional conflict that would affect every American. It is a pity that party confusion left little room for the development of experience in government and for the long-range planning that might conceivably have postponed or prevented the tragedy of civil war.

11

A Manifest Destiny

Expansionist Enthusiasm

By and large, citizens of the United States approved of territorial acquisitions, wanted to continue the expansion which had been a feature of American life since colonial days. They liked to think that this outward movement was inevitable, that the United States was driven on by a divine force that could not be denied. Many were aware that pushing outward might yield economic gains, such as the addition of good farming land. Others found political opportunity in promoting expansion programs popular with voters. But the "Manifest Destiny" concept was nearly always present, strengthening other expansion impulses. Persuaded of their higher duty, nineteenth-century Americans moved from interest to enthusiasm to unbounded zeal. This made for success in imperial ventures; and it tended to make Americans seem bombastic and high-handed.

Expansionists accomplished a good deal in the four decades after the War of 1812. They increased the size of the United States by half, adding more than a million square miles, including Florida, Texas, New Mexico, and California; and the republic also obtained a clear title to a large part of the Oregon country.

In pressing expansion, advocates of Manifest Destiny had to bear in mind two things: the need for agreement within the United States as to the desirability of annexing each new region; and the necessity of preventing European powers from securing control of areas in which Americans were interested.

The Threat from Abroad

In the long run expansionists encountered greater difficulty within the United States; but foreign complications loomed large immediately after the War of 1812. The Russians, established in Alaska, were showing interest in Oregon, which was claimed by both Great Britain and the United States. Even more serious was the situation in Spanish America, from Mexico to Argentina. There the colonists had revolted against Spain; and Spain, unable to suppress the uprising, hoped to get aid from the concert of Europe (France, Austria, Prussia, Russia, Britain). Formed at the end of the Napoleonic era, this was a combination of powers dedicated to the preservation of ruling monarchs. Having crushed Spanish and Italian revolutions of 1820, the concert could logically take an interest in colonial revolts.

The United States, of course, viewed these developments with concern. Action by the concert of Europe might reëstablish Spanish colonial monopoly or give France a foothold in former Spanish colonies. In either case, American merchants would be shut out of a growing trade with the new Spanish-American republics. And a French advance would establish a major power at the southern border of the United States, creating a security problem and blocking the territorial advance of the republic.

Fortunately, the United States did not have to stand alone. Britain also regarded the situation with disapproval. In the early 1820's, Britain was drifting away from the concert of Europe; and she desired to keep continental powers out of the New World. English businessmen were suspicious of French maneuvers in Spanish America. Those interested in furs were concerned about Russian ambitions in the Pacific Northwest. Strategic questions were also important. Britain's imperial stakes were large, and she wanted no European competitors in the Western Hemisphere.

Noting the common interests of the English-speaking nations, British Foreign Minister George Canning proposed that the United States join Britain in warning others to stay out of the Americas. This, however, could not be arranged. In those days of slow communication, Anglo-American negotiations took time; and quick action was essential. Besides, Anglophobia was strong in the United States; and Americans feared "entangling alliances."

The Monroe Doctrine

In the end, the two countries moved separately toward the same goal. In October, 1823, Canning served notice on the French through diplomatic channels. In December, President James Monroe included in his message to Congress a declaration to the same effect—the Monroe Doctrine.

Of the two warnings, the British was the more important. The United States was a new, relatively feeble state while Britain was a great naval power, capable of heading off any expedition which might start across the Atlantic. But, since Canning's pronouncement was not published at the

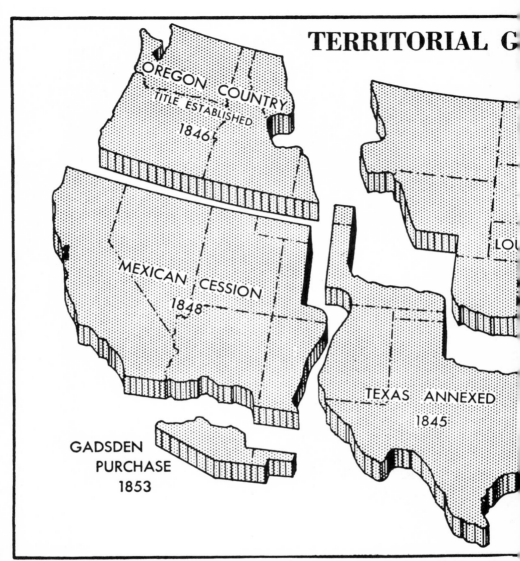

TERRITORIAL G

OREGON COUNTRY
TITLE ESTABLISHED
1846

LOU

MEXICAN CESSION
1848

TEXAS ANNEXED
1845

GADSDEN
PURCHASE
1853

In the seven decades after the War for Independence, the United States nearly quadrupled in size. Diplomacy accounted for some of these gains, military force for others

PURCHASE

03

THE UNITED STATES
1783

FLORIDA
PURCHASE
1821

Flannery

Also involved, in every case, was Manifest Destiny, an expansionist urge which was one of the major forces in American history before the Civil War.

time, Americans assumed that they and not the British had checked the Europeans. The Monroe Doctrine thus became a symbol of American power, conveying to Americans the idea that their republic could and should dominate the Western Hemisphere. This fitted neatly into expansionist blueprints for an enlarged United States.

The Monroe Doctrine was the work of President Monroe and his Secretary of State, John Quincy Adams. It stated that:

1. *The United States intended to stay out of European quarrels,* would not "interfere in the internal concerns" of Old World nations or take part in European wars.

2. In turn, *European powers should not establish new colonies or interfere with existing governments in the Western Hemisphere.* "Such interposition" would be "dangerous to our peace and safety," and would be considered as the "manifestation of an unfriendly disposition towards the United States."

Monroe and Adams made it clear that they were trying to protect the "rights and interests of the United States." At the same time they suggested that they stood on higher ground than self-interest, were working for the welfare of mankind. As they saw it, the United States was defending republicanism against monarchy, for the "political system" of the European powers was "essentially different . . . from that of America." Nor did they conceal their preference for republicanism. In referring to American governments, they used such terms as "wisdom," "unexampled felicity," "liberty and happiness." Mention of European policies brought forth other words: "oppressing," "controlling," "dangerous."

This assumption of superiority helps explain the lasting appeal of the Monroe Doctrine to the people of the United States. The Doctrine had another advantage. It was not a binding treaty or law. It was merely part of a presidential message. It could be used or ignored as circumstances warranted and could be reinterpreted at will. It was ignored in the late 1820's and 1830's, when Presidents overlooked European activity in Latin-American regions not vital to the United States. It was revived in 1845 and reinterpreted to justify the expansionist policies of President James K. Polk.

Anglo-American Conflict

The Monroe Doctrine of 1823 was closely linked to British policy; Canning boasted that he had "called the New World into existence to redress the balance of the Old." That statement, though, told only part of the story. The Monroe Doctrine was as anti-French and anti-Russian as Canning desired; but it was also anti-British.

This was in keeping with the spirit of the times. Territorial expansion was a ruling aim of Americans in the first half of the nineteenth century; and Britain blocked American expansion more often than did all other powers put together. Wherever Americans turned—Florida, Texas, Oregon, California, Cuba, Nicaragua—they encountered opposition from the British. Basically, Anglo-American conflict stemmed from the interest of American agrarians in areas where British influence was strong. American expansionists had their eyes on the Oregon country, where Britain had territorial claims and a flourishing fur trade. Americans coveted Texas, New Mexico, and California, provinces of Mexico, a republic in which Britain had a lion's share of the trade and diplomatic influence. Southern planters were interested in the West Indies, where Britain was the predominant naval power.

Resulting tensions caused several war scares. There was one in 1819, when Andrew Jackson, invading Spanish Florida, hanged two Britishers who had been working with the Seminoles. There was another upsurge of bad feeling at the end of the 1830's, when Canadians and Americans were squabbling over the Maine boundary. At the same time there was conflict over the African slave trade and the participation of United States citizens in the Canadian insurrection of 1837. Britishers were also irritated when, after the panic of 1837, American states defaulted on debts owed to English investors. Trouble flared up again in the 1840's, when Americans used the phrase "Fifty-Four Forty or Fight!" This meant insisting on American ownership of all the Oregon country, from California to Alaska. This was an extreme demand, for, by an arrangement of 1818, the United States and Britain were to occupy this region jointly.

Fortunately, war was averted on each of these occasions. In 1819 Britain decided not to press the Florida issue. The controversies of the 1830's were worked out in a conciliatory spirit by American Secretary of State Daniel Webster and Lord Ashburton, a British diplomat. Their Webster-Ashburton Treaty (1842) split the disputed territory along the Maine border. Four years after this northeast settlement, the English-speaking countries agreed on a northwest boundary. This was not drawn at 54°40', as Americans desired, nor along the Columbia River, as the British considered proper, but on the forty-ninth parallel.

In Florida and Oregon, Britain yielded a great deal. That is, Britain tried to stop the expansion of the United States; but when Americans pressed hard, London withdrew or accepted a settlement satisfactory to the American republic. Preoccupied with Old World problems, the United Kingdom could not give the Western Hemisphere full attention. Nor did the British think that a war with the United States would be worth the cost. In those years Britain was taking up the doctrines of Adam Smith and moving toward free trade. Her tendency, then, was to stress trade and put less emphasis on possession and enlargement of colonies.

In the year of the Oregon settlement (1846), Britain also gave ground in Mexico. Encouraged by British diplomats to resist United States encroachments on Mexican territory, many Mexicans concluded that England would aid Mexico in a Mexican-American conflict. But when conflict came (the Mexican War of 1846–48), Britain remained neutral. So the United States won an easy victory; and British prestige declined south of the Rio Grande.

During the colonial era, Britain had secured a foothold in British Honduras. After the Central American states won independence from Spain, British Honduras was enlarged at the expense of Guatemala; and British agents organized a puppet state in eastern Nicaragua, along the Mosquito Coast. Possession of this area yielded little trade but meant control of the Nicaraguan transit route across Central America. It was assumed that in time an Isthmian canal would be dug across Panama or Nicaragua, connecting the Atlantic and Pacific oceans. Control of possible routes thus became important. Nor was it altogether a matter for the future. There were land routes across Nicaragua and Panama, the possession of which promised much to a trading nation.

Citizens of the United States became interested in the transit routes in the 1840's. By then the United States had pushed west to the Pacific. But the Great Plains were not yet settled; and there was no transcontinental railroad. As a consequence, it was difficult to run the mail from the eastern United States to Pacific settlements. It was harder still for settlers to get from the Mississippi Valley to the west coast. Some took covered wagons across the unsettled plains, by the Oregon Trail and other routes. Many, though, preferred to go to New York or New Orleans, take a steamship to Central America, cross Nicaragua or Panama, then go by steamer to California. This remained the standard route until the completion of the Union Pacific Railroad in 1869.

To handle the transit business, Cornelius Vanderbilt and other Americans established ocean steamship lines, built a railroad across Panama, and provided a stagecoach and lake steamer service across Nicaragua. Inevitably, these activities caused Americans to take an interest in the local governments. In 1846 the United States made a treaty with Colombia (which then owned Panama), giving the United States the right to intervene in Panama to keep the transit route open. At the same time, Americans turned attention to Nicaragua, where the British were well established. As in Oregon, the possibilities of conflict were substantial. But, knowing they could not have complete control, the British were willing to make concessions. The Americans also gave some ground. In the Clayton-Bulwer Treaty of 1850, Britain and the United States agreed that neither would absorb territory belonging to Central American republics, and that neither would seek exclusive control of a future Isthmian canal.

The treaty was unpopular in the United States. Expansionists called it a surrender to the British. Actually, the pact showed that British diplomats were aware that they could not keep the United States out of the Isthmian area. And half a century later Britain would bow out altogether, leaving the United States free to construct and control the Panama Canal.

Conflict Within the United States: Texas

While dealing with European opposition to American expansion, advocates of Manifest Destiny also faced divisions within the United States. These splits delayed the annexation of Texas, created problems during the war with Mexico, and by 1850 halted the expansion movement.

In the Transcontinental Treaty of 1821, by which the United States acquired Florida, the American republic recognized Spain's title to Texas. Soon afterwards, Spain lost her mainland colonies in the New World. The new Mexican nation then took over the Spanish title to Texas, New Mexico, and California. Texas was settled only by local Indians and a few missionaries, ranchers, and officials from Mexico. Desiring to build up the region, the Mexican government offered large land grants to settlers. This brought in persons from the southern United States. Newcomers were expected to join the Roman Catholic Church and become citizens of Mexico. These requirements, the Mexicans reasoned, should make the immigrants loyal to Mexico. But nearly all the new settlers remained attached to the United States. Nor did they get along with the Mexicans in Texas. To the Americans, the Mexicans seemed ignorant and untrustworthy; and the Mexicans considered Americans vicious braggarts.

Mexican officials soon decided they had erred in encouraging immigration. At the end of the 1820's, they closed the border to prevent any more Americans from coming into Texas. But Americans already outnumbered Mexicans in Texas; and, despite prohibitions, immigrants kept coming in from the United States. Being from slave states, many American settlers favored Negro slavery. A few brought slaves with them; others planned to send for some after getting settled. But Mexico in 1829 specifically prohibited slavery. Disturbed, the Americans in Texas were further angered by the Mexican constitution of 1831, which centralized the government of the republic and withdrew from Texas previously enjoyed rights of local self-government. Settlers from the United States were willing to live under the flag of Mexico if they could run Texas as they chose. It was another matter if they were to be ruled from Mexico City.

In the end there was an armed uprising—the Texan War of Independence (1835–36). Mexico had military force enough to crush this revolt, even though the Americans in Texas were reinforced by volunteers from the United States. But Santa Anna, dictator-president of Mexico, mismanaged his campaign against the insurrectionists. Overconfident, he divided his forces in enemy territory and failed to guard against surprise attacks. Even so, the Mexicans defeated two units of Texas Americans— one at the Alamo, where Colonel James Bowie, Davy Crockett, and 200 others died fighting off the foe. One month later, in April, 1836, Texas forces under Sam Houston caught the Mexicans napping at San Jacinto, defeated them, and took Santa Anna prisoner. Although Mexico refused to acknowledge defeat, the war was over. Houston and his friends organized a republic of Texas, which asked for annexation to the United States, as West Florida had a generation earlier.

In some respects, annexation seemed in order.. The United States had remained technically neutral during the Texas uprising, but the revolt had been organized, fought, and won by men from the United States. Sam Houston was an old friend of Andrew Jackson, who was President of the United States when the Texans gained independence. The cause of Texas was popular all over the United States. Citizens gathered in mass meetings to offer sympathy, money, and recruits. And yet, though the Texans won independence in 1836, the region was not annexed to the United States until 1845.

Why the delay? One reason was the panic of 1837. Concerned about hard times, Americans gave less thought to Texas than would otherwise have been the case. More important was sectional division. Most of those who lived in the South wanted Texas added to the Union. Getting it meant securing cotton land, providing opportunities for Southerners who moved west. Those who stayed in older southern states could sell their surplus slaves to the new plantations. And Texas would strengthen the southern states politically, by giving them more votes in Congress.[1]

Many free-state citizens opposed absorbing Texas. Annexation would strengthen slavery. To abolitionists, this seemed morally wrong. Other

---

[1] Some seaboard Whig planters dissented. Fearing competition of virgin cotton soils in the Southwest, they opposed annexation of Texas, and later opposed the Mexican War.

Northerners objected on political and economic grounds. Bringing in Texas would increase southern votes in Congress, making it more difficult for free states to get legislation they desired. Specifically, northern politicians interested in the Clay program (internal improvements and a protective tariff) knew that southern Congressmen generally opposed such measures. Nor did northern farmers have much enthusiasm for Texas. In the main, these farmers were expansionists and believed in Manifest Destiny. But they were free-state men who did not want to compete with slave labor. Hence few cared to go to Texas; and they therefore had no strong desire for annexation.

Andrew Jackson, a slave-state expansionist, recognized Texas independence in 1837; but he left the White House before the annexation issue came to a head. Jackson's successor, Martin Van Buren, was a New Yorker who knew that many Northerners doubted the advisability of expansion southward. Besides, Van Buren had to give attention to deficits and other depression problems, and had little time for Texas. John Tyler, the Virginia planter who entered the White House in 1841 (after the death of Harrison), represented the slave-state view on Texas. So did John C. Calhoun, who became Tyler's Secretary of State in 1843. As a result, a treaty of annexation was submitted to the United States Senate. The Senate, however, refused to accept the treaty (1844). One factor was the unpopularity of Tyler; another was continuing northern opposition to annexation.

Democratic expansionists solved the problem in the presidential campaign of 1844. Their platform and candidate (James K. Polk) called for the annexation of *both Texas and Oregon.* Southerners approved, for they stood to gain Texas. But there was bait for the North as well—the great Northwest, with furs, forests, and farmland. In 1812, the expansionists had called for Florida and Canada, something for the South, something for the North. Now it was Texas and Oregon. Polk swept the polls, beating Henry Clay, who hedged on expansion.

In the dying days of the Tyler administration—after Polk's election but before his inauguration—Congress added Texas to the Union (January–March, 1845). Even then, friends of Manifest Destiny could not muster the two-thirds vote needed for Senate approval of an annexation treaty. They effected annexation by passing a joint resolution, this requiring only a majority in each house.

War with Mexico (1846–48)

In annexing Texas, the United States acquired a boundary dispute with Mexico. Texas claimed land as far south as the Rio Grande. Mexico, indisposed to yield any of Texas, was emphatically unwilling to give up the territory between the Nueces River and the Rio Grande.

President Polk saw this dispute as an opportunity. He proposed that the United States and Mexico, when settling the boundary dispute, make a further deal, transferring to the United States the Mexican territories of California and New Mexico, for $25,000,000. When Mexico refused, Polk ordered General Zachary Taylor to move troops from the Nueces to the Rio Grande (early 1846). As was expected, this produced a border skirmish between American and Mexican soldiers. Polk then cried that Mexico had "invaded our territory and shed American blood upon the American soil." Congress promptly declared (May, 1846) that "by the act of the Republic of Mexico, a state of war exists between that Government and the United States." Polk had planned to ask for a declaration of hostilities in any case, on the basis of some unpaid claims, plus Mexico's refusal to receive Polk's agents. The flare-up on the Rio Grande enabled the Chief Executive to strengthen his war message and make his appeal on "higher grounds."

The war did not win support of all Americans. The South approved of the conflict. Some Northerners caught the excitement. Others were doubtful, indifferent, or hostile. Whigs disliked the war partly because it was sponsored by a Democratic administration. And, since Polk was a Southerner, many Northerners concluded that this war was a conspiracy to get new cotton lands and add to southern strength in Congress.

Many Mexicans believed that their republic would win. The population of Mexico was only half that of her neighbor; but the Mexican Army was larger than the standing army of the United States. Mexico could fight near her center of population, while her opponent had to transport men and materials tremendous distances. As to fighting talent, many Mexicans felt that Americans ran to boast and bluster; and if the Americans did well, Mexico hoped for aid from Great Britain or France.

Americans were no less confident. Expecting easy victory, Congress voted no war taxes, though it did sanction borrowing. Despite the distance factor, the administration accepted short-term volunteers. Some ran out their terms before they reached the front. Others were lost in the middle of campaigns. Problems of supply were hopelessly mismanaged, and politicians without army training were given military jobs. The diplomatic record was little better. When the war began, the Mexican politician Santa Anna was in exile. He told Americans that if returned to power he would have Mexico make peace. Polk therefore helped Santa Anna get back to Mexico, whereupon that wily character helped organize resistance against the United States.

Still, the Americans did win. Mexico received no foreign aid, and her soldiers, though courageous, were poorly equipped and trained. Santa Anna was resourceful, sometimes brilliant; but he could not compare with the top American commander, Winfield Scott. The United States also had the edge in junior officers, Scott being aided by such young West Pointers as Robert E. Lee, Ulysses S. Grant, George B. McClellan, T. J. (Stonewall) Jackson, and William Tecumseh Sherman. Sea power also worked on the American side; the United States Navy transported an expeditionary force to Vera Cruz, blockaded the Mexican coast, and helped seize California.

The war was decided by two major thrusts into Mexican territory. The first was made by Zachary Taylor, who crossed the Rio Grande and pushed into northern Mexico. He was stopped by Santa Anna on the bloody field of Buena Vista (February, 1847). Badly punished, Taylor considered falling back; but the Mexicans, short of stores, withdrew first.

Had he been reinforced, Taylor might have driven on to Mexico City. But higher-ups had decided to try from the other side. One month after Buena Vista, an army of 10,000 was landed on the coast near Vera Cruz. Winfield Scott, commander of this force, quickly took that seaport, then marched into the interior. Driving Santa Anna before them, the Americans had made good progress by summer, 1847. Then the invaders cut loose from communications and took a rugged mountain road to Mexico City. "Scott is lost," said Napoleon's conqueror Wellington. But Scott made it, smashing Santa Anna's force and taking Mexico City in September, 1847.

While Scott and Taylor were moving into the heart of Mexico, other Americans were taking the outlying districts of New Mexico and California. The most spectacular work was done by Colonel Stephen W. Kearny, who led an expedition from Kansas to Santa Fe, New Mexico, then went on to California (June, 1846–January, 1847). Distance and the desert were the colonel's chief opponents, for Santa Anna was engaged elsewhere. Still, Kearny's contribution was real; he established claims to areas which the United States was never to relinquish.

Kearny took New Mexico alone. Others helped in California. Naval officers controlled coastal waters and were active on shore. An exploring party under John C. Frémont mixed in the struggle. So did Americans who had settled in California. In the approved West Florida–Texas fashion, they "revolted" and proclaimed a California (Bear Flag) republic, which, of course, asked to be annexed to the United States.

Results of the Mexican War

Triumphant everywhere the United States could dictate peace terms. Some Americans, swelling with the Manifest Destiny idea, favored taking all Mexico. Others were not so sure. Southerners like John C. Calhoun had welcomed war and approved of the annexation of California and New Mexico. Taking all Mexico was a different matter. Many parts of that republic were ill-suited to a plantation economy; and the Mexicans had specifically prohibited slavery. Brought into the Union, they might vote with the free states against the South.

As it turned out, citizens of the United States did not have to decide this basic question. Under the Treaty of Guadalupe-Hidalgo (1848), Mexico remained independent. The treaty recognized American claims to the area between the Nueces and the Rio Grande. Mexico also transferred California and New Mexico—half of prewar Mexico—to the United States. In return, the United States paid Mexico $15,000,000 and assumed some private claims of American citizens against the Mexican republic. This curious feature—the victor giving money to the vanquished—was the work of the American negotiator, Nicholas Trist, who also decided that the United States should be content with California and New Mexico. President Polk was displeased with Trist's decisions but, since his term was running out, decided not to change the treaty. The Senate agreed, and the war with Mexico was over.

When he left the White House in 1849, Polk could rightly boast of his accomplishments. In a single term he had squeezed maximum results out of boundary disputes involving Oregon and Texas. He had added California to the Union just as gold was discovered there. He had acquired New Mexico, a territory covering much of the area now included in Arizona, New Mexico, Utah, Nevada, Colorado, and Wyoming. At the same time, the war had increased animosity toward the United States in Latin America and contributed to the sectional turmoil that would produce the Civil War.

Polk had expected that his program would help the Democratic party. But, instead of acclaiming those who had engineered the war, American voters bestowed their favors on battlefield heroes. The two chief American commanders were Whigs. Winfield Scott was much the better general; but Old Fuss and Feathers was too pompous for the people. Zachary Taylor, though short on military talent, had real campaign appeal. The Whigs therefore nominated him for President in 1848, and he won at the polls.[2]

The conflict also disappointed southern planters who wanted new plantation lands. New Mexico did not fit well into the cotton culture. California offered greater possibilities; but the gold rush attracted free-state settlers who were in control by 1850.

---

[2] Taylor's success caused both major parties to nominate military heroes in 1852. The Whigs chose Scott, who was defeated by Franklin Pierce, a Democrat who had been a Scott brigade commander. Still another Mexican War figure, Frémont, became the first Republican presidential candidate, in 1856.

Not only that. The Mexican War marked the end of the expansion movement which had added Louisiana, Florida, Texas, Oregon, New Mexico, and California to the Union. Until this time, southern advocates of Manifest Destiny had been able to join forces with northern expansionists. After the war with Mexico, Northerners became less interested in foreign territory; and without aid from the free states, the South could not swing expansion projects. The northern attitude was understandable. After settlement of the Oregon question, there was little land that Northerners desired. Western Canada looked inviting, but to get it the United States would have to fight a costly war with Britain. And moving southward had little appeal to citizens of the free states. Northern farmers would not care to move into such areas, and their annexation might add to the political and economic power of the slave states.

Southern Expansion Schemes

Despite the discouraging outlook, many Southerners continued to support expansion. From the late 1840's down to the Civil War, they talked of taking or buying northern Mexico and Lower California, Nicaragua, Santo Domingo, and Spanish Cuba.

Cuba received most attention. Certain American politicians backed Cubans who were rebelling against Spanish authority. One Cuban insurrectionist, Narciso Lopez, discussed plans with such leading Southerners as John C. Calhoun and Jefferson Davis. In his last filibustering expeditions (1850–51), Lopez had the support of Governor John A. Quitman of Mississippi and enlisted recruits from southern states. Lopez, however, was captured and executed by Spanish authorities.

American advocates of Cuban annexation tried again during the Democratic administration of Franklin Pierce (1853–57). Like Polk, Pierce was an all-out expansionist; and, though a Northerner, he was influenced by Jefferson Davis and other Southerners. Pierce tried to persuade Spain to sell Cuba. Spain's refusal brought forth the Ostend Manifesto of 1854. This strange document was issued by three American diplomats in Europe —Pierre Soulé of Louisiana, John Y. Mason of Virginia, James Buchanan of Pennsylvania. It stated that if Spain declined to sell Cuba, the American republic might under certain circumstances "by every law human and Divine . . . be justified in wresting it from Spain." This statement increased Buchanan's popularity in the South and helped him win nomination and election as Democratic presidential candidate in 1856. But, despite the Manifest Destiny tradition, Americans were too divided on expansion to get together on a war for Cuba.

Southern expansionists were also interested in William Walker, a Southerner whose taste for adventure caused him to lead a filibustering expedition into northern Mexico. When that venture failed, Walker shifted activities to Central America and became dictator of Nicaragua in the mid-1850's. His movements there were of interest to Cornelius Vanderbilt and other businessmen who had invested in the transit routes across the Isthmus. No less interested were American proslavery leaders who saw some chance of annexing Nicaragua to the United States. Again, however, there was a lack of general enthusiasm for expansion. As for Walker, his luck changed, and he died before a firing squad.

Although unable to swing annexation of Cuba or Nicaragua, the southern expansionists did add one piece of territory to the United States—the Gadsden Purchase (1853), 30,000 square miles in what is now southern Arizona and New Mexico. Surveys had shown the importance of this area to the proposed southern route for a transcontinental railroad. Santa Anna, again on top in Mexico, and in need of cash, was willing to sell for $10,000,000; and the Senate finally allowed President Pierce to go through with the deal.

That, and no more. Northern Congressmen turned thumbs down at the end of the 1850's, when President Buchanan (1857–61) proposed further advances into Mexico. Citizens of the United States had worked together in pushing westward; but they were no longer agreed as to their country's destiny.

Backing the Merchant Marine

Manifest Destiny—the expansion urge—was the major impulse in American diplomacy from 1812 to 1850. But the government also continued to support the American merchant marine; and Americans did what they could to promote ideals abroad.

Expansionist activity varied with shifts in sectional and party strength. The merchant marine, however, was backed whoever was in power. For one thing, "national honor" was involved; it was patriotic to aid vessels flying the United States flag. Practical considerations were even more compelling. Shipowners constituted an important pressure group, for a good deal of capital was invested in old sailing vessels, in the faster clipper ships during the 1840's, and in the new steam vessels. And, since American vessels carried American goods to every corner of the globe, exporters handling southern cotton and northern wheat saw advantage in aiding the shippers.

Back in the days of Alexander Hamilton, the United States had tried to help American carriers by charging foreign ships higher tariff and tonnage duties in American ports. This worked out badly, for discrimination caused foreign countries to retaliate against American ships. So the United States shifted after 1815, offered to remove discriminatory duties in return for similar concessions abroad. The resulting arrangements benefited American traders.

During the wars of the French Revolution American ships had been allowed to trade with West Indian colonies of France, Spain, Britain, and the Netherlands. These privileges were withdrawn when Napoleon was beaten. Gradually, diplomatic and economic pressure forced the closed doors open—Spanish and British colonies by 1830, the Dutch and French in the generation following. Meantime, United States shippers were building commerce with the newly liberated Latin-American nations. The State Department helped by negotiating commercial treaties with these countries.

Americans developed other new trade areas in the Far East and the Pacific. New England whalers helped develop United States influence in the kingdom of Hawaii. Massachusetts merchants cornered Sumatra's pepper trade; American clipper ships competed with Britain for the China tea trade. Behind these trading pioneers was the influence of the United States. When possible, the American government worked through diplomatic channels, as when the Massachusetts merchant-politician, Caleb Cushing, negotiated the first treaty between China and the United States (1844). Not infrequently, however, there was a resort to force. When Sumatrans seized an American pepper ship, Andrew Jackson had a man-of-war shell a native village. Two decades later, when the hermit kingdom of Japan showed a reluctance to trade with the outside world, Commodore Matthew Perry obtained a treaty by making a naval demonstration (1854). On an earlier occasion this same officer had "disciplined" African natives who had interfered with commercial operations.

Most American carriers were in legal commerce, but a few were tied up in the African slave trade. The United States declared this traffic unlawful in 1808 and made it piracy in 1820. Nonetheless, the trade continued, much of it in vessels built in the United States.[3] Although conditions were indescribably bad, the American government did next to nothing to stop this illicit commerce. The few navy vessels assigned to the African coast were unable to handle the task of enforcement. The more efficient British Navy could have done the job. But, remembering past search and impressment controversies, the United States was unwilling to have English officials stop and examine vessels flying the Stars and Stripes. Not until the Civil War did the United States agree to joint Anglo-American action

---

[3] Most Negroes run across the Atlantic in these years were marketed in Brazil or Cuba. Planters in the United States did not want slaves fresh from Africa, for they were difficult to manage, and many died before they could adjust to the climate.

against slavers. Then and then only did this shocking business come to an end.

When the age of steam created a new situation in transatlantic trade, Americans resented the efforts of the British government subsidized Cunard Line to dominate the passenger business. Fighting back, American capitalists started a rival Collins Line, which began receiving government subsidies in the 1840's. In the 1850's, however, the subsidy program ran into the sectional conflict, that is, southern opposition to northern economic enterprises. Subsidies were stopped, and the Collins Line went out of business.

Exporting Democratic Ideas

Americans hoped that commercial and territorial expansion would spread American ideas and institutions. Most citizens of the United States regarded their culture as superior to that of the Old World. Did it not follow that every increase in American influence would help mankind?

Convinced that this was so, average Americans were glad to have their government use force to obtain territory and trade. They were no less pleased when their politicians cried that Europe represented the past, America the future. As they saw it, Old World monarchies stood for decadence and tyranny, and the republican United States, devoted to democracy and progress, was the hope of the world.

Some felt that the United States could peform its world mission simply by providing an example. Walt Whitman and Ralph Waldo Emerson so viewed American democracy, as a symbol of hope for all peoples. Others, not content with so passive a role, maintained that example would not cause European autocrats to yield to democratic forces. Action would be required—revolts for freedom or to establish democratic and republican rule. When revolutions came, Americans would give the rebels sympathy at least, perhaps active aid. Some said there would be a world showdown between monarchies and republics. Could the crowned heads of Europe feel secure while the spirit of democracy was spreading? Could American republicans be safe while monarchies remained? Self-seeking politicians took up the cry because they found it meant votes. But there was more than politics to the drive for world republicanism. There was belief among the people that the democratic United States had a world mission to perform.

In the 1820's attention centered on the Greeks, who were fighting to free themselves from the Turks. Freedom was involved. So was religion, with Christian Greeks lined up against Mohammedans. To Americans, this was a holy war, a people's war, a war of liberty against autocracy, right against wrong. Philhellenism swept the country. William Cullen Bryant dashed off poetry to help the cause. Daniel Webster and Henry Clay talked of mankind's debt to Greek culture. Ypsilanti, Michigan, took its name from a Greek soldier who came to the New World to fight in the American Revolution. His sons were heroes of the Greek War of Independence; and they were joined by Americans who crossed the Atlantic to labor for the Greek cause. Most prominent of these was Samuel Gridley Howe, later known for his work with the blind.

Though unable to give active aid, the United States government did what it could to help the Greek uprising. Friends of the rebels were allowed to raise money and secure supplies in America. Government officials made public statements of sympathy. Even the White House did its bit. President Monroe praised the Greeks in the message to Congress which contained the Monroe Doctrine—a doctrine which asserted that the United States did not meddle in European affairs.

After the Greeks had won independence, Americans expressed approval of the short-lived revolt of the Poles against the Russians (1830). There was even greater interest in the European revolutions of 1848. In France, Italy, Germany, and Austria, rebels demanded democratic rule, cried for national self-determination, overthrow of monarchs, and establishment of republican governments. To citizens of the United States it seemed that the European revolutionaries were following in the footsteps of their New World republic. They cheered the triumphs of the insurrectionists, and were disheartened when the revolutions failed.

The Kossuth Craze

The high point of excitement came in connection with the Hungarian bid for independence from the Austrian Empire. Americans were openly sympathetic with the rebels; and in 1849 the United States sent a diplomatic agent to the Hungarians. The revolt was crushed by Austrian and Russian troops before this agent reached his destination; but even defeat did not kill American enthusiasm for the cause. At the end of 1849 President Zachary Taylor publicly told Congress of his devotion to Hungarian republicanism. When Austria protested, Secretary of State Daniel Webster wrote a stinging reply. This "Hülsemann letter" of 1850 said that the Hungarian revolt was of course connected with American democracy. The rising interest in "republican liberty," said Webster, was the direct "result of the reaction of America upon Europe."

Louis Kossuth's visit of 1851–52 was part of the same pattern. Kossuth, a Hungarian revolutionary, was brought across the Atlantic on an American man-of-war, was publicly received by the Senate and House, and was entertained by President Millard Fillmore in the White House. To top things off, Secretary of State Webster publicly proclaimed his desire for Hungarian independence at the Congressional banquet given in Kossuth's honor. The whole country was gripped by a Kossuth craze as the visitor toured the northern states. Webster Whigs tried to make the Hungarian cause their own, only to be outdone by Stephen A. Douglas and his Young America Democrats. Douglas went beyond Webster in denouncing European despotism, and the Democratic Central Committee of New York resolved that "at the tap of the drum one hundred thousand armed men will rally around the American standard to be unfurled on the field when the issue between freedom and despotism is to be decided."

It was more talk than action. Much of the money raised for Hungarian aid was frittered away on bands and banquets. Nor did Kossuth obtain satisfaction when he asked Americans to save Hungary, "peaceably, if they may . . . forcibly, if they must." Interested though they were, citizens of the United States were not yet ready, physically or psychologically, to fight wars in Europe. Yet the excitement over Kossuth was important. It influenced American politics. It added to national self-consciousness. And it pointed toward the day when the New World republic would in fact be ready to play an active role in European affairs.

Antiforeign Feeling

Since colonial days, America had given asylum to political refugees. It continued to do so in the nineteenth century, and became a land of refuge and promise for individuals driven into exile by the failure of the European revolutions of 1848. Some of these men, like Kossuth and the Italian patriot Garibaldi, visited but did not remain in the United States. Others came to stay—for example, such German 48'ers as Carl Schurz. These refugees received a warm welcome, as men who had fought for the American ideals of liberty and democracy, hence could be expected to fit into the framework of American republican institutions.

The welcome did not extend to all foreigners. The nationalism which led Americans to favor republican revolts in Europe made citizens of the United States suspicious of foreigners. Americans believed that their republic boasted the best institutions known to man. It followed that European culture was inferior; therefore "foreign influence" was dangerous.

This nativist tendency increased when Americans read articles written by Europeans who had visited the United States. Some travelers praised American vigor and saw merits in American democracy. Nearly all, however, described the people of the United States as boastful and crude. Americans replied in kind. Stephen A. Douglas, the voice of Young America, called the Old World a "graveyard," and announced that Europe's day of glory was past.

Money was also in the picture. The young republic needed foreign capital; without it, the Erie Canal and Illinois Central Railroad could not have been constructed. Yet Americans disliked having foreigners for creditors. They resented being scolded for defaults after the panic of 1837. On another level, antiforeign feeling was associated with immigration. Only a tiny fraction of these immigrants were political refugees. Most were impoverished farmers from Ireland and Germany, seeking economic opportunities. These settlers were needed in the still underpopulated United States. Many native Americans, however, considered newcomers unwelcome competitors. The Germans did not seem so bad, for most of them became farmers in the thinly settled Middle West. But the Irish stayed in the East and took jobs from the native-born.

Along with the economic factor went language and religion. The Germans spoke English with a thick accent or not at all; and the Americans disliked the Irish brand of English. Besides, a large share of the Irish and German immigrants were Roman Catholic. This disturbed many Americans, for until this time the United States had been overwhelmingly Protestant. The result was that by 1850 "antiforeign" and "anti-Catholic" were virtually synonymous terms in the United States.

Strong in the 1830's and 1840's, nativism was to become stronger still with the rise of the Know-Nothing party of the 1850's. But, like other things, the antiforeign movement was then swallowed by the sectional conflict which produced the Civil War.

Part IV

The Triumph of American Nationalism

(1850-1877)

 *By the 1850's, it was evident that nationalism was increasing in importance in the United States; that commercial and industrial interests were making headway; and that the slave states would have less influence in the future than they had possessed in the past.*

Disturbed, Southerners opposed these trends. For a time, they worked within the Union. Then they tried secession. But the trends prevailed. Crushed in battle, the South had to give up slavery, and emerged from the Civil War with less national influence than ever before.

Meantime, the commercial and industrial forces of the North gained influence, pointing the way toward the industrial age. The sectional conflict thus coincided with the transition from an agrarian to a manufacturing economy. And, by weakening states' rights, the controversy between North and South hastened the triumph of American nationalism.

12

The Sectional Conflict

Rise in Nationalist Feeling

The expansion of the United States greatly increased nationalist feeling. Americans were pleased that their country had quadrupled in size between 1800 and 1850. No less impressive was the westward movement. Pleasing, too, was the fact that the United States was gaining population more rapidly than were Old World powers. Victory over Mexico was a further source of pride, as was the flow of immigrants into the United States. Even those who disliked newcomers saw in immigration a recognition of American superiority.

Americans soaked up patriotism at school and in church. Historians also helped; Jared Sparks corrected Washington's spelling errors, lest the General seem short of perfect. Newspapers were filled with similar sentiments. Longfellow turned out nationalist verse; novelists did their patriotic best in prose. From Daniel Webster on down to local spellbinders, politicians used nationalist appeals on the stump.

Most of the public found devotion to the nation emotionally appealing, and logical in a country with good transportation and a developing domestic trade. National patriotism also fitted in with the mobility of America. A Pennsylvanian who moved west into Ohio, later to Iowa, was unlikely to be completely devoted to any of his three states of residence; rather he would consider himself primarily an American.

Persistence of Other Loyalties

Nationalism did not destroy other loyalties. Most Americans felt attached to their villages, counties, or states. But the major challenge came from sectionalism. As travel and communication improved, residents of adjacent states became aware of common interests, looked at problems in terms of blocs of states. Individuals then came to think of themselves as New Englanders rather than as citizens of Maine or Rhode Island; as Southerners rather than as Carolinians or Georgians.

Sectional feeling, grounded in common interests, developed quickly

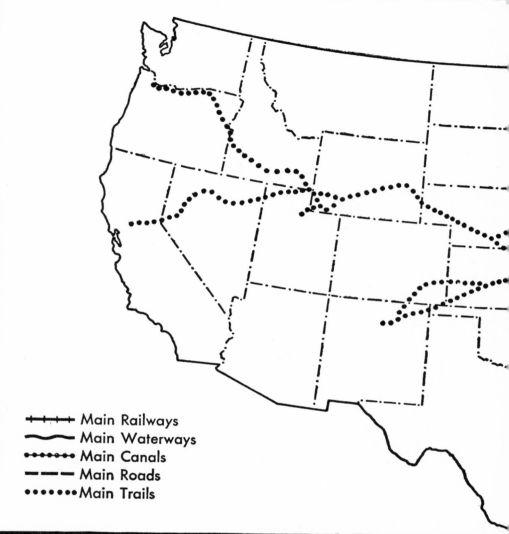

+++++ Main Railways
～～～～ Main Waterways
•••••• Main Canals
－ － － Main Roads
••••••Main Trails

This map shows the great economic progress of the United States between
1815 and 1860, for the great majority of the transportation lines here indicated were developed after the War of 1812. The map also shows the general east-west direction of the transportation lines. There were important
north-south lines, such as the Mississippi River and the Illinois Central Railroad. On the whole, however, the roads, canals, and railroads of 1860 tied
the Northeast to the Northwest, and the Southeast to the Southwest. This was
a fact of importance in the sectional struggle then coming to a crisis. In particular, the transportation situation helps explain why the agrarian states of

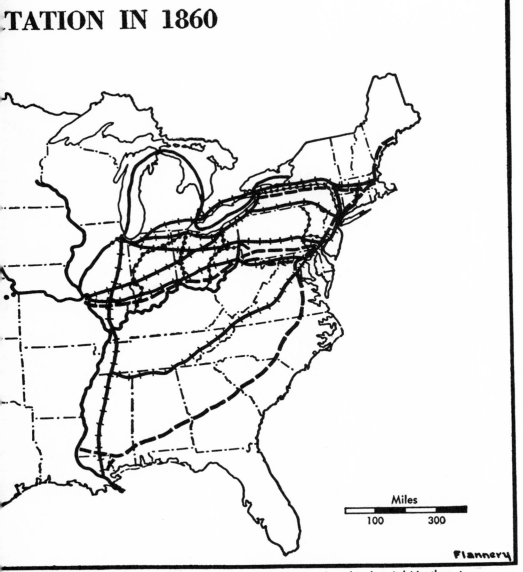

the Great Lakes region lined up with the commercial and industrial Northeast rather than with the agricultural South. It will be noted also that the transportation network of the South did not compare with that of the North. Southerners, disturbed at seeing their section falling behind the free states in economic progress, sought a remedy in secession. But when secession came, the northern transportation network helped the Union organize for victory, whereas the transportation deficiencies in the South seriously impeded the Confederate war effort. The destruction of southern railroads during the Civil War left the South weaker still after 1865.

when political conflicts touched those interests. Sectional consciousness in New England was increased by opposition to the War of 1812; southern sectional consciousness grew during the later slavery controversy. Sectional feeling was most acute when the states involved felt themselves a minority group opposed by a majority in the nation.

Sectional lines are not always sharply drawn. Besides, these lines shift from time to time; and there are subsections within each section. In the South there was a sharp contrast between the plantation lowlands and Appalachian highlands. The hill country might or might not coöperate with the rest of the South on a given issue. To increase complications, class interests cut across sectional lines, as when Jefferson and Jackson won the backing of western farmers and eastern workingmen.

Between 1800 and 1830, there was an East-West division in the United States. Interested in cheap land, easy credit, and improved transportation, western states were conscious of their common interest. They felt tied together, too, by the Mississippi River, which linked Northwest with Southwest, Ohio and Illinois with Louisiana and Alabama. Meanwhile, Easterners felt united in opposition to the West. Tidewater planters of Carolina and Virginia regarded with suspicion the rise of Southwest states like Mississippi and Alabama; New Englanders viewed the settlement of the Great Lakes region with distaste.

After 1830, East-West conflicts abated. New roads, canals, and railroads running west across the mountains brought the Northwest back into contact with the Northeast. Thus the Erie Canal shifted Ohio trade back to New York City, away from New Orleans. Sentimental bonds reinforced economic links, for the Northwest was settled largely from the Northeast. Family connections also helped to unite Southeast and Southwest. Expansion of the plantation economy into the Gulf states also put the Southwest and Southeast on one economic plane. Finally, east-west railroads brought southeastern states into effective contact with the Southwest. These developments produced a new sectional alignment. Southeastern and southwestern states represented southern interests against the northeastern and northwestern states, now joined in a northern combination. It was North against South, the division being increasingly evident in the 1840's and the 1850's.

North-South Conflict

Of the two sections, the North had the edge in wealth, population, transportation, commerce, industry, and (potentially) political influence. The North could in a crisis dominate the Union. Northerners, therefore, tended to be national-minded, to prefer national patriotism to sectional attachment. As the weaker section, the South became increasingly sectional-minded, conscious of its minority position and critical of a national government it could not control.

The North-South division featured agricultural contrasts. Northern agriculture was diversified, involving grains, livestock, fruits, produce. Farms were small and depended on improved transportation (roads, canals, railroads) to get goods to market. Southern agriculture centered on the large plantation, producing one money crop, usually cotton. Since many plantation areas were intersected by slow-moving streams, the staple could be shipped by water, and there was less need for transportation improvements than in the North. As for food, Southerners raised only what was needed for home consumption, mainly corn and pork.

Northern and southern farmers could not agree on policy. Northerners wanted Congressional appropriations for roads, canals, and railroads. Southerners, relatively satisfied with river facilities, objected to internal improvements. Northern wool growers wanted tariff protection from foreign competition. Southerners, facing no such competition, opposed tariffs. Northerners wanted regions suitable for small farms and diversified agriculture (Oregon, for example). Southerners were interested in Texas and other areas where plantation staples could be grown.

Most southern farmers were not planters. But many small farmers hoped to become planters, much as many small businessmen hope to become big businessmen. The tendency, therefore, was to adopt planter attitudes. There were exceptions. Soils and climate barred the plantation system in southern hill country. Owning few or no slaves, hill farmers resembled inhabitants of poor farming areas in the North. But this element exerted little influence on politics. Control rested with the planter and his allies.

The North-South division also represented labor contrasts. Northern farm and factory labor was free; the southern plantation system rested on slave labor. For this reason and because of climate, immigrants avoided the South. Some Irishmen worked on southern railroads, and immigrants settled in southern cities. There, however, they and native whites encountered competition from slaves. Northern abolitionists and labor leaders therefore condemned slavery as degrading and as unfair competition with free labor. Replying, Southerners claimed that northern factory workers were "wage slaves," forced to work longer hours than enslaved Negroes, paid a pittance, and junked when their usefulness was over. This was worse than slavery, cried Southerners. They employed "African barbarians"; but Yankee mill-owners degraded their own people.

Some Southerners favored uniting with northern manufacturers. John C. Calhoun said that the southern planter and northern textile manufacturer should coöperate, since they depended on each other and since both represented wealth and stability. Planter spokesmen also suggested that abolitionists were a threat to manufacturers as well as planters. One Southerner reported about 1850 that he had overheard Boston abolitionists plotting to wipe out planters' capital by abolishing slavery, then to attack northern capital on the ground that northern businessmen were exploiting wage earners. Abolitionists, in short, were socialists in disguise, and businessmen should suppress them to protect the capitalist system.

Some northern capitalists were impressed by these arguments. Had not William Lloyd Garrison called the Constitution a "covenant with Hell" because it recognized slavery? A man who would overthrow the Constitution might overthrow other institutions. Some northern businessmen held this view down to 1861. Others broke with the planter-politicians over the tariff. A fair number of them then joined the antislavery movement, lining up, however, with politicians less extreme than Garrison.

There was another effort to substitute class for sectional lines—a northern appeal to the small white farmer of the South. Free-state foes of slavery had long claimed that the institution not only hurt the Negro but also degraded the less fortunate southern whites. How could small farmers compete with a planter who could buy wholesale and use slave labor for large-scale operations? Should not small southern farmers join northern labor in a crusade against slavery?[1]

This presentation contained flaws. The degradation of the poorest southern whites was related to soil exhaustion, malaria, and hookworm as well as slavery. The same sort of hopeless people could have been found in poor-soil areas of free states. Moreover, many small white farmers managed well in plantation areas. Those who aspired to be planters were not likely to attack the slave system; and the rest were too anti-Negro to join a movement to liberate slaves.

The slavery controversy was not confined to economic factors. The most bitter foes of slavery, the abolitionists, attacked the institution primarily on religious and moral grounds. Slavery, they said, was against Christian principles. Though recognized by the Constitution, it violated God's "higher law"; it was evil for a man to own another man.

This indictment aroused Southerners more than economic criticism did. Answering, they pointed out that slavery was recognized in the Bible. Fur-

---

[1] Among efforts in this field, one stood out: *The Impending Crisis of the South* (1857), by a North Carolinian, Hinton R. Helper. Himself a small farmer, Helper shared the anti-Negro feelings of that class; but he also insisted that slavery was ruining the rank and file of the whites. Ignored in the South, his book was enthusiastically received in the North, and increased antislavery feeling.

ther, the fact that owners had money invested in Negroes made for good treatment. It did not pay to abuse or neglect one's slaves. Finally, ran the proslavery argument, Negroes had benefited by their transfer from barbaric and heathen Africa to civilized, Christian America. And emancipation would bring social chaos.

Efforts to Strengthen the South

Proslavery leaders blamed southern troubles on the North. They noted that the South, following Jeffersonian principles, had continued to put the emphasis on agriculture. The North, by contrast, had emphasized commerce and manufacturing as well as farming, thus obtaining the power to hold down and exploit the South.

The free states had, certainly, acquired great wealth in the half-century before 1850. Much of this wealth was liquid—banking capital easily shifted from one business to another. Northerners could thus increase business by investing in manufacturing and by building a steamship-canal-railroad network across the North from the seaboard to the Mississippi. Meanwhile, the South, with its wealth tied up in land and slaves, found it hard to raise funds for railroads or manufacturing. The results were reflected in population figures. In 1790, Charleston had a population of 16,000, half that of New York. By 1850, Charleston had doubled in population, but New York was fifteen times its former size.

With wealth came power. Southerners feared that the North would soon force Congress to adopt a protective tariff, thus taxing southern consumers for the benefit of northern manufacturers. Southern merchants were losing their overseas trade (even cotton) to richer, more aggressive New York companies. Southern banks had to borrow from northern institutions, Southerners bought goods from northern factories. The North, it appeared, was turning the South into an economic colony.

Paralleling economic subordination was cultural dependence. Northern cities could do more for arts and sciences than could small southern centers. Schools, learned societies, artistic organizations, publishing firms flourished chiefly in the free states. Southerners found themselves reading Yankee literature, accepting Yankee styles, sending their children to Yankee schools.

What to do about it? After 1840, many southern trade conventions sought solutions. Agricultural reformers urged new crops; but cotton was king, and few could be diverted from its cultivation. Some tried manufacturing. But, though successful mills were established in South Carolina and Georgia, the total was unimpressive. Lack of capital, plus distances and terrain, made southern railway mileage lag behind that of the northern states. And southern efforts to build shipping companies and reëstablish direct trade with Europe failed for lack of money and experience.

Southerners also tried the cultural approach. The best results were obtained by *DeBow's Review*, a New Orleans business journal, and the *Southern Review*, a Charleston literary publication. But few able southern writers appeared, and the greatest, Edgar Allan Poe, moved north. Indeed, all artists, authors, and musicians found their best opportunities in northern centers.

Any cultural program depends in part on the schools. Here Southerners lacked the necessary funds. By 1850, northern states had free public schools even in rural areas, and northern cities were starting free high schools. The South, by contrast, had few rural public schools, no free high schools. The South led the North in the state university field but lagged far behind in professional education. A good medical school needs a connection with a large hospital. This gave institutions in large northern centers a distinct advantage; New York and Philadelphia medical colleges drew southern students. Legal education followed a similar pattern. Trained at the North, and taking northern journals, southern professional men were as colonially dependent as southern bankers and brokers. Attempts to change the situation achieved only limited success by 1860.

Breaking the Bonds of Union

Southerners, then, had failed to free themselves from economic and cultural dependence on the North. Some felt further efforts were in order. Others said that the South, as a minority section, could expect no satisfaction within the Union. The one way out was to secede and form a separate confederacy, devoted to southern aims.

In the 1840's, few Southerners considered secession. Despite quarrels, there were ties which held North and South together—personal friendships; religious, educational, and business associations; loyalty to a common nation; national political parties. These were strong bonds; but one by one they snapped in the two decades before 1861.

Religious and educational ties were among the first to go. Differences on slavery split the Methodists and Baptists into northern and southern churches during the 1840's. The next decade saw the New School Presbyterians divide. Meantime, southern educators demanded their own, pro-slavery schoolbooks; northern books and teachers denounced slavery.

Business links remained. Intersectional trade helped explain the nation's prosperity in the early 1850's; many New York merchants were pro-southern to the end. But Southerners disapproved of northern economic penetration of the slave states and were distressed to see the North accumulating wealth more rapidly than the South. And northern businessmen increasingly resented southern opposition to a protective tariff, merchant marine subsidies, and a northern-based transcontinental railroad.

National patriotism? Southerners were proud of the American republic, which their ancestors had helped build. But, though attached to the nation of their fathers, they felt less affection for the nation of their day, a nation in which northern interests were growing stronger. Given the new conditions, Southerners tended to be loyal chiefly to the South, where an agrarian economy survived. Northerners remained nationalist. This, too, made for friction. Believing in the idea of progress, northern nationalists saw the future as a changing one. The factory meant progress; northern capital and free labor would create a better America. Did the South object? Well, then, the South was against progress, and must be opposed.

In 1850, one significant North-South bond remained—that of political organization. The major parties (Whig and Democratic) were national. When faced with sectional disputes, they sought compromise solutions, so as to hold together their parties and the nation. In 1850, as before, party leaders used compromise successfully. In the ensuing decade, the technique failed. The Whig party disappeared, the Democrats divided; and the nation split in two.

The Compromise Technique

Those who favored compromising sectional disputes won victories in the Constitutional Convention of 1787; in the Missouri Compromise of 1820; in the Compromise of 1833, involving Nullification; and in the Compromise of 1850. Each time the South feared a growing North; each time the North made concessions.

Southern delegates to the 1787 convention saw to it that the Constitution prohibited export taxes, which would hit southern staples. They also insisted on the requirement that treaties needed a two-thirds vote in the Senate, so that no administration could force through a treaty harmful to the South.

The next North-South crisis came when Southerners criticized Congressional legislation in the Kentucky and Virginia Resolutions of 1798 and 1799; but this problem was settled when Jefferson became President in 1801. Thereafter, southern influence was so strong that Northerners complained. Before and during the War of 1812, a few New England extremists declared that their section should withdraw from the Union and form a confederacy "exempt from the . . . oppression of the . . . South."

This, though, was temporary. When Missouri sought admission to the Union after 1815, there was an even balance in the Senate (eleven slave, eleven free states, each having two Senators). But the House of Representatives, where representation was based on population, had a northern majority. A New York Congressman's proposal that Missouri be admitted without slavery alarmed Southerners, for if accepted it would give the free states control of both houses. The result was the Missouri Compromise of 1820, Missouri coming in as a slave state, Maine as a free state. But the Compromise barred slavery from all future states carved out of territory north of 36° 30′ (Missouri's southern boundary). This meant that in time the free states would outnumber the slave states and the North would dominate the Senate as well as the House.

Not only that. The North was also tightening its hold on the House of Representatives. European immigrants, of no mind to compete with slave labor, avoided the slave states; and the South lagged in industrialization, which always tends to quicken the growth of population. Hence the North gained population more rapidly than the South, and the free states gained seats in the House. By the 1850's the free states had 144, the slave states 90.

Long before that it was obvious that the slave states were doomed to a minority position in the republic. As a result, the South turned to states' rights to protect sectional interests. But asserting states'-rights doctrine was not as easy as in Jefferson's day; the achievements of the United States had swelled nationalist feeling. The South found this out in the Nullification controversy. Under the direction of Calhoun, South Carolina declared the Tariff of 1832 unconstitutional, hence unenforceable in South Carolina. Calhoun maintained that sovereignty was indivisible and belonged to the states. In accepting the Constitution, the states had delegated powers to the federal government. If that central government went beyond its delegated authority, the states could step in and exercise their sovereign power.

Though sympathetic toward states' rights, President Jackson was also influenced by the new nationalism. He therefore denied the right of a state to nullify acts of Congress. Serious difficulties were avoided by the Compromise of 1833. To please Calhoun, the tariff rates of 1832 were reduced. A Force Act, however, upheld national authority, striking at Nullification and implying that national authority transcended state authority. As in 1820, the South had a short-run victory that pointed toward long-range defeat. The tariff had been cut; but, given the Force Act, Nullification could not be used again. The slave states would have to obey national laws while they remained in the Union.

Last Compromise: 1850

Though slipping, the South retained half the votes in the Senate. With Missouri and Maine, the Union contained two dozen states, half free, half slave. Six more came in during the 1830's and 1840's, three with slavery (Arkansas, Florida, Texas), three without (Michigan, Iowa, Wisconsin). Then came a real crisis, over the disposition of land acquired in 1848 as a result of the war with Mexico. During the war a Pennsylvania Democratic Congressman, David Wilmot, proposed that territory obtained from Mexico should be forever free. After a bitter struggle, the northern-dominated House of Representatives voted for the Wilmot Proviso (1846, 1847). But the Senate, in which slave states had half the votes, turned the proposition down. The Wilmot Proviso inflamed passions north and south; and it broke party unity. Southern Whigs voted against, northern Whigs for the Proviso. There was less division among Democrats, who generally opposed Wilmot's proposal. But quite a few northern Democrats, including Martin Van Buren, broke party ranks on the issue. The line-up of legislatures was even more impressive. All northern legislatures except one favored the Wilmot Proviso principle of excluding slavery from newly added territories. Southern legislatures unanimously condemned the proposed restriction.

Having defeated the Wilmot Proviso, Southerners hoped for a breathing spell. Instead, 1849–50 brought a new conflict. California, comprising half the territory acquired from Mexico in 1848, sought admission as a free state. This was logical, for the gold rush had attracted Northerners to California. Southerners, however, viewed the situation with dismay. The South had no region ready to come in as a slave state. Hence admitting California free would destroy the North-South balance in the Senate.

Southern extremists like Calhoun said that the South must press now or be forever humbled. He wanted a stringent fugitive slave law, protection of slavery in the territories (the exact opposite of the Wilmot Proviso), and a dual presidency, in which the South would be permanently represented and through which it could veto Congressional measures hostile to southern interests. If the North refused such concessions, Calhoun favored secession.

Northern extremists, like William H. Seward, a Whig Senator from New York, opposed making any concessions. Antislavery sentiment was increasing. So was sentiment for northern domination of the government, to assure adoption of legislation favorable to commercial and industrial interests. Many Northerners therefore stood on the Wilmot Proviso principle of barring slavery from the territories. Others demanded abolition of the slave trade and slavery in the District of Columbia.

Many sought a middle ground. Unionists defeated secessionists in election of delegates to a southern convention in Nashville. Compromise seemed best to many slave-state leaders, including the Whig leader Henry Clay, who had helped arrange the Compromises in 1820 and 1833. Northern advocates of adjustment included the old Whig Daniel Webster, and the rising young Illinois Democrat Stephen A. Douglas.

As worked out, the Compromise of 1850 offered something to free states, something to slave states. To please the North, (1) California was admitted as a free state; (2) the slave trade was barred in the District of Columbia; and (3) Texas was prevailed upon to give up its claims to New Mexico. To satisfy the South, (1) the Wilmot Proviso was shelved, and the principle of popular or squatter sovereignty was applied to the territories of Utah and New Mexico (Congress neither forbade nor encouraged slavery, but allowed the residents of each territory to vote for or against the institution when they sought admission to the Union); (2) slavery was retained in the District of Columbia; (3) the United States assumed certain Texas debts; and (4) Congress adopted a new fugitive slave law. The old statute of 1793 had not kept "underground railroad" abolitionists from smuggling runaway Negroes through the free states to Canada; and in Prigg vs. Pennsylvania (1842) the Supreme Court had held that state authorities were not bound to help slaveowners capture runaways. The new law required state officers and others to aid in rendition of fugitives. Negroes charged with being runaways were denied many legal safeguards. Disputes were referred to federal agents, who were paid small fees if claimed persons were released, larger sums if the Negroes were turned over to the claimants.

Although the Fugitive Slave Law irritated many Northerners, the Compromise of 1850 definitely favored the free states. They had won control of the Senate (with the admission of California, there were sixteen free and fifteen slave states, and two more free states were soon to come—Minnesota, 1858; Oregon, 1859). Popular sovereignty gave planters a chance in Utah and New Mexico; but a very slender chance, for those areas were not by nature suited to plantation agriculture.[2]

There was much southern dissatisfaction with the Compromise of 1850. Secession was too serious to be taken lightly. But how would the South fare in the Union? Typical of southern thinking was the Georgia platform adopted by a convention which accepted the Compromise, then warned the North that the Fugitive Slave Law must be enforced, and that Congress must impose no new restrictions on slavery in the territories. Otherwise, the South would resist, "even to the disruption of the Union."

In 1850 the whole country was concerned about the sectional conflict. Excitement then died down, and there ensued a brief period of peace. In the presidential campaign of 1852, both major parties upheld the Compromise. The Whig candidate, Winfield Scott, expressed antislavery opposi-

---

[2] The North was further aided by the fact that the Compromise of 1850 postponed disunion for ten years. During those years the free states increased their economic power and thus could crush the South in 1861–65. Things might have turned out differently had the slave states seceded a decade earlier.

tion to certain provisions of the settlement; but the Democratic nominee, Franklin Pierce of New Hampshire, accepted the Compromise as a finality. Pierce's victory suggested popular ratification of the Compromise and a general desire to end sectional hostility.

Good will was further promoted by prosperity. Southern cotton, sugar, hemp, and tobacco found markets in the North and overseas. The march westward of the plantation system provided new opportunities. The West found markets for foodstuffs in a South given over to one-crop staples. Western farmers also profited from new rail connections with the East. Industry in the Northeast flourished as factories found markets in the West and South. California gold forced up prices, feeding further the widening channels of trade. Prosperity clearly rested on economic interdependence of the sections. Outspoken nationalists therefore defended the Union both in patriotic terms and in terms of the economic advantages of a nation-wide market.

Sectional Hostility

Southerners, however, were not satisfied. The North, they said, was getting the lion's share of the nation's wealth. Southern fire-eaters said that an independent South would develop resources more rapidly than a South tied to northern apron strings. A southern nation might also reopen the African slave trade, thus reducing the price of field hands; and, unhampered by northern opposition, the South might snap up territory to the south. Some Southerners deplored this disunion talk; but they too saw danger in the growing antislavery movement in the North.

Sectional antagonism was growing in the North as well. True, antislavery agitation was opposed by northern business leaders who depended on the southern trade. But northern bankers disliked decentralized banking, maintained since Jackson's day by votes of southern and western agrarians. Iron and textile manufacturers blamed southern Congressmen for holding down tariff rates. Northern railroad and steamship promoters objected to slave-state opposition to their plans, as did free-state agrarians interested in homestead or cheap land legislation.

Linked to these economic attitudes was growing opposition to slavery on moral grounds. To be sure, Northerners discriminated against free Negroes in their own communities. But, year by year, more free-state citizens came to feel that slavery was incompatible with Christianity and the Declaration of Independence. Northern Baptists and Methodists gained followers in the 1840's, when they decided to fight slavery. The popularity of Harriet Beecher Stowe's novel, *Uncle Tom's Cabin* (1852), was a symptom and

310 A HISTORY OF AMERICAN CIVILIZATION

cause of the changing attitude. Hitherto, free-state people had thought little about the plantation economy. But now slavery, as depicted in blackest
terms, became a terrible reality.

Uncle Tom's Cabin influenced the South, too. The success of the novel
convinced Southerners that Northerners misjudged slavery and would do
no justice to the South. This view was reinforced by northern opposition
to the Fugitive Slave Law. To Southerners, this spelled treachery—free-
state unwillingness to carry out the bargain made in 1850. Northern foes
of slavery admitted that the law was on the statute books. But, they said,
it was unconstitutional in its denial of jury trial, and immoral (against the
"higher law"). Mobs rescued fugitives seized by authorities. A United
States deputy marshal was killed in the Anthony Burns case. To return this
Negro to bondage in Virginia it was necessary to reinforce the Boston police with 1100 militiamen at the cost of many thousand dollars. And to
prevent rendition of other runaways, northern legislatures passed personal-
liberty acts designed to turn the fugitive slave law into a dead letter.

Kansas and Nebraska

Lingering hopes of peace were dispelled
when the issue of slavery in the territories was reopened in 1854, when
Senator Stephen A. Douglas of Illinois, a Democrat, proposed that Congress organize territorial government in Kansas and Nebraska. Douglas and
his friends wanted a transcontinental railroad connecting St. Louis or Chicago with California. Territorial organization west of Iowa and Missouri
would make possible elimination of Indian claims and encouragement of
white settlement. Then the federal government might subsidize railroad
building with land grants.

The Missouri Compromise of 1820 had specifically barred slavery from
the Kansas-Nebraska region, all of which was north of 36°30'. As a consequence, southern Congressmen opposed territorial organization, so as to
head off settlement and the formation of new free states. Besides, organizing Kansas and Nebraska would thus hurt chances for a southern-based
transcontinental railroad, from New Orleans or Memphis to California.
The United States was not likely to subsidize more than one line.

By 1854, the South had lost control of both houses of Congress. Even
so, slave-state Congressmen retained enough power to delay or defeat measures they opposed. And if such measures passed, they were likely to be vetoed by President Franklin Pierce, who took advice from a Mississippian,
Secretary of War Jefferson Davis. To solve his problem, Douglas made concessions to the slave states. He moved repeal of the Missouri Compromise,
which barred slavery from Louisiana Purchase territory north of 36°30'

Kansas and Nebraska would then be organized under popular sovereignty, used in the Compromise of 1850 for lands recently acquired from Mexico. That is, the actual settlers of Kansas or Nebraska would decide for or against slavery when it was time for statehood. Backed by White House pressure, Douglas pushed the Kansas-Nebraska Bill through Congress, and it became law (1854).

Douglas figured that, after the first wave of excitement, the arrangement would satisfy both North and South. Slave states would have access to a region from which they had been barred by the Missouri Compromise of 1820. Free-state people should be satisfied, for they were almost certain to dominate the new territories. Geography would exclude slavery from Nebraska, probably from Kansas, too.

As it turned out, Southerners approved the law, Democrats and Whigs alike. But there was lasting opposition in the free states. Northerners had come to regard as sacred the agreement of 1820 reserving the plains country for free settlers. Changing the rules was "an enormous crime." Nor did excitement die when the bill was passed. Encouraged by the popular reaction, antislavery leaders adopted two new lines of strategy. One was to combine all opponents of the Kansas-Nebraska Act into a single antislavery party. The other was to win Kansas and Nebraska for freedom.

Free-state forces controlled Nebraska from the start. But Kansas adjoined the slave state of Missouri. Missourians were certain to push west into Kansas Territory, just as Iowans moved west into Nebraska. And that might make Kansas a slave state. To prevent this, political and business leaders of the North financed the free-state settlement of Kansas. Organizations like the New England Emigrant Aid Company established towns at Lawrence, Topeka, and elsewhere. Fighting back, the South also sent in settlers. Proslavery forces won the first territorial elections; and Democratic governors appointed by President Pierce worked with the proslavery legislature. Free-state settlers, however, refused to recognize these officials, and formed their own territorial government at Lawrence. The Lawrence group claimed that the opposition government was illegal, since many proslavery votes had been cast by "border ruffians"—Missourians who had come to Kansas just for the election.

Guerrilla warfare followed. A proslavery band sacked Lawrence. John Brown, a fanatic who believed himself divinely designated to end slavery, butchered five proslavery men on Pottawatomie Creek. Fighting had cost 200 lives and $2,000,000 worth of property when President Pierce established military law (1856).

The Kansas question rose again in 1858, when the proslavery faction tried to get Kansas admitted to the Union as a slave state, under the Le-

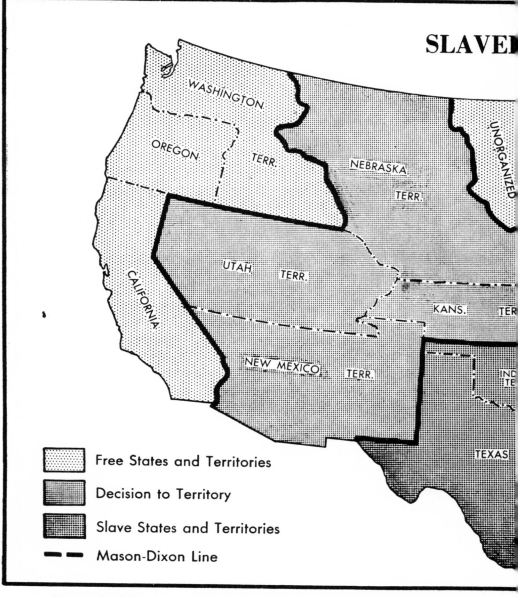

SLAVE

Free States and Territories

Decision to Territory

Slave States and Territories

━ ━ Mason-Dixon Line

During the half-century after the Revolution, slavery faded out in the states
north of the Mason and Dixon line (southern boundary of Pennsylvania).
Meantime, the Northwest Ordinance of 1787 excluded slavery from the
Great Lakes region. When Missouri was admitted as a slave state, the Missouri Compromise of 1820 barred slavery from all remaining Louisiana Purchase territory north of 36°30′ (southern boundary of Missouri). This held
for three decades, and was not changed by the annexation of Texas and
the settlement of the Oregon question (Texas entered the Union as a slave
state; and Congress barred slavery from the Oregon country). The Mexican
cession of 1848 raised new questions. The result was the Compromise of
1850. California became a free state, and the popular sovereignty principle
was applied to Utah and New Mexico—that is, the inhabitants could vote

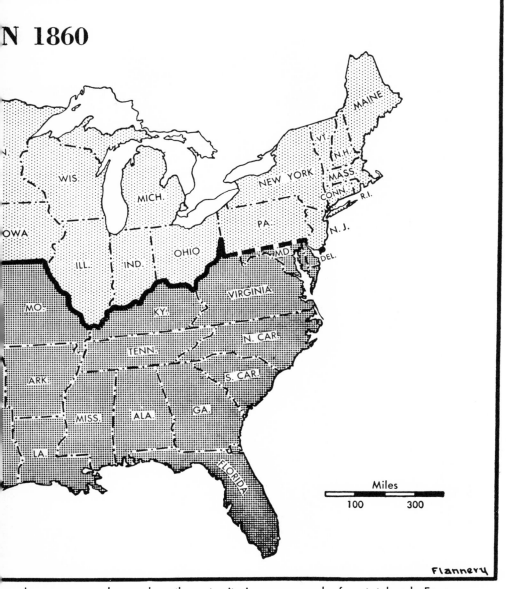

Miles
100   300

Flannery

slavery up or down when these territories were ready for statehood. Four years later Congress repealed the Missouri Compromise and applied popular sovereignty to Kansas and Nebraska. The Kansas-Nebraska Act did not apply specifically to the Indian country (Oklahoma), where slavery had long existed. Nor did it apply to Minnesota and Oregon (admitted as free states in 1857 and 1859), or to the Washington Territory and the unorganized territory west of Minnesota (both free by Congressional legislation of the 1840's). In the Dred Scott decision of 1857, the Supreme Court ruled that Congress could not exclude slavery from any territory; but many Northerners refused to consider themselves bound by this decision. In 1861, during the Civil War, Kansas was admitted as a free state; and in 1862 the Union Congress outlawed slavery in all the territories.

compton Constitution. By that time most residents of Kansas were against slavery. Nonetheless, Pierce's proslavery successor as President, James Buchanan, ordered all Democratic Congressmen to approve. Many northern Democrats refused; Stephen A. Douglas, for one, said that this was a violation of popular sovereignty. So the Lecompton Constitution was set aside.

Three years later, on the eve of the Civil War, Kansas came in as a free state. By then squabbles over Kansas had increased sectional animosities and weakened the national political parties, which had long served to hold North and South together.

Breakdown of National Political Organization: Collapse of the Whigs

The breakdown of the national political parties had begun before the passage of the Kansas-Nebraska Act of 1854. An early indication of the coming trend was the founding of the strongly antislavery Liberty party in 1840. The major parties (Whig and Democratic) bid for votes all over the country. The Liberty party largely confined its appeal to the free states. Concentrating on the single issue of slavery, it polled few votes in the presidential contests of 1840 and 1844. It then gave way to a stronger sectional organization, the Free-Soil party. The Free-Soilers attracted some farmers and urban workers by declaring for free homesteads. More important, they gained as the Wilmot Proviso controversy intensified the antislavery views of northern Whigs and Democrats. Thus the Free-Soil party was able to present a strong ticket in the presidential race of 1848—Martin Van Buren, a former Democrat, and Charles Francis Adams, an ex-Whig. (Van Buren had been President of the United States, Adams was the son and grandson of Presidents.)

The Compromise of 1850 checked the growth of the Free-Soilers, whose vote fell off in 1852. But the Compromise also shook the major parties. The Whigs suffered most. The old Whig leaders, notably Clay and Webster, had favored compromise. But both these leaders died in 1852. Their successors were more insistent on sectional programs, less willing to yield ground. Representing the new attitude were Thaddeus Stevens of Pennsylvania and William H. Seward of New York, both bitter antislavery men; and Alexander H. Stephens and Robert Toombs of Georgia, vigorous advocates of southern rights.

Here was no minor split; it was irreconcilable division. In the last Whig convention (1852) it took fifty-three ballots to name a presidential candidate. The party had already lost many southern Whigs to the Democrats. Others deserted during the campaign, when the Whig nominee, General

Scott, expressed mild antislavery views. Total collapse came two years later, when the Whigs proved unable to define party policy on the Kansas-Nebraska Bill.

When the Whig party died, some politicians wanted a new national party. One result was the American or Know-Nothing party, created in 1854 and based on antiforeign feeling. In the North the Know-Nothings attracted workers who feared job competition from immigrants; Protestants disturbed because most immigrants were Catholic; those who disapproved of the Democratic party's success with newly naturalized voters; individuals who enjoyed the secrecy of the Know-Nothing lodges; politicians who saw a new path to political preferment. Southern lodges also drew militant Protestants, power-hungry politicians, and those who loved secrecy; also persons weary of the slavery issue and not a few who hated immigrants because the flow of Europeans to free states had swelled the prosperity of the North.

Rising overnight, the Know-Nothings achieved impressive victories in 1854. Nearly half the Congressmen chosen that fall were members of lodges; and the Know-Nothings talked of carrying the country in the next presidential contest. But the party faded quickly. Prejudice against newcomers was a feeble basis for national political organization. What was more, northern and southern nativists split on slavery. Antislavery politicians left the lodges when the proslavery element won control of the national party machinery. Hence Millard Fillmore, first and last Know-Nothing presidential candidate, made a poor showing in 1856.

Former Whigs made still another effort to organize on a national basis —the Constitutional Union party, which opposed the current trend toward sectional division and stressed devotion to the nation and national unity. In 1860 the party nominated an old-Whig ticket (John Bell of Tennessee and Edward Everett of Massachusetts). But the party polled few votes, its approach being out of line with the sectional emphases of the day.

Breakdown of National Political Organization: Rise of the Republicans

The force of sectional antagonism was revealed in the failure of the Whig, American, and Constitutional Union parties to maintain successful national organization. Illustrating the same point was the success of the frankly sectional Republican party. This party was launched in 1854, as a result of the Kansas-Nebraska struggle. As early as February, 1854, a local gathering at Ripon, Wisconsin, foreshadowed the creation of a new antislavery party. On July 4, a mass meeting at Jackson, Michigan, set up a state-wide organization and, recalling Jefferson, proposed the name Republican. By fall there were enthusiastic workers in most free states. National organization was effected that winter, and the Republicans were ready to challenge the Democrats in 1856.

Like the Liberty and Free-Soil parties, the Republican organization was northern-based and opposed to extension of slavery. Free-Soilers like Charles Sumner of Massachusetts and Salmon P. Chase of Ohio joined the new party. The Republicans also appealed to northern voters who had considered the Free-Soilers too extreme. The party thus won antislavery Whigs like William H. Seward of New York, who became a Republican leader in the Senate; antislavery Democrats like John C. Frémont of California, the first Republican candidate for the presidency; antislavery Know-Nothings like N. P. Banks of Massachusetts, first Republican Speaker of the House.

In 1856, Republican spellbinders talked of "bleeding Kansas," and of the Sumner-Brooks affair.[3] They also wooed laborers, whom Horace Greeley of the New York *Tribune* had long befriended. They went after the votes of free-state farmers eager for cheap or free western land. They worked among newly naturalized immigrants, who, despite their Democratic affiliations, had no stomach for slavery. They courted nativists in centers of Know-Nothing strength, tried to annex the antiliquor vote in temperance areas. The Republican presidential nominee, Frémont, failed to defeat James Buchanan, the Democrat. But Frémont ran far ahead of Millard Fillmore, the Know-Nothing, and gave Buchanan a close race. The Republicans, then, had replaced the Whigs as a major party. The shift was significant. The Whigs had been a national party and had compromised sectional differences. The Republicans were a free-state group, and sought advantage for their section.

Breakdown of National Political Organization: The Democrats Divide

After 1856, all eyes were on the Democrats. So far they had weathered sectional storms to remain a national party. Could this continue? No one could be sure. The party had lost antislavery members to the Free-Soilers in 1848, when national Democratic leadership had condemned the Wilmot Proviso. Party endorsement of the Kansas-Nebraska Act had caused other northern Democrats to desert, to the Republicans. Meantime, southern Whigs had joined the Democrats, increasing slave-state strength within the party and threatening to turn the Demo-

---

[3] In the spring of 1856, Senator Sumner, a bitter foe of slavery, had denounced southern leaders in intemperate language. Aroused by these attacks, Congressman Preston Brooks of South Carolina had caned Sumner into insensibility. This episode made Brooks a hero in the South, a villain in the North. Republicans used the incident as campaign material, citing it as an example of southern "chivalry."

cratic organization into a southern instrument. Stephen A. Douglas and others still hoped to keep the party national. But the task was difficult. Although the Democratic Presidents of the decade were Northerners— Pierce, 1853–57, and Buchanan, 1857–61—both were under southern influence.

Then came the Dred Scott case, decided by the Supreme Court in 1857. Scott, a Negro slave of an army surgeon, had been taken from the slave state of Missouri to the free state of Illinois and to Minnesota Territory, from which slavery had been barred by the Missouri Compromise. Had residence on free soil made Dred Scott a free man?

At this time the Chief Justice was Roger B. Taney, a slave-state Democrat. Serving with him were four other southern Democrats and two northern Democrats, in a court of nine. By a party division (7–2), the Democratic justices decided that Dred Scott, being a Negro, was not a citizen; hence his case could not be considered in the federal courts. The judges might have stopped right there. But Taney and his colleagues chose to try to settle the thorny question of slavery in the territories. They ruled that temporary residence in Illinois or any other free state did not affect the status of a slave. As for Minnesota Territory, a majority of the Court held that Congress had no power to bar slavery from any territory. In other words, the Missouri Compromise was unconstitutional, since the Constitution forbade the federal government to deprive any person of property without due process of law.

President Buchanan hoped that the decision would settle the slavery controversy. But Republicans refused to accept Taney's views, and denounced the Supreme Court. Southern Democrats welcomed the decision as giving them the right to take slaves to any territory. Northern Democrats were less pleased, for it was difficult to reconcile the verdict with Douglas' popular-sovereignty principle.

The issue came to a head in debates held in Illinois in 1858, between two candidates for election to the United States Senate—Stephen A. Douglas, the incumbent Democrat, and Abraham Lincoln, his Republican opponent. Lincoln, then unknown to the nation, was a self-made lawyer who had served one term as a Whig Congressman. Taking the initiative at Freeport, Illinois, Lincoln asked Douglas if he still believed in popular sovereignty, and, if so, how he reconciled that belief with the Dred Scott decision. This put Douglas in a tight spot. If he junked popular sovereignty, he would alienate Illinois voters. If he rejected the Dred Scott decision, he would displease southern Democrats and lose all chance of getting a Democratic presidential nomination. Seeking a way out, Douglas said that the Supreme Court was right—slavery could not be barred from any territory.

But, by refusing to enact a slave code, a territorial legislature could effectively exclude slavery, since no owner would take his slaves into a territory where local police regulations did not protect his property. This Freeport doctrine satisfied Illinois, which reëlected Douglas to the Senate. Southerners, however, denounced the Little Giant as a traitor.

With this fight, and the struggle over the Lecompton Constitution, the Democratic party split wide open. The climax came in 1860, when the Democratic national convention met at Charleston. Southern Democrats wanted the party pledged to Congressional protection of slavery in the territories. Northern Democrats, committed to the Freeport doctrine, refused. A large number of slave-state Democrats thereupon walked out; and the Democratic party had divided on sectional lines.

There were two Democratic tickets in 1860. Douglas was backed by the party's northern wing and by some southern Democrats. The more ardent champions of southern rights supported John C. Breckinridge of Kentucky, who ran on a platform which asserted the beneficial character of slavery.

Lincoln Is Elected President

The division of the Democrats played into the hands of the Republicans. Seeing their opportunity, Republican managers set out to capture every vote they could. To win northern moderates, the Republican platform of 1860 condemned John Brown, who had led a raid into Virginia for the purpose of inciting a slave insurrection. The Republicans also said they would not interfere with slavery in the states where it existed. To please foes of slavery, the Republicans denounced the Dred Scott decision and declared against any extension of slavery. To catch farm and labor votes, the platform promised 160-acre homesteads free to those who wished to settle on the public domain. There was something for the northern industrialist and railroad promoter, too—endorsement of the old Henry Clay program of a protective tariff and internal improvements at federal expense.

The logical Republican candidate in 1860 was William H. Seward of New York. But, like other prominent politicians, Seward had many enemies. Then, too, he had offended moderates by speaking of an "irrepressible conflict" between North and South. In the end the Republicans nominated Abraham Lincoln, who, being less well known, had fewer enemies. Besides, as an Illinoisan, Lincoln would be likely to carry the doubtful states of Illinois and Indiana; as a self-made Westerner, he would have popular appeal.

There were four candidates in 1860: Lincoln, the Democrats Douglas and Breckinridge, and Bell, Constitutional Unionist. The first two were free-state men, the others from the slave states. One Southerner, Bell, and one Northerner, Douglas, sought votes North and South by stressing national ties, by talking of moderation and compromise. The other Southerner, Breckinridge, and the other Northerner, Lincoln, appealed chiefly to their own sections. The Breckinridge Democrats called on the slave states to unite against the northern foe. Lincoln Republicans told free-state voters that they needed control of the government to promote northern interests.

The outcome showed that Americans North and South had gone beyond compromise. Lincoln and Breckinridge, who used sectional appeals, polled more votes than did Bell and Douglas, who favored adjustment of sectional differences. Douglas and Bell picked up a few electoral votes in the border slave states; but Breckinridge carried the rest of the South and Lincoln triumphed in the free slates. Since the North was more populous than the South, this gave Lincoln a majority of the electoral votes and the presidency.

The Republican victory was not complete. The party failed to capture either house of Congress. What was more, Lincoln was a minority President. Although he had a majority in the electoral college, he polled nearly a million less votes than his opponents, in a total of less than 5,000,000. Lincoln was backed by only 40 percent of those who went to the polls. In the whole of American history, no other candidate has carried the electoral college with so small a percentage of the popular vote.

Such an analysis indicated that southern politicians had no reason for despair. But the distribution of votes showed one thing more. If all ballots cast for Douglas, Breckinridge, and Bell had been given to any one of these, Lincoln would still have won a majority in the electoral college. That is to say, the Republicans had won control of the free states; and controlling the free states meant controlling the nation. Realizing this, several southern states prepared to leave the Union.

The Secession Movement

During the 1860 campaign southern extremists declared that election of Lincoln would justify secession. In December, 1860, a month after the returns were in, South Carolina severed all ties with the Union. Georgia and the states bordering on the Gulf of Mexico followed suit, and in February, 1861, the seceded states formed a new union, the Confederate States of America. Jefferson Davis of Mississippi and Alexander H. Stephens of Georgia were chosen as President and Vice-President of the Confederacy. The Confederate Constitution in general resembled that of the United States; but there were key differences. The

Confederate government was denied the right to interfere with slavery in the states, or to pass tariff or internal improvement legislation.

In defending secession, the Confederate states said they were merely exercising their constitutional right to resume sovereign powers which they had delegated to the central government. This was necessary, they said, in view of the transformation of the federal Union into a centralized government dominated by the North. The northern reaction was one of bewilderment. A few free-state men said good riddance, that (in the words of Horace Greeley) the erring sisters should be permitted to go in peace. Some Northerners believed southern leaders were bluffing, that patience would bring the South back into the fold. Others argued that peace and the Union were worth some sacrifice. Perhaps the North should offer a new compromise—say, constitutional amendments prohibiting interference with slavery in the states where it existed, and permitting slavery in territories south of 36°30′.

Compromise also appealed to some Southerners, especially in the border states. Ex-president John Tyler of Virginia headed a peace convention which met in Washington in February, 1861. But the convention failed, for, despite talk of compromise, neither Northerners nor Southerners were willing to give way on vital points.

When the peace convention met, James Buchanan was completing his term in the White House. (Lincoln, elected in November, 1860, was inaugurated in March, 1861). Old and weary, Buchanan did his feeble best for compromise. He urged northern legislatures to repeal personal-liberty acts, which interfered with enforcement of the Fugitive Slave Law. The President also denied the right of secession. At the same time, he held that the Constitution gave the federal government no power to coerce the states. This was in contrast with the stand taken by Jackson in the Nullification controversy; and it was in contrast with the views of Lincoln.

President-elect Lincoln worked out his program at home in Springfield, Illinois. Yes, he favored compromise within limits. He would accept a constitutional amendment prohibiting interference with slavery where it existed. He would consider improving enforcement of the Fugitive Slave Law, if free Negroes were protected from possible enslavement. But that was all. Lincoln would not allow slavery in any territory whatsoever. He specifically opposed (thus killed) the Crittenden Compromise, proposed by a Kentucky Senator who, among other things, wanted slavery protected in territories south of 36°30′.

If Lincoln had been willing to give way on this point, would the South have yielded? Probably not. Proslavery extremists felt that no guarantee could protect the South in a Union dominated by Republican politicians and by the commercial and industrial forces of the North. The Crittenden Compromise, peace convention, and other last-ditch stabs at sectional adjustment had come too late.

Lincoln and the Union

The incoming President had to make one more basic decision. He had to decide whether he would use force to prevent disunion. Lincoln's answer stemmed from his background. Raised on the frontier, influenced by Clay and the American system, he was a nationalist who took pride in the union. He had only scorn for the states'-rights arguments of secessionists. He liked Jackson's Nullification Proclamation and rated Webster's supernationalist reply to Hayne as the "grandest specimen of American oratory."

Hoping to keep the border slave states in the Union, Lincoln avoided violent denunciation of the South in his inaugural address (March 4, 1861). But he made his meaning clear. He called the Union "perpetual." Secession, then, was unconstitutional; and it was Lincoln's intention to have the laws "faithfully executed in all the States."

Although he here hinted at coercion, Lincoln did not want to strike the initial blow. If the Confederates fired first, they would appear as aggressors. The North and possibly the border states as well would then forget petty squabbles and "defend the Union." So it turned out. When seceding, the Confederates had taken over most federal forts and arsenals in the South. A few, however, had remained in Union hands. Chief among these was Fort Sumter in Charleston Harbor. Lincoln finally decided to send a relief expedition to supply the garrison holding this fort. Meantime, South Carolina secessionists brought matters to a head by demanding immediate surrender of the fort. After brief resistance, the Union garrison surrendered (April, 1861). This incident aroused the people of the free states. Indecision disappeared; citizens rallied to the flag when (on April 15) Lincoln called for volunteers. The South also completed preparations. When Lincoln adopted coercive measures, Virginia, North Carolina, Tennessee, and Arkansas joined the deep South in the Confederacy and dug in for war. But the border slave states of Maryland, Delaware, Kentucky, and Missouri were kept within the Union by persuasion, economic interest, and force. So was West Virginia, a new state made up of Virginia counties opposed to the Confederacy.

Even at the end, few wanted war. Conflict came because existing machinery for settling controversies broke down under the pressure of conflicting interests and emotions. The machinery had worked before, because of devotion to the nation and the technique of compromise. But compromise called for some sort of balance between sections. With the rapid rise of northern power, sectional balance was destroyed and could not be restored. As the free states grew stronger, those in charge of northern interests felt their views must prevail. As the slave states grew weaker, those who controlled the South felt they must defend their institutions at any cost.

13

Trial by Combat

Significance of the Civil War (1861–65)

To most poets, novelists, and historians, the Civil War is still "our greatest war." Why so? In part, because it was a brothers' battle; the divided loyalty of border people provides a romantic theme. There is further appeal in field operations, for this struggle was full of dashing cavalry raids and hand-to-hand engagements. Casualty lists also show the impact of this conflict. Of the 2,500,000 soldiers involved, one in four was killed in battle or died of wounds or of disease. This was a very heavy toll. It is roughly equal to the total number of American soldiers and sailors lost in the American Revolution, War of 1812, Mexican and Spanish-American Wars, and two World Wars, all put together.

Nor is that all. The Civil War advanced American nationalism. It ended Negro slavery, forcing readjustments in race relations. And the conflict gave certain economic groups power they would long retain.

The last point was apparent even before hostilities began. The secession of southern states removed from Washington Congressmen who had long opposed bills designed to aid northern enterprise. Their departure cleared the way for adoption of such bills; and the Hamilton-Clay policy of favoring commercial and industrial development won out at last. Take the tariff. Southern agrarians had long opposed the protective principle, and had helped keep rates down. When the Southerners left Congress, protectionists rushed the Morrill Tariff bill through both houses early in 1861. Signed by Buchanan just before Lincoln's inauguration, this high tariff set the pattern for decades to follow.

Clay's American system coupled tariff demands with insistence on federal financing of internal improvements. Here, too, there had been opposition from the South, as when southern politicians had fought suggestions that the United States support the building of a transcontinental railroad across northern territory. With southern votes eliminated, northern sponsors of that program secured generous land grants from Congress; and by 1869 the Northeast and Middle West had their first rail connection with the Pacific coast.

The growing power of northern business is seen in other legislation. In 1864 Congress passed a contract labor law, aiding manufacturers who imported cheap foreign labor. The same year saw the creation of a national banking system. This system differed from that of the first and second Banks of the United States. Instead of a centrally controlled institution with branches, the national banking system of 1864 provided for separate national banks in different localities. Still, these banks were established on a single pattern; and after 1865 (when state bank notes were taxed out of existence) they had a monopoly of note-issuing power. The national banking system thus pointed toward that uniformity and stability which northern merchants and manufacturers desired.

Business groups were not the only beneficiaries of legislation adopted after secession. Western farmers as well as financiers, traders, and industrialists wanted the transcontinental railroad. The Lincoln administration also saw the creation of a United States Department of Agriculture and the passage of the Morrill Land Grant Act, under which the federal government gave land to universities which provided instruction in agricultural and mechanical subjects (1862). A homestead law of 1862 provided that in some western districts 160-acre farms would be given free to any who settled and improved those holdings. Here, as with the tariff, secession eased the way for passage. Southern Congressmen had opposed homestead legislation, fearing it would help free-state rather than slave-state farming interests.

Secession, then, made it easier for northern economic groups to obtain what they wanted. Why, in that case, did the South secede? Partly, no doubt, because Southerners felt that the northern groups were bound to win anyway. The South could be outvoted in either house of Congress; and, with Lincoln's election, a northern party had secured control of the patronage. Plainly, Southerners could expect little from Washington. In their own Confederacy, they could protect their own institutions, keep the tariff down and be sure their taxes were not used for another section's benefit. They could seek advantage in direct negotiations with foreign countries, and might embark on expansion southward.

That represented future possibilities. In setting up the Confederate States of America in 1861, Southerners had to concentrate on immediate aims. It was quite a job to create governmental machinery in a hurry. More difficult was the never-to-be-completed task of persuading all slave states to secede. Meantime, Confederates had to prepare for war.

Northern Advantages and Southern Hopes

At first glance it looked like an unequal struggle. There were 8,000,000 people in the seceding states, against 23,-000,000 in the states that remained in the Union. For military purposes the disproportion was greater, since more than a third of the South's population was in Negro slaves, rarely used as soldiers. On top of that, northern banks were stronger than southern institutions. Northern merchants had more ready capital than did Southerners, whose wealth was tied up in land and slaves; and the Union controlled California, with its gold supply. The free states were far ahead in industrial production, and many northern factories could be converted into war plants. As for transportation, the South had lagged in railroad building; and railroads had become a key to military victory.

Sea power also fought on the Union side. Although many Regular Army officers took Confederate commissions, Lincoln retained nearly all the ships, officers, and enlisted men of the navy. The North also had a great merchant marine and a long-established shipbuilding industry. Thus the North could secure goods from Europe and interfere with Confederate supply lines. Naval might also contributed substantially to Union striking power, as in the Mississippi River campaigns.

Yet the South did not despair. Some secessionists felt that the North would not fight at all. Even if it came to blows, the South could count on divisions and indifference in the free states. And the Confederacy would be fighting on the defensive, as had the colonies in the American Revolution. To emerge triumphant, the North would have to crush southern armies, occupy the southern states. The secessionists had no such need for total victory. They could establish independence merely by continuing resistance until the Union gave up the struggle.

Though the North was ahead in financial resources, the South had enough gold and supplies for a short war.[1] Confederate leaders counted also on the value of interior lines and the fact that they would be fighting on their own soil. That should draw southern whites together, make them feel that theirs was a fight for home rule, a struggle for survival.

King Cotton Diplomacy

Finally, the sponsors of secession hoped that Great Britain would help the South. Southern reasoning was based on King Cotton. British prosperity depended in good part on cotton textile

---

[1] In weighing southern attitudes, it should be remembered that there had been no major war in the Western world since 1815; consequently, the military importance of railroads and industrial resources was inadequately understood in 1861.

factories, which obtained raw material from the southern part of the United States. Could Britain allow itself to be shut off from its supply? Would not the British recognize the independence of the South and cut through a Union blockade, even if doing so meant involvement in the American Civil War?

To back up the King Cotton theory, Confederate agents went to Europe, talked to diplomats, and carried on a propaganda war. They stressed the desire of the Confederacy to trade with Europe. They denounced the Union policy of recruiting soldiers in Ireland and Germany. They played on the British businessman's dislike for the Union's new Morrill Tariff. They courted French Emperor Louis Napoleon, who had shown New World ambitions by invading Mexico in 1861. Winning sympathy in many circles, they were able to float loans on European money markets. And, despite Lincoln's objections, Britain and other countries accorded the secessionists belligerent rights. This was not outright recognition; but it was more than rebel status.

The Southerners were also able to buy supplies and a few ships in England. The vessels included the Confederate cruisers *Alabama*, *Florida*, and *Shenandoah*. Britain did not allow the Confederates to build armed ships. Still, it was easy to run unarmed vessels out of port and have them pick up armament from other ships at sea. Thus transformed into privateers, vessels built in Britain preyed on Union shipping. Insurance rates soared, and many Union shipowners transferred to British registry.

Promising though this seemed, it did not win the war. Reconsidering, Britain shut off the South's supply of vessels; and one by one the Confederate privateers were eliminated by Union men-of-war. Even at their peak effectiveness, the raiders were not able to take on the Union Navy, or break the blockade, or stop the flow of goods between the North and Europe.[2]

Plainly, the South had expected too much of King Cotton. Shortage of cotton caused suffering and an increased relief burden in British factory towns. But England had a good supply at hand when hostilities began, a carry-over from bumper crops of prewar years. As this supply dwindled, Brazil, Egypt, and India took up cotton growing—not too difficult a task, since cotton is an annual. And, as cotton textile output declined, manufacturers of woolen and linen goods increased production.

---

[2] British soil was again used when Confederates operating from Canada raided St. Albans, Vermont, in 1864. Such incidents, and a general feeling that Britain favored the Confederates, increased Anglophobia in the North. As a consequence, many Americans encouraged the Fenians, Irish revolutionaries who invaded Canada from the United States in 1866. But most Anglo-American problems were ironed out in the Treaty of Washington (1871). Among other things, this treaty settled the *Alabama* claims, Britain eventually paying $15,500,000 for having neglected her duties as a neutral in the case of the Confederate cruisers.

King Wheat was also in the picture. Britain needed grain for her urban population. American wheat was especially important in the 1860's because of disappointing crops in Europe. In addition, the Union provided a first-rate market for British manufactured goods. London was reluctant to sacrifice this trade by lining up with the South, and in any case preferred to avoid a costly war.

Northern diplomacy played along with this situation. The Union complained about British aid to the Confederacy but, where possible, tried not to force issues. Thus, when a northern naval officer removed two Confederate diplomats from a British vessel (the *Trent*), Lincoln released the envoys to avoid a diplomatic crisis. In like fashion, the North was careful to avoid a rupture with Louis Napoleon, despite French invasion of Mexico. Napoleon, in return, stayed out of the Civil War. (He withdrew from Mexico in 1867.)

So the South had to fight alone. With European allies, she might have won the war, just as the thirteen colonies had made good their secession movement eighty years before. Without European aid, the thirteen colonies could not have succeeded; and, lacking allies, the Confederacy failed.

War Plans

The Civil War was among the first conflicts in which railroads and ironclad vessels were used. The Union experimented with photography, military aviation (observation balloons), and machine guns; and the Confederacy boasted, in Robert E. Lee and T. J. (Stonewall) Jackson, two of the greatest military men of modern times. On the other hand, both sides made colossal blunders, threw away battles and campaigns. Far too frequently military efficiency yielded to personal ambition, petty greed, and party politics.

Confederate strategy was defensive. Southern armies made a few thrusts into the free states, as in the Gettysburg campaign. By and large, however, secessionists concentrated on defending frontiers, fighting until the Union became discouraged or Britain came in on the southern side. For four years the Confederates worked on this plan, under the guidance of Jefferson Davis. President Davis lacked the romantic qualities of Lee. Davis was nervous and irritable, offended subordinates and failed to inspire confidence among the people. Still, the Confederate President was a man of talent. A West Point graduate, he had fought in the war with Mexico, had wrestled with administrative problems while Secretary of War under Pierce. He had also been Senator from Mississippi, and one of his region's major politicians. This background proved of value in 1861, when Davis and men of his selection had to build an army overnight.

Considering the difficulties, they did well. In the states'-rights South, they created a national army—developed a uniform system of raising and organizing troops. Local-minded states did hold on to arms and men which the Confederacy could have used. Still, the record of the secession government compares favorably with that of the "national" North. In selection of commanding officers, Davis did better than Lincoln. The Southerners, of course, were hampered by shortages; but they made the best of their situation. They obtained goods through the blockade and captured supplies from the Union. Such factories as they had (for example, iron works in Richmond) operated full blast. This output was supplemented by blacksmith shops. Plantations and smaller farms shifted from cotton to subsistence crops, and the South fought on.

Given the Confederate strategy, it was necessary for the Union to plan its offensive skillfully. This was clear to the ranking Union general, Winfield Scott. Old Fuss and Feathers was in his seventies, so infirm that he could not mount a horse. Yet he retained the keenness he had demonstrated in the wars with Great Britain and Mexico. As Scott saw it, the Union should start with sea power—shut the Confederates off from outside aid by a tight blockade. Then, after careful preparation, the Union could smash in Confederate defenses, cut the enemy in half, and squeeze life out of what remained.

Scott's plans were not adopted; instead, the General was retired. He was an old man, discredited by political defeats; and he urged caution when others demanded speed. Scott, moreover, felt it would be necessary to conquer the whole Confederacy. Most Northerners considered this ridiculous, and maintained that the Davis government would collapse like a house of cards when Union regiments marched against Richmond, the secession capital.

The Eastern Theater

This was not the case. When hastily assembled Union regiments marched across Virginia in July, 1861, they were whipped in the first battle of Bull Run and fell back in panic. President Lincoln then gave the chief command to General George McClellan, a vain but competent commander who put the northern forces into fighting shape. McClellan planned to take Richmond from the rear in his Peninsular campaign of 1862. His movements, though, left Washington partly uncovered. Lee and Jackson took advantage of that, Jackson striking north into the Shenandoah Valley, where he overwhelmed an assortment of Union political generals (amateurs who had been given stars because of their political importance). So spectacular was Jackson's showing that Union officials feared for the safety of their capital. Hence troops earmarked for McClellan's Peninsular campaign were kept in front of Washington; and Little Mac's offensive failed (early summer, 1862).

Republican politicians had never liked McClellan, knowing him to be a Democrat. His failure to take Richmond gave them a chance to clamor for his removal. Yielding, Lincoln changed commanders; but John Pope, a favorite of the politicians, was badly beaten by Stonewall Jackson at second Bull Run (August, 1862). Lincoln next called back McClellan, who checked Lee when the Confederates invaded Maryland. But when McClellan failed to follow up his advantage after the bloody battle of Antietam (September, 1862), he was dropped for good.

After that, Lincoln relied chiefly on General H. W. Halleck, a bookish soldier stronger in military theory than in ability to meet real situations. Old Brains, as he was called, was General in Chief, roughly the equivalent of the Chief of Staff in World Wars I and II. That is, Halleck helped the President and Secretary of War organize military effort and set up campaigns. Details of operation were left to field commanders. In Virginia, this meant relying on such incompetents as Ambrose Burnside and Joseph Hooker. These generals were no match for Lee and Jackson, Burnside being soundly thrashed at Fredericksburg at the end of 1862, Hooker at Chancellorsville in May, 1863. (But the South, too, lost at Chancellorsville; Stonewall Jackson was mortally wounded.)

Encouraged by victories, Lee invaded the North. In July, 1863, he was stopped at Gettysburg, Pennsylvania, by George Meade. Meade, like McClellan at Antietam, failed to make the most of his opportunities; and the Confederates fell back into Virginia. At that time, the North and South had been at war for more than two years. The secessionists had done exactly as planned: they had defended their frontiers against attack. The Union, by contrast, had failed to conquer the seceded states. Lincoln's regiments were as far as ever from Richmond.

Time, though, worked with the Union. Despite conscription, Confederate man power was running low. Southern morale was ebbing, too, for it was now apparent that European powers would remain aloof, and that the North was in to stay. It was also clear that, after many blunders, the North had found out how to win the war. By 1863 the Union had given up its three-to-nine-months' enlistment policy and was recruiting men for three years or the duration. Trained officers, mostly West Pointers, were replacing the political generals. Supply and transport, though still mismanaged, were improved; and there was some effort to train recruits for combat rather than parade.

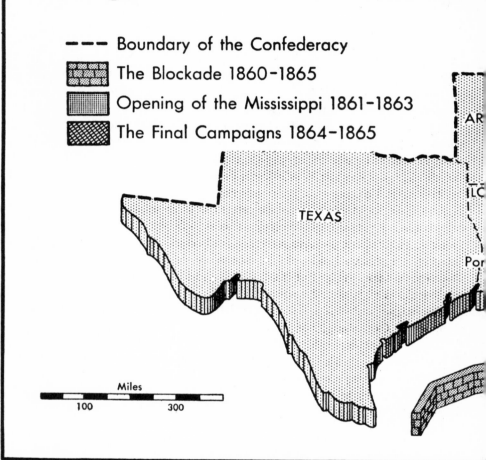

CONQUEST OF THE CONFEDERACY

- – – Boundary of the Confederacy
- The Blockade 1860-1865
- Opening of the Mississippi 1861-1863
- The Final Campaigns 1864-1865

AR

ILC

TEXAS

Por

Miles

100   300

Though never totally effective, the blockade greatly aided the Union cause. Then, in 1863, the northern forces took the Mississippi, cutting the Confederacy in

THREE STAGES

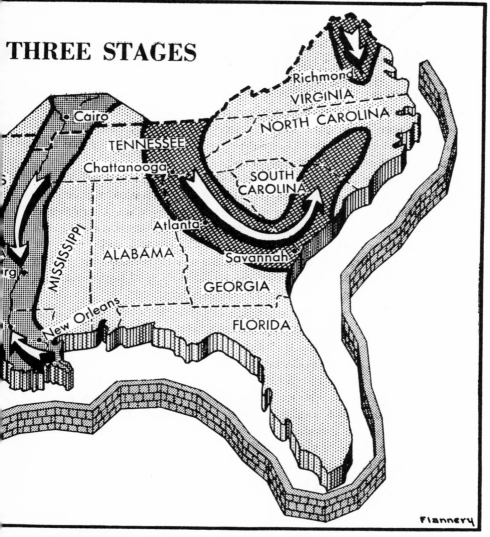

two. The stage was set for the inevitable final push. Grant next drove on Richmond, while Sherman pressed in from the other side; and the war was over.

Dividing the Confederacy

While improving on land, the Union made good use of sea power. The blockade of the South was never totally effective, for the Confederacy had 3000 miles of seacoast, and bordered Mexico. Still, Union operations made blockade running dangerous and sharply reduced southern trade with the outside world. Nor did naval activity stop there. Early in 1862, David Farragut established control of the mouth of the Mississippi River, enabling Union forces to take New Orleans. Northern gunboats were already active on the upper Mississippi; and in 1863 they helped clear the river of Confederates.

The campaigns on the Mississippi showed the changing Union concept of the war. Gone was the early notion that taking Richmond was enough; now northern leaders were giving their attention to the whole Confederacy. The Mississippi was especially important, since its possession would split the Confederacy in two. This would hurt southern morale and deprive the Southeast of products and man power of the trans-Mississippi area, not to mention trade with Mexico. Finally, the Mississippi would supply a starting point for a drive into the heart of the Confederacy.

Ulysses S. Grant was the chief figure in the western campaigns. Grant was not brilliant; he was outguessed by A. S. Johnston at Shiloh (1862), outmaneuvered by Robert E. Lee in the Wilderness (1864). But Grant was bold and daring. He cared less for supply lines than for a chance to strike the foe. Knowing that the North had numerical superiority, he insisted that the Union should advance and keep right on advancing. That would mean heavy losses but would save men in the end. It would force the South to use up her resources and, when they were gone, to surrender.

Early in the war, Grant took Confederate positions which controlled the Tennessee and Cumberland rivers (Forts Henry and Donelson). In 1863, he moved against Vicksburg. This fortified Mississippi town was a key to the Mississippi River and the western terminus of the vital Savannah-Vicksburg Railroad. Failing in two attempts to take the place by storm, Grant dug in for a siege. Those inside hoped that Confederate forces would come to their assistance. Hopes faded when the weeks went by, as the inhabitants of Vicksburg were reduced to eating rats and mules. After six weeks of resistance, Vicksburg surrendered (July, 1863), in the week Lee lost to Meade at Gettysburg. Now the North had a firm grip on the Mississippi. ("The Father of Waters," wrote Lincoln, "flows again unvexed to the sea.") In hard fighting in east Tennessee, Union forces then secured permanent control of the Chattanooga railroad center. The sands of the Confederacy were running out.

The Last Campaigns

At this juncture Grant was summoned east to take command of all Union armies. His plan was simple. He would take charge in the East, would smash through Lee's lines to Richmond. Meantime William Tecumseh Sherman, operating out of Chattanooga, would pound in from the other side.

It took a year to work this out—from the spring of 1864 to the spring of 1865. The Southerners contested every inch of soil. Defending Georgia, Joseph E. Johnston fought delaying actions, burned bridges, wrecked railroads, slowed Sherman's advance to less than two miles a day. Meanwhile, Lee gave ground slowly in Virginia, punishing Grant severely in the battle of the Wilderness.

Sherman broke through first, and in the summer of 1864 captured Atlanta. That fall he marched on through Georgia to Savannah by the sea, living off the country and wrecking what was left of the Confederacy's communications. Early in 1865 he swung north through the Carolinas, planning to join Grant in Virginia.

That proved unnecessary. Despite heavy losses, Grant had pushed Lee in close to Richmond in the summer of 1864. The Confederates held their ground in the fall and winter; but numbers finally told. The spring of 1865 saw Grant with 120,000 men, double the strength of his opponent. Lee then tried to pull out of Richmond, to join Joe Johnston to the south. It was too late. The Union cut off all lines of retreat, and on April 9, 1865, Lee surrendered. Confederate commanders in other theaters followed suit; and the Civil War was over.

Raising Troops

The average soldier did not think in terms of campaigns. His job was to fight, march, and fight some more. Many citizens took on this work with enthusiasm. Others were less eager, or lost their zeal in the months of struggle. Class lines had something to do with this. Many poorer southern whites fought with vigor, convinced that they were defending southern rights and their own homes. Others, including many hill farmers, grumbled that this was all to help the planters, a "rich man's war and a poor man's fight." Did not the Confederate conscription law of 1862 exempt from military service white men who supervised fifteen slaves? And should one fight to enrich southern cotton speculators and war-profiteering manufacturers? Such thoughts kept many from enlisting, caused others to resist the draft or to desert after induction. Disaffection grew as the southern cause faded; altogether there were a quarter-million desertions from Confederate regiments.

The Union figure was even higher. Most volunteers were given cash when they enlisted. Many enlisted for the bounty (several hundred dollars), then deserted to enlist again for another bounty in another state. Bounty jumpers were aided by bounty brokers, who bribed recruiting officers to accept the physically unfit. Enlistments being on a state and local basis, it was difficult to catch offenders.

The Union's conscription system, organized in 1863, made things worse. The idea was to encourage volunteering rather than raise a draft army; districts furnishing enough volunteers were given no draft quotas. Rich areas, offering large bounties, drew in recruits from poorer regions. These districts received credit for the enlistments and did not have to call on their own residents to serve. But poorer districts, without credit on the books, had to supply draftees from their already reduced man-power pools. This amounted to class discrimination. So did the rules of 1863, under which a man could escape service by paying $300 or hiring a substitute. Dissatisfaction flared up in the Draft Riots of 1863. A thousand persons were killed or wounded in New York City in a four-day uprising. Being Democrats, Irish-Americans of New York tended to be hostile to Lincoln's administration. Many were anti-Negro and antiabolitionist, and felt the war was being waged to benefit those hated groups. But most of all, opposition to the draft was due to favors given the well-to-do. The first draft lists were loaded with names of workingmen; and rioters cried "Down with the rich!" as they raced through the streets, smashing windows, burning houses, and lynching Negroes.

The Soldier's War

Those who bore arms found the Civil War no picnic. The South was so short of men that it rarely gave furloughs; and, since mails worked badly, southern soldiers could not keep in touch with home. Confederate units were short of locomotives, freight cars, wagons, mules, ordnance, and quartermaster stores. Most serious of all was a shortage of artillery. As for small arms, most southern regiments used smooth-bore muzzleloaders of the vintage of 1812. Moreover, secessionists had to husband caps and ammunition, and watch their food supply.

By comparison, the Yankees lived like kings. To weary Southerners, it seemed as though their enemies had an exhaustless store of ammunition, and dined on oranges and lobster. But Union troops had their problems. Lincoln's inefficient War Department bought shoddy uniforms which turned to tatters after a march; shoes with soles that fell off when one stumbled; tents which disintegrated in inclement weather. Although breechloading rifles were obtainable, the North's military leaders were content with old-fashioned muskets with a tenth of the rifle's fire power. General in Chief Halleck made a spirited defense of smoothbores as late as the winter of 1862–63. Although the Union spent enough to feed its men well, the average soldier often received moldy meat and hardtack. Some of the hardtack was marked "B.C." Not the manufacturer's initials, privates insisted, but the biscuit's age. After digging out worms, those with strong teeth could gnaw at what was left; but most preferred to soften the stuff by soaking it in coffee or boiling grease.

Both sides supplemented army rations by "living off the country," requisitioning supplies along the line of march. This practice had military merit —it increased mobility by reducing dependence on supply lines. But those who lived in devastated districts suffered deeply. Conditions grew worse as supplies dwindled. Philip Sheridan, who wrought great havoc in the Shenandoah Valley, boasted that a crow flying across that area would need to carry its provisions. Sherman did an even more thorough job in Georgia. The worst excesses were the work of stragglers and irregulars; the Union commander did not approve of indiscriminate looting. But Sherman did use destruction in a conscious attempt to wreck the Confederate economy and shatter southern morale. Not content with such halfway measures as pulling out railroad spikes, he had his men heat the rails and wrap them around trees. This helped the North win the war—and left the South in sad shape when peace came.

Although there were sieges, this was more a war of movement than of position. When possible, commanders moved troops and supplies by train or steamboat. But generally soldiers marched, stumbled along Virginia's plank roads, struggled through Louisiana mud. They picked their way across corn and cotton fields, cut through the tangled underbrush of southern woodlands. It was tough going. Some deserted. Others fell sick and died in the wretched shelters that served as camp hospitals. It was everywhere the same—dysentery, typhoid, scurvy, jaundice, syphilis, plain exhaustion, all sorts of unlabeled aches, pains, coughs, fevers. Camps were deadlier than battlefields; disease claimed twice as many as were killed in action or died of wounds.

Hoping to correct this situation, army doctors used quinine to protect soldiers against malaria, attacked smallpox with vaccination and revaccination. Union commanders fought yellow fever in occupied New Orleans by enforcing quarantine regulations and cleaning up the city streets. Voluntary bodies like the United States Sanitary Commission equiped and supplied hospitals; male and female nurses performed heroic labors. (One of these, Clara Barton, later organized the American Red Cross.) But both sides, and the Confederates especially, were short of physicians, nurses, and supplies. Neither made effective use of knowledge then available in sanitation.

The major battles were brief but bloody encounters involving from ten to fifty thousand on a side. Some engagements dragged out for a week. More commonly, battles were decided in part of a single day. Battles were normally preceded by cavalry maneuvers as scouts tried to determine enemy positions. The Confederate cavalry had the edge for most of the war. Since cavalrymen were the eyes of nineteenth-century armies, this was an important advantage, and helps explain some stunning southern victories.

As battle neared, each side sought a strong position, preferably an elevated location commanding an enemy flank. The foes then felt each other out in an artillery duel, lasting about an hour. Here the North had the advantage, with better guns and more ammunition. While the big guns boomed, skirmishers felt their way forward, using such cover as the area afforded. When they met stiff opposition, the skirmishers fell back, or called for reinforcements. Then the main forces worked into position, and the critical moment was at hand.

The more confident commander ordered an advance, by company or regiment or along the whole line. Sometimes there was an attempt to catch the enemy off balance, as in striking heavily on one flank. Often, however, the opposing forces met head on. The character of the advance varied with the terrain. It ended in a charge, with the advancing soldiers screaming as they ran. (Here came the rebel yell, and Yankee variants.) The purpose was to reach the enemy and whip him in close combat. If repulsed, the attackers moved back, re-formed, and tried again. Or the other side came forward, for both prized "possession of the field." In the crucial moments, the whole emphasis was on attack. Instead of seeking cover, advancing soldiers came on in formation, and fell back only when their lines were torn to shreds. Heavy losses were expected, and general retreat was thought of as disgraceful. "Honor and glory are before us," said one officer (later killed in action). "Shame lurks in the rear."

With such fierce fighting, the issue was quickly decided. Civil War commanders therefore tended to throw in all reserves at once, before the enemy could make its full force felt. And when the battle ended, both sides were exhausted. Rarely did a victor have strength to follow up his triumph by pursuit of his adversary.

War Finance

Although the North had ample economic resources, it was slow and inept in organizing war finance. The war began in a period of business uncertainty. After Lincoln's election most Pennsylvania, Maryland, and Virginia banks suspended specie payment. Even greater strain came when the outbreak of war lessened the value of southern state bonds, widely used as security for the currency of western banks.

Salmon P. Chase, Lincoln's Secretary of the Treasury, believed the war would be over in a few months. He therefore did not press for a large increase in taxes, and placed the main burden of financing on bond sales. But bonds sold slowly, forcing Congress to issue currency without specie backing in 1862—the so-called greenbacks.

Congress also increased taxes in 1862. An income tax was tried: 3 percent on incomes from $600 to $10,000, 5 percent on higher incomes. (The latter figure was later doubled.) This was an important precedent in fiscal policy; but repeal in 1872 left undecided the questions of the ethics and constitutionality of income taxation. The war Congress also raised tariff duties and imposed excise taxes. Little was overlooked—there were inheritance taxes, stamp taxes on legal papers, gross receipts taxes, taxes on the transfer of real estate, licenses for professions. But even in 1865 taxes were meeting only 25 percent of war costs. Borrowing by long-term bonds remained the Union's chief reliance.

To speed bond sales, Chase entered into a marketing agreement with Jay Cooke. This investment banker used two thousand house-to-house canvassers, who sold support of the war along with the bonds. Cooke's profits were enormous; but the government got its money's worth.

The problem of selling bonds was one factor behind the creation of a national banking system. The National Banking Act of 1863 provided for the creation of privately owned national banks—new institutions or state banks interested in taking out federal charters. National banks could issue bank notes, using Union bonds as security for note issue. This, it was thought, would promote bond sales. The law also aimed at a uniform currency. Fifteen hundred state-chartered banks issued 5000 kinds of notes, of which there were 7000 known varieties of counterfeits. Since all banks had suspended specie payments by the end of 1861, it was virtually impossible to distinguish sound from weak bank notes. Sponsors of the national banking system hoped that chaos would give way to order with the appearance of bond-secured notes of the national banks. The new system met with opposition, and was not well established until the war was over. Then, in 1866, Congress imposed a prohibitory 10 percent annual tax on the notes of state-chartered banks.

By twentieth-century standards, Union financing in the Civil War was only mildly inflationary. Banks created proportionately less credit based on government securities than in later wars. Bonds sold to individuals in return for real savings are not inflationary, and Cooke's selling policy operated in this direction. The supply of currency and credit was increased by the issue of $250,000,000 in state bank notes and twice that amount in United States government greenbacks; but there was no runaway inflation.

Nor did the Union have to meet any such strain on the national income as in the World Wars. The Civil War cost the North $3,000,000,000, a fifth of the national income for these four years. For an equal period World War II took nearly half the national income. Wholesale prices, unchecked by rationing or controls, did rise alarmingly during the Civil War (around 130 percent). But much of the upsurge was due to inefficient government purchasing rather than to monetary, loan, or taxation policies.

The Confederacy had more difficult problems. Southern money income came largely from cotton sales overseas. In 1861, the South withheld cotton, hoping a shortage would bring Britain into the war. Later, the Union blockade made exporting difficult. Moreover, the South shifted many acres from cotton to food crops. Inevitably, then, planters lacked current savings to invest in bonds, and lacked cash income which could be taxed for war purposes. The South did have a substantial supply of gold and silver in 1861—specie held by the banks, coins and plate owned by wealthy Southerners. The government obtained the bulk of the bank holdings, by the specie loan of 1861. Most of the privately held gold and silver, however, went into hiding and was of no use to the cause.

The Confederacy eventually explored every source of revenue. Southerners paid taxes on business and excess profits; on real and personal property; taxes in kind on farm produce. There were graduated income taxes, license and distillers' taxes, customs duties. All rates were raised in 1864, and Congress added a 30 percent sales tax. Still another raise was voted in March, 1865, as the secession government collapsed.

High though they were, the taxes produced little revenue. Collection was never easy, and became impossible as Union troops occupied southern areas. It was necessary, therefore, for the South to rely on borrowing and on the printing presses. Bonds sold in London and Paris enabled the South to secure some vital goods. But the totals were small, and were cut by mismanagement. Domestic borrowing also broke down. A loan of May, 1861, was less than half subscribed at the end of the year, though one could pay in cotton or produce as well as specie. By 1864 there was no market for Confederate bonds offered at six cents on the specie dollar. By then the Confederates were relying on unsecured paper currency. There was runaway inflation in the last days of the war; but it is hard to see how this could have been avoided.

The War Economy, North and South

In the long run, accumulation of savings in Union bonds made capital available for expansion. In the short run, however, the Civil War depressed the volume of investment in useful goods and delayed industrialization of the North. At the outset, war demands failed to compensate producers for loss of the southern market. There was a lively demand for war supplies: woolen textiles, shoes, munitions, and (especially) food. But much of this demand might have developed in peacetime, had there been a continuation of the economic expansion of the early 1850's.

In the South, the prospect was appalling, the result calamitous. Facing a powerful foe, the Confederacy concentrated with some success on increasing industrial output. But in speeding up production the Southerners used up existing equipment; and Union armies destroyed southern capital when they invaded the Confederacy.

Both contestants had to meet wartime needs with less than the usual number of workers. The armed forces drew off 15 percent of the labor force. This increased the desire for labor-saving machinery. Such machinery was not to be had in the Confederacy. Some was available in the North. Still, installing machinery took time, and high prices placed a check on this means of meeting demand. Western wheat farmers replaced harvest hands by mechanical reapers. Elsewhere, those in war production found it easier to use existing equipment and to attract workers from idle peacetime industries.

In spite of the need for labor, immigration remained at the low level to which it had fallen in the recession of the middle 1850's. In 1862, 72,000 immigrants arrived, the smallest number for any year from 1843 to 1932. Fear of the uncertainties of war was a factor. The Union Congress tried to increase the flow by the law of 1864, which reaffirmed the legality of importing foreign workers bound to labor contracts. This statute, however, did not change the situation.

North and South, inflation redistributed wealth. High prices shifted purchasing power from those living on wages, salaries, and interest to those able to secure profits. From 1862 on, entrepreneurs, including farmers, enjoyed prosperity. Shares rose on stock markets, inventories increased in value, debts diminished in importance. Many railroads were saved from bankruptcy by higher rates and increased army traffic. The temporary halting of construction also gave lines a chance to accumulate surplus funds for future development. Meantime, speculators and war contractors amassed fortunes. The concentration of wealth brought lower standards for less-favored classes. Despite trade-union activity and strikes, real wages in the Union were 25 percent lower in 1865 than in 1860. The urban middle classes also felt the pinch, as did government employees.

When fighting started, the South was short of industry, transportation, and food. Shifting to a war economy was too great a task for private enterprise alone. The Confederate government therefore set up mills, mines, and factories. The central and state governments also subsidized key private industries, and took a share in blockade running. At the same time public officials urged household production on each farm and plantation, and a shift of acreage from cotton to food crops. As a result, the South became almost self-sufficient. Her industrial structure, though, was primitive. There was ever a shortage of capital, materials, experience, and transportation. Branch-line railroads had to be torn up to repair main lines. Surplus food from remote districts never reached the Confederate armies; and in the end the secession movement failed. The failure cannot be called surprising. The surprising thing is that the South held out so long.

Politics in the Confederacy

On both sides, it was politics-as-usual during the Civil War. Many Confederates, like President Davis, had been lifelong Democrats. Even there, there were divisions, between Breckinridge and Douglas Democrats. Other Confederates, including Vice-President Alexander H. Stephens, were ex-Whigs. There were also former Know-Nothings, and moderates who had belonged to the Constitutional Union party in 1860. Old party wrangles were combined with personal squabbles. Politicians who failed to obtain good appointments complained that the Confederate cabinet was made up of nonentities, that Davis preferred mediocrity to talent. No love was lost between Davis and his Vice-President, and the southern Congress never learned that coöperation with the executive was a necessity in war.

Political quarrels also reflected sectional conflict. War did not wipe out the differences between the tidewater and interior, the contrasts between the upper and lower South. Local pride was linked with the states'-rights issue. Before secession, most Southerners had eagerly defended the rights of states as against the government of the United States. But did this mean the rights of southern states as a regional unit, or the rights of each state by itself?

The South as one unit, said Davis and other southern nationalists. The rights of individual Confederate states must not weaken the common cause. Victory was impossible without coöperation; seceding states must hold together to win the war. Many southerners took a contrary view. Vice-President Stephens and Governors Joseph E. Brown of Georgia and Zebulon Vance of North Carolina talked of states' rights in the Confederacy as they had in the Union. They tried to prevent Davis from controlling troops and supplies. They talked of tyranny, resisted martial law, interfered with conscription, and sabotaged impressment legislation. In the early fighting, governors withheld arms needed by the Richmond government. Later, governors refused to release state troops they did not need. Some gave way at the end, but others were still standing on principle when the Confederacy fell in ruins.

Politics in the Union

The rights of states also plagued the Union government. Maryland and other border states used states'-rights arguments in efforts to persuade the national government to restrict its activities within their borders. All through the North, state officials tried to control recruiting and equipping of troops and the commissioning of officers. Some governors, like John A. Andrew of Massachusetts and Horatio Seymour of New York, were openly critical of Lincoln's conduct of the war. There were efforts (as at the Altoona Conference of 1863) to form a united front of governors against the President. But the Washington government won out. Most Northerners saw the war as a fight for the nation. In addition, the governors quarreled among themselves and fell down on their job of raising and supplying troops. And a very able politician, Abraham Lincoln, was on the national side.

When he became President in 1861, Lincoln lacked the background of Jefferson Davis. Many Northerners considered him a crude, unpolished local politician too inexperienced to handle national problems. The Union President proved this estimate erroneous. Lincoln made mistakes, but demonstrated a real talent for holding the North's war machine together. He maneuvered carefully, balancing factions, now yielding, now insisting. He was cautious, patient, practical; and he usually had his way.

Much of Lincoln's work centered in the Republican party. In 1861, this party was a loose federation of state organizations. There was no real party leadership, and the Republicans were a miscellaneous lot. Personal ambition was another problem. At least two members of the cabinet— Secretary of State William H. Seward and Secretary of the Treasury Salmon P. Chase—hoped to shove Lincoln aside after a single term and succeed him as President. Instead of dropping these officers for insubordination, Lincoln kept them both. In time he managed to get Seward to work with him. Chase was more difficult, but Lincoln preferred to have him inside rather than outside of the administration. He was shelved in 1864 by an appointment as Chief Justice of the Supreme Court.

Deeper than individual discord was a struggle between the major Republican factions, the moderates and radicals. By modern standards, these terms are misleading. Neither faction was anti-business. Both favored a protective tariff, just as both favored homestead legislation to please farmers and laboring men. The basic conflict involved other matters, notably the Negro question, treatment of the South and control of patronage.

The radical Republicans included many who had long been bitter foes of slavery—Chase, Sumner, Benjamin F. Wade, Thaddeus Stevens. These radicals favored vigorous prosecution of the war and no compromise with southern whites. They felt that leading secessionists should be severely punished, stripped of land and political rights. The radicals also centered attention on the Negro, for they felt that the Civil War must be, not only a fight for the Union, but also a war for immediate emancipation of the slaves, without compensation for owners. In addition, the radicals believed that the North should allow Negroes to serve as Union soldiers—colored men from the free states, runaway slaves who reached Union lines, field hands in southern areas occupied by northern troops. And, as the war continued, the radicals were more and more inclined to extend the vote to men of color.

The moderate Republicans included Seward, and such border-state politicians as Attorney General Edward Bates of Missouri. They advocated caution and conciliation, felt that the question of the Negro should be subordinated to the issue of maintaining the Union. After all, they said, there was anti-Negro sentiment in the free states, and four border slave states were loyal to the Union. If emancipation proved desirable, the moderates were inclined to think that it should be gradual rather than immediate. They also favored compensation for owners, or loyal owners, anyway. Moderate Republicans tended to disapprove of Negro suffrage, since most free states barred Negroes from the polls. They were disinclined to favor use of Negroes as soldiers. Nor did they want all-out confiscation of the property of secessionists; harsh treatment might stiffen southern resistance and prolong the war.

Lincoln was a moderate. Though he chose coercion in 1861, he believed basically in adjustment and compromise. He stressed the Union, not the slavery question, and said he welcomed the support of loyal slaveowners. He refused to support John C. Frémont when that politician-in-uniform proclaimed emancipation of the slaves of Confederate sympathizers in Missouri, in August, 1861. When Union regiments took over southern territory, the President was more interested in winning over the inhabitants than in punishing secessionists. He was displeased when General Benjamin F. Butler irritated the citizens of occupied New Orleans; and he replaced Butler by a moderate, N. P. Banks.

Ending Slavery

By 1862 and 1863 political pressure and the necessities of war led Lincoln to adopt some radical measures. As volunteering fell off, the President came to favor the enlistment of Negroes; and by the end of the war there were 100,000 in the Union forces. Lincoln also moved against slavery. In a preliminary Emancipation Proclamation (September, 1862) he announced that he proposed to outlaw slavery in all areas still in rebellion at the end of the year. Three months later, Lincoln issued the final Emancipation Proclamation, effective New Year's Day, 1863.

The Proclamation did not in fact end slavery. For one thing, Lincoln was acting on doubtful constitutional authority, under powers as Commander in Chief. Then, too, the proclamation did not apply to areas under Union control—border slave states and Confederate districts occupied by northern armies. Beyond the Union lines, of course, Lincoln's authority was not respected. Hence it could be said that the proclamation freed no slaves and was a "declaration of purpose only."

The announcement pleased few except the radical Republicans. Southerners were more convinced than ever that they must fight to the end. Border-state citizens and Northerners grumbled that Lincoln was turning a war for the Union into a war for the Negro. Volunteering lagged after the preliminary proclamation, and there was a slump on the New York Stock Market. Lincoln's party lost ground in the elections of 1862 and looked like a poor bet for 1864. But in the longer view, the emancipation move helped the northern cause. The war remained primarily a struggle for the Union; but now it was also a fight for human liberty. This gave satisfaction to more and more Northerners as time passed.

As war dragged to an end, there was little doubt that slavery would go down. Since Lincoln's proclamations were of doubtful constitutionality, and limited to certain areas, it seemed best to have legislative action. Early in 1865, Congress proposed a Thirteenth Amendment, banning slavery and involuntary servitude, except as a punishment for those convicted of crime. Emancipation was to be immediate, uncompensated, and universal, there being no exception for Union areas or loyal slaveowners. Ratification by the states was completed after Lee's surrender, the Thirteenth Amendment being added to the Constitution in December, 1865.

In declaring for emancipation, Lincoln satisfied the radical Republicans; but he did not join them. He was especially opposed to radical plans for the postwar treatment of the South. Lincoln and his moderate Republicans favored reconciliation and reunion after fighting was over, with a quick restoration of southern states to their former position in the Union. Radicals preferred to postpone restoration, to treat the states which had seceded as conquered provinces pending a general reorganization of the South's political and economic structure. Radicals did all they could to wreck Lincoln's program, as set forth in his Ten Percent Plan of December, 1863. The President, in turn, killed by pocket veto the Wade-Davis Bill of 1864, embodying a radical reconstruction program. The sponsors of that measure then denounced the Chief Executive in the violent Wade-Davis Manifesto.

The Election of 1864

The radical Republicans also tried to prevent Lincoln's renomination for President in 1864. They talked of the "salutary one-term principle," no President since Jackson having served two terms. They backed fellow radicals for the succession. Though Chase was their favorite, they also boomed Ben Butler and Frémont. In the ante-bellum era, Frémont had been a moderate Republican, Butler a doughface Democrat. Political ambition and quarrels with Lincoln changed them during the Civil War; and in the spring of 1864 Frémont allowed one group of radicals to nominate him for President. He withdrew later, and the radical Republicans generally supported Lincoln for reëlection. But they did so with ill grace, and criticized the President during the campaign.

While wrangling with the radical Republicans, Lincoln also worked on the war Democrats. When war broke out, the Union President sought the backing of Democrats as well as Republicans. He gave military jobs to Democrats, brought a Democrat (Edwin M. Stanton) into his cabinet as Secretary of War. This worked so well that the Republicans chose a Democrat as Lincoln's running mate in 1864—Andrew Johnson of Tennessee. And for that campaign, the Republicans changed the party's name to National Union. This made possible a broad appeal, and contributed to Lincoln's triumph.

Most Democrats, however, remained in their own party. While they backed the war effort, they were very critical of the administration. Some raised the cry of inefficiency, or claimed that the Republicans represented business rather than the common people. Others concentrated on the war-weariness of many Northerners. Although they lacked outstanding leaders, Douglas having died in 1861, the Democrats did have some able chieftains, including Horatio Seymour of New York. They were thus able to make a strong showing at the polls in 1862; and with General McClellan as their presidential candidate, they nearly defeated Lincoln two years later.

In fighting Democrats, the Republicans sometimes used force. Lincoln having suspended the writ of habeas corpus, some members of the administration felt that they were free to arrest whom they chose and to clamp down on opposition newspapers. The New York World was seized for a time in 1864. Out in Ohio, General Ambrose Burnside, objecting to a speech made by Clement Vallandigham, arrested that antiadministration Democrat. Although civil courts were open, Burnside proceeded by court-martial; and, by Lincoln's order, Vallandigham was expelled from the country.

In general, the Republicans used words instead of violence. They appealed to patriotism, denouncing Democrats as "Copperheads," Northerners whose hearts were with the Confederacy. Although the accusation was unjust, it made some impression, and helped protect the administration's narrow margin of control. The Republicans were further favored by soldier ballots. Furloughs were arranged for election time, and there was in addition a good deal of absentee balloting, voting in the field.

Victorious in November, 1864, Lincoln began his second term as President in March, 1865. By then, the war was drawing to a close. Immediately ahead was the problem of the treatment of the conquered Confederacy. The radical Republicans, strong in Congress, were determined to have what they would call "thorough" reconstruction. The President was just as insistent that there must be "no persecution, no bloody work, after the war was over." So he said in his last cabinet meeting, just after Lee's surrender. But the job of reconstruction would be left to others, for on that same day, April 14, 1865, Lincoln was shot by John Wilkes Booth.

14

Reconstruction

Union soldiers occupied parts of the former Confederacy for a dozen years (the Reconstruction era, 1865–77). And military occupation ended long before Americans had solved the problems which had grown out of the Civil War.

The Republicans Plan Their Future

In the Reconstruction period the Republicans of course wanted to control the patronage. They also desired legislation favorable to the economic interests which they represented. To effect these ends, it was necessary to control the presidency and Congress, and as many state governments as possible.

In 1865 it was far from certain that the Republicans would be equal to the task. They were divided among themselves. More important, they had been a minority party before secession, Lincoln owing his first election to a divided opposition. Although they had managed to control the loyal states during the war, their margin had been small. In 1865 the Democrats were strong in New York, Ohio, and Indiana. The Republicans were none too well established in the border states; and their party had virtually no strength further south.

What to do? The Republicans decided (1) to strengthen their hold on northern states; (2) to work for admission of new states likely to vote Republican; and (3) to keep secession states out of the Union until a Republican party was built in the South.

In the North traders, industrialists, and financiers helped the Republicans by providing funds, votes, and newspaper space. In return, Republican legislators saw to it that the United States retained the protective tariff policy established in 1861. More than that; Congress increased protection by repealing certain war taxes without repealing compensatory tariff duties. The income tax was dropped, as were other measures unpopular with businessmen. The Republicans also pleased their economic allies by taking a "sound money" stand, supporting the new national banking

346

system, resisting debtor demands for inflation, and seeing to it that holders of government bonds were paid off in gold (that is, with a handsome profit).

While bidding for business backing, the Republicans also appealed to the veteran, farmer, and laborer. A Republican-sponsored eight-hour law of 1868 reduced the working day for laborers employed by the government. Republicans pointed with pride at the establishment of a Department of Agriculture; the Morrill Land-Grant Act, promoting agricultural education; the Homestead Bill. To please northern veterans, Republicans pushed through pension laws. The Grand Army of the Republic, the chief organization of Union veterans, was predominantly Republican. Party orators also wooed the boys in blue by "waving the bloody shirt." That is, they charged that the Democratic party was the party of secession and rebellion.

Meanwhile, Republicans brought in states likely to vote Republican. Kansas had become a state in January, 1861. West Virginia, carved out of Virginia (1863), and Nevada, brought in during 1864, added strength to the Republican cause during the war. Reconstruction saw the addition of Nebraska (1867) and Colorado (1876). Except for West Virginia, which went Democratic one time out of four, these states were Republican in presidential contests from 1864 to 1876.

Some Republicans wanted to add other states, agitated for annexation of all or part of Canada. If successful, this drive would have brought in additional Republican states, besides adding to the national wealth. The movement failed but, failing, had significance. To keep Canadians content within the British Empire, London gave Canada dominion status (1867). And, although they did not acquire Canada, Republican annexationists in the United States picked up votes with the issue—notably from Irish-Americans, ever anxious to embarrass Britain.

Reconstruction and Political Alignments

While the Republicans bid for northern votes, the Democrats were far from idle. They retained control of the political machines in New York and other northern cities. Seymour and other northern Democrats had personal followings. Although the party contained men of wealth, it appealed to workingmen who disapproved of the tie between Republicans and businessmen. What was more, certain Democrats were mild inflationists, and won support from debtor farmers. As an example, George H. Pendleton of Ohio urged that the United States use greenbacks to redeem Union bonds which did not specifically call for payment in specie.

Having strength in the North, the Democrats felt they could recapture the federal government as soon as the South came back into the fold. The South was more likely to vote Democratic than Republican; and it promised to be stronger than ever in Congress. Before secession, a slave had counted as three-fifths of a free person in figuring representation in the lower house. After emancipation, each Negro, like each white person, counted as a full individual (five-fifths); and southern representation was proportionately increased.

Given this situation, the Republicans felt that their retention in power depended on ability to handle the southern question. But how? Lincoln moderates insisted that the southern states had never left the Union and should be readmitted to representation in Congress as soon as possible. Southerners should be required to abandon secession and slavery, and repudiate the Confederate debt; that was all. Moderates hoped thus to reunite North and South and build a strong Republican party in the South. Lincoln and his moderate Republicans felt that such a party should be based on the poorer southern whites. Negroes could be brought into the picture gradually. Lincoln felt that the vote should be extended first to literate Negroes and to men of color who had served as soldiers. Progress must be slow, said the moderates. Former slaves were "not ready" for full participation in politics. It was also feared that giving the ballot to all Negroes would antagonize southern whites and drive them into the Democratic camp.

The moderate view was set forth in Lincoln's proclamation of December, 1863, concerning Confederate areas occupied by Union troops. Lincoln offered pardons to nearly all secessionists who would take an oath of allegiance to the Union. When 10 percent of the qualified voters had taken the oath in any state, this group could form a Union government, which would be recognized by Lincoln. Louisiana, Arkansas, and Tennessee set up state governments under this proclamation, and elected Congressmen. When Lincoln died, his successor, Andrew Johnson, recognized the Ten Percent governments and continued the moderate program. His amnesty proclamation of May 29, 1865 pardoned the bulk of those who had fought for the Confederacy. There was no general pardon for high-ranking Confederate officials, officers above the rank of colonel, and property owners worth $20,000. These leaders, though, could obtain individual pardons from the President; and many of them participated in the formation of new state governments after the cessation of hostilities. By the end of 1865, such governments existed in nearly all the ex-Confederate states; and Southerners were clamoring for admission to Congress.

Radical Republicans objected to the moderate program. To begin with, the Lincoln-Johnson plan did not provide punishment. Quite a few Northerners felt that the "rebels" should be made to pay for northern lives lost in the war; southern leaders should be imprisoned, or at least stripped of civil rights and property. Second, radicals said that the moderate formula was unfair to the Negro. Thaddeus Stevens, Sumner, and other radical Republicans felt that the liberated slaves should have a real chance to get ahead in the postwar South. The Negro should have civil rights, perhaps land as well—say, up to forty acres and a mule, to be provided by confiscation of property of white secessionists.

Finally, the radical Republicans said the Lincoln-Johnson approach was politically unworkable. The moderates hoped that conciliation would cause southern whites to abandon old leaders and join the Republicans. But these white Southerners had long been Democratic. Many were sworn enemies of the urban capitalist allies of the radical Republicans. Were such Southerners likely to change overnight? Were ex-Confederates likely to flock to the party of the Union? The radicals thought not; and events of 1865 bore out their judgment. Southern governments set up under Lincoln-Johnson auspices renounced slavery, condemned secession, and embraced the Union. But the governments were not controlled by Republicans. They were run by Democrats, many of the leaders being planter-politicians who had guided the destinies of the South before and during the Civil War.

To radical Republicans, this spelled catastrophe. Were "traitors" to rule the South? Slavery was abolished; but southern legislatures adopted "black codes" that limited the liberty of Negroes. Was that to be allowed? Could "unreconstructed" southern Democrats be permitted to enter Congress and oppose the financial and industrial measures sponsored by radical Republicans? Could Republican politicians let southern voters throw their party out of national power? No, said the radicals, southern states must be kept out of the Union until they were Republican. Having doubts about Lincoln's Ten Percent scheme, the radicals set forth a program of their own in 1864. When Lincoln rejected this (pocket veto of the Wade-Davis Bill), the radicals attacked the state governments set up under the President's plan. All was deadlocked at the time of Lincoln's assassination. Executive authority, as represented by Lincoln, was behind the South's new Union governments. But the radicals, strong in the Senate and House, had not allowed the representatives of these governments to take their seats in Congress.

Johnson and the Radicals

Had Lincoln lived, he might have triumphed on the reconstruction issue. But even Lincoln would have had his hands full. With his death the job passed to Andrew Johnson, who occupied the White House from 1865 to 1869. Johnson was an able, well-meaning man. Though a product of the slave states, he was no ally of planters. Rather, he was an east Tennessee Unionist who spoke for the small farmer. In this he agreed with the radical Republicans. But Johnson was hostile to the northern business leaders who supported the radical Republicans; and, unlike the radicals, he felt that the southern states should be full members of the Union as soon as the war was over.

Johnson could not handle the radicals. Firm to stubbornness, he lacked Lincoln's talent for accommodation and compromise. Johnson also lacked Lincoln's prestige, labored under the handicap of being an accidental President. Then, too, he was not really a Republican; he was a southern Union Democrat who had been put on the Lincoln ticket to attract Democratic votes in 1864. The issue was soon decided. The Congress that met in December, 1865, rejected the state governments set up by Lincoln and Johnson. The President fought back in 1866, vetoing such radical measures as the Freedmen's Bureau and Civil Rights bills. The radicals, however, overrode these vetoes. A showdown followed, in the Congressional elections of 1866. In these contests, Johnson worked with northern Democrats as well as with some moderate Republicans. But the radical Republicans scored a smashing victory, winning control of the Republican party and of Congress.

After that the radicals had their way. They curbed the Supreme Court by limiting appeals from lower courts. They overrode Johnson vetoes and jammed through legislation to reduce presidential power. One law shifted military authority from the White House to the ranking general, Ulysses S. Grant. Another, the Tenure of Office Act, specified that the President could not discharge executive officials without Senate approval. Johnson considered this unconstitutional (and so it was, said the Supreme Court, in the Myers case of 1926). But when Johnson dismissed a radical cabinet member, Secretary of War Edwin M. Stanton, the House impeached the President. Johnson was then tried before the Senate; and, although the charges were absurd, the radicals came within one vote of obtaining the two-thirds necessary for removal (1868).

Radical Reconstruction

Johnson stayed in office; but the radicals had the power. They used it to adopt their own reconstruction program. Having destroyed the Lincoln-Johnson governments, they divided the South into five districts, each under military rule (Reconstruction Act of 1867). This meant that southern states were to be treated as "conquered provinces" and would have no representation in Congress. Southerners would not be able to join northern Democrats in an attempt to overthrow Republican rule.

The radicals did not plan to keep the South out of the Union forever. Readmission was expected after the acceptance of certain conditions, notably ratification of the Fourteenth and Fifteenth amendments, added to the Constitution in 1868 and 1870 respectively. These amendments were designed to curb the old planter-politicians and pave the way for new southern political combinations based partly on the liberated slaves. The Fourteenth Amendment was designed primarily to protect Negroes. It guaranteed all citizens equal protection of the laws, and specified that no person should be deprived of life, liberty, or property without due process of law.[1] The amendment also barred high Confederate officials from officeholding, and ruled that states which barred adult male citizens from voting were to have their representation in Congress reduced. Thus, if the South blocked Negro suffrage, it would lose political strength in proportion. The Fifteenth Amendment centered directly on suffrage, stating that no American could be denied the right to vote because of race, color, or previous condition of servitude.

Republican machines were now organized throughout the South. They centered around the now-enfranchised Negroes, some southern whites from lower economic levels, and persons newly arrived from the North. Leadership was provided by the latter. Protected by the Union's occupation troops, these "carpetbaggers" operated through the Freedmen's Bureau, a war agency that lasted until 1868, and through privately controlled Union Leagues. As organization improved, state after state became Republican. New constitutions were adopted, new legislatures set in motion. Most of the new constitution makers and officeholders were carpetbaggers and southern whites; a few were Negroes. White or black, they were inexperienced and often fumbled badly. Their record was also marred by corruption and extravagance. Still, these new lawmakers did much that was admirable in their brief period of rule. They launched needed public works, encouraged immigration, and planned prison reform. They set about reforming the South's archaic taxation structure. They provided government relief and institutional care for the unfortunate. They gave their attention to the school problem, and laid the foundations for a system of free and compulsory public education.

When "reconstructed," southern states were "readmitted" to the Union (1868–70); and southern Republicans took seats in Congress. Southern states helped elect the Republican Ulysses S. Grant in the presidential campaign of 1868, helped reëlect Grant in 1872. Finally, in the close, dis-

---

[1] This section, written to protect the Negro, was later used to protect the business groups which coöperated with the radical Republicans. In law a corporation is a person. The Fourteenth Amendment thus protected corporations against various reform statutes adopted by the state governments.

puted presidential election of 1876, the electoral votes of military-dominated southern states provided the margin of victory for Rutherford B. Hayes, the Republican, over the Democrat, Samuel J. Tilden.

Democrats Regain Control of the South

That was the end. State by state, control went to the Democrats, and to prewar leaders of the South. At first, the Republicans lost by narrow margins; then they were snowed under, and became a party of no consequence in the South. In 1877, when Hayes removed the last occupation forces, the solid South was a reality. The Republicans maintained an organization, so as to control federal patronage when Republicans were in the White House; but Democrats won all southern election contests.

There were many reasons for the failure of the Republicans in the South. Their organization was known as the party of the Union. In the North, this was an asset; in the South, it was a liability. Quality of leadership was another factor. Many southern Republicans were corrupt. Others were well-intentioned but politically inexperienced.

But above all, Republican failure was associated with the Negro question. To win elections in the South, the radicals had to turn out the Negro voters. Indeed, most of the Republican votes in the ex-Confederate states came from Negroes. The Republicans hoped also to appeal to small white farmers and thus form a combination against the old planter leaders. But this was hard to do. For one thing, the Republican party, with its upper-class business ties, was not the perfect rallying point for a lower-class organization. More important, the proposed combination ran into race prejudice. In the ante-bellum South the white man who owned no slaves had sided with the planters against the enslaved Negro. During Reconstruction, this same white man resented and was reluctant to coöperate with the emancipated black man.

Taking advantage of this situation, the old leaders of the South drove a wedge between the Negro and poorer whites. By the 1870's, small white farmers were joining old planter leaders in ousting carpetbaggers and re-establishing "home rule." Home rule meant white rule, for, despite the Fifteenth Amendment, the southern Negro was kept from voting after Union troops left the South. This was done by force, by such terrorist organizations as the Ku Klux Klan; later, by laws designed to keep Negroes from the polls.

For a time, northern Republicans fought back. They had Congress outlaw the Klan (1871); and they talked of using force to protect the Negro's right to vote. But nothing came of this; and northern Republicans gradually lost interest. The business backers of the party had the legislation they desired—high tariffs, transcontinental railroad measures, and the like. It was not probable that this would be overthrown, for commercial and industrial leaders had strength among the Democrats as well as the Republicans. As for the Republican politicians, they had become so powerful in the North and West that they no longer needed southern votes as desperately as a decade earlier. A Republican, James A. Garfield, was elected President in 1880 without a single electoral vote from the states that had belonged to the Confederacy. So why worry about the solid South?

The Postwar South

Those who controlled Congress during Reconstruction looked on southern problems from the northern point of view. To Southerners, white and black alike, the problems were quite different. In 1865, the great, overpowering fact about the South was devastation. The cotton economy had been disrupted by war, further jarred by emancipation. Southern banks had gone down with the Confederacy. Invasion had meant wholesale destruction, and the South faced the future short of capital, livestock, farm equipment, roads, railroads, factories, and stores.

Some southern leaders gave up. Edmund Ruffin, the agricultural reformer, wrapped himself in the Confederate flag and committed suicide. Others fled. Judah P. Benjamin of the Davis cabinet practiced law in England; and a few moved to Brazil, where slavery survived. But most leading Southerners who lived through the Civil War stayed on in the South. Though reconciled to emancipation, they clung to the plantation system; in their new South, the Negro was to be subordinated though not enslaved, and the small white farmer was to work with the planter to keep the freedman "in his place."

Putting through this program was not easy. Planters lacked animals and seed; and their former slaves had left the plantations. Many owners had to sell part of their land for taxes; even so they could not raise enough capital for efficient operations. Then, too, many persons were demanding the breakup of the plantations. Liberated slaves and landless whites wanted small farms of their own. Yet the planters won. The plantation system could have been eliminated by use of Union confiscation acts, and by new tax legislation, combined with division of tax-delinquent properties. But this was not accomplished. The radical Republicans were so obsessed with politics that they had little time left for the economic problem of the South. (Perhaps, too, they were not so friendly to the Negro as they claimed to be.) Northern capitalists who invested in southern lands also

THE NORTH AND SOUTH IN 1880

PER CAPITA WEALTH

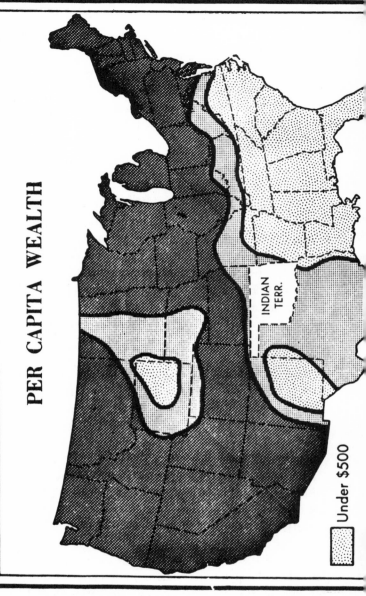

INDIAN TERR.

Under $500

The Civil War and Reconstruction changed, but did not solve, the "southern question." In the years before secession, Southerners had been disturbed because their section lagged far behind the North in economic progress. In 1880 there was a noticeable imbalance of wealth.

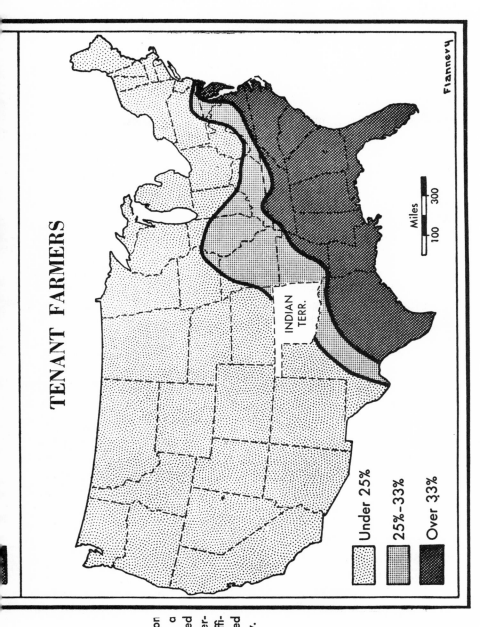

TENANT FARMERS

The end of Reconstruction saw the South, as before, a depressed region. Unsolved race problems were inter-twined with economic difficulties; and the South faced the future with uncertainty.

INDIAN TERR.

Miles
100   300

Under 25%

25%-33%

Over 33%

Flannery

opposed breakup of large holdings. Northerners who lent money to Southerners, or handled cotton transactions, preferred to deal with a few units rather than many. Finally, there was the race question. Small white farmers and Negroes both stood to gain by wrecking the plantation system; but prejudice prevented them from coöperating.

The result was survival of the plantation system, even its expansion, with the opening of new cotton lands in the Arkansas delta country and in Texas, which in time became the leading cotton state.[2] Sharecropping was the key. The owner supplied the land and, generally, seed and equipment, and a shack out in the fields. The sharecropper worked the land and divided the proceeds with the owner. Being without capital, tenants had to borrow or use store credit during the winter and growing season. Slavery was gone, but in its place there was debt servitude.

Some sharecroppers were white. But, though on an economic level with Negroes, white tenants considered themselves superior. As evidence, they pointed to the segregation system, which meant separate though not equal facilities for whites and blacks. There was segregation in the schools, on trains, and on the streets. Negroes could not vote or serve on juries. Intermarriage was prohibited; colored people were excluded from most hotels and restaurants, from the better residential districts, and from most professions. When Northerners criticized this system, southern whites pointed out that there was discrimination in the North, and that segregation was the "solution" to the Negro question. More properly, it was a new and none too satisfactory approach to a race problem which Americans have not yet solved.

Under the sharecrop system, the leading Southerners held their tenants in control. Yet they themselves were far from free. Short of cash, they had to borrow to buy land and move their crops. To make sure of repayment, lenders required borrowers to raise a money crop—in most cases, cotton. This, with other factors, fastened one-crop agriculture on the South, preventing beneficial diversification.

In 1877, Union troops left South Carolina, Louisiana, and Florida, thus completing their withdrawal from the South. By then, cotton production had passed prewar levels. Railroads had been rebuilt and extended, and Southerners were getting ready for a bid in the industrial field. But, to offset these gains, the South had less political influence than ever before. The area was handicapped by a one-party system and a one-crop system. Edu-

---

[2] The United States Census indicated that the South was being broken up into small holdings. But the census counted each sharecrop unit as a separate farm; and the sharecropper was not an independent operator.

cation, though improving, lagged. The bitterness of war remained; and the South was a tributary region, serving an ever-stronger North.

Politics Hits a New Low

Reconstruction was the leading issue after the Civil War. But Americans had other interests during the administrations of Andrew Johnson (1865–69) and Ulysses S. Grant (1869–77). Attention was focused on corruption and reform, business expansion, the westward movement, and diplomacy.

Corruption was standard in southern legislatures, notably during radical rule. Conditions were as bad in the North, where thievery was less open but involved larger sums. These were the years of the Philadelphia Gas Ring; of William H. Tweed, the Tammany boss who fleeced taxpayers of $100,000,000; of railroad magnates who corrupted judges and legislators. National officeholders drained profits from the Union Pacific, through a concern called the Crédit Mobilier. Congressmen voted themselves back pay in the Salary Grab of 1873. The Whiskey Ring, Star Route frauds, and others looted the Treasury. Several of these affairs involved persons high in the Grant administration.

There were signs of what was coming in Grant's first administration. Moreover, Grant was unsympathetic with growing demands for civil service reform. Consequently, some Republicans refused to support Grant for reelection in 1872. Organizing as Liberal Republicans, they backed Horace Greeley, who was also nominated by the Democrats. But Grant won.

As Grant's second term closed, the Republicans chose Rutherford B. Hayes of Ohio as their candidate for 1876. Hayes was abler than Grant, and favored civil service reform. His Democratic opponent, Samuel J. Tilden, was also a reformer, having helped overthrow the Tweed Ring. The political climate seemed to be improving; but the contest ended in a shameful political dispute. At first glance, it appeared that Tilden was elected. The Republicans, however, juggled figures in southern states still under military rule. Congress referred the conflicting returns to an electoral commission, which by a party vote favored Hayes, who was inaugurated in March, 1877.

A National Economy

While squabbling about politics, Americans were celebrating national achievements at a Centennial Exposition at Philadelphia (1876). It was not a perfect year for celebration. Just at this time, Sioux Indians wiped out a detachment under George Custer, at the Little Big Horn. And there was general suffering because of the depression which had followed the collapse of Jay Cooke and Company and the resulting panic of 1873.

Even so, Americans had much to boast about. In 1776, the United States had been thirteen feeble agricultural units strung along the Atlantic seacoast. A century later, there were thirty-eight states, industrial as well as agricultural and, stretching from the Atlantic to the Pacific. Moreover, these states constituted a nation, tied together by bonds of sentiment and economic interest.

Much of the nation's economic progress had been made during the sectional conflict. Before 1845 there were no railroads beyond the Appalachians. There was no telegraph, and express service was confined to the Northeast. Postage rates, charged on a zone basis, ran up to twenty-five cents an ounce. Business tended to be regional rather than national. But by 1861 railroads reached every major city east of the Mississippi and went beyond into Iowa, Minnesota, and Missouri. A transcontinental railroad was completed in 1869. Telegraph lines were strung across the continent even before secession. Express service spanned the nation by 1860, and a three-cent postage rate was in force except for the Far West.

This created a national market. Traveling salesmen were on the first trains of new railroads. New agencies supplying credit information made it safe to do business at a distance. Goods from eastern factories broke down local price agreements. Nation-wide competition brought new sales methods and national advertising. With orders coming in by telegraph, with shipments moving by fast freight, the tempo of business quickened.

Central commodity exchanges—the Chicago Board of Trade (grain), the New York Produce and Cotton exchanges—established national markets. The New York Stock Exchange assumed new importance as railroad corporations increased in size and as industrial firms became corporations with publicly owned stocks. Quotations were carried by telegraph all over the country, and Wall Street became the center of American finance.

Settling the West

In 1850, when California was admitted to the Union, an enormous gap separated that state from the others. Filling the gap contributed to making the American economy national.

As early as 1844 Asa Whitney sought a Congressional land grant to help finance a transcontinental railroad. By 1850 such a plan seemed sensible; but politics delayed action. Proslavery forces wanted the railroad to run from New Orleans or Memphis. Antislavery men preferred a railhead in Iowa or Minnesota. The impasse was broken by secession. In 1862 Congress chartered the Union Pacific, to build west from Iowa, and the Central Pacific, to build from California east. Both roads received grants of alternate sections of federal land on both sides of the track to a distance of twenty miles. (The public would benefit by increase in value of intervening acreage.) In addition, Congress granted second-mortgage loans ranging up to $48,000 a mile.

These charters were followed by a dozen more between 1864 and 1872. The later acts did not provide for mortgage bonds. Land grants, however, were standard. In return, railroad companies had to carry government freight at reduced rates. From an economic standpoint, transcontinental roads were built too fast, too far ahead of potential traffic, over too many routes. Hence they needlessly dispersed population and capital. Still, they reflected the national spirit; and completion of the Union-Central Pacific in 1869 was a great landmark in American nationalism.

California's gold strike of 1848 was followed by one at Pike's Peak in Colorado (1859) and others in Nevada, Idaho, and elsewhere in the 1860's. Boom towns sprang up and became ghost towns when deposits were exhausted. Not until 1866 did land laws take account of the miner's desire to claim a few hundred square feet of ground. Until then, miners enforced their own codes. Ultimately federal and state authorities legalized most of their acts.

Few prospectors became rich. Those who did owed success to ability to organize mining companies. Surface deposits were limited, and deeper penetration called for expensive machinery. Corporations with mining engineers made the great strikes like the "Big Bonanza" at Comstock, Nevada (1873). This, with nearby properties, produced $300,000,000 in gold and silver. Stockholders holding shares in such companies became rich; but for every profitable company, a dozen failed. In seeking gold, geologists discovered deposits of most of the base metals. Ultimately copper, lead, zinc, tin, and iron constituted the chief mining wealth of the Rockies, but exploitation awaited the coming of railroads in the 1870's.

Western railroads built a new business on the prairies: cattle raising. When the Kansas Pacific, the Atchison, Topeka and Santa Fe, and other lines built to points beyond the settled farm frontier, it was easy to drive cattle from Texas and sell to dealers at the railroad stations. Then local cattlemen and agents of eastern and British investors enclosed the prairie with barbed wire and established ranches in western Kansas and Nebraska, in eastern Colorado and Wyoming. Where the grass was too short or sparse for cattle, ranchers raised sheep. In the late 1880's, the boom was ended by dry summers and cold snowy winters; but stockmen had achieved permanent settlement of an important region.

The last to move onto the prairies were farmers raising wheat and corn.

They followed rivers or railroad lines, buying land from railroad and real-estate companies or homesteading if good tracts were available. Lack of lumber necessitated sod houses. Uncertainties of climate made crops speculative; long railroad hauls ate into profits. But, despite obstacles, the farmer's frontier touched the eastern edge of the cattle country by 1890, and the nation was settled from coast to coast.

Toward a New America

While some Americans went west, others found employment in manufacturing. The factory and not the farm would hereafter be the center of the American economy; and the United States would be a great industrial power. So, as the republic emerged from civil war, it entered a new phase of its history.

The new economy, coupled with the Union victory in the Civil War, spelled triumph for American nationalism. To be sure, nationalism would have triumphed had there been no Civil War. The conflict, however, speeded up the process. The necessities of war reduced states' rights in North and South; and the defeat of the Confederacy was a victory of national power.

While he lived, Lincoln stressed national loyalty. After his assassination he became a symbol of devotion to the nation. Lincoln's mistakes were forgotten; he was pictured as the unparalleled example of democracy, humanity, and Americanism. This helped cement the bonds of nationalism. So did Memorial Day orators, and the G.A.R., and those who wrote about the Civil War. Meantime, Francis Lieber and others were developing a new nationalist philosophy. The older nationalism had stressed the contractual relationship between the states and central government. The new writers saw the nation as a living organism, which thought as a great, collective person, commanded as a father, and was to be obeyed. The Civil War was a great crisis in the life of this organism. Having come through with flying colors, the nation would go on to greater glories.

Most Americans did not read these intellectuals. But, as the sectional era gave way to the industrial age, the ordinary citizen felt a great pride in his republic. He was glad to be an American, he was devoted to his nation. He was pleased about his country's past; and he viewed the future with optimism.

Part V

The Triumph of Industry

(1850-1896)

 *In the middle of the nineteenth century, the economy of the United States was still predominantly agrarian. By the end of the century, the American economy was basically industrial. Given world trends, and the natural resources of the United States, the transformation was inevitable. Just as logically, the change profoundly affected social and economic institutions in the republic and led American farmers to protest—rather ineffectively—against the dominant trends.*

15

Industrial Expansion

In the whole of world history, there are few movements as important as the industrial expansion of the United States from 1850 to 1900. The rise of manufacturing in those years transformed American agrarian society into the urban and industrial civilization of today. The shift affected American political, economic, and cultural interests, and changed the role of the United States among the nations of the globe.

Why the United States Became Industrialized When It Did

The industrialization of the United States was in line with world trends. The industrial revolution was at first confined to Great Britain and a few small regions on the European mainland. By 1850, however, citizens of many nations felt that prosperity and power were associated with manufacturing. Hence Germany became industrialized between 1850 and 1900. France, Austria, Italy, and other European countries also built factories; and Japan and the United States entered the industrial competition.

Desire alone could not create a factory economy. Industrialization was impossible without raw materials. (In particular, there was need for coal, the basic source of power, and for iron ore, the key to heavy industry.) Capital was also necessary, as was a good labor supply. Well-developed transportation was essential, for raw materials had to be taken to factories, finished products to market. There was need, too, for technological and managerial skill and a government favorable to industrialization.

Before 1850 the United States did not meet these requirements. Technological difficulties and deficiencies of transportation had prevented the exploitation of mineral resources. Despite an inflow of capital from London and immigrants from Germany and Ireland, the United States in 1850 was short of capital and labor. Population was still too small to provide a satisfactory market for a large industrial structure; and the scattered character of settlement aggravated transportation problems. There were too few trained engineers and factory managers; and the agrarian-dominated government did little to encourage manufacturing.

After 1850, a high birth rate, a declining death rate, plus heavy immigration from Europe trebled the population of the United States in fifty years. It stood at 75,000,000 in 1900, exceeding that of any state in western Europe. The increase yielded labor needed for industrialization and presented a market for factory products. The supply of capital was also growing. British money continued to pour in, and was supplemented by domestic funds, accumulated through the piling up of profits. With capital and labor available, businessmen were able to improve transportation and exploit natural resources. Improvements in science and technology (notably the rise of the engineering profession) speeded the process, as did the development of managerial efficiency. To top things off, the federal government favored manufacturing after 1860. The industrialization of the United States thus became possible.

Railroads Change the Nation

Railroads played a key role in the transition from an agricultural to a manufacturing economy. Railroads hauled raw materials to factories, factory products to consumers. Railroad securities attracted foreign capital; railroad promoters drew immigrants to the United States by advertising cheap land. Railroad profits provided capital for manufacturing plants; railroads were the best customers of the iron and steel industry. Besides that, the rise of the engineering profession was tied to railway building, as was much technological advance. And railroad promoters were among the first to persuade government officials to support the new economic trends.

These were the great years for American railway builders. In 1850 the country had less than 10,000 miles of first-line track (mileage omitting yards, sidings, double track). By 1900 the total was almost 200,000—roughly the mileage of all European nations combined.

Much capital was required, for costs ran up to $50,000 a mile. The railroads therefore dominated the security exchanges. In 1900 Americans had as large an investment in railroads as in all types of manufacturing put together. Everyone seemed to regard railroad investments as sound. Bankers would lend money on railroad bonds but not on industrials. Foreign investors, though reluctant to risk money in American manufacturing schemes, bought enormous quantities of American railroad securities.

The new railroads made business national by broadening marketing opportunities and by putting manufacturers all over the country into competition with each other. Such western centers as Omaha, Denver, and Billings were products of the railroad. Eastern manufacturing cities at junction points profited from their rail connections and waged wars of extermination against competitors on less accessible branch lines. Thus the railroad system tended to locate industry in larger towns, reinforcing trends established in the days of water transportation. But uniformity was lacking. Some lines promoted manufacturing in smaller cities along their rights of way by offering special rates and other concessions.

Some railroads relied on connections with the new factories. Others fared well without such ties. A good many lines made profits by hauling coal. Even more served purely agricultural communities, as in Illinois, Wisconsin, and Iowa. The coming of the railroads gave many western farmers their first chance to make profits. Besides, railroad construction jobs took workingmen westward. A substantial number stayed on, settling down as farmers.

The railroads themselves were often involved in the settling process, for national and state governments gave railroad entrepreneurs great gifts of land. By selling the land, the entrepreneurs obtained funds to build their lines; and the purchasers then provided freight for the railroad. In consequence, railroads stressed land operations. Advertising for settlers at home and abroad, selling on credit, and directing settlement, the railroads became, in a sense, regional development organizations, not unlike the chartered companies of colonial days.

Railroad influence was many-sided. When railroads came, farmers who had previously been unable to market their products shifted from subsistence to commercial agriculture. This often meant an expansion of operations, with new credit relations and mortgages. Many rural communities went into debt to buy railroad bonds, this being one way of attracting a branch line.

As soon as the railroads arrived, grain elevators were constructed, and new banks and stores. Local businessmen expanded their horizons, and grew rich or went broke speculating on what the railroad would do for real estate, crops, or trade. Life lost its easygoing seasonal timing and became geared to the schedule of daily trains and the speed of telegraph communication. By the middle 1870's the local sundial was obsolete: time had been standardized in zones, and the station clock was the local authority.

Most lines were started as small ventures to connect inland communities with existing railroad centers or with lake or river ports. Finding that they could not swing the deal themselves, the local sponsors went hat in hand to New York, Boston, or Philadelphia financiers. Since money was hard to raise, terms were usually harsh. Big-city financiers were likely to insist on retaining the controlling stock as a bonus; and they insisted that the inland

HHHHHH Railroads Built by 1850
———— Railroads Added by 1890

| 100 | 300 |
Miles

When railroad building began, most Americans felt the new lines would be useful chiefly as a means of hauling agricultural products to market. They did prove important in that field. At the same time, the railroads were able to carry coal and other raw materials to industrial areas, and to transport manufactured goods to consumers. Railroad construction thus played a key role in the transition from an agrarian to an industrial economy. It was no accident that the great era of railroad building (1850–90) coincided with the industrialization of the American republic.

There were few miles of railroad in the United States of 1850, and most of

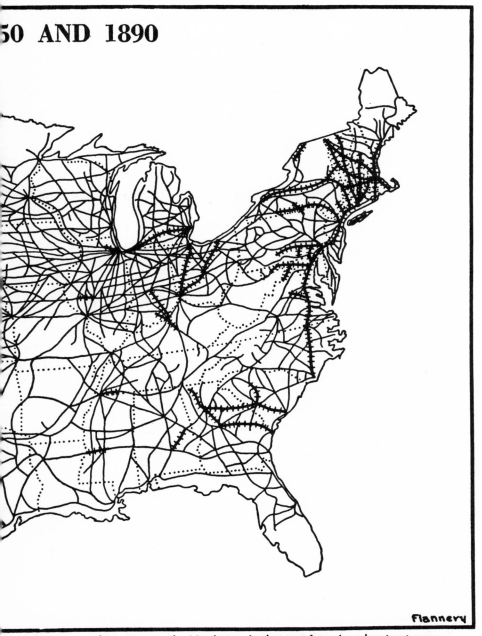

Flannery

the existing mileage was in the Northeast. In the next four decades, track was laid down in all parts of the country. The areas of heaviest concentration, however, were the Northeast and the Middle West. The South, held back by the Civil War and Reconstruction, continued to lag behind the northern sections of the country. And most major lines ran east-west rather than north-south.

Relatively few new lines were laid down after 1890. Existing roads were improved, and (in the West especially) companies built branch lines. But the major part of the work was done by 1890.

communities take a good share of the bonds. The inland promoters had to accept these terms; but they found ways of getting even. Construction had to take place far from Wall Street; and local men provided much of the supervision, labor, and materials. Building costs were difficult to estimate, and those on the ground tried to make sure that they would not lose money on construction contracts. So while the local people complained that they were being exploited by eastern capitalists, the capitalists moaned that they were being fleeced by small-town associates.

Many railroad financiers behaved very badly. Some raised money without any intention of building railroads. Others laid track parallel to existing lines, the aim being to profit from construction contracts, then force the older railroad to buy them out. A large percentage of the most unsavory figures were associated with minor lines. But the trunk lines had scoundrels, too, like "Jubilee Jim" Fisk and Jay Gould, who manipulated stock and politicians and milked the Erie Railroad dry.

Other railroad financiers were well intentioned. Good intentions did not always mean efficiency, for many honest promoters—including Henry Villard of the Northern Pacific—were overoptimistic or extravagant. But there were those who combined integrity with good judgment. John Murray Forbes, whose group financed the Michigan Central and the Chicago, Burlington and Quincy, dealt fairly with stockholders and built efficient railroads at minimum cost. In the process he enriched himself; but he also added to his nation's wealth.

A chief incentive in railway building was the value added to nearby lands. Virtually every group of railroad promoters organized land companies to buy up property along the proposed right of way. Much of the net profit in the early years came from these operations. Western roads that received federal or state land grants were directly in the real-estate business. Their main problem was price. Selling land quickly to settlers brought traffic for the road; but this meant bottom prices. Holding out for high prices meant delay in settlement and little freight for the railroad. High prices also caused the public to attack the railroad as a monopoly that retarded land development. Most roads, therefore, finally decided to sell at low rates.

Various types of abuse entered into government land grants. One involved holding land off the market. The original land-grant acts set broad limits, within which the railroads could claim a certain amount of land. Until they made their choice all land between the designated limits was off the market. Some companies which ran into construction difficulties failed to indicate the land they wanted for a decade. Some never made a choice, the land eventually reverting to the government. But meantime citizens were deprived of the opportunity to acquire much valuable western land. When lines were built, insiders were able to find out where stations and yards would be located. Then, with the connivance of company officials, they bought land from the railroads at minimum prices and made huge profits. This practice deprived stockholders of legitimate profits from land sales; and it made the public suspicious of the railroads.

Rates and Regulations

Many citizens disapproved of the financial and land policies of the railroads. But demands for government regulation after 1870 centered on the rate question. One side of the rate problem was the short haul–long haul differential. A large part of the cost of hauling freight by rail or water is for loading and unloading. This is as expensive for a ten- as for a thousand-mile trip. Consequently, railroads charged a higher rate per mile for short hauls than for long ones. This was understandable; but it did not tell all the story. Rates for long runs were also affected by competition. Long-haul freight (say, Chicago to New York) could go by different routes. With several railroads bidding for business, rates went down—far down during rate wars like that of 1874. There was no such competition, no such rate reduction on short hauls. Normally a farmer had access to only one railroad. The line did not need to cut rates to keep the farmer's business. On the contrary; it could use its monopolistic position to boost the rate, thus making up for losses on long hauls. It cost more to ship wheat a few miles from Nora, Illinois, to Chicago than to send the same product the much longer distance from St. Paul, Minnesota, to Chicago.

Naturally, farmers and merchants who had to pay the high rates complained. They also objected to the special favors given big shippers. To get the business of such giants as the Standard Oil Company, railroads offered bargain rates or gave rebates. When the railroads themselves began to suffer under the pressure of shippers and cutthroat competition, the stronger roads formed pools to maintain rates and share business. But, since pooling agreements were unenforceable at law, secret rate cutting continued. And many Americans regarded pooling as additional evidence that railroads thought in terms of monopoly rather than the public interest.

As criticism mounted, citizens demanded government regulation of railroads. At first (1865–85) focus was on state action. As early as 1869 Massachusetts set up a commission to investigate abuses, and an Illinois constitutional convention empowered the legislature to set maximum rates. Thereafter Illinois and other states tried to fix rates by legislative act or through state commissions. The movement centered in the Middle West and reached its peak in the depression of the mid-1870's, when the Grangers had great political influence. In the end, however, state rate fixing failed.

Some commissions were so anti-railroad that a reaction set in—after all, the Middle West was still trying to attract new lines. The Grangers, chief sponsors of regulation, lost ground after 1875; and the railroads fought regulation tooth and nail, using money and working through friendly journalists and politicians. So by 1880 many regulatory laws were repealed or ignored. Then the federal courts stepped in. During the 1870's the United States Supreme Court upheld the right of state legislatures to regulate rates (the Granger cases, notably Peik vs. Chicago and North Western Railway, 1876). But in the Wabash case of 1886, the Court took different ground, ruling that states had no power to fix rates on routes that involved interstate commerce. Since most routes fell in this category, the decision was a paralyzing blow for regulation.

With state regulation a failure, there was increasing demand for action by the United States government. Small shippers pushed the movement, and in 1887 Congress passed an Interstate Commerce Act. Theoretically, the law gave an Interstate Commerce Commission the right to declare rates unjust, to prevent long haul–short haul discrimination, and to outlaw pooling. Actually, the statute was not effective at the start. The I.C.C. had to work through the courts; and federal judges found loopholes in the 1887 law. Even so, the creation of the I.C.C. was a landmark in the advance of national power and the movement toward government regulation of economic life.

Meanwhile, technological improvements, expansion of routes, and a general price decline forced rates down from 1873 to 1896. By 1900 there were half a dozen transcontinentals, plus a dozen other long lines from the Mississippi to the Rockies. There had been much building in the South; and the East and Middle West were crisscrossed by rails seldom more than twenty miles apart. This meant that farmers and other small shippers were likely to be near competitive points.

Although the essentials of railroad technology remained unchanged in this period, heavier rails, more powerful engines, and the Westinghouse air brake speeded service. So did the combination of short lines into railroad empires like Cornelius Vanderbilt's New York Central system. In the 1850's a trip from Chicago to New York took three days. By 1900 express trains were covering the distance in less than a day. Crossing the continent by train and stage had required a month in 1860. By 1900 the transcontinentals had cut this time to less than a week.

Production of Raw Materials

Over half the tonnage hauled by the railroads consisted of a single item, coal. From the beginning of the industrial revolution to the present, coal has been the most important raw material.

The emergence of the United States as the greatest industrial power is closely related to the fact that this country possesses half the world's known coal reserves. Coal not only supplied freight; it also provided fuel for the locomotives. As the years went by, coal warmed more and more American homes, stores, and offices. In manufacturing, coal was the major source of power, running far ahead of water power and petroleum. Manufacture of iron and steel required more coal than iron ore. Coal heated the blast furnaces, drove the steam engines that made the factories function.

The first commercial coal in America was the anthracite (hard coal) of eastern Pennsylvania. Annual production doubled each decade after 1850. But geologists found no important new deposits of anthracite; so bituminous (soft coal) became the chief source for heat and power. From 1850 to 1900, anthracite production rose from 4,000,000 to 60,000,000 tons per year; but bituminous jumped from 3,000,000 to 200,000,000 tons. Unlike anthracite, bituminous coal was found in every major region of the United States. The largest and best-quality veins are in the Appalachian Mountains, extending from western Pennsylvania through Virginia, West Virginia, Tennesssee, and Kentucky. But many other areas contain commercially valuable deposits. The location of coal in Illinois, Missouri, and Alabama promoted a westward and southward movement of heavy industry after 1880.

Coal was basic in the power picture; but water was not to be ignored. From colonial days, millers had located by waterfalls and used water power. With the development of the electrical industry after the Civil War it became possible to transform water power into electrical energy, supplementing the supply of electricity obtained from coal. By the mid-1890's, the hydroelectric industry was firmly established, and power was being transmitted twenty miles. The future appeared promising. The main difficulty was the fact that the major untapped sources of water power were in the Rocky Mountains, far from the industrial centers.

In the twentieth century, petroleum has become an important source of heat and power. From the 1850's to the 1890's, however, the petroleum industry centered attention on kerosene, used chiefly for illumination. Later, petroleum-powered internal-combustion engines would transform transportation, though coal and the steam engine would continue to dominate the factories.

There are, of course, other sources of power—wind, animal, man power. But as industrialization continued, the accent was on mechanical power. Between the late 1850's and late 1890's population of the United States increased 150 percent. The number of draft animals increased in proportion. But installed mechanical power went from less than 5,000,000 to more than 40,000,000 horsepower, an increase of 700 percent.

Besides power, an industrial nation needs iron ore. Here again the United States was fortunate, having more and richer ores than competitors. Eastern seaboard ores, scattered from New York to Alabama, had been worked on a small scale since the colonial period. As the nation moved into large-scale iron production, around 1850, Pennsylvania took the lead. Her supremacy came from a strategic combination of resources, for she had both iron ore and coking coal. Virginia had the same combination, but made less headway because she was not so close to the chief markets for iron.

The discovery of iron ore around Lake Superior (in upper Michigan, Wisconsin, and especially Minnesota) added to the advantages of Pennsylvania. Since there was no coal in the Lake Superior region, and since iron manufacture required twice as much weight in coal as in ore, it was logical to send the ore to the coal. This meant shipping iron ore down the Great Lakes by steamer to the Pittsburgh coal area. The opening of the Mesabi Range in Minnesota provided mountains of ore; and by 1900 the Lake Superior mines were supplying ore for most of the nation's iron and steel production. Besides western Pennsylvania, ore went to new furnaces along the Great Lakes in Ohio, Indiana, and Illinois. Meantime, ore deposits of lesser importance had been opened in other states, from Alabama and Tennessee to California and Oregon. Factories sprang up near each local field.

In 1850 the American iron and steel industry specialized in iron. Blast furnaces produced 600,000 tons a year, whereas steel output was negligible. Fifty years later, concentration was on steel. Nearly 70 percent of the 15,-000,000 tons of pig iron produced by furnaces in 1900 was turned into steel. The change-over came in the 1870's, and was linked to the introduction of technological processes from Europe.

The years from 1850 to 1900 saw increased production of other minerals —lead, zinc, copper, silver, gold. Gold and silver were very significant in politics; but in industry copper counted most. It was the basic metal of the electrical industry, important after 1870. Copper had been mined in colonial New Jersey, and in Michigan during the 1850's; but there had been no incentive for large production until the need for copper wire. By then copper ore had been located in the West, from Montana to Arizona. This became the great producing area as production increased tenfold from 1880 to 1900, and the United States took the world lead in copper mining.

Aside from cement, stone, sand, and other materials generally available locally, lumber was the remaining vital raw material. The cutting of hardwoods moved across the North from Maine and New York to Michigan and Wisconsin, then to Minnesota and by the 1890's to the Pacific Northwest. Production continued in the older areas also, and a new soft-pine industry developed in the South. Coal was replacing wood as fuel, but the new industrial system needed lumber in a thousand ways. In 1900 lumber products had approximately the same value as pig iron.

In raw materials as in railroads, these were days when one could "get rich quick." Cornelius Vanderbilt, Jay Gould, Leland Stanford, C. P. Huntington, and others made fortunes in railroads. At the same time, Marcus Daly and William A. Clark went from rags to riches in copper. The Weyerhaeuse.s made a lumber fortune in the Great Lakes region, later increased it by operations on the Pacific coast. John D. Rockefeller's wealth came from another raw material, petroleum, though his control was at the refining rather than the producing level. Similarly, Henry Clay Frick's first successes were in coke, a coal product of importance to the steel industry. (Frick was financed by the Mellons of Pittsburgh. In the twentieth century, the Mellons secured control of a newly important raw material, aluminum.)

Many were lost along the way. Leonidas Merritt, with brothers and other relatives, opened the Mesabi iron range. For a time the "seven iron men" seemed on the way to wealth. Then they were caught short in the depression that followed the panic of 1893. The wealth of Mesabi went to other men—to John D. Rockefeller, Andrew Carnegie, Henry Clay Frick, James J. Hill.

These names tell how raw materials were interrelated, and how all were linked to transportation. Carnegie and Frick were iron and steel magnates. Frick had started out in coal, Carnegie in railroads. Coal, railroads, ore, and iron and steel thus formed a single pattern. Hill was another railroad man, the builder of the Great Northern. Rockefeller was in oil. That meant transportation, too, including control of pipe lines. Rockefeller moved into the iron ore business by lending money to the Merritts and acquiring lake steamers which transported ore to steel centers.

Land grants greatly speeded the building of the western railroads. In like fashion land policy influenced exploitation of raw materials. In 1850 much of the nation's mineral and timber wealth was located on government land. By 1900 most of this land had been transferred to private hands, often for absurdly low prices. The transfers were in line with long-established land policies. From the beginning Congress had been anxious to shift public lands to private hands as rapidly as possible. The tendency from the 1790's on was to reduce the price. After the passage of the Homestead Act in 1862, some lands were given away to settlers; and, of course, enormous tracts were assigned to railroad promoters. A series of laws in the 1870's did set lands of special value outside the provisions of the Homestead Act; but these lands were sold far below their true value. Under the Mining Act of 1872 mineral lands were to be sold at from $2.50 to $5.00 an acre. In 1873 Congress set a price of $10 to $15 an acre for coal lands. A Timber and

Stone Act of 1878 set a $2.50 to $5.00 price per acre. Although these were minimum figures, government officials made virtually no effort to get more than the lowest permissible price. Nor did the government try to enforce all provisions of the statutes. The Timber and Stone Act called for development of the property by the purchaser; but much of the land acquired under this legislation was transferred to big lumber companies.

Most nineteenth-century Americans assumed that individual self-seeking would produce public gain. The exploitation of natural resources did not point to that conclusion. Lumber companies were unbelievably wasteful, and took no interest in reforestation. Poverty-stricken, unproductive "cutover" lands were their gift to later generations. Petroleum producers were even more prodigal with that irreplaceable raw material. Owners of coal mines skimmed the cream, seeking quick profits and leaving properties in bad shape for their successors. Yet few Americans objected. The conservation movement would not take hold until the republic had wasted much of its heritage.

New Locations for Industry

Americans had long used food preprocessed in mills or factories. In value of product, flour milling was in 1850 the nation's chief industry. Meat packing also ranked high; and factory-packed food in cans and jars, first appearing in the 1820's, had a small market among those not afraid to experiment.

As urban needs increased, and as transportation improved, processing became big business. Minneapolis won ascendancy in flour through new milling processes introduced in the 1870's. Chicago came to dominate meat packing because of rail connections and efficient stockyards. The introduction of refrigerator cars in the 1870's enabled Chicago packers to ship fresh beef to eastern and foreign markets. Simultaneously, other processed foods won popularity. City dwellers tried canned salmon and soup, prepared cereals, and bottled pickles. Advertising slowly broke down resistance to each new product.

Food was not all the story. The commercial adaptation of the sewing machine to cloth, then to leather, lowered the price of factory shoes and ready-made clothes. Furniture from plants in Grand Rapids, Michigan, and elsewhere began to displace products of the local cabinetmaker. Homemade rugs slowly gave way to factory-produced floor coverings; mass production reduced the price of stoves, brooms, matches, and scores of other household articles.

For heavy industry the main problem was cost of transportation. In locating a steel plant, Andrew Carnegie had to balance cost of transporting coke, iron ore, and finished steel in such a way as to produce the lowest total. This kept the industry centered in western Pennsylvania. But in industries where value added by manufacture was large and weight of product small, supply of skilled labor might be the vital factor. New England is far from the geographical center of the United States—far, too, from the center of population and from the key raw materials. Yet, in defiance of the pressure of transportation costs, New England remained a manufacturing center from 1850 to 1900, specializing in hardware, clocks, firearms, silverware, and other products which required skilled labor.

As in earlier decades, New England led the nation in textile production. That industry, however, required few skilled workers; the call was for cheap, unskilled labor. Hence the industry began to migrate to southern states, where manufacturers employed back-country farm families at low wages. New England had no comparable labor supply; her back-country districts had been depopulated by the westward movement. Attempting to hold on, New England businessmen brought in French-Canadian and European immigrants. But the southward trend continued.

Since textile manufacturing required bulky machinery and large buildings, cheap land was a factor in locating textile establishments. The manufacture of furs, clothing, jewelry, novelties, and notions, on the other hand, needed very little land. Producers of these items also wanted to be near the markets so as to predict fashions. Hence these industries stayed in the heart of big cities, particularly New York, and employed immigrant labor. By 1900 such enterprises plus those that used cheaper land on the outskirts had concentrated 15 percent of the value of the nation's manufactured products in this one big city.

Despite this concentration, industry was spreading out. By 1900 all five of the states of the Old Northwest (Ohio, Indiana, Illinois, Michigan, Wisconsin) ranked among the first ten states in number of people engaged in manufacturing. Only New York, Pennsylvania, and Massachusetts ranked ahead of Illinois and Ohio. Factories were also springing up in other traditionally agricultural regions. Georgia, California, and North Carolina stood fourteenth, fifteenth, and sixteenth in number of industrial wage earners. This spread of manufacturing was not caused by economic forces alone. Impressed by the wealth that came from industrial operations, states and cities offered cash or tax exemption over a period of years to those who would build factories.

Technological Advance

The phenomenal growth of American industry after 1850 would have been impossible without a major advance in technology. Technical progress of these years was linked to practical inventions, worked out by empirical (trial-and-error) methods. But, to an ever greater degree, progress was tied also to theoretical (basic) science.

Since nineteenth-century Americans neglected theoretical science, technologic improvements developed in the United States were generally the result of trial-and-error experimentation. Elias Howe's sewing machine (1846) is an example. A stitching machine had been patented in England in 1780, a workable sewing machine in France in 1830. Adding an eye-pointed needle and double-lock stitch, Howe turned out a highly efficient machine. His work required no basic research, but it solved the problem of finding an automatic equivalent for the complicated finger motions of sewing. When marketed, the sewing machine lightened labor in the home; and in factories it made possible rapid and cheaper production of woolen, cotton, and leather products.

Or take the linotype, created in 1884 by a German-trained American mechanic, Ottmar Mergenthaler, in response to a definite need. The earlier invention of the rotary press enabled newspapers to turn out rapidly great numbers of sheets; but the hand-setting of type held back the presses. Mergenthaler's linotype solved the problem. It operated through a keyboard; and molten lead poured into a mold so as to cast an entire line of type at a time. Printing promptly became cheaper as well as more rapid. This happened just when advertising brought increasing income to periodicals, making mass circulation possible.

The same years brought the typewriter. "Writing machines" had been made between 1820 and 1870, but none operated as rapidly as handwriting. But as the tempo of business increased, the advantages of rapid writing became apparent. Then (1873) Christopher Sholes produced a typewriter which was more rapid than the hand and simple enough for commercial production. The machine was marketed by Remington, and by 1890 typewriters were selling briskly. In time, other office machines were invented— mimeographs, addressographs, calculators. With them came improved office procedures such as systematic filing and indexing, and the correlation of typing with the old process of shorthand. Later, the phonograph (Dictaphone) was used in business. These devices produced a revolution in office management, related as both cause and effect to the evolution of large-scale business. The old-fashioned merchant's office, with a few clerks on high stools handling written accounts and correspondence, could no more carry on a modern business than could stagecoaches handle present-day transportation.

Other inventions rested on knowledge of basic science. Here American contributions were less impressive; American developments came generally after Europeans had laid the foundations. Lighting illustrates the point. Here there was little improvement from classical times to 1800. Although people would have enjoyed better light, there had been no strong demand for it. Trial-and-error experiments offered few possibilities, save in such minor advantages as the use of whale oil in lamps. But by 1800, growing knowledge of the chemistry of gases suggested to European scientists the possibility of gas lighting. This was tried in London, later in America; by 1860 New York's Broadway stores were so illuminated. A Canadian geologist obtained kerosene from petroleum in the 1850's; and the kerosene lamp was soon used all over the world. Meantime, chemists had opened an even more promising field. Early in the nineteenth century Sir Humphry Davy, an Englishman, found that an electric current generated by chemical decomposition in a battery would decompose other chemicals, giving off light. This led to his invention of the arc light (1809). Davy also found that some metals burned very slowly when a current was passed through them, and in so doing gave out light. Following this line, English and French scientists developed incandescent lights in the middle of the century, and lighted rooms on an experimental basis, using carbon filaments and partial vacuums in the bulbs. That is to say, the basic theory had been established, and some technologic paths explored.

Thomas Alva Edison then entered the field. Edison was a self-trained American who lacked, at least in his earlier career, basic scientific knowledge. He was, however, ingenious and persevering. Given a problem, he came up with solutions that baffled more original thinkers. Incandescent lights had "worked" abroad but were neither cheap nor durable. What metals were best for wires, what degrees of vacuum? What substances made the toughest and best filaments? The problem, in other words, was in the trial-and-error stage. Taking it up there, Edison produced in 1879 an effective light that used carbon filaments, platinum wires, and a high-vacuum bulb. Simultaneously, others were developing incandescent bulbs in Britain.

Edison cared little for abstract problems. If such questions arose, he could "hire a mathematician." Nor was Edison's the "pure" curiosity of the scientist. Rather his was a zeal for turning out products that could be made available to the public. He felt that democracy had a mission to use technology for the welfare of the people. This helps explain Edison's interest in the phonograph. It also helps explain his interest in producing and distributing his products. He was, of course, interested in personal gain; but he was even more interested in aiding his countrymen. Unlike many inventors, he had the ability to put his inventions into commercial production. He showed this when he opened the famous Pearl Street power plant in New York City in 1882 to supply current for electric lights.

Edison's success was linked to American conditions. Relatively low living standards cut down the market for new inventions in Europe—most

Europeans could not afford the gadgets. Although many Americans were far from prosperous, average income was higher than in Europe, providing a large market for new inventions. Not that new inventions were accepted right away. Older people resisted Edison's lights and Alexander Graham Bell's telephone. Even with younger citizens, time and salesmanship were required. Sometimes delay was a matter of price and quality, for it took a decade to make many new devices cheap and efficient.

There is a popular belief that inventors starved while predatory corporations made millions from their inventions. Sometimes it was this way. But many inventors made fortunes on their patents; and often businessmen lost heavily in backing particular inventions. Successful inventors won great popular acclaim from 1850 to 1900, at a time when Americans ignored theoretical scientists. Thus Edison became the "Wizard of Menlo Park" while the great mathematical physicist Willard Gibbs remained unknown.

Technology in Iron and Steel

Europeans had used iron since remote times and had gradually acquired knowledge of different grades and alloys. Ore was smelted in charcoal furnaces, and rule-of-thumb methods produced cast and pig iron (hard and brittle), wrought iron (soft and malleable), and steel (hard and tough). The differences depended largely on the amount of carbon present. Relatively brittle grades of iron were at first the only ones that could be produced reasonably in large quantities. Hence the rails on early railroads had a habit of breaking and tearing through the floor of the cars. Iron boilers were also unreliable; boiler explosions accounted for most of the "Great Steamboat Disaster" headlines of the 1840's. Plainly needed was a cheap, reliable steel.

Part of the answer was found by the trial-and-error method. William Kelley (United States, 1846) and William Bessemer (England, 1856) found that when one melted pig iron (high in carbon) the carbon would burn under an air blast and thus provide its own fuel. The burning could be stopped when enough carbon remained to provide the qualities of steel. It was no longer necessary to remove nearly all the carbon to make wrought iron, then add carbon to make steel. Bessemer also invented a converter to control air blasts; and cheap steel became a possibility, especially after a merger of the Kelley and Bessemer groups solved American patent problems in the 1860's.

Science helped eliminate remaining difficulties. Chemists found that quality of steel depended in part on the amount of phosphorus and manganese in the original iron ore. With this knowledge, manufacturers could tell just when to turn off the blast with each ore. Chemists also learned how to improve steel by adding silicon and manganese; and their research made it possible for producers to grade the product.

There were further technologic improvements, many of them brought from Europe. Notable was the German-developed open-hearth process, in which gases escaping from the furnace were combined with air to form a super-hot flame which was played over the surface of the molten metal. This made it possible to determine even more exactly what the quality of the steel would be. Andrew Carnegie used this technique to advantage, and after 1900 it became more widely used than the Bessemer process.

For improvements based on scientific research American steel manufacturers leaned on Europe. American supremacy was in mass production. By the 1880's the steel production of the United States had surpassed that of Britain. By 1900 Americans were making a third of the world's steel. Production on this scale was made possible by expanding uses—locomotives, battleships, railroad rails, business machines, wire, cans, bicycles, and rivets and girders for the new skyscrapers.

The Power Engine

In 1850 the steam engine was replacing horses in long-distance land transportation and wind power in ocean transport. Steam power was also being substituted for water power in textile mills and for man power in printing. Even greater gains were ahead. In the 1840's an English physicist had defined the mechanical equivalent of heat. It became known that energy as well as matter was indestructible and that all forms of energy (heat, electricity, mechanical energy, and so on) were mutually convertible. One could now compare the amount of heat generated in the firebox with the amount of mechanical power actually delivered at the wheels. One could measure the relative efficiency of boilers, valves, and governors. With such yardsticks and by experiment, engineers by 1900 produced locomotives and stationary engines far superior to those of 1850.

The future of technology, however, did not lie entirely with the steam engine. By 1890 scientists and inventors were also harnessing electrical power and were using the energy that bound together the atoms of chemical combinations. (Later, with the development of atomic physics, the much vaster energy which held together the interior systems of atoms would also be liberated for man's use or misuse.)

The energy locked in chemical combinations had long been employed in exploding gunpowder. Thus the cannon may be called an early internal-combustion engine. A spark or flame raised the gunpowder to a temperature at which it would combine with air (sudden oxidation or explosion). The resulting gases expanded rapidly, forcing the cannonball out with great speed. In a steam engine, by contrast, heat raised water to a temperature producing steam, and the expansion of steam forced out a piston. A chief difference between these two heat engines is that in a steam engine the fuel is burned in a separate furnace. In cannon and other gas engines the fuel is burned within the tube or motor cylinder. In other words, the combustion is internal.

The development of the internal-combustion engine was tied to basic scientific research. When chemists discovered hydrogen, they found that this gas, when ignited, united explosively with air. Why not utilize the force of these explosions to drive pistons? Experimenters in England, France, and Germany worked along this line and produced commercially practicable internal-combustion engines by the 1870's. The use of gasoline as a fuel made these new engines very efficient, notably in transportation. Gottlieb Daimler and other Europeans built practical automobiles in the 1880's. Americans followed suit; in the United States the Duryea brothers, Elwood Haynes, and Henry Ford produced gasoline-powered internal-combustion-engine automobiles between 1892 and 1895. These vehicles looked like buggies (some even had whip sockets), just as the first railroad cars resembled stagecoaches. In many early automobiles the engine was under the seat, and was connected with bicycle-type tires by chains.

Despite its ultimate triumph, the internal-combustion car did not at first seem as promising as steam and electric automobiles, which dominated the market until 1900. To be sure, it was a nuisance to handle the fire in a steamer; and the batteries of electric cars needed recharging after a few miles. But the first gasoline cars had problems, too. Hand cranking was necessary to turn the flywheel over and compress the "mixture" for the initial explosion. This was not eliminated until the invention of the self-starter just before World War I.

In time, the gasoline engine won. It was the same with small vessels—steam and electric launches were superseded by gasoline-driven motorboats. So, too, in a new field, aviation. Early experimenters had tried to use man power (wings) and steam power. But man power was too feeble, and steam engines were too heavy. The internal-combustion engine was the answer. It was used by the Wright brothers in 1903. Hence the internal-combustion engine had brought forth the modern automobile and the airplane in the same generation.

Basic research, so important in the history of the internal-combustion engine, was no less vital in the harnessing of electrical energy. The discovery that electricity produces electromagnetic fields led early in the nineteenth century to the invention in England of the electromagnet. This helped bring about the invention of the telegraph. It also pointed toward the invention of the electric motor. Could not magnets be arranged so as to pull a bar or turn a wheel (that is, to do work)? Following this line, the American Joseph Henry built a primitive electromagnetic motor in 1831; but, being a "pure" scientist, he did not try to make the machine practical.[1]

Both Joseph Henry and Michael Faraday of England also found that, just as current would produce magnetism, so magnetism would produce current. If a coil of wire were revolved between the two poles of a magnet, a current was induced in it. Here was a way of producing electricity without recourse to chemical decomposition (batteries). Thus the discovery that current would create magnetism led to the invention of the electromagnetic motor; and the discovery that magnets would produce current contained in germ the idea of the electromagnetic generator or dynamo, with which electric power came into its own. Faraday constructed a primitive dynamo, which produced alternating current (AC). This type of current proved very useful later; but nineteenth-century experimenters were accustomed to the continuous or direct current (DC) produced by batteries. By 1870 European technologists (an Italian and a Belgian) had made the necessary adjustments, and there were dynamos capable of producing direct current. Edison used such a machine in setting up his New York power station in 1881–82.

Other inventors now operated motors by wire connection with distant dynamos. In 1882 Frank J. Sprague, an American, worked out the trolley device for supplying electric current from wires to streetcars. Five years later he gave Richmond, Virginia, the first electric street railway system. Trolleys were so obviously superior to horsecars that a hundred other cities sought Sprague's service in the next two years. Meantime, an alternate method of supplying current to cars appeared in the invention of the third rail, used in subways and elevated railways.

In time internal-combustion engines and electric motors competed with steam power in the stationary-engine field (for such jobs as pumping) and in railroad transportation (Diesel and electric locomotives replacing steam locomotives). On the whole, however, steam continued to do most heavy work on steamships, for railroads, and in industry. Electric and internal-combustion engines did jobs for which steam engines were too complicated or heavy.

There was, in any case, no sharp division among the sources of power. Electrical devices like the self-starter eventually made internal-combustion

---

[1] After seeing Henry's electromagnet operate, Thomas Davenport, a Vermont blacksmith, actually built electric motors in the 1830's and by 1850 applied these to running an electric car and a player piano. But, lacking capital, he failed to achieve commercial success.

engines operate efficiently. And electrical energy was produced by both steam and water power. From the 1840's on, engineers developed turbines, these being elaborations of the vanes long employed in water wheels and windmills. Water or steam could be forced into these turbines in such a way as to utilize more of the original energy than had been possible with clumsy wheels. Then the turbines could revolve the coils of dynamos and create electric current. A spectacular application of this was in the harnessing of Niagara Falls (1895). Steam generation of electricity, though less dramatic, was even more important.

Science and Invention

In photography as with power machines, Europeans had done basic investigational work by 1850. The next half-century saw the commercial development of the photographic industry. The chief American figure was George Eastman, who at the end of the 1880's marketed the first roll-film camera (Kodak). Like other American producers, Eastman used mass production methods and made his product available to a large public. At the same time, others were applying electrical devices to photography to produce the moving picture.

Photography illustrates the impact of physics on technology. So does the discovery of X-rays in 1895 by the German physicist Roentgen. In like fashion analytic chemistry was becoming increasingly valuable in metallurgy, pharmacology, and other fields. By isolating the key ingredients in plant drugs, chemists made an enduring contribution to medicine. Geologists became more important, for they could help locate newly significant mineral deposits. Meteorologists, using many observation points and bringing together data by telegraph, evolved fairly accurate methods of weather prediction. The rise of medical bacteriology led to the use of antiseptic techniques in surgery; and genetics, the science of heredity, began in the 1890's to have meaning for plant and animal breeders.

Noting this activity, Americans gradually came to appreciate the need for trained scientists and engineers. The educational system slowly responded to the new needs. Meanwhile, colleges and corporations gave greater attention to basic research. In 1850, most American inventors were self-trained mechanics who worked in homemade laboratories. By 1900, science had become much more complex; would-be inventors found that they needed educational background and money for staff, equipment, and materials. The money would come, increasingly, from universities and business concerns. Most American business leaders remained skeptical about the value of basic research. But German corporations were finding that laboratory work in theoretical science (as in chemistry and optics) paid off in profits. American businessmen would eventually reach that same conclusion; and in 1900 the General Electric Company would establish a research laboratory.

The new trend would mean that future inventors would have basic science training and would exchange the fame (and uncertainties) of private invention for the secure anonymity of the scientific employee. The inventive process, like the production and distribution of goods, would become less an individual matter than before.

The Business Cycle

The boom-and-bust cycle had been bad enough in a farming nation. Industrialization made things worse, for the economy was more complex, and the urban unemployed faced actual hunger in hard times.

There were four major Wall Street panics between 1850 and 1900, each followed by an economic depression. The panics came in 1857, 1873, 1884, and 1893. All involved a reaction to overinvestment, particularly in railroads. Each was preceded by a period of rising prices, wages, and interest rates, and by speculative booms in land and securities. Then the boom broke, amid spectacular business failures. Confidence evaporated, stocks and bonds declined, prices and production slumped, and the country entered an economic depression (1857–62, 1873–79, 1883–85, 1893–96), with widespread industrial unemployment, gloomy forecasts as to the future, and a temporary slowing down of physical progress. A depression normally spelled national political defeat for the party in power. But political reactions were only one sign of the discouragement felt by citizens in an age when federal and state governments took no steps to prevent bankruptcies and provided no unemployment relief.

After a while, good times returned. Factories went back into production, freight car loadings increased, laborers were called to work. Prices moved upward, as did stocks and bonds. The nation soon had an inflationary boom (1850–54, 1863–65, 1869–72, 1880–83, 1890–92), to be ended by another crash.

Rise of the Corporation

Although factories grew in size after 1850, the average plant remained small. A typical factory of 1900 yielded $25,000 in gross annual income. This had to be divided among the proprietor, one or two salaried assistants, and a score of workers. These "average" factories made tools, stoves, textiles, house furnishings, jewelry, books, luggage, drugs, and other products that sustained the American standard of living.

Larger plants were required for manufacture of locomotives, sheet steel, heavy machinery, and refined oil.

Within industries dominated by small business there were great variations in size. Although the average textile mill employed a few dozen workers, some hired a thousand. There were small shops staffed by the proprietor's family and giant department stores like those of Marshall Field in Chicago and John Wanamaker in Philadelphia and New York. Sometimes small units grew into big ones. In the early 1870's Lydia Pinkham bottled a vegetable compound in her own kitchen. Two decades later production required a factory with many employees.

Excluding farms and household manufacture, there were 500,000 American business enterprises in 1850, and more than twice that number in 1900. Most were individual proprietorships or partnerships; but for large undertakings the corporation was becoming increasingly popular. By the 1870's most states had general incorporation laws, enabling businessmen to launch a corporation with a minimum of trouble, after registering and paying a moderate fee. Corporations had one great advantage—limited liability. Proprietors and partners normally had unlimited liability, were personally responsible for debts of their firms. The liability of stockholders in corporations was limited to the stock held; debts of the company could not be assessed against stockholders personally.

The stock of most corporations, even the large ones, was closely held by the founders and their families. These persons owned and ran the corporation. So it was with the Rockefeller-dominated Standard Oil Company and with Andrew Carnegie's steel combine. So it is today with such concerns as the Ford Motor Company. But there was another trend, discernible by 1880. Persons with stock in several corporations had little time for each company. Nor, as minority shareholders, could they wield much influence. They ceased, therefore, to try to be "owners" in the old sense, and became passive investors. Much property came to be held this way, the nominal owners having less control over their property than did managers, bankers, customers, and even workers. The owners' (stockholders') claim was just one of many; and management decided what the owners should receive.

The first general incorporation laws did not give corporations the right to own stock of other corporations. Pennsylvania, Kentucky, and other states did grant this right in special cases; but the privilege was not generally extended until, in 1888, New Jersey passed its famous holding company law. This statute made it easy for businessmen to form holding companies in New Jersey. That done, they could secure control of any industry anywhere by buying a controlling share of the voting stock of the leading producers.

Business and the Market

While corporate structure was changing, the railroad was revolutionizing marketing. Traveling salesmen took the orders of inland merchants and saw to it that goods were supplied quickly by freight or express. Hence the merchant could buy less at a time and make payment more rapidly. Credit terms of six months to a year shrank to sixty or ninety days. Improved credit information and credit ratings worked out by Dun and Bradstreet enabled manufacturers and wholesalers to grant short-term credits with greater liberality, which meant a better selection of goods, fresher wares, and all-around improved service.

Before the railroad era there had been many local and regional agreements for control of competition. The railroads shattered these agreements by introducing nation-wide trade. Shoemakers of Lynn, Massachusetts, were put into competition with those of Chicago; and a New England trade association could not regulate an industry that had spread into Ohio. Many manufacturers complained of the resulting national competition. Others were pleased to be able to move outside the local market.

Building a nation-wide market for soap or sewing machines called for national advertising. Advertising agencies, appearing before the Civil War, grew rapidly after 1865. They dealt in space in dailies and weeklies, and advised clients as to types of display and the probable circulation of various journals. It was no accident that a leading advertising agent, George P. Rowell, prepared a pioneer newspaper directory.

Technological advance also aided advertising. The rotary press, the linotype, and a sulfite process for making cheap wood-pulp paper virtually ended limitations on newspaper space. Previously editors had frowned on elaborate pictorial displays as a waste of precious paper. Now a new world opened; and advertising agencies added art departments. In improving techniques, Americans studied methods worked out in Europe. Partly as a result of that study, "reason why" copy began to replace extravagant overstatements and meaningless jingles by the 1880's. And advertising, previously associated largely with patent medicines and local stores, began to gain the dignity of bigness. By 1900 sedate magazines like *Harper's* contained full-page histories of great moments in beer consumption; slick-paper monthlies including the *Ladies' Home Journal* were read for advertisements as well as for copy. Billboards lined railroad tracks, posters appeared on roads used by bicyclists. Railroads, circuses, department stores, buggy manufacturers, producers of shoes, cereals, books, and liniments launched elaborate campaigns. Bible societies and politicians joined the procession. Everything seemed to be advertised.

Limiting Competition

Producers who did not sell directly to the public were slow to see the value of advertising. The more efficient, who could force the pace, used price warfare to secure the lion's share of the market. Price cutting, they said, would force the feeble out of competition and leave the field to the strong. But in price warfare even the efficient suffered. In a competitive situation prices quickly dropped to a point that barely covered operating expenses and paid little if any return on invested capital. Yet no one would leave the field willingly, for closing down meant even greater losses. Aggravating the situation was a long-run, world-wide decline in prices from the 1860's to the mid-1890's.

Efficient trade associations might have checked this warfare. But national trade associations were difficult to organize, harder still to keep in operation. "Gentlemen's agreements" were always being broken; and the American courts (in contrast to those of Europe) were hostile to contracts controlling prices or production.

Pools were also tried. Finding they could produce double what the market could absorb, the whiskey distillers formed a selling pool in 1881. Each distiller paid an assessment based on production, and the pool used the money to finance the sale of surpluses abroad. But pools, like gentlemen's agreements, broke down. There was no legal basis for prosecuting a member who cheated on assessments or sold secretly outside the pool. And American courts interpreted selling agreements as conspiracies in restraint of trade. Rockefeller's Standard Oil Company publicized the trustee device (1879). Let each producer incorporate, then turn his stock over to a group of trustees. The trustees (or "trust") would hold the stock of all competitors and could run an industry as though it were one big company. Ultimately, this method ran afoul of the courts; whereupon those anxious to eliminate competition would bring rivals together in one big corporation, like United States Steel, or would control competitors through holding companies. The "trust" was just one method of control; but in popular language at the end of the century all big companies were called trusts. As size increased, the term became a synonym for monopoly and lack of consideration for the public.

The consolidated company or group could make profits by holding prices artificially high. It could also increase efficiency by closing highcost plants and operating those with lowest costs at full capacity. Eighty distillers entered the Whiskey Trust, but the trust kept only a dozen plants in operation. Partly offsetting the gains of such operations was overcapitalization. It cost a lot to buy the stock of individual properties and to market additional securities to pay high legal and financial fees and obtain more working capital. Many early trusts failed to earn satisfactory dividends on their inflated capital structures.

Mergers were sometimes arranged openly. Control could also be secured by a secret stock-purchasing campaign. Jay Gould was expert at this, buying carefully through many brokers until he controlled railroads from New York to Texas, and the nation-wide Western Union Telegraph Company. By using corporate leases he made his money go a long way. That is, he bought control of a corporation, then used control to lease the company's property to another of his companies. After that he could unload stock of the leased corporation and invest his money elsewhere.

Establishing control of an industry called for effective promotion and operation, up-to-date technology, tariff protection, political influence, and control of key patents. It was also necessary to have a cost per unit that decreased as volume increased, so that one could take advantage of mass production economies. Important, too, were willingness and ability to take advantage of every opportunity to crush one's competitors. Here depressions were useful. Almost anyone could survive in a boom, but only efficient producers with strong credit could keep going in a shrinking market.

Standard Oil illustrates these points. John D. Rockefeller, the man behind this company, was determined to secure complete control of oil refining. He therefore made his company efficient, introducing cost accounting and employing experts who improved refining techniques. He secured political connections, built good credit ties by borrowing from many banks, and obtained control of such subsidiary operations as cooperage and carting. But he stayed out of well drilling, a risky, uncertain business. Producing was so highly competitive and producers were so weak and divided that it was easy to keep the price of crude oil down.

Rockefeller's location in Cleveland was a great advantage. He was as near the oil fields as were the Pittsburgh refiners. Pittsburgh, moreover, was a "captive town" of the Pennsylvania Railroad; those who shipped oil out of Pittsburgh had to use that railroad and pay the rates it chose to charge. Cleveland, by contrast, was served by more than one line. Rockefeller could play one railroad against another, or play the water routes against all the railroads, forcing rates down. Nor was that all. Once in the lead among Cleveland refiners, Rockefeller pressed home the advantages of mass production. Standard's reliably large freight shipments increased its bargaining power with the railroads; the "magnitude and regularity" of Rockefeller's business made it worth while to cut rates to the bone to get him as a customer. Later, Rockefeller reduced transportation costs still more by laying pipe lines.

Standard had a commanding position in Cleveland by 1870. The depression after the panic of 1873 enabled Rockefeller to bid for national monopoly. The plan was simple: Take in efficient producers through mergers arranged on generous terms and force the less efficient to sell out at bargain rates. Naturally, weaker competitors resisted. But Standard could use control of transportation against competitors. It could persuade producers not to sell to some refiners, could hire away the best officers of rival firms, could wreck competitors in price wars. So, by 1880 Rockefeller controlled all major refining centers.

It was similar in other fields. Henry Clay Frick used the panic of 1873 to dominate the coke industry. Andrew Carnegie did much the same in iron and steel. Frick presently joined Carnegie and, as manager of the Carnegie enterprises, squeezed out competitors after the panic of 1893. Such victories were possible because the Carnegie-Frick enterprises were efficient, employed the best machinery and best minds, and reduced unit costs. By underselling rivals, they could get the business in hard times, when there were not enough orders to go around. In addition, Carnegie and Frick, like Rockefeller, plowed profits back into the business. This made for financial strength, all-important in a crisis.

So in sugar refining, where the Havemeyers secured a stranglehold; in meat packing, with such men as Philip Armour forging to the top; in sleeping cars, dominated by George Pullman; in Frederick Weyerhaeuser's lumber kingdom. Many failed. Those who succeeded built great economic empires.

Rise of Finance Capitalism

Many of the industrial monopolies were owned by individuals who managed their companies. In consequence, 1875–1900 was a period of highly independent captains of industry. But these same years also witnessed the rise of investment bankers, who dealt, not in factories, but in stocks and bonds. By the 1890's these finance capitalists controlled a sizable portion of the nation's wealth.

At first, investment bankers were less active in manufacturing than in other fields. In the 1850's, trading in securities centered around government, railroad, bank, and utility issues, railroads leading. By then stocks and bonds were regarded as a normal investment for the upper-middle-class Northerners, prosperous southern planters, and western real-estate operators. Activity was increased by purchases made by European investors.

New York was the center of trading, and telegraphic quotations from the New York Stock Exchange set prices on exchanges in other cities.

Investment in securities increased enormously during the Civil War. Merchants and professional men who had previously kept their savings in real estate were cajoled into showing their patriotism by investing in Union bonds. Prosperous citizens thus fell into the habit of trading in securities. When the war was over, many sold their government bonds to banks and insurance companies, then sank the proceeds in the securities of private companies, which promised a better return on investment. This meant a more active market, and easier financing for the railroads, utilities, and mining companies.

Unfortunately, many of the new investments turned out badly. Daniel Drew, Jim Fisk, Jay Gould, Cornelius Vanderbilt, and other stock manipulators fleeced unwary investors. Since the most reprehensible practices concerned common stocks, this type of security obtained a bad reputation. Conservatives preferred to deal in bonds, where the return was relatively small but relatively certain. The degradation of common stock continued until about 1907. This was unfortunate, for stock represented ownership. The unwillingness of investors to buy stocks forced railroads and utilities to finance largely through bonds. This meant heavy interest payments, for bondholders were creditors, not owners, and had to be paid regularly, whether times were good or bad. Companies that had raised large sums of money through bond issues found it difficult to meet fixed charges in periods of depression; many went into bankruptcy.

As the sale of securities increased, the investment banker took on new importance. He was the wholesaler who marketed securities. There had been a few American investment houses before 1860. The number increased during and after the Civil War, but the panic of 1873 eliminated the smaller and weaker houses, particularly those without close foreign connections. Even larger houses were affected. Jay Cooke and Company, which had borne the brunt of Civil War financing, failed dramatically in its attempt to carry the burden of constructing the Northern Pacific Railroad. But the houses that survived were stronger than ever. Among these were Lee, Higginson and Company of Boston; August Belmont and Company, a New York concern connected with the Rothschilds of Europe; and Drexel, Morgan and Company of New York and Philadelphia. This last firm was the American side of an Anglo-American combination. Renamed J. P. Morgan and Company in 1895, it became a major influence in American life.

Each company tended to do its financing through one banking house. This did not exclude other bankers from a share in the profits. To speed

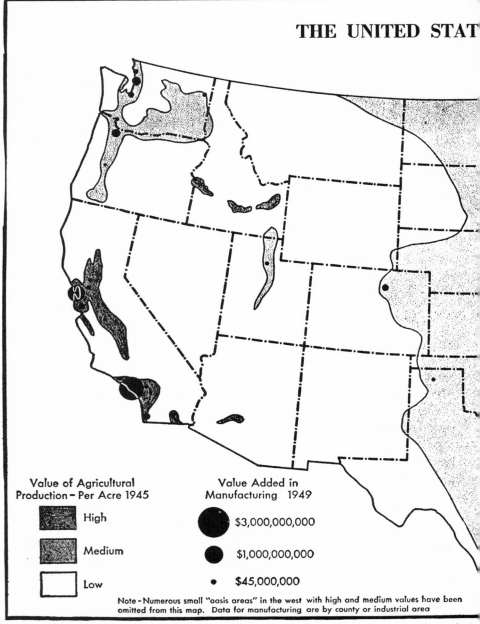

Value of Agricultural
Production – Per Acre 1945

High

Medium

Low

Value Added in
Manufacturing 1949

$3,000,000,000

$1,000,000,000

• $45,000,000

Note – Numerous small "oasis areas" in the west with high and medium values have been
omitted from this map. Data for manufacturing are by county or industrial area

Much of the history of the United States during the past century is reflected
in the development, character, and location of economic enterprises. This
map clearly shows the concentration of manufacturing between Boston and
Chicago-St. Louis, with the heaviest concentration in the Northeast (Boston
to Baltimore). Note the great industrial activity in New York's Mohawk Valley
and around Pittsburgh, and the rise of a factory area on the Pacific coast.
Manufacturing in the "new South," notable Piedmont textile development, is
indicated; but, as can be seen, southern industry does not yet approach
northern factory areas in value-added-by-manufacture.

ECONOMIC ACTIVITY

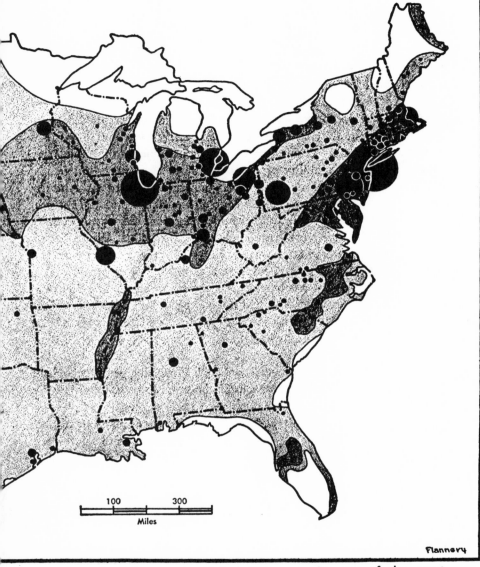

Flannery

In the industrial age, the United States remains one of the great farming nations. This map shows the location and relative importance of the various farming regions: the tobacco area of Virginia, the Carolinas, and westward; the cotton belt, with the high production of the Mississippi River and Texas cotton regions emphasized; the citrus fruit areas of California and Florida; the dairy and truck gardening of the Northeast; the corn-and-hog and dairy production of the Great Lakes area, with the wheat region to the west, and the cattle kingdom beyond.

the sale of securities and spread the risk, leading houses formed syndicates for the marketing of large issues of securities. Friendly bankers and brokers were invited to take some of the stocks and bonds for sale and to participate in the anticipated profits. Consequently, the financial community became more of a unit than other types of business. All members of the community shared a common interest in maintaining the group practices, which were called "sound finance."

What was "sound finance"? The banker saw his role as that of physician to patient. He helped bring a company into being by selling its securities. He gave advice for its continuing health, injected new capital to speed growth, operated when serious trouble developed. The latter emergency usually resulted from inability of the company to pay interest on bonds; the operation consisted of reorganizing capital structure. Creditors—mostly bondholders—took their case before a court in the state where the corporation had its home office. The judge could appoint a receiver temporarily to manage the defaulting company and conserve its value. While the receiver ran things the creditors met, usually under the leadership of the investment bankers, to find a formula that would satisfy everybody.

Now the ordinary relations in a company were reversed. The common stockholders, who normally controlled the company, had little to say. First mortage bondholders, ordinarily passive creditors, had the power of life and death. If no compromise suited them, they might try to recover their investments by selling the property at auction. But few railroads and utilities were actually put on the auction block. Normally, receivership led rather to reorganization than to foreclosure and sale in bankruptcy. In the reorganization, security holders might have to make some sacrifice in income. The investment houses would market a new bond issue to pay off the floating or unfunded debt due to suppliers, banks, and employees. Fixed charges were reduced by the slash in interest rates; but the new issues tended to increase total indebtedness.

The investment bankers, then, were in command in good times and in bad. In company after company the tendency was to ask Wall Street advice at every step. By the 1890's, J. Pierpont Morgan (the most important investment banker) was one of the most influential persons in the United States. Having mastered transportation, he and his financial colleagues were moving into manufacturing. And the nation was entering an era of finance capitalism that would continue until 1929.

Commercial Banking and Insurance

After 1850, as before, small, weak local banks and conflicting state banking laws continued to be the rule. Bank failures after the panic of 1837 had led nine southern and western states to pass laws prohibiting banks. The boom of the 1850's caused repeal of these laws, and new state-chartered banks entered the field. Regulatory legislation held up standards in some states; but in most regions there was no adequate supervision.

When the National Banking Act was passed (1863), conservatives hoped a new day had dawned. There was now a system of national banks, privately owned but subject to inspection and regulation by the United States government. In 1865, when Congress imposed a prohibitory tax on paper money issued by state-chartered banks, the national institutions obtained a monopoly of bank-note issue. This, it was felt, would force all state banks to take national charters, so that they could issue paper currency; and they would thus become subject to regulation by the national government.

For a time, this was the trend. By 1868 there were 1600 national banks, against less than 250 others. But then the rising market value of government bonds led many banks to sell these securities. Since note issue was based on bond holdings, this made it necessary for them to contract their bank-note circulation. As a substitute for bank notes, they urged depositors to use checks. This worked so well that many banks decided they could get along without issuing bank notes; they could use coin and checks, and the paper currency of other institutions. If a bank no longer issued bank notes, it no longer needed a federal charter, no longer needed to submit to inspections and regulations of the United States government. So by 1887 state and non-chartered banks were more numerous than were national banks. The confusion and uncertainty of the 1850's had returned to the banking field. States seeking to encourage business expansion permitted individuals or groups to organize banks with as little as $5000 in capital; and these institutions were not adequately inspected. In 1893, 228 failed.

In urban communities a new type of bank gained ground. This was the trust company. Trust companies originated as organizations for managing estates (one was chartered as early as 1828 in New York). Gradually the trust company came to do a commercial banking business. Its advantage was the fact that it could invest in stocks as well as bonds. State-chartered banks, by contrast, were usually restricted by law to certain types of bonds. With their broader base, trust companies became customers of the investment bankers and shared in the growth of finance capitalism.

Marine insurance had long been important in America and in Europe. Fire insurance became significant after 1815, particularly after the New York fire of 1835. Meantime, a few businessmen pioneered in life insurance. They encountered difficulties, for many thought it immoral to "gamble" on human life. In 1860, life insurance policies in force came to less than $200,000,000, one-fifteenth the figure for marine and fire insurance. Thereafter, life insurance boomed; in 1890 $13,000,000,000 in life insurance policies were in force. Needing to build large reserves against claims, life insurance companies bought bonds; and, like the trust companies, they drew close to the investment bankers. By 1900 "pooled savings" in trust companies, banks, and insurance companies provided the principal market for American transportation and industrial bonds.

New Employees

The nineteenth century saw office employment increasing throughout the Western world. But in the United States the white-collar group was larger than in any other nation and possessed more purchasing power than it did elsewhere. This reflected the triumph of mass production—the American industrial machine required proportionately fewer workers and proportionately more administrators than the hand-labor processes still used in many European nations.

By 1900 American clerical, sales, professional, and managerial employees were half again as numerous as were men in business for themselves. They were outnumbered by the farmers and urban laborers; but there were nearly a third as many office workers as there were nonagricultural manual workers. It would be a mistake to look on white-collar workers as a single class. Still, there was no sharp break in the social and economic hierarchy between the $12-a-week clerk and the $200-a-week vice-president. Both were office workers; both were administrative employees. Furthermore, business was expanding so fast in the 1890's that able clerical employees had many chances for rapid advancement.

Conditions of Manual Labor

White-collar opportunities weakened the labor movement at the top, while competition from low-paid immigrants weakened it at the bottom. Nevertheless, workers made progress from 1850 to 1900, gaining shorter hours and somewhat higher wages.

Wage scales varied widely from place to place, even between neighboring cities like New York and Albany. Regional variations were greatest in businesses that produced for local markets: breweries, bakeries, construction, the service trades. In such activities there was no national labor market but a host of separate local markets. Theoretically, workers would move to the area of highest pay until the resulting surplus of labor at that point reduced rates to the common level. In practice, this happened slowly, if at all. Home, family, friends, security, and inertia kept workers tied to their communities; and newcomers from Europe went to cities where their relatives were already located. Migration, therefore, did not wipe out local wage differences.

Nor were wage scales uniform within a local area. Polish and German

Jews who poured into New York at the end of the century were employed in the garment industry at near-starvation wages. At the same time, in the same city, electrical and some construction workers obtained wages far above the national average. Similarly, Negroes received less than whites for the same jobs, women less than men. Many better-paying jobs (especially those involving supervisory functions) were closed to all except native-born white males.

In 1850 there was a clear distinction between skilled and unskilled workers. The unskilled were common laborers; the skilled were journeymen who had served an apprenticeship and learned a special trade. As factories became mechanized, the call was for workers with intelligence but no special skill. Subdivision of operations made it possible to assign a man to operations at which he might become proficient in a few days. The truly skilled crafts were gradually disappearing save in such strongholds as the building and railroad industries.

By 1900 20 percent of working Americans owned or operated farms. The professional and business group, with clerks, accounted for 25 percent. Subtracting 5 percent for servants, the remaining 50 percent represented labor, divided fairly evenly between skilled, semiskilled, unskilled, and agricultural. For all types of manual workers, except some of the skilled crafts, real wages increased from 1865 to 1896, after a decline in the previous decade and a half. In many industries $1.50 was the daily wage for all this period. But, with prices on the decline, that amount would buy more in 1896 than in 1865. Meanwhile, the working day dropped from nearly eleven to about ten hours.

These gains were somewhat offset by less convenient working and living conditions. Machines went faster; the worker of 1900 might be as tired after ten hours of labor as the worker of 1865 after eleven. The growth of cities was another complication. If it took a man half an hour longer to get to work each day, an equivalent reduction in the working day would give him no added leisure. If trolley fares, higher rent, and more expensive amusements raised his living costs, he lost his increase in real wages. In addition, his children were likely to be brought up in undesirable locations, surrounded by disease, crime, and vice. Thus it is difficult to conclude that the big-city worker of 1900 was as well off as the small-town laborer of fifty years before.

The Labor Movement

In Europe, the labor movement grew by leaps and bounds. In the United States, the movement lagged. Organizers were hampered by conflicts among workers (native Americans versus immigrants, whites versus Negroes), by antiunion policies of employers, by indifference or opposition of the public and government. In 1896 trade-union members numbered only 3 percent of the nation's nonagricultural labor force. Most labor leaders were associated with skilled craft unions, organizations of the "aristocrats of labor." As was natural, these craft unions were basically interested in aiding their own members, only incidentally concerned about the needs of the great mass of less skilled workers.

There was no nation-wide labor association in 1850; and few crafts had organized on a national basis. The strength of organized labor was in local craft unions. During the prosperous 1850's and 1860's these unions gained strength. Some of the strongest (typographers, iron molders, locomotive engineers) created national organizations. There were two dozen national labor organizations in 1873, with a quarter-million members. The ensuing depression, however, reduced this number by more than half.

For a decade before his death in 1869, William Sylvis of the Moulders Union was the chief American labor leader. As spokesman for the Moulders (well-organized skilled workers in a key industry), Sylvis could win the attention of other workers, and of businessmen and politicians. In the secession crisis Sylvis opposed coercion of the South; but when war came, he vigorously backed the Union cause. After the war, Sylvis and others formed a short-lived National Labor Union (1866). Here he worked with such leaders of the shorter-hour movement as Ira Steward; Wendell Phillips and other intellectuals interested in labor reform; and even the woman-suffrage advocates, including Elizabeth Cady Stanton and Susan B. Anthony. With 500,000 members, the National Labor Union was in part responsible for establishing an eight-hour day for United States government workers (1868), and for agitation for state laws extending this principle further. The movement also led to Labor Reform victories in local elections in the Northeast, and an unsuccessful attempt to name a National Labor Reform presidential ticket in 1872. But in the end the National Labor Union failed. The death of Sylvis removed one able leader. More important, the union had paid too much attention to political reform and producers' coöperatives, too little to strengthening union organization and raising workers' standards. Workingmen had lost interest even before the panic of 1873 cut into labor strength; and the union in its final stages was run by kindhearted but ineffectual intellectuals.

There was no immediate effort to form another national labor association. It was hard enough to keep local craft unions going during the depression years. Organized labor suffered further in the railway strikes of 1877—strikes caused by wage cuts and the black-listing of union members. Federal and state officials sided with the employers, and the strikers were defeated.

Then came the Order of the Knights of Labor. Founded in 1869 as a secret society of Philadelphia tailors, the Order in 1878 became a national organization for all workers, skilled and unskilled, male and female, native and immigrant, white and Negro. Under a new leader, Terence V. Powderly, the Knights grew rapidly, to 700,000 in 1886. Success was related to the improving economic situation, which helped all labor organizations; the willingness of the Knights to welcome anyone interested in labor; the low initiation fee (one dollar); the abolition of the oath of secrecy (1881); and the success of the Knights in a clash with Jay Gould's railroad and telegraph empire.

But then came trouble. Members poured in too fast to be assimilated, too fast to be disciplined in union practices. Powderly gave too much time to such side issues as temperance, coöperatives, and local politics. He presently found himself unable to control his men. The rank and file undertook unwise strikes. Skilled workers in the Order quarreled with the common laborers in the mixed locals. By 1887 the membership had melted away. The great day of the Knights ended as suddenly as it began.

The collapse of the Knights discredited the one-big-union idea, and the craft unions again took hold. For greater strength, these unions of skilled workers formed an American Federation of Labor (1886), under able young Samuel Gompers of the Cigarmakers. Beginning with 100,000 members, the A.F. of L. grew to 250,000 ten years later. In the A.F. of L., each union had autonomy. Hence there were substantial differences among the unions. The United Brewery Workers and United Mine Workers had an industrial union basis and took in all workers in their fields. More typical were craft unions like the United Brotherhood of Carpenters and Joiners, the International Brotherhood of Teamsters, the Cigarmakers International Union. Most of these excluded not only unskilled workers but also women and Negroes.

It is possible to criticize the A.F. of L. for its policies of exclusion. The Federation failed to help those who needed help the most, and concentrated on skills when machines were eliminating skills in industry. But the Knights of Labor, by trying to do too much, had ended by accomplishing nothing at all. Attempting less, the A.F. of L. achieved limited success. Its victories were in large part the work of its president. Although Gompers did not try to dominate the member unions, he did set standards. In particular, he kept his unions out of politics and emphasized negotiations with employers, aiming at contracts for higher wages and shorter hours.

Although the A.F. of L. attracted most of the craft unions, it did not get them all. The strongest outside the fold were the railroad brotherhoods. Formed from 1863 to 1883, these embraced the men who rode the trains: engineers, firemen, conductors, trainmen. Skilled and relatively well paid, members of the brotherhoods preferred to handle their problems in their own way, and not to affiliate with any national organization.

Employers and Unions

Opportunities for advancement, competition from immigrants, and the narrow interest of skilled crafts helped explain the failure of labor organizers from 1850 to 1896. In addition, organizers faced opposition from employers. Nineteenth-century businessmen were generally so opposed to unions that they were ready to fight labor organizers to the death, with every available weapon.

When workers organized, employers also combined. The emergence of strong craft unions in the 1860's led to the formation of local employers' associations, like the New York Typothetae (1862), in the printing field. Twenty-five years later this and other regional associations formed the United Typothetae, a national employers' association. Such associations, with a view of a whole industry, could give useful advice in labor crises.

The method used depended somewhat on the times. If business was good it was best to compromise, or to hire strikebreakers to maintain the flow of goods. If business was poor little was lost by a shutdown. One could ask a court for an injunction against strike activity as a threat to property. But since courts were slow, and lawyers expensive, most employers and employer associations preferred lockouts or the hiring of strikebreakers.

Violence was always a possibility in labor disputes. It might hurt the employer (by destroying his property) or help him (by bringing public support and government troops). Employer associations maintained contact with the Pinkerton Detective Agency and other concerns that supplied armed guards to guard property and protect strikebreakers from attacks by pickets. Sometimes guards deliberately created disturbances, causing government authorities to send in troops to help defend the plant.

When strikes attracted national attention (as in the strike at Carnegie's Homestead, Pennsylvania, plant in 1892), middle-class opinion usually supported the employer. Often, too, employer associations and newspapers misled the public on a labor question. This happened in the Haymarket case. Anarchists were then bidding for support, urging direct individual warfare against the tyranny of bosses and the government. This had a certain appeal in the mountain states and Far West, in recently settled areas accustomed to weak law and strong personal action. Elsewhere the movement made little headway. But the anarchists preached violence; and in 1886 a Chicago court connected them with a Haymarket Square bomb outrage. Four anarchists were hanged and others imprisoned after a trial featured by disregard for legal rights of the accused. Having no sympathy for anarchists, and being forced to rely on distorted press accounts, the public generally approved of the verdict. The affair hurt the anarchists. But then, the anarchists would not have been important in any case. The significant point was the influence of this episode on the union movement. Few labor leaders were anarchists; and anarchist doctrines made no impression whatsoever on the union rank and file. Nevertheless, employer associations and many editors blamed the labor movement for the Haymarket outrage. For years thereafter, foes of labor called union organizers "anarchists."

Or "socialists." Here the antilabor forces were on sounder ground. Many European and some American labor leaders were influenced by socialist doctrine. Early in the 1890's Daniel DeLeon and other members of the Socialist Labor party tried to get control of the American Federation of Labor. Working with other groups, they managed for one year to have antisocialist Samuel Gompers dropped as president of the A.F. of L. But Gompers came back stronger than ever, and socialist influence declined. Although antiunion agents continued to denounce labor as "socialistic," the overwhelming majority of union members voted Democratic or Republican.

In general, the United States government stayed out of labor disputes; but when it did intervene, it was on the side of the employers. The most celebrated case was that of the Pullman strike of 1894. This involved a new, industrial-type American Railway Union, headed by Eugene V. Debs, and strong on midwestern railroads and in the Pullman Company. A defensive strike against pay cuts by this sleeping car company forced Debs to test his strength in 1894, during a deep depression. To help the strikers, members of the American Railway Union refused to handle Pullman cars in the Chicago yards. Maintaining that Debs was interfering with the mails, a federal district judge issued a sweeping injunction against all types of activity needed to maintain the strike. President Grover Cleveland then rushed in federal troops to guard the trains. This was done over the protests of the governor of Illinois, John P. Altgeld. Like Cleveland, Altgeld was a Democrat; but he did not share the President's antilabor views. Cleveland, however, persisted. The strike and the American Railway Union were broken, and Debs was sent to jail.

This strike is interesting for several reasons: crushing of an industrial union; use of an injunction and federal troops against organized labor; conflict between state and federal governments, resulting in defeat for states' rights. Most interesting of all was the public reaction. Altgeld partisans and labor leaders denounced Cleveland's actions. But most citizens felt that the President had acted wisely. Organized labor had not yet come into its own.

16

Urban Growth
and Culture

Industry Creates Large Cities

Industrial expansion was an urban development. As centers increased in size, their possession of banks and transportation and a labor supply attracted still more industrial establishments. Immigrants and native workers came in to claim the new jobs; and the cities became ever bigger. New York City, a town of 20,000 in Revolutionary days, had passed 500,000 in 1850 and jumped to nearly 3,500,000 by 1900. Cleveland, with 17,000 in 1850, boasted 400,000 by 1900; Chicago soared from 30,000 to 1,700,000.

Urban growth lagged in the agricultural South. Even so, new textile factories did bring workers to Georgia, Carolina, and Alabama mill towns. New Orleans, the southern export center, grew moderately from 100,000 to 400,000. The Rocky Mountain and Pacific coast areas also had few large cities. An exception was San Francisco, a port which mushroomed from 34,000 to ten times that figure.

Growth was not confined to metropolitan districts. Improvements in transportation and establishment of small factories turned villages into towns, towns into cities. Connecticut, for example, developed many industrial centers ranging from 10,000 to 100,000 in population. Plainly, the republic was becoming urbanized. In 1850 urban population was only 15 percent of the total. By 1900 it was nearly 40 percent.

In the mad rush of industrial expansion, cities poured out into adjacent territory without seriously considering problems of housing, traffic, recreation, and public safety. Local authorities were then faced with needs for street paving and maintenance, police and fire protection, water supplies, health services, and sewage disposal. Expansion of these services was paid for by increased tax income, based chiefly on mounting real-estate values. In the process, city officials handled ever greater funds—just when numbers of citizens became so large that the average individual lost touch with City Hall. Treasuries were now worth looting, and corrupt officials enriched themselves by awarding contracts to friends. Corruption left little money for needed services. But the poor, who suffered most, lacked influence; the upper classes were prosperous anyway, so why worry?

Most American cities were laid out in squares and rectangles, following such early models as Philadelphia. City streets were cleaner than in colonial times, and rough cobblestones were being replaced by asphalt pavements; but dirt and trash testified to the inefficiency of municipal collecting services. Water-front areas were crowded and filthy, in contrast to some western European harbors. American business streets were usually narrow and noisy, overhead networks of telegraph and telephone wires adding to their ugliness. Residential neighborhoods had a monotonous appearance, with their rows of buildings all looking much alike. Separate houses predominated in small cities, but solid blocks became the rule in metropolitan centers. Population pressure forced the less prosperous into large tenements and "flats." Skyscrapers were yet to come. Low urban skylines were relieved by church spires, but the general appearance was unimpressive.

As cities grew, the poor crowded into the older parts of town. Congestion was worst in New York, swamped by waves of immigrants. By 1900, 1,500,000 persons lived in New York City's slums. Here and in other large cities national groups crowded into adjacent blocks, creating a "little Greece" or a "little Italy," which so segregated special elements as to delay their Americanization. Meantime, business sections moved back from the water fronts, and middle- and upper-income residents (largely of native stock) escaped uptown. By the 1890's many were moving out into new suburbs.

The wealthy provided themselves with elaborate suburban homes (as along Chicago's North Shore) or built expensive residences on aristocratic avenues and squares in town. By walking a few blocks, the poor could compare their misery with the luxury of the rich. This experience was especially bitter during hard times, when families dependent on soup kitchens saw the conspicuous waste associated with elaborate entertainments in the mansions of plutocrats. How could this be reconciled with American traditions of equal opportunities and the rights of the common man?

Middle-income families, a relatively large class, lived in fairly comfortable houses on side streets uptown. Since they could not afford carriages, these citizens rode bicycles or streetcars to work. They mingled in the business section with the poor, returning to their quiet neighborhoods at nightfall.

The Urban Family

City dwellers had far more modern conveniences than farm families. By the 1890's, prosperous urban citizens were lighting their homes by electricity or by improved Welsbach gas mantles; a few had telephones. Immigrant maids relieved the housewife of much drudgery. Summer vacations for mother and the children were becoming more common, although father could not tear himself away from the desk except on week ends. Boys enjoyed these vacations into their teens, for schooling was being extended. Formerly, many destined for business had left school at the end of the elementary grades. Now a high school education seemed desirable. Prosperous families were also coming to feel that boys (and even girls) should go to college.

College education for girls reflected continued improvement in the position of women. True, the husband still insisted on being head of the household. But women by 1900 had almost complete control of their own property, and a half-century of agitation for women's rights had begun to change middle-class family patterns. Poor women, without property or advanced education, were less able to assert themselves.

Women were increasingly employed outside the home. Girls had invaded factories long before 1850. Industrial expansion increased such employment after mid-century, especially in textile mills. Education also provided openings; by 1890 a man teacher was a curiosity in elementary public schools. Technologic innovations brought new opportunities in business. The telephone, the typewriter, the new filing systems called for additional employees; and most employers found girls as efficient as men, and cheaper.

Employment of wives and daughters was necessary to supplement lower- and even middle-class family income. But when there were young children, the trend produced problems. The new compulsory attendance laws kept children at school a good part of the day. Nevertheless, the absence of the mother from the home was unfortunate; it left children on the streets outside of school hours in the very neighborhoods where this environment was most demoralizing.

The Slums Breed Crime and Disease

The evils of urban life were of course most obvious in the slums. Parks were few. Neither the public nor the parochial schools provided recreational facilities. The churches could do little, for Catholic parishes in the slums were poor; and the Protestant churches had fled the slums with their parishioners. Children could play only on the streets or in back yards; and adults were driven to the saloons.

There were plenty of these; New York had 7500 in 1890, one for every 200 citizens. The saloon served as a sort of poor man's club, where one could relax, talk to friends, and purchase forgetfulness. Drunkenness often resulted, leading to street brawls and to the beating and neglect of wives and children. (In middle-class neighborhoods drinking had been discouraged by the temperance movement. By the 1890's, the foes of alcohol were beginning to demand complete prohibition of liquor; the Anti-Saloon League was organized in 1895 to carry forward this aggressive campaign.)

Children growing up in slum dwellings lacked normal outlets and restraints, and life on the street led easily to delinquency. It was a short step from petty thievery to robbery, then to murder. In 1881 there were 25 murders per million population in the United States; by 1898, 107. New York and Chicago each listed more crimes of violence per year than did all England and Wales. Why so? Some blamed the American frontier tradition and passion for individualism. Others talked of culture conflicts growing out of immigration, or the inefficiency and corruption in police and court systems.

A long-inadequate prison structure now had added burdens. Earlier experiments with solitary confinement were abandoned as too severe and too expensive. But even with two or more inmates per cell, new buildings were needed. And social reformers and prison officials urged reconsideration of the whole penal system. Private charities were multiplying at this time, settlement houses were established in the slums, societies took interest in poor children. Supplementing voluntary efforts, state boards of charity coördinated the activities of such tax-supported welfare agencies as poorhouses, orphanages, and hospitals. Prison reform was closely related.

A National Prison Association, organized in the 1870's, asked for better buildings and less brutal discipline; also, emphasis should be on reformation rather than punishment. The idea was to help human beings and save taxpayers money. In that decade, Massachusetts began placing minor offenders on probation. Thereafter, many states liberated prisoners on parole, continued freedom being based on good behavior. In 1877 New York established special reformatories for youthful offenders. (Reformation was more likely if young delinquents were kept separate from habitual criminals.) These experiments brought encouraging results on the state level. It was more difficult to modernize city and county jails. Since prisoners were committed to these institutions for short terms, there was less concern about their treatment. Besides, jailers and other local officials were almost always untrained and frequently corrupt. Average citizens were indifferent, and unwilling to have their taxes increased to improve the situation.

In or near the slums were "red-light districts" of commercialized prostitution. Always an urban phenomenon, these districts flourished in cities which contained large numbers of unmarried men. Because of the moral issue, prostitution was not legalized in this country as in Latin Europe. Hence it expanded as an illegal business. Management of brothels was often tied to saloons and gambling interests. Since the houses had to pay for protection, the police and local politicians were drawn into the complex underworld picture. Patrons were mostly poor or of moderate means; wealthy men could maintain mistresses. Prostitution spread venereal diseases. Since infection was a social disgrace, and since Victorian prudishness placed a taboo on discussions of sex, a conspiracy of silence prevailed. This made it impossible to enlighten the public on medical aspects of the situation and prevented health authorities from dealing with venereal diseases by notification and isolation.

The slums were breeding places for all infectious diseases. Overworked and undernourished, the poor were ill equipped to resist illness. Crowded, unsanitary surroundings spelled danger. Lack of fresh air increased the risk of tuberculosis; filth brought vermin and the threat of typhus fever. In 1900, when the gross national death rate was seventeen per thousand, it was twenty for New York City, and as high as sixty-two for that city's tenement districts.

Disturbed by epidemics especially, physicians and engineers launched a sanitary movement in the 1850's. Unfortunately, the chief sanitarians are now forgotten—Lemuel Shattuck, who in 1850 planned in Massachusetts the first state board of health; Dr. Wilson Jewell, who inspired the first national health association (1857). National sanitary conventions by 1860 were urging cities to clean their streets, supply pure water, and provide proper disposal of garbage and sewage. An American Public Health Association took up the work in 1872.

As late as 1877, such large places as Providence and Milwaukee had no public water supplies, and Philadelphia still possessed over 80,000 private vaults and cesspools. Thereafter, sanitary arrangements began to catch up with urban expansion. Only 600 cities had public waterworks in 1878; six times that many possessed them two decades later. Sewage systems also extended into long underground networks. But still cities dumped sewage in rivers and harbors, contaminating their own and their neighbors' water supplies.

By promoting cleanliness, the new water systems reduced such diseases as typhus. Water also made better fire protection possible. Fire risks mounted with urban congestion and the installation of electric wiring. In the early 1870's great conflagrations nearly destroyed Chicago and Boston; and by 1883 the annual property loss from fire exceeded $100,000,000. To combat this menace, large cities replaced excitable volunteers with uniformed, professional firemen. Horse-drawn fire engines were improved; inventors produced automatic sprinklers and experimented with fireproof building construction.

Technology had limitations when it came to protecting public health. When a water supply was contaminated, improved engineering systematically pumped typhoid germs into homes. What was needed was medical as well as mechanical knowledge. This came after 1885, when European discoveries in bacteriology stressed the need for safe as well as sufficient water supplies. Boards of health took notice, and the annual death rate of major cities, constant between 1870 and 1890, fell from twenty-five per thousand in 1893 to twenty in 1900. This improvement came from conquest of the chief infectious diseases—typhoid, typhus, scarlet fever, smallpox, tuberculosis. Typhoid mortality in New York City fell from thirty-seven per 100,000 in 1893 to twenty-one in 1900 (by 1920 it was only two).

The decline in city death rates in the 1890's was double that of the country as a whole. Urban death rates remained a little higher than the rural, but the margin was closing. No longer could the cities be condemned as the graveyards of mankind.

Religion and Urban Life

During the Civil War the Protestant churches provided for the spiritual and physical well-being of the armed forces. After 1865, they planted churches in the new West. Significant, too, was a growing interest in foreign missions. But each of these trends was in line with traditional, evangelical aims of rural Protestantism; none struck at problems of urban society. The hold of the older evangelism was again shown in the 1870's and 1880's, in the revival led by Dwight L. Moody, a lay preacher, and Ira D. Sankey, his singing assistant. Addressing huge urban audiences, Moody urged all to cast aside sin and find peace and salvation in Jesus. The concentration, however, was on reclaiming erring souls among the middle classes rather than on making converts in immigrant-crowded slums.

Exponents of old-time religion looked with alarm on the secularization of the Sabbath in American cities. European immigrants regarded the Sabbath as a day of recreation; and many native American workers also sought pleasure on their one free day. Interpreting this as evidence of a decline in faith, orthodox Protestants tried to enforce Sunday-closing ordinances. To fit the changing times, an American Sabbath Union (1888) shifted the argument from a religious to a humanitarian basis. That is, Sabbath-breaking was condemned less as a sin against God than as an offense against man's need for rest. But, save in strictly rural areas, it was a losing struggle. Such urban states as New York and Massachusetts relaxed Sunday-closing laws, and the old-time Sabbath retreated as American life was urbanized.

Protestants did try new approaches in an effort to hold the urban middle classes. The Young Men's Christian Association, which migrated from England to the United States in 1851, grew rapidly after 1865. Its early emphasis was on temperance and on providing a religious atmosphere for country boys working in the cities. Without abandoning this interest, the Y.M.C.A. gave increasing attention to providing recreational and educational facilities. The Young Women's Christian Association (1866) did similar work for young women, concerning itself from the start with the welfare of working girls.

This period also saw the rise of Christian Science, founded by Mrs. Mary Baker Eddy. In *Science and Health* (1875) she taught that disease and poverty were illusions that could be dispelled by working in harmony with Eternal Mind as revealed by Jesus. Since it rejected poverty as an illusion, Christian Science had little appeal for working people. It did, however, attract an urban middle-class following. Adherents found comfort in its therapeutics and solace in a doctrine which, without rejecting the advantages of material well-being, disparaged the urban middle-class emphasis on materialism.

The rural heritage of Protestantism and the financial support it derived from the comfortable urban classes caused many Protestant leaders to ignore industrial workers. When the bakers' union petitioned 500 New York clergymen to preach sermons against compulsory labor on the Sabbath, all but six ignored the appeal. As late as 1894 a church at Oshkosh, Wisconsin, excluded trade unionists on the ground that the law of God forbade membership in a labor organization.

Yet this was only one side of the picture. These years witnessed growing concern for the problems of the poor. Temperance led some Protestants to the new position. After 1850 many foes of liquor saw the saloon as an escape from, rather than the cause of, slum conditions. Observers then recalled the doctrine of Horace Bushnell, a Connecticut Congregationalist who taught that the churches, while converting sinners, must also eliminate from the community factors that led individuals astray.

English example was even more important. At this very time certain Anglican clergymen were maintaining that the church must fight the evils of industrialism. Following their example, a few American Protestants began in the later 1880's to work for the poorest industrial workers. The Reverend W. D. P. Bliss, an Episcopalian, founded a Church Organization for the Advancement of the Interests of Labor (1887) and a more radical Society of Christian Socialists (1889). Bliss also joined a union and established a Church of the Carpenter in a working-class neighborhood. Early in the 1890's, the Baptists and Congregationalists formed committees to study social and economic problems; and at least one Protestant clergyman, Washington Gladden, mediated in disputes between employers and employees. Gladden, a Congregationalist, also investigated industrial conditions in Ohio as a step toward working out a program of profit sharing for workers.

Many books helped popularize the new movement, which was called social Christianity or the social gospel. Two became best sellers: Our Country (1885), by Josiah Strong, a Congregationalist home missionary; and In His Steps (1896), by the Reverend Charles M. Sheldon, of Topeka, Kansas. In His Steps sold 7,000,000 copies. It told about a congregation that resolved to live for one year in full accord with the teachings of Jesus. "If the church members were all doing as Jesus would do," asked Sheldon, "could it remain true that armies of men would walk the streets for jobs, and hundreds of them curse the church, and . . . find in the saloon their best friend?"

Social Christianity also inspired the founders of the new social settlement houses. Another example of awakening social conscience was the institutional church, featuring day nurseries, recreation centers, and vocational courses for those who lacked the "advantages." Meantime, interdenominational coöperation increased. The Y.M.C.A. and Y.W.C.A. were pioneer experiments, as was the United States Christian Commission, which ministered to the needs of soldiers during the Civil War. The Woman's Christian Temperance Union (1874), led by Frances Willard, drew support from all evangelical bodies. So did the Evangelical Alliance, which combated skepticism, rationalism, and Catholicism in the Old World and the New.

The secularization of society made a united religious front almost a necessity. Coöperation was made easier by a decline of traditional rivalry among Protestant sects. Minor theological points seemed less important than before when clergymen faced the immense challenge of the new industrialism. Critical Bible scholarship was also significant. Study of existing Christian texts in the light of archaeological discoveries and an improved philology compelled religious leaders to reverse long-accepted authorities, including the King James Version of the Bible. Involved, too, was the Darwinian theory of evolution, which cast doubt on the Biblical account of creation. At first, this theory increased conflict within church ranks; but in the long run widespread acceptance of Darwinism would further break down denominational lines. These trends were far more noticeable in the cities than in rural areas, where the traditional, individualistic type of Protestantism continued to be the rule.

Catholic Advance and the A.P.A.

While the Protestants adjusted themselves to urban life, Roman Catholicism flourished in the immigrant-packed districts of the cities. In 1865 Catholics accounted for 9 percent of the population—3,000,000. By 1900 there were 15,000,000, nearly 16 percent of the population. No less striking was the fact that the Catholic Church, which owed its rise to the influx of immigrants, was augmenting its property holdings even more rapidly than its membership.

The church did not maintain its hold on all Catholic immigrants; but the great majority stayed in the fold. One factor in the situation was the failure of Protestants to establish churches in lower-class neighborhoods. More important was the Catholic policy of having immigrant priests take care of immigrant groups. This meant that religion was closely associated with Old World experience and culture. No less significant was the establishment of parochial schools for elementary education. A Plenary Council, meeting in Baltimore in 1884, commanded Catholic parents to send their children to parochial rather than to public schools. The Council further ordered that a parochial school be built beside each parish church within two years. There followed a campaign to raise funds for this purpose.

In these years most American Catholics belonged to the working classes. Members of the Catholic hierarchy in the United States were therefore disturbed when the Canadian Catholic bishops had the Knights of Labor condemned (as a secret society). Backed by a number of American bishops, Cardinal Gibbons of Baltimore noted that the head of the Knights, Terence Powderly, was a Catholic, and held that the Order was not a secret society in the canonical sense. In 1886, the Vatican accepted the Cardinal's view. Five years later, Pope Leo XIII issued his famous "labor encyclical," *De Rerum Novarum*. While rejecting socialism, this document pleaded for justice to the workingman. Thanks to this stand, the more progressive members of the American Catholic hierarchy developed a policy comparable to that of the social gospel within Protestantism. Archbishop Ireland of St. Paul mediated two railway strikes, and other prelates helped movements for social justice. From 1882 on, the Catholic Church also sponsored the Knights of Columbus, which, like the Y.M.C.A., provided recreational and educational opportunities for urban youth.

The growth of Catholicism revived the traditional religious fears of old-stock Protestants. Catholic immigrants competed with American-born Protestants for jobs. Rural Protestants distrusted urban political machines run by Irish Catholics. Catholic newcomers were different from most native Americans in language and customs; and many Protestants looked askance at Catholic parochial school policy. One result of friction was the rise of the American Protective Association. Formed in Clinton, Iowa, in 1887, the A.P.A. picked up 70,000 members in five years and made further gains during the depression of the mid-1890's. Members pledged themselves not to vote for or employ Catholics if Protestants were available. The A.P.A. won a few city elections and for a time held the balance of power in several rural areas. But it ceased to be of consequence after 1896.

Many Protestants criticized the A.P.A. as intolerant. Catholic leaders, too, worked for good will. Tension did not disappear; but by 1900 many writers were emphasizing common spiritual traditions rather than ancient sources of conflict.

Education and the City

By 1850 the states in the Northeast and Middle West required all urban and rural areas to provide tax-supported elementary schools. Some also set a minimum school term—generally twelve weeks a year—and a few required larger towns to maintain public high schools. This loosely organized state system of locally run public schools spread westward after 1850. The Civil War cut short a promising public school movement in the South, and Reconstruction plans failed to materialize. But there was great progress by 1900.

Rural schools improved after 1850. Teachers were somewhat better, partly because of new state requirements for certification. In the 1880's, Massachusetts pioneered in developing consolidated schools to replace rural district schools. This movement spread, but very slowly. In many states the dispersed character of population made consolidated schools expensive. Besides, many farmers were not interested in education or did not want their children to go into town to school. Not until after 1900 did rural leaders see that the city would lure an undue proportion of farm youth until country schools became more attractive, and more effectively prepared boys and girls for rural living.

Education changed more rapidly in the city. There the basic economic processes took place, not in and around the home (as in the country), but in the factory, shop, and office. Thus the city home did not give children the skills they would need in later life. Increasingly, the task of providing these skills was assigned to education. Frequently the impetus came from employers. Massachusetts manufacturers attending the London Exhibition in 1851 were impressed at the way in which the British were applying art and science to industry. Returning home, they demanded that drawing and design be taught in public schools. As a result, the Massachusetts legislature permitted (1860), then required (1870) schools to introduce these subjects. A Normal Art School was set up to train teachers. In like fashion, businessmen were responsible for the founding of the nation's first manual training school (St. Louis, 1880).

Commercial training had long been available in private schools ("business colleges"). T' en, in 1871, John Eaton, head of the new United States Bureau of Educatioi, urged public schools to add commercial subjects. Taxpayers objected, since adding manual training and commercial subjects meant extra costs. Conservative educators said the trend involved debasing standards. But the movement steadily gained ground.

The need for child labor declined as hordes of immigrants arrived. Humanitarian considerations also reduced the employment of children. This in turn led to demands for statutes to require school attendance, to lengthen the school year, and to provide better opportunities for children to continue studies into high school. Massachusetts enacted the first compulsory attendance law in 1852, requiring all children from eight to fourteen to attend school twelve weeks a year. By 1895 most northern and western states had some such statute. Industrial states also led the way in increasing the length of the school year. As late as 1880 the average American received less than four years of schooling; by 1896 the amount was almost five. Compulsory attendance helped; so did the development of the kindergarten at one end of the system and the addition of the high school at the other. In 1870 there were 500 high schools in the country; by 1890 there were five times that many.

In asking for better schools, reformers noted the special problems of urban areas. Community restraints on the individual counted for less in the city than in the country. Could not schools provide the needed restraint, thus checking juvenile delinquency? Church and family had less hold on many city people than on the rural population. Might not schools instill the moral values which religion and the home could not adequately provide? Immigrants, many felt, did not understand American institutions, hence fell prey to unscrupulous politicians and radical agitators. Could not educators combat these influences, turning the children of immigrants into useful, loyal Americans?

The traditional classroom, wedded to rote learning and "mental discipline," was under fire in these years. Darwin's evolutionary theory, by stressing individual differences, challenged the assumption that rigid uniformity was necessary in education. American educators returning from Germany introduced the Herbartian psychology, which stressed the importance of arousing a child's interest by making schoolwork meaningful in terms of past and potential experiences. Refusing to be bound by the traditional curriculum, Herbartians helped introduce such subjects as literature, history, economics, typewriting, and cooking. Others echoed Herbert Spencer's view that education must prepare young people for an urban, industrial society.

Colleges and Universities

Some 260 new colleges and universities opened their doors between 1860 and 1890. Meantime, older institutions grew in strength. This was definitely related to urbanization and industrialization. To be sure, most colleges were in rural areas; but, save for a few state universities, the largest, most progressive, and most prosperous were tied to urban centers. Upper-middle-class parents were finding it desirable to send their children to college.

In this period state and federal governments poured substantial sums into higher education. So did businessmen. A Pennsylvania coal operator founded Lehigh, a New England industrialist planned Clark. Railroad promoters like Cornelius Vanderbilt and Leland Stanford endowed universities, as did Ezra Cornell (telegraph and lands) and Johns Hopkins (trade and finance). John D. Rockefeller gave liberally to the new University of Chicago. Vassar, Wellesley, and Smith owed their foundation to well-to-do citizens who wanted to give women better opportunities.

Even before 1850, college presidents and professors had debated the issue of classical versus practical education. The coming of the industrial age settled the debate; the classical curriculum with its prescribed course of study for all students gave way with the introduction of the natural sciences, the social studies, and the elective system. The new trend was aided by the Morrill Land-Grant Act of 1862, designed to encourage mechanical and agricultural education. Lack of experience, personnel, or funds held the lang-grant colleges back for a while; but they soon made up for lost time. The University of Illinois pioneered in introducing shop courses. Cornell University (which combined land-grant support with private benefactions) gave scientific and practical education equal status with liberal arts. Nor were the land-grant colleges alone. The older private institutions added science and engineering courses. New technical colleges were established to meet the needs of the urban age: Massachusetts Institute of Technology, Case, Drexel, Armour. Most of these were designed to train engineers needed in transportation and industry.

Business also wanted personnel trained in social science. In 1881 the banker Joseph Wharton gave the University of Pennsylvania a liberal gift for establishing a school of finance and commerce—the first modern institution of its kind. Other institutions introduced courses in economics, sociology, and political science. Some of the new social scientists ran into trouble when their teachings did not square with ideas generally accepted in business circles. Tariff protectionists tried to have William Graham Sumner ousted from Yale. One economist was compelled to leave Cornell when he expressed himself frankly on the Gould strike. Another was virtually dismissed from Chicago when he criticized certain corporations. Nevertheless, social scientists increased their influence and won the right to air their views.

Adult Education

The lyceum reached its height in the 1850's. After the Civil War James Redpath, an enterprising journalist, opened a central booking office. Lecturers could secure engagements through this agency, and local lyceums could engage speakers. This was convenient on both sides. But quality was sacrificed to efficiency. As older stars like Ralph Waldo Emerson died or retired, Redpath pushed less serious entertainment —humorous readings, travelogues, musical varieties.

As the lyceum changed character, Chautauqua took its place. This movement was launched in the 1870's, one of its founders being John H. Vincent, later a Methodist bishop. Interested in training Sunday School teachers, the sponsors staged summer camp meetings at Lake Chautauqua, New York. Then they broadened their approach, in a democratic, Christian effort to supply plain people with a rich cultural fare. Presently, touring companies reached townspeople and farmers who were unable to attend the summer assemblies. Study groups were supplied with syllabuses and books, to supplement the lectures.

There were lectures in the cities, too. In addition, cities had evening schools. The first of these were private; later, many won public backing. The public library movement was also city centered. Here the major figure was the self-educated iron and steel magnate, Andrew Carnegie. His first gift in the field was made in Pittsburgh in 1881; and by 1900 he had given $6,000,000 for library purposes. The community furnished the site. Carnegie then built the library, which the community agreed to maintain. Thanks to Carnegie and others, the free public library was to become a great bulwark of American democracy.

Literature for Everybody

The new reading habits and growth of urban population brought prosperity to American publishers. As before, books were sold on a subscription basis, through traveling book agents, and through bookstores. Editions became larger; books were advertised more widely than before. As in other businesses, growth brought concentration; and publishing became centered in New York.

Until 1891 American legislation protected native but not foreign authors. Many publishers therefore ignored American writers (to whom royalties had to be paid) and brought out cheap editions of English novels (paying nothing for the privilege). Both European and American authors were better off when Congress finally extended protection to foreigners, in an international copyright law of 1891.

From 1850 on, there was an enormous increase in the production of "literature for the masses." Hack writers ground out this material in quantity; Harlan P. Halsey, creator of the *Old Sleuth* series, penned 650 dime novels. Publishers sold such products by the tens of thousands. Love and adventure were major themes. Juveniles went for Buffalo Bill Wild West titles and for Horatio Alger's stories about country boys who made good in the city. Adults liked suspense and sugary sentiment.

Critics rightly held that few of these items had enduring literary value. These same critics, however, underrated Samuel L. Clemens (Mark Twain), mistakenly identifying his humor with the "low tradition." Many public libraries even refused to stock *Huckleberry Finn*. More acceptable were the local-color writers: George Washington Cable, who wrote of Louisiana Creoles; Joel Chandler Harris, whose stories concerned southern Negroes; Thomas Nelson Page (a bygone Virginia); Edward Eggleston (backwoods Indiana); Hamlin Garland (prairie frontier); Bret Harte (Far West); Sarah Orne Jewett (down-east Maine).

Many writers dealt with the new urban regions. Walt Whitman found inspiration in bustling city crowds. William Dean Howells probed problems of urban life, including divorce. Stephen Crane handled another city type in *Maggie, A Girl of the Streets*. John Hay's *Breadwinners* dealt unsympathetically with trade unions; Edward Bellamy's utopian *Looking Backward* described an urban society under socialism.

Magazines sold better than before, especially in the cities. The reasons were various: the rise of mass advertising; improvements in printing and the reproduction of illustrations; the second-class mailing privilege granted by Congress in 1879. The quality periodicals included *Harper's Monthly*, which first appeared in 1850, and the *Atlantic* (1857). More spectacular was the rise of the mass-circulation magazine. The *New York Ledger*, launched in 1855, quickly soared to the then-unheard-of circulation of 400,000. Its publisher, Richard Bonner, became a millionaire; and the high prices paid for contributions made the writing profession more attractive than before. Henry Wadsworth Longfellow and Harriet Beecher Stowe were glad to write for the *Ledger*. Also popular were the illustrated weeklies, *Leslie's* and *Harper's Weekly*, both of which backed reforms. *Leslie's* crusaded against the pollution of milk; Thomas Nast's cartoons in *Harper's* helped expose Boss Tweed's corrupt New York City machine.

In 1865, 700 magazines were published in the United States. In 1885 there were 3300. Many appealed to special groups. The *Independent* used a religious approach, E. L. Godkin's *Nation* aimed at the intellectual elite, *Popular Science* was for those interested in new technological discoveries. New magazines for women overshadowed the venerable *Godey's Lady's Book*, which gave up the fight in 1898. The new pacemaker was the *Ladies' Home Journal*, especially after the crusading Edward K. Bok became editor in 1889.

The number of daily newspapers doubled from 1880 to 1900, and circulation went up even faster. Technological improvements enabled publishers to get out larger, more frequent editions at lower cost. To reach more customers, journalists stressed reader appeal. Editorials were played down. News was presented in a livelier style, headlines became bolder, and there were pages for homemakers, sports sections, comic strips, cartoons, health hints, columns for theatergoers and the lovelorn. As circulation increased, papers bought outside services. In 1884 S. S. McClure set up the first agency to provide syndicated features. At the same time the growth of such news-gathering agencies as the Associated Press added to the efficiency (and uniformity) of the American press. Since advertising helped pay for the new services and features, and since newspapers were themselves big businesses, editorials often reflected ideas of industrial and mercantile leaders.

Horace Greeley had used his New York *Tribune* to air his economic and political views. The new journalists cared less for this than for sensation. Charles A. Dana of the *Sun* and the James Gordon Bennetts of the *Herald* pointed the way in New York journalism by playing up scandals and human-interest stories. Out in the Middle West, the Scripps brothers also favored sensationalism. In addition, they demonstrated the possibilities of the evening paper, which appealed to office workers and laboring men. The Scripps brothers further blazed a trail in the chain newspaper field.

Still more influential was Joseph Pulitzer, an immigrant who bought the St. Louis *Post-Dispatch* in the 1870's. Pulitzer championed civic causes, exposed bribery and corruption. At the same time, he featured crime and sex and introduced departments designed to appeal to average readers. Later he used the same formula to build up the run-down New York *World*. From 1895 on, Pulitzer had a rival in New York—William Randolph Hearst, who had started out in California, with the San Francisco *Examiner*. Branching out, Hearst acquired the New York *Journal*, the second link in what would become a nation-wide newspaper-and-magazine chain. Soon Hearst and Pulitzer were locked in a circulation war, each trying to outdo the other in news coverage, features, sensations, and reforms. In the process, both influenced diplomacy by playing up the Cuban insurgent cause (1895–98) and demanding that the United States drive Spain out of the island of Cuba.

An Age of Specialists

Industrialization and urbanization brought a need for all sorts of specialists. Colonial doctors had given medicine, pulled teeth, and treated animals. Now these several jobs were divided. Colleges of dentistry were founded after 1850, veterinary schools after 1875. Specialties also developed within medicine proper—obstetrics, surgery, and so on. Each group set up its own professional organization, such as the American Otological Society (ear specialists, 1869) and the American Surgical Society (1880). Engineers formed many special groups: civil (1852), mining and metallurgical (1871), mechanical (1880), electrical (1884). Specialists did not neglect the larger view. Members of the American Surgical Society continued to back the American Medical Association, which represented physicians in general. The American Association for the Advancement of Science (1848) won the support of many different disciplines.

The professional associations stressed formal education. Motives varied. Protection from competition was involved; a college-training requirement reduced the number entering a given field. Also, the professional bodies wanted to eliminate charlatans who fleeced the public and dragged down the reputation of the specialty. And, obviously, specialized preparation was more necessary in a complex urban culture than in the simpler agrarian society of an earlier age.

By developing interest in special problems, the new professional societies encouraged basic research. Here the colleges led the way. President Charles W. Eliot of Harvard appointed research men to his faculty and provided laboratory equipment. The Johns Hopkins University in Baltimore, established in 1876, devoted itself primarily to research. Modeled on German institutions, this university had no undergraduate liberal arts college. Its professors therefore could give their time to original research and the training of a few advanced scholars. The Hopkins experiment had great influence, and by 1896 several institutions had men and laboratories capable of basic investigations.

The new enthusiasm for research affected the humanities and social disciplines as well as the natural sciences. Approaches changed as the "scientific spirit" made its impact felt on language studies, history, economics, sociology, and law. Investigators borrowed methods of the natural scientists. They tried to observe phenomena systematically and to be objective, that is, to study without bias ("scientifically").

As in science, there was a tendency to rely on European leadership. Historians introduced the seminar technique from Germany; and college-trained "scientific historians" who strove for objectivity replaced the earlier, literary historians. Statistical methods developed in Europe and America enabled economists and sociologists to study institutions more analytically than before. But it was difficult to observe human behavior with the calm detachment that one applied to chemical combinations. Those who studied history, economics, sociology, and government generally elaborated doctrines which justified the systems they preferred. Some, like the Englishman Herbert Spencer, used available knowledge to defend laissez-faire capitalism. Others, including the German Karl Marx, used much the same information to attack existing institutions. In choosing sides, American thinkers were guided by their view of national interests. Marxian socialism, with its doctrine of class struggle, made little impression. Spencer had a great vogue, partly because his Darwinian slant pleased businessmen who felt that they represented the "survival of the fittest" in a free-for-all economic struggle.

The Natural Sciences: Darwinism

These were years of great advance in the natural sciences. Physicists expanded their knowledge of energy, thus making possible many technological improvements. Chemists learned how to proceed by analysis and synthesis—how to break down substances into their constituent elements and how to build up products by combining elements. Physics gave physicians improved microscopes and cameras; chemistry revolutionized physiology and pharmacology. Meanwhile, the theory of evolution transformed the field of biology. Back in the eighteenth century, zoölogists and botanists had collected and classified thousands of specimens of plants and animals. Some scientists had then become intrigued by the close resemblance of certain species to others. It was discovered that closely related species of animals and plants could be cross-bred, producing hybrids in some cases superior to one or both of the parent species.

This posed a problem: If breeders could produce new types, might this not have occurred in nature? Several scientists worked on this early in the nineteenth century. A few, including American-born Dr. William Charles Wells, suggested that all animals faced disease and competition, and that only the fittest would survive to perpetuate their kind. Animal types ill suited to the struggle for existence would become extinct, whereas successful competitors would survive and gradually evolve new species. In 1860 Charles Darwin and Alfred Russel Wallace, two Englishmen working independently, presented this same basic theory and supported it with a mass of evidence from comparative anatomy, natural history, animal breeding, and geology. Darwin's book, *The Origin of Species*, was especially notable.

Many churchmen condemned Darwin on the ground that his view implied that men as well as animals were descended from lower forms—the most immediate ancestor of man being some sort of prehistoric ape. Just as astronomers had dethroned the earth from a central position in the universe, so biologists were tumbling man from his unique position. Darwin was defended by the American writer John Fiske and others, who said that evolution was God's design for producing man; and by 1900 Darwinism had won general acceptance among educated Europeans and Americans. Biological research was greatly stimulated by the theory. Specialists in the new field of genetics gave their full attention to the mechanism of heredity. (Here Americans took the lead after 1890.) Evolution also influenced social thinkers, for the concept of the survival of the fittest could be applied to social classes, business competition, and even conflicts between nations.

Medical Advance

By the second half of the nineteenth century physicians had begun to identify diseases. No longer did they say simply that a patient was "bilious"; instead, they tried to diagnose his disease, as indicated by special symptoms. To perfect the new technique, medical scientists had to perform many autopsies and observe symptoms very closely. Hence they invented instruments to make bedside observations precise—the stethoscope, for example, and clinical thermometer. Using exact measurements, medicine was finally taking advantage of quantitative procedures, as the physical sciences had much earlier.

Knowledge obtained through autopsies was especially useful to surgeons. For centuries, surgery had been largely limited to amputations and the setting of fractures. After 1850, surgeons operated on the abdominal organs, finally (by 1900) on the chest and brain. Meanwhile, effective anesthetics had been developed. And, discovering that infections were caused by microörganisms, surgeons were using antiseptic dressings that eliminated these organisms, and were stressing absolute cleanliness (antiseptic and aseptic surgery).

Dental surgery deserves particular mention, as a specialty in which Americans excelled. In the 1840's American dentists gave the world the first effective anesthetics; and by 1870 even Europeans regarded American dentists as the best on earth. Dentistry affected appearance as well as health. It therefore appealed to a practical people like the Americans, who at the same time were in a relatively good position for paying dental bills.

Having identified many diseases, medical science now began to seek the causes of disease. Some blamed "noxious airs"; but a search for particular poisons in the atmosphere led to no result. More fruitful was another old theory, that diseases were caused by minute animals or plants ("germs"), which upon gaining access to the body attacked it as parasites. Using the improved microscope, French and German scientists demonstrated that certain diseases could be traced to particular microörganisms. Investigators found that typhoid and cholera germs were carried through water and food, and that these diseases could be prevented by purifying water and pasteurizing milk. In other cases, including diphtheria, it was learned that germs spread by contacts between persons. These diseases called for isolation. Pasteur also discovered that killed or weakened germs, when injected into the body, stimulated defense mechanisms in the blood. The germs could not multiply and cause disease; but they protected the body against later invasion by live and virulent organisms. A few protective vaccines were known by 1900; others (notably against typhoid) were developed soon thereafter.

In these years of progress, little was done for the mentally ill. Thanks to Dorothea Dix, government institutions for the insane had been set up by 1860. Study at these and European institutions enabled doctors to distinguish between mild conditions (neuroses) and more serious ones (psychoses). Investigators, however, were unable to discover any physical basis for mental illness. The tendency, therefore, was to commit to an asylum—and forget—serious psychotic cases, and dismiss neurotic patients with the remark that "it is just your nerves."

Between 1820 and 1870, many Americans lost confidence in physicians. Medical research was then concentrating on identifying disease; but doctors had few cures. Earlier, they had been sure that bleeding and purging were "good for what ails you"; and patients had been encouraged by this confidence. But as physicians discarded traditional techniques, patients felt that they were receiving little aid. Many turned to medical sects whose practitioners promised cures (for example, homeopathy, imported from Germany after 1830). In the 1850's it looked as though the medical profession might be broken into a number of warring sects, of which the "regulars" would be only one. Thereafter, medical progress cleared up the confusion.

American physicians who studied in Germany brought back news of discoveries that held out real hope for suffering mankind. Public confidence revived. Following the trend, many states limited practice largely to regular physicians, and required these to pass a state examination before starting practice.

Down to 1890 Americans benefited from, but played little part in, medical research. This was because of indifference to basic science and because Americans had an aversion to the autopsies essential for pathological studies. After 1890, Americans would see the utility of basic science and support it with enthusiasm.

The Fine Arts: Painting

In the fine arts as in science, nineteenth-century Americans leaned heavily on Europe. Trained in Europe or by European-trained masters, American artists tended to use Old World techniques. They did pick native themes, but only a few (like the painter Thomas Eakins and the architect Louis Sullivan) took up the challenge of the city. Urbanization did, however, affect the arts in another way. The accumulation of wealth in urban areas enabled individuals and city governments to pay substantial fees to architects, sculptors, and artists, and to establish art museums and patronize good music. This stimulated all the fine arts.

In the generation before 1850 the most significant development in painting had been the rise of the Hudson River school of landscape painters. Members of this school employed European techniques. They were, however, American nationalists who combined a romantic interest in the countryside with the conviction that the American scene offered inspiration and subject matter. Several painters continued this tradition into the 1870's. Chief among these was Frederic E. Church, a world traveler who painted icebergs, waterfalls, and mountain ranges.

In emphasis on detail members of the Hudson River school failed to catch the overall impression. A vital defect, said William Morris Hunt, who in the 1850's brought to America the technique and points of view of the French Barbizon school. Like his European masters, Hunt looked for "the big things first," tried to capture mood as well as detail. The same trend was seen in the work of George Inness, perhaps the greatest American landscape painter. Self-taught, Inness did his first work under influence of the Hudson River school. His early canvases, therefore, were literal, detailed representations of what he saw. Later association with members of the French Barbizon school led him to subordinate detail to feeling, and his romantic landscapes of the 1880's caught the moods of nature.

Meanwhile, other painters were rejecting romanticism and demanding realism. This group included James McNeill Whistler, Winslow Homer, and Thomas Eakins. All were influenced by the French realists and tried to paint what they saw. But they did not return to the literal representation of detail of the Hudson River school. Rather they suppressed irrelevant details and gave their paintings unity and force as well as accuracy. Though an American, Whistler lived abroad. Homer and Eakins, however, lived in the United States and gave their work an American character. Homer was most successful with pictures of fishermen and the foaming surf. His was a talent for making the usual seem fresh and unexpected. Eakins presented aspects of the new urban society: a medical clinic, prize fighters, a dancing Negro boy, business leaders. The pictures show the scientist's knowledge of anatomy and the poet's feeling for color and rhythm.

Although Homer was popular with the public as well as the critics, there was generally a distinction between the work of the great artists (the high tradition) and art by and for the people (the low tradition, or genre art). The great artists painted for themselves, the critics, and posterity. Genre art was for the average citizen. "Never paint for the few, but the many," said William Sidney Mount, who produced cheerful pictures of Negro life. Though influenced by European models, Mount and other genre artists gave their work a distinctively American character—were, in this, more successful than painters in the high tradition. And some popular artists did very good work. An example is George Caleb Bingham, who caught the spirit of life on western rivers and the frontier. Though primarily a genre artist, Bingham painted portraits in the high tradition; and he also served as professor of art at the University of Missouri.

Much popular art reached the public in lithograph form. In 1857, Nathaniel Currier (a businessman) and J. Merritt Ives (an artist) combined talents to become "print-makers to the American people." Employing a crew of artists, they put out thousands of lithographs illustrating public disasters, sporting events, national progress, and regional peculiarities. Many rivals challenged Currier & Ives, but the firm held its own until the end of the century.

Magazine and book publishers also distributed popular art. They, like Currier & Ives, took advantage of improved techniques of reproduction, from wood engravings to process blocks, and finally to half-tones. There were so many able artists in the field that this period has been called the golden age of American illustration. Among the leaders were Joseph Pennell, one of the great figures in American graphic arts, and Frederic Remington, sculptor, illustrator, and chronicler of the old West.

As in earlier times, the plain people created artistic objects for themselves. The Pennsylvania Dutch and Shakers maintained their folk art traditions. Even after 1850 New England whittlers carved handsome figureheads for clipper ships. Limners (though in diminishing numbers) roamed the countryside making portraits. Sign painters remained active; and housewives kept on making bedspreads and decorating wallpaper. But new recreational opportunities absorbed time formerly spent on folk arts. Machines replaced whittlers; and lithographing processes made good prints available at a low cost. So the old traditions faded in a changing age.

The Fine Arts: Sculpture

The equivalent of genre painting in sculpture was the popular work of John Rogers, whose low-priced composition statuettes sold widely. Some Rogers groups concerned everyday living ("Going for the Cows"); others represented military action ("One More Shot") or great political events ("The Emancipation Proclamation").

Sculpture in the high tradition fitted in with the upsurge of nationalism and the increase of urban wealth. Cities and states provided commissions for Civil War memorials, libraries, and capitol buildings; and the new-rich began patronizing sculptors. The result was a large increase of activity, signalized by the formation of the National Sculpture Society.

In 1850, American sculpture was under Italian neoclassic influence. By 1900 the chief influence was that of the French modernists. A key figure in the transition was Henry Kirke Brown. Italian-trained, Brown at first worked in the neoclassical tradition; but as he turned to American western themes, his work took on a new boldness and vitality. Brown's pupil John Quincy Adams Ward went further in the same direction. So did Daniel Chester French, who studied very briefly with Ward. French prepared "The Minute Man" for the centennial of Lexington and Concord in 1875; he later created the great statue in the Lincoln Memorial in Washington.

But it was Augustus Saint-Gaudens who dominated American sculpture. Like Brown, Ward, and French, Saint-Gaudens helped liberate his art from the arid neoclassic conventions. Irish-born and European-trained, Saint-Gaudens nevertheless captured American ideals in his statues of Farragut (New York) and Lincoln (Chicago). Outstanding, too, was his memorial for Mrs. Henry Adams, a bronze figure which suggested the brooding mystery of death. Saint-Gaudens also directed the sculptural harmonies at the Chicago World's Fair in 1893.

The Fine Arts: Architecture

The Greek revival in architecture was on the way out in 1850. It was succeeded by a romantic confusion of styles. The rich increasingly preferred the hodgepodge which architects called Gothic. Interiors, darkened by stained-glass windows and dark woodwork, presented a bewildering array of heavy, ornate furniture, inlaid tiles, and fancy mantles groaning under the weight of bric-a-brac. "Italian Gothic" public buildings, featuring varicolored stone and terra-cotta decorations, also reflected the new enthusiasm. The emphasis, all around, seemed to be on ugliness and discomfort.

Yet many signs pointed to progress. The Philadelphia Centennial Exposition of 1876 made Americans aware of the superiority of European designs in the decorative arts. Then two architects raised American standards. Richard Morris Hunt (brother of William Morris Hunt, the artist) built French Renaissance chateaux for the well-to-do. Though showy and ill suited to the American environment, these were at least good imitations of the originals. Hunt also founded the first American training center for architects and helped organize a professional association, the American Institute of Architects. Henry H. Richardson revived the Romanesque form of southern France and Spain; and his massive solid masonry structures with rounded arches dealt a blow to the Gothic revival. In his later years, Richardson put up office buildings in Boston, Chicago, and elsewhere, and moved toward the modern idea of adapting the form of a structure to its function.

Ultimately, urban and industrial needs would necessitate the creation of a new American architectural style. One can trace the origins back to factory buildings erected before 1860. More important were the post-Civil War suspension bridges which made use of steel. The Roeblings, in building the Brooklyn Bridge, and James B. Eads, who bridged the Mississippi at St. Louis, made notable use of new materials. Another American innovation was the elevator, which made it possible to build tall structures in downtown districts where real-estate values were high.

Combining European and American discoveries, Americans produced the skyscraper. William LeBaron Jenney's ten-story Home Insurance Building (constructed in Chicago in the 1880's) is generally regarded as the first skyscraper. Until this time builders had been unable to achieve height without using heavy walls. Jenney solved the problem by supporting walls and floor on a metal framework. Heavy walls were no longer necessary; all one needed to do was to cover the steel skeleton with a veneer of bricks or glass.

Louis Sullivan, who worked for Jenney for a time, felt that the new steel construction called for a revolutionary style of architecture. Form, said Sullivan, should follow and be determined by use. That is, the use of a building should be shown in its appearance. Sullivan developed his theory partly from Walt Whitman's democratic ideology and Darwin's principle of adaptation to environment. And it was more than theory. Sullivan showed what he meant when he built the Transportation Building at the Chicago World's Fair of 1893. At the time, though, his was a minority voice. The governing committee for the Fair turned down his proposed scheme of functional architecture. It accepted rather a design submitted by McKim, Mead and White, three French-educated partners who were promoting a classical revival. As a result, classical influence would be strong on into the twentieth century; but in time Sullivan would be heard.

The Fine Arts: Music

The second half of the nineteenth century saw a growing appreciation of good music in the United States. Music-loving immigrants, especially Germans, helped. These newcomers taught piano, organized singing societies and orchestras, founded conservatories and manufactured instruments (Knabe, Steinway). Most important of the German immigrants was Theodore Thomas. Arriving in 1845, Thomas made his way against great odds. He gave one-man concerts in the South. He directed the Cincinnati School of Music, conducted the New York Philharmonic Society and the Opera, and in the 1890's provided leadership for the Chicago Symphony Orchestra. Leopold Damrosch, another European-born missionary of musical taste, organized musical festivals and was conductor for the New York Symphony Society. In 1884 he successfully introduced German opera at the Metropolitan Opera House—the first challenge to the dominant Italian school. Damrosch's sons, Frank and Walter, carried on their father's work, introducing young Americans to good music.

Choral societies, symphony orchestras, and opera owed much to civic pride and to the support of wealthy patrons. Opera, which appealed both to music lovers and to "society," required large subsidies. These came in time from the urban rich; and by the 1880's New York's Metropolitan Opera gave promise of permanence. The rise of music education was also associated with the cities. Here the pioneer was Lowell Mason, a composer of hymns who began his musical career in Savannah, Georgia. Mason early became interested in having music taught in the public schools. He succeeded in Boston in the 1830's. Later, he pushed teacher training in music. Progress was rapid. By 1896 (a generation after Mason's death) many urban public schools and some in smaller towns offered instruction in music.

In composition, a few Americans ventured into opera, and many composed orchestral and choral works. Some of the most successful were immigrants, like Dublin-born Victor Herbert, of light-opera fame. Most American-born composers (for instance, Ethelbert Nevin and Edward A. MacDowell) did their chief work after studying in Europe.

As for popular music, the minstrel show, firmly established by 1850, continued to be successful in later decades. The Civil War produced famous songs. In the South, "Maryland, My Maryland" was a favorite, as was "The Bonnie Blue Flag." Union composers produced the spirited "Battle Hymn of the Republic" and "Marching Through Georgia." The postwar years brought cowboy and immigrant songs, and songs of urban America. By the 1890's the new urban tempo produced sprightly tunes oddly in contrast with the slow music of Stephen Foster, who had caught the spirit of an earlier agrarian America. Such songs as Barney Fagan's "My Gal Is a High-Born Lady" heralded a new fashion for syncopated scores. Presently labeled "ragtime," this music embraced the whole of city life and pointed the way toward twentieth-century jazz.

The Image of America Overseas

The United States had always interested those who lived in other lands. There had, however, been no single image or mental picture of the New World republic. To kings, nobles, great landowners, and the higher clergy of established churches, America spelled defiance of authority and tradition. It presented a picture of lawlessness, of a crude and culturally mediocre democracy in which the rule of the masses debased standards and jeopardized morality and religion. Emigration to America disturbed landlords and factory owners eager to have a cheap labor supply, and clergymen who wished to keep their flocks intact. Consequently, these groups joined government officials in discouraging emigration, circulating stories about the misery of those who had chased the rainbow across the Atlantic.

Champions of liberalism, democracy, and reform praised America as the successful example of a constitutional republic based on the will of the people. They hailed American separation of church and state as a triumph of religious freedom, applauded American manhood suffrage and free public schools. The Chartists in Britain repeatedly cited the American example; and the revolutionary governments temporarily in power in many European countries in 1848 frankly adopted American principles of government. When the revolutions collapsed, the United States welcomed refugees. Americans also welcomed European missions which came to study American institutions. The American jury system influenced Norwegian practices; the American public library movement stimulated the adult education program in Sweden. American prison theories influenced several European countries.

Latin America was closer to Europe than to the United States. Yet Latin-American liberals were often inspired by the example of the republic north of the Rio Grande. United States success in overthrowing a transatlantic overlord encouraged Latin-American leaders who wanted to win freedom from Spain. The Declaration of Independence and the Constitution circulated in Latin-American ports. Although it would be easy to overemphasize the American influence on the federal system of Mexico, Colombia, and Argentina, these countries all owed something to the example of their northern neighbor. Domingo Sarmiento modeled Argentina's public school system on that of the United States.

When the Civil War broke out in 1861, European liberals took the Union side. Conservatives, by contrast, called secession proof of the "fundamental weakness" of republican institutions. They sympathized with the Confederacy, based as it was on slavery and a landed aristocracy. When Union agents appeared to recruit immigrants to replace workers who had gone into military service, the established classes sourly insisted that immigrants would be sucked into the army and come to a bad end. Northern victory confounded conservative Europe and justified the faith of liberal leaders and plain people in the Union. But government officials, clergymen, landed aristocrats, and industrialists kept on discouraging emigration by belittling America, pointing to the chaos of Reconstruction, the race problem, the recurrent depressions, and the backwardness of social legislation.

Liberals continued to praise the United States. The abolition of slavery removed an institution that had long troubled European admirers of America. Thoreau, Emerson, and Whitman were admired by democratic writers of the Old World, as were Henry George, the American champion of land reform, and the socialist novelist Edward Bellamy. Later, the American device of commissions to fix the rates of public carriers and control the practices of corporations found favor in Britain. Even so, European liberals and radicals were disappointed in certain American trends. They deplored American abandonment of the low-tariff policy after 1861. They expressed alarm at the growing inequalities in distribution of wealth in the United States, the rise of trusts, the disappearance of cheap land, the sluggishness of the movement for social legislation in the interest of workers. American expansion overseas in the 1890's convinced many Europeans that the United States was following Old World paths of empire. And Latin Americans, long suspicious of United States diplomacy, spoke of the "Yankee peril."

These misgivings did not change the image of America cherished by Europe's common people. To them, the United States continued to seem a land of incredible opportunities. Steamship companies and railroad agents, anxious to sell tickets or land, spread this picture throughout Europe. To many America meant economic advancement. Others thought in terms of religious freedom, exemption from compulsory military service, educational opportunities for their children. Remittances and letters from immigrants to relatives in the Old World gave credence to such views. The same impression was conveyed when immigrants returned to their native villages with good clothes and spending money. American philanthropy further reinforced the image of the United States as a land of milk and honey. For Americans poured money into Europe when there were famines in Ireland in the 1840's and in Russia five decades later.

Meantime other images of America were developing. The opening of the last frontiers and the use of new machinery increased American agricultural production. This meant sharp competition for the grain- and cattle-producing countries of Europe, causing Germany (1879) and other nations to erect tariff barriers and use other devices to keep out American farm products, especially meat. American factories also provided competition. By the 1880's European manufacturers were clamoring for tariffs to protect home markets and were complaining of the difficulty of competing with mass-manufactured American goods in the markets of the world.

European industrialists recognized the many advantages of their American competitors: a great home market; rich farmlands; abundant coal, iron, and copper. Old World observers also noted that Americans had great technical skill or "know-how." American exhibits at world's fairs featured labor-saving devices, mass production items, and machines with interchangeable parts. Interested in American methods, the British Board of Ordnance in 1854 sent a committee to visit Colt's Connecticut factory. This group recommended that Britain order a full set of American machines for the making of small arms and import American workers to set up and demonstrate the use of the machines. At this same time a British parliamentary commission sought the secrets of American success. It found that Americans adapted tools and machines to the specific purpose at hand; that they experimented continually; and that many American employers gave attention to the comfort of workers and the satisfaction that high wages brought.

American technology excited criticism as well as admiration. Europeans rightly noted that the United States neglected basic research. They claimed that Americans wanted quantity rather than quality. But many industrialists, alarmed at the American threat to their markets, saw the need of changing methods to meet the competition. "The American invasion of Europe" was a term heard even before American demonstration of industrial power in World War I. Thus by 1900 the United States had begun to export, not only liberal ideas and farm surpluses, but also industrial goods and techniques. The new image of America was one of industrial and technical power.

17

Farming in the Industrial Age

Farmers viewed the new urban culture with suspicion. Rural living, they felt, was more healthy and desirable than city life. Older farmers deplored the tendency of children to seek their fortunes in the city. Rural clergymen and educators denounced the corruption and worldliness of urban society. Perhaps this was conscious propaganda to stay the tide of migration cityward. Or a defense mechanism associated with the uncomfortable fact that urban prestige had replaced the traditional leadership of rural America.

Nonetheless, urban ways influenced rural areas. Farm journals and agricultural colleges urged farmers to imitate city businessmen, study market conditions, keep accounts, adopt a business outlook. Village editors read and copied metropolitan newspapers, and city magazines like the *Ladies' Home Journal* invaded rural districts, familiarizing farmers with city customs. Better merchandising, faster deliveries and low prices led country people to buy soap, overalls, carpets, and other items formerly made at home. Farm boys who had moved to the city talked of metropolitan ways when home for visits. Rural free delivery (R.F.D.) of mail and, in the 1890's, telephones and improved roads were further links between town and country. Taken together, these factors gradually urbanized rural America.

Many Farmers, Many Problems

At the same time, farmers had their special problems. After prospering in the Civil War era, they ran into serious difficulties in the years of price decline, from 1865 to 1896. The plight of middle western farmers (a quarter of the nation's agriculturalists) received most attention. But the tenth who lived in New England and the middle states, and the half in the old South, also had problems.

Unable to compete with Westerners in grain and livestock, New Englanders had to supply chicken, eggs, milk, and fresh vegetables to nearby urban centers. Changing over was difficult. Dairy cows were expensive. Truck gardening called for new techniques. Chicken raising was arduous, uncertain, and despised as "women's work." Hence many New Englanders abandoned agriculture. From 1850 to 1900 improved acreage in the section fell by more than a third. The better soils, climate, and terrain of the middle states and their superior agricultural traditions enabled them to fare better. They also developed profitable specialties, such as fattening western beef cattle for market. But, save for local use, wheat and corn became unprofitable.

The Pacific states had a distance problem. They could produce out-of-season fruits and vegetables. But not until the 1890's did transcontinental freight become cheap and fast enough to enable west coast shippers to invade eastern markets. Transportation also plagued western cattle and sheep ranchers. They, too, had products much demanded in the East—and in Europe as well. Their fortunes suffered, though, until there was a satisfactory rail network in the area from Texas to Montana. When the railroads came (in the 1870's), the range enjoyed a few prosperous years. Then Argentine competition and European tariffs and prohibitions cut into foreign sales. Blizzards, droughts, and locusts caused heavy losses. Freight rates were high; and by the 1880's wheat farmers were invading the cattle kingdom.

Down to 1900 half the nation's farmers were located in the South. Their difficulties were part of the pattern that produced the Civil War. Reconstruction brought changes without solutions. The South had a higher percentage of tenants (mostly sharecroppers),[1] a lower standard of living, and less immediate prospect of improvement than agricultural areas elsewhere.

Southern agriculture centered around staples: tobacco, rice, sugar, and (especially) cotton. But subsistence farming held on, too. Hill people kept on trying to scratch a living from their submarginal land. They suffered the woes of their ancestors, and more besides, for the woodlands no longer contained the game that had supported early settlers.

Tobacco planting remained concentrated in Virginia, North Carolina, and Kentucky. Rice and sugar cultivation declined during the Civil War. Southern sugar production did not reach the 1860 level until the 1890's; and in that decade sugar beets (grown in such northern and western states

---

[1] Under the sharecrop system, the owner provided land, the tenant's cabin, and perhaps farm equipment, livestock, and seed. The sharecropper supplied labor. At the end of the season, the crop was split into shares. The tenant received a third or more, the amount varying with the area, time, and extent of the sharecropper's contribution. (He received more, of course, if he had his own livestock and farm equipment.)

as Michigan, Colorado, and Utah) became more important than Louisiana cane. Meantime, the center of rice production shifted from South Carolina and Georgia to Texas and Arkansas. The great southern crop, cotton, also moved westward, Texas becoming the leading cotton state. But by using fertilizer, the Southeast kept in competition. Cotton production reached the prewar level before the end of the 1870's. Thereafter it soared far beyond slave-day totals, finding a ready market in England and in textile factories of New England and the South. But prosperity eluded the cotton belt. World prices were low because of high production in the United States and elsewhere. Unlike wheat farmers, cotton growers did not cut costs by using new machines. Nor did they diversify crops; creditors called for a cash crop, and sharecroppers lacked the education and incentive to experiment. And after 1892 there was a new enemy, the boll weevil.

In 1860, seven-eighths of the cotton crop was produced by Negro labor. Whites accounted for a higher proportion after emancipation, especially in newly opened lands west of the Mississippi. But whether whites or Negroes were involved, the plantation system persisted. To be sure, there were more individually owned small cotton farms than before the Civil War (and a fair number were owned by Negroes). Even so, the large landowning unit was the rule in many areas. The owner cut his land into small pieces, these being assigned to Negro or white sharecroppers. Borrowing from the owner, and buying at his store, these tenants quickly slipped into debt servitude. And the owner, too, was a debtor, pressed for payment on his mortgage or bank loans.

Southern whites contended that they had "settled" the Negro question after Reconstruction, by establishing "white supremacy" and adopting segregation. Under this system, Negroes were denied the vote and had separate—and inferior—accommodations in the schools, on trains, and in theaters and churches. Deprived of equal economic opportunity, the Negro had little incentive to build a better South. And many white men, concentrating on "control" of the Negro, also failed to give adequate attention to economic problems.

Farmers from Ohio to Nebraska raised wheat or corn-and-hogs for distant markets. Generalizations, however, are difficult, for there were many contrasts. While eighty-acre wheat growers were eking out a bare existence in Dakota Territory, Oliver Dalrymple was clearing $200,000 a year on his 100,000 acres. Well-located Iowa corn-hog producers did well while mid-Kansas farmers were ruined by drought.

After 1840 cheap transportation opened world markets. Wheat was second to cotton among American exports, and pork products (representing corn) ranked third. On the one hand, exports allowed American farmers to expand operations with little fear of permanent overproduction. On the other hand, the situation geared American agriculture to world prices and destroyed the possibility of gain from a protective tariff. Returns were generally good until about 1883. Thereafter Kansas, Nebraska, and Dakota suffered from severe winters and from summer droughts, and all American farmers encountered increased competition and declining prices. Fortunately, production costs fell, too. Machinery and the increasing size of prairie farms improved the efficiency of wheat farmers, and in 1896 wheat could be produced for half the dollar cost of 1850. But mechanization and large-scale production made grain farming more complicated and hazardous.

Land, Transportation, and Credit

Much government land remained unsettled in 1850. Theoretically, an individual might "squat" on land not open for sale, then preëmpt it under the law of 1841—that is, buy it for the standard price of $1.25 or $2.50 an acre. Or, after 1862, the settler might acquire his farm free under the Homestead Act. But when the government granted land to railroad companies, areas adjacent to the new routes were withdrawn from preëmption and homesteading. Other grants to states, and the sale of Indian, timber, stone, and mineral lands removed enormous tracts from the operation of laws designed to aid the small farmer. The key fact was that commercially usable land was worth more than the government maximum ($2.50 an acre). It therefore paid corporations and wealthy individuals to buy land for investment. These purchasers operated ahead of the small settler, who could neither homestead nor preëmpt the better land; instead he had to buy from the private owner.

Homesteading, then, was not of major importance (only 10 percent of new farms from 1862 to 1890). Most farms were bought from individual or corporate landlords, many of whom were connected with land-grant railroads. These men knew where the railroads were to go, and profited accordingly. One can, however, overstate the evils of railroad and corporation sales policies. The western migrant needed transportation, credit, and protection from Indians, claim jumpers, and corrupt land office officials. Railroads could supply these along with land. Some railroads also gave agricultural advice to newcomers and aided farmers when crops failed. The line, of course, hoped to take a good share of the farmer's profit through freight rates. But that very interest made the railroad interested in attracting farmers and having them produce large crops.

By 1850 settlers had built up the first tier of states west of the Mississippi; and a few citizens had located along the Pacific coast. Thereafter, lines of settlement pushed westward from the Mississippi and eastward from the

Pacific. By 1890 these two movements had joined, and the census showed that there was no longer a continuous frontier line. There was unsettled land, but it was in isolated patches rather than in one big block of western territory. Thus, with the passing of the frontier, old opportunities were fading. Soon farmers would be unable to improve their lot by going west. Instead they would need to move to the city, or tackle and try to solve their problems where they were.

Of these problems, none was more serious than transportation. Western grain farmers found their profits eaten up by freight rates. Southern and eastern producers also cried out against high rates. On the short haul to the nearest primary grain market most farmers paid high noncompetitive rates. On the long haul from such primary markets as Minneapolis to the East or Europe rates barely covered railroad and steamship operating expenses. Farmers could not calculate the benefit they derived from the cheap long haul. They were aware, however, of the adverse effects of local rates; and after 1865 the railroads became the prime target of agrarian reformers.

In the East and South, farmers used little machinery. Plows, hoes, rakes, and hand cultivators remained standard equipment. Threshing was done by portable machines, moved from farm to farm. But on the prairies, large-scale operations were essential; and the mechanized farm became a reality.

Mechanization meant that the farmer had to understand machinery and keep it in repair. He found, too, that one cost led to another. In addition to expensive machines, he needed horses or mules to pull the equipment, and a large acreage to make efficient use of his mechanized power. This meant buying land or equipment on credit. Moving crops to market involved further outlays, calling for bank loans or mortgages.

Down to 1880 it was hard to borrow money on farm mortgages. Then, in the early 1880's, financiers interested eastern investors in long-term farm mortgages. For half a dozen years prairie farmers were literally coaxed into borrowing money. Drought hit the West just as this boom reached its peak. Thousands of mortgages were foreclosed, and both farmers and investors suffered. The supply of eastern funds dried up overnight; and in the West the experience built a long-lasting suspicion of eastern money men.

Despite difficulties, western and southern farmers remained optimistic. The price of land was still rising. Hence even if he made little profit from farming, the landowner would be reasonably well off when he reached middle age. But the rise in land values stimulated speculation. Much land therefore came to be held by absentee landlords who would rent but not sell. The richest soils (as in central Illinois and the Mississippi delta) were the most likely to be farmed by tenants. Tenancy was less common in the southern hills and in the poorer regions of the Dakotas. In the country as a whole, tenancy rose rapidly after 1865. After unsuccessful experiments with hired labor, southern owners put sharecrop tenants on old plantations and new southwest lands. In the upper Mississippi Valley, farmers went down the line to tenancy when they were broken by floods, droughts, and price declines. Farm hands and immigrants became tenants on farms held by banks, insurance companies, or individuals. Farmers' sons, who in earlier generations would have gone west, started out as tenants. Some tenants in the corn and wheat country became wealthy. As a rule, however, renters did less well than owners; and it was increasingly difficult with rising land and equipment costs to move up to ownership.

Every farmer had marketing problems. Wheat will serve for illustration. In each locality hundreds of farmers had to sell through a few grain dealers, who could combine in setting prices. A farmer could buck the combination by shipping to some central elevator (storage company). But that took cash and time. Most farmers could not wait, for they had borrowed harvesting expenses on short-term notes from local banks.

Besides the dealers, railroads, elevators, and millers made profits from handling grain. The farmer, in fact, often received less than a quarter of the price paid by the consumer; and he appeared to be the one man in the chain who had no direct control over price.

Seeking a Way Out

In general, American farmers avoided the laborious tasks associated with intensive farming as inconsistent with high living standards. This explains why Italian and Polish immigrants replaced Yankees in eastern truck farming. Among older settlers the Pennsylvania Germans were successful because (unlike most Americans) they were devoted to farming as a way of life. In addition, close religious bonds provided morale. Religion was also a vital factor in Mormon communities, where organization brought agricultural success even in semiarid lands of the Rocky Mountain area.

These groups were exceptional; the average farmer was isolated and individualistic. On occasion, though, crises forced him to modify his attitude. Such a crisis came in the 1870's and 1880's, a period of acute distress for many farmers. Seeking a solution, some moved to town. Some went west; but this took them to the western plains, where they encountered thin soils and an unreliable climate. Others favored improving agricultural techniques, coöperating in joint business ventures, entering politics. Did not businessmen use improved technology, coöperate effectively, and take part in politics in their own interest? Even with farmers the process was not altogether new. "Scientific farming" had been tried before 1860; and southern planters had defended their interests by political action. Their defeat in battle was a setback for agrarianism. When farmers again sought favorable legislation after 1870, they had to start all over; and they found themselves opposed by business interests more powerful than before.

Coöperatives

The first post-Civil War attempt of farmers to combine came through the Granges. These were at first secret societies, stressing social activity. The Patrons of Husbandry, launched in 1867 and commonly called the Grange, was a national body tying together such local groups. Hard times after 1873 increased membership to more than 2,000,-000 and drove the Grangers to action. Businessmen eliminated cutthroat competition. Why not farmers, too? Grangers therefore set up coöperative banks and insurance companies to relieve credit shortages and provide lower premiums and interest charges; coöperative stores and farm-equipment factories to cut the cost of manufactured goods; coöperative marketing agencies to eliminate middlemen's profits and the charges of monopolistic elevators.

Unfortunately, most of these ventures failed. Coöperative stores and factories, unable to secure bank loans, shut down for lack of working capital. Discriminatory freight rates made it difficult for coöperative marketing bodies to compete with private grain elevators. Defeated in politics, too, the Grangers went back to their old social role. But new farm organizations appeared when price decline and drought increased agrarian distress in the 1880's. The Southern and Northwestern Alliances, like the Granges, brought farmers together, then tried coöperative enterprises, and finally moved into politics (as Populists). But their business ventures, like those of the Grangers, usually failed. This is not surprising. It was difficult for isolated farmers to coöperate. Even when they did combine, inexperience, lack of capital, and business opposition made defeat almost certain.

Technology and Science

More successful were efforts to improve farm techniques. Scientific farming was too complex, mechanization too expensive for those who most needed help. Yet improved methods did aid many agriculturalists to hold their own. The reaper replaced labor lost to military service in the Civil War. Harvesters and binders were introduced during the next generation. These machines worked best in level areas and were most economical on large farms. Mechanization therefore made the greatest progress in the corn and wheat empires of the Middle West. There was less progress in the South and East. New England farms were too small or stony for machines to be used with profit; and no devices were invented to revolutionize cotton and tobacco planting. Only recently has a mechanical cotton picker been developed; and most cotton and tobacco is still harvested by hand.

The need for irrigation became apparent when semiarid western regions were opened to settlement. Here quality of soils was high, but rainfall did not provide enough water. The Mormons showed the possibilities of large-scale irrigation in Utah after 1850. Then Congress passed the Desert Land Act of 1877, offering arid lands at bargain prices to persons who would launch irrigation projects. Although 50,000 irrigators filed for land under this statute, the results were unsatisfactory. It was difficult for individuals to finance irrigation projects; and the act prevented purchasers from getting title until they had actually brought in water. In 1894, therefore, Congress offered land to states that would irrigate a portion of any area settled. Colorado, Nevada, Wyoming, and other mountain states accepted the terms, then arranged for private companies to build irrigation works and lease water rights to settlers. Settlers applied for 7,000,000 acres under this arrangement; but only one-fifteenth of this was actually reclaimed. Private companies hesitated because of the uncertainty of returns. Concerns that did operate had trouble apportioning water and securing payment from landowners. The farmer, on his part, found it hard to add the cost of water to other expenses. Apparently the problems of irrigation were too great to be solved by private initiative alone.

Irrigation and mechanization involved application of technology to agriculture. Equally important were the contributions of chemistry and biology. In 1850, "scientific farming" meant little more than careful trial-and-error experimentation. By 1900, it was possible to apply certain scientific principles to farm processes. Since these applications were of a technical nature, they were developed, not by farmers, but by a new professional group of agricultural scientists. The rise of these scientists was tied to the establishment of the federal Department of Agriculture in 1862 (elevated to cabinet rank in 1889). The Morrill Act of 1862 provided land grants to states for the support of agricultural and mechanical (A & M) colleges. After 1890 Congress voted annual subsidies for the land-grant schools. And with the Hatch Act (1887), Congress began to subsidize state agricultural experiment stations. These stations coöperated with the agricultural colleges and the United States Department of Agriculture to increase the output of American farms.

Nor was this all. State governments and private agencies were active.

Wisconsin is an example. In 1860, this state specialized in grain. When states further west began growing wheat, Wisconsin suffered. Many of the state's farmers then shifted to dairy farming. Research at the state land-grant college (the University of Wisconsin) helped make the transformation profitable. Short courses at the university familiarized farmers with improved techniques. *Hoard's Dairyman*, a privately-owned farm journal, also spread the word; and a state dairymen's association located markets and publicized Wisconsin cheese.

The scientific approach to agriculture was many-sided. Chemistry, geology, and biology coöperated in developing "soil science." When soil or climate made it difficult to raise a common cereal in a certain region, botanists sought varieties more adaptable to the area. Geneticists later produced strains of hybrid corn which resisted adverse conditions and increased yields. The study of plant and livestock diseases assumed great importance.

Still, change came slowly. Old-time farmers distrusted new methods. They also feared that scientific training would make their sons give up dirt farming to become teachers and experts. This did happen in many cases. What was more, graduates of agricultural colleges sometimes found it difficult to apply general principles to the operation of small farms. But by 1900 science was moving into agriculture, just as it was moving into industry.

The Farmer Turns to Politics

In the long run, science would provide the answer to many American farm problems. Humans, however, live in the short run. The debt-ridden farmer of 1890 saw no quick salvation in science. Scientific farming would, in fact, call for a larger cash outlay. Coöperatives and migration west also failed to provide much help. The farmer therefore turned to politics.

Agriculturalists had done this before. The Jefferson and Jackson movements had been made possible by a union of western and southern farmers, coöperating with some city workers. Might not these triumphs be repeated? Some thought they could. But the republic was no longer predominantly agrarian. Hence success depended on efficient organization. This was not easy to obtain, for sectional conflict had shattered the old Jeffersonian-Jacksonian combination of western and southern farmers. After 1865 most western farmers were Republicans, most southern rural voters Democrats. Split between the major parties, and unable to control either, the farmers had a dim outlook.

In the 1860's the Republicans bid boldly for the farm vote. They attracted western agrarians by passing laws popular with rural voters: the

Homestead and Morrill Land-Grant laws, transcontinental railroad legislation, the act establishing a Department of Agriculture. After the war, Lincoln planned to add southern farmers, by appealing to Negroes and poorer southern whites. This, though, did not work. Sectional hatred, race conflict, and political accidents kept the Republicans feeble in the South. And, though Republicans held the midwest farmers, the party was obviously run by urban leaders.

Meantime, the Democrats, assured of the southern rural vote, sought farm backing elsewhere. Their most effective leader was George H. Pendleton, whose Ohio Idea called for payment of most of the Union debt in unsupported paper currency (greenbacks). This appealed to western farmers. First, it involved an attack on eastern bondholders, long unpopular with rural citizens. Second, it called for currency inflation, which would raise farm prices, giving farmers more cash with which to pay debts or buy equipment or additional land. The Democratic national convention of 1868 endorsed this plan. But, instead of nominating Pendleton for President, the party chose Horatio Seymour, who disapproved of inflation. And Democratic leadership, like that of the Republicans, was overwhelmingly urban. In six of the seven presidential campaigns from 1868 to 1892 the Democrats picked a New Yorker to head their ticket.

Grangers and Greenbackers

Unable to control either major national party, the farmers tried working on a local or sectional basis. Thus the Grangers, active in the Middle West in the 1870's, centered attention on the states rather than the national arena. For a time they were successful; seven state legislatures adopted Granger legislation. These laws regulated rates charged by railroads and grain elevators, prohibited pools, rebates, and other monopolistic devices, restricted the granting of passes (which railroads used to influence politicians). And the United States Supreme Court called Granger legislation constitutional (Munn vs. Illinois, and Peik vs. Chicago and Northwestern Railway, 1876).

Then came reverses. Better economic conditions temporarily took the edge off farmers' grievances. Regulation proved less effective than had been anticipated, partly because transportation problems went beyond the confines of any single state. The railroads, fighting hard, had secured repeal of many Granger laws even before the Supreme Court, reversing itself, declared most Granger legislation unconstitutional (Wabash case of 1886, on the ground that states could not regulate rates on interstate carriers).

Some farmers went from the Granger movement to the Greenback party, which ran presidential candidates from 1876 to 1884. The Greenbackers made an interesting but unsuccessful effort to form a farmer-labor party. Their appeal to rural voters centered around their demand for inflation, which would increase farm income. In addition, they reflected Granger interest in transportation problems; however, instead of concentrating on the states, they asked for federal regulation of the railroads. But they entered national politics before they had enough effective local machines; and it was difficult to buck the major parties. Besides, the Greenbackers made two strange presidential nominations, picking an industrialist, Peter Cooper, in 1876, and an unpredictable professional politician, Benjamin F. Butler, in 1884. General James B. Weaver of Iowa, the 1880 nominee, was a happier choice. Weaver polled a respectable vote in the Middle West. But, as an agrarian, the General won little backing among workingmen.

That, in fact, explained the situation. Like farmers, city workingmen opposed monopoly. Like rural voters, urban laborers stood to gain if a farmer-labor combination secured political power. But such a combination was not forthcoming. As always, city and country people viewed each other with suspicion. Farmers wanted to raise prices; city workers wanted to hold them down. Laborers took little interest in railroad rates, which deeply concerned agrarians; and farmers were indifferent to the labor-sponsored shorter-hour movement.

The Populist Crusade

As the Greenback party died, the Alliance movement took its place. There were two National Farmers' Alliances, both formed in the 1880's. A Northwestern Alliance, in old Granger country, reflected midwest reaction to drought and dwindling prices. A Southern Alliance united several groups that represented the growing dissatisfaction of white farmers of the South and Southwest. Since the Southern Alliance drew the color line, there was also a National Colored Farmers' Alliance. In politics from the beginning, the Alliances did well in the state and Congressional elections of 1890. They then formed a national political organization, the Populist or People's party, launched in Omaha in 1892.

Like the Grangers, the Populists were against the railroads. Like the Greenbackers, they felt that inflation would help agriculture. The Populists also attacked the tariff and demanded tax reform, including use of a graduated income tax. They denounced grain speculation and the national banks, called for government ownership of the railroads, telegraph, and telephone. They wanted a postal savings system, direct election of United States Senators, and government aid to agriculture, through extension of credit to farmers.

Here at last was a fighting program for rural voters. Farmers flocked to hear the movement's fiery orators: Tom Watson of Georgia, spokesman of the hard-pressed cotton farmer; Mary Ellen Lease, who told her Kansas followers to "raise less corn and more hell"; Jerry Simpson, another Kansan, the "sockless Socrates of the prairies"; Ignatius Donnelly of Minnesota, a veteran champion of the wheat farmer; Davis H. ("Bloody Bridles") Waite of Colorado, who pleaded the cause of ranchers and miners of the Rockies.

In 1892 the Populists chose as their presidential candidate General James B. Weaver, who had been Greenback nominee in 1880. Weaver did well, polling a million of the 12,000,000 votes cast and picking up electoral votes in a half-dozen states. This was the strongest showing made by a third party since the Civil War, and many predicted that there would hereafter be three major parties.

But this was not to be. From the beginning, the Populists had certain shortcomings, notably a weakness in the Northeast and failure to capture the votes of city workers. The People's party was essentially a combination of southern and western farmers. In the national convention of 1892, Texas had more votes than New York, North Dakota more than Pennsylvania. The presidential nomination went to an Iowan (Weaver), the runner-up being from South Dakota. A Virginian was chosen over a Texan for the second place on the ticket; and the platform stressed agrarian demands. As a sort of afterthought, a Populist committee on resolutions bid for labor votes by praising the eight-hour movement and criticizing strikebreaking tactics of employers and the government. But there was scant response. Some small-town members of the Knights of Labor joined the Populists. The Knights, however, had passed their period of strength; and other workingmen showed little interest in the cause. In 1892 the Populists ran behind the feeble Prohibition ticket in most industrial states. In New York, they also trailed an even weaker minor group, the new Socialist Labor party.

Failure to attract workingmen was not the only problem. Also significant was the fact that most Americans were attached to the two-party system. The Populists did best in states where they captured or coöperated with a major party. Thus Weaver polled his biggest vote in 1892 in Kansas, where the Populists had taken over the Democratic machine. In the South, Populists found it useful to form coalitions with the Republicans. Such a combination carried North Carolina in 1894. It followed that the Populists might give up the fight if a major party adopted their views. In a way, this happened in 1896. By then, the nation was in the depression that followed the panic of 1893. There were cries for reform within both major parties. In the end, the Republicans chose to remain conservative. But the conservative (Grover Cleveland) Democrats lost control of their party to William Jennings Bryan's free-silver agrarians. The Populists thereupon endorsed Bryan for President; and the People's party slid into oblivion. A handful of determined Populists continued the struggle, and named tickets on into the next century. But for all practical purposes the Democrats swallowed the Populists in 1896.

Bryan and the Election of 1896

To put it in another way, the farmers had recaptured the Democratic party. Southern and western farmers had been two of the strongest elements in the Democratic organization back in the days of Jackson. Coöperation had been maintained on into the 1850's, with Southerners led by Jefferson Davis working with western followers of Stephen A. Douglas. After the Civil War, the Pendleton forces had tried to reëstablish the old southern-and-western-farmer control, only to meet with defeat. Thereafter, the Democratic party was run by city bosses and businessmen, working in league with conservative Southerners. But by 1890 agrarian distress had brought new Democratic leaders to the fore. Down in South Carolina "Pitchfork Ben" Tillman denounced the party's national leadership and said that Democrats must back reform. The same call sounded in the West, where "Silver Dick" Bland of Missouri and young William Jennings Bryan of Nebraska demanded Democratic action for the farmer. And at long last, in 1896, these southern and western agrarians secured control of the Democratic party and named the golden-voiced Bryan as candidate for President.

In some ways this strengthened the agrarian cause. Unlike the Populists, the Democrats were organized the nation over. They were strong in labor circles, where the People's party had been extremely weak. There were well-oiled Democratic machines in northeastern cities in which the Populists had polled next to no vote at all. The Democrats also controlled the solid South. Although the Populists had done well in the South, they had run into the race question. When they had allied themselves with Republicans (as in North Carolina), the Populists had been denounced as Negrophiles. Elsewhere, as in Alabama, Democratic politicians had marched Negroes to the polls to vote against the new party. Alarmed at such developments many white Southerners had concluded that new parties might be danger-ous, and that agrarian reform should be sought through the Democratic organization. Finally, the decision of 1896 gave the farmers a much more vigorous and effective leader than old General Weaver. The late nineteenth century produced many politicians of greater intellect than William Jennings Bryan, and some with better insight. But Bryan had the magic touch. As they looked at Bryan's young and handsome person, as they listened to his rich, persuasive tones, the country people felt that now at last they had their spokesman, a new Jefferson, a new Jackson. Indeed, Bryan was closer to the farm voters than either of those leaders of an earlier day.

Yet much was lost when the People's party joined the Democrats. Most of the Populist program was sacrificed in the process. The Bryan Democrats put all their weight behind inflation. To them, free silver was the cure-all for the farmers' woes. That is, Bryan wanted the United States to base its currency system on silver as well as gold. Silver was to be given an artificially high value (sixteen ounces of silver were to be considered worth an ounce of gold, though one could buy twice that much silver with that amount of gold). Since silver was plentiful, the result would be expansion of the paper money in circulation. The downward trend of farm prices would be reversed. Rural people could pay their taxes and debts and buy equipment; and the crippling depression would pass away.

Focusing on free silver, the agrarian Democrats pushed aside other Populist demands: government ownership of transportation and communication agencies; tax reform; credit for the farmer. Some Populists believed that these things could be obtained later, after the farmers had won control of the government and taken care of the immediate problem of farm prices. Others felt that inflation was a snare and a delusion and did not get at the basic problems of agriculture in an industrial age.

Most farmers, though, were willing to give Bryan a try. Perhaps the Nebraska Democrat did overemphasize free silver. Still, the average farmer was most concerned over prices. And Bryan won rural voters by telling them what he himself believed—that the American economy was based on the farm, not on the factory. He said this eloquently in his cross-of-gold address, made at the Democratic convention just before his nomination: "The great cities rest upon our broad and fertile prairies. Burn down your cities and leave our farms, and your cities will spring up again as if by magic; but destroy our farms and the grass will grow in the streets of every city in the country."

In the 1896 campaign, Bryan covered 20,000 miles and spoke 600 times. He won the hearts of farmers everywhere . . . but William McKinley, the Republican candidate, won the election. Bryan had most of the rural vote; but farmers were in a minority in the industrial age. McKinley swung the urban, industrial Northeast and the newly industrialized states of the Middle West. That turned the contest, and showed that the farmers were no longer strong enough to carry a national election.

In defeat Bryan looked forward to a "second battle" in 1900. He would lose that, too. But the agrarian crusade would not altogether fail. The embattled farmers had made an impression. When the progressive movement flowered after 1900, its leaders would try to help farmers as well as city workers. And though the rural voters could not carry national campaigns alone, they had learned how to operate politically in an industrial society. After the 1890's farmers would use pressure politics to influence politicians in both major parties, thus obtaining consideration from the government. Farmers would become an ever smaller part of the nation's population; but they would be heard.

18

Politics and Politicians

The Quest for Power

As agricultural history shows, the coming of the factory age profoundly influenced politics. Those who opposed industrialism carried their fight into political channels, attacking monopolies and demanding governmental regulation of business. At the same time, those who approved of industrialization sought influence in politics to speed the transition to a manufacturing economy, and to defeat anti-business groups.

In the days of Jackson, agrarian control of politics had defeated Clay's American system, a plan designed to promote manufacturing. By 1850, the factory age was at hand, but the political influence of southern agriculturalists still acted as a restraining force. Southern votes prevented northern businessmen from geting a protective tariff, railroad land grants, subsidies for ocean-going steamships. Secession of southern states in 1860–61 enabled northern commercial and industrial interests to secure legislation to their liking. In rapid succession they obtained from Congress a protective tariff (Morrill Tariff of 1861), land grants for a transcontinental railroad (the Union-Central Pacific, completed in 1869), contract labor and national banking laws (1864). In the next three decades, business interests sought to retain and extend political influence. They were willing to grant favors to farmers and workingmen—homestead laws, for instance, and pensions for Union veterans. But, as was natural, the captains of industry were chiefly interested in obtaining government backing for their own projects and in heading off attempts to regulate their enterprises.

On the whole, they succeeded from the 1860's to the 1890's. They had more influence than they had possessed before the Civil War, more than they would have in the twentieth century. As a result, they succeeded in postponing effective government control of economic life. In the states they obtained favorable corporation laws, such as the holding company legislation of New Jersey. They won state and national land grants for their railroads, tariff protection for their industries, currency and tax legislation that they considered satisfactory. Finally, in disputes between employers and

442

labor, local, state, and national governments almost always favored the employer.

Businessmen were a small minority of the American people. The South and West were traditionally opposed to eastern business domination. In all sections, farmers, laborers, white-collar workers, and small businessmen regarded financial and industrial giants with suspicion. Confidence in business was shaken by panics in 1873 and 1893. Yet business continued strong in politics. Why? Partly because farmers lacked effective national organization; differing party loyalties and Civil War memories kept western and southern agrarians from coöperating. Labor, too, was weak; even in the heyday of the Knights of Labor, unions reached only a small fraction of the workers. Organized labor was divided; and labor chieftains did not coöperate with farm leaders. Other foes of big business were still less effective. White-collar workers, small merchants and manufacturers, and professional people failed to organize for political purposes. All wished to improve their lot; but all were reluctant to join hands politically with labor or agriculture.

Business control of politics was also linked to public indifference. Down to 1860, politics was an honored calling, and those in public life were objects of admiration. After 1865, the accent was on business success; ambitious young men looked to industry or the professions rather than the Senate. Politics seemed increasingly corrupt, and run by sordid professionals. Citizens were disturbed by scandals associated with Grant Republicans and Tweed Democrats. But instead of rising to correct the situation, many turned away from politics in disgust. This enabled bosses and pressure groups to run the show.

Political Techniques

Political standards were distressingly low after 1865. It was the same at every level. City trolley franchises and state land grants frequently went to those who lined politicians' pockets. State legislators and judges often sold their influence to such businessmen as Gould, Fisk, Drew, and Vanderbilt. Congressmen of both parties made personal profit out of land grants to railroad promoters. Sometimes, legislators were given opportunities to buy valuable securities at bargain rates. Often the operation was more direct. "Enclosing a check which I hoped you would accept . . . ," wrote a manufacturer of watches to his Congressman in 1867. "What probability is there that the tax on Manufactures will be lowered?"

When reformers exposed such relationships, the public was apt to turn against briber and bribed. In the long run, therefore, bribery was less effective than were campaign contributions. Farmers, laborers, and small businessmen were not yet well enough organized to make large contributions. Big business, though, could supply substantial sums. A politician receiving such aid took no pledge to obey contributors. But if he wanted support in future campaigns, he was unlikely to bite the hand that fed him. Party discipline often operated in the same fashion. Many of the largest contributions went to political parties rather than to individuals. Depending on this money to finance state and national campaigns, bosses set party policy in such a way as to insure a continuing flow of funds. Party officeholders were expected to coöperate. Those who did won political favors. Those who did not found it difficult to secure patronage or nomination for better jobs.

Campaign contributions were tied closely to the lobby system. Industrialists, financiers, and others who desired to influence public officials maintained paid agents at the seats of government. These lobbyists checked on the activities of lawmakers and executive officials; and campaign contributions often depended on their reports. Lobbyists also testified before Congressional and state legislative committees, as experts on the needs of their employers. They supplied facts and wrote speeches for friendly legislators. They tried to persuade others, combining arguments with pressure from the politician's home district. They provided entertainment; they furthered their cause by supplying newspapers with copy.

In time both labor and the farmers would have effective lobbies. But, save in a few state capitals, neither group was adequately represented before 1890. The efficient lobbies were those of the Union veterans, the temperance people, and rising business groups. A typical successful lobbyist was John L. Hayes of the National Association of Wool Manufacturers. Hayes worked chiefly through Republican Congressmen from New England and the Middle Atlantic states, making sure that Congress retained high tariff duties on woolen goods. During the Civil War tariff schedules had been forced upward, partly because domestic producers were carrying an extra burden of manufacturing and income taxes. The taxes on income and manufactures were eliminated after the war, but (partly because of lobbyists like Hayes) tariff duties were not reduced. Later, when Ohio growers demanded protection, Hayes obtained still higher duties on manufactured woolens, to offset the expected rise in price of the raw material.

Businessmen also controlled newspapers; and they and their partisans wrote books and articles promoting their ideas. Industrialists swung votes by advising, even threatening their employees. Sometimes men of capital themselves entered politics, seeking to add to wealth prestige and political power. Two who represented this trend were Abram Hewitt, iron and steel manufacturer who was elected mayor of New York City, and Mark Hanna, Ohio traction magnate who became a Senator and is best remembered as the power behind William McKinley. Such men tried to identify business leadership with basic American ideals. As citizens of a rising nation, Americans had long prized the opportunity of every man to improve his economic status. Recognizing this, business spokesmen made much of the fact that Andrew Carnegie and other industrialists were self-made men. The industrial community, in other words, was run by democratic-minded leaders who understood the people; and every hard-working laborer had a chance to reach the top. So said Carnegie, in essays that associated industrialism with democracy. So said Horatio Alger, Jr., whose rags-to-riches yarns sold 20,000,000 copies. Other appeals stressed the American tradition of individualism. Americans loved freedom. How, then, could they favor governmental regulation of business? Patriotic appeals were equally important. After the Civil War, Union bondholders insisted that the honor of the nation required that they be paid in gold, not in depreciated greenbacks. Likewise, the tariff was defended on patriotic grounds, as a device to protect American workers from unfair competition with impoverished foreigners.

The Two-Party System

After 1861, industrialists, financiers, and merchants tended to line up with the Republicans. This was logical, for the Republican party was tariff-minded and interested in a national banking system and in land grants for railroads. Then, too, the Republicans were stronger than the Democrats, better able to achieve results in Washington and in most state capitals. But business did not limit its attention to Republicans. That would have been suicidal. To be sure, the country was "normally Republican" in the half-century after Lincoln's election to the presidency. But the Democrats were always strong. The Republicans controlled both houses of Congress only a third of the time from 1867 to 1897; and the Democratic popular vote exceeded the Republican in four of the nine presidential contests in those years. Hence business made contributions to Democratic as well as Republican campaign funds.

On the whole, this program worked. Take iron and steel. Carnegie, Frick, and most other major figures in the industry were Republican. But Abram Hewitt was an influential Democrat; the industry had a voice at court whichever party was in power. If the Republicans controlled the House of Representatives, iron and steel's need for tariff protection could be set forth by Representative William D. ("Pig Iron") Kelley, a Pennsylvania Republican. When the Democrats took over, the same arguments could be presented by Representative Samuel J. Randall, a Pennsylvania Democrat.

Nor did it matter which party occupied the White House. There were railroad strikes in the 1870's and in the 1890's. In each case the government helped the employers. In the 1870's, troops were ordered in by a Republican President, Rutherford B. Hayes; in the 1890's, by a Democratic Chief Executive, Grover Cleveland. So, too, on state and local levels. In the North, industrialists and financiers generally obtained franchises and land grants through Republicans. In the South, businessmen worked through Democrats. Yet many of these southern Democratic businessmen were agents of northern Republican financiers. Party labels meant less than did lines of power.

Those who desired a change could try to capture a major party; or they could launch a minor or third party. The first alternative was generally preferred. Some, though, felt that the old parties were beyond redemption, and that reform-minded citizens must make a new start. ("We denounce the Democratic and Republican parties as . . . corrupt, and, by reason of their affiliation with monopolies, equally unworthy . . . ," said one group of extremists. "We therefore . . . sever all connection with both.")

The most persistent minor party was the Prohibition party, which nominated presidential candidates regularly after 1872. Besides attacking liquor, Prohibitionists denounced gambling, speculation, prostitution, polygamy, and nonobservance of the Sabbath; and they worked for woman suffrage, cheaper postage, educational and civil service reform. Some Prohibition candidates were able politicians—for example, Neal Dow of Maine, nominee for President in 1880. Still, the Prohibition vote was always light, and did not begin to reflect the strength of the temperance movement. Most foes of alcohol opposed the third-party approach and preferred to work as a pressure group, influencing major-party politicians through such agencies as the Woman's Christian Temperance Union (W.C.T.U.).

Early efforts to form a labor party met with almost complete failure. After achieving local successes in Massachusetts and elsewhere, the Labor Reform party held a national convention in 1872. The delegates nominated Lincoln's old friend David Davis for President, hoping that Davis would also be acceptable to the Liberal Republicans, who had broken with the regular Republicans for this campaign. Instead, the Liberal Republicans lined up with the Democrats. Judge Davis refused to run; and the candidate finally chosen by the Labor Reformers made a poor showing. The party expired in the depression that followed the panic of 1873.

After that, some Labor Reformers tied in with the Greenback party, which tried to build a farmer-labor combination (1876–84). In this effort, the Greenbackers endorsed labor demands: they opposed child and contract labor, asked for Chinese exclusion, shorter hours, government inspection of mines and factories. But the Greenback movement, with its inflation emphasis, appealed to farmers rather than laborers. Only in 1884 did the Greenbackers show urban strength; and that was because of the personal appeal of Ben Butler, the party's popular but shifty presidential nominee.

When the Greenback party died, some of its sponsors brought forth a Union Labor ticket in 1888. This, like the Greenback organization, did best in Mississippi Valley rural districts; and it gave way naturally to the Populist or People's party. As has been noted, the Populists developed amazing strength in the early 1890's, only to be swallowed by the Democrats in 1896. This 1896 (Bryan-McKinley) contest saw many minor tickets in the field. Although the Populists endorsed Bryan, they would not accept Bryan's Democratic running mate, and ran their own vice-presidential candidate, Tom Watson. Anti-inflationist Democrats refused to support Bryan, and nominated General John M. Palmer on a Gold Democratic ticket. The Prohibitionists also divided on free silver, and split their tiny vote between two candidates. Rounding out the field was the Socialist Labor party, a feeble left-wing group that had first entered the arena four years before.

There were, then, six presidential candidates in 1896. But just two counted; all efforts to form a powerful third party had failed. Nonetheless, minor parties had influenced politics. More than once they had spearheaded reform drives, pressing ideas rejected by the major parties. As public interest mounted, one or both of the major parties took over the issue. The activities of Labor Reform and the Socialist Laborites forced Republican and Democratic leaders to pay more attention to workingmen. Prohibition gains in rural districts affected the attitude of major-party workers. The Greenbackers caused some leading politicians to reconsider their views on public questions; and both Republicans and Democrats were deeply influenced by the Populist crusade.

The Major Parties

Even so, most of American history must be told in terms of the major parties. They controlled the offices; they passed, enforced, and interpreted the laws. Pressure groups and average voters both operated within the framework of the major-party system. Many Americans backed one party consistently, regardless of the current issues and candidates. Others shifted from time to time, because of hope, disgust, or the personalities of leading candidates. Major-party politicians therefore used pressure and persuasion to get all their regular supporters to the polls; and they did all they could to attract undecided voters. The politicians also studied those who regularly voted the opposition ticket, searching or useful openings.

The regular strength of the Democrats from the 1850's to the 1890's was concentrated in the solid South and in a few northern cities. The opposition did its best to break this combination. Republicans tried to secure power in northern cities by exploiting Democratic scandals and appealing to special-interest groups (Irish-Americans, for example). Sometimes they succeeded. In 1888 they turned enough urban Irish voters against President Grover Cleveland to insure his defeat for reëlection. Again, in the 1890's, a Republican-dominated "good government" group defeated the Tammany Democrats of New York City. (Young Theodore Roosevelt became police commissioner in the reform administration.) These victories, though, were impermanent. Tammany regained control the next time out; and the Irish and other "immigrant groups" in northern cities generally remained Democratic.

The Republicans had even harder sledding in the South. Reconstruction (1865–77) gave them a chance to try to build Republican machines around carpetbaggers, newly emancipated Negroes, and the poorer whites. By the 1870's, however, the latter group had lined up with the Democrats; and the old slave states were lost to the Republicans. Disenfranchisement of the Negro tightened the Democratic hold, and in the 1880's Republican strength in the South was largely confined to such border states as Missouri and Delaware. The Republicans kept trying. Some backed Henry Cabot Lodge's Force Bill, which would have used federal power to protect the voting rights of southern Negroes. This bill passed the House in 1890, only to die in the Senate. Meantime, some southern Republicans were flirting with the Populists. But by the late 1890's southern Democrats had reëstablished one-party rule. The Populists were gone; and disenfranchisement of the Negroes was made virtually complete by new laws. A typical statute barred those who could not read and write, and "understand" the Constitution. Since white election officers interpreted "understand," Negroes could be excluded easily. Illiterate whites, however, were allowed to vote under "grandfather clauses," which opened the polls to descendants of those who had voted in slavery days.

Weak in the South, the Republicans were strong elsewhere. Most big and little businessmen of the North and West were regular Republicans. So were many professional people. A large percentage of the Union veterans consistently backed the Republican candidates, as did nearly all northern Negro voters. Some northern cities were run by Republican machines, the party being especially strong in such industrial areas as Pittsburgh. The Republicans had some strength among skilled workers, including those who disliked the foreign-born voters controlled by the Democratic machines. Finally, the Republicans were well organized in northern and western farm districts. When invading Republican territory, the Democrats aimed chiefly at the workers and farmers. Success was limited until the 1890's, when William Jennings Bryan took thousands of farm votes away from the Republicans. But, as an agrarian leader, Bryan had limited appeal to workers. That fact, and great activity on the part of business groups, gave the Republicans the crucial election of 1896.

Congress and the White House

The political history of the national government is bound to center around the White House. For one thing, the President has great constitutional powers. For another, he and his running mate are the only American officials chosen on a national basis. And, by virtue of his position, the President is head of one major party and the target of the other. Presidential power, though, has shifted from time to time. Party strength, personal ability, and crisis situations have made some Chief Executives the dominant figures of their day; others have been ineffective.

The decade before the Civil War was one of weak Presidents: Millard Fillmore (1850–53), last Whig occupant of the White House, an accidental President who moved up from Vice-President when Zachary Taylor died; Franklin Pierce (1853–57) and James Buchanan (1857–61), Democrats chosen because of their lack of enemies rather than for qualities of leadership. No one of these three was renominated for President, let alone reëlected. The strongest national figures were members of Congress—such men as Stephen A. Douglas, the Illinois Democrat, and William H. Seward, the New York Whig who turned Republican.

Then Abraham Lincoln, the first Republican President (1861–65), brought back Andrew Jackson's concept of the strong executive. The war crisis and Lincoln's ability made this possible. But the White House lost prestige under Lincoln's successor, Andrew Johnson (1865–69). Under the leadership of Thaddeus Stevens, radical Republicans rejected Johnson proposals, overrode his vetoes, and tried to remove him from office. Although they failed to get the two-thirds vote necessary to convict at Johnson's impeachment trial before the Senate (1868), the radical Republicans did sharply reduce presidential power. Not until the twentieth century (and the age of Wilson and the Roosevelts) would there be a return to effective executive leadership.

Four Republican Presidents (1869–85)

After Johnson's term, the Republicans controlled the presidency for sixteen years. For the first half of this period (1869–77) the occupant of the White House was Ulysses S. Grant, the only Republican ever to serve two full terms as President. The prosperity of the day helped Grant win election in 1868 and reëlection in 1872. Important, too, was Republican control of southern states still under military rule. These factors would have benefited any Republican nominee. Grant, however, had an additional point of strength: his military reputation. This meant votes, and meant that Grant, as a national hero, was in a position to reëstablish presidential leadership. But the General, new to politics, did not know how to use his popularity. He never discovered how to present issues so as to impress the public. He accepted the spoils system but did not know how to turn it to his political advantage. He chose some good subordinates, then failed to work in harmony with many of these individuals. Often he relied on incompetent or corrupt advisers who looted the Treasury. And his efforts to influence the legislative branch of the government were singularly unsuccessful. In 1870, when his party controlled both houses of Congress, Grant was badly beaten in his effort to effect annexation of Santo Domingo.

Despite his status as hero, Grant began to lose support. Carl Schurz, Charles Francis Adams, Charles Sumner, Horace Greeley, and other prominent Republicans left the party in 1872 to fight against Grant's reëlection. As Liberal Republicans, they nominated Horace Greeley for President. Although Greeley was also endorsed by the Democrats, the Republican managed to pull Grant through to victory. But then the panic of 1873 ushered in a long depression. Voters who had given the Republicans credit for prosperity now blamed them for the downward turn in the business cycle; and the Democrats gained in the Congressional elections of 1874. Scandals such as the Crédit Mobilier affair further damned the Grant administration. In addition, many citizens were saying that Grant's reconstruction policies had failed and that the Republicans had neglected to heed demands for tariff and civil service reform.

Given this trend, it seemed probable that the Democrats would win the presidential election of 1876. Republican defeat seemed the more likely when the Democrats named a reform candidate, Samuel J. Tilden of New York. But the Republicans also had a reform nominee, Rutherford B. Hayes, an Ohioan not connected with the Grant gang. Hayes would have the regular Republican vote. Having been a Union officer, he was sure to do well among veterans (Tilden had not been in uniform). As a foe of the spoils system, Hayes won the backing of Schurz and other Liberal Republicans who had deserted Grant in 1872. Would that be enough? First returns indicated that Tilden had the edge in popular votes and would have a majority in the electoral college. Some Republican managers, however, refused to concede defeat. The contest ultimately turned on electoral votes in Oregon and in three states still held by federal troops—Louisiana, South

Carolina, and Florida. There were double returns from these four states. By counting all against Tilden, a Republican-dominated electoral commission gave the victory to Hayes by a single electoral vote (185–184). Tilden men felt that their opponents had stolen the election; but Hayes was inaugurated and served out his term (1877–81).

As President, Rutherford B. Hayes labored under several handicaps. A conscientious, honest man, he was not outstanding in ability. Many of his countrymen considered him illegally elected. The Democrats controlled one house of Congress all through the administration, both after the mid-term elections. Finally, Hayes' own Republican party was torn by dissension between the Stalwarts and the Halfbreeds. Both factions were headed by self-seeking politicians—Roscoe Conkling (Stalwart) and James G. Blaine (Halfbreed).

Hayes, though, did his best, and tried to restore dignity to the presidential office. Grant had lacked the will and competence to challenge the Senate on patronage. Hayes, by contrast, specifically refused to follow the wishes of Stalwart Senator Roscoe Conkling, a vain, dictatorial spoilsman from New York. In the end, Hayes won. He thereby struck a modest blow for presidential leadership and to some slight extent advanced the cause of civil service reform. Hayes took decisive action in other matters, too. He ended Reconstruction by withdrawing the last occupation troops from the South (1877). Disturbed by labor conflicts in that same year, he used federal troops to help break railroad strikes. He also employed his veto power to prevent Congress from barring Chinese immigrants, which said Hayes, would violate treaty obligations. Congress proved unable to pass the bill over Hayes' veto, and Chinese exclusion legislation was delayed until 1882.

Hayes, however, did not always have his way. When he asked for civil service reform, Congress pointedly refused to act. And when Hayes vetoed the Bland-Allison Act of 1878, Congress passed the measure over the veto. This statute involved the currency. During the Civil War the Union had issued unsupported paper money (greenbacks). After 1865, some farm politicians urged continuation of this policy, as a means of raising prices. Business opposition, however, caused Congress to vote against increasing the number of greenbacks. What was more, those outstanding were made redeemable in gold (resumption of specie payments, 1879). By then, farm inflationists were adopting a new approach. Down to 1873, the United States was on a bimetallic standard. In other words, the monetary system theoretically rested on both gold and silver, an ounce of silver being rated as worth one-sixteenth as much as an ounce of gold. Since silver brought more on the commercial market, and since gold was in good supply after the California gold rush, the United States came to rely almost exclusively on gold. Silver was therefore demonetized by Congress in 1873; and the country was on a single (gold) standard. But just at that time, vast quantities of silver became available with the opening of new western mines. The result was a sharp drop in the price of silver. Silver miners then desired to sell their product to the government, preferably at the old price (one-sixteenth that of gold). Southern and western farmers also demonstrated interest. If the government bought silver, and issued silver coins or paper money on the basis of these holdings, there would be more currency in circulation, and prices would rise—a development much desired in the hard times after 1873. Bimetallism would thus have the same inflationary result as the issuance of greenbacks. Hence demonetization was termed the "crime of '73," and there were cries for "free silver," "16:1," and "the dollar of our daddies." As a result, Congress passed the Bland-Allison Act, which provided for a limited coinage of silver.

Hayes did not seek renomination in 1880. Conkling suggested nominating Grant for a third term. Blaine and other foes of Conkling checked this strange movement, and the Republican nomination went to James A. Garfield of Ohio, a party regular who had a distinguished war record and had been a capable Congressman. To placate the Grant forces, the second place on the ticket was awarded to Conkling's political crony, Chester A. Arthur of New York. The Garfield-Arthur team went on to win. Returning prosperity worked for the Republicans, for in good times voters favor the party in power. Besides, the Democrats had an unusually weak ticket, headed by General Winfield S. Hancock. The Democrats carried the solid South, New Jersey, and two far western states; but northeastern and middle western votes took the Republicans to victory. It was close. Garfield was only 7000 ahead of Hancock in popular votes (4,449,000 against 4,442,000), and the shift of New York would have meant a Democratic triumph in the electoral college.

In his few months in office (1881), Garfield showed energy and competence. Like Hayes, he wanted to increase presidential influence and to modify some of the worst features of the spoils system. Like Hayes, Garfield locked horns with Conkling; and in the contest Conkling was driven from the Senate and out of politics. But Garfield was killed by a frustrated office seeker; and the presidency went to Conkling's friend Arthur.

Chester A. Arthur was not so bad a president as might have been expected. All his life, Arthur had been a party hack. Elevation to the White House (1881–85) seemed to change his standards. He took on dignity, prosecuted the star-route mail frauds, declared for civil service reform (helping to effect passage of the Pendleton Act of 1883). His term also saw the beginnings of the modern navy. But, as an accidental President, without much prestige or ability, Arthur was frequently ignored by Congress and by leaders of his own party. The public gave him only a fair rating; and the Democrats gained in the mid-term elections of 1882. So in 1884, Arthur was dropped, and the Republican nomination went instead to James G. Blaine.

Cleveland and Harrison

Now, for the first time since 1856, the Republicans were to lose a presidential contest. James G. Blaine, the Republican candidate in 1884, was a master politician. Though not a veteran, he was popular with the "boys in blue." Though a foe of reform, he won the support of many humble citizens. Though a political spoilsman exposed in the "Mulligan letters," he was famed as the "Plumed Knight." As Speaker of the House, as Senator from Maine, as Secretary of State under Garfield, he had impressed his magic personality on other politicians and the public. His was a logical nomination, and many guessed that he would coast to victory. Instead, he was beaten. In a long political career he had accumulated many enemies. Some were spoilsmen who envied Blaine's success (Conkling, to mention one). Others were reformers who disliked Blaine as a machine politician and corruptionist. When Blaine was nominated in 1884, some liberal Republicans ("Mugwumps") bolted and threw their support to the Democratic candidate, Grover Cleveland, who had been a reform governor of New York.

Though sorry to lose the mugwumps, Blaine did not consider the loss irreparable. He could make it up, he thought, by attracting voters who disapproved of Cleveland's Civil War record (he had hired a substitute) or disliked Cleveland's reputation as one who drank and was the reputed father of an illegitimate child. Since Blaine was anti-British and had Roman Catholic relatives, the Republicans also expected to pick up some normally Democratic Irish-Americans. But here they failed. At the very end of the campaign, Blaine antagonized the Irish when he allowed one of his Protestant backers to call the Democrats the party of "rum, Romanism and rebellion." In a close election, Blaine lost New York by less than 1200 votes; one-tenth of one percent of the total cast in that state. Had he carried New York, he would have been elected President. It could be said, therefore, that the loss of a few Irish voters in New York cost Blaine the election. Or one could say that the shift of a few mugwumps to Cleveland had determined the result. Putting it another way: Cleveland carried the southern states from Maryland and Delaware to Texas. He also won four northern states: Indiana, New Jersey, Connecticut, New York, just enough for victory.

The first Democratic President since the Civil War (1885–89) was a cut above the average occupant of the White House. Stolid, heavy-set, and unexciting, Cleveland had little popular appeal. He was, however, a determined and intelligent man more attached to principle than to political expediency. A conservative, he felt that the government should limit its activities. Within the sphere of governmental action, though, he favored vigorous policies, above the level of party politics. Thus he was a reform mayor of Buffalo, a reform governor, a reform President.

Even so, Cleveland did not greatly alter American political patterns. There was a substantial job turnover, with an increase in the number of Southerners holding posts in Washington. Cleveland also showed his courage by establishing a new veto record. (Most vetoes were of private pension bills. General legislation covered Union veterans disabled in service, and Cleveland rightly felt that many of the private bills involved unworthy cases.) Still, Cleveland lacked the party strength, public backing, and political finesse to dominate Congress.

At the end of 1887 Cleveland dramatized the tariff issue by devoting his entire annual message to a plea for lower rates. This was in preparation for the 1888 campaign. As in 1884, Cleveland polled more popular votes than his Republican opponent. As in 1884, he carried the solid South and picked up a few northern states. But this time Cleveland lost New York; and again New York turned the tide. As in 1884, the New York vote hinged on less than one percent of the state's ballots. Among the reasons for Cleveland's defeat was the loss of Irish-Americans who considered him too favorable to Britain.

The Republican victor in 1888 was Benjamin Harrison, an Indianian whose grandfather had been President in 1841. Harrison was a Union veteran, a proved vote getter from a doubtful state, a decent, respected individual. His friends thought him capable and forceful; others found him cold and undistinguished. As President (1889–93), he tried to build a vigorous foreign policy. Otherwise, he made little effort to provide leadership. He let Congress run the government.

Congressional activity was very apparent in the winter of 1889–90. It was then that the Republican Speaker of the House, Thomas B. ("Czar") Reed, streamlined the rules so that business could be handled quickly, in line with the wishes of the dominant party. Another member of the House, William McKinley, gave his name to a new high-tariff bill. There had been tariff changes from time to time since the passage of the Morrill Tariff of 1861, notably a slight reduction in 1883. The McKinley bill of 1890, however, was the most significant revision of rates since the Civil War. By moving levels sharply upward, it demonstrated how committed the Republicans were to a high protective policy.

In the same year, Senator John Sherman's name was attached to an antitrust law designed to curb monopoly and a silver-purchase act intended to pacify the western inflationists. With the Interstate Commerce Act of 1887, the Sherman Antitrust Act of 1890 indicated that the national government was beginning to see the need of regulating certain aspects of economic life. The Sherman Silver Purchase Act was an effort to conciliate silver owners and farm inflationists by stepping up the silver-buying program of the Bland-Allison Act of 1878. Like the earlier measure, the 1890 law helped the silver interests more than it did the farmers.

In addition, this "billion-dollar Congress" spent money lavishly. Income from the tariff and from liquor and tobacco taxes had created an embarrassing surplus. The Republicans, however, did not want to cut the tariff. They therefore chose to spend the surplus, passing pork-barrel river and harbor bills, voting a bounty for domestic sugar growers, increasing silver purchases, appropriating money for a big navy, increasing the number of veterans on the pension rolls. Once formed, the spending habit proved hard to break; and the government ran into difficulties when surpluses evaporated after the panic of 1893.

Republican leaders thought the laws of 1889–90 would increase their party's strength. They hoped, too, that Republican fortunes would be advanced by the admission of new western states. Colorado had been brought in during 1876. North Dakota, South Dakota, Montana, and Washington followed in 1889, Idaho and Wyoming the next year. But there were unexpected results. Some of the new states developed an interest in Populism; later, all espoused Bryan-style Democracy. Nor did the Republicans fare well elsewhere. In 1890, halfway through the Harrison administration, they suffered a crushing defeat, dropping many Senate seats and losing control of the House. Two years later, in another Cleveland-Harrison contest, Cleveland increased his popular lead and carried the electoral college. In this 1892 campaign, Cleveland captured New York by a substantial margin. He could have won the election even without the Empire State, for he carried, in addition to the solid South, three states in the Middle West (Indiana, Illinois, Wisconsin). Further west, the Populists showed strength, and the Republicans received their smallest electoral total since their first presidential race in 1856.

Back in the White House for a second stay (1893–97), Grover Cleveland faced an economic depression, ushered in by the panic of 1893. Here was an opportunity for presidential leadership. But Cleveland, basically conservative, felt he should not step in to lessen the effects of depression. The people should support the government, he said, but the government should not support the people.

Not that Cleveland was inactive. He urged tariff reduction, and obtained it, after a fashion, in a Wilson-Gorman Tariff of 1894. But the President was hostile when Jacob Coxey's army of the unemployed marched on Washington, demanding a public works program to provide jobs for the needy and to get money into circulation. When the marchers reached the nation's capital, leaders were arrested for walking on the grass. In the same year (1894) Cleveland had federal troops help crush the Pullman strike. The President also opposed agrarian demands for higher prices. Instead of espousing free silver, he persuaded Congress to repeal the Sherman Silver Purchase Act, which was draining the Treasury of gold. And Cleveland used his influence inside the Democratic party against such rural leaders as William Jennings Bryan.

Mark Hanna's Victory (1896)

For a generation before the panic of 1893 the major parties had been much alike. Depression and the Cleveland policies finally brought a change. Southern and western agrarians captured the Democratic convention in 1896. Junking the conservative Cleveland crowd, they demanded that something be done for the depression-ridden farmers; and they named for President the Populist-influenced Bryan. This was more than a normal party change. Bryan's nomination shifted control of Democratic machinery from eastern cities to the West and South. It changed party emphasis from laissez faire to a demand for government participation in social and economic reform. It provided leadership such as the Democrats had not know, for decades. Bryan would move from inflation in 1896 to anti-imperialism and an assault on the trusts four years later; and the Democrats would help bring in the progressive era (1901–17).

The Republicans met the challenge of depression in a different way. Their nominee of 1896 was William McKinley of Ohio, author of the high-tariff bill of 1890. McKinley and his manager, Marcus Alonzo Hanna, lined up with hard money against free silver; with big business against the farmer; with the *status quo* against reform. Using techniques developed in earlier campaigns (1888 in particular), Mark Hanna collected an enormous campaign fund from business leaders. Bryan obtained what he could from silver miners and farmers; but he was hopelessly outclassed by Hanna. And Bryan lost the election, his rural strength being offset by Republican influence in the growing cities.

There were many party changes in this 1896 campaign. The Populists endorsed Bryan and were absorbed by the Democrats. Bryan lost many Cleveland Democrats. Some, like President Cleveland himself, sat out the election without endorsing any candidate. Others went to McKinley, or backed John M. Palmer, a gold Democratic presidential candidate who helped the Republicans by drawing votes from Bryan. Meantime, Henry M. Teller of Colorado and other inflation-minded Republicans from farm and silver states lined up with Bryan. The contest resulted in a triumph of gold over silver, manufacturing over agriculture. It also centered attention on the national character of political and economic questions. Interesting, too, was the fact that Congressional leadership was fading. Each party stressed the leadership qualities of its presidential candidate; and after 1896 the White House would have new prestige. And, though the conservatives won, a revitalized Republican party would presently, like the Democrats, begin to weigh the possibilities of progressive reform.

Role of the Courts

Congressional influence was the major force in the national government from 1865 to 1896, despite an occasional show of presidential strength. But these years also witnessed an increase in the power of the judiciary.

The federal courts fared badly in the 1850's and 1860's. When the Supreme Court took a stand on slavery (Dred Scott case, 1857) many Northerners refused to respect the verdict. Antagonism toward the courts lasted a full decade. Suspecting that many judges were pro-Confederate, Lincoln suspended the writ of habeas corpus and sometimes operated through military tribunals. Congress reflected the same attiude when it increased the number of Supreme Court justices, enabling Lincoln to alter the complexion of the Court. During Reconstruction, Congress by-passed the regular judiciary when it established military courts in the occupied South. Further legislation limited appeals to higher courts, lest reconstruction laws be declared unconstitutional. And judicial prestige suffered another blow in 1870–71, when the Supreme Court reversed itself overnight in the Legal Tender cases.[1]

From then on, the federal courts gained in prestige. Most judges were exceedingly conservative, disposed to protect property rights against any form of public interference. Although the Supreme Court upheld some state regulatory legislation in the Granger cases of the 1870's, the Wabash

---

[1] At first, the judges expressed doubt as to the government's right to issue unsupported paper currency. Then, after Grant had filled two vacancies with jurists of another turn of mind, the Court, in a case involving slightly different circumstances, upheld the constitutionality of Civil War greenbacks.

PATTERN OF REPUBLICAN VICTORY IN 1896

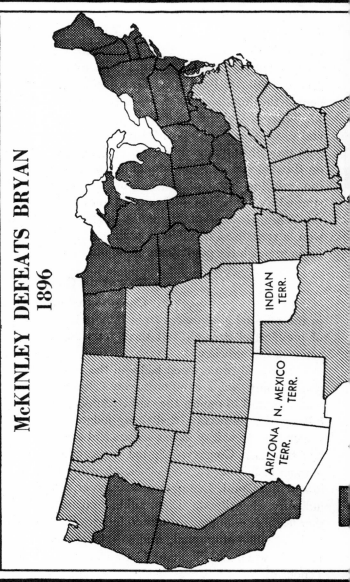

McKINLEY DEFEATS BRYAN
1896

INDIAN TERR.

N. MEXICO TERR.

ARIZONA TERR.

Presidential contests seldom present clear-cut issues. The election of 1896, however, saw the agrarian forces, under the Democratic presidential candidate, William Jennings Bryan, lined up against the urban and industrial backers of the Republican nominee, William McKinley. The Republicans won by carrying the industrial Northeast and the newly industrialized states of the Middle West. Bryan carried the southern and western farm states, and the mining states of the Rocky Mountains. This, though, was not enough to bring him victory.

CHIEF MANUFACTURING STATES

PER CAPITA VALUE OF MANUFACTURING IN 1900

INDIAN TERR.

N. MEXICO TERR.

ARIZONA TERR.

Flannery

$120 and Over

Under $120

Miles

100   300   500

Miles

The campaign showed plainly that the agrarian economy traditional to America had given way to an industrial one, and that there would be no turning back. It was clear, too, that agrarian politicians could not hope to win national contests without support from the cities—for example, from urban workers. By attracting city laborers, Woodrow Wilson and Franklin D. Roosevelt were to succeed where Bryan had failed.

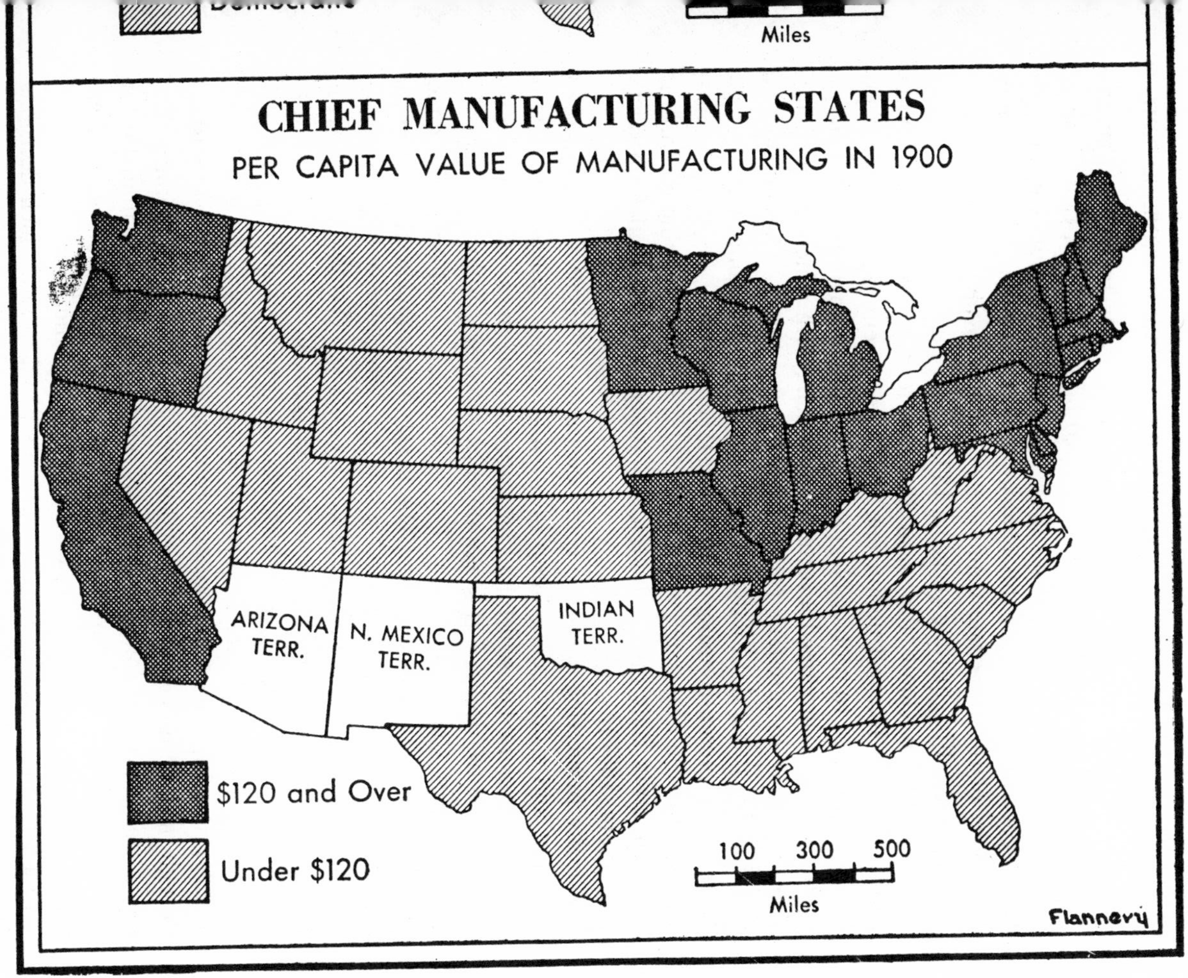

decision of 1886 severely limited the right of states to regulate railroad rates. In this decision the judges hammered home the point that Congress had exclusive power to regulate interstate commerce. But when the national government entered this field in 1887, the courts interpreted away the power of the Interstate Commerce Commission to adjust rates (as in the Maximum Freight Rate decision, 1897).

The Supreme Court also used the Fourteenth Amendment. When adopted in the Reconstruction era, this amendment was considered primarily as a device to protect Negroes against discrimination. Nevertheless, southern whites developed a segregation system, with which federal courts were reluctant to interfere (Civil Rights cases, 1883). The amendment therefore became a dead letter so far as the Negro was concerned. But the courts were presently using it to protect corporations (legal "persons") against regulation by state governments. This was the doctrine set forth in the Minnesota Rate case (Chicago, Milwaukee and St. Paul Railroad vs. Minnesota, 1889).

Equally interesting were the court decisions on taxation and trusts. A tariff cut and a depression slump in revenues caused Congress in 1894 to revive the income tax, which had been used during the Civil War. But the Supreme Court declared this tax unconstitutional (Pollock vs. Farmers' Loan & Trust Company, 1895). The legal problem concerned the direct tax provision of the Constitution. The judges, however, also thought of the tax as an "assault upon property," a threat to conservative interests which the judges desired to protect; that is, they correctly saw the income tax as a dangerous weapon against those with large incomes.

The Sherman Antitrust Act of 1890 also ran into judicial difficulties. This law outlawed combinations in restraint of trade. In the E. C. Knight case of 1895, the Supreme Court refused to crack down on the sugar trust, although that combination had a virtual monopoly of sugar refining. This was a manufacturing combination, said the Court, not a combination in restraint of trade. But simultaneously the judges used the Sherman Act against labor, in the Debs case, which grew out of the Pullman strike.

In a way, the McKinley victory of 1896 seemed to ratify such decisions But they would not satisfy twentieth-century Americans.

Part VI

The New World Power

(1896-1919)

 *By the 1890's, the United States had become one of the greatest manufacturing nations on earth. The triumph of industry had, however, aggravated old problems and created new difficulties. Reform was necessary because of humanitarian considerations, and to make sure that discouraged citizens would not turn toward radicalism. As a consequence, the early years of the new century brought a progressive movement, aimed at eliminating corruption from politics and aiding labor, agriculture, and small business. At the same time, an expansion drive increased the world power and influence of the United States.*

19

The Industrial Nation

Economic Trends

By 1896 the United States was in population and production the leading industrial nation of the world. It had passed Germany and Britain in production of iron and steel and had pulled level with Britain as a producer of coal. The new power sources, oil and electricity, would soon give the United States an even more striking supremacy.

In 1900, as before, coal, iron-and-steel, lumber, textiles, and railroads were the country's largest industries. But changes in technology were already pointing industry in new directions. Electricity for light, power, and communication, together with the internal-combustion engine and new alloyed metals, would presently alter American economic and social patterns.

As has been seen, inventors had done the foundation work by 1896. Europeans had worked out the gasoline-powered internal-combustion engine, creating the automobile and pointing toward the day when the Wright brothers would fly an airplane at Kittyhawk, North Carolina (1903). By 1895 Old World experimenters had done the basic research in wireless telegraphy (radio), and in alternating-current electricity, the type suitable for long-distance transmission. The electric trolley, incandescent lamp, telephone, motion picture, phonograph had all come into being.

There remained the job of development. Here Americans excelled. A typical American contribution was a new method of treating high-speed tool steel, worked out at the turn of the century by Frederick W. Taylor (better known as the "father of scientific management") and Maunsell White. This doubled the speed of cutting machinery, and encouraged experimentation with other alloys.

The key to American industrial success was mass production. Improvements in machine tools helped make this possible. Rods, shafts, and bearings were machined to closer tolerances (less variation in measurement), and continuous, mechanized assembly lines were introduced. A century after Eli Whitney had shown that he could put muskets together from piles of similar parts, three Cadillac automobiles were dismembered in a test in London. The parts were shuffled, and three good new cars were assembled from the assortment. In 1917 800,000 Ford chassis moved through the assembly line, each interchangeable with every other.

Meantime, there opened a new world of reproduction of sight and sound. By improving the vacuum tube, Lee De Forest (an American) opened the way for the commercial success of radio. Phonograph records brought Americans classical and popular music; and the movies became the nation's chief entertainment medium.

New Industries

The revolution in technology brought new industries that ultimately displaced the old leaders. The automobile industry went beyond steel in value of product in the 1920's; the electrical industry by the 1930's exceeded steam railroads in capital investment. Furthermore, the automobile led by 1919 to a $300,000,000-a-year government outlay for highways.

Urban areas were electrified between 1896 and 1910. Since there were few big hydroelectric stations, most electric current for power and light was supplied by coal-powered steam-generating plants. By 1912 there were 5000 of these local power stations. The telephone spread even more rapidly. In 1895 there were less than 350,000 phones. By 1910 there were nearly 8,000,000, or about one for every ten persons. This ratio changed slowly thereafter, and stood at one telephone for every four persons by 1950. Meantime, electricity had revolutionized urban transportation. By 1900, electric trolley lines extended into suburban areas and connected major cities. This brought new areas into the commuting zone and threatened the short-haul passenger service of steam railroads. Electric subways and elevated lines became common in the largest centers.

The automobile industry advanced with equal rapidity. Instead of copying the expensive French models, Americans set out in the late 1890's to build cheap, light cars. The time and place were admirably suited to the new industry. No other major Western nation needed the automobile so badly to overcome distances; no other contained so many persons who could afford a thousand-dollar machine. American manufacturers of bicycles, wagons, and machinery could easily supply the parts required. And the Dingley Tariff of 1897, with its 45 percent import duty on foreign cars, helped keep European competitors out of the low- and medium-price market.

Small producers dominated the new industry at first. In 1900 4000 American cars were turned out by a host of small firms, each selling in a local area. Failures and consolidations gradually reduced the number of manufacturers. The two giants, Ford and General Motors, and some twenty smaller companies accounted for the great bulk of the 1,600,000 cars and trucks turned out in 1916.

Henry Ford introduced his standardized Model T in 1909, and never varied its essential specifications until he abandoned it in 1927. After 1914 Ford cars were made on a mechanized assembly line by men receiving the then-phenomenal minimum wage of $5.00 a day. As Model T sales climbed to over 500,000 a year, Fords became an international symbol of American mass production and a part of the national folklore.

Toward Bigger Business

Large-scale operations benefited industries using heavy power machinery and assembly line techniques. Small companies were able to compete with big plants only because they bought from large suppliers who had in turn the advantages of mass production. Small plants disappeared in industries where such arrangements were impossible. In iron, for instance, the capacity of the most efficient blast furnaces increased tenfold from 1885 to 1919, and the big furnaces were beyond the means of a small producer. Consolidation thus tended, not only to increase efficiency, but also to eliminate competition.

Oddly, judicial interpretation of the Sherman Antitrust Act of 1890 promoted consolidation. In 1895, in the E. C. Knight case, the Supreme Court held that a monopoly of manufacture was not necessarily a restraint of trade under the 1890 statute. Four years later, in the Addyston Pipe decision, the justices held that a voluntary association of producers for the regulation of prices (what Europeans might call a cartel) was a conspiracy in restraint of trade and hence prohibited by the Sherman Act. The lesson seemed clear: it was legally safer for competitors to form one big company than to control the market by agreements. So the Sherman Act was, in a way, "the mother of trusts."

Consolidation came so fast at the end of the century that the republic seemed headed toward some form of monopoly capitalism. In 1897 there were only a dozen manufacturing companies with as much as $30,000,000 in capital; by 1903 there were forty-one. Following the panic of 1893 financiers combined the most important railroads into half a dozen systems, each held together by common ownership of strategic blocs of stock. Meantime, the communications field was coming under domination of such giants as American Telephone and Telegraph (A.T. & T.) and Western Union.

The aim of many of these companies was complete monopoly. When Presidents Theodore Roosevelt (1901–09) and William Howard Taft (1909–13) set out to enforce the Sherman Antitrust Act, major capitalists decided that it would be best to leave some competition. The Supreme Court suggested as much in 1911. In ordering the dissolution of the Standard Oil combination, the justices used the "rule of reason." That is, they distinguished between "reasonable" and "unreasonable" restraint of trade (the judges to define the terms). Presumably complete domination of the market by one concern would be "unreasonable"; but domination by a handful might be regarded with less disfavor.

As a consequence, the monopolies of 1900 gave way to domination of industries by few companies. The almost complete control of Rockefeller's old Standard Oil trust was replaced by leadership of around a dozen companies. A like situation developed in tobacco after the breakup of James B. Duke's American Tobacco Company by Supreme Court order (1910). In steel, the giant United States Steel Company came to be content with about half the market. The result was neither free competition nor monopoly, but a mixture that economists call monopolistic competition. Competition was maintained in advertising, service, and quality, but not in price. In other words, the decline of single-company control did not restore a free market. The drift was rather toward an era of "stable prices," set by intercompany understanding.

The Money Trust

Consolidations involved exchange of stocks and bonds and the marketing of new securities. This was the business of investment bankers, who gained importance as mergers increased. Nor was banking influence confined to the marketing of securities. J. Pierpont Morgan and other financiers kept an eye on the management of reorganized or refinanced corporations.

J. Pierpont Morgan engineered the biggest mergers. In 1901 he combined the Carnegie interests and smaller steel companies into United States Steel. Capitalized at $1,400,000,000, the new company was by far the biggest manufacturing concern ever organized anywhere on earth. Other Morgan creations included General Electric and International Harvester; and the firm was active in transportation, finance, and public utilities (as with the Southern Railway, the Bankers Trust, and A.T. & T.).

Big corporations had large bank accounts, which they placed in the big banks. Hence fewer and larger producers meant concentration in financial resources. As telephones and fast trains enabled trusts to control their business empires from New York, that city became more than ever the center of American finance. Within the city a group of already large banks grew until they overshadowed financial interests elsewhere in the nation. Among commercial banks National City took the lead. It handled the accounts of oil, meat, copper, and other raw material producers, forging far ahead of its competitors. Holding the largest gold reserves outside the Treasury, National City ran the principal market in government bonds and held the reserve deposits of 200 out-of-town banks. Its aggressive president, James Stillman, was a leader among the New York bankers, who informally set discount rates, eased or restricted credit, granted or withheld large loans.

The minor panic of 1907 illustrated the operation of the New York combination. Backed by Stillman and by George F. Baker (of the First National), J. Pierpont Morgan assumed responsibility for the entire financial community in time of crisis. Morgan and the Committee of the New York Clearing House decided which banks could be permitted to fail and which had to be saved. The United States Treasury coöperated by entrusting funds to this group. Morgan did the rest, using his personality and economic power.

Although Morgan and his friends lessened the impact of the panic of 1907, the episode indicated an alarming concentration of financial power. Exposures by reforming journalists (muckrakers) further alarmed the public, as did the haughty manner of J. Pierpont Morgan. The national House of Representatives therefore had a special subcommittee headed by Arsène Pujo of Louisiana investigate the concentration of financial power. The hearings and report of this committee (1912–13) convinced many citizens that a "money trust" dominated the American economy.

In support of this view, the Pujo investigators named as the inner group the house of Morgan, their affiliates, the Bankers Trust and the Guaranty Trust, together with the National City and the First National. The officers of these institutions held 341 directorships in 112 corporations with resources of $22,000,000,000. It was implied that through these posts the inner group dominated banking, railroads and public utilities, and influenced ocean shipping and heavy industry. Morgan and George F. Baker were each directors in forty-eight companies. Besides the inner group, the Pujo subcommittee identified an outer circle of bankers whose aims were generally in harmony with those of the Morgan bloc: Kuhn, Loeb; Kidder, Peabody; Lee, Higginson; August Belmont; J. W. Seligman; and Brown Brothers.

The Pujo investigators ascribed to Morgan more power than he possessed. There was much internecine warfare in the financial world, and little of the careful planning of efficient monopolists. Morgan and Baker were so overloaded with duties that they frequently failed to use the power at their disposal. And when they did give advice, it was likely to be confined to matters related to the securities market. Still, banker influence was increasing; finance capitalism had replaced industrial capitalism in many fields. When Morgan or Stillman spoke up at board meetings, their opinions were close to decisive. Though bankers competed for business, nearly all represented the same conservative Wall Street point of view. And Morgan's opinions strongly influenced the entire banking world.

Good, said Morgan partisans; this meant economic stability. In defense of this position, it was pointed out that there were no long or severe depressions between 1896 and 1919. But the bankers could not claim exclusive credit for the industrial expansion, rising farm prices, and war boom of these years. Nor did the bankers always operate with discretion. In the name of "sound finance" they increased bonded indebtedness enormously and advised the issue of common stock in foolishly large quantities. Morgan felt that monopoly or community of interest would guarantee profits notwithstanding this watering of securities. But sometimes (as with the New Haven Railroad) the heavy capital burden led to receivership and bankruptcy.

The Federal Reserve System

Many thought that creation of a central banking system would reduce the power of the finance capitalists, by providing an alternative supply of credit. At the same time, a central bank might issue currency in periods of crisis, when there was a desperate shortage of money.

Congress became interested in this demand for a more elastic currency after the panic of 1907. As a temporary expedient the House and Senate passed the Aldrich-Vreeland Act of 1908, designed to provide extra bank notes in a crisis. The long-range problem was handled during the administration of Woodrow Wilson (1913–21), by passage of the Federal Reserve Act of 1913. In keeping with the American tradition of localism and fear of federal power, this law established a decentralized system rather than a national bank. The one central agency was a Federal Reserve Board composed of the Controller of the Currency, the Secretary of the Treasury, and five members appointed by the President. The act divided the country into twelve districts, each with a Federal Reserve Bank. The Federal Reserve Banks were bankers' banks, serving member institutions, which in turn served the public. Local banks supplied the capital and two-thirds of the directors of each Reserve Bank. All national banks had to join the system, and other banks could do so by subscribing to Federal Reserve Bank stock (6 percent of their capital and surplus). Only members of the system could use the twelve Reserve Banks.

The Reserve Banks provided a more elastic currency because they could issue paper money in return for certain kinds of agricultural or commercial paper offered as security by the member banks.[1] The Federal Reserve notes had to be backed to the extent of 40 percent by cash. But since member institutions had to keep their reserves on deposit at the Reserve Banks, cash on hand was sufficient to permit a very large note expansion during emergencies.

Reserve Banks could encourage or discourage member-bank borrowing by raising or lowering the rediscount rate. If the rediscount rate were only 2 percent, and customers of member banks were anxious to borrow on eligible paper at 5 percent, local bankers could profit by lending at 5 percent and rediscounting at 2 percent. If the rediscount rate was raised to 5 percent, lending would be discouraged. The Reserve Banks could also influence the money market by dealing in government bonds. Buying bonds added to the Federal Reserve notes in circulation; selling bonds reduced the quantity of circulating currency. Normally each Reserve Bank regulated these matters to suit itself, but the central board could override local decisions.

Since membership involved submitting to federal regulation, most state banks stayed outside the system. But, though only a quarter of the country's banks were members in 1917, the members controlled two-thirds of all banking resources.

In providing an elastic currency, the Federal Reserve Act in no way interfered with the investment activities of the money trust. Even the death of J. Pierpont Morgan in 1913 did not reduce the influence of the house of Morgan. In 1914, the firm became American purchasing agent for France and Britain.

Workers in the Factory Age

For businessmen able to share in the profits of ownership, and for farmers selling at ever higher prices, the early twentieth century was a period of prosperity. For white-collar and industrial workers it was an era of frustration. For in the two decades after 1898, the rich became richer, the poor poorer. An upper-middle-class standard of living featured by automobiles, telephones, phonographs, and electric lights grew up alongside the unimproved tenements and shanties of the "other half." Advertising created acute dissatisfaction among those unable to afford the new luxuries. Schools also improved, widening the horizons of

---

[1] Local banks lent to individuals on a short-term basis, taking as security a claim on goods moving to market. The banks obtained profit by "discounting" the promissory notes. The local bank could then borrow on these notes (have them "rediscounted") at a Federal Reserve Bank. In this transaction the Reserve Bank lent paper money (Federal Reserve notes) to the member bank. The amount of paper money in circulation would depend, then, on business activity and needs as well as on gold supply.

the multitude just when jobs became increasingly monotonous and promotion slow, unless one had good family connections.

Americans had long boasted of their equality of opportunity and democratic rule. In consequence, they were unwilling to accept the new order without protest. A progressive movement threatened the old guard of both major parties. Radical movements gained strength, socialism and anarcho-syndicalism picking up many supporters. White-collar workers turned to such movements because their annual income rose only 80 percent from 1896 to 1918, when the cost of living went up 150 percent. Since standards of living are relative, the situation would have been more tolerable had all classes been held back by some failure of productivity or international calamity. But in these same years of hardship for clerical employees, businessmen and farmers did very well.

Industrial workers also suffered. In the 1890's less than a third of the population lived in cities of over 8000 inhabitants. By 1919 the number approached a half. Partially effective tenement-house legislation prevented overcrowding from becoming any worse than before in New York and a few other places. In most cities, however, the slums continued to spread, unchecked and unregulated. The average work week declined, from fifty-eight to fifty-two hours from 1896 to 1918. But the minute subdivision of labor in big plants led to tedious, repetitive operations that gave the employee little of the pleasure of good workmanship.

Since most employees worked for firms employing over 100, the employee lost contact with those in ultimate authority. His immediate superiors were foremen and straw bosses, many of whom were petty tyrants. Foremen could discriminate against Negroes and foreigners, could give the best jobs to friends and relatives. Unless the results clearly reduced productivity, higher officials did not interfere.

Would owners and managers have run things differently had they been informed? It is hard to say; but it is clear that top management was concerned with finance and the market rather than with labor. And bankers, who controlled some big-company policies, regarded employee relations as beyond their sphere of interest.

During the 1880's Frederick W. Taylor was impressed by the low efficiency—the lost motion, wasted time, listless work—of American shops. Resigning an executive post, Taylor became in 1893 the first specialist in "systematizing shop management and manufacturing costs." He sold his services to many companies; others picked up his scheme of incentive pay for higher production.

Taylor used time-motion studies to analyze jobs and set standards of performance. He urged the proper placing of machines and careful division of labor under trained foremen. To achieve maximum exertion from each worker he favored paying wages on a piece-rate basis. Unions had no place in the Taylor system.

Although no company adopted all of Taylor's ideas, workers disliked what they saw of scientific management. If employees responded well to piecework rates and doubled their wages, the company cut the rates. If workers went all out in some competition for bonuses, the employers expected them to maintain the accelerated rate thereafter. To workingmen Taylorism spelled speed-up, and they wanted none of it.

The A.F. of L.

Throughout this period the mass production industries were able to prevent the unionization of the rank and file of their workers. The great area of union growth was in the building trades, mining, and transportation, notably in small and medium-sized cities. Union success was generally associated with the skilled craftsmanship that fitted into the traditional organization of the American Federation of Labor. Yet at this time the trend was away from skills, toward machine production. Thus the main pattern of unionism represented the past rather than the future and was highly vulnerable to the advance of the machine.

Union membership grew rapidly after 1897, and stood at 2,000,000 in 1904. Although this was only 6 percent of the labor force, it represented a fivefold increase in eight years. If the trend continued, a majority of the workers would soon be organized. But the trend did not continue. Employer opposition and the limitations of the craft approach kept membership stationary for the next five years. Then unionization of clothing workers caused a rise, but less than 6 percent of the labor force was unionized in 1914.

Shortage of workers during World War I paved the way for a great gain in trade-union strength between 1916 and 1919. Also important was the passage of the Clayton Antitrust Act of 1914, which specifically exempted unions from prosecution under antitrust laws. The attitude of President Wilson also helped. During the war Samuel Gompers of the A.F. of L. gave Wilson a no-strike pledge. In return the President saw to it that manufacturers who held war contracts allowed Gompers to approach their workers. The results were spectacular. By 1919 there were 4,000,000 union members, nearly 10 percent of the labor force. But then came a decline, owing to employer activity, collapse of war industries, loss of strikes in 1920, the Big Red Scare, and A.F. of L. insistence on skilled-craft organizations.

Some independent unions rebelled against the strictly defined craft unionism of the A.F. of L. The opposing plan was to organize all workers of one industry regardless of skills, into one big union (industrial unionism). This was vertical unionism, running from top to bottom of a plant, as contrasted with the horizontal type, which attached each kind of skilled worker to a different union and left the unskilled unorganized. The Western Federation of Miners and later the Amalgamated Clothing Workers broke away from the A.F. of L. and maintained industrial organization. But the strength of Samuel Gompers in union politics, and threats of jurisdictional warfare kept most unions from attempting industrial organization.

The I.W.W.

Disgusted by the "aristocratic" craft unionism and conservative politics of the A.F. of L., radical leaders in 1905 formed the Industrial Workers of the World (I.W.W., nicknamed "Wobblies"). The plan, like that of the Knights of Labor, was to include all workers in one big union. But membership was probably never over 70,000.

The Wobblies had their chief influence in fields neglected by the A.F. of L. Big Bill Haywood and other I.W.W. organizers worked in textile centers, staging bloody strikes in Lawrence, Massachusetts, and Paterson, New Jersey, just before World War I. They built up a following among migratory farm workers. They organized northwestern lumber camps and aided the Western Federation of Miners in the Rocky Mountain region.

I.W.W. activity was everywhere associated with violence. For this the union was partly responsible; it used sabotage, sit-down strikes, and slowdowns ("poor work for poor pay"). Employers and government officials in turn employed violent measures against the I.W.W.

Vaguely anarchosyndicalist (believing in internationalism and individual perfectionism), Wobbly leaders opposed American entry into war in 1917. They were arrested in wholesale lots, tried, convicted, and given long prison sentences. Disorganized by loss of leaders and seizure of offices, the organization failed to recover its strength after the armistice. The I.W.W. doctrines of extreme individualism, coöperative production, and a negligible state belonged in any case to an older America and had little place in the state-dominated large-scale industrialism of the twentieth century.

Employer Attitudes

The I.W.W. was of course condemned by businessmen. But even the conservative A.F. of L. failed to alter employers' opposition to collective bargaining. As unions gained, employers combined in opposition. Take the closed shop issue. In many cities the A.F. of L.

had succeeded in restricting the building trades and other skilled crafts to union men. Then the Citizens Industrial Alliance, representing 250 employers' associations, took up the fight. The Bureau of Education of the C.I.A. mobilized local business leaders against the closed shop. Lectures and articles, reinforced by the antiunion attitude of most newspapers, brought middle-class support. As a result, the spread of unionism was checked.

Meanwhile, the League for Industrial Rights used the Sherman Antitrust Act to keep the A.F. of L. from circulating "We Don't Patronize" lists of firms unfair to labor. After years of litigation, the Supreme Court held in the Danbury Hatters' case (1908) that such nation-wide boycotts violated the Sherman Act. The hatmakers' union was ultimately fined $200,000.

Employers' associations were chiefly useful to medium-sized and small businesses. Large concerns needed no outside advice as to where to hire armed guards or strikebreakers and how to secure injunctions against labor unions. Until menaced by the New Deal of the 1930's, many industrial giants did not even join the National Association of Manufacturers or support the League for Industrial Rights. Rather, big companies took care of their own problems through specialized staffs. In a strike of 1901, United States Steel defeated the Amalgamated Association of Iron, Steel and Tin Workers; and in electricity, motors, foods, and chemicals, unionism was confined to a few skilled workers. The labor wars of this era mainly involved smaller employers in construction, mining, textiles, and clothing.

Labor Legislation

As machinery grew more complicated and operated at higher speeds, there was a sharp rise in industrial injuries. Injured workers could sue for damages. But this meant lawyers' fees and costs that the poor man could not advance. If he went to court the laborer had to prove that he had not been negligent. Further, if another employee was to blame, the common law assigned responsibility to this impecunious fellow worker rather than the employer. The need, plainly, was for compulsory workmen's compensation legislation.

Child labor, long hours, and bad factory conditions also affected health. Nearly 2,000,000 children under sixteen were employed in 1900. Many men and women still worked twelve hours or more at a stretch, in dusty, humid, and ill-ventilated plants. The nations of western Europe had already brought such evils under control. Only the United States, once the great center of reform, had failed to act.

Why so? Partly because individualistic industrialists opposed regulation on principle. Partly because conservative labor leaders like Samuel Gompers failed to fight hard for social legislation, preferring to devote their energies to bargaining with employers for higher wages. Little was done until urban upperclass reformers, concerned over public health, brought pressure on state legislatures.

Some employers tried to ward off state action by improving conditions in their plants. The majority, however, did nothing but fight the reform lobbies. In these battles, James A. Emery of the National Association of Manufacturers developed many of the techniques of modern pressure politics. He deluged legislators with telegrams from constituents, and told politicians about the power of the interests affected by their acts. Still, between 1901 and 1917 the legislatures of many industrial states passed laws compelling employers to insure against accidents to workers; prohibiting child labor; requiring school attendance; and limiting hours of labor for women.

Many apparent gains for labor were undone by the courts. Conservative judges threw out compulsory-insurance laws, saying such statutes deprived employers of property without due process of law. Laws regulating hours of labor were scrapped because, it was said, they violated freedom of contract. Gradually, though, the picture changed. Regulatory laws were rewritten to meet constitutional objections. Liberal judges replaced conservatives. In 1908 the United States Supreme Court approved state legislation limiting hours of work for women (Muller vs. Oregon). It took nine years more to bring approval of a state law limiting the working day for men (Bunting vs. Oregon). By 1913 state workmen's compensation and child labor laws were generally meeting the judicial test.

In labor disputes the courts usually adhered to traditional interpretations. The Clayton Antitrust Act of 1914 tried to limit the use of injunctions in labor cases. Nevertheless, judges kept on issuing court orders against strikers, saying this was necessary to protect property. In Coppage *vs.* Kansas (1915), the Supreme Court declared unconstitutional a state law prohibiting employers from forcing workers to sign yellow-dog contracts (pledges not to join a union). In 1917 (Hitchman Coal and Coke decision) the Court denied union delegates the right to organize workers where such contracts were in effect.

Welfare Capitalism

In time employers found that social legislation did not hurt them as much as they had feared. Workmen's compensation laws caused businessmen to install safety devices, which reduced accidents and brought increased production. Statutory limitation of the work day saved light and fuel; and workers turned out about as much product in nine hours as they had in ten. Some managers further discovered that cafeterias, clean washrooms, rest periods, and recreational facilities attached workers to a particular plant and cut down the need for training replacements. Shortage of labor in the World War I boom emphasized these matters and led to personnel studies aimed at picking the right man for the job, and keeping him at it.

A few industrialists experimented with annual bonuses based on profits. Others tried the installment sale of common stock to workers. Neither was successful. Workers preferred good wages to unpredictable windfalls. Workers could not save enough to buy any meaningful stock holding, and the installment plan tied them to the company, often to a nonunion contract.

Meantime some business leaders noted the workers' desire for self-expression. As early as 1904 the American Rolling Mills established a work council to represent employees. Then a system established in the Rockefeller-owned Colorado Fuel and Iron Company, after a bloody strike in 1914, attracted general attention to the "company union." The spread of such unions was aided during World War I by the attitude of government boards which held that companies receiving war contracts should bargain with their employees. As a consequence, General Electric and 125 other large companies instituted their own unions.

At first Gompers approved, feeling that company unions would presently swing over to affiliation with the A.F. of L. But they did not. Company union leaders could not work for affiliation with the A.F. of L. without forfeiting chances for promotion and perhaps losing their jobs. Company unions, therefore, were often a bar to true collective bargaining.

The dilemma of the company union was typical of the problem of the relations of labor and management. Even in the factories where welfare plans were tried, managerial emphasis was on lowering costs. Plant superintendents defended welfare programs on a moneymaking basis. Workers therefore suspected that each improvement was a device to stall off pay increases or a subtle means of increasing production. When companies provided improved housing and model towns, workers sensed a loss of independence and felt the company was giving pleasant conditions only in return for harder work.

Like other humans workers value prestige as well as pay. The companies that did most for their workers were strongly antiunion, and unwilling to admit labor to any real participation in policy or planning. Able management sought rapid change, displacement of labor by machines, a dynamic situation in which no job could be guaranteed. Unions stressed fixed rules and the right of the worker to his job. Most managers could see no way of bringing these views together, no hope of treating organized labor as a partner in the enterprise. Yet the worker was taught in school to believe in majority rule and the importance of individual rights. How could one reconcile administrative efficiency with social democracy? Great complex business machines had been built under aggressive, autocratic leaders. How could the structure be fitted to the traditions of majority rule?

Better Times for Agriculture

For farmers, these were years of relative prosperity. They were years, however, in which little was done to attack fundamental problems. Hence farmers would be ill prepared for the difficulties which would press down on them after World War I.

Rural problems had gone from bad to worse after the Civil War, reaching a climax of calamity in the drought and depression of the early 1890's. Then, suddenly, rain returned to the prairies. Farm prices rose as gold supply increased and as the growth of urban population swelled demands for food and textiles. Wholesale prices of manufactured goods went up 30 percent between 1900 and 1914; farm prices went up 60 percent. Higher income paid off mortgages and bought equipment. The discouragement of 1896 gave way to optimism. New roads brought farmers nearer to market. New machines increased production. And a whole new world was coming into being, with the telephone, automobile, electric lights, and septic tanks.

Urged on by science and by improved markets, farmers turned to new crops: citrus fruits, for instance, in Florida, California, Texas. At the same time, agrarians took up new lands, continuing the traditional westward movement. Although 1890 marked the end of the frontier as a continuous line, there remained much unsettled land, including enormous tracts on the plains, from the Dakotas and Montana to Oklahoma and Texas. Wheat and cotton both moved westward. There was much land speculation; and there was more homesteading from 1900 to 1910 than in the preceding decade.

The Grangers had experimented with coöperation, as had the Populists. Success, however, had been very limited. There were less than a thousand farmers' coöperative societies in the nation in 1896. By 1921 there were 11,000. Coöperatives were especially strong in the Middle West, notably in marketing. Of the several groups behind the movement, two stood out: the American Society of Equity, started in Indiana in 1902; and the Farmers' Union, organized in Texas that same year.

Though disappointed by Bryan's defeat in 1896, the farmers stayed in politics. Many stuck with the Democrats; others built influence among the Republicans. In 1910, at long last, an effective farm lobby was set up in the national capital.

A Nonpartisan League, founded in North Dakota in 1915, became influential in several wheat states. Not exactly a political party, the League endorsed major-party candidates who favored government warehouses, easier credit, and the like. Under Arthur C. Townley, the League captured the Republican machinery in North Dakota and strengthened a new Farmer-Labor party in Minnesota. But after 1920 the League lost ground.

Meantime, the more conservative Farm Bureau Federation came into being (1920). Working through county agents, it improved agricultural methods and pushed coöperatives. It also became a lobbying agency. Through its efforts and those of other interested associations a bipartisan farm bloc was organized in Congress in the early 1920's.

Working at all government levels, the farmers secured better roads, first from state and local governments, then (in Wilson's administration) from the United States as well. Congress and state legislatures voted increased sums for agricultural research and education. A Congressional Smith-Lever Act of 1914 provided for demonstration work through county agents; a Smith-Hughes Act of 1917 promoted agricultural education through the high schools. The Hepburn (1906), Mann-Elkins (1910), and Valuation (1913) acts made federal regulation of the railroads more effective. The credit situation improved, with the creation of a Federal Farm Loan System in 1916. United States government support of irrigation became significant with the adoption of the Reclamation Act of 1902.

Unsolved Problems

Yet farmers did not solve their basic problems. With rising costs, it became more difficult to acquire a farm. Tenancy therefore increased; and a young man starting out as a renter was likely to remain one. As in earlier years, the situation was at its worst in the South, where the sharecrop system was tied to racial as well as to economic questions.

Large-scale farming became the rule in wheat and in some fruit-growing regions. This brought a demand for farm labor—mainly migratory harvest hands. Mexicans as well as natives did this work, which paid little and made a settled life impossible. Yet almost no one tried to help these unfortunates.

Farmers could have used the good times of 1900–19 to diversify their crops. But diversification called for skill in planning and in execution. Tenants and hired hands lacked the desire or the ability to experiment. Owners, too, preferred soil-exhausting staples, because they feared change and wanted a cash crop.

Cotton and tobacco commanded a good European market after 1900.

Meat and wheat did not do so well. Americans were producing more pork, beef, and wheat than ever. But simultaneously production was soaring in Canada, South America, Australia, and New Zealand. After 1900, foreign markets for American meat and cereal products began to melt away; but neither the government nor the farmers gave much study to the matter.

American agriculturalists also failed to take care of their land resources. One-crop agriculture exhausted the soil. Erosion went unchecked. Forest fires destroyed much of value. President Theodore Roosevelt and his successors developed a conservation program, as did many state officials. But other government officials encouraged waste of natural resources. Congress made homesteading easier between 1900 and 1914 by increasing the amount of land one could homestead and by allowing settlers to obtain title in a shorter time. This meant settlement of land that should have been left for grazing. For in many areas, plowing the plains led to wind erosion; and the topsoil blew away.

20

The People and
Maturing Capitalism

A New Standard of Living

Rising prices from 1896 to 1919 added to the appearance of national prosperity. Gold from Yukon mines increased bank reserves and credit. Export surpluses improved the terms of dollar exchange. More important still was the increased variety of goods for sale at moderate prices. Here was an age of marvels in consumers' goods.

The range was wide. Prepared cereals, canned fruits and vegetables added variety to the American diet. So did improved transportation. In the 1890's citrus fruits came east from California, and new railroads developed orange growing in Florida. By 1900 one could buy at low prices ready-made women's clothing of the latest Paris style (put together by immigrant labor in New York loft buildings). One could select sports equipment from an increasingly wide and cheap assortment. Installment plans brought more expensive goods like pianos within the reach of working-class families.

Down to 1880, farmers seldom traveled more than a dozen miles from home, except when changing residence. The city dweller's world was even more restricted. Then the "safety bicycle" revolutionized travel. Urban families pedaled twenty miles on their multiseated machines for picnics in the country. Bicycle clubs lobbied for better roads, and induced New Jersey and other states to start hard surfacing operations. Electric trolleys also broadened the daily range of travel in and around cities. After 1915, buses became significant. The trolley then declined in importance; and eventually much of the 45,000 miles of track was torn up or abandoned.

Of all the consumer utilities, the automobile was the most important. By 1910 cars were sufficiently cheap and reliable to encourage long trips and regular use for commuting purposes. Ten years later there were 7,000,-000 passenger automobiles in the United States, one for every four families. Through highways were already relocating country towns and diverting local business from small-town general stores to the bigger establishments in nearby cities. Farmers enjoyed a new range of markets, schools, and recreation. Suburban areas accessible only by automobile drew upper-class families away from Main Street mansions.

Population Trends

In 1896 the nation's population was 70,000,-000. Twenty-five years later it stood at 105,000,000. Immigration accounted for half the increase. The rest represented the excess of the birth rate over the death rate.

Although the increase was substantial, the rate of increase was declining. In the generation before 1896 the population nearly doubled. It took two full generations after 1896 for it to double again. Part of the explanation for this could be found in the slowing down of immigration after 1914. Fully as important was the relationship of the birth rate to the rise of cities.

In 1896 less than two-fifths of the people lived in places of 2500 or more inhabitants. By 1921, the figure was more than half. In 1890 there were fewer than sixty cities with a population above 50,000. The census of 1920 listed 150 such places. Los Angeles, barely 50,000 in the early 1890's, was beyond half a million three decades later. Atlanta and Cleveland trebled; Detroit increased by 400 percent, and joined New York, Chicago, and Philadelphia in the million class by the 1920's.

As in earlier periods, the children of old-stock American farmers left rural areas to seek their fortunes in the city. In the nineteenth century, many European immigrants had settled on the land. In the twentieth, nearly all newcomers crowded into the industrial cities. They came in quantity, a million a year by 1910. Every northern and western city had its immigrant community; and in the early 1920's more than 30 percent of the population of New York, Boston, Cleveland, and Chicago was foreign born.

Meantime, Negroes who saw no future in southern agriculture moved to southern and northern cities. Impressive by 1900, this migration became even more so after 1914. Altogether, 1,700,000 Negroes moved to urban areas between 1896 and 1919, nearly half going to northern cities.

The movement cityward contributed to the slump in the rate of population growth. The urban birth rate was less than that of rural areas. City people found it difficult to bring up big families in crowded surroundings. The economic insecurity of urban life was also a factor, as was the middle-class belief that small families were associated with higher living standards.

The decline in birth rate among middle and upper classes in the cities caused public comment as early as the 1840's. Children were becoming more of an economic burden, what with mounting bills for medical attention and for education. Besides that, the health of mothers was better assured if they did not bear children too frequently. Thus an increasing number of couples limited the size of their families. The middle-class tendency to delay marriage until one had a little money saved affected the situation. Also significant was the use of contraceptive devices.

Reactions to the declining birth rate were varied. Catholic authorities and conservative Protestants condemned as sinful the use of contraceptives even by married couples. On the other side was Margaret Sanger, a nurse who had witnessed the suffering of poor women burdened by frequent childbearing. After her arrest for circulating a pamphlet on family limitation (1914), this advocate of birth control organized a national association which led to the creation of the Planned Parenthood Federation of America. In 1921 Mrs. Sanger opened a birth control clinic in Brooklyn. Although this was closed by the police, a higher court ruled that in New York physicians could give contraceptive information when childbearing would impair a patient's health. Similar victories followed in other states.

Critics of birth control noted that the family limitation idea had most influence with the upper- and middle-class parents best able to support large families. The poor, both in the cities and in the country, continued to have many children. There was some point to this argument; but after World War I the birth rate would decline even among the poorest urban and rural classes.

The decline in birth rate was partly offset by a drop in death rate. The national rate went down from seventeen to thirteen from 1900 to 1920. (By 1948 it dipped below ten.)

The death rate was not uniform. It was higher for males than for females; higher for the colored population than for whites. Down to 1915, rural areas had a somewhat lower death rate than did urban regions. Thereafter, several large cities brought their rate down as low as that of nearby country districts. Within cities, the lowest death rates (like the lowest birth rates) continued to obtain in wealthier neighborhoods.

The drop in death rate was related to diet, better medical care of small children, sanitary improvements, and preventive measures against infectious disease. Since little progress was made against the degenerative diseases of older age groups (cancer and heart trouble, for example), it was chiefly children and young adults who benefited. The death rate for infants under one year declined dramatically between 1900 and 1920 from 162 per thousand population of that group to ninety-two.

Despite improved life expectancy for children, the drop in birth rate reduced the percentage of children in the total population. The median age of the population rose from less than twenty-three in 1900 to more than twenty-five two decades later. American, on the average, were becoming an older people. In time this trend led to conscious efforts to improve the lot of elderly people. Senior citizens who could afford it migrated in the winters (or permanently) to Florida and California, where they could associate with others of their generation. At the same time professional groups and some larger corporations organized retirement plans. Others began to hope for old-age pensions.

The New Immigration

Until the 1880's most of those who crossed the Atlantic to settle in the New World came from northern and western Europe, especially from the British Isles, Germany, and Scandinavia. After 1890, eastern and southern Europe provided the majority of immigrants.

Several circumstances explained the shift. Standards of living improved in Britain, Germany, and Scandinavia, and social legislation provided increased security. At the same time, many citizens of Italy, Austria-Hungary, Russia, and the Balkans found economic conditions increasingly difficult and encountered burdens associated with anti-Semitism and militarism (which involved conscription and new taxes). Steamship lines made migration easier by opening direct connections between southern Europe and the United States. These firms circulated propaganda stressing the attractions of the New World. So did American employers who wanted cheap labor. Even more impressive were the messages which immigrants wrote back home. These described America in glowing terms; and often they enclosed passage money for those left behind.

The arrival of Poles, Italians, Greeks, Hungarians, and Russians alarmed many native-born Americans. There had been opposition to the old immigration, too. But the north Europeans who had come in before 1890 represented a culture not essentially different from that of the United States. Save for the Irish and south Germans, the immigrants of 1840–90 had been overwhelmingly Protestant, as were most old-stock Americans. Few of the immigrants who came after 1890 belonged to Protestant churches active in the United States. Instead, the newcomers were mainly Roman Catholic, Greek Orthodox, or Jewish. Many of the newcomers desired to become Americanized; but the process was retarded by the conditions under which they lived and by their Old World heritage of poverty and ignorance. Too often the new arrivals took on only the superficial aspects of American culture. This resulted in psychological conflicts, which became more pronounced as the gulf widened between the first generation and their children. In school and elsewhere, the children learned that European ways were a handicap. Such discoveries brought cultural disorganization, which in turn produced unhappiness and, sometimes, delinquency and crime.

The melting pot, said some Americans, no longer worked.

Immigrants accustomed to a low standard of living accepted wages that the native American worker spurned. Newcomers with peasant backgrounds failed to understand the advantages of trade unions (most were excluded anyway, as unskilled workers). Then, too, employers hired immigrants as strikebreakers. Finally, the few immigrants who did enter the labor movement included socialists and anarchists, whom the native American workers disliked heartily.

As a result trade unionists early favored partial or complete exclusion of immigrants. The Knights of Labor fought for exclusion of Orientals in the 1870's. The American Federation of Labor stood for curtailment of immigration from the 1880's on. Many American-born workers, in the unions and out, backed the anti-Catholic, anti-immigrant American Protective Association in the 1890's.

The exclusionists won their first victories in connection with immigration from the Far East. Chinese coolies had been brought in to provide cheap labor in the construction of western railways. Gradually, they had turned to other pursuits, working for a pittance and thus undercutting native laborers. In addition, Orientals did not prove easily assimilable in a social sense. Hence there were disgraceful anti-Chinese riots in western states (twenty-eight Chinese were killed in the Rock Springs, Wyoming, massacre of 1885). And political agitators like Irish-born Denis Kearney of California shouted that "the Chinese must go!" Responding, Congress suspended Chinese immigration in 1882, and made exclusion permanent in 1902. By then feeling was developing against immigrants from other Oriental areas— a Japanese and Korean Exclusion League was organized on the west coast in 1905. To prevent the passage of further exclusion legislation, President Theodore Roosevelt worked out a gentlemen's agreement (1907) under which Japan agreed to limit the emigration of laborers to America. This, though, did not satisfy the exclusionists. California and other states passed laws discriminating against Orientals. Congress followed suit, specifically excluding most Asiatics in 1917, and Japanese as well seven years later.

In the 1880's, Congress also began to restrict immigration from Europe. In a series of statutes passed then and later, the United States excluded contract laborers, convicts, prostitutes, anarchists, the mentally ill, and others likely to become public charges. Restrictionists also persuaded Congress to pass bills requiring a literacy test. Feeling that illiteracy reflected lack of opportunity rather than inferiority, Presidents Cleveland (1897), Taft (1913), and Wilson (1915, 1917) vetoed such bills. The last, however, was passed over Wilson's veto and became law. This indicated the growing strength of those who wanted to abandon the historic policy of welcoming foreigners. Riots against aliens (as in Omaha in 1915) were

THE COUNTRIES OF ORIGIN OF THE
NEW AND OLD IMMIGRATION

1840–1860

North and West

The immigrants who came to the United States before the Civil War were largely from northern and western Europe —from Germany and Ireland in particular. This "old immigration" continued on a large scale until after World War I. Meantime, however, there developed a "new immigration" from eastern and southern Europe. The "new immigration" reached its peak after 1900.

1900-1920

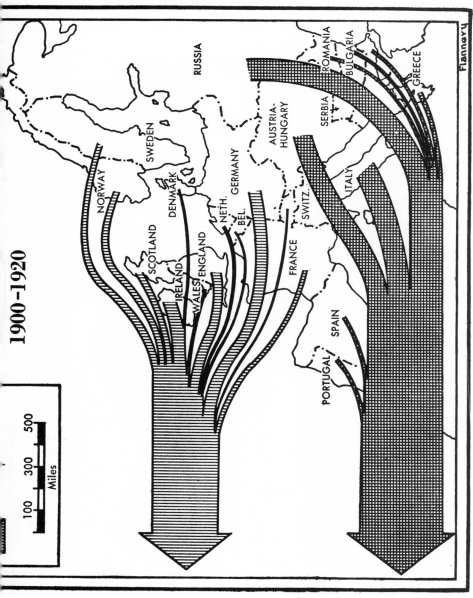

Miles
100 300 500

Flannery

As cheap land disappeared, and opportunities for employment declined, demand for immigration restriction increased. Some restrictionists favored reducing immigration from all foreign countries. Others wanted a selective quota system, designed to favor north European countries ("old immigration"), since most Americans were of north European stock. The immigration law of 1924 followed this line.

another sign of the changing times. So was the organization in 1915 of a new Ku Klux Klan, which included in its program definite opposition to immigration.

Just before World War I an effort was made to speed up the Americanization process by a vast educational program. When this failed, many favored barring outsiders, as a way of safeguarding the American way of life. Exclusionists won further converts by claiming (in the face of evidence to the contrary) that immigrants were likely to be disloyal in wartime. More telling still were claims that immigrants from an impoverished postwar Europe would threaten American living standards. The 1920's, therefore, would see the exclusionists triumphant.

Increasing Inequalities

The United States had long known a wealthy class. Before the Civil War, however, fortunes rarely exceeded a million dollars. Post-Civil War business expansion produced far greater wealth. Every large city had its millionaires, divided into the established aristocracy—those who had inherited wealth—and the newly rich, most of whom were social climbers. Both groups spent money lavishly; an 1897 ball cost the Bradley Martins of New York $369,000.

Such displays of conspicuous waste defied the traditions of democracy and mocked the middle-class Americans who tried to emulate the rich. But high society mocked even more bitterly the mass of citizens. A study of 1890 indicated that seven-eighths of the families held only one-eighth of the wealth. A later examination of estates probated in five urban and rural counties in Wisconsin showed that the top 1 percent owned half the property probated, the bottom two-thirds less than 6 percent. Clearly, a few Americans enjoyed luxury while many were barely able to make ends meet.

Even so, Americans clung to the belief that courage and industry would produce success. The tradition of the success story as set forth by Horatio Alger had surprising vitality. Newspaper writers, educators, and industrialists helped keep this cult of the self-made man alive, by way of insisting that the American system offered equal opportunities to all. The doctrine was not discredited until the great depression that set in in 1929.

Family Patterns

As has been seen, urbanization broke up the family's economic unity. Wives remained economic assets among the poor since they often worked in factories; and children also took jobs. But father, mother, and the children no longer worked together as on the farm; they separated early in the day and most of their time was spent away from home. If the mother worked, small children were likely to be neglected and the older ones grew up on the streets.

Concerned, industrial states adopted compulsory-education laws. Most of these required children to attend school until they reached the fourteenth year. Hence even poor children gained educationally from the urban location, where schools were ordinarily better and sessions longer than in rural districts. Since city youngsters spent more time at school and less at home, schools took over some of the family's function in disciplining and supervising the younger generation. Some municipal authorities recognized this responsibility by 1919 and provided gymnasium facilities and baseball diamonds for use after school hours.

Mothers and children ceased to be direct economic assets to families of middle and upper station. Housewives took care of the home and children but no longer had to perform the extra tasks required of their mothers on the farm. Yet household drudgery was greater around 1900 than it is now. Houses occupied by those in comfortable circumstances were of considerable size. There was endless dusting, cleaning, and washing to be done by hand. A servant was therefore more necessary than in the present day of vacuum cleaners and electric washers.

Relieved of much routine, and possessing increased legal rights, the middle-class woman of 1910 fared better than her ancestors. Improved opportunities for education and employment also affected her situation. So did the trend away from the father-centered farm economy. Increasingly aware of her rights, the city woman began demanding absolute equality with men. She did not get it in this generation. She did, however, get the ballot, first in school, municipal, and state elections, finally on a nation-wide basis (Nineteenth Amendment to the Constitution, 1920).

Though long legal in most states, divorce had been rare in the nineteenth century. Economic factors had worked against it in an age when the woman who left her husband had few job opportunities. Religious attitudes had also made divorce undesirable even for an "innocent party."

Points of view were shifting by 1910. Religious condemnation of divorce lessened among Protestants. At the same time economic barriers were being reduced. Divorce also was viewed as one of "women's rights" since the wife suffered more than the husband in the typical unhappy marriage. Catholics and conservative Protestants and Jews continued to condemn divorce on theological or moral grounds. They claimed that the availability of divorce tended to weaken family ties, and that divorce broke down moral standards. Those who favored more liberal divorce laws recognized the problems of broken marriages, especially where children were involved.

They argued, however, that the maintenance of totally unsuccessful unions helped neither parents nor children.

Americans became increasingly child-conscious after 1900. Legislators required school attendance and prohibited the labor of young children. Schools as well as homes were becoming "child centered." Other organizations, such as the Boy Scouts and the Girl Scouts, provided training and relaxation for the younger generation. Churches also increased their concern for the young.

The new attitude was related, no doubt, to the growing influence of women, who undermined the old, father-centered household. The humanitarian interests of the progressive era also counted, as did the declining birth rate (with fewer children, each could receive more attention). Significant, too, was the rise in the city of specialists who gave their full attention to children's problems: educators, writers, manufacturers, psychologists. Physicians who specialized in child care (pediatricians) impressed on parents the importance of proper attention. So did city health officials bent on reducing child mortality. Psychological clinics for children with mental difficulties were set up in universities after 1900; and soon special magazines began to instruct middle-class parents along medical and psychological lines.

Fashions, Diet, Etiquette

A few wealthy American women bought their dresses at the fashion capital, Paris. Many more patronized American dressmakers who followed the French styles; and housewives who made their clothes used Paris-influenced patterns supplied by the women's magazines. The commercialization of women's fashions accelerated changes in style, for dressmaking concerns profited from any new look which necessitated frequent purchase of new garments.

Hoop skirts, always impractical, disappeared after the Civil War; but garments remained full for a generation thereafter. Elaborate with buttons and bows, dresses revealed the same taste for the ornate that expressed itself also in the gingerbread details of interior decoration and architecture. Costumes of the 1890's also reflected nineteenth-century moral attitudes. A relatively prudish age dictated that the fair sex be completely clothed from neck to ankle, regardless of convenience or safety. Long, heavy skirts were perfect devices for tripping their wearers and sweeping the streets; and they made ladies somewhat helpless in emergencies. Seashore costumes were daring by comparison: short sleeves, knee-length skirts, long stockings.

Yet even by 1896 there were signs of change. Health reformers had long criticized women's styles. Feminists urged that young ladies be permitted exercise more violent than croquet. In apparent response, undergarments became less cumbersome, and the tight lacing of rigid corsets was gradually relaxed. The upper-middle-class ideal of the early 1900's was the Gibson girl, an outdoor type who was ready for yachting or tennis. There was a trend toward informal dress at resorts and summer camps after 1910; and teen-age girls would soon revolt against corsets altogether. The costumes of working-class women were less elaborate than those affected by the gen-teel—a contrast related to price and practicality. (Millworkers had never worn hoop skirts, for obvious reasons.) But there were no distinctive class costumes in America. The equalitarian tradition prevented that.

Masculine costumes changed slowly. Trousers became narrow and short (to the shoe tops) in the 1890's and the wing collar and broad tie of the 1880's gave way to long four-in-hand ties and high, stiff collars. Other changes pointed toward greater simplicity and comfort. Thus, high shoes began to give way to low oxfords at the end of this period. Belts replaced suspenders, canes and detachable cuffs went out, and lightweight Palm Beach suits were introduced for summer wear.

Feminine hair styles changed frequently, as now; the early 1900's saw such forms as the high pompadour. On the male side, the full beard of 1880 gave way to the handlebar mustache, then (by 1910) to the clean-shaven face of pre-Civil War days. Advertisers of safety razors and shaving cream speeded the transition, arguing that the fair sex liked men with smooth faces, and that "Adam did not wear a beard."

Until after the Civil War children were viewed as "little men" and "little women," and were dressed accordingly. Distinctive costumes for youngsters were introduced by the 1890's. Little girls now wore short dresses quite different from their mothers' cumbersome garments; boys shifted from miniature long pants to short trousers fitting tightly at the knees. Store clothes came in for children as well as adults, and there were vogues in children's styles. One was the Little Lord Fauntleroy costume, which involved velvet blouses and long curls. The protests of the boys themselves had something to do with the passing of this style, which disappeared by 1910.

Food habits, like clothing, changed more rapidly in the city than in the country. Farmers continued the heavy diet inherited from colonial days, with emphasis on meat and starchy vegetables. This was marked in the rural South, where many whites and Negroes depended largely in winter on "hog and hominy" (salt pork, corn meal, molasses). Meantime, urban Americans were making concessions to the sedentary life of the cities. Only one meat was now served at dinner, and there was more interest in fruits and green vegetables. This period saw the introduction of foods heretofore unknown to or little used by Americans: tomatoes, bananas, grapefruit, broccoli. The old plea for whole wheat and green vegetables was now reinforced by the biochemical discovery of vitamins. The advantages of a balanced diet were, however, largely confined to the prosperous. Ignorance and poverty made a good diet less accessible to low-income families.

The growth of equalitarian feeling in the days of Jackson had led to some decline in formality in American social functions. But the rise of a new superwealthy class after 1865 brought a revival of formal etiquette. Elaborate customs in dining and other entertainment were again introduced, in imitation of those observed by European aristocrats.

Most Americans rejected such formalism and preferred traditional American informality. Middle-class citizens did, however, buy and study the new etiquette books ("Consume soup quietly"), as part of their effort to "keep up with the Joneses."

Customs associated with marriage, birth, and death changed slowly. The tendency in cities was to remove these matters from the home, just as education and recreation were being separated from the family. Couples were married in church or city halls. More and more urban children were born in hospitals; and the upper classes were turning from dependence on general practitioners to the skilled services of obstetricians. Funeral ceremonies were shifted from the home to funeral parlors, operated by undertakers who now called themselves morticians.

Commercialization of Leisure

As city residents enjoyed reduced hours of toil, they demanded facilities for recreation. But they did not expect the government to supply these for nothing, as ancient Rome had provided its famed circuses. Most municipal governments confined their activities in this sphere to improving city parks and constructing parks and parkways on the edge of town. Most urban citizens therefore relied chiefly on commercial amusements.

Much popular entertainment centered around music. Ragtime and the blues were the folk songs of the machine age. Ground out along New York's tin-pan alley, pieces were available as sheet music and on phonograph records, and could be heard at vaudeville performances and in music and dance halls. Irving Berlin started his professional career as a singing waiter in such a resort.

Many theater owners bid for lower-class patronage, offering melodrama, burlesque, and vaudeville at reasonable prices. Emphasis was on sentimental romance and wild West themes; on girl shows; on acrobatics, juggling,

magic, animal acts, and what passed for humor. There were chains of theaters, organized bookings, and well-advertised productions. Combination
and efficiency, the watchwords of manufacturing, trade, and transportation,
had invaded entertainment.

Burlesque and vaudeville finally met their match in the motion picture.
This developed from Thomas Alva Edison's kinetoscope, a peep-show
machine which for a penny or nickel revealed tiny figures dancing, bathing,
or sneezing. The projector next made it possible for people to see moving
pictures on a screen. The first commercial show exploiting this device was
staged in New York in 1896. Proprietors of penny arcades began to show
the new moving pictures in darkened back rooms. Then, in 1905, an enterprising promoter opened in McKeesport, Pennsylvania, a special movie
theater, named the Nickelodeon. In no time there were nickelodeons everywhere.

The early movies flickered badly, and were confined to simple episodes.
The Great Train Robbery broke new ground by presenting a real story
(1903). Then, as producers discovered the boy-meets-girl theme, the star
system emerged. Movie-goers became acquainted with Mary Pickford,
Charlie Chaplin, and William S. Hart. These performers received more
pay than established stage actors. Directors, producers, and exhibitors also
profited, for by 1910 the movies earned more than all other types of commercialized amusement put together. Some 10,000 theaters boasted 10,000,-
000 attendance every week.

The movies encountered strong opposition from moral leaders and the
intellectual and artistic elite. Not until D. W. Griffith made *The Birth
of a Nation* (1915) did the critical-minded discover how well the movie
makers could use the closeup, fadeout, switchback, and flashback. It was
apparent, too, that the movies had social impact. *The Birth of a Nation*
dealt with Reconstruction in such a way as to nourish race hatreds.

Meantime, spectator sports flourished. Professional prize fighting gained
limited respectability as bare-knuckled bouts gave way to contests with
gloves, and as "Gentleman Jim" Corbett demonstrated that pugilism could
involve skill as well as brutality. Large crowds attended fights in states
which legalized this "sport." Heavyweight champions like James J. Jeffries
and Jack Johnson drew substantial purses, and there were even greater profits for promoters such as "Tex" Rickard.

Most Americans, however, preferred baseball. This national pastime was
played by amateurs on city sand lots and country pastures. It was also a
highly organized spectator sport. With the launching of the American
League in 1901, there were two major professional organizations, the National and American leagues. League champions staged a play-off for the

"world's championship" at the end of each playing season. Minor leagues fed talent to the majors, and leading players like Christy Mathewson and Ty Cobb became nationally famous. Profits mounted. The 1913 World's Series, in which Connie Mack's Philadelphia Athletics defeated John Mc-Graw's New York Giants, drew 150,000 spectators and $325,000 in gate receipts. Organized baseball fought outside competition much as did big business combinations. When a new Federal League (1913–15) challenged the domination of the American and National leagues, the intruder was quickly forced out of existence.

Certain sports remained largely amateur, and confined mainly to the rich. This group included yachting, tennis, and golf, the latter two introduced from Britain in the 1870's. There was professional competition in golf and tennis, however, by World War I. Horse racing, patronized by the rich, became thoroughly commercialized, with betting increasingly important.

The colleges helped build interest in spectator sports. Football, an American adaptation of English Rugby, caught on quickly after Rutgers and Princeton played the first intercollegiate game (1869). By World War I, the game attracted large crowds. Well-paid coaches and costly stadiums, emphasis on gate receipts and winning teams, plus talent scouting all suggested a quasi-professional outlook. At first, football was highly dangerous —there were forty-four fatalities in 1903. Protests led to rule changes, better equipment, and a shift away from close-formation mass plays.

College rowing and track and field, which drew few spectators, avoided commercialization. So, also, did college basketball, which was invented at the Y.M.C.A. College at Springfield, Massachusetts, in the early 1890's. Eventually, however, basketball would also develop spectator interest, leading to the construction of huge gymnasium buildings and concern about the gate.

The Quest for Personal Security

Americans were findings the problem of security more pressing than ever. The income of city dwellers fluctuated with the state of business. Farmers likewise became dependent on the business cycle as they turned to money crops. Inevitably, then, individuals tried to provide their families with some degree of security against major financial risks.

What to do? Fraternal organizations offered some health, unemployment, and life insurance. Most such plans, however, yielded insufficient sums for large emergencies. Nor was commercial life insurance common until after 1890. Thereafter, the habit of taking out life policies gradually spread. One factor was the decline of rates, tied to increased business and longer life expectancy. Life insurance became safer, too, with state supervision, which became general after the New York insurance investigations, conducted in 1905–06 by Charles Evans Hughes.

Although increasingly popular with the middle class, life insurance did not help the poor (save for burial policies, paid for with small, weekly payments). Nor did life insurance adequately protect any class against the risks of unemployment, illness, and old age. These risks became acute in urban society, for crowded city families were less able (and perhaps less willing) to care for the sick and aged than patriarchal farm families of an earlier generation. The panics of 1893 and 1907 convinced some that American states should consider extending the insurance principle by law. European countries were doing this, Germany having adopted social security legislation even before 1880.

But little was done. Humanitarian sentiment did secure laws regulating labor of women and children in nearly forty states by World War I. Almost as many states required compensation for industrial accidents. But both labor and capital opposed suggestions for unemployment insurance, on the ground that this would sap the rugged independence of workers. When social reformers urged the enactment of compulsory health insurance, the opposition was supplemented by that of the medical profession, which felt that its own freedom would be threatened by a public program. A compulsory health insurance bill did pass one house of the New York legislature in 1915; but the movement went no further.

Conservation of Natural Resources

While city families were increasingly concerned about individual security, the more thoughtful began to worry about national security. For two centuries Americans had acquired wealth by a ruthless exploitation of natural resources. Although these at first seemed endless, it eventually appeared that they could be and were being exhausted. Soils, forests, and fur-bearing animals were being destroyed over large areas; and the long-run threat to the national economy was very real. Individuals took the short-run view, in the interest of profits. (Why worry if Alaskan fur seals became extinct, provided one had made his pile in the process?) Only the states or federal government could stop destruction. So said the American Association for the Advancement of Science as early as 1873, when it demanded government conservation of natural resources.

The efforts of scientists and naturalists finally impressed legislators. States passed fish and game laws and established forestry departments. In 1891 a forest service was set up in the Department of Agriculture, and a national forest reserve was organized. Theodore Roosevelt was the first President to display a marked interest in the program. He saved much public land from reckless exploitation by withdrawing it from entry under the land laws. He appointed a national Conservation Commission (1909), and called a special White House conference on the subject.

The concept of conservation presently came to include human as well as natural resources. Was it not as important to save American children as to protect soil and seals? In 1909 Professor Irving Fisher of Yale and other private citizens issued a *Report on National Vitality: Its Waste and Conservation*. This volume urged the importance of public health programs and called attention to the need of the poor for more adequate medical care. The wasting of human resources was dramatized in 1917–18, when the examination of military recruits revealed how widespread were preventable illness and remediable defects, even among young men. It was apparent that many of these youths could have been in good health had they received proper medical attention. In this case, the federal government as well as the health reformer was interested, because illness reduced the man power available for military service. Thus the old humanitarian concern about the public health was supplemented by the modern motive of national interest.

Improving Educational Opportunities

By 1896 the American people were committed to the democratic ideal of equality of educational opportunity. But much remained undone. The next generation witnessed an impressive expansion in education, linked to growing wealth and to industrialization and urbanization.

Expansion was greatest in the elementary day schools, enrollment increasing 6,500,000 between 1896 and 1921, to 22,000,000. In percentages, there was an even more spectacular increase in evening schools for adults. Barely 150 cities provided evening schools in the late 1890's. Two decades later the number approached 500, enrolling two-thirds of a million persons. The number of free public high schools trebled from the mid-1890's to the early 1920's. Instead of enrolling 5 percent of those of high school age (as in 1896), these schools in 1921 took care of 30 percent of that age group.

Growth stemmed partly from child labor and compulsory-attendance laws. (When Mississippi passed a compulsory-attendance law in 1918, all the states had such statutes.) The rapid development of the public school system of the South after 1900 also helped account for the general upswing. So did recognition of the educational needs of the new industrial civilization. Immigration burdened the schools with responsibility for "Americanizing" children of newcomers. The waning influence of home and church imposed new obligations on the school. The crowded slums cried for new approaches, such as the conversion of the school into a community service center, a guardian of the health and hygiene of the poorer classes. Job opportunities promoted manual training, commercial courses, and evening classes. Finally, the humanitarianism of the progressive movement created special classes for the handicapped—the deaf, blind, crippled, feeble-minded.

Inequalities persisted. Opportunities were better in the city than the country, better for middle classes than the poor, better in the North than the South, better for southern whites than southern Negroes. Illiteracy (inability to read and write) declined from 13 percent of the population in 1890 to 6 percent thirty years later. But the First World War revealed that many classified as literate actually possessed no adequate command of language. And, notwithstanding more years of school attendance, the average was only just above six in 1919.

In the early 1890's, only three out of every hundred young men and women attended college. By the 1920's the proportion was eight in a hundred. Financial support for the colleges increased fivefold. Western state universities built extension programs, enabling adults to attend college classes near home or to pursue university-level work through carefully supervised correspondence courses. The period also saw the rise of junior colleges, there being fifty by World War I.

New buildings and longer terms involved added expense, as did the gradual increase in the shamefully low pay for teachers. In 1910 the country spent slightly over $200,000,000 on public education. A decade later expenditures reached the $1,000,000,000 level. Most of the money came from local taxation, chiefly taxes on real estate. States increased their contributions, especially in higher education. The state universities, imbued with the ideal of service to the commonwealth, flourished as never before.

The federal government also helped. As before, United States funds were poured into land-grant colleges. In addition, the central government entered vocational education. Under the Smith-Lever Act of 1914, the central government supplemented state funds used for disseminating knowledge of agriculture and home economics. In 1917 a Smith-Hughes Act offered states federal aid for vocational training programs in the schools. This made possible a national system of vocational education unsurpassed by that of any other nation.

Private funds also flowed into education. In 1867, the banker George Peabody created a trust fund to promote public education in the South. At first, the Peabody Fund helped school systems in southern cities; after 1890, it aided teacher training. Meantime, Samuel Slater, a New England manufacturer, gave money for Negro education (1882). In the twentieth century others provided aid—Julius Rosenwald, for example. Colleges and universities profited from liberal gifts. Rockefeller bounties to the University of Chicago amounted to $13,500,000 by 1910. Meanwhile, dozens of other private institutions used gifts from philanthropists to improve plant and build large endowments. Also of moment was the establishment of a Carnegie fund to provide retirement pensions for professors.

The Practical Approach

The emphasis on practical education found justification in the teachings of John Dewey, an educator-philosopher who rejected the old concept of education as memorization of traditional bodies of knowledge. Instead, students should learn how to live by meeting conditions of life in the classroom. This meant project work involving solution of problems. Working together and building on experience, children could then move naturally to the next level of learning. By reconsidering methods and materials constantly, schools could reflect a changing society. Education could thus become closely related to the building of democracy. Dewey, however, disapproved of vocational education that was geared only to job training. Children who learned vocations should also understand the social and economic patterns in which the vocation operated. Such ideas caught hold slowly; but elementary education showed the influence of Dewey's ideas by 1920.

Higher education also adjusted itself to the needs of the day. The social studies (especially economics) and natural sciences boomed. So did engineering, industrialization bringing a shift from civil to mechanical, electrical, and chemical engineering. There was also great interest in law and the new field of business administration. The women's colleges, having won their uphill fight for recognition as sound educational ventures, clung to the liberal arts curriculum. So did many smaller coeducational and men's colleges. But by 1919, many were following the general trend.

The age of industry changed higher learning in other ways as well. Businessmen now dominated many boards of trustees. This brought money, and sometimes other results. Now and again trustees and administrators refused to continue on their faculties men whose social and economic ideas were at variance with those of the business community. To give just one example, the University of Pennsylvania dismissed Scott Nearing, an economist of socialist convictions. Disturbed over such trends, academicians formed the American Association of University Professors (1914), which would strike many a blow for academic freedom.

Developing Interest in Science

The needs of the industrial age turned educators away from traditional subjects (Latin, for example) and toward the natural sciences. By 1910 nearly every secondary school required at least one science course. Such courses were not always taught well; and science, alive in the laboratory, often became dead in the classroom. But by the 1930's—as high school students of the early twentieth century came to direct the destinies of the republic—Americans would show a mounting interest in science.

By 1900 most biologists and some churchmen accepted the doctrine of evolution. Yet controversy persisted, as conservative clergymen used their pulpits to accuse the evolutionists of undermining Christian doctrine. Replying, evolutionists wrote about the "warfare between science and theology" and said churchmen opposed the free search for truth. This debate gave science much publicity. The evolutionists gradually gained ground, and by 1921 only fundamentalist churches continued to fight Darwinism. As other religious groups accepted the new biology, Darwinians found less reason to oppose theology; and there was a partial reconciliation of science and religion.

Simultaneously, Americans were becoming aware of the close relationship between science and technology. Citizens did not change their basic values—they still prized utility more than "pure" research. But as basic research yielded useful results, practical people became interested. Corporations and universities gave more attention to basic research after the 1890's; and the government became interested by 1919.

In business, General Electric led the way, establishing a permanent research laboratory in 1900. The Du Ponts, Eastman Kodak, the A.T. & T. were not far behind. Basic studies in bacteriology and pharmacology were started in the applied laboratories earlier established by pharmaceutical houses. By 1919, such investments in research had "paid off"—the acid test in business. The ensuing years therefore saw business-supported research expanded both in corporation laboratories and through subsidies extended to university scientists.

The same conditions that encouraged research in industry also stimulated it in universities. Attracted by the reputation of German schools, many chemists, physicists, and medical men migrated to them after 1870 and were trained in original research. Returning home, they maintained these interests in American universities and trained new scientists to carry on their work.

The increasing wealth of American colleges made money available for laboratories, instruction, and scientific research. Medicine furnishes an example. A few medical schools, including Harvard, Michigan, and Pennsylvania, established research laboratories as early as the 1870's. Then a medical school was set up at the Johns Hopkins University (1893) for the primary purpose of advancing original research. Under such men as William Osler and William H. Welch, this school did much to encourage medical research throughout the country.

Welch and other organizers of research were aided by large private foundations, which channeled funds of philanthropic millionaires into science and scholarship, generally through fellowships and research grants. Of key importance was the Rockefeller Foundation (1913), which was to pour $10,000,000 a year into research, chiefly in medicine and public health. At first this and other foundations were attacked because of their connection with the rich. But, whatever the motivation of the founders, the foundations made possible a great expansion of university research activities.

Science and the Government

Although private support of science was the dominant pattern between 1896 and 1919, government backing was significant. State universities became major scientific centers. These institutions drew support both from state legislatures and from the federal government —notably the land-grant schools connected with the agricultural experiment stations set up under the Hatch Act of 1887.

Meantime, state and federal bureaus, long active in applied science, were turning to basic research. The United States Bureau of Fisheries did creditable work in biology, the Bureau of Standards in the physical sciences. In studying Texas fever among cattle, Dr. Theobald Smith of the Department of Agriculture found (1889) that the disease was spread by an infected tick. This discovery was basic to the control of any disease (of animals or man) which was carried by a so-called secondary host. Smith's work opened the way to later demonstrations of the manner in which mosquitoes served as carriers of malaria and yellow fever. A Cuban, Dr. Carlos Finlay, supplied the leads in the case of yellow fever. Dr. Walter Reed and other members of an American military commission provided the final proof (1901).

Such findings led to Congressional support of basic studies. In 1912 the Public Health Service was authorized to study "the diseases of man." Here was a charter for research comparable to that being carried on in universities, significant because federal funds provided resources greater than those of the wealthiest universities and foundations.

Relations between government and science became closer during World War I. Lincoln had established a National Academy of Sciences during the Civil War in an effort to enlist scientific knowledge in the Union cause. The Academy had survived as a small and largely honorary body, ill prepared to make the studies needed in an age of aircraft and poison gas. At President Wilson's request, therefore, this National Academy set up a new National Research Council in 1916. Once organized, the Council brought the ablest scientists into a planned program of turning scientific knowledge to military use. University and government scientists coöperated to good advantage.

Science and Society

As the achievements of science became increasingly impressive, Americans wondered if science and scientific methods might solve social problems. Certainly help was needed; most social problems remained unsolved. Biologists and physicians knew how to improve food products and how to prevent many diseases; but social difficulties still made it impossible to avoid famine and epidemics in many parts of the world. Although technology had enabled men to build and supply large cities, crime and poverty persisted in those great urban centers. In the past, such matters had been dealt with in terms of moral enthusiasm rather than calm analysis. Why not try a scientific approach—collect facts systematically, interpret the data rationally, in attacking such problems as business depressions, divorce, and race relations?

A few persons had tried this approach by 1896. For one thing, they had collected social statistics. But scholars differed widely in interpreting this material. It was fairly easy for a natural scientist to view his data on planetary orbits with impartiality. It was more difficult for a social scientist to view with detachment the race question or the rights of labor unions.

As a consequence, social scientists developed conflicting "systems." Some used Darwinian theory to defend the existing economic order. The English thinker Herbert Spencer saw the history of civilization as an evolution from simple societies to the complex. Modern industrialism, then, was the highest, most desirable state of society. Taking over from there, William Graham Sumner of Yale stressed the role of an unchecked struggle for existence in business competition. Sumner felt that if the government stopped this struggle, Americans would lose desirable incentives to thrift and initiative. Sumner's analysis, phrased in scientific language, was really a defense of the industrial capitalism of his day.

Others who accepted Darwinism opposed Spencer and Sumner. Were all save the masters of capital "unfit" in an evolutionary sense? Traditional

American sympathy with the common man inspired the sociologist Lester F. Ward to defend the rights of the majority. Ward was convinced that man, as a free agent, could guide the evolutionary process in terms of such old ideals as the greatest good for the greatest number. Like Sumner, Ward used scientific language; but his conclusions justified future government control of business.

Learned though they were, the writings of Sumner and Ward could be criticized as based on preconceived views. Many intellectuals felt that such partisanship was improper—that social scientists, like chemists, should interpret data in a cold-blooded or objective manner. Science would simply present the evidence. Politicians or reformers could carry on from there.

As they came to stress exactitude and objectivity, some social scientists felt disdain for welfare workers and reformers. These "do-gooders," said social scientists, still displayed emotional attitudes and worked without benefit of scientific principles. (This resembled, in a way, the aloof attitude of some "pure scientists" toward practical inventors.) Eventually, however, the two groups moved closer together. Sociologists became consultants for welfare organizations, and economists were employed by banks and by the government.

The Rise of Psychology

After 1850 neurologists began to study the behavior of the nervous system; and a group of professional psychologists emerged. Unlike most social sciences, psychology could often employ experimentation. This was true even in educational psychology. Thus one could experiment with a method of teaching arithmetic to one group, and compare the result by testing a "control" group using another method. Measurements became useful in practice even before there was agreement as to the principles of the learning process. After introduction from Europe, the Binet tests and concept of the intelligence quotient (IQ) proved useful in rating students. They were used by the United States Army in World War I, by business later.

Psychiatry had had a long history as a branch of medicine. Physicians, however, had given little attention to mental illness between 1850 and 1900. Engrossed in the strictly physical approach to disease, medical men had ignored mental troubles except those ascribed to some physical ailment. Then came Freud, an Austrian physician who associated neurotic symptoms with long-suppressed desires, particularly those of a sexual nature produced in childhood. Although repressed by social taboos or inhibitions, these thoughts became embedded in the subconscious, and produced tensions which caused nervous behavior. This could be cured, said Freud, by psychoanalysis—questioning the patient until he recalled the original circumstances. Once memory was brought to the conscious level, the tensions and neurotic behavior would disappear.

Many medical men were skeptical, especially since experimental verification was not immediately forthcoming. But, whatever its limitations, psychoanalysis appeared to offer hope to patients who feared a nervous breakdown. Ordinary medicine seemed of little help in most such cases. In addition, Freud's emphasis on sex aroused curiosity; and after 1910 Freudianism became almost a cult in America. Talk about inhibitions produced a daring feeling of escape from the prudishness of Victorian grandparents. Novels and plays appeared with such titles as *Suppressed Desires*. "Realistic" writers offered amateur analyses of their characters, and some sought hidden sex motivation in the lives of Napoleon and other historical personalities.

These trends show the influence of science on literature. This was not new; literary men had discussed science since the days of Newton. Interests had changed with the times. Walt Whitman, a nineteenth-century writer, had spoken of the "learned astronomer." Sinclair Lewis, a twentieth-century novelist, exploited the dramatic possibilities of bacteriology (in *Arrowsmith*). This literary treatment reached readers who would otherwise have been unaware of the growing significance of science.

Science and the Universe

As has been noted, some sociologists interpreted social evolution as a predetermined, inevitable process. Others held that man was a free agent who could direct evolution toward his own welfare. This raised the old problem of free will—now presented in scientific form instead of in the earlier theological terms of predestination. The question was of more than abstract interest; for the answer affected conduct. Thus Herbert Spencer, viewing evolution as inevitable, adopted a fatalistic or indifferent attitude toward reform. Lester F. Ward, believing man to be a free agent, favored social reforms in the interests of the masses.

The central philosophical problem was the relationship of man to the universe. Physicists and astronomers pictured the universe as a vast clockwork mechanism. The earth was a mere speck, man a minute accident destined for extinction when the universe ran down. Even on his tiny planet, man was not a unique creation, but the product of a brutal process of evolution from lowest animal forms. Disturbed at finding no suggestion of divine concern about man, orthodox religious thinkers refused to accept the evidence set forth by scientists. Idealistic philosophers, like Josiah Royce, did not deny scientific findings. They insisted, however, that this field of science was one of surface appearances. Behind the natural phenomena with which scientists dealt lay an ultimate spiritual reality. Man himself was not merely an animal but was endowed with a spark of that divine principle which animated the entire universe. The historian John Fiske wrote in similar vein. He maintained that evolution was true, but added that evolution was the process by which God had brought man into existence as the highest of His creations.

Less hopeful thinkers became skeptical of spiritual reality and pessimistic about life. Some took refuge in the old philosophy of Epicureanism—man should enjoy his brief existence by cultivating the good life. *The Rubáiyát of Omar Khayyám*, which featured this outlook, had a vogue in the United States. "Eat, drink, and be merry, for tomorrow you die."

Spurning both pessimism and idealism, some thinkers held that science would replace religion as a guide in life. Was not science doing more for mankind than the churches had ever done? Rejecting religion and most philosophy, the French thinker Auguste Comte held that, since the human mind could not understand the ultimate nature of reality, all thinking along such lines was a waste of time. Philosophers should devote themselves simply to questions raised by science itself.

Theologians and others opposed this positivist view. Henry Adams pointed out that science was cold, impersonal, and certainly not an unmixed blessing. Factory techniques destroyed the old joy of craftsmanship; and science gave men weapons with which to destroy themselves. Perhaps science was a Frankenstein's monster, made by man but destined to destroy him.

As new generations accepted science, the cosmic problem became a less intense issue, and philosophers stressed social questions. Such intellectuals as William James and John Dewey felt it unnecessary to worry much about the problem of the universe. Man was a part of nature, and he should make the best of it. One should neither worship nor condemn science, but direct it toward social betterment—the goal of the eighteenth-century Enlightenment. In choosing social goals, humans did not need to deal in absolutes. Things were true, said William James, if they were pragmatic—that is, if they worked well. If an ideal proved illusory, or a process unfortunate, it was not really good or true; and something more practical must be found.

Both James and Dewey sought to apply their principles in socially useful ways, as in improving education. As a psychologist, James felt that an understanding of the learning process was basic to teaching procedures. This prepared the way for Dewey's emphasis on the child-centered school, in which subjects would be fitted to children's needs, rather than (as heretofore) the children to the subjects.

The pragmatism of James and Dewey was a logical outgrowth of New World experience. Americans had always been practical people. Practical they remained in the age of science.

Money and the Arts

As before, Old World influences were strong in music, sculpture, painting, and architecture. At the same time, these arts reflected the new urbanism and industrialism.

With the rise of industrial wealth, the arts obtained added financial support. The prestige value associated with liberal patronage of the arts counted for a good deal. Some wealthy persons also developed a genuine aesthetic interest. Simultaneously, civic pride in public buildings was on the upgrade; and the economic development of the nation permitted that pride to find expression.

Symphony orchestras and opera won many new patrons after 1900. The very largest cities now had much good music; and symphony orchestras were organized in such smaller centers as Seattle and Minneapolis. Eager to emulate the rich, the middle classes also cultivated music. Daughters took piano lessons, providing a $75,000,000 yearly business for the piano manufacturers by 1914. Phonograph sales were even higher.

Although European classical influence remained strong, Theodore Thomas and others felt that a native American music might emerge from Indian, cowboy, and Negro themes. Edward A. MacDowell and other composers experimented with these materials, though with only limited success. More impressive in many ways was the new popular music. Irving Berlin caught the public fancy with his "Alexander's Ragtime Band" (1912), the most famous of the new ragtime songs. Meanwhile, Negro bands in New Orleans, Memphis, and St. Louis were improvising sad, lovesick blues and a pioneer form of jazz.

Besides patronizing opera, the super-rich filled their mansions with paintings and other art objects. Money was no object with such collectors as J. Pierpont Morgan and Andrew W. Mellon. Private wealth also flowed into the endowment of art galleries. Although many of these galleries were architectural monstrosities, their collections helped develop aesthetic interests among Americans. And several museums established art schools.

The richest Americans occupied uncomfortable Romanesque or Renaissance palaces—quite out of harmony with an industrial America. The new factories and office buildings, however, suited the changing times. They used the new materials (concrete, steel, glass) and were built to serve the purposes of modern life. To save expensive space in downtown districts, structures became ever taller. Chicago led the way. New York and other cities followed suit, and the metropolitan skyline took on a twentieth-century appearance.

Louis Sullivan generalized the emerging trend in the slogan "Form follows function." Although he did not completely forgo decorative effects, this Chicago architect emphasized substance and utility rather than frills. Sullivan's student, Frank Lloyd Wright, carried functionalism still further. His Larkin Building in Buffalo protected workers from the smoke, dirt, and noise of the railways at the rear by a massive, unbroken wall. At the same time, Wright provided ample light by a generous use of glass. Wright also designed homes exemplifying the principle that a home should grow out of the soil and the surroundings. His clean vertical lines and jutting horizontals showed that true simplicity and functional use need not be the simplicity of the side of a barn. For massive Victorian furniture, Wright substituted built-in shelves, tables, and benches. His work, though, took hold slowly. Most wealthy people preferred traditional houses that suggested a remote time or place. After 1900 they turned from European-style castles to American regional traditions: the colonial style in New England and New York, the Spanish mission type in Florida and California.

In public architecture, the accent was on the classical. Here a major influence was that of the Chicago World's Fair of 1893, which featured glistening white classical temples of imitation marble. Consequently, builders of new state capitols copied classical forms and used classical allegories in their murals. So did railway stations, conceived in the image of the Roman baths.

The Gothic style dominated ecclesiastical and collegiate architecture. John La Farge's experiments with stained glass added to the popularity of this style. So did the work of Ralph Adams Cram, an architect with a religious devotion to the Middle Ages. The Tudor Gothic used by many colleges had attractive features; but when applied to the library, it resulted in reading rooms that required artificial lights even on the brightest days.

The sculpture at the Chicago Fair (under the direction of Augustus Saint-Gaudens) also reflected the classical taste. So did the painting, classical murals being used in the classical temples. And the gallery of art excluded the rising French moderns—Manet, Degas, Cézanne.

Though mistreated at the Fair, these French artists set a stamp on American painting. French influence had been growing in the United States since the 1870's. The landscapist George Inness had changed his style as he came to appreciate the French Barbizon school; Whistler had learned much from the French impressionists. After 1900, French leadership pointed Americans first toward realistic presentation of industrial society, then toward experiments in abstraction.

Realism first centered around Philadelphia painters, notably Thomas Eakins. Later, New Yorkers took the lead—Robert Henri, one of The Eight, who publicly crusaded for the new art; Henri's pupil, George Bellows; and John Sloan. These artists painted pictures of the new skyscrapers; street urchins in alleys strewn with ash cans; barroom, pushcart, and tenement scenes. They painted in oils, made etchings, used the lithograph form. Their work was admired by discerning critics; but they were also genre painters, artists to the people.

French artists, meantime, were experimenting with geometric abstractions. Postimpressionists, cubists, futurists felt that they were discovering a more profound aesthetic experience than that revealed by traditional forms, colors, and lines. Even before World War I the trend had influenced a number of American painters (John Marin and A. B. Davies, for example) and some sculptors, including Jo Davidson. Davies, who was one of The Eight, was the major figure behind the spectacular Armory Show (New York, 1913), which introduced Americans to European and native painters who were working with symbols and abstractions. Conservative critics and the bewildered public condemned what they saw. There was no "picture" here; one could not even tell what the artist was trying to do. But perhaps the defiant lines and broken colors were no more confusing than other aspects of the new industrialism. And in any case, this "modern art" had come to stay.

Literature

In letters, popular taste still ran to sentimental romance, like the "molasses fiction" of Mrs. Gene Stratton-Porter (five of her novels went over a million copies each). Equally successful were the sermonized melodramas of the Reverend Harold Bell Wright. But not all best sellers were conformist. Zane Grey put a note of brutality in some of his wild West novels (15,000,000 copies); and Elinor Glyn's wretchedly written *Three Weeks* became a best seller because it dealt with sex.

While most writers were grinding out escape literature, Henry James, William Dean Howells, and Samuel L. Clemens (Mark Twain) were moving toward realism. They and other American authors were influenced by French and Russian naturalists, who tried to describe life just as scientists described what they saw under the microscope.

Several of the ablest of the new writers were women. Edith Wharton, a disciple of Henry James, wrote of the New York elite. Willa Cather, reared in Nebraska, told of pioneers on the prairie, concealing neither heroism nor insecurity. Some of Ellen Glasgow's Virginians were uncouth, some genteel; nearly all were poor.

Many of the new authors stressed the faults of the new industrial civilization. Frank Norris, a disciple of the French novelist Zola, wrote about monopolistic railways and ruthless speculators (*Pit, Octopus*). Jack London, impressed with Darwinism, turned out adventure stories about the struggle for survival on the last frontiers (*Call of the Wild*). He also developed the themes of class struggle in industrial society (*Iron Heel*). Upton Sinclair's *Jungle* dealt in gory detail with the faults of Chicago meat-packing concerns. Intended as a plea for socialism, this novel failed on that score, but helped bring effective meat-inspection legislation.

Among the new writers Theodore Dreiser deserves special notice. Careless about style, Dreiser nonetheless showed great power in laying bare the bewildering character of urban life. His *Sister Carrie* was the tale of a village girl in the city. There followed *The Financier* and *The Titan* (the second virtually suppressed by the publisher), novels picturing the corrupt capitalist. *The American Tragedy* dealt with problems associated with the traditional American struggle to get ahead.

Many writers were less extreme in their criticism of the evils of their day. Booth Tarkington, for example, viewed the struggle for business success with less cynicism than did Dreiser. But Tarkington did attack political corruption. So did the historical novelist Winston Churchill, who wrote fiction about corruption in high places (*Mr. Crewe's Career*) and himself entered politics in New Hampshire.

Poets, too, treated social problems. In "The Man with the Hoe," Edwin Markham pictured exploited labor. William Vaughn Moody warned against the new slavery to materialism and the machine. Carl Sandburg celebrated in Walt Whitman fashion the strength and dignity of the common man amid urban confusion and smoke. Vachel Lindsay caught the spirit of the social gospel and the humble and poor. All this helped provide background and support for progressive reform.

There were magazines for every taste—professional, religious, and literary organs, periodicals devoted to science, humor, and romance. The circulation giants were Edward Bok's *Ladies' Home Journal* (2,000,000) and George Horace Lorimer's *Saturday Evening Post*. Not far behind were *Munsey's*, *Collier's*, *McClure's*, and *American*. The "quality" magazines (*Harper's*, *Scribner's*) also increased sales. One factor in the circulation increase was price—*Munsey's* led the way in the 1890's by cutting to a dime. New printing and distributing techniques made mass circulation possible. So did advertising. Finally, *McClure's* and other leading periodicals won new readers after 1900 by attacking corruption in government and business. This meant profits, except when advertisers were offended; and it advanced the progressive cause.

With improved news-gathering methods, newspaper readers obtained information sooner than before. Coverage was also better, in both foreign and domestic fields. Newspapers joined progressive novelists and magazine writers in exposing fraud. Much good was done by such journalists as Joseph Pulitzer of the New York *World* and St. Louis *Post-Dispatch*.

But there was also a continuing trend toward standardization and sensationalism. The old ideal of the editor as a molder of opinion retreated before the new concept of journalism as a profitable business. This involved deferring to advertisers and catering to the public taste. It meant playing down issues and building up feature sections: women's pages, with recipes, shopping hints, and advice to the lovelorn; comic strips; sports; romantic serials. Some of this was slanted toward local interests. But as time went on, newspaper chains and feature syndicates spread the same fare all over the nation.

Religion: Church Membership

In numbers, the Baptists and Methodists led the Protestant procession at the beginning and the end of this period. The Presbyterians, Lutherans, Disciples of Christ, Episcopalians, and Congregationalists followed. Several smaller groups grew at a more rapid rate than the larger bodies. The Mormons (who abandoned polygamy in 1896) remained dominant in Utah and showed missionary vitality in surrounding states and even in foreign lands. Christian Scientists also advanced, with the founder, Mrs. Mary Baker Eddy, providing leadership until her death in 1910.

More than a dozen new Protestant sects were started in these years, many being holiness or pentecostal groups organized among the rural poor. In the main, the new bodies represented a protest against the older denominations, which were abandoning revivalism and substituting an educated clergy for the more exciting leaders of yesteryear. The new sects were bent on recapturing the emotional spirit of camp-meeting days.

The Roman Catholics gained rapidly after 1896. By 1919, the Catholic Church claimed about a third of the church members in the country, substantially its percentage of 1950.[1] The major factor in the rise to this level

---

[1] This does not mean that the Catholics numbered a third of the population. Nearly half of the persons who considered themselves Protestant had no formal church connection. Hence in 1919 and afterward approximately one-sixth of the inhabitants of the United States were Catholic.

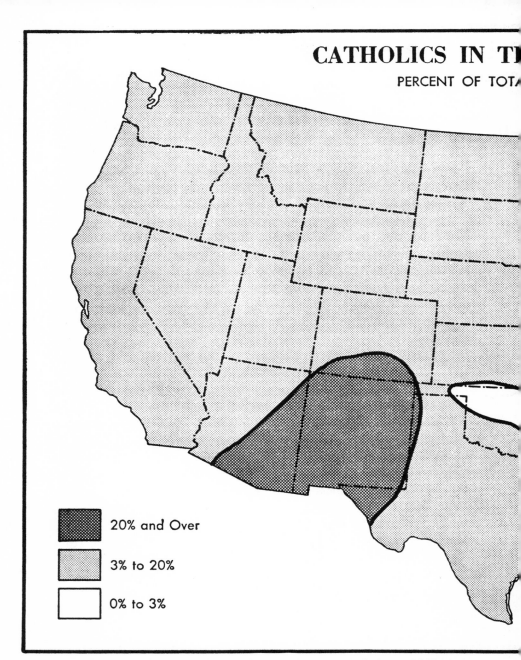

20% and Over

3% to 20%

0% to 3%

In 1850, five out of every hundred Americans were Catholic; in 1950, sixteen
out of every hundred. The Catholic increase is closely related to the history
of immigration. Hence the southern states, which attracted few immigrants,
have a very small percentage of Catholics even today. (Louisiana, first settled by the French, furnishes an exception.)

The Catholic Church in the United States has been stronger in urban than
in rural areas. Many German Catholics settled in Middle West farm communities in the nineteenth century; and twentieth-century Mexican immigrants

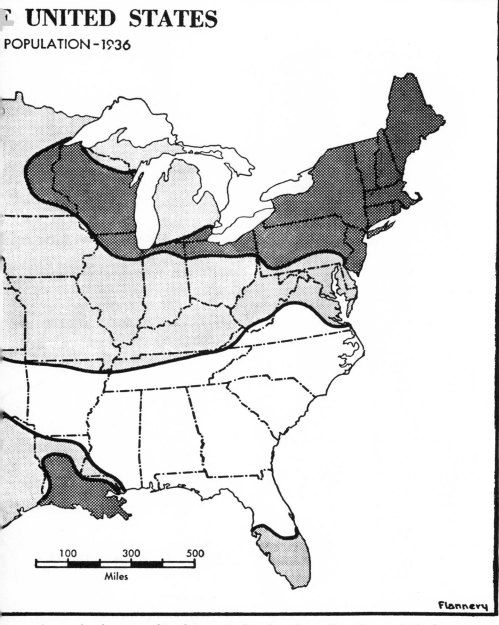

Flannery

have also been employed in agricultural regions. (Americans of Mexican background bulk large in the Catholic population of the Southwest.) In the main, however, Catholic immigrants settled in urban districts. The Irish, who arrived from the 1840's on, located in and around the northeastern cities. So did the Italians, the Poles, and the French Canadians, all of whom came in large numbers after 1880. Economic factors were more important than religious ones in this situation, for non-Catholic immigrants followed the same pattern.

was the arrival of Catholic immigrants. Able leadership, as of Cardinal James Gibbons, was also in the picture. As the Catholic population increased, new dioceses were formed at the rate of about one a year. More religious orders were set up; and there was a large increase in the number of and enrollment in Catholic educational institutions. The growth was especially marked on the elementary (parochial school) and college levels.

Although some Protestants viewed these trends with alarm, there was less organized anti-Catholic activity in this era than in the years before and after. Having failed in its bid for influence in the Republican party, the anti-Catholic American Protective Association was fading out by 1896. In 1915 the Ku Klux Klan would be organized as an anti-Catholic, anti-Negro, society; but the Klan would not reach its peak until after 1919.

The Catholics were not alone in profiting from immigration. Some Protestant bodies (the Lutherans in particular) obtained reinforcement from this quarter. The new immigration also brought in a substantial number of Jews, many of them refugees from persecution in Russian Poland and elsewhere. The number of Jewish congregations in the United States doubled in the fifteen years after 1890, doubled again in the next fifteen years. In New York City the Jews made up a considerable fraction of the population by 1920. But in the country as a whole the Jews remained a very small part of the population—less than 4 percent in 1919.

Religion and Social Problems

Religious leaders continued to wrestle with the problems of industrial civilization. One by one Protestant groups followed the example of the Episcopalians in recognizing labor—the Congregationalists in 1901, Presbyterians in 1903, Methodists in 1908, and so on. Protestant clergymen read such books as *Christianity and the Social Crisis*, by Walter Rauschenbusch of the Rochester Theological Seminary, a leader of the social gospel movement. Rauschenbusch asked the churches to help create a more humane social system. The general public made best sellers out of Winston Churchill's *Inside of the Cup*, and *That Printer of Udell's*, by Harold Bell Wright; and Street and Smith, the pulp publishers, found a good market for paper-backed volumes with such titles as *Would Christ Belong to a Labor Union?*

Important in the new movement was the Federal Council of Churches of Christ in America. Organized in 1908, the Council represented thirty-three Protestant bodies with 17,000,000 communicants. It endorsed the social gospel, stressing the obligations of Christianity to work for social legislation and a more equitable distribution of the profits of industry.

These Protestants had support from other groups. Judaism, especially its liberal wing, actively extended its historic interest in charities by cultivating closer affiliation with working people. Among Catholics, the encyclical *De Rerum Novarum* of Pope Leo XIII (1891) pointed toward social reform. One Catholic prelate who did active work along that line was Archbishop John L. Spalding, whom President Theodore Roosevelt named as one of the arbitrators of the anthracite coal strike in 1902. Another was Father John Ryan, who published a spirited book, *A Living Wage*, in 1910.

Strong though it was, the movement toward social reform did not affect all. Many Catholic prelates, Jewish rabbis, and Protestant clergymen were not interested. In many rural areas, interest in social issues was confined to one problem: the liquor question. Granting the importance of this matter, the fact remained that concentration on it turned attention away from other vital questions.

Long in the field, the foes of alcohol were better organized than those interested in other social problems. Until the 1890's, the key work was done by the Woman's Christian Temperance Union, which was run by Frances Willard from the late 1870's until her death in 1898. In her day many rural and small-town areas "went dry"; and, with Kansas leading, some states followed suit.

During the 1890's, the Anti-Saloon League spearheaded a nation-wide drive to ban the sale of liquor. Backed by nonurban Protestants, the League forced newspapers to give it space. It enlisted the aid of clergymen and employers, it browbeat and converted legislators. Wayne B. Wheeler, the League's "legislative representative," was one of the ablest lobbyists in American history.

Although the Anti-Saloon League met opposition in the cities, it won many victories in village and rural local-option contests. Then it worked at state capitals, securing state prohibitory laws. By the time of World War I, much of the United States was dry, though the industrial Northeast still held out. War brought a need for grain conservation, adding a patriotic argument. At the end of 1917 Congress adopted a proposed Eighteenth Amendment to the Constitution, banning the manufacture, transportation, and sale of intoxicating beverages. When approved by three-quarters of the state legislatures, this became effective (1919); and the nation began its experiment in national prohibition.

Interdenominational Activity

As Protestant doctrinal quarrels subsided, the possibility of coöperation among sects increased. Meantime, the need for it was becoming acute. In rural areas depleted by migration to the city, financial necessity pointed toward some form of interdenominational activity. The repeal of Sabbath-observance laws and the increase in secular interests (as in motoring) also thinned church attendance, reinforcing the movement for unity. Under such pressures, many small towns and farm areas formed community churches. Several rival groups within the larger sects joined hands. Others discussed union, paving the way for such later combinations as that of the Methodists. Interdenominational activity increased in the W.C.T.U., Anti-Saloon League, Y.M.C.A., Y.W.C.A., Home Missions Council. The new tendency was to divide foreign mission fields, rather than to insist on competition. The establishment of the Federal Council of Churches of Christ in America in 1908 was a still more important interdenominational move.

There were efforts, too, on a broader basis. A World Congress of Religions at the Chicago Fair in 1893 tried to bring together all religious-minded people. Somewhat the same end was served by scholars interested in comparative religion. Protestants, Catholics, and Jews coöperated in many causes, as in denouncing Russian persecution of the Jews. Suspicions remained. Many Protestant clergymen looked with disfavor on the growth of Catholic strength; and most members of the Catholic hierarchy were very cautious about coöperating with Protestants. Jewish-Christian coöperation was also difficult to arrange. But those who tried achieved some success, which testified to the continuing vigor of the American tradition of toleration.

Modernists and Fundamentalists

There were doctrinal controversies in all churches, despite a tendency away from theological disputation. Orthodox Jews believed in strict observance of dietary laws and other age-old religious customs. Reformed Jews felt that many of these traditional beliefs had outlived their usefulness. Conservatives took a position in between. Catholics differed among themselves on such questions as coöperation with Protestants, and as to how far doctrine should be adjusted to fit the changing times. Addressing the American hierarchy in 1898, Leo XIII felt called upon to condemn a tendency to modify traditional beliefs.

Protestants continued to be plagued by the modernist controversy. Liberal Protestants kept on trying to reconcile Biblical criticism and the new science with the essence of Christian teachings. On the whole, they were successful, partly because of the influence of the Chicago Divinity School and New York's Union Theological Seminary. But in the rural West and South, conservatives denounced the liberal tendencies of urban preachers. In 1909 these champions of the historic position organized. In 1910 they issued a booklet entitled *The Fundamentals, a Testimony to the Truth,* setting forth their belief in the literal truth of the Bible, the divine birth, bodily resurrection, the imminent second coming of Christ.

The fundamentalists were a powerful voice in every large Protestant denomination. They had influence in theological seminaries, many votes at annual conventions. In the South they controlled a majority of the pulpits. And they had mighty champions: William Jennings Bryan and William A. ("Billy") Sunday. Sunday's racy preaching and athletic behavior in the pulpit attracted huge crowds (80,000,000, he estimated). He and other traveling revivalists covered country districts and pitched tents in cities to fight skepticism, sin, liquor, and liberalism.

The fundamentalists won some victories in the World War I decade. But even in 1910, when *The Fundamentals* appeared, most of them knew they were fighting a last-ditch stand; and not a few suspected that their cause was already lost.

21

The Progressive

Movement

When Bryan went down in 1896, some felt
that reform was indefinitely postponed. Actually, reform came soon, reaching a climax in the progressive movement of 1901–17. This movement,
though, was different from the agrarian crusade of Bryan and the Populists.
The progressives had urban as well as agrarian leadership. Most progressives
were disinclined to follow Bryan's 1896 condemnation of urbanization and
industrialization. (They accepted city-and-machine civilization as a fact,
and tried to make it serve the average man.) And the progressives included
many who had considered Bryan and the Populists dangerous radicals. Conservative in outlook, these individuals felt moderate reform would keep the
people from turning to extremes.

Among other things, the progressive movement was a protest against
corruption. To be sure, the 1890's saw no Grant-type scandals. Corrup-
tionists had learned how to be discreet. But votes were openly purchased
in key states during the 1888 campaign, in which John Wanamaker, the
department store magnate, passed the hat among industrialists. Bribes were
used in the 1890's to secure federal land grants. State governors sold pardons, used the military to break strikes in plants of friendly industrialists,
vetoed social legislation distasteful to campaign contributors. Conditions
were still worse on the local level. Schools, roads, public health, law enforcement provided a paradise of peculation in the nation's 3000 counties.
In the cities, contractors and politicians made profitable deals in transportation, gas and electricity, sewage disposal, paving, and public buildings.
Hazen S. Pingree, reform mayor of Detroit, was offered a trip around the
world by one group of franchise hunters, a $50,000 bribe by another. An
inquiry directed by State Senator Clarence Lexow in 1894 revealed that
appointments to the New York police force were openly sold, and that
officials exacted a percentage of the profits of streetwalkers, pickpockets,
gamblers, and saloonkeepers.

Why all this crime? Some said that the separation of legislative, executive, and judicial powers promoted corruption by division of responsibility, and the multiplicity of political offices responsible to no central control invited chaos. Others blamed the very richness of American natural resources, or the rapidity of industrialization and urbanization, which made regulation difficult. Public indifference was no less important.

Yet there was resistance. Some came from agrarian and labor reformers, who opposed monopoly and special privilege. Rather more came from well-to-do citizens with a sense of civic decency—liberal clergymen, professional leaders, small businessmen, members of women's clubs.

Reforming Mayors

Middle-class votes helped elect reform mayors in scores of cities after 1890. Some were Republicans, some Democrats, some independents. All tried to cleanse the Augean stables and establish good government. A number stressed municipal home rule, to end the reign of state bosses. Others emphasized civil service, or concentrated on breaking corrupt alliances between private interests and city officials.

Many reform mayors were well-to-do businessmen. Hazen S. Pingree, a shoe manufacturer who was elected mayor of Detroit in 1889, used his office to insure competition among private interests bidding for public favors. He also tried to regulate utility rates and to establish a municipally owned electric plant; and he helped the poor by providing vacant lots for potato patches. Samuel ("Golden Rule") Jones, chosen mayor of Toledo in 1897, was a machinery manufacturer who had introduced democratic methods in his own plant. As mayor, he established civil service and vetoed renewals of trolley franchises to a private corporation. Seth Low, a tea importer and president of Columbia University, won a mayoralty race in New York in 1901, defeating Tammany. He then checked patronage excesses by extending the merit system.

Most spectacular reform mayor was Tom Johnson. A trolley magnate and iron manufacturer, Johnson entered politics after reading Henry George. Elected mayor of Cleveland in 1901, he held tent meetings to educate the citizenry in municipal affairs. He overhauled the city government and promoted municipal ownership and operation of street railroads. And he lessened the grip of state machine politics by fighting for home rule.

These were four of many. A Minneapolis grand jury forced prosecution of a graft ring. In Jersey City Mark Fagin fought to free the city from the coils of utilities, railroads, and spoilsmen politicians. In St. Louis Circuit Attorney Joseph W. Folk prosecuted many bribery cases. A National Municipal League, founded in 1894, worked for simplification of governmental machinery, publicity of accounts, protection against franchise grabbers, administration by experts. Municipal research bureaus (modeled after one established in New York in 1906) trained administrators and studied urban problems.

Significant, too, was the commission form of government, used in Galveston, Texas, after the flood of 1900. It substituted an elected commission of five for the cumbersome mayor-and-council plan. Four commissioners ran city departments; the fifth (a mayor-president) coördinated the work of his colleagues. With many variations, this scheme spread to 200 cities by 1912.

Frequently reform administrations ended in defeats at the polls, the old gang of politicians regaining control. Even when the reformers hung on, the bosses found new methods of getting what they wanted. Nonetheless, there was more competence and decency in city government in 1919 than in 1896.

Progressive Governors

Reformers were also active in state politics. After four terms as mayor of Detroit, Hazen Pingree was twice elected governor of Michigan. Joseph W. Folk, first a reform politician in St. Louis, later became reform governor of Missouri, securing anti-lobby and utility regulation laws, the initiative and referendum, state-wide primary, compulsory-education and child labor statutes, and appropriations for highways ("Get Missouri out of the mud").

There were some reform governors in the 1890's—John Peter Altgeld of Illinois and James S. Hogg of Texas among the Democrats, Theodore Roosevelt among the Republicans. But the great era of state reforms came after 1900. Progressive Republican governors included Robert M. La Follette of Wisconsin, Albert B. Cummins of Iowa, Charles Evans Hughes of New York, Hiram Johnson of California; among Democrats there were Folk of Missouri, Hoke Smith of Georgia, Woodrow Wilson of New Jersey.

Many progressive governors concentrated on political devices. One victory was achieved before 1900, with the adoption of the secret official ballot. In earlier years parties had printed and distributed at the polls their own lists of candidates. Thus voters had little chance for privacy. Massachusetts in 1888 introduced secret, uniform, officially printed ballots. Within a decade all but four states had followed suit.

In 1890 New York adopted a statute regulating the use of money in elections. By 1900 sixteen states had followed her example. Three prohibited corporations from contributing to campaign funds. Then in 1903, Governor Robert M. La Follette persuaded Wisconsin to adopt the direct primary. The idea was to have party nominees chosen by the voters rather than by machine-ridden conventions. All states had the direct primary in some form by 1915. Unfortunately, bosses controlled the primaries much as they had controlled party conventions. Still, the primary did on occasion serve democratic ends—as when it helped bring victory in the fight for direct election of United States Senators. Under the Constitution, Senators were chosen by state legislatures. Often legislators chose machine politicians or men of wealth. Taking advantage of the new direct primary, a number of states allowed voters to indicate preferences as to senatorial nominees. Legislators were bound to respect these views. Finally, in 1912, the Senate reluctantly joined the House in submitting to the states a proposed constitutional amendment providing for popular election of Senators. A year later, the necessary three-fourths of the states had approved, and the Seventeenth Amendment was added to the Constitution.

Noting Swiss practice, American reformers also agitated for the initiative and referendum. Under the initiative, a small percentage of the electorate could force the legislature to consider a measure. The referendum enabled a similar group to compel submission of a measure to the people. South Dakota enacted this program in 1898. Four years later William S. U'Ren persuaded Oregon to do the same. Within a decade, fifteen more states fell into line. Meantime, in 1908, Oregon adopted the recall. Colorado and other states followed suit. Dissatisfied citizens could now challenge the right of an official to stay in office. If enough voters were interested, the officer could be forced to submit to the test of a new election.

Many states changed their constitutions after 1900. Many of the new constitutional provisions curbed the power of the legislature, which was suspected of being the seat of corrupt influence. Executive power increased. A number of states created commissions of nonpartisan experts for regulating railroads, insurance companies, and utilities. Under La Follette's leadership, Wisconsin made wide use of such machinery, which was a central aspect of the Wisconsin Idea.

In 1910 the state of Washington followed the example of Wyoming, which had granted votes to women in territorial days. California then climbed on the bandwagon, as did other western states—a dozen, all west of the Mississippi, by World War I. Proponents of woman suffrage argued that women were as competent as men to make public decisions. Denial of the ballot, they said, was a denial of democracy. Reformers further felt that women voters could help check corruption and secure social legislation. This very point led some conservatives to take the other side. But the objectors gradually lost ground. The National American Woman Suffrage Association, led by Carrie Chapman Catt, pressed for national action. Success came in World War I. Congress submitted a proposed amendment to the states; and in 1920 the Nineteenth Amendment gave votes to women all over the land.

Social and Economic Reforms

Many progressives were humanitarians who backed political reform as a means of securing economic and social benefits for the plain people. Moderate reformers rather than left-wing radicals, these people felt that industrialization and urbanization had brought a social crisis which right-thinking people could not ignore. They therefore organized many effective associations, including a National Consumers League, an Association for Labor Legislation, a National Housing Association, a National Association for the Advancement of Colored People.

The humanitarians operated in many ways. Clergymen like Washington Gladden developed the social gospel in preaching and writing. Lester F. Ward, the sociologist, publicized the idea that knowledge and wealth, being socially created, must be socially shared. Richard T. Ely, Thorstein Veblen, and other economists undermined the classical economic theory of laissez faire, and as experts helped frame laws regulating private enterprise in the public interest. Such novelists as Frank Norris and Upton Sinclair stressed the need for reform.

Jane Addams, Lillian Wald, and other social workers were at this time developing social settlements in the slums (Lillian Wald also organized nursing service for country districts). Simultaneously, these social workers demanded reforms to eliminate slum conditions. Florence Kelley, who did settlement work in Chicago, also helped enforce Illinois factory inspection acts; and she organized consumers and secured improved labor legislation.

These and other citizens (including labor leaders) worked for tax reform; factory legislation to protect workers; insurance against sickness, accidents, and unemployment; old-age pensions; maximum hour and minimum wage laws; regulation of tenements; public playgrounds; public health clinics; and better public education. Some politicians joined the movement because of their humanitarian sympathies. Others saw that the public was becoming interested, and that it would be politically unwise to resist the tide.

A large body of social legislation was the result. Massachusetts enacted a factory inspection law as early as 1867. She extended this legislation in the next decade, and limited the working day for women to ten hours. By 1907 nearly half the states had statutes reducing the working day for miners and others engaged in dangerous pursuits. Virtually all industrial states were regulating working conditions in mines and factories. New York took a further step when it added a constitutional amendment authorizing accident insurance legislation. These laws reflected the conviction that private interests must submit to some government control in the public interest. Many of the laws, however, were not carried out effectively; and some were declared unconstitutional by the courts. This in turn strengthened the movement to nationalize the reform impulse.

The extension of reform to the national stage owed much to writers whom Theodore Roosevelt disparagingly christened "muckrakers." Henry Demarest Lloyd had anticipated the muckrakers with his *Wealth Versus Commonwealth* (1894), an exposure of Standard Oil. But the great era of muckraking began in 1902, with the appearance in *McClure's Magazine* of Ida Tarbell's history of the Standard Oil Company. The public displayed interest; and *McClure's* "exposed" railroad and insurance companies and had Lincoln Steffens describe the corrupt dealings of city bosses with franchise seekers.

Other magazines joined the parade. *Everybody's* did a series on stockbrokers ("Frenzied Finance"). *Collier's* had Samuel Hopkins Adams expose patent medicine frauds; David Graham Phillips attacked the Senate in *Cosmopolitan*. In due time, there were series on banks, packing houses, distilleries, immoral traffic in women, child labor, and the Negro.

The muckrakers spared no names. Though sensational, the exposures were accurate, as the relatively few libel suits indicated. In time, the public tired of reading all the sordid details; and advertisers used pressure to curb the literature of exposure. But, while it lasted, the muckrake crusade increased interest in reform and made possible much progressive legislation.

The National Scene

As the muckrakers gained strength, it was clear that the progressive movement was taking on a national character. Young progressives were obtaining seats in Congress: George W. Norris of Nebraska, Miles Poindexter of Washington, Albert J. Beveridge of Indiana. Reforming governors like La Follette of Wisconsin and Cummins of Iowa went from their state capitals to the Senate. Joseph W. Folk, who had begun as a municipal reformer, and had then entered the state arena in Missouri, ended his public career as a federal officeholder. And two men who had sponsored progressive legislation in state politics (Theodore Roosevelt and Woodrow Wilson) became Presidents of the United States.

For this nationalization there were precedents—the Jeffersonian and Jacksonian movements, the national appeals of the Populists and Bryan. The inability of states to control railroads led Congress to pass the Interstate Commerce Act (1887). Failure of the states to check business monopoly led the federal government to adopt the Sherman Antitrust Act (1890). In emasculating these laws, the courts merely inspired reformers to agitate for more effective national legislation and, if need be, amendments to the Constitution. Moreover, the tendency of higher courts to nullify state social legislation reinforced the conviction that the next great battle must be fought on the national stage.[1]

In national as in state politics, the progressive movement cut across party lines. Reforms were sought by progressive Democrats like Bryan and Wilson, by progressive Republicans like La Follette and Theodore Roosevelt. The opposition, too, found adherents in both major parties. Conservative Republicans who opposed change—men like Senator Nelson Aldrich of Rhode Island—worked with conservative Democrats who clung to doctrines of states' rights and laissez faire.

Although grounded in economic factors and desire for political success, progressivism also possessed a strong moral appeal. Most reformers of this era subscribed to the doctrine of progress, which fired them with optimism and zeal. The progressives also appealed to the patriotic beliefs that identified Americanism with the well-being of the common man. Nineteenth-century Americans had believed in a basic law of right. Belief in this higher law had provided emotional support for reform movements from abolitionism to Populism. The progressive crusade was, in a way, heir to these doctrines embedded in the American faith.

Another factor was Socialist strength. Brought into the country by immigrants, Socialism at first had little appeal for old-stock Americans. Then, around 1900, new leaders, including Eugene V. Debs of Indiana and Victor Berger of Wisconsin, put Socialism into the American idiom and attracted a large following. In the presidential election of 1912 Debs polled almost a million votes—7 percent of the total cast. Many Americans were disturbed by this rise of the Socialists. The Socialist doctrine of class war repelled both conservatives and progressives, as did Socialist demands for

---

[1] Many, in fact, called the movement broader than national. For the American progressive drive was part of a world movement. Many states of the United States modeled their reform legislation on English and German statutes providing for factory inspection, compensation of injured workingmen, and the protection of women and children in industry. The British Parliament was expanding control over business and was revamping the tax structure in the interest of such enlarged social services as slum clearance, public health, and old-age pensions. France, Germany, and the Scandinavian countries were taking similar steps, and New Zealand and Australia were in many respects leading the world in social improvements under government auspices. Returning from a round-the-world trip, Bryan declared in 1906 that citizens everywhere were demanding that the government help the people. Hence Americans were in step with world trends when they looked to the central government to take up the movement begun in the cities and states.

public ownership of the means of production and distribution. Defenders of the existing economic order were still more frightened by the I.W.W., which preached sabotage and revolution. What to do? Faced with a similar problem, Bismarck and other European conservatives had made concessions to the workers. That is, European defenders of the *status quo* had backed reform to please workers and keep them from turning radical. The same thing might work in the United States. Thus thoughtful conservatives joined the humanitarians after 1900, supporting progressive legislation as a means of opposing radicalism.

From McKinley to Roosevelt

In 1896, the candidates stressed currency. The hard-money forces won, the Republican William McKinley defeating the Democratic Bryan. As President (1897–1901), McKinley supported legislation to aid the groups which had elected him. The Wilson-Gorman Tariff of 1894, passed in Cleveland's second term, was replaced by a highly protective Dingley Tariff of 1897. The currency question was settled in favor of the hard-money forces, with the passage of the Gold Standard Act of 1900.

The public was more interested in the war with Spain (1898). Victory in this conflict added greatly to McKinley's prestige. At the same time, there was a revival of business activity, and the country pulled out of the depression that had followed the panic of 1893. This meant jobs for workers; and, as gold poured in from the Yukon, farm prices rose. The result was general satisfaction with the Republican administration. Also in the picture was the personal popularity of McKinley, who was a kindly, religious man. Inevitably, then, McKinley was renominated by the Republicans in 1900. Just as naturally, he was victorious at the polls. His most effective slogan was "The Full Dinner Pail," which called attention to the prevailing good times. Prosperity enabled McKinley to hold the states he had won in 1896, and to add half a dozen states west of the Mississippi.

As in 1896, McKinley's Democratic opponent was William Jennings Bryan. In 1900, Bryan continued to advocate free silver. He also set himself against imperialism, opposing retention of the Philippine Islands, which McKinley had acquired from Spain. But, as the campaign proceeded, Bryan put increasing emphasis on opposition to monopoly. This antitrust issue did not bring victory; but it publicized what would be a key demand of the progressives.

Although Bryan Democrats launched the antitrust campaign, quite a different group of politicians pressed the issue into service. For, after 1901, the fight against the trusts was taken up by Theodore Roosevelt, a Republican. And Roosevelt, not Bryan, was to be the leading progressive for the first dozen years of the twentieth century.

Theodore Roosevelt came from an old New York family. Being well-to-do, he could have coasted through life. Instead, he chose to be unceasingly active. He cultivated manly sports, ranched in the Dakotas, became a popular writer. Fascinated by politics, he served in the New York legislature. Although defeated for mayor of New York City (running third behind Abram Hewitt and Henry George), he secured various appointive jobs: United States Civil Service Commissioner; New York Police Commissioner; Assistant Secretary of the Navy under McKinley. He then led a highly publicized group of "Rough Riders" in the Spanish-American War. His military reputation helped him win election as governor of New York in 1898. Finding Roosevelt hard to control, New York's Republican bosses had him "kicked upstairs." That is, they had him nominated for Vice-President in 1900 (McKinley's running mate of 1896 had died in office). The vice-presidency was generally regarded as a political graveyard. But soon after McKinley was inaugurated for his second term, the President was shot by a fanatic. When McKinley died in September, 1901, Roosevelt became President. Elected in his own right in 1904, he occupied the White House from 1901 to 1909.

Only forty-three when he took office, the new Chief Executive was a man of bursting energy and buoyant personality. Roosevelt had a gift of turning phrases; and, despite his upper-class origin, he could express the yearnings of the great middle class. He could also dramatize himself. Dramatic speaking tours helped, as did striking newspaper interviews; and T. R. was publicized as no preceding President had been. This enabled him to use his office as one of leadership. For Roosevelt believed that a President could do anything in the public interest not specifically prohibited by the Constitution.

To vigorous progressives, Theodore Roosevelt seemed somewhat superficial, a compromiser who lacked spiritual insight. Conservative Republicans, on the other hand, regarded the new President as too much on the impulsive, reforming side. Yet Theodore Roosevelt managed to get on pretty well with both groups. He cultivated the support of such progressive Republicans as Albert Beveridge, while he remained intimate with Republican conservatives, including Henry Cabot Lodge and Nelson Aldrich.

In the White House years inherited from McKinley (1901–05), Roosevelt proceeded cautiously in championing the reforms long advocated by Bryan and others. Then, in the presidential contest of 1904, Roosevelt won an overwhelming victory, defeating an undistinguished Democratic candidate, Alton B. Parker. Parker carried only the solid South. Thereafter (1905–09) Roosevelt moved more vigorously along the path of reform.

The Roosevelt Reforms (1901–09)

Of the issues facing Theodore Roosevelt, none was more important than the growth of monopoly. In 1900 a Congressionally appointed Industrial Commission revealed that ninety-two great business combinations had been organized in the preceding year. These included Standard Oil of New Jersey, a Rockefeller holding company with far-flung properties. Soon there appeared a billion-dollar United States Steel Corporation, followed by the International Harvester Company, made up of the five leading units in the industry. Organized by profit-minded bankers, many of the new trusts were fantastically overcapitalized, with consequent ill effects on the purchasers of securities. Some of the new combinations engaged in practices definitely against the public interest.

Sensitive to mounting public criticism of monopolies, Roosevelt decided to enforce the long-neglected Sherman Antitrust Act of 1890. He therefore ordered his Attorney General to start proceedings against the Northern Securities Company. This holding company was a creation of J. Pierpont Morgan and James J. Hill. The intention was to combine the railroads of the Northwest—the Great Northern, the Northern Pacific, the Chicago, Burlington and Quincy. In 1904, by a bare majority, the Supreme Court declared the merger a violation of the Sherman Act, and ordered the Northern Securities Company dissolved. In 1905 the Court handed down a decision against the beef trust; and by 1909, when Roosevelt left the White House, the Department of Justice had prepared twenty-five indictments against trusts.

For this record, Theodore Roosevelt was acclaimed as a "trust buster." But, as the President himself recognized, no number of antitrust suits could unscramble the omelet of monopoly. Roosevelt refrained from attacking many combinations, saying some trusts were "bad," some "good." The Supreme Court took the same line. In the Standard Oil case of 1911, the justices used the rule of reason, holding that monopoly was not necessarily undesirable, and that the government could break up trusts only when the companies involved pursued policies that were clearly unfair and unreasonable. Unreasonable, that is, in the eyes of the judges.

Besides suits against trusts, Roosevelt sponsored legislation establishing a Bureau of Corporations. Set up in 1903, the Bureau had power to investigate and publicize business practices. Roosevelt also helped push Meat Inspection and Pure Food and Drug acts through Congress (1906). These laws provided for the regulation in the public interest of the products of packing houses and patent medicine firms engaged in interstate commerce.

The railroad problem was even more pressing. Congress grudgingly bowed to a White House demand that the Interstate Commerce Commission be given increased power. Striking at the rebate evil, the Elkins Act of 1903 prohibited variations from published freight rates, and provided fines for shippers as well as carriers.

Then came demands for further action. Congressional reformers led by Senator La Follette insisted that the I.C.C. be empowered to fix rates on the basis of fair earnings on actual investment. The House passed such a bill in 1906, but it met with vigorous opposition from the old guard in the Senate. Much to the disgust of La Follette, Roosevelt compromised. The resulting Hepburn Act increased the power of the I.C.C. by requiring that railroads, rather than the Commission, initiate litigation testing the validity of I.C.C. orders in rate matters. The law also brought express and sleeping car companies within the jurisdiction of the I.C.C.; and it banned free passes, a notorious source of political influence. The I.C.C. was further authorized to prescribe uniform accounting methods, making it difficult for carriers to conceal expenditures for improper activities.

In the same year, 1906, Congress also passed an Employers' Liability Act. This statute, recommended by Roosevelt, required the railroads to compensate employees injured in the course of duty. Although the Supreme Court declared this law unconstitutional, a similar act of 1908 was upheld.

Roosevelt did little in the general field of labor; but he did favor a "square deal for labor." This led him to intervene in the coal strike of 1902. In 1894, President Cleveland had used federal troops to help the Pullman Company break a strike. In 1902 President Roosevelt used his influence to effect a compromise settlement between John Mitchell's United Mine Workers and the Morgan-connected coal operators. Plainly, the government's relation to business was changing.

Theodore Roosevelt's most notable contribution to the movement for controlling private property in the public interest was in conservation. He began at once; his first annual message to Congress (1901) stressed the need for conserving such natural resources as forests, coal, oil, water sites, and the soil. The demand for conservation was not new. John Powell, founder of the United States Geological Survey, had warned that the republic would exhaust its priceless heritage within the predictable future. The achievements of German conservationists, featured at the Chicago Fair of 1893, impressed those ready to learn. Roosevelt took up this movement, working through such able lieutenants as Gifford Pinchot, who had studied forestry in Germany. State governors also helped, as did a Roosevelt-appointed National Conservation Commission, which made a natural resources inventory.

One achievement was the Reclamation Act of 1902, which provided for construction by the federal government of irrigation projects. Financing was to come from proceeds of public land sales. A new Reclamation Service initiated significant projects, including, ultimately, the Roosevelt Dam in Arizona, Boulder Dam on the Colorado River, the Grand Coulee project on the Columbia. Millions of acres of arid land were reclaimed for cultivation; hydroelectric power was made available, flood control was promoted, reforestation advanced. Swamp lands were also reclaimed; and inland waterways were developed.

Roosevelt withdrew from sale tens of millions of acres of public land. Here he acted under authority of a hitherto little used Forest Reserve Act of 1891. More lands were withdrawn from entry when the National Conservation Commission recommended that the government retain (and lease for limited periods) lands containing phosphates, natural gas, oil, and coal. Congress at first refused to confirm the retention by the government of mineral and water-power sites; but the conservationists ultimately won their point.

By dramatizing the need for a new policy, T. R. made the public conservation-minded. The advocates of ruthless exploitation would win further victories. But at long last, after three centuries of waste, Americans were beginning to see the need for conservation.

Then Came Taft (1909–13)

Roosevelt's talent for combining crusade and compromise enabled him to control the Republican machinery during his presidency (1901–09). He could easily have obtained the party nomination for President in 1908. But, after winning in 1904, Roosevelt had announced that he would not be a candidate in 1908 for what in effect would be a third term. Adhering to this promise, T. R. persuaded his party to nominate William Howard Taft of Ohio. Progressive Republicans were surprised at Roosevelt's choice. Charles Evans Hughes, liberal governor of New York, would have been a logical selection. Taft had shown conservative tendencies as a judge in the 1890's, before his appointment as Commissioner in the Philippines and Secretary of War under Roosevelt. Besides, Taft obviously lacked Roosevelt's energy—he was an easygoing, genial man of 350 pounds. Roosevelt, however, believed that Taft was loyal and would continue the Roosevelt policies. Besides, T. R. did not like Hughes.

In the campaign of 1908, Taft sounded like a progressive. He was 100 percent for the Roosevelt record, was against monopoly, for conservation.

He was even for tariff reform (Roosevelt had avoided the tariff issue as politically dangerous). But in private, Taft seemed to side with conservative old-guard Republicans, and to favor slowing down the reform crusade. Taft was progressive, he insisted, largely to prevent the radicals from taking hold. "If the tyranny and oppression of an oligarchy of wealth cannot be avoided," he said, in denouncing the money trust, "then socialism will triumph, and the institution of private property will perish."

Having failed with the unexciting Alton B. Parker in 1904, the Democrats in 1908 turned again to Bryan. In his third presidential campaign, Bryan denounced the protective tariff—the "mother of trusts," the "cause" of the soaring cost of living. Bryan demanded government ownership of railroads; asked for elimination of injunctions in labor disputes; favored the income tax and direct election of Senators. Long a rural favorite, Bryan now gained some labor support, winning official backing of the American Federation of Labor, which had never before endorsed a presidential candidate. But Bryan lost. This time he made his poorest showing, carrying only three states outside of the South. Taft swung middle-class votes by insisting that his Democratic foe was "irresponsible," that a Bryan victory would mean unjust punishment of the rich. Besides, times were good, despite the minor panic of 1907. That, and Roosevelt's popularity, gave Taft victory, and one term in the White House (1909–13).

Unlike his predecessor, Taft stressed the legalistic restrictions on executive power; and, more than Roosevelt, Taft worked with conservative Republicans. He was close, for instance, to reactionary Senator Aldrich, and to Joseph G. Cannon of Illinois, autocratic Speaker of the House. Yet Taft kept pushing the Roosevelt program. He saved public coal and petroleum lands from private exploitation. He enlarged the national forests. In one term under Taft the Justice Department instituted almost twice as many antitrust suits as it had in Roosevelt's two terms. And a Mann-Elkins Act of 1910 gave the Interstate Commerce Commission authority over telegraph and telephone lines, and facilitated immediate execution of Commission orders for rate reduction.

Taft also struck out in new directions. He urged Congress to submit to the states a proposed constitutional amendment enabling the federal government to impose an income tax. (This Sixteenth Amendment went into effect at the end of Taft's administration, in 1913.) Another movement resulted, just after Taft's retirement, in the Seventeenth Amendment, providing for the direct election of Senators (1913). And, with Taft's approval, Congress enacted legislation limiting and publicizing expenditures in Congressional campaigns.

Even so, the Taft regime was generally considered a failure. The President could not hold his party together. Republican progressives like George W. Norris broke party ranks to join Democrats in curbing the arbitrary power of "Uncle Joe" Cannon, conservative Republican Speaker of the House (1910). In this revolt, the Speaker was shorn of his power to appoint committees and dominate legislation.

The tariff also split Republicans apart. The platform of 1908 called for tariff revision, which Taft said meant revision downward. This view was shared by western Republicans (mostly progressives), who felt that the Dingley Tariff of 1897 favored eastern industrialists. A House bill therefore cut rates. But the Old Guard took over in the Senate. Senator Aldrich, a wealthy New England industrialist, introduced 800 amendments, most of which increased duties. Republican progressives—La Follette, Cummins, Beveridge, William E. Borah of Idaho—joined Democrats in opposing the Aldrich proposals. Taft at first backed the progressives. Then he switched, and his influence gave Aldrich the victory (Payne-Aldrich Tariff, 1909).

The Payne-Aldrich bill contained many commendable features: a Tariff Commission to gather facts on costs of production at home and abroad; a flexible clause enabling the President to raise or lower duties in response to discriminations of a foreign country; a one percent tax on corporation earnings above $5000. Basically, however, the law was a standard high protective tariff, like the McKinley Tariff of 1890 and the Dingley Tariff of 1897. Its passage was a victory for conservative Republicans. But, since the tariff was unpopular, enactment actually strengthened the progressives. Taft found this out when he defended the Payne-Aldrich measure as the best tariff ever enacted.

Hoping to regain lost ground, the President sponsored a tariff-cutting reciprocity treaty with Canada (1911). This provided for the admission of Canadian farm produce into eastern markets previously dominated by agricultural goods from middle western states. In return, American industrialists would receive favorable treatment in Canada. Middle western voters, naturally, were far from pleased. To make matters more embarrassing for Taft, Canada rejected the treaty, fearing it would mean domination by the United States.

Republican difficulties were increased by the Ballinger-Pinchot controversy. Taft's Secretary of the Interior, Richard A. Ballinger of Washington, reflected the western desire to use natural resources now; and he regarded Roosevelt's withdrawal of land from private entry as wanting in legality. Hence Ballinger restored to private entry valuable timber and water-power sites. Which, of course, brought criticism from Roosevelt conservationists. Then came more serious charges. A Land Office investigator, Louis R. Glavis, claimed that Ballinger was blocking investigation of allegedly fraudulent corporation claims to Alaskan coal lands. Taft authorized the dismissal of Glavis, who publicized his story in *Collier's*. Glavis was then supported by Roosevelt's friend Gifford Pinchot, who still headed the Forest Service in the Department of Agriculture. When Congressional investigators found Ballinger innocent of the Glavis-Pinchot charges, Taft dismissed Pinchot. To clear the air, Ballinger also resigned. But progressives insisted that Taft had betrayed the conservation cause.

The Bull Moose Campaign (1912)

Dissatisfied with Taft, the progressive Republicans opposed the President's renomination in 1912. Instead, a National Progressive League (1911) backed La Follette. The League stood for direct election of Senators, preferential primaries, the initiative, referendum, and recall, corrupt-practices acts, and control of big business in the public interest.

At this point Theodore Roosevelt reëntered the political arena. After bowing out as President, he had gone to Africa to hunt, and to Europe to visit leading dignitaries. When he returned to the United States in 1910, it was clear that he and Taft were less friendly than before. The Ballinger-Pinchot row was one factor. Roosevelt's exclusion from the inner councils of the Taft administration was another. Then, too, progressive strength was rising. Taft was cautious. Roosevelt, however, tended to go along with the tide of reform. He spoke out for the initiative and referendum, and for recall of judicial decisions. He moved sharply to the left in a speech at Osawatomie, Kansas, in 1910, when he tried to balance the old individualism of free enterprise with the movement for social control. He would allow a man to gain wealth, he said, "only so long as the gaining represents benefit to the country." This, he added, "implies a policy of a far more active governmental interference with social and economic conditions in this country than we have yet had." In this "new nationalism," Roosevelt favored increasing the power of the federal government, so that it could control corporations, abolish child labor, introduce unemployment insurance, old-age pensions, minimum wages, workingmen's compensation.

Thus Roosevelt was lining up with the progressive Republicans. Would he, then, support La Follette for the Republican nomination in 1912? Or would he himself seek the designation, despite his 1904 renunciation of a third term? Roosevelt finally tossed his own hat into the ring. La Follette was understandably irked at this, and the progressive Republicans went into the 1912 campaign divided. Moreover, Taft controlled the party machinery. Roosevelt won convention delegates in states which had presidential prefcrence primaries; but Taft won elsewhere. Controlling the nominating convention, the Taft forces renominated the President, rejecting Roosevelt's bid for consideration. The progressives were also ignored in the platform, and Taft ran as a conservative.

Terming these results a machine victory, Roosevelt's supporters created a new Progressive party. Roosevelt was nominated for President, with Hiram Johnson of California as his running mate. The bull moose became the Progressive symbol, as the elephant was the emblem of the Republicans. The Progressives called for the democratization of political machinery, social legislation, monetary reform, control of big business in the public interest. There were prolabor planks, too, but the A.F. of L. withheld endorsement, perhaps because the Bull Moose party was heavily supported by George Perkins, a wealthy industrialist who had been a J. P. Morgan partner.

Meantime, the Democrats also adopted a progressive platform. They demanded tariff reform; strict enforcement of the Sherman Antitrust Act; new laws to check such business practices as the watering of stock, price discrimination, interlocking directorates, the monopolistic suppression of free competition; rural credits and a flexible banking system to aid farmers; and, to please workers, legislation against injunctions in labor disputes. After a long contest for the nomination, Bryan threw his support to Woodrow Wilson, progressive governor of New Jersey, who won nomination on the forty-sixth ballot.

Southern-born, of strict Presbyterian background, Woodrow Wilson had been a professor and president of Princeton before he entered politics in 1910. His conversion to progressivism came late; in the early years of the century he was anti-Bryan, anti-union, a defender of property rights who said much that was pleasing to big business. But as governor of New Jersey (1911–13) he opposed machine politics and fought for laws to curb big business and benefit workingmen. As presidential candidate in 1912, Wilson set forth a political philosophy which he called the "New Freedom." Differing from Roosevelt's New Nationalism in approach rather than in essence, the New Freedom aimed to restore the older freedom of competition which corporate wealth had all but eliminated. T. R. proposed using a strong central government and stressed the difference between good and bad business combinations. Wilson leaned toward the states as instruments in advancing social reform; and he felt that bigness in itself was dangerous, in business or government.

In dividing votes between Taft and Roosevelt, the Republicans lost the election. Wilson received 6,000,000 votes; Roosevelt 4,000,000; Taft 3,500,-

000; Eugene V. Debs, the Socialist, just under 1,000,000. Carrying forty states,[2] Wilson had a large majority in the electoral college; and his party won control of both houses of Congress. Wilson was, however, a minority President who polled fewer votes than Bryan had obtained in any of his three unsuccessful campaigns. Yet the Wilson program unquestionably represented the views of most Americans. The conservative Republican, Taft, carried only two states, Utah and Vermont, and polled a smaller percentage of the total vote than any other major-party nominee since the Civil War. Voters flocked rather to the protest candidates, Wilson, Roosevelt, and Debs. The country was in a reform frame of mind.

Wilson and the New Freedom

Wilson at first considered departing from normal patronage patterns. Instead of giving jobs to deserving Democrats, he would surround himself with experts and use his appointive power to convert the Democratic party into a truly progressive instrument. But Colonel Edward M. House of Texas, Wilson's chief political adviser, persuaded the incoming President that he must play ball with party managers if he wished to get his bills through Congress. So Wilson straddled, giving some jobs to professional politicians, some to nonpolitical experts. In the end the Democratic bosses controlled a large share of the patronage.

Early in his academic career Wilson had become impressed with the merits of the British constitutional structure. In a book, Congressional Government, he had urged that the United States borrow certain English institutions. Specifically, Wilson felt that Americans had overstressed the separation of powers, and that Congress had too much influence. In his view, a President should be virtually a Prime Minister, should not only administer laws but also participate in the lawmaking process. Wilson's ideas were in line with those of progressive constitution-makers who had enlarged the governor's power in the states; and, on the national scene, Theodore Roosevelt had built up presidential prestige. Wilson carried this trend further. Breaking a century-old precedent, he delivered his message to Congress in person. And when his proposals met opposition—as in the tariff fight of 1913—Wilson himself acted as party whip. He continued to assert presidential leadership for most of his two terms in the White House (1913–21).

The first Wilson administration (1913–17) brought the most significant

---

[2] Forty-eight states participated. The wholesale admission of western states in 1889–90 had raised the total to forty-four. Utah was admitted in 1896, Oklahoma in 1907. New Mexico came in during January, 1912, Arizona one month later.

reform program since the American Revolution. As Wilson himself admitted, the achievement was not merely Wilsonian and Democratic. Rather it was the culmination of a generation of effort. On domestic reform, Wilson was supported by progressive Republicans as well as by his own Democratic followers. He also had the support of the bulk of American farmers, laborers, small businessmen and white-collar workers.

Wilson lost no time in getting started. In his inaugural address he asked "all forward-looking men" to help him "abolish . . . even the semblance of privilege." The appeal caught hold. Wilson had given the public an emotional lift. "It seemed as if we had climbed mountain heights," said Louis Brandeis, recalling the Washington of 1913. (Brandeis, incidentally, influenced Wilsonian legislation. In 1916, over conservative objections, Wilson appointed him to the Supreme Court.)

The Underwood Tariff

Calling Congress into special session in 1913, Wilson demanded repeal of the Payne-Aldrich Tariff of 1909 and substitution of a law that would reduce the cost of filling a market basket. When Democratic protectionists pleaded the cause of special interests, Wilson used his control of patronage to bring them into line. When lobbyists attacked tariff reform, Wilson publicized their activities. The President, therefore, deserved much of the credit for the passage of the Underwood Tariff of 1913.

This was not a free-trade measure. It modified instead of junking protection. But the act shifted hundreds of items to the free list: wool, paper, steel rails, lumber, wood pulp, sugar. There were reductions averaging 10 percent for nearly a thousand other products. The country as a whole approved. Had the period been a normal one, the measure might have had significant long-range influences on overseas commerce. But the outbreak of World War I in 1914 dislocated normal trade; and it was never possible to judge the effect of the Wilsonian tariff cuts.

The ratification of the Sixteenth Amendment in February, 1913, enabled Congress to add an income tax clause to the new tariff act. The tax ranged from 1 percent on annual earnings over $3000 (with a further exemption for married men) to 6 percent on income above $500,000. These rates were very moderate. Still, the introduction of the graduated income tax marked a turning point in American financial history. Traditionally, the federal government had relied on tariff revenues, excise taxes, and income from sale of public lands. After 1913, there would be heavy reliance on the income tax, with the highest rates applying to those best able to pay.

Finance and Business

After the panic of 1907, even conservatives admitted the need for greater elasticity than was provided by the old national banking system. A commission headed by conservative Republican Senator Aldrich therefore favored a centralized national banking system controlled by private financiers. Conservative Democrats approved. There was opposition, though, from Bryan Democrats and progressive Republicans. Heirs of the old Jacksonian and Populist fears of centralized banking, these groups were impressed with the findings of the Pujo Committee, which had reported the existence of a money trust. Would not a privately owned centralized banking system be dominated by New York financiers? After consulting Brandeis, Wilson swung over to the progressive side. The result was compromise. The Federal Reserve Act of 1914 deferred to Bryan's opposition to a centralized system. Instead of one national institution, there were to be twelve Federal Reserve Banks. A measure of centralization, however, was achieved by the creation of a Federal Reserve Board to supervise the whole system.

Bankers and other citizens were pleased that the new organization could expand or contract the currency in relation to changing need. Yet many reformers felt that the Federal Reserve Act did not go far enough. State banks could remain outside the system; and the 1914 law did not prevent officers of some national banks from speculating recklessly with deposit money. But the Federal Reserve law did increase business efficiency, and without undue concentration of power in the hands of one group of financiers.

Like Theodore Roosevelt, Wilson said he was not the foe of legitimate business; rather, he favored reform as a safeguard against revolutionary change. Wilson disapproved of government ownership; he wanted no monopoly, government or otherwise. Suspicious of bigness, he hoped to curb the largest combinations, restore competition, and see that business was regulated in the public interest. His program found expression in the Clayton Antitrust Act of 1914. The Sherman Antitrust Act of 1890 had prohibited combinations in restraint of trade. The Clayton Antitrust Act was more specific. It forbade interlocking directorates of competing corporations capitalized at over $1,000,000. Also forbidden were price discriminations designed to lessen competition, and tying contracts under which manufacturers forced dealers to handle only one line of goods. The act made corporation officials personally responsible for failure to observe the rules.

Closely tied to the Clayton Act was a Federal Trade Commission Act, establishing a board of five, to be appointed by the President. Inheriting the investigative functions of the old Bureau of Corporations, the Federal Trade Commission could publicize dishonest business practices. It could also issue cease-and-desist orders to firms violating antitrust legislation or engaging in unfair competition in interstate trade. The commissioners could further follow up court decrees in antitrust cases. Although the Federal Trade Commission failed to realize all expectations, it did much in its early years to eliminate unfair business practices.

Labor and the Farmer

The New Freedom also aided workingmen. The Clayton Antitrust Act declared that strikes, peaceful picketing, and boycotts were not violations of federal law; and unions were exempted from the provisions of the Sherman and Clayton Antitrust acts. (This exemption was set down because of the antiunion record of federal courts.) Finally, the Clayton Act limited injunctions in labor disputes to cases in which there was danger of irreparable injury to property rights. As it turned out, this provision helped the unions very little. By seeing grave danger in almost any strike, conservative judges were able to issue injunctions much as before. Not until 1933 did legislation close this loophole.

The prolabor record of the Wilson administration included other acts. One set up a cabinet-level Department of Labor; another provided for mediation of railway labor disputes (both 1913). In 1916, Wilson persuaded Congress to pass the Adamson Act, which conceded the eight-hour day to railway employees whose work touched interstate commerce. Congress also passed two child labor acts, both later declared unconstitutional by the Supreme Court; and the La Follette Seaman's Act, which improved working conditions in the merchant marine.

There were also laws for farmers. A Farm Loan Act of 1916 supplemented the Federal Reserve Act by setting up federal land banks authorized to extend long-term loans to farmers on terms more favorable than those prevailing in private banks. The Smith-Lever Act of 1914, to promote agricultural extension work, and the Smith-Hughes Act of 1917, for vocational education, helped farmers. So did the new federal system of matching state road-building funds.

End of the Progressive Era

The legislative record helped Wilson win a second term. The Republicans ran only one candidate in 1916, Taft conservatives and Roosevelt progressives uniting behind Charles Evans Hughes. Wilson's reform record, however, brought him the backing of many citizens who normally voted Republican, some who had voted for the Socialist Debs in 1912. Friction in Republican ranks (particularly a misunderstanding between Hughes and Hiram Johnson) also helped the Democrats; and Wilson was chosen for a second term (1917–21).

The victory was narrow. Wilson lost the three most populous states— New York, Pennsylvania, Illinois. But he swept the South, picked up Ohio and New Hampshire, and carried eighteen of the twenty-two states west of the Mississippi. This gave him the victory in the electoral college, 277–254. The popular vote stood at 9,000,000 to 8,500,000. Thus the margin of triumph was small. But one could look at the figures in another way. Wilson drew a much larger percentage of the total vote in 1916 than he had. obtained in 1912—a larger percentage of the total vote than any Democratic candidate since before the Civil War.

When he won reëlection in 1916, Wilson had virtually stopped pressing for domestic reforms. His pace-forcing on progressive legislation had begun to slow down by 1915. Why? For one thing, it was difficult to control Congress for a long period of time. Second, Wilson was a moderate who did not want to go "too far." Finally, war in Europe was turning attention to world affairs. So the liberal drives of the New Freedom days came to an end. In some areas, the progressive trends were actually reversed. Supreme Court decisions emasculated the labor gains of the Clayton Antitrust Act; and child labor laws were pronounced unconstitutional. The Federal Trade Commission lost its initial energy and became increasingly pro-business. Even before the United States entered World War I (1917), Wilson brought businessmen into his administration; and in Republican ranks liberals lost ground to conservatives. The progressive era was grinding to a close.

Despite this, the reform movement had been important. Wilson showed that traditionally states'-rights Democrats, with a Jeffersonian tradition of as-little-government-as-possible, could enlarge the scope of the central government in the interest of public welfare. In other words, the final doom of states' rights was pronounced by Wilson, a southern-born advocate of individualism. From this time forth, reform movements would function primarily on a national basis.

By 1916, the progressive urge was slackening. But what had once been done could be done again. And the progressives had done a good deal. The plan of federal grants-in-aid to the states (highways, agricultural education) remained a significant feature of the American system. The banking reforms were important, as was the establishment of the Federal Trade Commission. Labor received legislation on which it could build later; and the farmer obtained more than that. The progressives had not worked in vain.

22

The Expanding Nation

A New Manifest Destiny

It was decreed by fate that the great United States should be greater still. So thought Americans as they pushed their country's frontiers outward. In the process, they created a philosophy of expansion. By the 1850's, "Manifest Destiny" had become part of American patriotism, folklore, political philosophy, and ideals. The sectional crisis turned attention away from diplomacy but strengthened the foundation on which expansion concepts rested. In defending territorial gains, Americans had used nationalist arguments; and the Civil War was a great triumph for nationalism. Prophets of expansion had always pictured Americans as a chosen people, guided toward conquest by the hand of the Almighty. An accurate description, thought most Northerners when their armies had humbled the Confederates. The new Darwinian theories also strengthened the expansionist philosophy. Darwin had shown that the fittest would survive in the biological struggle. By the 1880's, John Fiske and other American popularizers of Darwinism were applying this formula to world affairs. They claimed that through natural selection the United States had become superior and that Americans, having shown themselves to be more fit, would naturally rule feebler, less fit peoples.

Thus the expansion flames still burned. But national interests were changing. Down to 1850, American expansion had been largely agricultural. The aims had been protection and new lands for farmers, and outlets for farm products. After mid-century, the agrarian expansion urge had become less strong. Having acquired California and Oregon, the United States had spanned the continent. Canada beckoned, but could not be won without a costly fight with Britain. Southern planters were interested in Cuba, northern Mexico, and Central America. But defeat in the Civil War reduced their influence, and, with slavery dead, the planters were less interested in territorial additions.

As the drive for agrarian expansion lost its vigor, there developed an urge for an overseas expansion in which businessmen would figure more than would the farmer. The old Manifest Destiny had pointed to acquisition of nearby regions suitable for farming. The new imperialism looked far afield, and sought commercial and strategic rather than agricultural opportunities. Farm expansionists had insisted on outright ownership. Advocates of commercial expansion, planning no mass migration, were often satisfied with influence or control.

Efforts to build trade were not new. Back in the eighteenth century, Federalist foreign policy had featured efforts to aid the merchant marine. After 1800 the Jeffersonians had fought the Barbary pirates to protect American trade in the Mediterranean and had used diplomatic machinery to get new markets for American farm products. President John Tyler had sought commercial agreements with Germany and China. Congressional subsidies had helped the Collins steamers compete with the British Cunard line for passenger traffic on the Atlantic in the 1840's and 1850's. All this was of secondary interest to a people concentrating on domestic developments and agrarian expansion. But from 1850 on, Americans turned toward manufacturing; and the pressure for overseas expansion increased with the emergence of an industrial economy.

The trade balance provides a key to the new imperialism. For a century after independence the republic had an import or "unfavorable" balance of trade. That is, the country bought more products than it sold—a natural situation for a young agricultural nation. In the 1870's the pattern changed; thereafter the republic sold more than it purchased. This was a fundamental change, for the United States has retained an export or "favorable" trade balance to the present.

When the balance turned, imports were soaring and exports were going up still more rapidly. The nation had long imported manufactures and exported raw materials (chiefly wheat and cotton). Trade continued in these lines; but export lists began to show more manufactured articles—textiles, farm implements, machines, railroad equipment. Imports included proportionately fewer finished goods, proportionately more raw materials like wool, sugar, copper, petroleum, coffee, rubber. Such items were demanded by factories and by the urban population tied to the new industrialism.

Expansionist Groups

The trade shift did not change foreign policy immediately; merchants and manufacturers of the 1870's and 1880's concentrated on domestic problems. But the National Association of Manufacturers, organized in 1895, gave half its ten-point program to expansion of foreign trade. By then, export-conscious producers were seeking government aid in capturing markets overseas. Those who wanted raw materials from abroad felt that the United States should have influence at the source of supply. Activity of European competitors had increased demands for action, notably in the so-called "backward areas" of Latin America, Asia, Africa, and the Pacific. There were raw materials, also potential markets for manufactured goods.

American businessmen did not insist on territorial acquisition. Rather they stressed trade promotion. They asked for (and in 1906 obtained) reorganization of the traditionally inefficient consular service. They wanted the government to collect trade information, fight discrimination against American products, subsidize the merchant marine, dig and control an Isthmian canal. Many felt that business expansion could be promoted by strengthening the navy; and there was growing sentiment among exporters for reciprocal trade agreements. Those who favored reciprocity held that the United States could afford to reduce tariff rates without losing the home market. Cuts, then, could be used to get tariff concessions abroad, forcing open needed foreign markets.

Exporters were not alone in planning a broad national future. Shipowners saw in expansion a chance to revive the faltering merchant marine. In clipper-ship days the United States had been a power in the carrying trade. Then came decline, as wood gave way to iron, sail to steam. Britain led in the new construction, for she had a well-established iron industry, and her coal and iron ore were near together, and close to the sea. The British government assisted English shipping interests, whereas the American subsidy system collapsed in the 1850's. The next decade brought the Civil War, with Confederate privateers sinking some Union vessels and causing others to shift to foreign registry. This flight from the flag was permanent, for when war ended in 1865, Congress refused to allow these ships to transfer registry back to the United States. So decline continued until, in 1900, less than 10 percent of American foreign trade was carried in American bottoms. Aware of their weak position, American carriers sought government assistance. They secured some, in the Ocean Mail Subsidy Act of 1891. This was not enough to bring back the old-time glory. Still, merchant marine lobbying and publicity activities increased public interest in overseas affairs.

In a few cases, shipowners more directly influenced expansion. American power on the Isthmus was linked to steamship companies. In gold-rush days, the United States did not rely exclusively on covered wagon and pony express routes to California. Mail, express, and passengers normally were routed by steamer from the eastern United States to Panama and Nicaragua, then by land and inland waterways across to the Pacific, and by steamship up to California. William H. Aspinwall, whose Pacific Mail Steamship Company dominated the Pacific part of this traffic, added to his profits by constructing a railway across Panama; and from the 1850's on, the Panama Railroad helped the United States dominate this region. Meantime, Cornelius Vanderbilt controlled routes to and across Nicaragua. This took him into Nicaraguan politics and into conflict with English interests. When bloodshed followed, the United States Navy backed American interests, destroying Greytown, center of British influence in Nicaragua (1854).

During Reconstruction, William H. Webb started steamship service from San Francisco to Australia. New Zealand put up money; but Webb, as a shoestring operator, also needed American support. To get it, he stressed the value of Samoa, one of his ports of call. Webb's venture collapsed; but out of his efforts came notice for Samoa, especially in naval circles. And in 1889 the United States moved into Samoa to stay.

Recognizing that influence and investment went hand in hand in many "backward areas," the State Department eventually developed dollar diplomacy, the use of financial strength to build diplomatic power. The big deals came in the twentieth century, when industrial profits created large surpluses of capital and when declining interest rates in the United States tempted financiers to look for openings abroad. But even before 1900, American promoters were interested in special opportunities overseas. Well-established bankers held back, allowing shoestring promoters to operate. If the wildcatters succeeded, conservative financiers could step in later and work with or replace the pioneers.

Some schemes were too ambitious for immediate realization. Hinton Rowan Helper (of *Impending Crisis* fame) tried in vain to promote a railroad from Chile to Alaska. Less ambitious projects, like the Panama Railroad, brought profit and influence. Take Minor Keith, who began building Costa Rican railroads in he 1870's. Keith gained fame when he planted bananas to provide freight for his lines. His United Fruit Company, organized in 1899, did much to make northern Latin America a sphere of influence for the United States. At the same time, the Guggenheims acquired copper and silver mines in Canada, Mexico, and South America. Other Americans developed sugar plantations in Spanish Cuba. The United States government helped, securing a treaty which gave Americans better commercial chances in Spain's colonies (1887). Sugar was also in the picture in Hawaii. A reciprocity agreement of 1875 tied that kingdom to the United States, stimulating American investment and helping determine Hawaii's future.

The United States remained a debtor nation until World War I. That is, there was more European capital invested in the United States than American capital invested overseas. But the American stake abroad grew rapidly, especially after 1900. Americans put money in Mexican oil lands and Argentine packing plants, lent money to foreign governments. They provided funds which helped Japan defeat Russia (Russo-Japanese War, 1904–05). They took over the foreign debt of the Dominican Republic and several Central American countries. Each such step increased American influence abroad.

Backing up economic interests were powerful religious groups. Christianity has always been a missionary religion. The first white settlers of the New World tried to convert the Indians; and by 1812 American Protestants were sending agents into Asia. From 1850 on, mission work was the chief American enterprise in the Orient. Mission boards thus obtained large influence with the State Department. Missionaries created interest in expansion by writing books about distant lands. They advanced American influence by demanding rights of trade and residence in regions closed to foreigners, and by teaching Asiatics to use and desire Occidental goods. They called for American political influence, as preferable to European imperialism or misrule by native despots. Some religious leaders took an even bolder view. In his best seller, *Our Country* (1885), Josiah Strong called the Anglo-Saxon the favored child of destiny, picked by the Lord to Christianize and control backward peoples.

It was a missionary-diplomat, Peter Parker, who in the 1850's arranged to have Americans seize Formosa. (Superiors chose to let China keep the island.) Four decades later, Dr. Horace N. Allen, another missionary-diplomat, obtained for Americans railroad, mining, and other concessions in the kingdom of Korea. Meantime, missionary-founded Robert College in Constantinople became a center of American influence in the Near East. In Hawaii, missionaries served as royal advisers, and paved the way for absorption of the islands by the United States. The American Asiatic Association, organized in 1898 to build American influence in the Far East, had missionary as well as commercial backing.

The new navy—launched with appropriations of 1883 and 1890—was product and cause of expansion. As foreign interests grew, there came demands for fighting ships to protect the American stake abroad. The navy found that it helped itself by working for economic expansion. The navy bills, by requiring the use of domestic materials, started the manufacture of armor plate and big-gun forgings in the United States (1887). These enterprises, once launched, became centers of big-navy and expansion sentiment.

One advocate of American sea power was young Theodore Roosevelt, whose *Naval War of 1812* (1882) argued for a larger navy. More important was Captain Alfred T. Mahan, who in 1890 began publishing studies of the influence of sea power on history. In Mahan's view, national power and welfare depended on naval strength. In the early days Americans had been satisfied with a navy designed for coast defense. But, having become a major exporting nation, the United States now needed a world fleet built around modern battleships. The republic would further need such coaling stations as Pearl Harbor in Hawaii, Pago Pago in Samoa. Also an Isthmian canal, said Mahan.

Mahan explained, others executed. They worked along the lines of Commodore Matthew Perry, who in 1854 had used naval might to force the hermit country of Japan to deal more actively with the Western world. The Perry trick was duplicated in Korea by Commodore Robert Shufeldt (1883). At that same time the navy showed its growing interest in diplomacy by improving its attaché system, assigning naval officers to watch foreign trends. Action tended to be more direct in such out-of-the-way places as Haiti, Samoa, and Hawaii, where actual force was used to build American influence.

It is the job of politicians to reflect the interests which they represent, to anticipate the wishes of their constituents. In the late nineteenth century, business had much influence on politics. Politicians, therefore, sought to satisfy the expanding needs of manufacturers, traders, and financiers. Besides, like other Americans, political leaders were affected by the swelling tide of nationalism. Many politicians were active in religious groups and sympathized with missionary views. Others saw expansion as good campaign material. Increased activity meant competition with the British, affording opportunities to catch Irish votes by twisting the lion's tail. Politicians in the State Department and on diplomatic missions stood to gain more by urging expansion than by maintaining the *status quo*. If things stayed as they were, there would be little publicity. Expansion activity, by contrast, might catch the public fancy and help the politician to improve his position.

Opposition to Expansion

Although strong, the expansionists were not able to persuade the government to adopt their program until just before 1900. Even then, they ran into difficulties. The most serious problem was indifference. Having long concentrated on domestic affairs, Americans cared little about diplomacy. Nor was it easy to learn. Foreign news coverage was inadequate, and American educators paid little attention to international developments. Even interested parties found it difficult to concentrate on the subject. Most of the manufacturers who wanted foreign markets sold the bulk of their product at home. They thus gave most of their energy to domestic sales. Foreign problems were neglected until companies began assigning special officers to give full attention to such matters (generally after 1890).

Overseas expansion was specifically opposed by the peace societies. Seeing the tie between expansion and naval construction, pacifists denounced both. They also said that an increase in American activity would bring conflict with Germany, Britain, France, or Russia. Weakened by the Civil War, the peace movement was feeble when expansion agitation gathered force in the 1880's. By 1900, however, the pacifists had gained, especially among religious leaders and educators. Successful peace congresses, the partial success of the government-sponsored Hague peace conferences (1899, 1907), and the establishment of the Nobel Peace Prize added to pacifist strength. Meantime, increased financial support (as from Andrew Carnegie) enabled peace organizations to publicize their views.

Besides pacifists, the foes of expansion included many public figures who feared that overseas adventures would hurt the United States. Some (the Populists, for example) wanted to concentrate on domestic reform. Others felt that control of tropical areas would present race problems. (This helped explain the Senate's rejection of Grant's proposal to annex the Dominican Republic in 1870.) Humanitarians held that expansion always resulted in mistreatment of "subject peoples." (Among the most active anti-expansionists were officers of the Indian Rights Association, and Moorfield Storey, an organizer of the National Association for the Advancement of Colored People.) And many citizens, including Grover Cleveland, Carl Schurz, and Thomas B. ("Czar") Reed, felt that control of distant areas would strike at the principle of self-government and thus adversely affect democratic institutions in the United States.

Some economic groups fought expansion. Growers of sugar (cane and beets) opposed annexation of areas where cane could be grown cheaply. Tobacco farmers also feared competition. Farmers in general saw no gain in expansion. The new imperialism centered in tropical regions, where American farmers could neither sell goods nor settle to advantage. Agrarian spokesmen like Bryan therefore tended to be critical of expansionist activity.

The new Manifest Destiny also met opposition in labor ranks. Conservative labor leaders like Samuel Gompers and left-wingers like Eugene V. Debs denounced imperialism. Both were anti-navy and anti-militarist, partly because they feared the use of the military to break strikes. Like many Socialists, Debs was a pacifist, and felt that expansion would aid Wall Street, not the people. Gompers said control of colonial areas would not help American workingmen; moreover, such acquisitions might result in flooding the United States with immigrants who would take jobs away from native workers.

Pierce, Seward, Blaine

War with Spain in 1898 brought the expansion issue to a head. But expansionists had long since prepared the ground. President Franklin Pierce (1853–57) linked the old, agrarian expansion with the new, commercial kind. He added a final scrap of territory to the continental United States, the Gadsden Purchase of 1853. Three years later Congress authorized Americans to take over uninhabited guano islands (guano being used for fertilizer). Under this law, the United States obtained its first overseas possessions, including such islets as Navassa in the Caribbean, Baker and Howland in the Pacific. In the Ostend Manifesto of 1854, diplomats chosen by Pierce demanded that Spain cede Cuba to the United States. Also in 1854, American naval forces bombarded British-controlled Greytown in Nicaragua. Meantime, Perry was forcing the Japanese to trade more actively with the outside world; and, also in 1854, the United States negotiated a treaty of annexation with Hawaii. But the Senate rejected the treaty, and domestic difficulties (as in Kansas) prevented Pierce from continuing expansion.

Sectional complications also restrained William H. Seward, Secretary of State under Presidents Abraham Lincoln and Andrew Johnson (1861–69). A New York politician who worked well with business, Seward looked forward to American economic domination of the Caribbean and Pacific. By opposing French designs in Mexico, Seward added to his country's influence in Latin America; but Congress rejected his program of annexing the Danish West Indies, Haiti, and the Dominican Republic. He was also unsuccessful in Hawaiian and Korean projects. He did, however, snap up the Midway Islands; and in 1867 he bought Alaska from Russia for $7,200,000. Though some Americans thought Alaska worthless ("Seward's Folly"), most citizens considered the area worth the purchase price. Russia, too, knew that Alaska had value. For that very reason, the colony was likely to tempt enemies of Russia. It seemed better, therefore, to sell to the friendly United States than to lose Alaska to a European power. Snatching at the opportunity, Seward signed a treaty, which the Senate then approved. The House finally voted the purchase money in 1868, after the Russian minister in Washington had invested some cash in publicity and bribes.

A key expansionist was James G. Blaine, who emphasized trade promotion while Secretary of State (1881–82, 1889–92). Blaine knew that Latin America sold to the United States twice as much as she bought from this country. That is, the republics to the south marketed sugar, wool, coffee, and rubber in the United States, then used the proceeds to buy European goods. To change this, Blaine proposed forming an organization that would include the United States and the Latin-American nations, but not the European states or their New World possessions. As the one industrial country in the Pan American group, the United States would be in a favored position as against Old World competitors. Blaine therefore organized the first Pan American conference (1889–90). The delegates formed what in time became the Pan American Union, and adopted resolutions calculated to develop inter-American relations.

That was a start; but little more. Trade, investment, and tradition linked Latin America to Europe, and those who lived south of the Rio Grande had long viewed the United States with suspicion. To many Latin Americans, Blaine seemed more foe than friend. For, good will notwithstanding, the Secretary of State used a heavy hand in dealing with Central America and the island republics. United States interference in local politics, and a drunken brawl involving sailors from the U.S.S. *Baltimore* brought Chile and the United States close to war (1891). Although hostilities were averted, the bullying technique of Blaine and President Harrison increased Latin-American doubts as to the desirability of accepting leadership from the United States.

Pan-Americanism was only one aspect of Blaine's expansion program. During Blaine's second period as Secretary of State, the United States gained its first foothold on Samoa (1889). The Navy Bill of 1890 reflected developing ambitions, as did the Ocean Mail Subsidy Act of 1891, designed to aid the merchant marine. Also in 1891, Congress protected markets by empowering the President to retaliate against European countries which discriminated against American meat products. And the McKinley Tariff of 1890 contained so-called reciprocity provisions, aimed at increasing American exports to Latin America.[1]

---

[1] The President could impose penalty duties against countries not providing satisfactory openings for American goods. This brought concessions but (since the United States gave nothing in return) also built ill will. The program died when the Democrats repealed the McKinley Tariff in 1894. Back in power in 1897, the Republicans put reciprocity provisions in the Dingley Tariff. Steel manufacturers and others approved— they had little need for tariff protection, and wanted to get into foreign markets. But there were objections from small manufacturers (toys, jewelry, etc.). As a result, Congress let the President cut duties on only a few items, e.g., tonka beans. When J. A. Kasson negotiated broad reciprocity agreements, the Senate rejected them. President McKinley supported reciprocity until he died, saying that American manufacturers must give concessions to win foreign markets. But the National Association of Manufacturers, pressed by small manufacturers, withdrew its endorsement of reciprocity; and President Theodore Roosevelt, save in Cuba, did not press the point. Franklin D. Roosevelt would revive the subject in 1934.

Pierce, Seward, and Blaine accomplished a good deal. But when Blaine left the State Department in 1892, the major period of expansion lay ahead. In the quarter-century before American entry into World War I (1892–1917), the United States would acquire a colonial empire, build a sphere of interest in northern Latin America, and abandon isolation to become an important factor in the world balance of power.

Hawaii

The reciprocity treaty of 1875 made the Hawaiian Islands an economic dependency of the United States. Hawaii could send sugar to the United States below the normal tariff rates; and American products received special treatment in the Pacific kingdom. As a result, nearly all of Hawaii's foreign trade was with the United States. What was more, Americans invested in Hawaiian sugar lands; and when reciprocity was renewed in 1884, the United States also obtained control of Pearl Harbor.

Then the situation changed. The McKinley Tariff of 1890 put sugar on the free list and voted a subsidy to sugar growers within the United States. Americans who owned plantations in Hawaii (a foreign country) could not qualify for the subsidy. Nor did reciprocity assist them now; with sugar duty-free, they had no advantage in the American market over planters from Spanish Cuba and other sugar-producing regions. At the same time, Queen Liliuokalani, who believed in Hawaii for the Hawaiians, set out to reduce American influence in her kingdom. Disturbed, the Americans in Hawaii revolted, early in 1893, much as the Americans in Texas had revolted in 1836. A prominent rebel was Sanford B. Dole, whose family represented both missionary and business interests. He and fellow insurrectionists received support from the American minister to Hawaii, John L. Stevens. Stevens, a Blaine man and a pronounced expansionist, summoned American marines to Honolulu. Theoretically, the marines were to protect American property. Actually, their presence helped persuade Queen Liliuokalani to give way to a Hawaiian republic, headed by Dole.

This republic, naturally enough, petitioned for annexation to the United States, as the Texas republic had six decades before. President Harrison was coöperative, and tried to rush an annexation treaty through the Senate. But, having been defeated for reëlection in 1892, Harrison was a lame duck when he took up the Hawaiian question. He was unable to effect annexation before he left the White House in March, 1893; and his successor, Cleveland (1893–97), withdrew the treaty from the Senate. As a Democrat and an anti-imperialist, Cleveland disapproved of the methods used by Republican Minister Stevens.

Annexation efforts were renewed by President McKinley in 1897. When it proved impossible to get the two-thirds vote needed for Senate approval of an annexation treaty, the administration brought forth a joint resolution. This device, used in the case of Texas a half-century before, made it possible to effect annexation with only a majority vote in each house. The required votes were obtained in June, 1898, and Hawaii belonged to the United States.

The Cuban Question

When Hawaii was annexed, the United States was engaged in a war with Spain (April–August, 1898). This was a curious conflict. Although it added colonies to the United States, the war of 1898 was not originally a territory-grabbing venture. Although it yielded results which pleased businessmen, it was not at first desired by business. And although victory over Spain would help McKinley win re-election, the President long delayed asking Congress for a declaration of hostilities.

The war centered around Cuba. After five centuries of Spanish rule, the residents of the "ever faithful isle" were clamoring for independence. It took Spain a full decade to put down one revolt (Ten Years' War of 1868–78). Then came a new insurrection, in 1895–98. With few exceptions, citizens of the United States sympathized with the rebels. Spain was a traditional enemy and to many Americans symbolized monarchy and absolutism. Being weak, the Cubans won sympathy as underdogs. More important, they were fighting for goals which Americans approved: independence, republicanism, self-government. In addition, American religious leaders felt that missionary activities could be expanded if Cuba broke away from Spain. Businessmen guessed that Cuba libre would be a better customer than a Cuba controlled from Europe. The cause attracted humanitarians impressed by propaganda which the Cubans circulated in the United States. Some politicians saw political opportunity in the question; and some expansionists felt that intervention in Cuba would make the United States expansion-conscious.

All these groups were brought together by sensational journalists who increased circulation by backing the popular Cuban cause. William Randolph Hearst of the New York *Journal* and Joseph Pulitzer of the New York *World* were two of many in this field. Mixing appeals for liberty with stories about Spanish atrocities, these newspapermen turned American sympathy for Cuba into a crusade to save the Cubans. By 1897 aroused citizens were contributing money, volunteering for service in Cuba, and petitioning Congress and the President to take action against Spain.

Grover Cleveland was in the White House when the Cuban insurrection broke out in 1895. Although opposed to annexing overseas possessions,

Cleveland nonetheless believed in extending American influence. So he demonstrated in his endorsement of the Olney Doctrine, set forth by his Secretary of State, Richard Olney, in 1895. Intervening in a boundary dispute between Venezuela and British Guiana, Olney demanded that Britain arbitrate the dispute, and stated that the United States proposed to be dominant in the northern part of Latin America. In supporting Olney, Cleveland took expansionist ground. The President, however, would not go so far in Cuba; he refused to endorse interventionist schemes.

McKinley, who succeeded Cleveland in 1897, was at heart a cautious, peaceful man. Moreover, he was backed by Mark Hanna and other business leaders who did not want war with Cuba. Business desired expansion; but it preferred peaceful methods. War, it was feared, would bring inflation. Business had gone to some pains to defeat Bryan's inflationists in 1896. Why, then, have war and get inflation anyway? The depression was lifting in 1898, and business was content to leave well enough alone. Americans with money invested in Cuba inclined to the same view. These individuals prized law and order (essential for economic operations), and felt a Spanish-dominated Cuba was likely to be more peaceful than one run by Cubans.

McKinley, however, eventually asked Congress to declare war against Spain. As a religious man and humanitarian, the President was impressed by the anti-Spanish views of religious leaders. As a professional politician, he was aware that the people wanted war. This was notably the case after the publication of the DeLôme letter, a foolish communication from the Spanish minister in Washington, denouncing McKinley. Even more important was the sinking of the Maine, an American warship blown up while visiting Havana. Although the explosion remains a mystery to this day, Americans blamed the Spaniards, and called for war.

In a last-minute effort to head off conflict, Spain offered major concessions. But the offer came too late; Americans burned with war fever. In April, 1898, McKinley asked and obtained a declaration of hostilities. The President's appeal stressed humanitarian motives; and, in the Teller Amendment, Congress asserted that the United States intended, not to annex Cuba, but to set the island free. (Teller, incidentally, was from the beet sugar state of Colorado, which preferred to keep sugar islands outside American tariff walls.)

War with Spain (1898)

Businessmen feared that a Spanish-American conflict would wear on for a long time and force the United States to adopt inflationary measures. They were needlessly concerned. Beating Spain proved an easy, relatively inexpensive job. Congress took care of some of the expense by voting a few war taxes (an inheritance tax, stamp duties on legal documents, sales taxes on chewing gum and patent medicine). This brought in $100,000,000 the first year. The government also floated one war loan, for $200,000,000. Though this bond issue carried only 3 percent interest—half the Civil War rate—subscriptions were seven times the amount requested. The war's popularity also made it easy to raise troops. There was no need of a draft, for McKinley obtained without difficulty all the volunteers desired (200,000). The government also increased the size of the Regular Army and Navy; and this sufficed to win the war.

The Union army of 1865 had been broken up in a demobilization that was almost complete; the army in 1898 was small and poorly supplied. Nor had the War Department bothered to acquire up-to-date weapons and the new smokeless powder. Soldiers were sent to tropical Cuba wearing the heavy blue uniform of Civil War days; and they were given rations unsuited to the climate. Medical and sanitary needs were woefully neglected; fourteen-fifteenths of the 5000 enlisted men who lost their lives in this war died of disease.

In addition, the armed services were shot through with politics. Theodore Roosevelt, a young Republican, obtained a good command and became a military hero; William Jennings Bryan, a young Democrat, had only a Nebraska state commission, and served out the war in Florida. W. T. Sampson and W. S. Schley, ranking naval officers, spent much of the war, and years thereafter, deciding which should get the credit for winning the battle of Santiago. (Neither deserved very much.) Nelson A. Miles, the ranking general, was ready to accept a presidential nomination from either the Republicans or the Democrats. (All he got was a feeler from the Prohibitionists.)

Nor were operations carefully planned. The United States assembled troops in Tampa, Florida, a town served by a one-track railroad. War had been a possibility for two long years; but neither army nor navy had good plans. Having failed to consider transportation and supply problems, the military was able to transport to Cuba only a fraction of the soldiers assembled in Florida. This expeditionary force was landed clumsily on an exposed beach; only Spanish weakness prevented heavy loss.

Yet the United States won a quick, smashing victory. Commodore George Dewey overwhelmed Spain's Pacific fleet at Manila Bay in the Philippines. Sampson and Schley crushed the enemy's Atlantic squadron off Cuba (battle of Santiago). Guam surrendered without a struggle, and Miles took Puerto Rico by marching across the island. Working with the Cuban rebels, General William R. Shafter defeated the Spaniards in Cuba.

Meanwhile, American and Filipino soldiers took Manila. Spain then asked for an armistice, and, in August, 1898, hostilities ended.

In the weeks of action, the United States had made blunders. Mistakes are to be expected, however, in the opening months of war. Had the conflict lasted longer, the American forces would have developed greater efficiency. Even as it was, the republic accomplished its mission, with much to spare. Especially noteworthy was the way in which the navy had established control of the approaches to the Spanish islands. In sea power, the United States held a key to further overseas expansion.

The Peace Settlement

Only a few Americans had urged war with Spain as a means of acquiring territory. But when war came, opinions changed. Businessmen who had opposed declaration of hostilities now felt that the United States should get as much as possible out of the struggle. Religious leaders like Lyman Abbott favored annexation projects to aid missions. The expansion cry was taken up by journalists, including Whitelaw Reid of the New York *Tribune* and Henry Watterson of the Louisville *Courier-Journal*. A. T. Mahan noted the need for coaling stations. Enthusiastic young politicians like Theodore Roosevelt, Henry Cabot Lodge, and Albert J. Beveridge called for empire, as did older Republicans who felt that acquisition of the Spanish islands would increase McKinley's chances for reëlection in 1900.

Under the circumstances, territorial additions seemed inevitable. The armistice agreement of August, 1898, specified that Spain would cede to the United States Puerto Rico and Guam. The final peace settlement, signed at Paris at the end of the year, transferred the Philippine Islands to the United States. Spain did not want to make this cession, and argued that the Americans occupied only a tiny part of the islands. The question was finally settled when the American negotiators agreed to pay Spain $20,000,000.

The peace treaty further specified that Cuba was to be set free. Americans affected by the new Manifest Destiny would like to have annexed the island. Here, however, the Teller Amendment blocked the way. So the Cubans were allowed to set up a republic. But American troops occupied Cuba until 1902; and when they left, the island was a protectorate of the United States. Cuba granted land for an American naval base. Besides that, the United States secured the right to intervene in Cuba to maintain order (in the Platt Amendment, which was incorporated into American law, into the Cuban constitution, and into a Cuban-American treaty). Ties were made closer still by a special reciprocity agreement of 1902, which gave Cuban sugar special advantages in the United States and enabled American manufacturers to dominate the Cuban market.

While expansion sentiment was rising, the anti-expansionists were also forming their lines. An Anti-Imperialist League organized in 1898 had as vice-presidents Samuel Gompers of the A.F. of L.; such farm spokesmen as Herbert Myrick; humanitarians like Jane Addams and Moorfield Storey; Mark Twain and other intellectuals; such anti-imperialist Democrats as Grover Cleveland; and anti-expansionist Republicans like "Czar" Reed, who disliked seeing the Republican party falling into the hands of Lodge, Roosevelt, and other young imperialists. Coöperating closely with the League was William Jennings Bryan, who controlled the Democratic machinery.

For tactical reasons, the anti-imperialists raised no objection to the annexation of Puerto Rico and Guam. They concentrated rather on opposing acquisition or retention of the Philippine Islands. Opponents of expansion felt that it would be impossible to allow the Philippines statehood—doing so would give Filipinos the balance of power in the United States. Annexing the Philippines without giving them statehood would involve denying Filipinos the right of self-government, which would undermine American democracy. Further, Filipino laborers and goods would compete with American workingmen and products.

The anti-imperialists came close to defeating ratification of the treaty of peace with Spain; the Senate approved the treaty in February, 1899, with just one vote to spare. Two factors influenced the result. Bryan, though anti-imperialist, urged ratification so that the Philippine question could be threshed out in American politics rather than in diplomatic discussions. And just at this time armed conflict broke out between American troops in the Philippines and Filipinos under Emilio Aguinaldo. Many Senators felt that approval of the treaty was necessary to give the McKinley administration support against Aguinaldo.

Undaunted by defeat, the anti-imperialists tried again, in the presidential election of 1900. In that contest McKinley, the Republican, sought reëlection on an expansion platform. Bryan, the Democrat, ran as a foe of expansion, with the special endorsement of an anti-imperialist convention. The diplomatic issue was only one of several in the campaign. Still, McKinley's triumph was a victory for expansion.

Retreat from Empire

Having won all along the line, the imperialists might well have clamored for more colonies. In fact, they did not. Although the United States later picked up the Canal Zone, Virgin Islands, and some naval bases, the Philippines were the last large-scale addition of territory by the republic.

Why so? Partly because European powers had grabbed most of Africa and Asia before the United States became a competitor. Going after what was left would involve greater expenditures and risks than most Americans were willing to take. Besides, the colonies acquired proved less valuable than had been expected. Investment openings helped only a few Americans. Farmers within the United States became increasingly aware of competition from the islands. On the strategic side, it gradually became apparent that the Philippines were as much liability as asset (an "Achilles heel," admitted Theodore Roosevelt). Nor did Manila become a second Hong Kong, as many had predicted.

The Filipino insurrection was an even greater reason for discouragement. For three years (1899–1902) Aguinaldo's Filipinos waged guerrilla warfare against the United States. Putting down the rebels cost more men and money than the war with Spain. In fighting the Filipinos, American commanders found it necessary to use concentration camps and strong-arm tactics—the very things Spain had used in Cuba. Thus a movement started as an effort to liberate Cubans ended in a drive to subjugate Filipinos. Meanwhile, Congressional investigations uncovered corruption and inefficiency in the armed services. Imperial operations thus seemed less glorious than before.

At the same time, American expansionists were coming to feel that annexation of colonies was an inefficient method of building American influence abroad. Cuba, which was not annexed, brought the United States more profit and less trouble than the Philippines, which were acquired outright. Might not control be preferable to ownership? This did not mean abandoning expansion. The United States could continue to push outward in trade and investment fields, to seek diplomatic influence and strategic control. But the republic would stop short of actually annexing overseas areas. This was the ruling policy after 1900.

The government failed to work out a well-coördinated colonial policy. Alaska was handled by the Department of the Interior. Samoa and Guam were under the Navy Department, and the Canal Zone (after 1903) was controlled by the War Department. Hawaii, Puerto Rico, and the Philippines were under no cabinet official; and each was governed by a separate set of officers.

In the Insular cases (1901–03), the Supreme Court gave Congress virtually a free hand in dealing with newly acquired possessions. Holding that the Constitution did not necessarily follow the flag, the justices said that Congress could withhold constitutional guarantees from the colonies and could force the islanders to pay tariff duties. The legislators at first charged 15 percent of the Dingley duties on goods coming in from Puerto Rico

(Foraker Act, 1900). Then, in 1902, these duties were dropped. But in that same year, Philippine goods were required to pay three-fourths of the Dingley rates. These charges were wiped out in 1909, although there were restrictions as to sugar and tobacco until the passage of the Underwood Tariff of 1913.

Stirred by humanitarian motives and anti-imperialist criticism, McKinley and his successors tried to create model governments in the new possessions. Despite a painful lack of overall plans, the effort was partially successful. Most administrators sent to the islands were well-meaning, and quite a few were efficient. Schools were established, disease was reduced. Natives were brought into the administration, and local voters were given a measure of home rule.

Problems remained. Much of the wealth of the colonies was controlled by outsiders, notably American businessmen. Then, too, there was a continuing desire for self-government. In Hawaii and Alaska, both settled largely from the United States, the cry was for statehood. In both cases low population was an obstacle; but ultimately, after World War II, global strategy added strength to the statehood movements.

The Spanish-speaking Puerto Ricans and Filipinos were more interested in independence. During World War I, President Wilson, an anti-imperialist, tried to work out a solution. One Jones Act, passed in 1916, promised the Philippines eventual independence. A second Jones Act, adopted the next year, made Puerto Ricans American citizens and gave them increased powers of self-government. Under Wilson's successors the trend toward home rule was arrested. It was resumed after the crash of 1929. The ensuing depression made American farmers and laborers protection-minded; they wanted to exclude all competitors for their markets and jobs. Beet and cane sugar, tobacco, hemp, and dairy farmers joined the A.F. of L. in urging that the Philippines be given independence and put outside American tariff and immigration walls. These economic groups accomplished what humanitarian anti-imperialists had been unable to do. A Tydings-McDuffie Act, passed in 1934, gave the Filipinos political independence as of 1946.

With Philippine independence a reality, the empire of 1898 seemed to be breaking up. In 1947, Congress increased home rule in Puerto Rico—among other things, local citizens were permitted to choose their own governor. Here was evidence that the United States had moved away from emphasis on colonies. There were other indications along the same line—for example, the refusal of the United States to take territory, even on a temporary, mandate basis, after World War I. This was not a matter of withdrawing from the scene. The United States was much more of a world power after the world wars than before. But the weight had shifted from territorial to economic, strategic, diplomatic, and even moral factors.

The Far East

Nineteenth-century annexations had given the United States strong positions in the Pacific. Hawaii, with its great Pearl Harbor base, was the key to the mid-Pacific. To the north was Alaska; to the south, Samoa; to the west, the Philippines; to the east, the Pacific coast states, and, presently, the Panama Canal. Naval officers also wanted a base or two on the Asiatic mainland. They therefore had the State Department ask China for a naval base (1902). The request was denied, largely because of opposition from Japan.

At that time, Americans underrated the Japanese. Shortly, however, Japan won a major victory in the Russo-Japanese War (1904–05); and she followed up the war by taking control of south Manchuria and Korea. Thereafter, American concern over Japan's naval strength increased. This could be seen in statements of Congressman Richmond P. Hobson of Alabama, the navy spokesman in Congress; the Navy League (organized in 1902); west coast labor leaders who led the fight to exclude Japanese immigrants; and the Hearst newspapers, much worried about the "yellow peril."

American Far Eastern policy depended more on economic than on strategic factors. American textiles, cigarettes, and kerosene had a good sale in the Orient in the 1890's, and Americans were getting interested in Chinese railroads. Manufacturers and financiers, organized in an American Asiatic Association, hoped for even better business in the future. Their efforts centered on the Chinese Empire. China, however, was very weak. Taking advantage of that weakness, Japan and the European powers were marking out spheres of interest. Given the normal policies of great powers, it seemed likely that the United States would be squeezed out of China's economic life, and that American missionaries, too, would have hard going.

Hoping to protect the future, McKinley's Secretary of State, John Hay, issued the Open Door Notes in 1899. The notes indicated that the United States hoped China would remain territorily intact. But even if the empire was divided into spheres, the United States still wanted equal economic opportunity. Despite some support from the British, Germans, and Japanese, Hay failed to gain general acceptance of his proposal. Yet the Open Door Notes marked a turning point in American diplomacy; the United States would hereafter play a more active role in world affairs. The notes also set a pattern; American diplomats would soon be demanding equal economic opportunities all over the world. Finally, the notes improved American relations with commerce-minded Britain and the grateful Chinese.

The next year, 1900, saw the rise in China of an antiforeign Boxer movement, backed by government officials. When the legations in Peking were besieged, Japanese, American, and European troops invaded China and crushed the Boxers. In this crisis, American missionaries suffered heavily. The United States, however, made few demands for punishment. Rather American emphasis was on maintaining Chinese integrity—essential for American trade, investment, and mission work, and for the Asiatic balance of power. Like other nations, the United States accepted monetary damages from China. Later, the American republic returned most of this Boxer indemnity, earning the good will of China and starting a heavy flow of Chinese students to the United States.

At first American financiers, traders, and diplomats felt they could coöperate with the Japanese. Japan, after all, was allied to Britain, and claimed to favor the open door. Certainly the Japanese were less obstructionist than the Russians, who consistently opposed American enterprise. In the Russo-Japanese War, therefore, Wall Street joined English bankers in helping to finance Japan. Being pro-Japanese and anti-Russian, President Roosevelt and the American people approved this development.

Presently, however, coöperation broke down. American traders met difficulties in Chinese areas under Japanese control. E. H. Harriman found himself blocked by Japan when he tried to buy into Manchurian railroads (he saw these as a link in his projected round-the-world transportation system). Japan also wrecked a J. P. Morgan-sponsored Anglo-American financial project and joined Russia in defeating an American proposal for international control of Manchurian development (the neutralization project of Philander Knox, Taft's Secretary of State, 1911). Despite such rebuffs, the United States continued to try to work with Japan, partly to please Britain, partly because President Theodore Roosevelt was pro-Japanese. A secret Taft-Katsura understanding of 1905 specified that Japan had no designs on the Philippines and that the United States would give Japan a free hand in Korea. The Root-Takahira agreement of 1908 half-recognized Japan's "special interests" in Manchuria.

Unable to make headway against Japan and Russia in north China, American financiers fared better in central and southern China. Here the bankers had the enthusiastic backing of President Taft, who knew that investment and trade were closely connected. Taft used his influence to get Americans a share in the Anglo-French-German Hukuang Railway project (1909). Later he helped create the first consortium, an international combination of government-supported bankers, who proposed to lend money to China and supervise currency and other reforms. But the overthrow of the Manchu dynasty in the Chinese Revolution of 1911 prevented the consortium from being very effective.

When Wilson became President in 1913, he condemned the policies of his predecessors, particularly Taft's support of the consortium. In Wilson's view, Taft was helping the money trust—the American group in the consortium was dominated by Morgan. Besides, the consortium had monopolistic aims, and seemed more interested in controlling than helping China. When Wilson announced that he would not support Wall Street in China, the American group withdrew from the consortium. But this weakened American influence without helping China. With the United States inactive, and Europe engaged in World War I, Japan increased her influence. Wilson did what he could. He asked Japan to soften her Twenty-One Demands against China (1915). He tried to work with Japan, and granted that the Japanese had "special interests" in China (Lansing-Ishii agreement, 1917). Since this helped neither China nor America, Wilson eventually went back to dollar diplomacy. At the end of World War I, Wilson's Secretary of State invited the house of Morgan to organize a second consortium.

Latin America: The Panama Canal

In the Far East, the expectations of 1898 were not realized. In Latin America, by contrast, the early part of the twentieth century saw an enormous increase of American influence. Part of the time emphasis was on strategic considerations (as under Theodore Roosevelt and during World War I). Again, as in the Taft administration, economic approaches were stressed. Either way, influence soared.

Much of the story involved the Panama Canal. Mahan and other naval men had long demanded an Isthmian canal, through either Panama or Nicaragua. So had merchants, who hoped to increase trade with western South America. The war with Spain dramatized the strategic need—the U.S.S. Oregon had to go all the way around South America to join the American fleet off Cuba. After the peace settlement, therefore, the American government moved ahead.

First, Secretary of State John Hay took care of the British. Under the Clayton-Bulwer Treaty of 1850, the United States and Britain had agreed to approach the canal problem together. By the end of the century Britain was willing to let the United States go ahead alone. The first Hay-Pauncefote Treaty (1900) canceled the Clayton-Bulwer agreement; but it specified that the United States could not fortify an Isthmian canal or adjust rates so as to favor American ships over British vessels. When the Senate objected to the terms, the British gave way on the fortification question (second Hay-Pauncefote Treaty, 1901), and the matter was settled. A decade later, Congress tried to aid American shipowners by passing a Panama Canal Tolls Act in apparent violation of the 1900 treaty. But President

Wilson secured repeal of this statute before the canal was opened in 1914.

Having decided to dig a canal, the United States had to choose between Panama and Nicaragua. The Panama route was shorter; but it was more rugged. In either case, it was a job for public rather than private enterprise. An American company had failed in Nicaragua. There had been a similar failure in Panama, where Ferdinand de Lesseps' French Panama Canal Company had been unable to overcome promotional and geographical difficulties, not to mention yellow fever. But the French company had maintained its organization, and hired William Nelson Cromwell as lobbyist. Cromwell's job was to persuade the United States to buy the rights and property of the French company. The lobbyist did his work well, earning his $800,000 fee. First, he helped persuade American officials that the Panama route was better than the one through Nicaragua. Second, he finally obtained a high price ($40,000,000) for the French company's franchise and assets.

Meantime, the United States had been dealing with the republic of Colombia, which owned Panama. President Roosevelt and Secretary of State Hay offered Colombia $10,000,000 and an annual rental for a Canal Zone (proposed Hay-Herran Treaty, 1903). This was rejected by Colombia, which wanted more money. Roosevelt and Hay could raise the offer, turn to Nicaragua, put off the project, or use force. The first two possibilities seemed most logical. But T. R., irritated with Colombia, chose to make no concession whatsoever. Instead, he took matters into his own hands. ("I took the Canal Zone.")

It was almost that crude. The French Panama Canal Company helped organize a Panama secession movement. The movement was supported by Panama patriots who had long desired home rule. If left alone, Colombia could have crushed the revolt with ease. Roosevelt, though, sent naval vessels to the Isthmus. They supported the revolution, making it possible to organize a republic of Panama. The new state was at once recognized by the United States. A canal treaty was immediately negotiated (the Hay-Bunau-Varilla Treaty, 1903). The United States secured full rights in the Canal Zone; and a canal was dug (opened in 1914). Panama became a protectorate of the United States, rights of intervention being similar to those stated in the Platt Amendment in Cuba.

Roosevelt's high-handed policy won public approval—after all, the President did get canal rights. What was more, the administration claimed to have acted legally, under a Colombian-American treaty of 1846, which gave the United States the right to intervene to protect the Isthmian transit route. But, in bullying Colombia, the United States won the animosity of many Latin Americans. United States diplomats encountered more opposi-

The United States acquired a few guano islands even before the Civil War, Navassa being the first of these. Congress, however, rejected presidential proposals for the annexation of the Virgin Islands (Danish West Indies) and the Dominican Republic in the Reconstruction era.

After the war with Spain in 1898 the United States annexed Puerto Rico, secured a naval base at Guantanamo, and a protectorate over Cuba. During Theodore Roosevelt's administration, the United States won control of the Canal Zone (1903), with a protectorate treaty covering all Panama (1903–39). Roosevelt set up a "financial protectorate" over the Dominican Republic

THE UNITED STATES
IN MIDDLE AMERICA
1898-1918

THE BAHAMAS

CUBA

GUANTANAMO   HAITI

JAMAICA   NAVASSA IS.

DOMINICAN
REPUBLIC

PUERTO RICO   VIRGIN IS.

CARIBBEAN   SEA

CURAÇAO

TRINIDAD

IS.

CANAL ZONE

PANAMA

COLOMBIA

VENEZUELA

(1905–41, there being armed intervention, 1914–24). Occupation of Nicaragua (1912–33) began under Taft, who also tried to arrange a financial protectorate of Honduras. Wilson continued the intervention policy, occupying Haiti (1915–34), holding Vera Cruz briefly (1914), leasing the Corn Islands from Nicaragua (1914), and purchasing the Virgin Islands from Denmark (1917).

Finding that force diplomacy brought resentment and opposition in Latin America, the United States abandoned the direct intervention method after 1930.

tion than before; American businessmen found it difficult to get economic concessions. Finally, in 1921, the United States gave Colombia $25,000,000. Although the sum was not accompanied by apologies, it was plain that the United States was asking Colombians to forget the Panama affair—and consider Americans for oil concessions. All this might have been avoided if Theodore Roosevelt had been less impulsive, or more generous, in 1903.

Intervention as a Policy

From this time on, the Canal Zone loomed large in American diplomacy. The Canal, when opened in 1914, helped turn the trade of western South America from London to New York. No less important were strategic factors. Britain had long been the dominant naval power in the West Indies. The rise of American naval strength and acquisition of the Canal Zone by the United States changed this age-old pattern. Recognizing the new situation, the British in 1906 broke up their Caribbean fleet. This strengthened Britain against Germany in European waters; and it made the United States unchallenged master of the New World.

Constant vigilance was necessary to protect the new position. Theodore Roosevelt felt that even that was not enough. It was necessary, he said, to make a display of strength. Quoting an African proverb, he claimed it was wise to "speak softly and carry a big stick." Actually, Roosevelt rarely spoke softly. But he did favor a big navy; and he used force and the threat of force as an arm of foreign policy. He called attention to American power by sending the navy around the world (1907). In Latin America he used naval strength to develop the intervention policy which centered around the Roosevelt Corollary to the Monroe Doctrine. Under this Corollary the United States claimed the right to intervene in a Latin-American republic to prevent the intervention of an outside power. Only in this way, said Roosevelt, could the United States defend the approaches to the Panama Canal and carry out the responsibilities of world power.

Roosevelt was concerned even before the acquisition of the Canal Zone —as in 1902, when Britain, Germany, and Italy used pressure to collect debts from Venezuela. In 1904, Roosevelt moved into the Dominican Republic, taking over the customs. At the time, the Dominicans were deep in debt to European creditors; and Roosevelt (who was anti-German) feared that Germany might intervene if the United States did not. Once in control, the President had American bankers take over the Dominican foreign debt. When the Senate failed to approve a treaty providing for a financial receivership, Roosevelt carried on under executive authority. The Senate finally gave way in 1907. Despite American supervision of revenues, political turmoil remained constant in the Dominican Republic; and in 1916

American troops occupied the country. The armed intervention lasted for eight years.

By then, Theodore Roosevelt had sent troops into Cuba, under authority of the Platt Amendment. Inexperienced in government, the Cubans had moved into political chaos after the end of the first American occupation (1902). Since Cuba was an American protectorate, Roosevelt felt obliged to see order maintained. In addition, the President was again concerned about Germany. Charles E. Magoon was in charge of the occupation, which lasted three years (1906–09).

Roosevelt's successors continued his policies. William Howard Taft and his Secretary of State, Philander Knox, relied on dollar diplomacy—the use of financial influence to determine diplomatic policy. Many Latin-American treasuries depended heavily on tariff revenues. Those who controlled the customs, then, controlled the country. Taft therefore felt that American banks should lend money to Latin-American governments, and that, to assure repayment, they or the State Department should get control of the customs. The Senate refused to agree to financial receivership treaties which Taft and Knox negotiated with Honduras and Nicaragua; but, even without the treaties, the bankers and State Department made the necessary arrangements. Taft defended this by saying it meant more trade, and that using finance was better than using force ("Dollars not bullets"). Yet the Taft-Knox program led to employment of troops. In 1909, the United States Navy helped overthrow the Zelaya regime in Nicaragua. Three years later, American marines moved in. Save for a few months in the 1920's, they were there until 1933.

As a Democrat and anti-imperialist, Wilson condemned the interventionist policies of his predecessors (as in his Mobile speech of 1913). In practice, however, Wilson continued the intervention program, using both financial influence and military force. He kept the marines in Nicaragua, and negotiated an agreement that made Nicaragua virtually a United States protectorate (the Bryan-Chamorro Treaty of 1914, which gave the United States exclusive canal rights and permission to build Atlantic and Pacific naval bases). He tightened control over the Dominican Republic by sending in troops, and had Haiti occupied by American naval forces, inaugurating an armed intervention that lasted until 1934.

These developments took place during World War I; and Wilson felt that he was protecting the approaches of the Panama Canal against possible German moves. In the same spirit, he bought the Virgin Islands from Denmark (1917), for the high price of $25,000,000. Germany, it was thought, might coerce her neighbor Denmark into ceding the islands to her, for a submarine base.

Wilson followed much the same line in Mexico. The Mexican Revolution of 1910 had been followed by turmoil, involving difficulties for foreign capital. This disturbed Wilson, who also disapproved of the chief Mexican politician, Huerta. Refusing to recognize Huerta, Wilson would not let that dictator buy arms in the United States; arms could, however, go to Huerta's foe Carranza. A minor incident concerning American sailors at Tampico led to the occupation of Vera Cruz by American naval forces in April, 1914. Again, the Germans were in the picture; the occupation prevented Huerta from getting arms from German sources. The ABC countries of South America (Argentina, Brazil, Chile) then arranged a sort of compromise, with Huerta going into exile and the United States withdrawing from Vera Cruz. Carranza, whom Wilson had supported, became President of Mexico.

More troubles followed. In 1916 Pancho Villa, a bandit-politician, slaughtered Americans in Mexico and across the border in New Mexico. Since Carranza was unable to catch Villa, Wilson sent General J. J. Pershing and 15,000 troops on a punitive expedition into Mexico. Pershing did not catch Villa; and the affair embittered Mexican-American relations. In a constitution of 1917, the Mexicans made new attacks on Americans who owned oil properties south of the Rio Grande. On the American side, Wilson became convinced that the Mexicans were under German influence; and after World War I he saw to it that Mexico was not invited to join the League of Nations.

The intervention policy of 1900–20 fell short of success. True, the United States obtained the Canal Zone; and these years saw American influence increase in the northern part of Latin America. United States trade, investment, and naval power rose sharply. Diplomatic influence went up, too; and when the United States entered World War I in 1917, several Latin-American states followed suit. (Not only such United States-dominated states as Cuba, but also the larger republic of Brazil, which depended on the United States for its coffee market.) But, along with the rise of influence, there was a rise in animosity toward the United States. During the generation to follow, citizens of the United States would find that abandonment of the intervention policy would increase their effectiveness below the Rio Grande.

Europe: Isolation Fades

In 1898, most Americans still believed that their republic should steer clear of European quarrels. But even then, the old isolation ideology was breaking down. By 1914 the United States would be very close to Europe's quarrels.

There were many aspects to the new trend. Greater wealth and improved transportation caused well-to-do Americans to visit Europe. These travelers were frequently regarded with contempt by European intellectuals; and the Americans in turn sneered at European culture (see Mark Twain's *Innocents Abroad*). Still, the closer contact made many realize that American and European cultures were closely related. European-trained American scholars had even more influence; and the same end was served by the gradually improved foreign correspondence of American newspapers. In the International Copyright Act of 1891, Congress eliminated book pirating, and to that extent cut the circulation of European books in the United States. At the same time, the statute indicated that the United States was at last recognizing its responsibilities in international cultural relations.

Simultaneously, the economic and naval expansion of the American republic brought new commitments. As early as 1865, the United States joined European nations in maintaining the Cape Spartel lighthouse near Gibraltar. From the 1880's on, Americans took part in many international conferences. Some concerned distant areas—the Congo, Morocco, Spitzbergen. Others dealt with subjects which the United States would not earlier have considered to be matters of international concern: the slave trade; liquor traffic; patents and trademarks; weights and measures; sanitary regulations; peace, disarmament, and international arbitration; rules of war. In 1900, American troops served as part of an international military force in China; and in the Boxer Protocol that followed, the United States joined other nations in determining the fate of China. Beginning with the 1880's, the United States signed many multilateral agreements and joined international organizations, including the Universal Postal Union and Pan American Union. There was semiofficial and unofficial activity, too, as in the China consortium agreements; when Congress chartered the American Red Cross (associated with the International Red Cross); and when, from 1896 on, Americans took part in the Olympic games.

Presidential Influence

Presidential power increased with diplomatic activity. The Chief Executive had broad constitutional powers in the international field: the right to appoint diplomats; control over recognition of foreign governments; power to negotiate treaties; authority as commander in chief of the nation's armed forces. Twentieth-century Presidents used these powers to the full, as when Taft sent marines to Nicaragua, and when Wilson determined Mexican policy by withholding recognition from Huerta.

Not stopping there, Presidents added to their authority. Theodore

Roosevelt acted as a kind of mediator at the end of the Russo-Japanese War. Normal diplomatic appointees (ambassadors, for instance) required Senate confirmation. But Presidents could by-pass the Senate by using executive agents, responsible only to the President. The peace treaty with Spain in 1898 was handled in this fashion. Presidents could also get around the constitutional requirement that the Senate approve treaties, by making executive agreements which were not submitted to the Senate. Important Far Eastern commitments fell into this category: the Boxer Protocol; the gentlemen's agreement with Japan on immigration; the Taft-Katsura, Root-Takahira, and Lansing-Ishii agreements. The Taft-Katsura understanding, worked out in Theodore Roosevelt's time, was kept secret from the public. Moreover, it was negotiated by an executive agent, who was not confirmed by the Senate. And yet, apparently, the terms bound the United States.

Under the circumstances, the personal attitude of the President was bound to influence the diplomatic alignments of the United States. It is significant, therefore, that Roosevelt, Taft, and Wilson, despite their differences, agreed on many points of diplomatic policy. All felt that the United States must have increasing influence overseas. All believed in presidential diplomatic leadership. And all were enthusiastically pro-British.

Anglo-American Friendship

The four decades before World War I saw a great upsurge of nationalism in Europe, a new interest in imperialism, an enormous increase in armaments, and the formation of new alliances. Being part of one world, the United States was involved at every point. Nationalism was a mighty force in America. The American republic sampled imperialism, and became a great naval power. Only in the matter of alliances did Americans seem different from Europeans. Even there the difference was not so great, for in the generation before 1914 the United States became the informal partner of Great Britain.

Anglo-American friendship developed slowly. Old claims-and-boundary difficulties were removed in the Treaty of Washington (1871). Some controversies remained, as over fisheries; and the United States and Britain continued to be commercial rivals. But, as earlier quarrels subsided, Americans and Englishmen became increasingly aware of their ties of blood and language, similarities of government, and common cultural heritage. These bonds were keenly felt by such Britishers as Joseph Chamberlain and Rudyard Kipling, by such Americans as Hay, Roosevelt, and Wilson.

Diplomatic trends also counted. With the rise of Germany, Britain needed friends. She therefore built new alliances, with Japan, France, and Russia. Before any of these had been arranged, the British government suggested an Anglo-American combination in the Far East (1898). President McKinley replied that the United States had a tradition against alliances. But that, of course, did not rule out friendly coöperation.

Britain made every effort to effect that coöperation. When Cleveland's Secretary of State Olney scolded Britain in the Venezuela boundary dispute of 1895, British diplomats restrained themselves, and did what the United States desired. Britain took the American side in the Spanish-American War, and told European powers that they could not intervene to save Spain. By that time, Britain was working with the United States in Samoa. Soon afterward, Great Britain advanced American canal ambitions by voluntarily giving up most of her Isthmian rights in the Hay-Pauncefote treaties (1899–1900). When Canada and the United States differed over the Alaska boundary, a British arbitrator sided with the Americans against the Canadians, giving the United States the victory (1903). Three years later, Britain withdrew her fleet from the West Indies, turning strategic control of the Carribbean over to the United States.

Some felt that the United States gave little in return. Despite pro-British sentiment in the White House, Anglophobia remained strong in the Senate, especially among Senators with Irish-American constituents. In Cleveland's day and again in Taft's, the Senate rejected Anglo-American arbitration treaties. Anti-British sentiment figured in the rejection of the first Hay-Pauncefote Treaty and the passage of the Panama Canal Tolls Act. Twisting the lion's tail still paid off in Irish-American and German-American districts. And some progressives were suspicious of the British because of the close relations between Wall Street and British bankers.

Still, Anglo-American coöperation did become a reality. Hay's Open Door Notes of 1899 were drafted by a Britisher. The United States, Britain, and Japan worked together during the Russo-Japanese War, against France and Russia. At the Algeciras Conference of 1906, the Americans worked with the French and British against the Germans. And on both sides of the Atlantic, citizens said that war between Britain and the United States was unthinkable, that the English-speaking nations would stand together in the future.

By 1914, Britain was allied to France, Japan, and Russia. Franco-American relations were improving at the time, partly owing to French efforts to win American friendship. Japanese-American relations, traditionally good, were taking a turn for the worst. There was even greater friction between Russia and the United States. Fairly friendly in the nineteenth century, these nations ran into difficulties in the twentieth. There were economic clashes in northeast Asia, where America favored and Russia opposed the open door. No less significant was Tsarist persecution of Russian and foreign Jews. Russian unwillingness to give passports to American Jews finally resulted in termination of a Russian-American commercial treaty in 1911.

Though sometimes irritated with Britain's allies, most Americans emphatically preferred the Anglo-Russian-French entente to the opposing alliance (Germany, Austria-Hungary, Turkey, the Central Powers). During the nineteenth century there had been much pro-German sentiment in the United States. Some was associated with German immigrants, some with Americans who had studied in Germany. But German unification had changed the pattern after 1870. The new German empire was aggressive and efficient; and Americans were concerned.

Friction developed at several points. Government-subsidized German firms captured Latin-American markets which Americans desired. Americans ran into German competition in Samoa and China. Germany plainly preferred Spain in the Spanish-American War of 1898. After that conflict, the German empire bought Spain's remaining islands in the Pacific and thus secured potential naval bases close to America's Pacific strongholds. In addition, citizens of the United States were alarmed by the violent public statements of Kaiser Wilhelm II and were impressed by the anti-German views of leading Britishers.

To most Americans, the trend toward Britain and away from Germany did not matter much, one way or the other. Actually, it was exceedingly important. As a great power, the American republic had great influence. And in a world that would soon be torn by war, few facts would be more telling than the American alignment with Britain.

23

In World War I

On April 6, 1917, the United States declared war on Germany and became a belligeren· 'n the First World War. Americans had mixed in European wars since colonial days. Normally, however, they had confined their participation to the "American phase" of these conflicts. In 1917–18, however, the United States was a world power, able and ready to play an active role in the war in Europe as well as outside. Involvement was economic as well as military, the American industrial and agrarian economy being geared to war production.

Why did the United States go to war in 1917? President Wilson and other Americans felt that their republic was called on to save democracy, to crush autocracy as represented by the German Kaiser, Wilhelm II. Historians supported this position, noting that Germany had broken treaty obligations by invading neutral Belgium and had offended further by taking American lives with the new submarine weapon. Postwar disillusionment brought forth other views. By the 1930's revisionist historians were suggesting that the United States had been drawn into war in 1917 by British propaganda, or by American bankers who had lent money to the Allies, or because trade with the Allies gave the United States an economic stake in Allied victory. In the 1940's, World War II caused some writers to reconsider their revisionist views and to defend the earlier claim that declaration of war in 1917 was a matter of defending democracy.

Sympathy for the Allies

Despite conflicting interpretations, it is clear that the basic sympathy of most Americans was with the Allies. The United States was bound to one of the Allies, Great Britain, by ties of blood and culture. Americans spoke English, read and appreciated English literature, had a government and society based in large part on British institutions. Trade and investment further linked the English-speaking nations, notably Canada and the United States. Finally, a generation of diplomacy had pointed toward Anglo-American coöperation.

Relations with the other Allies were less intimate. There was, however, a tradition of Franco-American friendship, dating back to the American Revolution and symbolized by the French gift of the Statue of Liberty to the American people (1886). In contrast, the leading Central Power, Germany, was regarded with suspicion by many Americans. Particularly disturbing were the Kaiser's saber rattling and German-American competition in Latin America and the Orient.

During the years of American neutrality (1914–17), sympathy for the Allies and distrust of Germany increased. Being well organized for war, the Germans scored heavily at the start, occupying most of Belgium and smashing into France. Meanwhile, Germany's partner, Austria-Hungary, went after little Serbia. This aroused traditional American fondness for the underdog, the more so since Belgium had been neutralized by international agreement. Americans were also influenced by the German use of the U-boat, or submarine. Though strong on land, Germany could not match the British fleet. But the Germans could and did challenge British sea power by using submarines to sink merchant vessels bound for British shores. Striking without warning, the U-boats took a heavy toll in ships and lives. The dead included women and children as well as men, neutrals as well as belligerents. Many Americans thereupon concluded that undersea warfare was improper, and that the Germans were breaking the rules of international law and fair play.

News treatment supported this position. The Central Powers had no way to send information quickly to America. (Britain cut German-American cable connections early in the war, and the radio was not yet a very satisfactory medium.) Germany established a propaganda unit in New York under Dr. Dernburg; but the job was bungled, and, in any case, Americans were not receptive to the German point of view. With the Allies it was another story. Britain had access to the cables, and censored news as it went through to the United States. To this was added a publicity campaign, skillfully directed by Sir Gilbert Parker. British propaganda stressed German activities in Belgium ("Hun atrocities") and the "inhumanity" of the U-boat campaign. Use was made of names well known in America—Rudyard Kipling and James Bryce, for instance.

The British blockade prevented American trade with the Central Powers; hence the United States had no economic stake in German victory. Trade with the Allies, on the other hand, increased enormously during the years of neutrality. This commerce headed off a threatened depression in 1914 and gave prosperity to American farmers and industrialists. Some citizens felt that this association with the Allies was unfortunate, especially in munitions. But most Americans approved of the trend, because of pro-Ally attitudes and profits.

To finance purchases, France, Britain, and other Allies borrowed $2,000,-000,000 from private American investors by 1917. Citizens who bought French and British bonds were of course already pro-Ally—many were businessmen who were selling goods to Britain. In all probability, however, their bond purchases increased their concern for Allied victory. Fearing this, neutral-minded Secretary of State William Jennings Bryan refused to allow belligerents to float bond issues in the United States in 1914–15, though he did allow banks to extend short-term credit. But when Bryan left the State Department, in 1915, long-term loans were authorized.

Concerned over American aid to Britain, Germany protested. When this approach proved ineffective, German agents in the United States organized water-front strikes to delay loading of ships bound for Britain. They used dummy corporations to corner key raw materials. Franz von Papen, the German military attaché, also tried direct action—blowing up munitions plants. Being poorly organized, these activities did not materially affect American production; but anti-German sentiment soared when Americans learned about sabotage operations.

Some of the most effective pro-British work was done by a League to Enforce Peace, organized in 1915 to build sentiment for a postwar League of Nations. The League to Enforce Peace was also, and emphatically, pro-Ally. It received good publicity in most newspapers (the Hearst chain being an exception). In addition, Germany was condemned in pulpits, classrooms, business, farm, and labor periodicals, and in a great flood of pro-British books.

The Other Side

Though general, anti-German sentiment was not unanimous. German-Americans were critical of the Allies. So were the Irish-Americans, who cared little for Germany but harbored a deep hatred for the Englsh. Many middle-western agriculturalists were also affected by Anglophobia. Farm leaders who had long disliked the tie-up of Wall Street with British finance now noted that J. P. Morgan and Company was Allied purchasing agent in America. The Socialists and the I.W.W. condemned both sides in this "imperialist" war; and pacifists opposed any step likely to take the United States into battle.

Had they pulled together, these groups might have had great influence. Working separately, they were ineffective. It was easy for the opposition to dismiss the pacifists as cranks, to call the Socialists dangerous radicals, to denounce the immigrant groups as disloyal. In 1916 both President Wilson and ex-President Theodore Roosevelt attacked citizens of Irish and German ancestry as "hyphenated Americans."

By then, Americans were overwhelmingly anti-German. Still, few desired war. A popular song was "I Didn't Raise My Boy to Be a Soldier." In the campaign of 1916, Democratic managers found that voters gave Wilson little credit for his anti-German utterances but were definitely interested in the slogan, "He kept us out of war." Americans were not neutral "in thought," as Wilson had advised them to be in 1914. They preferred the Allies. But there was little of the "get-in-the-fight" feeling that had swept the country in 1898.

Wilson and Neutral Rights

Nonetheless, the United States did get in the fight. As early as 1915, President Wilson took a firm stand on German violations of neutral rights. At the time, Germany yielded. When the Germans changed policy early in 1917, Wilson severed diplomatic relations with Germany; and war soon followed.

Actually, both sides infringed on neutral rights. The British interfered with United States mail; seized American property under doubtful interpretations of the international rules of contraband and continuous voyage; limited trade between the United States and Europe; prepared black lists of American firms suspected of trading with Germany. Although the United States protested against these practices, Wilson considered them less serious than the acts of Germany. Why? Partly because Wilson and his chief advisers were pro-British. Also, apparently, because British interference with property rights seldom cost life. German submarine activity, on the other hand, resulted in the loss of over 200 American lives.

Under international law, belligerent warships are supposed to give notice before they sink enemy merchant ships. The German U-boats sank without warning, which made for heavy losses on the vessels that went down. Defending their practice, the Germans said that submarines were frail. If they came to the surface to give warning, they could be rammed, or destroyed by fire from an armed merchant vessel's deck guns. To avoid trouble, neutral citizens should travel on neutral ships. Some Americans agreed —Bryan among the Democrats, La Follette among the Republicans. In 1916, Congress nearly passed the Gore-McLemore resolution, designed to keep Americans off belligerent vessels. But the resolution was defeated, by White House pressure.

The first submarine crises came in 1915, when U-boats sank several Allied ships on which Americans were traveling. The chief case was that of the *Lusitania*, an English merchant vessel sunk off the Irish coast. Of the thousand passengers who lost their lives, 128 were Americans, nearly half being women and children. The *Lusitania* was a belligerent vessel traveling in a war zone; and it was carrying contraband (cartridges). But the ship was unarmed and was not carrying troops. As might have been expected, the *Lusitania* affair created a great furor in the United States. Nevertheless, Secretary of State Bryan felt that if the United States protested German actions, it should at the same time crack down on Britain's violations of neutral rights. When Wilson insisted on a firm stand against Germany, Bryan resigned. Wilson thereupon gave the State Department post to Robert Lansing, a pronounced Anglophile.

Having overruled Bryan, Wilson ruled that U-boat commanders should safeguard American lives, even on Allied ships. Not desiring to have the United States enter the war, the Germans gave way, and stopped unrestricted submarine warfare. It was resumed on February 1, 1917, when Germany set out to sink all belligerent and neutral vessels heading for the British Isles or France. The hope was to bring Britain to her knees before the United States could give effective aid to the Allies.

Woodrow Wilson was definitely pro-British. In 1916 he permitted his personal agent Colonel House to intimate to Britain that, under certain circumstances, the United States might join the Allies against Germany. Yet the President really hoped that the United States would not have to take up arms. As late as the end of 1916 he talked of settling the war by compromise ("peace without victory"). Early in 1917, when the Germans announced resumption of unrestricted submarine warfare, Wilson gave the German ambassador his passports. But even then the Chief Executive hoped against hope that a declaration of hostilities would not be necessary.

Declaring War (April, 1917)

The nation, however, rapidly moved toward war. In February and March, 1917, U-boats sank Allied ships with American citizens aboard, and sank American vessels, too. Wilson asked Congress for authority to arm merchant craft, only to run into a Senate filibuster led by Senators La Follette and Norris. Denouncing the filibusterers as eleven "willful men," the President had the ships armed anyway, under authority of a statute of 1797.

Just then—March, 1917—the British gave the United States an intercepted German message to Mexico. This Zimmermann wrote proposed a German-Mexican-Japanese alliance in case war broke out between the United States and Germany. Germany would help Mexico (how, was not clear), and Mexico would regain her "lost territory" of Texas, New Mexico,

Arizona. When set before the American public, this astounding dispatch inflamed opinion against Germany and took the United States closer to war.

In this same month came news of the overthrow of the Russian czar in the March Revolution. Eight months later, the Provisional Russian government would be overthrown by Communists; but in March, 1917, it seemed that Russia would have an American-type republican government. Hence one could say that all the Allies believed in democracy, and that World War I was a conflict between democracy and autocracy. So Wilson felt; so he said when, early in April, 1917, he asked Congress to declare war against Germany. The House and Senate responded, 373–50 and 82–6. The votes roughly reflected public opinion. Although some Americans held back, most had come to consider war inevitable.

Economic Conversion to War

American industry was unprepared for war in 1917. This is not surprising, for the United States had fought no major war for a half-century. Then, too, modern war calls for governmental planning. Despite progressive reforms, American business still regulated its own affairs in 1917. In some industries control rested with a few monopolists; in others there was sharp competition. Either way, businessmen ran the show, and prized freedom from the governmental control that is essential in military crises.

During the neutrality years (1914–17), a few leaders unsuccessfully urged industrial preparation for war. In 1916—rather late—Wilson created a Council of National Defense, made up of cabinet officers, with an advisory committee of business and labor leaders. By April, 1917, the Council had made some suggestions; but most of these had been disregarded by both business and government. Such preparation as there was stemmed from Allied war orders, channeled through the house of Morgan. Between 1914 and 1917 Britain and her partners spent $3,000,000,000 in the United States; and American industry expanded to meet the demand. This increased American ability to produce war goods.

Still, American declaration of war necessitated a tremendous industrial reorganization. Since businessmen could not effect the reorganization alone, government controls, quotas, and administered prices came in overnight. Later in the century, such phenomena would be familiar to all Americans. But they were strange in 1917, and came as a shock to business.

The difficulties were many. A new airplane engine or artillery weapon required months of planning and thousands of blueprints. New machines needed to make the parts called for much consideration. Solution of these problems still left questions of labor, materials, and transportation. Allied purchasing in the neutrality period had brought Americans close to full employment. Hence the diversion of man power to war production meant abandoning some civilian activities. This in turn necessitated government-directed allocation of materials, capital, and labor.

Confusion reigned in 1917. The Council of National Defense established a War Industries Board in July, 1917, but failed to give the Board sufficient power. Priorities were established with little regard to time schedules or the quantity of goods available. Raw materials delivered to processors ahead of schedule were left on sidings in freight cars, while those cars were urgently needed elsewhere. Army and navy, American and Allied priorities were in conflict with each other, and no one had final power to control allocations. The transportation situation was worst of all. Too many contracts were let in areas where traffic was overcongested. The thirty-two major railroad systems, held apart by the Sherman Antitrust Act, could not unsnarl the tangle. Conditions became worse each month, as shippers routed orders through bottleneck port areas, particularly New York. By the end of 1917 the jam of freight cars and cargo boats in that city was threatening to halt the movement of supplies to Europe.

Would inefficiency mean defeat? Fearing that it might, President Wilson exercised the sweeping war powers conferred on him by the Constitution and by acts of Congress (e.g., the Lever Act of August, 1917, the Overman Act of May, 1918). In December, 1917, he seized the railroads and coördinated them into one vast government-administered system under Secretary of the Treasury William G. McAdoo. In January, 1918, Wilson took over the telephone and telegraph lines. Two months later he gave the War Industries Board control over prices and allocations, and vested power in its chairman, Bernard Baruch. By summer, 1918, America at last had a smoothly functioning war machine.

Industrial productivity depended on the very men whom the progressives had denounced. In 1917 and 1918, leading capitalists were recruited for government service, many as "dollar-a-year men." Examples are Daniel Willard of the Baltimore and Ohio Railroad; Julius Rosenwald of Sears, Roebuck; and Charles M. Schwab of Bethlehem Steel. The presence of these men in government gradually changed the tone of the Wilson administration.

The key man in the structure was Bernard Baruch, a successful member of the New York Stock Exchange. Baruch's War Industries Board leaned heavily on manufacturers' trade associations and on the United States Chamber of Commerce. These organizations reported on who could make what and how soon. Some effort was made to reach medium-sized and even small producers. But, since drawing up many contracts was time-consuming, the tendency was to rely heavily on industrial giants. Wilson, long a foe of bigness, helped make the largest producers larger yet.

To insure maximum supply, the government set prices high enough to cover costs of production in inefficient plants. Inevitably, then, the larger, more efficient companies made huge profits. Nevertheless, profits for business as a whole were lower in 1917 than in 1916, and lower still in 1918 (after the imposition of excess-profits taxes). War was less rewarding than neutrality.

The most serious shortage was in ships. Sinkings far exceeded launchings in early 1917, when the U-boats were most effective. To handle the problem, America and Britain worked out antisubmarine devices. The United States seized and pressed into service enemy and neutral cargo ships. Meantime, new construction was pushed. High rates had stimulated American building even before the American declaration of war. A third of a million gross tons had been completed in 1916. This doubled in 1917. Knowing that still more was needed, the Wilson administration encouraged shipbuilding concerns, and also went directly into business. The Shipping Board established a government-owned Emergency Fleet Corporation and authorized it to construct freighters. But building ships is a slow job. The government was just getting into production when the war ended (November, 1918). Building was continued after the armistice; and by 1921 the United States had 9,000,000 gross tons of slow, uneconomical freighters, for which there was little peacetime use.

Raw materials also presented problems. Food and fuels were placed under federal administrators in the summer of 1917. These administrators, like Baruch of the War Industries Board, bought at prices high enough to bring out maximum production. As an illustration, Food Administrator Herbert Hoover announced that his Grain Corporation would pay $2.20 a bushel for wheat produced in 1917, $2.26 for the 1918 crop. In 1913, the price had been 97¢.

Encouraged by price trends and government appeals for top production, farmers expanded their operations. Wheat acreage in 1919 was 20 percent above any previous year. (For various reasons, however, the total yield was below that of 1915, the only billion-bushel year before World War II.) Unfortunately, much of the land added to cultivation was marginal—unlikely to show profit in peacetime. Much of this acreage was bought with funds borrowed from government Farm Loan Banks; and the war boom was too short to enable farmers to repay the money.

Efforts to control civilian consumption were on a voluntary basis. Price fixing and rationing were not applied directly to consumers. Automobiles, tires, and gasoline went unrationed, although motorists were asked to avoid unnecessary driving. There were wheatless, meatless, and heatless days. Enforcement, though, was limited to individual action and the force of community opinion.

Paying for War

American banks and investors financed the Allied cause in the neutrality period (1914–17). With American entry into the war, the government assumed this function. During and after the war the American Treasury advanced $10,000,000,000 to the Allies. Including these war loans, the direct cost of World War I to the United States from April, 1917, to June, 1920, was about $32,000,000,000.

Although these sums seem large, war costs approached a quarter of the national income only in 1918. Had Congress imposed high taxes in April, 1917, the United States could have financed World War I on a pay-as-you-go basis. Doing so would have spared the aged and salaried groups the economic distress of postwar inflation. But Congress rejected pay-as-you-go, feeling it would be politically unpopular, might discourage business, and would reduce war enthusiasm. Congress did, however, vote moderate taxes in the spring of 1917. These were increased during the year, again in 1918. Income taxes were sharply increased, the government taking three-quarters of 1918 incomes above $1,000,000. Tobacco and liquor taxes, inheritance duties, and postal rates were stepped up, and the government taxed express, railroad, telephone, and telegraph charges, automobiles, insurance, theater admissions and club dues, and many "luxury" items (yachts, cosmetics, jewelry, chewing gum, sporting goods). The yield, however, was only $11,000,000,000 for 1917–20, one-third of the cost of the war.

Two-thirds, then, had to be obtained by borrowing. This reënacted Civil War history—but with a difference. In the Civil War, greenbacks had been needed. The creation of the Federal Reserve System just before World War I enabled the Wilson administration to raise money by selling short-term certificates and bonds directly to the banks. Although inflationary, this was not as upsetting as unsupported paper money.

To retire the certificates held by banks, the Treasury sold long-term bonds to the public. Liberty Bonds were marketed at local rallies and movie houses, and advertised in poster campaigns. Bonds were sold through employers and in door-to-door canvasses; war savings stamps were marketed in the schools. Volunteer committees exerted pressure on those reluctant to coöperate; hence the government netted $21,000,000,000 in four Liberty Loans and a post-armistice Victory Loan. The smaller bonds ($100 and less) were bought largely from savings. The larger denominations were purchased by banks, which then created deposits to the government's account, or by businessmen who used the bonds as security for loans. These operations did not represent real savings, and were inflationary. Here was a basic cause for the 85 percent rise in living costs between 1916 and 1920.

Civil War inflation had hurt workers. Organization and labor shortages made the World War I situation somewhat better for workingmen. For all workers, wage increases nearly kept pace with the rise in cost of living through 1918, and forged ahead in 1919–20. White-collar workers and those living on savings and annuities were less fortunate. Living costs nearly doubled between 1916 and 1920; but clerical salaries advanced only 25 percent, and teachers' pay remained virtually stationary. Citizens living on pensions or fixed salaries lost nearly half their purchasing power.

Meanwhile, war profits were aiding the more fortunate. In 1910 the top tenth made 34 percent of the national income, the bottom tenth 3½ percent. Ten years later, the figures were 38 percent and 2 percent. The average member of the top group received ten times as much income as the average in the bottom group in 1910, nineteen times as much a decade later. World War I had made the rich richer, the poor relatively poorer.

The Labor Force

Samuel Gompers of the American Federation of Labor became a member of the Advisory Commission to the Council of National Defense even before the United States entered the war. He lost no time in pledging labor's coöperation in the war effort. A.F. of L. unions would not strike. Workers would buy Liberty Bonds, and would stick to the job, not drift from plant to plant. In return, Gompers hoped employers would not interfere with organizing drives.

Results were generally satisfactory. There was antilabor sentiment, as indicated by the passage of work-or-fight laws in half a dozen states. In addition, the federal Espionage Act was used to imprison radical labor leaders. But a War Labor Board kept the peace in manufacturing centers. Workers set production records; many employers agreed to bargain collectively. The war also established the basic eight-hour day (overtime extra). Applied to railroads by the Adamson Act of 1916, the principle was extended by application to war contracts of a 1912 statute which had fixed eight hours as the working day for government employees.

During the war, Gompers refrained from pushing hard to unionize the most vital war industries (steel, motors, chemicals). In consequence, union membership increased moderately, about 25 percent, between 1916 and 1918. After the armistice (November, 1918) organizational and strike activities were increased. Union strength went up 50 percent in 1919–20. Some 4,000,000 workers went on strike in 1919—a larger number and higher percentage of workers than in any other year in America's history. Some strikes failed, as in steel. Others succeeded; and labor's real wages went to a new high. The new level prevailed in the 1920's, despite the relative inefficiency of labor leadership.

American participation in World War I accentuated the characteristic American tendency to move. Two million American men crossed the Atlantic, and almost as many more moved about the United States, from camp to camp. Job opportunities in war plants lured rural citizens to urban centers. Wages were high, even in terms of soaring prices, because of the drain of man power to the armed forces and the virtual cessation of immigration (except from Mexico).

No aspect of country-to-city migration was more dramatic than the movement of southern Negroes to industrial centers. This began before World War I and continued afterward; but the war brought the trend to climax. Many Negroes who left the soil went to nearby southern cities. Others took the longer trip north. In doing so, they sought not only good pay but also the social freedom and cultural opportunities that the North was said to offer. So the 1920 census, as compared with that of 1910, showed a proportionate decrease of colored population to total population throughout the South. There was a corresponding gain in such northern states as Illinois, Michigan, Pennsylvania, and New York.

But all did not go well. Negro migration to the cities presented the usual problems of adjustment of rural people to urban ways. Difficulties were heightened by bad conditions in the slums into which the Negroes necessarily moved. There was discrimination, too, in the North as well as the South, and bloody race riots in East St. Louis and Chicago. Disheartened, some Negroes went back home. But the great majority stayed. Opportunities were limited, North and South. Negroes could not get into unions. They met with discrimination in employment (last hired, first fired). Even a prosperous, educated Negro could not buy a house in the better residential areas, be he in the South or North. Most clubs and restaurants were closed to him. But, both in northern and southern cities, educational and economic opportunities were better than on share-crop farms. The political outlook was better, too. Negroes could vote in some southern and all northern cities; and they had substantial influence in the latter.

World War I opened jobs to women. In many cases, children suffered. But pay was good; and employment gave women a feeling of independence. Besides, it was considered patriotic to work in a war plant, as a million women did.

By demonstrating the capability of women in industry, the war emphasized the absurdity of denying women the vote. The point was the more clear in view of Wilson's claim that this was a war to make the world safe for democracy. Suffragettes, while shouldering their full share of war duties, made it plain that they expected the vote when the shooting stopped. Earlier, Wilson had believed in leaving this matter to the states. Now he decided that the nation must act. In September, 1918, he announced that successful prosecution of the war required ratification of the proposed woman-suffrage amendment. Thanks to his prodding and other influences, the Nineteenth Amendment became a part of the Constitution soon after the armistice.

War Attitudes

Some Americans opposed the declaration of war in 1917. Many more, though willing to accept Wilsonian leadership, thought of the conflict as little related to their lives. Volunteering lagged. The government therefore adopted conscription; and it also set out to sell the war to the people, through a Committee on Public Information, directed by an able journalist, George Creel. The C.P.I. promoted hatred of the enemy. Creel had 75,000 volunteer speakers who gave short patriotic talks at every sort of public meeting. The audience total for these "four-minute men" was nearly a third of a billion. The C.P.I. also had artists prepare huge posters depicting the brutality of the "Hun" foe and the idealistic nature of the Allied cause. Journalists, clergymen, and professors wrote pamphlets detailing German atrocities and ambitions. A hundred million of these pamphlets reached the public. Creel also had handouts for daily and weekly newspapers; and the movie industry turned out such films as *The Beast of Berlin*.

This propaganda aided the war effort. But it so excited the public that Americans considered it disloyal to speak German, play German music, or retain German place and family names. Colleges and schools dropped German courses. Musicians of German background had to endure public insults—Fritz Kreisler, for example.

Most of this was unnecessary. Virtually all immigrants from enemy countries wholeheartedly supported their adopted land. So did the overwhelming majority of native Americans, including those who had been active in the peace movement. Such dissidents as there were, a tiny minority, hardly justified the widespread hysteria. And this emotionalism, carrying over into the postwar period, would help create antiliberal and antilabor movements.

The question of pacifism came to the fore when religious objectors were called in the draft. About 4000 refused, on grounds of conscience, to put on the uniform. Nine-tenths of these finally agreed to serve, e.g., in the Medical Corps. Those refusing any sort of service, or declining to obey military orders after induction, were tried and sent to prison. Some were given cruel treatment; and nearly all were kept behind bars for years after the war.

Some left-wingers also opposed the war. A Socialist convention said the conflict stemmed from capitalist and imperialist exploitation; but Upton Sinclair and many rank-and-file Socialists backed the war effort. There was prowar feeling even among the Industrial Workers of the World. I.W.W. leaders, though, condemned Wilsonianism and would not join the A.F. of L. in taking Gompers' no-strike pledge. Rather the Wobblies saw the war as a chance to undermine capitalism. But when they staged strikes in western copper and lumber camps, they met with determined opposition from local officials and an enraged citizenry. A Montana crowd lynched an I.W.W. leader; and Wobbly strikers in Arizona were forcibly deported beyond the state line.

Some moves against opponents of the war were worked out in coöperation with the federal government. Wilson's Justice Department sponsored an American Protective League, with 250,000 members. These patriots watched their neighbors, ostracizing, insulting, or reporting those deemed insufficiently ardent in support of the war. As for legislation, Congress in 1917 adopted an Espionage Act, fixing fines and imprisonment for those guilty of inciting disloyalty or interfering with recruiting. Later in 1917 a Trading-with-the-Enemy Act broadened Wilson's censorship powers. In 1918 came Sabotage and Sedition acts, the latter authorizing punishment of anyone using disloyal language or attacking the government, Constitution, flag, uniform, or war effort.

In enforcing these statutes, the government arrested 2000 persons. In most cases, the charges collapsed of their own weight, and the individuals were discharged. But Eugene V. Debs, the Socialist, went to prison. Nearly a hundred I.W.W. organizers were convicted after a sensational trial before Judge Kenesaw Mountain Landis; and their movement was broken. Meantime, the Postmaster General barred from the mails some Irish-American and German-American periodicals, and such Socialist publications as Victor Berger's Milwaukee Leader. Berger was also convicted under the Espionage Act; and when Wisconsin voters elected him to Congress at the end of the war, he was not allowed to take his seat.

Although a few religious leaders took pacifist positions, the great majority endorsed World War I as a holy crusade. Yet, curiously, the war brought no great religious revival. The stress of the times, the imminence of death, the strength of Wilsonian idealism turned some—but not many—people to the churches.

Education also rallied to the war effort. Colleges ran officer-training units; and a Student Army Training Corps was being set up in 500 institutions at the time of the armistice. The SATC was disliked by most of the military men who controlled it and the professors who provided instruction. Still, the program saved some colleges from bankruptcy and provided experience useful in later crises. More important was the contribution of scholars to the war effort. Many professors rushed off to jobs in Washington; others did military research on campus.

The schools, too, did their part. Teachers sold war savings stamps and used C.P.I. materials in their classrooms. School children were urged to persuade parents to buy more bonds, to accept the war aims, to observe meatless and wheatless days. Children saved tin foil and increased the food supply by working in school and home gardens.

Besides contributing propaganda pieces, artists, composers, actors, and authors entertained soldiers in camp. They also tried to interpret the war to the public. This effort brought forth many war songs ("Pack Up Your Troubles in Your Old Kit Bag"). Soldiers' narratives had a brisk sale; and Joyce Kilmer wrote moving war lyrics. Yet in neither music nor literature did the war bring forth much of enduring merit. The more impressive work came later, in the era of postwar disillusionment. Then deglamorized accounts of war would be presented by such writers as Ernest Hemingway (*Farewell to Arms*) and Maxwell Anderson and Laurence Stallings (*What Price Glory?*).

Winning the War

In entering the war against Germany, the United States did not declare war on the other Central Powers. To Wilson, German Kaiserism was the great threat. The American republic did, at the end of 1917, declare war against Austria-Hungary, doing so because one of the Allies, Italy, needed help. The United States also broke relations with Turkey. Here, though, there was no formal declaration of hostilities (such a declaration would have hurt American missionary interests in the Turkish Empire). Diplomatic relations with Bulgaria were maintained through the war.

The United States was not, then, an all-out participant in World War I. Along the same line, the American republic did not become one of the Allies. To have done so would have irritated citizens who were attached to the old no-alliance principle. Nor could America have become an Ally without raising the question of the secret treaties, which provided for postwar division of enemy territory. Preferring to postpone discussion of peace problems, Wilson called the United States an Associated Power.

This did not mean that the United States was uncoöperative. Far from it. Wilson appealed to neutrals everywhere to join in the crusade against Germany. Many did—China, Liberia, Brazil and other Latin-American countries. The United States also set aside isolation notions to insist that all the foes of Germany work together, instead of competing with each other for control of money, munitions, and transportation. Americans also had much to do with the creation in 1918 of an overall (Franco-British-American) command on the western front, under French Marshal Foch.

Yet there were many quarrels. John J. Pershing, who commanded the American Expeditionary Force (A.E.F.) in France, disliked trench warfare, which the English and French regarded as necessary. Pershing differed from his colleagues in his high rating of the rifle and low rating of the machine gun. The British had felt the same way until the battle of the Somme (1916). Thereafter, they had developed a caution that irritated the offense-minded commander of the A.E.F. French and British military leaders also felt that the inexperienced American troops should be worked into veteran Allied units. This would provide badly needed reinforcement. It would train the Americans quickly and reduce American casualties. (Trench-wise English and French soldiers could guide the newcomers.) National pride made Pershing and his superiors reject these suggestions. The French and British had separate parts of the western front: let the United States have its sector, too. It might take a little longer to train the Americans that way; but they would be effective when the war reached its decisive stage (late 1919, estimated the Americans, or 1920).

In fact, the crisis came sooner. Having gained victories to the east and south, against Russia and Italy, Germany in 1918 drove against the western front. As the French and British lines bent back, Pershing set aside his demand for a separate sector and rushed American troops into the lines. Green though they were, these Americans helped stop the German offensive in the second battle of the Marne.

When the Germans had been checked, the Americans were finally given a separate part of the western front. In the first distinctly American operation, Pershing pinched out the St.-Mihiel salient (September, 1918). Other engagements followed, in the Meuse-Argonne, as Americans joined the British and French in an advance that brought German surrender (November 11, 1918).

What was the American contribution to victory? At first, relatively little; later, a great deal. President Wilson was not converted to preparedness until 1916, and the United States was not ready to fight in April, 1917. It took many months to raise, equip, and train an American army and transport it to Europe. Only 300,000 reached France in the first year of American participation. After that, American troops poured in at the rate of 300,000 a month. All in all, 2,000,000 got to France; and if the war had lasted on into 1919, the American republic could have added at least as many more. This reinforcement boosted sagging Allied morale and turned the tide on the battlefields. When Germany's 1918 offensive failed, the German High Command knew their cause was lost. They were reaching the bottom of their man-power barrel, whereas the Americans were just coming into action. The Germans thus saw little use in fighting on; and they surrendered before Germany was invaded.

Americans heard more of General Pershing than of Admiral W. S. Sims. Yet World War I was also won at sea. One factor was the Allied blockade of Germany, established before American entry into the war. Germany's surface fleet failed in its one attempt to break the blockade (battle of Jutland, 1916). The U-boats also failed to cut Britain's supply lines. The submarines were most effective during 1917, and for a time the British cause was in grave danger. Then, with the development of antisubmarine devices, the United States and Britain reëstablished control of the Atlantic. Triumph was complete by the end of the war, as is indicated by the transportation of 2,000,000 American troops across the ocean without loss.

American vessels operated in the Mediterranean, and a few troops were sent to Italy, to help that limping Ally. Another handful went with Allied forces to north Russia in the summer of 1918, under the mistaken theory that such an operation might help the White Russians overthrow the Bolsheviks (who had seized power in November, 1917, and had made peace with Germany). This north Russian intervention lasted until after the armistice, and was closed out in the spring of 1919. Another contingent of Americans served with Allied forces in Russian Siberia, down to January, 1920. In this case, the main American purpose was to see to it that Japan did not seize Asiatic territory.

The United States Navy had done well in the war with Spain. It did better in World War I, making use of up-to-date equipment and new ideas. The army, too, made a good record. Army blunders in 1898 had led to a general overhauling, much of which took place while Elihu Root was Secretary of War under Theodore Roosevelt. A feature of this reorganization was the creation of a General Staff. In 1916 there were further changes. The old state militia system, now known as the National Guard, was fitted into the national military pattern. Inefficiency still reigned in many military bureaus; but the mistakes were not to be compared with those of former years.

Modern war depends heavily on equipment—ships, tanks, trucks, airplanes, the power of infantry and artillery weapons, the supply of food, clothing, and medicine. Starting slowly in 1917, the United States made a poor showing in some lines. Americans had to use European planes, British transports. But by war's end, the United States was in full military production and was turning out more and better goods than any other belligerent. American manufacturing was, clearly, a major factor in the world military picture.

In 1898 the military had made insufficient use of what was generally known about medicine and sanitation. During the next two decades, the armed forces caught up with and helped extend medical knowledge. Army research in Cuba aided in conquest of yellow fever; military application of these findings saved countless lives during the construction of the Panama Canal (1903–14). The army's medical experts were ready for World War I. Despite an influenza epidemic in the closing months of the war, only 60,000 men died of disease during the conflict—less than 2 percent of those mobilized. Forty thousand were killed in battle, losses being heavy in the few battles in which Americans were engaged. But improved methods of treatment saved six out of seven of the 200,000 wounded, an exceptionally high ratio.

While fighting World War I, the United States also spread propaganda. George Creel's Committee on Public Information, which whipped up war excitement at home, also functioned abroad. It explained American views in areas controlled by Allied and Associated Powers. It developed anti-German sentiment in neutral countries. It functioned behind enemy lines. Here the aim was to separate the German government and people, to persuade German soldiers and civilians that they could avoid postwar punishment if they overthrew the Kaiser and sought peace. This appears to have contributed to the breakdown of morale in the Central Powers, helping hasten the end of the war.

The Treaty of Versailles

The Allies wanted an old-fashioned peace, with the Central Powers to cede territory and pay a huge indemnity. Wilson stated different objectives in a fourteen-point peace plan of January, 1918. The Central Powers would get out of Belgium and restore territory earlier taken from France (Alsace-Lorraine). In general, though, the emphasis was on national self-determination rather than punishment. Subject peoples in the Turkish and Austro-Hungarian empires would have the right of self-government; and those who lived in German colonies would be consulted as to their future. A just peace would also establish freedom of the seas, end secret diplomacy, reduce tariff barriers, and provide for disarmament. A League of Nations would enforce the just peace and point toward a better future.

The Fourteen Points were well received in the United States. The reception was not so good in Allied countries. Wilson seems here to have made a tactical mistake. Back in April, 1917, when entering the war, the President could have insisted on Allied acceptance of his postwar plans. If the Allies refused, Wilson could then have threatened to withhold money, goods, or men. Wilson, however, had thrown his full weight into the cause without exacting any promises. This reduced his bargaining power later.

When the German offensive of 1918 failed, those who took control of Germany sought peace on the basis of the Fourteen Points. Britain, though, insisted on dropping the point relating to freedom of the seas. France asked for the inclusion of a reparations clause. That done, the armistice agreement of November, 1918, was concluded.

During the formal negotiations that followed, other Wilson points were dropped. The President himself stopped insisting on open diplomacy, and worked out the Versailles Treaty of 1919 in secret meetings with Lloyd George of Britain, Clemenceau of France, and Orlando of Italy (these being the Big Four). The point about removing economic barriers was forgotten. Disarmament was to be confined to the defeated nations. Instead of asking colonial peoples what they wanted, the Big Four assigned colonies to the victors, under the mandate system. Wilson's demand for national self-determination found expression in creation of such states as Poland and Czechoslovakia; but the settlement put Austrians in Italy, Germans in Czechoslovakia and Poland, Hungarians in Rumania. Japan won control of Shantung in China. Germany was required to accept war guilt, and to pay reparations to the Allies; and the Central Powers were not invited to join the League of Nations.

Though disappointed in the Versailles Treaty, Wilson felt it the best obtainable. The settlement did recognize the principle of national self-determination; it did set up a League of Nations, which could consider unsolved problems. So Wilson asked the Senate to approve the treaty and take the United States into the League (July, 1919). But the Senate refused.

The Senate and the League of Nations

In his first term (1913–17), Wilson had controlled Congress. As he turned his attention to world affairs, he seemed to lose touch with domestic developments. This was important, for Wilson had won reëlection in 1916 by the narrowest margin. Hence if neglecting home affairs meant losing ground, it meant losing control.

The declaration of hostilities in 1917 was supported by both major parties. War measures were backed by Republicans as well as Democrats. Wilson, however, refused to set up a bipartisan war cabinet; and in the fall of 1918 (just before the armistice) he asked the people for a Democratic Congress. Wilson's Republican foes then accused the President of playing politics in war time. This swung some votes. More shifted because of dissatisfaction with wartime controls. Leadership was involved, too. Will Hays, chairman of the Republican National Committee, healed wounds in his party, persuaded progressives and conservatives to work in harmony. Success crowned his efforts; the Republicans won the Congressional elections of 1918 and control of both houses of Congress.

This meant that the peace treaty would go before a Senate run by Wilson's opponents. That being the case, Wilson should have let the Republicans share in the peacemaking process. That is, he should have put a leading Republican like Elihu Root on the commission to negotiate the Versailles Treaty. Instead, Wilson headed the commission himself, and took with him to Paris his Democratic Secretary of State Robert Lansing and his Democratic adviser Colonel House. One obscure Republican participated; but it was Wilson's treaty; and, as the Republicans knew, its acceptance by the Senate would be a Wilsonian, Democratic victory.

Only fifteen of the ninety-five Senators (one vacancy) opposed the treaty and the League outright. These were the irreconcilables, many of them progressive Republicans who had long regarded Wilson with distrust (La Follette, Norris, Hiram Johnson, William E. Borah of Idaho). The other eighty Senators favored the treaty and the League. Half of the eighty were Wilson Democrats who wanted the treaty as it stood or with Wilson-approved amendments. (John Sharp Williams of Mississippi and Gilbert M. Hitchcock of Nebraska are examples.) The other forty were Republican reservationists, like Frank B. Kellogg of Minnesota. Though friendly to the League, they insisted on tacking on Republican reservations, so that their party could get credit.

With eighty for and fifteen against, victory for the treaty seemed probable. But the fifteen irreconcilables had their way. One reason was the position of Henry Cabot Lodge, Republican chairman of the Senate Foreign Relations Committee. Formerly a League man, Lodge swung to the irreconcilables, partly for political reasons, partly because of personal dislike for Wilson. Another factor was a popular anti-League campaign, financed by Henry Clay Frick and Andrew W. Mellon. Party politics was even more important. Republican reservationists who wanted the League felt that, for party reasons, they could not accept the Versailles Treaty as it stood, or with Wilson-sponsored amendments. They therefore joined the irreconcilables in voting against the treaty in those forms. Wilson Democrats were just as unwilling to yield to their political opponents; so they voted against the treaty with Republican amendments. In consequence, the treaty and League were beaten all around.

Wilson then appealed to the people. This was an old method of his, and it had worked before. But the President broke down on a 1919 speaking tour; and he was an ineffective leader thereafter.

He might have failed in any case. For the people, though moderately pro-League, were unenthusiastic. During the war Americans felt that beating Germany would save the world for democracy. But when the war was over, they felt let down, disillusioned. With war excitement gone, France and England seemed less attractive partners than before. The Kaiser was defeated; but there were new dangers to democracy. Communists had taken hold of eastern Europe; the Japanese were rising in the Orient; distress and want haunted the Western world. International problems, apparently, were less simple than they had seemed to George Creel's four-minute men. And in 1919, Americans were concerned over rising prices and strikes. These matters absorbed attention and made the average man indifferent to the fate of the League of Nations.

Campaign of 1920

The lack of interest in the Versailles Treaty was apparent in the campaign of 1920. The Democrats nominated for President James M. Cox, who had made a progressive record as governor of Ohio; for Vice-President, Franklin D. Roosevelt, who had a magic name and had been an efficient Assistant Secretary of the Navy. Cox and Roosevelt ran on a pro-Wilson, pro-League platform; but they won little backing. The voters seemed tired of Wilson, tired of the Democrats, tired of talk about the League.

If Theodore Roosevelt had been alive, he would probably have been Republican nominee in 1920. His death in 1919 left the field wide open. After some jockeying, the political managers arranged in a smoke-filled room to give the nomination to Senator Warren G. Harding of Ohio. Second place went to Governor Calvin Coolidge of Massachusetts, who had achieved some notice for opposing a Boston police strike. Harding staged a quiet ("front porch") campaign, in the McKinley tradition. He stressed opposition to the Wilsonian war controls and asked for a "return to normalcy." Harding had an anti-League, Coolidge a pro-League record. Both made confusing statements during the campaign; and their supporters added to the uncertainty. Some Republicans, including Hiram Johnson, were sure that Harding was anti-League. Others, like Taft and Herbert

Hoover, announced that they considered Harding pro-League. Take your choice.

The campaign of 1920 ended with a smashing victory for Harding and Coolidge. Most League supporters found the result disheartening. They hastened to state, however, that the election really proved nothing, in view of Republican hedging on the League question. But if Americans had really wanted the League, and had considered the issue important, they would have gone to Cox. The Harding victory did not show that Americans hated the League; but it indicated that they did not take the matter very seriously.

Rejection of the Versailles Treaty meant that the United States would not form close political relations with major European powers. Much the same decision was made when other issues came to the fore. Wilson proposed, and the Senate rejected, an Anglo-French-American alliance. The Senators also refused to consider having the United States take mandate control over Armenia; and they would not approve of the United States' joining the World Court (Permanent Court of International Justice), even though this was favored by Wilson and his three Republican successors.

Yet the American republic was not abandoning its world power position. For the United States remained a great military nation and, on the economic side, pushed outward more vigorously than before.

Part VII

Contemporary America

(Since 1919)

The period since World War I has brought a succession of crises. After prosperity in the 1920's there were ten desperate years of depression (1929–39), during which the whole American economy seemed to be on trial. Then came involvement in global war. The collapse of Germany and Japan brought an uneasy peace, featured by Russian-American conflict, and, after 1950, fighting in Korea.

At mid-century, the United States was the wealthiest nation the world had ever known. Most Americans enjoyed a high standard of living, and there were indications that it would be higher still. But, living in a troubled world, many felt confused and uncertain. In three and a half centuries, Americans had accomplished a great deal; but much remained undone.

24

Business and the
General Welfare

Depression and war divided the years after World War I into three parts. From 1919 to 1929 life seemed to resume nineteenth-century patterns. But the stock market crash of 1929 ushered in a decade of depression. The outbreak of World War II in 1939 inaugurated a third period, which covered the war (1939–45) and its aftermath. Business trends in this third period seemed to reëstablish ordered prosperity. Yet Americans knew their world had changed. All now saw what a few intellectuals had noted in the 1920's—the subtle problems of urban life, the insecurity of an industrial economy. Men and women now groped for certainty rather than for new adventure. College graduates hoped for comfortable, secure lives rather than the opportunity to get rich. Businessmen accepted security at the expense of salary and profits. Workers, enjoying the highest standard of living in history, demanded the additional assurances of state support in old age and adversity. Concern over atom bombs merely symbolized the deeper fear of the ruthless impersonality of an urban industrial society.

The Business Cycle

Immediately after the armistice in November, 1918, there was a sharp upswing in American business. Then came a collapse, caused mainly by overbuying of inventories (material for manufacture or sale). After 1921 came seven relatively prosperous years. Real per capita income rose 13 percent from 1923 to 1929. There was suffering because of technological unemployment, and depression in farm areas and declining industries. But most Americans shared in the gains.

In contrast with earlier booms, the upswing after 1923 did not see overexpansion of production and transportation. The productive area of the economy was in balance. Wholesale prices and long-term interest rates rose little. Wages were steady; and until 1927 there was no great boom in the stock market. Then came peculiar developments. Beginning in 1927, there was a slowing down of activity in building, automobiles, and foreign lending. Yet the stock market boomed. Had a depression come in 1927, it might have been moderate. The unsound stock market boom of 1927–29 led ultimately to more serious difficulties. In earlier decades, unstable prosperity had been prolonged by land booms. Now, it was speculation in stocks.

In the twentieth century, automobiles, radios, and electric refrigerators had become increasingly important. These consumers' goods had an indefinite length of life. If times were good, householders bought new models. If times were bad, the old model was kept in use. Which meant that depression cut production (and employment) more than in earlier periods. Once begun, the downward spiral affected all commodities. Hence heavy consumer buying of durable goods introduced an explosive element into the economy.

The depression that set in after the crash of 1929 was complicated by European difficulties. The cost of World War I had never been adjusted in a way that would permit a general return to prosperity. The Old World economy was held up in the 1920's by American loans—by foreign bond issues floated on Wall Street and sold to private American investors. When the New York stock market crash of 1929 stopped the flow of money from America to Europe, Old World nations suspended international debt payments. This upset trade relations; and by 1932 the entire Western world was in a desperate situation.

At this juncture John Maynard Keynes gained new followers. This British economist saw the problem in the relation between new investment and savings. If savings were invested in new labor-employing ventures, prosperity was possible. If this investment lagged behind savings, there would be unemployment and depression. In such a situation, the government should redress the balance by investing in public works.

Putting it another way: Keynes felt that the poor (who had to spend their income) received too little, and that the rich (who could save) received too much. Thus savings accumulated, instead of going into new labor-employing ventures. The way out was to get rid of the savings of the rich by heavy taxation of upper-bracket income. The proceeds could be distributed among the poor for relief or for work on government construction projects. And government spending would stimulate business activity in general, thus encouraging private capitalists to invest what savings they retained in new ventures, which would mean more jobs.

Closely related was the belief that the national debt could be an economic stabilizer. In depression, the government could use deficit financing —increase the debt and spend money on relief and public works employment. During prosperity, the debt could be paid off by higher taxation.

Keynes was, of course, providing a theory that fitted the practical situation. In spite of the old rule that revenue and expenditures should be roughly equal, government budgets of the 1930's were unbalanced all over the world. President Herbert Hoover (1929–33) deplored deficits, but had them just the same. His successor Franklin D. Roosevelt (1933–45) was less bothered by mounting governmental debts; and his advisers gradually taught him the Keynesian language. But F. D. R. never entirely approved of the new doctrines.

Nor were results spectacular. Despite large-scale spending, unemployment and economic stagnation lasted for a decade (1929–39). Only with the outbreak of World War II (1939–45) did full employment and prosperity return. But then came victory for the Keynesians. Most American legislators had now accepted the major tenet of Keynes: that government financial policy could regulate the economy. Congress applied the new doctrine when economic recession threatened in 1949. Appropriations were increased, unbalancing the budget by a record peacetime sum. Spurred by the promise of federal outlays exceeding taxes by $5,000,000,000, business and the stock market started upward.

Such a policy of acquiring debt might alter the nature of American capitalism. But it might also prevent the unemployment and depression which had plagued Americans before World War II. The trend also seemed to commit America to an active world role. Government spending on public works within the United States might compete with private business. There was no such competition when it came to spending on armaments and on loans or gifts to foreign countries. There was, therefore, an increasing preference for such expenditures, which linked American prosperity to the world economy.

The Quest for Normalcy

The big job of 1919 was the termination of World War I price controls, priorities, and contracts. The army was cut to a low peacetime level in a year; and Congress sharply reduced naval construction. Government employment agencies were closed; and the Transportation Act of 1920 ended government administration of railroads. Save for shipping and aviation, World War I brought few permanent changes in the size or functions of the national government.

In 1919 and 1920 there was a world-wide scarcity in manufactured goods and raw materials. Businessmen bid against each other for commodities, acting as though high prices and shortages would continue indefinitely. They should have known better. The fantastically high exports of 1914–19 were bound to decline. With fighting over, Europe came back into normal production. As the shipping crisis eased, Europe could buy from Australia and Argentina as easily as from the United States. At the same time, the credit situation was acute. European countries, deep in debt, were reluctant to float more long-term loans on Wall Street. American exports in 1920 were therefore carried by banks on short-term loans. As bank reserves dipped toward the legal minimum that summer, lending slackened and prices broke. The resulting depression of 1921 hit manufacturers and farmers alike. But the very rapidity of the price break raised real wages; and the physical volume of American consumer purchases kept on expanding. Business confidence returned by 1922, and business leaders hailed the return of "normalcy."

But there would be no return to the "good old days." The Liberty Loan drives had put securities in the hands of people who had never before purchased stocks or bonds. When patriotic ardor cooled, many of these investors exchanged their government bonds for something paying higher interest and offering more chance of a rise in value. This helped create a gigantic market for securities.

The demand for new issues had unfortunate results. Commercial banks established security-selling affiliates. Young salesmen from these agencies and from countless brokerage firms sold securities from door to door in prosperous neighborhoods. As sales mounted, dealers ran short of good domestic issues representing solid capital investment. They then resorted to speculative stocks and weak foreign bonds. The securities of holding companies were popular, which aided smart stock managers. Small buyers turned their savings over to investment trusts. By pooling the savings of many citizens, these trusts had large sums at their disposal and could secure control of large corporations. Sometimes the power was used for the benefit of the general stockholder, sometimes to further the aims of insiders.

Meanwhile, big business was expanding operations. Traditionally, new working capital had come from bank loans. Now practice changed, because of the ease of raising money by issuing securities. Banks participated in the trend; bank assets shifted from sixty-day commercial paper to "demand loans" backed by stock. Few dreamed that all stocks would fall so fast that the banks would be unable to cover their largest loans.

Although urban banks expanded in the flush 1920's, banks in depressed farm regions had hard sledding. Some failed in the 1920's, more in the 1930's because of inability to realize on nonliquid, declining agricultural assets. And city banks would fail after 1929 by reason of large, uncollectible loans on stocks.

Growing Industries

In the period between the world wars, automobiles and allied industries (oil, rubber, glass, concrete) forged ahead in amazing fashion. Far behind, but moving up, were electrical appliances for home and factory, chemicals, and processed foods.

World War II continued these trends. Save for ships and munitions, war needed the same types of goods as the peacetime economy. Auto companies turned from passenger cars to airplanes and tanks. Electrical companies developed new electronic devices, many of which would be useful in peace. The chemical industry produced munitions and expanded production of plastics and synthetic fabrics. Food manufacturers found new methods of processing.

The auto industry had changed American life before World War I; but the key period was 1919–29. At the end of World War I, there was one passenger car for every sixteen people. A decade later it was one for six. With some crowding, all Americans in 1929 could have ridden simultaneously in automobiles. (Often, on Sundays, it seemed as though they were trying to do so.) Meanwhile, trucks increased fourfold and by 1929 were nearly half again as numerous as railroad cars.

This great expansion was made possible by installment credit. Families with middle incomes cut down on food and clothing to keep up payments on new or used cars. But once the installment market had been thoroughly exploited (as in the late 1920's), a limit to easy expansion had been reached. And the depression after 1929 would bring wholesale defaults. The weaker automobile companies were unable to endure the collapse of sales after the stock market broke in 1929. By 1932 only big firms remained, with General Motors leading and Ford and Chrysler following. These companies produced 80 to 90 percent of all passenger cars. The remaining business was divided among a half-dozen smaller concerns. Some of these smaller firms would have gone down if the leaders had set out to eliminate competition by price wars. But if that had been done, the Antitrust Division of the Department of Justice might have cracked down on the victors. So a policy of live-and-let-live was pursued by the big companies.

Up to 1925 auto patents had been pooled. From then on firms controlled their own research. It was difficult, however, to keep trade secrets in a mass production industry where novelties had to be tested before application. And it was so costly to introduce important changes in machinery that no company sought any major advantage from technologic advance. In any case, the pioneer era was over by the 1930's. The eight-cylinder, enclosed car with a rigid steel top, four-wheel brakes, and low-pressure tires was altered only in minor details from then on.

With 8 percent of the value of finished commodities in 1929, automobile manufacture was the leading American industry; and Detroit, the auto center, had become a major manufacturing city. But this was only one aspect of the auto age. The new machines transformed street and highway construction, relocated shopping and residential areas, consolidated schools, affected advertising, recreation, and service industries.

When rubber and other shortages forced the rationing of gasoline in World War II, the whole pattern of American life was affected. Millions of employees could reach their jobs only by automobile. Others found that almost all their recreation required the use of a car. City deliveries and short-haul freight traveled chiefly by truck. Buses provided most urban passenger transportation and took rural children to school. King Cotton had never attained the power of King Gasoline; and even the tightest restrictions could reduce gasoline consumption no more than a third.

Household electrical equipment was another major newcomer. The vacuum cleaners and electric irons of pre-World War I days were just a slight forerunner of the later flood of appliances. Radios, electric phonographs, refrigerators, and washing machines by the 1930's represented 10 percent of all consumer expenditures for durable goods. The radio led. By World War II nearly every family had at least one radio; and the slightest rumor (true or false) could be spread in a few minutes from Atlantic coastal cities to mountain farms.

Down to 1914 Westinghouse and General Electric—the dominant electrical equipment companies—had dealt largely with commercial users. By the 1930's, every housewife knew these names. By then, however, dual monopoly of the leaders had given way to competition. Since it took relatively little capital to manufacture radios, dozens of small companies tried their luck. Refrigerators and the other large machines fitted the pattern of the auto industry; hence subsidiaries of motor firms went into production. This knitted manufacturers of the new durable consumers' goods together into a major industrial group.

American chemical firms had grown rapidly in the late nineteenth century. Greater expansion came with the seizure of German patents during World War I and the later rise of synthetic fibers and plastics. Allied Chemical and Dye, Union Carbide, and Du Pont led in the threefold increase of production between 1914 and 1939. Rayon was the most important new synthetic. Used first in women's wear, it was tried elsewhere, as in cords for automobile tires. As it grew, rayon hurt domestic cotton and Japanese silk. The addition of nylon in the 1940's heralded the day when synthetic fibers, made with just the qualities desired, might replace natural threads and yarns. This would pose problems for cotton states.

Processed food also expanded phenomenally. Flour and packed meats, of course, are manufactured food products as old as America. The nineteenth century added canned goods and prepared cereals; the twentieth, dehydrated and frozen products.

After 1919 small urban families wanted to avoid cooking; and they were being educated to eat more fruits and vegetables. Food processors took pains to capture this market for millions of little orders. Long-distance shipments (even by air), fancy packaging, and brand advertising all helped. Canners offered a wider variety and better quality. There was sharp competition in food; but there was combination, too. The retail end saw the growth of great food chains like the A & P (Great Atlantic and Pacific Tea Company). At the producing end mergers created such giants as General Foods, spreading across many fields.

Declining Industries

Textiles, coal, and construction were principal areas of decline between the world wars. Some textile manufacturers were hit by the shift from cotton and silk to rayon. All were affected by the declining bulk in men's and (particularly) women's clothing. This was tied to urban living, improved heating, and style. The Gibson girl of 1905 wore three to five pounds of underclothing; her daughter in 1930 cut this to a few ounces. The resulting readjustment in the textile industry depressed both wages and profits. Seeking a way out, owners moved their factories from New England to the cheap-labor South. But the cutting and stitching of outer garments remained a city industry, centered in New York.

Coal suffered most from increased efficiency in fuel utilization. Electric power stations cut their use of coal per kilowatt-hour by half in the 1920's. In addition, homeowners shifted from coal to oil or gas furnaces. Some factories switched from coal to hydroelectric energy (water power). Petroleum products were even more important, fuel oil superseding coal for heating and hauling. In the middle 1940's the steam railroads—backbone of demand in coal—began converting to oil-burning Diesel engines. By 1949 one major southern road operated no coal-burning engines. Anthracite and bituminous coal production in 1947 was about the same as in 1920, whereas hydro-, oil- and gas-generated electric power had doubled, and oil production had quadrupled.

Between the wars, building construction spurted for a decade, then lapsed into a dozen years of low activity. For the whole period the industry consumed 3 percent of the national income as against 8 percent around 1900. Quite apart from depression, a slower rate of physical expansion and restricted immigration limited demand for new building. And although many Americans were poorly housed, the government was reluctant to enter this field. During the depression of the 1930's, the United States government helped owners save and repair their homes; but Franklin D. Roosevelt's New Deal was less active in housing than in many other fields. Most government-financed World War II housing construction (1939–45) was of an emergency nature. Hence Americans ran into a severe housing shortage in the postwar years. Since times were good in the late 1940's, private building thrived. Prices were high, but credit was available to most middle-class citizens. Banks and loan companies did an active business; and the government underwrote many loans, especially for veterans. The construction boom was finally checked in 1950–51, by skyrocketing costs, shortages of material, and tightened credit (all connected with the international situation).

A New Pattern of Transportation

The mileage of surfaced roads increased four-fold between 1919 and 1949. Four-lane concrete highways, some having over- and under-passes for crossroads, connected metropolitan centers. Large cities built throughways to their central sections; and outlying parkways avoided the suburban towns. The speed of motor traffic on such routes nearly equaled that of fast passenger trains, and trucks easily outdistanced slow freights. Besides, cars could go to places never served by railroads.

Government-owned, the new highways were built and maintained with income from license and gasoline taxes. The need for work relief stimulated construction in the 1930's. World War II was an interruption; but large-scale building was resumed in 1945, at over a billion-dollar-a-year rate. Since no private industry steadily attracted capital in such quantities, it could be said that gasoline transportation socialized the chief single segment of investment.

Aviation also looked to the government. Without public airports, beacons, and mail subsidies, civilian flying would have remained a rich man's sport. Commercial mail and passenger service grew very slowly until Air Mail Commerce Acts (1925–26) granted many mail contracts on a subsidy basis. Soon after that, in 1927, Charles A. Lindbergh's flight from New York to Paris increased public confidence in air travel. Thereafter air-line transportation boomed; and in 1929 fifty companies were flying 30,000 miles of route.

Like other luxury services, air transportation suffered heavily in the depression. Air lines also contended with shifting government policies. A Republican statute of 1930 gave the Postmaster General broad powers over the creation of routes and the granting of subsidies. In 1934 the Democrats accused favored lines of corrupt political bargains and canceled all contracts. The army was called in to fly the mails. Unaccustomed to night and instrument flying, and given no time to plan, military aviators suffered heavy losses for three months. Then, after the private companies dropped certain officials, the Post Office awarded new contracts. Later, in 1938, Congress passed a new Civil Aeronautics Act. This vested regulatory powers in a six-man Civil Aeronautics Board; mail rates were to be set by negotiation.[1]

The rush of World War II business pushed air passenger travel to heights undreamed of in the 1930's. Wartime experiments improved designs; and the trend toward air travel continued after the war. Air freight and express, insignificant before World War II, became important.

Auto and air competition hurt the railroads. Trucks made small branch rail lines unprofitable, and when regulatory authorities would permit, tracks were torn up or abandoned. For the first time in a century, no important new routes were opened. Still, there was progress. Main-line track was improved to handle more and faster traffic. With economies in operation, railroads of 1950 did half again as much business as in 1920 with a third fewer employees. The trend in passenger-miles was downward; but freight and operating revenues had increased. Though less important than formerly in the nation's economic life, railroads still dominated long-haul freight and many types of passenger business.

Though their policies were under government supervision, railroads were owned and run by private interests. The government took over during World War I; and a Plumb Plan, for continued government operation, was endorsed by the railway brotherhoods. Congress, however, returned the railroads to private ownership (Transportation Act of 1920). When the owners ran into trouble during the depression, the government extended loans through the Reconstruction Finance Corporation (RFC). But the railroads remained in private hands, through the depression and World War II.

Opposition to government ownership was seen in ocean shipping, too.

---

[1] Meantime, Congress was increasing the authority of the Interstate Commerce Commission. Originally designed for railroad regulation, the I.C.C. by 1919 also had supervisory power over pipe lines and express companies. Later (notably in the Motor Carrier Act of 1935), I.C.C. jurisdiction was extended to bus lines, interstate truckers, and certain water carriers. Thus all long-haul transportation was under the jurisdiction of government commissions.

Total tonnage for the American merchant marine engaged in foreign trade climbed from 1,000,000 tons at the outbreak of World War I to eleven times that much in 1921. Most of the new vessels were government-owned, built for the wartime "bridge to France." Unfortunately, the construction program had stressed quantity, not quality; American ships were slower than European competitors. American vessels carried nearly half the American foreign trade of 1920, as against 10 percent six years earlier. Thereafter, the figure dropped to one-third.

Being devoted to private enterprise, Congress chose to sell government vessels to private owners (Jones Act of 1920). Sales were at bargain rates, credit was extended liberally, purchasers were given special tax consideration. Even so, the ships moved slowly, and a tenth were never sold. Raising postal subsidies (1928) did not help materially, and in 1936 Congress found it necessary to direct the new United States Maritime Commission to hand out direct subsidies for construction and operation. Only in coastwise shipping and the Great Lakes ore trade did the American merchant marine prosper.

Had it been an economic matter only, the United States might have given up the struggle. Shipping, however, has military as well as commercial value. Strategic considerations played a part in passage of the Merchant Marine Act of 1936; and in World War II the United States again turned to construction. As a result, the American republic emerged from the war with the world's largest ocean-going merchant fleet (over 25,000,000 gross tons). Yet there was little evidence that Americans had learned how to fit their vessels into an efficient peacetime economy.

The Role of Technology

Economic progress depended largely on technology. The automobile did not revolutionize transportation until it was mechanically perfected to a point of cheapness and dependability. The chemical, electrical, and food industries reflected scientific and engineering progress.

The main tendency was toward larger plants. But concrete highways, pipe and power lines divorced plants from the need to be near coal-carrying railroads; and in some industries, decentralization of operations became profitable. Technology helped here, too, by enabling officials to manage many plants from one central office. The railroad, telegraph, and telephone helped, as did the punch card, teletype, telephotos, and microfilm. Top executives could be in a financial center, while plants were scattered through low-cost rural areas.

Technology usually affected labor. New machines threw men out of work in one industry and created opportunities elsewhere. The adjustment was far from automatic. Often the displaced worker had the wrong skills or experience for the new type of job. Similarly, it was hard for an unemployed head of family in New York to take advantage of opportunities in California. An active federal employment service would have helped; but prejudice against government activity stood in the way. Technological unemployment therefore remained a problem.

Business and the Market

Although improved technology made bigness efficient, better control of the market remained the strongest incentive to growth. By 1929, less than 1000 companies did most of the nation's business in manufacturing, transportation, and finance. Plenty of small concerns remained in the field. There were 200,000 manufacturing companies in 1920, half again that many in 1950. But 97 percent of these companies employed less than half the industrial workers.

Small enterprise was most successful in trade. There little capital was needed; and the energy and personal appeal of the owner-manager could compensate for the operating economies of big distributors. Also, emphasis on service opened new fields for small business (catering, diaper service, radio repair).

In the nineteenth century, price warfare was considered the heart of the competitive system. After 1900 this view gave way to the older—indeed, medieval—doctrine of a just price based on costs and a reasonable profit. The shift away from price competition was encouraged by the trade associations. There were a thousand-odd of these, one or more for each industry. They became strong in World War I, when they helped Bernard Baruch's War Industries Board regulate production. After the war, trade associations tried to maintain uniform prices by exchange of information among members. This open-price policy was endorsed by Secretary of Commerce Herbert Hoover (1921–28), and was not wholly condemned by the Supreme Court. But the trade associations could not require their members to work together. After 1929, therefore, the depression brought desperate price cutting. Business leaders then demanded something stronger than open-price policy to protect profits. The Franklin D. Roosevelt administration responded with the National Industrial Recovery Act of 1933, which permitted agreements for uniform prices (NRA codes). Although the Supreme Court killed NRA in 1935, the price-maintenance idea survived. Many states passed "fair practice" statutes to maintain prices.

Congress extended the state systems under certain conditions to trade-marked articles in interstate commerce (Robinson-Patman Act, 1936, and Miller-Tydings Act, 1937).

The biggest businesses needed neither trade associations nor acts of Congress for regulation of prices. In steel, motors, glass, and cigarettes—where a few companies turned out most of the product—prices were maintained by informal agreements. Such arrangements proved effective even in depression.

Was it wise to hold up prices? Had there been no effort to do so, production might have been maintained during the depression at low wages and prices. To hold up prices and pay union wages it was necessary to cut production—which meant reducing employment. Rigid price policies therefore tended to shift the major force of depression from prices to unemployment. Depression and war then added the rigidities of government supports and regulation to the existing rigidities of union wages and controlled prices. Clearly, the American economy was unlikely to move back toward old-fashioned price competition.

Advertising

In 1900 American advertising outlays were under $100,000,000. By 1929 they were ten times that figure. After a dip during the depression, the upward movement was resumed; the total was $2,000,000,000 in the boom after World War II.

Everybody advertised—big companies and small. The giants came out better in the deal. An advertising budget that was moderate for a big firm would be ruinous for one a tenth that large. And big business used advertising both to protect its share of the market and to prevent interlopers from invading the field.

Even before World War I the automobile joined drugs, cosmetics, and liquor as a mainstay of periodical revenue. Driving also helped outdoor displays; and auto sales demonstrated the business value of advertising expensive consumers' goods. Manufacturers of household appliances took the hint.

As business mounted, advertising agencies improved their techniques. Their experts studied psychology. No longer was a citizen urged to buy mouthwash because it was a good product; he was told that bad breath might cost him his girl or his job. Talented artists and photographers supplied illustrations. Consumer buying habits were studied; and after 1913 periodicals were forced to allow regular audits of their circulation.

From 1922 on, the radio was the important new element in advertising. Money spent on broadcasts was small until 1929. Then, in the depression, radio advertising increased while expenditures for other media fell. In 1943, when advertising as a whole had regained its pre-depression position, radio advertising stood at eight times the 1929 figure.

Public-relations and institutional advertising also assumed new importance. Busy with war production, many companies had little to sell to the public from 1917 to 1919. It seemed wise, however, to insure future markets by advertising the social utility of the product. United States Steel publicized the contribution of steel to American welfare. When the war was over, some companies continued this tactic. Advertising agencies kept newspapers supplied with items showing their client's industry in a favorable light. Some editors threw this material away. Others, courting advertisers, published some releases. Again, many editors toned down or suppressed news that might offend their principal clients.

Managerial Enterprise

While public-relations officers were selling big business to the public, management was taking control of corporations away from the owners. In practically all leading companies 95 percent of the owners had been divorced from any control of the property. Company officials ran the company, and those who owned the stock had become passive investors sharing in net profits.

This situation had been shaping up for a long time. Even before 1900, the ownership of stock in many companies was widely scattered, making it difficult for the owners to act in harmony. But very large stockholders sat on the board of directors. After 1900 control often went to the Wall Street bankers who marketed the company's stock. But finance capitalism faded after World War I. In the 1920's, the great debt-free industrial companies had less need for Wall Street advice. They had funds for expansion, or could obtain money easily from the public. Banker influence further declined in the depression, when the government divorced investment from commercial banking, and when the RFC lent money. By the 1940's, some industrial companies had no bankers and no large stockholders on their boards—only salaried officials representing management.

The typical manager cared little about paying large dividends to thousands of unknown stockholders. He was interested rather in building personal prestige by creating a successful concern. This meant watching the market, and keeping labor, suppliers, consumers, and fellow officers reasonably content. Since profits meant prestige and high salaries, management was profit-minded. As a rule, though, managers were more interested in avoiding risks than in seeking enormous returns. In consequence, business put less emphasis than before on radical change.

A great increase in university-level schools of business heightened interest in managerial problems during the 1920's; and personnel studies, cost accounting, and social psychology all came to the aid of the overburdened executive. But the difficulties remained great. Twentieth-century business hierarchies turned out few empire-builders. Success went rather to agreeable conformists who accepted routine practices.

Owners of stock might not set policy; but they could be important as public friends. The ownership of even a few hundred dollars' worth of utilities stock made citizens critical of public regulation. Many companies, therefore, instructed branch managers to seek more local stockholders. In this way A.T. & T. by the early 1930's had acquired 700,000 owners. Managers signed letters welcoming new members of the stockholder family. Annual reports grew into illustrated booklets which made the stockholder feel that he was a recognized member of the organization.

While wooing stockholders, managers appealed to the public through advertisements and speeches. The response was good in the 1920's. Business became more popular than ever before; and Bruce Barton (a public-relations expert) won acclaim when he interpreted Jesus Christ as a businessman, in *The Man Nobody Knows*.

The prestige of business declined when the stock market collapsed in 1929 and when Congressional investigations revealed evidence of recklessness among industrial and financial leaders. The breakup of Samuel Insull's holding-company-based utilities empire left Americans gasping. So did the trial and conviction of Richard Whitney, who had been president of the New York Stock Exchange and had talked about business honesty. Plainly, if business leaders hoped to regain the confidence of the American people, they would have to do more than talk about the virtues of private industry and free enterprise. Yet no new approach was forthcoming. The return of prosperity in the 1940's did not bring back public confidence in business leadership.

What, then, of the future? Business obviously needed better roots in the community. In 1950 there were 6,000,000 stockholders in the United States —an average of one to every six families. To broaden the base, brokers favored selling stock more widely. Some friends of business suggested that companies could reach the people better by including labor and community representatives on their boards. But management was not sure it wanted that.

The Standard of Living

The nation as a whole enjoyed great prosperity in two of the three decades after World War I. But the depression of 1929–39 was a terrifying experience. Even those who stayed at work suffered, wondering how long their jobs would last or how long they could stave off bankruptcy, seeing their children grow up with scant hopes of employment. World War II brought better times, without erasing the memory of the dark days. And there was the new insecurity of the atomic age.

The best measure of the general welfare is real income—dollar income adjusted in line with the changing value of money. This shows purchasing power of the pay check. In broad outline, labor and the self-employed gained most in the "good times" of the 1920's and 1940's, while the salaried middle class lost ground. In the depression of the 1930's, citizens on salary fared well if they held their jobs. Workingmen and the self-employed had a hard time.

In 1900, clerical employees had earned much more than manual workers. The spread was still substantial (a third) in the early 1920's. But by 1950, much of this difference had disappeared. In 1948, hand bookkeepers received about $60 a week, whereas workers in automobile plants averaged four dollars a week more than that. To compensate, white-collar employees had a little more prestige and were a little less likely to be dropped overnight.

In this shift, real wages for clerical workers had not declined—they were about as high in 1950 as in 1920. Meanwhile, however, the real income of manual workers had increased sharply. In 1939 dollars, earnings of the average worker in manufacturing were $18 in 1918, $30 in 1948. Despite higher taxes, the laborer was ahead of the game.

Before World War I, increases in real wages had been caused largely by declines in prices. When prices had advanced (1843–57, 1897–1918), wages had lagged or barely kept abreast of living costs. But after 1919, union activities and government policies were the basic factors in increasing the worker's share of the national income.

Workers also acquired leisure through a shorter working day. The work week was close to fifty hours through the prosperous 1920's. In the depression of the 1930's share-the-work and spread-employment appeals cut the figure to thirty or thirty-five hours. When World War II provided full employment after 1941, the government helped the unions keep forty hours as the normal week. Since overtime meant pay-and-a-half or double pay, forty hours became standard after the war.

While the hour-and-income picture improved, workers continued to face other problems. By 1950 half the population lived in cities of 50,000 or more inhabitants. Most of these centers had inadequate housing, too many automobiles for roads or parking places, and living quarters remote from places of work. By the later 1940's, government planning and financing was bringing some improvement. But there seemed no way of restoring the old-fashioned town community.

Related to this and the world situation was the general feeling of insecurity. In the 1950's, with wages and employment at all-time highs, with the government ready to care for the unfortunate, most Americans worried about the future. Industrialism had produced change more rapidly than man's social organisms could adjust to it.

One cause of weak community relations was as old as America itself—continuous movement of population. Some moved in the prosperous 1920's. More shifted in the depression, in an often fruitless quest for jobs. War production in the 1940's and 1950's brought further migrations.

As they moved, Americans changed their occupations. There was a spectacular decline in domestic servants. Equally striking was a reduction of workers in rural areas. The percentage of farmers and hired farm laborers in the nation's working force was cut in half (to 13 percent) between World War I and 1950. Meantime, the percentage of clerical and sales employees in the working force rose by a third; the fraction in business and the professions grew two and a half times. Professional people, proprietors, and managers now outnumbered farmers and farm workers; and they were nearly as numerous as clerical and sales employees. The urban upper middle class was the fastest-growing element in America. Next came the middle class as represented by sales and clerical forces.

Family (father-to-son) patterns were disturbed more often than before. Millions worked at jobs remote from their early training. Added to displacement of depression and war were the great government-subsidized programs of military and veterans' education designed to fit men and women into new careers. Government funds trained some young people for fields where there were too few employment opportunities. But the cycle of change was in keeping with the spirit of democracy.

The Decline of Trade Unionism

In the nineteenth century it had been proper to organize workers in craft unions according to their skills; men were carpenters, boilermakers, cigar makers, or glass blowers. Then subdivision of labor and assembly line techniques eliminated skills. In automobile, steel, rubber, and electrical equipment factories, most men had no specialized skill; and organization along craft lines left out most workers.

The obvious solution was industrial organization—putting all auto workers into one union, rubber workers into another. But there were obstacles. One was the power and antiunion point of view of manufacturers in mass production industries—Detroit auto makers, for example. Equally difficult was the attitude of certain A.F. of L. craft unions, which were determined to oppose industrial unionism. When the Carriage Workers tried to organize auto workers, there were complaints from many craft unions, although these unions had made little headway in the industry. In 1913 the A.F. of L. ordered the Carriage Workers not to organize workers who might be classified as painters, blacksmiths, upholsterers, sheet-metal workers, patternmakers, metal polishers, machinists, carpenters, or electrical workers. Later, the Carriage Workers were expelled from the A.F. of L. Had they been encouraged rather than denounced, they might have made Detroit a union area. As it was, it remained nonunion until the depression.

In the World War I era, union membership increased to 5,000,000 workers. The increase was largely in such older areas of union strength as the building trades, printing, and railroads, and in war-stimulated industries soon to be doomed to inactivity—shipping, for instance, and metal trades. Nowhere did organizers gain a secure footing in the expanding mass production industries. Gompers of the A.F. of L. gave half-hearted support to an effort to organize steel; but this broke down after the unsuccessful steel strike of 1919.

In line with historic trends, union membership had grown in wartime prosperity. It declined during postwar depression (1920–22). The decline, though, was more than cyclical; it was tied to a national employer-backed campaign against the closed shop. Trouble began with President Wilson's Industrial Conference of 1919. Employers refused to accept the closed shop; and labor representatives withdrew. Then and later, employers organized groups to fight for the open shop as "the American way." No one should be denied the right to a job because he refused to join a union. To the antiunion speeches and advertisements of an earlier day were added labor spies to report on organizers; trade association agreements specifying the open shop; banker pressure on employers; letters to stockholders urging them to help.

The success of these antiunion measures was increased by the red scare of 1919–20. The rise of communism in Europe and the use of bombs by extremists in the United States led many to feel that revolution was at hand. Playing on this fear, employers stressed the great increase of strikes and the presence of a few radicals and foreigners in the labor movement. The government sided with employers. Although the war was over, wartime legislation was used to end the coal strike of 1919. A number of states passed laws prohibiting the closed shop or limiting strike activity. Federal and state courts granted injunctions to prevent strike action.

Considering the antiunion movement and the downward trend of the business cycle, it was natural that A.F. of L. membership should drop from over 4,000,000 to below 3,000,000 by 1923. More disheartening was the failure of the Federation to come back in years of prosperity. In 1929 the membership totals for A.F. of L. and independent unions were about the same as for 1923, although the nation's labor force had grown by 10 percent. The only significant gains in the decade were in company unions, which doubled and came to have a membership half as large as that of the Federation. Many company unions departed from the craft approach and organized on an industrial basis. To this degree they represented the needs of the new manufacturing economy. But, since they were influenced by management, they helped little in wage and hour disputes.

Unable to gain during prosperity, A.F. of L. craft unions suffered heavily after the stock market crash of 1929. In three years, they lost a quarter of their members. By 1933, the A.F. of L. represented only 4 percent of the labor force. All labor's organizing efforts of a half-century seemed to have been in vain.

The New Labor Movement

In the nineteenth century and after World War I, the government helped employers check organized labor. During World War I and in the 1930's, the government took the other side, and actively aided union organizers.

The labor policy of the Franklin D. Roosevelt administration (1933–45) first found expression in 1933 in Section 7a of the National Industrial Recovery Act, which stated that employees had the "right to organize and to bargain collectively through representatives of their own choosing." Protected by this and by a National Labor Board, unions regained their depression losses in two years. But company unions grew even faster; by 1935 their strength was two-thirds that of other unions. Then the National Labor Relations (Wagner) Act of 1935 checked the spread of the company union, by prohibiting employers from using coercion or giving financial support to company unions, and by specifying that the employer must bargain with the union representing the majority of his employees. The law also created a permanent National Labor Relations Board.

Calling the Wagner Act a complete victory for labor, employers were reluctant to abide by it. Most did so, however, after the Supreme Court upheld the constitutionality of the law (Jones and Laughlin Steel case, 1937). Even before that, the act had added notably to union strength and had helped effect a major improvement in wages and working conditions.

Opportunity to organize mass production industries under protection of law pointed to the need for industrial unions. John L. Lewis of the United Mine Workers and a few other A.F. of L. leaders organized a Committee for Industrial Organization and began recruiting workers on an industry-wide basis (1935). Craft-minded Federation leaders, including Gompers'

successor, William Green, complained that Lewis was crossing jurisdictional lines; and in 1938, the C.I.O. was expelled from the Federation. The
expelled officials promptly called a national convention and established the
Congress of Industrial Organizations, with John L. Lewis as president.

When formed, the C.I.O. had as members several old A.F. of L. unions,
including the Mine Workers and Sidney Hillman's Amalgamated Clothing
Workers. The greatest strength, however, came as the C.I.O. organized the
mass production industries: steel, motors, rubber, textiles.

Warfare between the A.F. of L. and C.I.O. harassed labor leaders, government officials, employers, and the public. Yet the competition brought
heroic organizing efforts. To defeat its younger rival, the Federation re-
modeled many of its unions along industrial lines. This put a final stamp
of approval on the industrial idea; and it increased union membership from
4,000,000 in 1935 to 16,000,000 in 1950. Half of these belonged to Green's
A.F. of L., one Federation union (Dan Tobin's Teamsters) claiming over
a million members. Two C.I.O. unions, the United Steelworkers and
United Automobile Workers, had just short of a million each; and Philip
Murray, who headed the C.I.O., had 6,000,000 followers. The other 2,000,-
000 union members were in independent unions—the railway brotherhoods, for instance, and the United Mine Workers, which John L. Lewis
took from the A.F. of L. to the C.I.O., back to the A.F. of L., then out
of both.

Compared with 1933, these numbers were enormous. But much remained undone. Organizing drives slowed down by 1945; yet of the 40,-
000,000 nonagricultural workers, the union share was far less than half.

Union victories were not achieved easily. In the 1930's, employers used
company unions, propaganda, even force ("service" units) against organizers. Sixteen workers were killed when police and strikers clashed in the
Republic Steel strike of 1937. Die-hard employers tried the Mohawk Valley formula to beat strikes—close the factory, ship away machinery, hint
that operations would be suspended forever. But labor won. United States
Steel, traditionally antilabor, gave in without a strike. Detroit became a union center. Unions carried the electric and rubber industries, organized government and office workers, penetrated antiunion districts of the South.

In 1936, labor tried the sit-down. Instead of going "out" on strike, workers stayed in the plant, while wives and fellow unionists brought them food.
For labor, the sit-down had the advantage of preventing operation by strikebreakers; and it forced company officials to resort to violence if they wanted
to expel the strikers. Opponents claimed the sit-down was an improper invasion of property rights. While the debate wore on into 1937, Governor
Frank Murphy of Michigan protected General Motors sit-down strikers at

Flint; and the employers eventually negotiated contracts for their major plants. Later, in the Fansteel case, the Supreme Court held the sit-down illegal.

After World War II there was a reaction against labor. Franklin D. Roosevelt's successor, Harry Truman, took an antilabor attitude when a national railroad strike was threatened in the spring of 1946. Thereafter, Truman moved toward labor. But the fall of 1946 brought Republican victories at the polls. Republicans and conservative Democrats then passed the Taft-Hartley law over President Truman's veto (1947). This act imposed restraints on unions. While the union or preferential shop was permitted, the closed shop was prohibited. A worker could stop paying dues, yet keep his job. Unions could be sued for breach of contract and could be forced to pay for damages suffered through jurisdictional disputes (as when C.I.O. and A.F. of L. unions fought for control of a plant). Labor organizations were held accountable in cases of secondary boycott—say, the refusal of workers to handle the products of a firm involved in a labor dispute. A sixty-day negotiating period was required between the calling and start of a strike. Union funds could not be used for political purposes; and union officials had to swear that they were not Communists. Although there was a swing toward labor in the 1948 election, the unions were unable to secure quick repeal of the Taft-Hartley law. But labor still retained its rights of collective bargaining, as established under the Wagner Act of 1935. It retained as well many other New Deal gains—wage and hour legislation (1938) and a social security system. As prices rose at mid-century, labor secured several rounds of wage increases; also many "fringe benefits" (retirement and hospitalization plans, and the like).

In 1951, labor leaders asserted that those in charge of the new military production program were not giving sufficient consideration to the claims of labor. But labor was, generally, faring well and had strong support in Washington. Early in 1952 President Truman supported his Wage Stabilization Board's recommendation that steel workers have substantial wage increases. At the same time, he used his price-control powers to block as inflationary price increases for the steel companies. When the companies rejected this settlement, Truman seized the companies (April, 1952) so as to prevent a strike that would cripple defense production. The Supreme Court soon held that the President had exceeded his constitutional powers in the seizure, and restored the companies to their owners (Youngstown Sheet & Tube vs. Sawyer, June, 1952). In the ensuing strike, Truman sided with the workers, and refused to use his anti-strike powers under the Taft-Hartley Act. A settlement was effected in July, 1952, with wage increases for the workers and price increases for the companies.

Organizing Office Workers

Among the new fields invaded by union organizers was office work. In earlier days clerical employees had boasted special skills and the "opportunity for rapid advancement." Adding machines, card sorters, and other devices gradually eliminated skills; and by 1929 many clerical positions were "dead end," rather than steps on a ladder. But, since paper work goes on even in slack times, the office staff could count on year-round employment; and white-collar workers had paid vacations, and more security and higher social status than manual workers.

Then came the depression. Office staffs were cut almost as drastically as factory employees. Many of those retained were forced to take payless vacations and deep salary cuts. Stenographic pools and dictating machines eliminated much secretarial work; and "opportunity for rapid advancement" disappeared altogether. This situation beckoned to the labor leader. The Newspaper Guild led the way. Government workers were organized. A Teachers Union sought members in that unorganized calling. Draftsmen, clerks, stenographers, and office boys joined unions and engaged in collective bargaining.

White-collar discontent increased in the 1940's. Price inflation hurt. Also, organized manual workers gained pensions and paid vacations—privileges hitherto confined to the office. In addition, social distinctions were slipping away. To gain higher pay, young people with good education often took factory jobs in preference to clerical positions. The trend seemed to foreshadow disappearance of a sharp class line.

The Self-Employed

Although most Americans were employees, the self-employed (including farmers and tenants) remained as numerous as the white-collar workers. The number of farmers declined from 1920 to 1950 by 1,500,000. Other proprietors—notably retail merchants—and those who performed "services" (hotel owners, repairmen, lawyers, physicians) increased by an equal amount.

These self-employed citizens had influence beyond their numbers. In villages and smaller cities, successful lawyers, doctors, insurance agents, merchants, and restaurant owners ran the local clubs, selected the local politicians, spoke for the "people." Often, too, they set the tone in state and national politics, for small city and country areas are more heavily represented in Congress and state legislatures than are metropolitan districts. The self-employed had less social uniformity in the large cities. Retailers and those who provided service were, on the average, too small and insecure to be regarded as members of the upper middle class. Leadership was largely in the hands of professional politicians, journalists, and top executives of big companies.

The self-employed were much affected by economic fluctuations. Good times brought substantial fees or profits; poor business meant reduced income. Many went bankrupt. But the self-employed also hoped for wealth, if they struck the right location or product. The self-employed thus differed from manual workers and white-collar employees in their hopes for the future. They were, in a sense, the spiritual descendants of the optimistic boomers of an earlier America.

There was little reduction of the citizen's opportunity to go into business for himself. Excluding banks, railroads, and the professions an average of 375,000 new firms were founded annually between 1900 and 1920. The figure rose to 425,000 in the next two decades, despite depression and a general trend toward the concentration of economic power. This testified to the continuing desire of many an American to be his own boss.

Little capital was needed to make a start in retailing, service, or certain lines of manufacturing. Some began with no capital at all, by securing credit from landlords, wholesalers, and finance companies, or by renting machinery. The mortality of these shoestring enterprises was high, the average life of the small business being less than seven years. Lack of capital, lack of business education, inexperience, and incompetence were common causes of failure. The real degree of insecurity, though, was not so great as the figures indicate. The shoestring operator often risked only the savings of two or three years. If he failed, he could take a job and save enough to try again. "Failure" might mean simply a reorganization with new loans, a new location, perhaps a new partner. And, at all events, there were plenty of men and women willing to assume the risks.

Farmers in the Twenties

New machines made it possible for farmers to expand wheat and corn acreage at small extra cost. But the machines displaced horses and mules, important consumers of grain. Before the tractor, a fifth of the grain raised had been fed to work animals on the farm, at no cost for shipping and marketing. Now the farmer had to sell the grain and buy gasoline, in an age of shrinking grain markets. Urban living and better knowledge of diet caused Americans to eat more dairy products, fruits, and vegetables, less grain, potatoes, and meat. This brought profit to farmers who could enter new lines. Many cereal farmers, however, could not manage the shift. The decline of foreign markets after 1925 (partly owing to competition from Argentina, Canada, and Australia) brought still heavier pressure against domestic grain prices. The price of wheat therefore fell more than 50 percent between 1925 and 1930.

It was the same with the other major market crop, cotton. Poor yields after World War I set a price of 29¢ a pound in 1923. Then everything went wrong. Rayon displaced cotton. Egyptian and Indian cotton undersold American in the export market. Production mounted, prices fell; in 1931 the biggest crop in history brought only 5.7¢ a pound.

Farmers with money to buy the new machines and acreage enough to put them to efficient use made a fair living in the late 1920's. So did agriculturalists with enough capital and skill to diversify crops. But 60 percent of American farms had less than 100 acres in 1925; and their owners lacked cash or credit. Many larger farms were in semiarid areas, where growing seasons were uncertain, mortgages common, transportation costs high. Their owners could do well enough when wheat brought $1.25 a bushel. It was different when the price was half that, especially with those who had purchased land at high World War I figures.

Conservative politicians like President Calvin Coolidge (1923–29) hoped that coöperative marketing might cure farmers' ills. There was hope, too, that farmers could act as a unit to capture foreign markets (under a Webb-Pomerene Act of 1918, the Sherman and Clayton Antitrust laws did not apply to combinations for export purposes). But overseas markets dwindled away; and, save for certain perishable commodities, marketing coöperatives added little to the farmer's net return.

Agriculturalists demanded something else. Working through farm lobbies—especially the American Farm Bureau Federation—they created a bipartisan farm bloc in Congress in the 1920's. In 1923, pressure brought Federal Intermediate Credit Banks, where farmers could get loans running from three months to five years. (Loans for shorter terms were available through the Federal Reserve System; long-term credit through banks set up by the Federal Farm Loan Act of 1916.) The farm bloc also pushed McNary-Haugen bills through Congress. Plan was for the government to pay farmers compensation for protective tariff rates on other commodities. But President Coolidge vetoed these bills (1927, 1928).

Farmers and Depression

Hard-pressed in the 1920's, farmers ran into serious trouble after 1929. To begin with, the crash caused over 1,000,000 unemployed workers to return to the land. In addition, workingmen who had done farming on the side turned entirely to agriculture when they lost factory jobs. Southern Agrarians and a few Northerners (including F. D. Roosevelt) spoke hopefully of this "return to the soil." Actually, the move-

TENANT FARMERS
PERCENT OF ALL FARMERS

1880

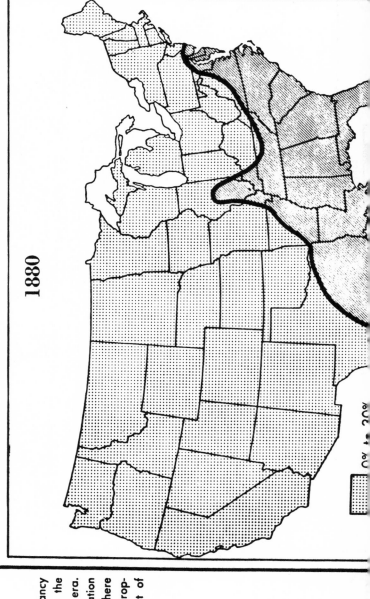

The pattern of farm tenancy was well established by the end of the Reconstruction era. The heaviest concentration was in the cotton belt, where white and Negro sharecroppers accounted for most of the tenant population.

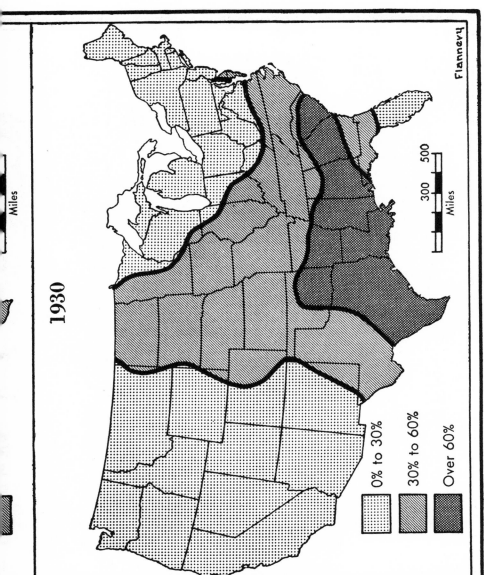

1930

0% to 30%

30% to 60%

Over 60%

300 500
Miles

Flannery

in the half century between 1880 and 1930, tenancy increased in every section. In the cotton belt, more than three-fifths of the farmers were tenants by 1930. Meanwhile, there had been a heavy increase in tenant farming in the cash grain areas of the middle section of the country.

Although some tenant farmers obtained good returns (in the Middle West especially), the average tenant was in an unenviable position. His plight would become worse during the depression; yet the government would do less for tenant farmers (and for migratory farm workers) than for other depressed groups. After the late 1930's, however, there would be a trend away from tenancy, because of better times and the changing character of American agriculture.

ment to the country increased production, cutting prices below already low levels. And the migration added to the number of farms that were too small to support families even in good times.

As income dwindled, many farmers could not pay taxes or interest on their part of the $8,000,000,000 farm mortgage debt. Foreclosures followed, and owners became tenants of banks and insurance companies. By the mid-1930's, managers or tenants operated over half the farm acreage. This created acute dissatisfaction; farmers took over foreclosure sales, forcing those in charge to sell to the old owners at a low figure. Here were reënacted scenes played out in the days of Daniel Shays.

Calamity piled on calamity. Rural local governments went bankrupt. Schools were closed; roads fell into disrepair. Dairy farmers organized milk strikes—refused to market milk and used road blocks to enforce coöperation. But, lacking national organization, these protesting groups were generally unsuccessful.

Just as the depression began, the presidential administration of Herbert Hoover (1929–33) established a Farm Board. The idea was to raise prices by lending to marketing coöperatives, which could store surpluses and release them only in times of scarcity. Had abundance and scarcity alternated frequently, the Hoover plan might have worked. But scarcity never came in the depression years; and the Farm Board used up its funds supporting a sinking market.

Franklin D. Roosevelt, who became President in 1933, raised farm prices by limited inflation and planned scarcity. Under the Agricultural Adjustment Act of 1933, farmers were offered payments for cutting acreage, the money to be raised by taxes on processing of farm goods. In addition, the government refinanced farm mortgages at a low rate of interest (4½ per cent), and offered to help the most unfortunate farmers move to better locations. The whole program was threatened in 1936, when the Supreme Court held the processing tax of the AAA unconstitutional (Hoosac Mills case). Congress hastily passed a Soil Conservation and Domestic Allotment Act; but this had little restrictive force.

Meantime, nature temporarily restored a better balance between production and consumption. In 1934, the prairie and plains states suffered a drought more severe than that of the late 1880's. Western Kansas, Oklahoma, and Texas became a vast dust bowl. One third of the nation's grain crop was lost, and "Okies" abandoned their burned-out farms to seek work picking fruit in California. Although 1935 brought some rain, 1936 was almost as bad as 1934. As a result of these short crops, farm prices rose, and by early 1937, real farm income was as high as in the late 1920's. But 1938 saw bumper corn and wheat crops and the old problem of overproduction.

The government then passed the Agricultural Adjustment Act of 1938.

The plan was to (1) fit production to market demand and (2) insure a constant supply of major commodities by government storage of surpluses. Marketing quotas would be imposed on basic crops if two-thirds of the producers agreed. Farmers who conformed to designated acreage quotas and planted soil-conserving crops on their remaining land would receive federal payments (an effort to avoid constitutional objections to direct subsidies).

The main controls, however, were in marketing. The administration set a "just" or parity price for major crops, based on the relation of farm to industrial prices in a prosperous agricultural era (1909–14). If market prices fell below 75 percent of these arbitrary levels, the farmer who had conformed to his quota would have the difference restored by parity payments. If he did not want to market his crop, he could store it in a government warehouse and borrow half to three-quarters of the parity price. If he did not redeem this no-interest loan, the government merely took over the produce.

With the establishment of the permanent AAA program in 1938, farms were added to railroads, shipping, and public utilities in the area of the economy that was partly government controlled. At first farmers were disturbed by the curtailment of their freedom and denounced the measures that boosted their living standards. In the Middle West especially, the late 1930's saw the farm vote shifting away from the Democratic sponsors of the AAA. But in time, the arrangements became routine and customary. By the late 1940's, a large number of farmers had come to support government aid policies with their ballots. It appeared unlikely that farmers as a whole would voluntarily relinquish government support. For they were getting more security and a larger share of the consumer's dollar than ever before.

War Brings Boom Years

In World War II (1939–45) American farmers benefited from increasing domestic prices and consumption. Large shipments of food to wartime allies (1942–45), and to postwar friends thereafter, insured a market for record-breaking crops. In 1944, for the first time since 1915, American farmers produced over 1,000,000,000 bushels of wheat. This crop went at the high price of $1.40 a bushel. More billion-bushel years followed, with prices soaring above $2.00. Corn-and-hog farmers fared even better. In 1931 the corn crop had brought less than $1,000,-000,000. Returns exceeded $5,000,000,000 in 1946 and 1947. Cotton production remained below the level of the 1920's and 1930's; but prices reached more than 30¢ a pound, five times the depression low.

All through American history, farmers had seen land values appreciate. But from 1920 to 1933 values declined (by 60 percent). Then came a rise, and by 1948 farmland had regained its record-breaking level of 1920.

The city people who had flocked to the country during the depression returned to urban centers as soon as the job market permitted. Military service further cut the supply of agricultural labor; and farm hands wanted better pay than before. Farmers therefore speeded up mechanization, so as to reduce dependence on labor. While production rose 20 percent in the 1940's, the number of workers on the land decreased. In corn and wheat states 90 percent of the acreage was cultivated with tractors.

Advance of Science

The 50 percent increase in productivity after World War I stemmed from better knowledge of soils, use of lime and fertilizer, new varieties of seed, scientific breeding and feeding of animals, and new machinery. Research workers developed new types of wheat, corn, cotton, and other crops with greater yields and more resistance to disease. Meantime new demands brought new products. Cultivation of soybeans, used in oils and plastics, jumped from 200,000 acres in the early 1920's to 10,000,000 in 1949.

There were improvements in every field. Veterinary medicine reduced hog and cattle disease such as cholera and tuberculosis, protecting raiser and consumer. Better nutrition and selective breeding added to the weight of hogs and cattle and the milk yield of dairy cows. Chickens confined in "chicken hotels" were bred for meat or eggs rather than legs and wings. Small, cheap tractors, new corn cultivators, field hay balers, and numerous other devices increased productivity per worker. Mechanical cotton pickers proved successful on some cotton lands by 1950, a fact of great social significance in the South.

This evolution of agriculture into a scientific, mechanized industry threatened the small, inefficient farmer. During the early 1940's the value of farms between 30 and 99 acres rose only half as fast as that of farms between 100 and 499 acres. With favorable prices after World War II, small farmers did well; but leaner years and further mechanical and scientific advances would renew the economic pressure for their elimination.

In the prosperous 1950's, serious farm problems remained. The cotton belt still had the single crop, debt, tenancy, and race difficulties. Southern hill sections, northern cutover areas, submarginal lands in New England remained depressed. Successful farmers remembered the troubled 1920's and calamitous 1930's. Would such things come again?

The General Welfare: A New Conception

As they entered the second half of the twentieth century, Americans worried about their economic future. But along with concern went a sort of confidence in the government. Now at last

Americans believed that they could rely on the government to prevent dire distress for any major part of the population.

All groups recognized that government had become the central mechanism in economic stability. A drastic reduction in government spending would undermine prosperity, whereas old-style depressions seemed unlikely if government activities were rapidly expanded. Very evidently, the clause of the Constitution giving Congress power to "provide for the common Defense and General Welfare" had come to have a meaning far broader than the founders could have dreamed. Welfare now seemed to mean the personal welfare of each citizen. Similarly, common defense appeared to include not only Americans but a large part of the people of the world.

25

Social and Intellectual Reactions

Immigration

Population trends after World War I were affected by the virtual cessation of immigration. This, in turn, was linked to new restrictive legislation. As earlier, there was antiforeign feeling; also special opposition to the "new immigration." World War I strengthened the labor unions that opposed the influx of low-wage workers. The war increased nationalist feeling, which added to suspicion of foreigners. And citizens who sympathized with the newcomers felt that immigration must be slowed down if assimilation was to be effective.

Emergency quota laws of 1921 and 1922 were followed by permanent legislation in 1924. This cut annual immigration to 150,000; and it favored northern Europeans over southern and eastern Europeans. From 1924 to 1929 annual immigration from each country was limited to 2 percent of its immigrants living in the United States in 1890. Since the foreign born of 1890 were predominantly north Europeans, this formula favored that area. The national origins system used after 1929 (as in the McCarran Act of 1952) operated in much the same fashion. Average immigration from northern Europe just before World War I had been 175,000. Under the quota rates of 1929, the limits were set at 130,000. But eastern and southern Europe, which had averaged 700,000 before World War I, were cut to 20,000. Most Asiatics were barred altogether until after World War II, then were assigned very tiny quotas.

Canadians and Latin-Americans were exempted from these restrictions, as were residents of American insular possessions. Thousands of Puerto Ricans crowded into New York slums; and 45,000 Filipinos entered the country during the 1920's. Many Mexican laborers crossed the border, as employers in the Southwest sought cheap labor. By the depression the number was 1,500,000.

Despite entry of these groups, and a very small amount of smuggling, the restrictive statutes were effective. The depression after 1929 reduced im-

618

migration below quota levels, for the President could exclude anyone likely to become a public charge. This could cover everybody in the 1930's. Such an interpretation cut the flow to a trickle (35,000 in 1935, against 800,000 in 1921). Emigration exceeded immigration in the early 1930's, for the first time. When business improved, after 1939, World War II prevented migration. The trend was upward after the war but was held within narrow limits by the quota system. After 1920 there was a steady decline in the percentage of foreign born in the United States.

In closing the door after 1924, Congress reversed a long-standing American tradition of welcoming newcomers. Unless policy is changed again (which seems unlikely), the United States will develop in the future a population based on that which existed here before 1930. This means a people who are, in greatest part, descended from British, Irish, Scandinavian, and German forebears. British stock (including Scots-Irish) made up just short of half the total. A sixth had German background, a ninth Irish. Americans of African background were about as numerous as those with Irish ancestors. Eastern and southern Europeans furnished very little of the total: Poles 4 percent, Italians less.

Migrations Within the United States

Migration westward, long significant, continued. There was a heavy movement into Texas, Oklahoma, and the western plains just before World War I, and to Texas and the Pacific coast during and after the depression of the 1930's. California nearly trebled in population from 1920 to 1950 and became the second most populous state. Oregon practically doubled, Washington and Texas increased by one-half. In each of these areas growth came primarily from new industrial activity.

Nonetheless, the westward movement was slowing down. Despite growth of total population between 1910 and 1940, the number of eastern born who lived west of the Mississippi declined, from a little more than 5,000,-000 to a little less. Meantime, a reverse movement back to the East gained momentum. In 1910, 700,000 western born had lived in the East; by 1940 this had risen to nearly 2,000,000.

There was North-South movement, too. Migration southward increased after 1890, as industrialization in Dixie stimulated growth of cities. By 1940 2,000,000 Northerners lived in the South. This movement was facilitated by declining opposition of Southerners toward Yankees, especially in cities.

More striking was the northward movement of Southerners. The chief motive was to escape the poverty that followed the Civil War. As early as 1870, 1,000,000 southern born were located in the North. The movement was increased in World War I when northern war industries needed work-

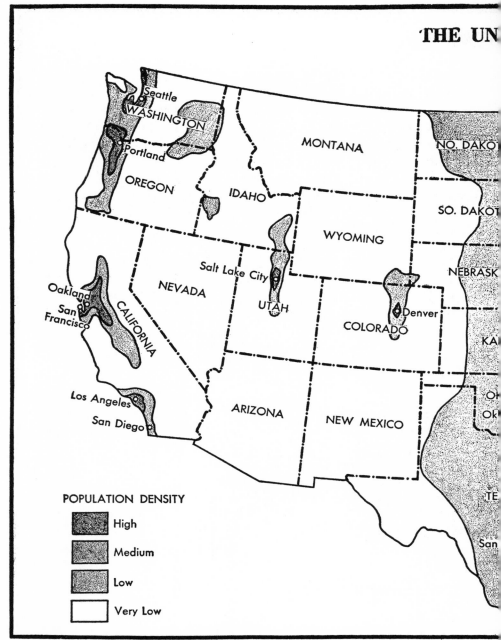

POPULATION DENSITY

High

Medium

Low

Very Low

Despite a continued westward movement, toward Texas and the Pacific coast, most Americans still lived east of the Mississippi River at the middle of the twentieth century. The heaviest concentrations of population were in New England and the middle states (roughly, the area from Boston to Washington, D. C.); in upstate New York; and in the Pittsburgh-Cleveland and Chicago areas. Further west, there were significant and rapidly growing population areas in the Pacific coast states. In spite of concerted efforts to develop in-

Flannery

dustrial centers in the South, that region still lacked the concentration of population that reflected large-scale manufacturing. Equally interesting was the contrast between the substantial population density of southern and Great-Lakes farming districts with the sparser settlement of the mid-continent agricultural belt from the Dakotas to central Texas. Striking, too, was the very low population density of most areas from there west-ward.

ers. By 1940 there were 3,500,000 southern born in the North. Many were white people from the southern hills, where the birth rate was high and economic opportunities were limited. In addition, southern Negroes moved to large northern cities. By 1950 a third of the nation's Negroes lived outside the South.

Despite the advantages which technology bestowed on rural life (telephones, automobiles, radio), the tendency of country people to move to the city continued. This migration sometimes involved long distances, as when Negroes went North or Middle Westerners retired to California. Except during war years, however, most of the influx into large centers came from the surrounding territory.

The coming of the automobile encouraged all internal migration. In the 1920's, thousands of Easterners motored south for winter vacations; and a speculative boom ensued in Florida real estate. The bubble burst even before the stock market crash of 1929; but winter migration south continued. In addition to the seasonal movement, some moved to Florida or California for good. Elderly people (now more numerous because of the declining death rate) preferred a warmer climate during retirement.

Meanwhile, a reverse flow moved northward in summer. New England advertised itself as Vacation Land. Other northern areas shared in the business, as longer vacations and the growing popularity of sports took more people out of doors. Summer camps and hotels shared in the profits. New England even cultivated a minor opportunity as a winter resort, with the advent in the 1930's of a vogue for winter sports.

Migration to California was in a class by itself. Retired midwest farmers, lured by the climate, took up permanent residence there. Besides, large numbers of poor farmers moved to California during the 1930's, desperately seeking jobs of any sort. Driven from their farms on the plains by low prices, exhausted soils, and dust storms, these people reached the west coast in dilapidated Fords, destitute and at the mercy of fruit ranchers who exploited their casual labor. The tragedy was dramatized in John Steinbeck's memorable novel, *The Grapes of Wrath.*

Migratory farm labor was not new. For years, gangs had moved with the wheat harvest from Kansas north to the Canadian plains. Migratory workers were also employed in northwest lumber camps; on sugar beet farms; on truck farms near eastern cities. Living arrangements among the families of such workers were shocking from the point of view of any normal standards. Child labor persisted here, after it had been largely eliminated in the cities.

As auto travel became widespread, railroads improved their schedules and introduced streamlined trains on main routes. This came mainly in the

1930's, when low-fare buses were cutting deeply into railroad passenger service. By then the major bus networks (the Greyhound Lines, for instance) rivaled those of large railway systems. In the 1940's commercial air lines entered competition, challenging both railroads and steamship companies. The net result was to provide unexcelled travel facilities.

When quota laws cut off most immigration in the 1920's, steamship lines turned to American tourists as their chief source of passenger revenue. The depression after 1929 limited overseas travel, as did World War II except for military personnel. After the war tourist business revived rapidly. By 1950, 1,000,000 Americans were spending summer vacations in Europe, and steamship companies were taking up the winter slack by conducting special tours in Latin-American waters. But most Americans confined their trips to the United States. Here one could move about over an enormous, picturesque land without worrying about passports, baggage inspection, and changing currencies. Americans formed the travel habit, for business and pleasure; and as they moved about, their horizons broadened.

Postwar Nationalism

The upsurge of nationalism after World War I was not without precedent. Earlier periods had witnessed a comparable glorification of American institutions and the identification of Americanism with conservative ideas. But never before had such nationalism been so intensified and so efficiently organized, never so strongly supported by government action.

Involved in the new nationalism was repudiation of Wilsonian internationalism and restriction of immigration to north Europeans—peoples considered racially superior. In the name of 100 percent Americanism, some citizens turned against all radicals and liberals, on the assumption that they were plotting to extend the Bolshevik Revolution from Russia to America. Simultaneously, aliens, Negroes, Catholics, and Jews were made special targets of discrimination. Opposition to these minorities was led by a new Ku Klux Klan, pledged to keep America safe for "true Americans." Safe, that is, for native white Protestants who rejected radical and liberal philosophies.

Why this departure from the American tradition of tolerance? For one thing, World War I accustomed Americans to rely on force rather than reason. Besides that, the wartime propaganda put out by Wilson's C.P.I. had stressed the possible disloyalty of left-wing labor and of immigrants from central Europe. This had created feelings of suspicion and insecurity. It was natural that the fury against the Germans should be transferred to fury against the Bolsheviks, whose revolution seemed to threaten the family, religion, democracy, and private property. And as the anti-Bolshevik excitement grew, it seemed logical to regard American radicals and liberals as advance agents of the world revolution emanating from Moscow. America was not alone in these trends. The war intensified nationalism everywhere; and, as always, the United States was affected by world movements. In addition, American prosperity aroused envy and resentment in war-impoverished Europe. Struggling to rebuild their shattered economies, the Allies expected the United States to cancel war debts and otherwise aid their rehabilitation. When the United States did not do so, America was denounced as selfish and materialistic. Such attacks on "Uncle Shylock" intensified nationalistic reaction in the United States.

Labor disturbances also contributed. Postwar inflation and the determination of management to make no more concessions caused a wave of strikes in 1919, involving 4,000,000 workers. Americans already worried about the possibility of revolution looked on these strikes with concern. Early in 1919, the walkout of 30,000 Seattle shipyard workers led to a general strike. Mayor Ole Hanson advertised the affair as an effort to overthrow the government; and the strike was broken.

Meantime there was a dramatic effort to organize the steel workers. This was sponsored by Samuel Gompers, the anticommunist, antisocialist president of the A.F. of L. But the drive itself was led by William Z. Foster, a left-wing labor organizer who would soon announce his conversion to communism. In September, 1919, a third of a million steel workers left their jobs in plants around Chicago and Pittsburgh. Because of Foster and the temper of the times, newspapers portrayed the strike as a Bolshevik plot. Many citizens accepted this interpretation when they heard of the high proportion of recent immigrants among the strikers and read news reports of violence in strike areas. There was general satisfaction, therefore, when martial law was proclaimed, and the strike collapsed, early in 1920. Later, there was some shift in sentiment, owing in part to an investigation by the Interchurch World Movement. The investigators stated that, despite Foster's presence, the strike was not Bolshevik controlled or designed to overthrow the government. It was, basically, an effort to improve the lot of steel workers, many of whom toiled twelve hours a day, seven days a week, under unenviable conditions. Company officials broke up union meetings and promoted bad feeling between Serbian and Italian workers. Negro strikebreakers were brought in, causing riots; and the steel companies organized a gigantic publicity campaign against the strikers.

September, 1919, also brought a walkout of Boston policemen. The strike immediately concerned suspension of leaders of a unionization drive. Left without effective protection, Boston suffered property loss. Public sentiment was strongly against the police. President Wilson called the strike a "crime against civilization"; and Governor Calvin Coolidge found himself a national hero when he belatedly sent state troops to patrol Boston. ("There is no right to strike against the public safety," said Coolidge.)

Next came raids organized by A. Mitchell Palmer, Wilson's Attorney General. Palmer suspected a nation-wide Bolshevik plot to murder officials who had offended labor. There was reason for alarm, for packages containing bombs had been addressed to several government officials; and Palmer's own house was bombed. Determined to deal summarily with the unknown criminals, the Attorney General proceeded with a minimum of regard for constitutional guarantees. Agents of the Federal Bureau of Investigation raided meeting places and private homes, arresting several thousand persons. Most were subsequently released; but a few hundred were deported. In violating civil liberties, Palmer had gone too far, alarming Americans who had no sympathy for radicals. In 1920, therefore, there was a reaction against the raid technique. The Department of Labor refused to give Palmer full coöperation in his deportation plans. Some prisoners were then released. Others were given counsel and, after fair trials, were set free. Congressmen criticized Justice Department methods; and President Wilson said suppression was not the answer to America's problems.

In this period, many states passed criminal syndicalist laws which forbade writing or speaking words that implied revolutionary intent. The effect was to outlaw membership in left-wing parties. The New York legislature expelled five Socialist legislators, on the ground that no Socialist could be a loyal American. There was bloodshed in an I.W.W.-American Legion clash at Centralia, Washington. The Legion was an organization of World War I veterans, set up to work for pension legislation and to protect the republic against radical ideas. (Theodore Roosevelt, Jr., and other Legion founders had the anti-Bolshevik goal clearly in mind.) On Armistice Day, 1919, Legionnaires attacked an I.W.W. meeting hall in Centralia. In the ensuing riot, four Legion men were killed. Mass arrests of Wobblies followed; and the I.W.W., already declining, practically ceased to exist.

Somewhat different was the case of Nicola Sacco and Bartolomeo Vanzetti, Italian immigrants of anarchist views. These men were charged with a robbery and murder that took place in South Braintree, Massachusetts, in April, 1920. Evidence was contradictory; and many felt that the court was unduly influenced by prejudice against the political views of the defendants. When the men were electrocuted (April, 1927), the case had become a world symbol of the bitter conflict between conservatives and radicals.

By then, the Big Red Scare had run its course. It was apparent that the

Bolshevik Revolution was not coming to America. After a Wall Street explosion of September, 1920 (costing thirty-eight lives), there were no more bomb outrages. American radicals, and liberals, too, had retreated into silence; and conservatives were reconsidering their positions.

Was repression wise? In attacking the expulsion of Socialists from the New York legislature, Charles Evans Hughes (a Republican and no radical) said that this was not the proper way to protect democracy. New York's Governor Alfred E. Smith (a Democrat and no radical) took the same position in vetoing repressive legislation proposed by the witch-hunting Lusk Committee. Conservative President Warren G. Harding (1921–23) released Socialist Eugene V. Debs from prison; and Harding seems to have advised the steel industry that one way of combating radicalism was to get rid of the twelve-hour day.

As excitement died down, liberals and radicals again spoke out. These groups were very vocal in the 1930's; and, as before, some conservatives raised the cry of revolution. This was done when World War I veterans marched on Washington to demand bonus money (1932–33); when a general strike paralyzed San Francisco (1934); when workers tried the sit-down. The public, though, did not become alarmed until the late 1940's, when Russian-American relations raised disturbing questions.

Treatment of Minorities

The anti-Bolshevik drive of 1919–20 reflected a sense of insecurity which was especially marked among the lower middle classes—persons hit hard by post-World War I inflation. Rural Protestants blamed the cities, which contained Catholics, Jews, foreigners, and radicals. Native white laborers North and South saw the Negro and foreigner as their competitors. A swimming-beach incident in 1919 led to a virtual race war in Chicago (three dozen dead, 500 wounded). There were race riots in Omaha, Tulsa, and elsewhere. All of which helped the Ku Klux Klan.

Founded at Atlanta in 1915, the Klan was in effect a revival of the nativist Know-Nothing party of the 1850's and the anti-Negro Ku Klux Klan of Reconstruction days. The new Klan differed from its predecessors in its commercialization. (Proceeds from ten-dollar memberships were divided among Klan officers, called Kleagles, Goblins, and the like.) Many who joined the Klan did so to find escape from village boredom in secret rituals and burning of great wooden crosses. Others found in the exclusion of aliens, Negroes, Jews, and Catholics the emotional satisfaction that comes from the sense of being of the elite. Klan hoods gave protection to the brutally inclined. In some states the Klan was a political power. But influence faded fast when Indiana's Klansman governor, David C. Stephenson, went to prison for murder. By 1926 Klan power everywhere was on the wane.

In the South the Klan was primarily anti-Negro; in the North and West, chiefly anti-Catholic. Only incidentally was it anti-Semitic. But immediately after World War I, Henry Ford's Dearborn *Independent* campaigned against the Jewish "money power," Jewish "radicals," and Jewish "monopoly" of the professions. The paper even professed to believe in the discredited "Protocols of the Elders of Zion," a forgery purporting to be an agreement for Jewish subjugation of Gentiles. Although Ford publicly repudiated anti-Semitism, these articles did much harm.

In the 1930's, Adolf Hitler's brutal treatment of the Jews in Germany shocked most Americans. But Hitler's propaganda also found ears in America. Part of this was owing to the depression—job competition increases discrimination. Some who attacked the Jews were pro-Nazi—Fritz Kuhn of the German-American Bund, for example, and William Dudley Pelley of the Silver Shirts. Anti-Semitism was also voiced by Father Charles Coughlin, a Detroit radio priest with a large following. (Coughlin was ultimately silenced by superiors; and most Catholic leaders, including the Pope, condemned anti-Semitism.) Anti-Semitism persisted even in the 1940's, in the midst of war against the race-persecuting Nazis.

During World War II Japanese citizens in the United States were badly treated. So were Americans of Japanese descent. Those located on the Pacific coast had to wind up their business affairs at once, generally at great sacrifice. Then they were sent inland, to government camps. This mass uprooting was associated with the shock Americans felt after Pearl Harbor, and with the fear of espionage and sabotage along the Pacific coast. Also, Americans who had long been anti-Japanese used the occasion to get rid of Japanese and Japanese-Americans. In other words, the evacuation of 1942 was a sequel to the California land laws of the World War I era, which prohibited aliens from owning land; a sequel, also, to the immigration law of 1924, which barred Japanese from entering the United States.

These attacks on minorities did not go unchallenged. The Ku Klux Klan was denounced, not only by radicals, but by liberals and conservatives, including conservative Southerners. Although many politicians sought Klan support, few acknowledged being Klansmen. The Klan was strong; but anti-Klan sentiment was always stronger. This was very evident when bigots tried unsuccessfully to revive the Klan in the 1940's. In like fashion, anti-Semites of the 1930's drew little backing from the public. When Charles A. Lindbergh criticized Jews at an America First rally in 1941, that utterance hurt the America First cause. Even during World War II many Americans criticized the treatment of Japanese-Americans. An even friendlier gesture toward a minority group was seen in the repeal in 1943 of Chinese exclusion legislation. This made Chinese-born residents of the United States eligible for citizenship; and it ended Chinese exclusion, putting China on the quota list (105 a year).

Still more significant was an antidiscrimination movement after World War II. States passed and tried to enforce fair employment practice laws. Efforts were made to reduce discrimination against minorities in federal employment. Laura Z. Hobson's *Gentleman's Agreement* (dealing with anti-Semitism) sold well as a novel and was an effective moving picture. The same could be said for William L. White's *Lost Boundaries*, which dealt with the Negro question. Radio and school programs urged elimination of discrimination.

This trend reflected humanitarianism. Involved, too, were intellectuals who believed in cultural pluralism and therefore stressed the contributions of minority groups to American culture. Rather more important was a mounting conviction that the United States would be judged abroad partly by its treatment of minorities at home. Finally, thoughtful Americans felt that if minority groups were treated well they would be unlikely to be interested in extremist views.

Negro Americans

These were important years in the history of American Negroes, who composed a tenth of the population. This was an era of Negro migration, from southern farms to southern and northern cities. It was also a period when Negroes became more outspoken, more insistent on their constitutional and human rights. And, despite the Ku Klux Klan, the Negroes made substantial gains, especially in the North.

Not that all was well. Poverty and restrictive real-estate covenants kept northern Negroes jammed into urban slums. There was friction between Negroes and whites in northern schools and factories, and on the streets. But Negro professional men became more prosperous and effective. At first politicians paid little attention to the Negro vote, which was solidly Republican (the party of Lincoln). During the depression, though, many Negroes shifted. As the Democrats tried to hold, the Republicans to regain, Negro support, the Negro vote became important. Negroes were elected to Congress from New York and Chicago.

What the Negro wanted was elimination of discrimination in employment, education, housing, and other fields. Striking victories were achieved after 1920, especially after 1945. These included adoption of state anti-bias and fair employment practice acts; increased opportunities for Negroes in federal service; espousal of national fair employment legislation by President Harry Truman and leading Republicans; partial breakdown of segregation in the armed services after World War II; admission of Negroes to organized baseball (when Jackie Robinson joined the Brooklyn Dodgers in 1948); the less unfriendly attitude of labor toward Negroes; the decision of leading newspapers to stop giving undue attention to crimes committed by nonwhites; appointment of Negroes to high positions (as with Ralph Bunche of the United Nations); popularity of books and moving pictures dealing with race discrimination (Richard Wright's *Black Boy;* *Kingsblood Royal,* by Sinclair Lewis).

In the South the tenancy system survived, except where white and Negro sharecroppers were thrown off the land to make way for large-scale production. (Croppers then became farm laborers, if they were employed at all.) Segregation persisted; and in depression, Negroes on relief received less consideration than unemployed whites. But the situation did get better, all the same. There was an increase in the number of Negro landowners. And, humble though they were, the Negro sections of southern towns provided opportunities for Negroes to rise in the economic scale and become merchants, dentists, realtors, and insurance salesmen.

Gradually, too, dents were made in the segregation system. In Nixon vs. Herndon, 1927, and Smith vs. Allwright, 1944, the Supreme Court upheld the right of Negroes to vote in Democratic primaries—the only important elections in most southern states. In the Ada Sipuel case of 1948 the Court ruled that, in fields where there were no adequate educational facilities for Negroes, southern state-supported "white" institutions had to admit qualified Negroes. By 1950 a handful of Negroes had been admitted to the medical and law colleges of southern state universities. By then judges were questioning the legality of agreements designed to keep nonwhites out of certain residential neighborhoods (District of Columbia Covenant cases of 1949). Some southern whites tried to stop the tide. Southern legislators rewrote restrictive laws so that they would hold up in court. Some conservative states'-rights Southerners went so far as to break with the national Democratic party in 1948 and run a separate (Dixiecrat) presidential candidate. But, though the movement for Negro rights gained slowly, it nonetheless advanced.

The Indians

According to the census, there were forty Negroes to every Indian in the United States. Despite a recent increase in population, Indians numbered less than 400,000 in 1950—one-quarter of

THE NEGRO IN THE UNITED STATES

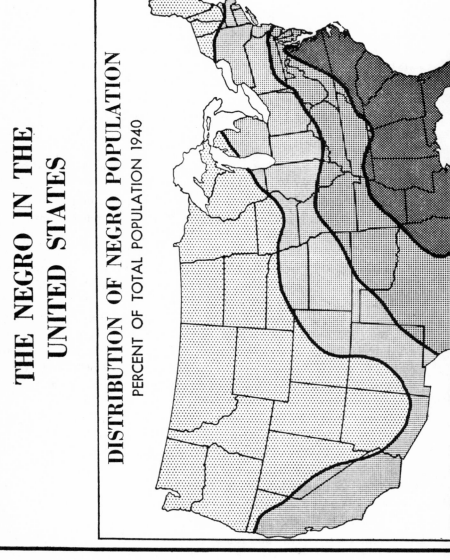

DISTRIBUTION OF NEGRO POPULATION
PERCENT OF TOTAL POPULATION 1940

In the twentieth century, as in slave days, most American Negroes lived in the southeastern part of the United States, and especially in the cotton-producing states. It will be noted, however, that whites outnumber the Negroes even in the states of the deep South. (Negroes make up most of the population in many lowland cotton-growing counties, but the hill counties are predominantly white.)

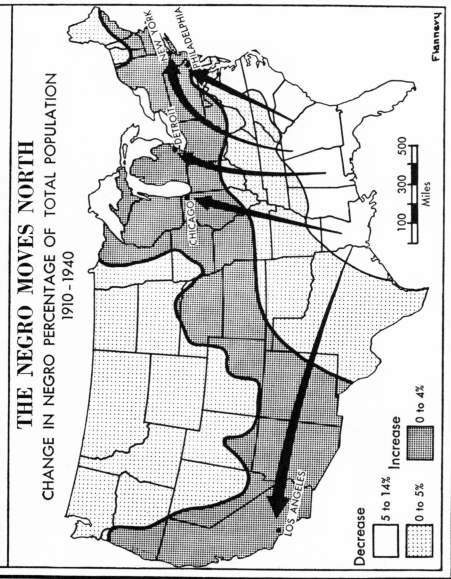

THE NEGRO MOVES NORTH

CHANGE IN NEGRO PERCENTAGE OF TOTAL POPULATION
1910-1940

NEW YORK
PHILADELPHIA
DETROIT
CHICAGO
LOS ANGELES

Miles

100   300   500
Miles

Decrease

5 to 14%   Increase

0 to 5%   0 to 4%

Flannery

were dissatisfied with their role in the southern plantation economy. Some therefore migrated to southern and border cities—Atlanta, New Orleans, Birmingham, St. Louis, Baltimore. Others moved to northern or far western industrial centers. As a result, the Negroes made up a smaller percentage of the southern population in 1940 than in 1910. In like fashion, Negroes formed a larger percentage of the northern population in 1940 than in 1910.

It will be noted that the Negro showed a greater tendency to leave the deep South than the border states, and that the Negro, a farmer in the South, did not move into northern farm areas. The Negro population of the wheat states showed a relative decline in this period.

one percent of the population. Many persons with some Indian blood were not included in this figure; but even their inclusion would not have made the total large.

Before the Civil War the government had driven the Indians west and herded them into reservations. Theoretically, reservation lands were granted in perpetuity; in practice, the whites continually cut down the Indians' share of the national domain. The Dawes Act of 1887, designed to prepare the Indian for citizenship, did that job badly. Citizenship was not extended until 1924. The Dawes Act, however, led to the loss of much tribal land. Contrary to popular belief, only a very few Indians profited from oil strikes on their property. Most red men remained extremely poor; they had lost the old ways without picking up the new.

An Indian Reorganization Act of 1934 proposed to keep remaining reservation lands intact and improve these properties through long-range planning. This did some good. But some reservations were too small, barren, eroded, or overgrazed to be redeemed. In 1948 the public was shocked to hear of widespread malnutrition among the Navahos. The news was the more impressive in that it came just when the United States was getting ready to help foreign nations through the Marshall Plan. Congress hastily voted emergency funds; but it was clear that three full centuries had not solved the Indian problem. Perhaps, however, time would provide a solution. Many an Indian had left the reservation by 1950 to become absorbed in the general population. And, despite efforts to preserve and revive Indian arts, the reservations also felt the impact of the white man's ways. Absorption in blood and culture seemed the long-run outlook for the Indian.

Prosperity and Depression

During the 1920's many Americans felt that prosperity was permanent. The great crash of 1929 came as a sickening shock; and the shock helps explain the turmoil of the 1930's. As if domestic woes were not enough, the same decade saw the rise of totalitarian fascism in Europe—a challenge to the American way of life.

All this time, Americans faced technologic change. Most welcomed the new machines as keys to comfort; but few saw the dislocations caused by the machine age. Men change their values slowly. Hence there was little planning of the social adjustments called for by mechanization. Machines gave control over time and distance; but they made men more interdependent, robbing the old individualism of much of its meaning. Machines brought leisure; but they also threw the economic system out of gear by producing more than could be consumed under prevailing patterns of income distribution.

The prosperity of the 1920's was shared unequally by the urban classes and only slightly affected the farmer. Yet there was a substantial increase in real per capita income. Much of the increase was spent on cars, radios, and other mechanical gadgets. The number of automobiles trebled in this decade. By 1929 every third home had a radio. Equally spectacular were increases in sales of cigarettes, rayon clothing, and cosmetics.

But there was another side to the picture. Even at the end of the 1920's most city homes lacked electric refrigeration, and many had neither electric lights nor furnace heat. Textile workers and coal miners suffered from the chronic depression that plagued these industries; tenant and sharecrop farmers enjoyed few of the luxuries of the prosperity decade. In some industries, workers over forty-five had difficulty holding jobs. Besides that, new machines threw perhaps 2,000,000 men out of work each year. Some 7,000,000 families had less than $1500 annual income; another 15,000,000 received less than $2500. None of these enjoyed what experts called an adequate standard of living; but they included most of the population.

Moreover, much of the decade's prosperity rested on insecure foundations. Paper fortunes, "made" on the stock market, melted away after 1929. Installment buying reached $7,000,000,000 in 1929, 15 percent of retail purchases. It should have been clear that if installment buyers suffered a shrinkage of income, the economy would sustain a serious blow. But mass advertising, success stories in the magazines, and the pronouncements of business and government leaders reassured the people. Prosperity had come to stay; every American was to enjoy an increasingly high standard of living. A chicken in every pot, said Herbert Hoover; two cars in every garage.

A few questioned these statements—novelists like Sinclair Lewis and John R. Dos Passos; liberal journalists; some academicians; a handful of politicians; spokesmen of the submerged left. Ignored in the 1920's, these critics won a larger audience during the depression. For a brief period in the 1930's, Americans listened to Howard Scott and other Technocrats who favored turning the economy over to a managerial-engineer elite. The Marxists enjoyed a longer period of influence; but they too failed to convince many Americans. Nor did citizens long listen to the Southern Agrarians, who reacted to the depression by repudiating the technological basis of society and by advocating an impossible return to an idealized agrarian culture.

While rejecting such views, Americans of the 1930's refused to accept business leadership. A great many took up the thesis behind Franklin D. Roosevelt's New Deal (1933–38). Americans, said F. D. R., could work out a way of life mid-point between the old uncontrolled business economy and European-type collectivism. The economy might be held in proper balance by moderate state subsidies and controls. But world crises made it difficult after 1939 to concentrate on domestic problems. The postwar years (after 1945) still saw most Americans badly housed and unable to afford many of the comforts created by modern science and technology. Productivity increased; and the economy was still capable of turning out more than could be absorbed easily by normal domestic peacetime consumption.

By 1950, however, the average citizen fared better than in the 1920's. In 1929 every third family had a radio. Two decades later nearly every family had one, and the average was two. Few farms and city residences lacked electricity; and more and more working-class Americans were thinking in terms of electric refrigerators and washing machines.

Crime

In the 1920's the accent was on conservatism and order. Such an age might have been expected to produce reverence for traditional values and obedience to the law. But it did not. The corruption of highly placed officials during the presidency of Warren G. Harding (1921–23) was paralleled by misdeeds in states and cities. The national homicide rate was sixteen times that of England. Theft cost Americans a quarter of a billion dollars a year, little being recovered and few culprits apprehended. More serious still, crime came to be organized in an efficient manner. The organizers—men like Al Capone and John Dillinger—received much newspaper space and were half-admired by many law-abiding citizens.

One feature of the crime wave was violation of the Eighteenth Amendment, which prohibited manufacture, transportation, and sale of intoxicating beverages. The Volstead Act and other enforcement measures never worked well, chiefly because of the determined resistance of millions of urban Americans. Citizens who had seldom touched liquor were intrigued with the desire to do what the law prohibited. Others, accustomed to drinking, did not propose to stop. Some brewed and distilled in their cellars and bathrooms. Others patronized speak-easies and bootleggers. Supplies came partly from industrial alcohol channels; partly from rumrunners who smuggled in liquor from Canada, Mexico, and the West Indies; partly from farmers who produced corn, grapes, wheat, and hops directly for illicit liquor manufacturers.

Bootlegging became a big business. To protect profits, the liquor interests paid protection to the police, and corrupted journalists and legislators. Using machine guns and armored cars, they forced goods on retailers and crushed rivals in gang warfare. Many bootleg gangs expanded their empires to include gambling houses and brothels. In some cities garages and laundries were required to pay substantial sums for "protection" of their establishments against hoodlums.

The depression brought repeal of the Eighteenth Amendment, by adoption of the Twenty-First Amendment in 1933. This came because of failure of enforcement efforts, plus a depression-inspired desire to raise money with liquor taxes. When prohibition died, some bootleg gangs turned to gambling: slot machines; policy; betting halls that quoted odds on horse races, prize fights, basketball games, and elections. Others tried politics or wormed their way into small business or labor unions.

Gradually, however, the public became aroused. The press printed stories about the fixing of athletic contests; the beating of restaurant owners and furriers who would not pay protection; the tie-up between politics and crime. Kidnapings (notably that of the son of Charles A. Lindbergh) shocked the public into action. As a result, new laws were passed. Improved law-enforcement agencies used science and technology to track down criminals. The Treasury Department closed in on Al Capone for nonpayment of income tax. Government agents (G-men) from J. Edgar Hoover's Federal Bureau of Investigation replaced racketeers as folk heroes of young Americans. Local prosecutors like Thomas E. Dewey built reputations as racket busters. Dewey put behind bars the notorious "Lucky" Luciano; also Jimmy Hines, a Tammany politician with underworld connections.

Although results were impressive, this was no job that could be done and laid aside. World War II saw criminals penetrating into war production. Then and later there was an alarming increase in juvenile delinquency. And in 1950–51 a committee headed by Senator Estes Kefauver unearthed much about the new racketeers—mostly politically influential gamblers anxious to appear "respectable." Hearings of this committee, broadcast by television, much impressed the public. Impressive too were the findings of other Congressional investigators. While examining the Reconstruction Finance Corporation, a Senate committee under J. W. Fulbright uncovered many a sordid tale of influence peddling in the Truman administration (1951). Senator J. J. Williams and a House committee headed by Cecil King showed how many Treasury and Justice Department officials had enriched themselves by aiding tax-dodgers (1951–52).

The Jazz Age, and After

The defiance of prohibition was in line with other trends of the jazz age. In the 1920's it was fashionable for women to emancipate themselves by smoking cigarettes, wearing "boyish bobs" and dresses that barely reached the knees, and talking freely about sex. It was "smart" to look down on traditional values, to appear cynical and disillusioned, to defy the old double standard of morals by open displays of affection and by drinking bootleg liquor in mixed gatherings. Dancing became a matter of intimate embraces to the tune of syncopated jazz rhythms; popular songs stressed sex and "sophistication."

Many writers echoed the sentiments of the jazz age. One example was Ernest Hemingway, who wrote hard-boiled stories about drinking, bullfighting, and sex. But the real voice of the era was the *American Mercury*. Edited by H. L. Mencken, this organ poked cynical fun at politicians and businessmen, belittled religion and conventional morality, and set forth a gospel of an emancipated, sophisticated elite. Not until the depression did Americans realize that Mencken's approach was negative, that he sneered at reform as well as at reaction.

The jazz age made its impact felt on many college campuses. F. Scott Fitzgerald overdrew the picture in *This Side of Paradise*, a novel that pictured the reckless gaiety and dissipation of well-to-do college students. But many undergraduates did take their studies lightly in the 1920's. The depression after 1929 had a sobering effect. College students had to economize, find odd jobs, rely on the help of the government's National Youth Administration. Confronted by harsh realities, an increasing number showed concern over current problems.

So, too, with most middle-class Americans. A new seriousness characterized the American mood in the 1930's. "Proletarian novels" attracted attention. *Tobacco Road*, a play about southern poor whites, broke records on Broadway. John Steinbeck's book about migratory workers, *The Grapes of Wrath*, became a best seller, rivaling the detective mystery stories and escape-into-the-past historical novels. Even Hollywood experimented cautiously with serious themes.

Some features of the jazz age survived. Women and girls continued to spend a good deal on cosmetics and at beauty parlors. Smoking habits persisted, as did informality of manner. Skirts became longer, but women refused to return to the confining garments of their grandmothers. Jazz and the movies remained popular.

During World War II and after, there was some effort to recapture the carefree spirit of the jazz era. But Mencken cynicism did not fit the atomic age. Besides, what had seemed sensational in the 1920's now appeared routine and commonplace (scanty bathing costumes, for example, and frank discussions about sex). The flask-toting "flaming youth" of the jazz age had considered themselves sophisticated and daring. But the young people of the 1950's would have thought them superficial and naïve.

The Triumph of Sports

At mid-century, old-timers looked back on the 1920's as the golden age in sports. Was it not the age of Babe Ruth in baseball, Bill Tilden in tennis, Bobby Jones in golf, Red Grange in football? Certainly it was the decade of big gates. Some 100,000 people paid over $2,500,000 to see Gene Tunney defend his heavyweight championship against Jack Dempsey in 1927. Newsreels, sports magazines, and radio made Americans more sports-conscious than ever before. And, although gate receipts dropped during the depression, the trend was upward again during and after World War II.

Commercialization and professionalization inevitably increased. College and high school football and basketball became more commercialized. So did amateur tennis and golf, even track-and-field events. Professional football, relatively unimportant before the 1920's, became profitable at the end of that decade. Organized baseball, with a livelier ball calculated to produce home runs, did so well that owners could pay large bonuses to talented teen-agers. Professional basketball, hockey, tennis, auto racing all became profitable to leading participants and to promoters. Horse and dog racing boomed when depression-haunted state governments permitted the installation of betting machines (the state's cut going for relief or for the aged). Professional wrestling degenerated into farce—professional, profitable farce. Interest declined only in six-day bicycle racing, which did not appeal to people-in-a-hurry.

As sports became big business, the trend was toward monopoly. The key was the reserve clause, which bound an athlete to one club until he was dropped or traded ("sold"). It was difficult to challenge Madison Square Garden control of big prize fights. It was all but impossible to buck organized baseball, which was presided over by a powerful commissioner, aptly called "czar." An effort to unionize big-league ballplayers after World War II failed; but the attempt did help the players get a pension system. Meantime, National League control of professional football was challenged by an All America conference. But after four years of expensive competition, the new circuit was merged with the old.

Interest was not limited to spectator sports. Thanks to municipal courses and courts, golf and tennis were no longer for the rich alone. Motoring, swimming, and boating were also within the reach of ordinary people. Every village had its ball teams; and there was a steady increase in the number of fishing and hunting licenses sold by the states. This helped sporting goods manufacturers, auto and boat makers, owners of resort hotels.

Where would it all lead? One could not make a living writing poetry; but one could make ends meet as a billiard champion or as an "amateur" in certain sports. Gambling brought unfortunate results, as in the fixing of college basketball games in Madison Square Garden (revealed in 1951). Defenders said that, thanks partly to sports, Americans were the healthiest people in the world. Moreover, the growth in sports did not prevent a simultaneous increase in interest in good literature and music. Sports enthusiasts further insisted that international competition (as in the Olympic games) made sports fans more international-minded than other Americans.

Changing Family Patterns

As commercialized leisure-time activities multiplied, recreation became less focused in the family. Other functions, such as canning, laundering, sewing, and dressmaking, declined with the advent of processed foods and commercialized services. Even child care moved in part into the multiplying nursery schools.

Some women used their new leisure at country clubs, movies, and bridge luncheons. Others tried civic uplift. More found jobs. In the 1920's middle-class circles buzzed with the question: Marriage, a career, or both? More and more frequently, the answer was both. Before and after marriage, women worked in department stores, beauty parlors, souvenir shops, tearooms, and business offices; and a few entered the professions. Factory employment was most important of all. World War I provided jobs; and the good times of the 1920's continued the trend.

The long struggle for woman suffrage ended in 1920 with ratification of the Nineteenth Amendment. But politics changed little. Women's groups did fight for laws to improve health standards, especially for children; and such groups worked for honest local government. But few women entered politics, and women rarely voted as a bloc. Voting by women neither wrecked the home nor made the world much better.

The divorce rate continued to rise. In 1914, one marriage out of ten was ending in divorce. In 1939, it was one in six; in 1945, one in four. The rate did go down early in the depression (though not as far or as fast as the marriage rate). The sharp rise after World War II was due partly to hasty war marriages. Largely, however, it reflected the long-range trend. Although many deplored the situation, it received less notice at mid-century than it had thirty years before.

The birth rate declined in the prosperous 1920's and depressed 1930's. Immigration restriction was one factor—immigrant families ran large. Increased interest in birth control was even more important. The Catholic Church continued to oppose the use of contraceptive devices; and in Massachusetts and Connecticut it continued to be illegal even for physicians to disseminate information about birth control. Some Protestants agreed with the Catholics. But most Americans took family limitation for granted by 1950. When the birth rate fell to a record low in 1933, some predicted that the population would soon be stationary. But the curve turned sharply upward during and after World War II, as the marriage rate reached an all-time high. (The rate in 1946 was double that of 1932.) The birth rate climbed back to World War I levels; and schools faced overcrowding in the 1950's.

Women were the first to lose their jobs in the depression. Back in the home, many tried to economize by reviving the arts of baking, canning, and sewing. But on the whole hard times still further weakened family patterns. Many families disintegrated during depression-caused migrations. Friction developed when two or more families had to double up in one home; and the atmosphere of the depression sharpened personal antagonism.

World War II brought new problems, with husbands away in service or working overtime on war jobs. Wives found employment again; and sometimes children were neglected. Many war marriages could not be well established, despite efforts of wives to follow their husbands from one camp to another. Once the war was over, the housing shortage subjected family life to still other strains. Alarmists expected disaster; but the family came through very well. The tendency toward early marriages, the high birth rate, the permanence of the great majority of unions all pointed to that conclusion.

Religion

In the 1920's the "smart set" sneered at religion. Yet there were fewer indications of militant agnosticism than in the late nineteenth century, when Robert Ingersoll stumped the country with his agnostic lectures. The American Association for the Advancement of Atheism, founded in 1925, attracted only the merest handful of members. Polls suggested that most Americans gave at least lip service to basic religious belief. Church membership grew. (It would decline in the depression, come up again in the 1940's.) Radio took sermons to many who did not attend church.

There were evidences, however, that religion was losing ground in this secular age. The collapse of prohibition hurt the prestige of the Protestant leaders who had supported that experiment. The decline of missionary activities in many parts of the world, together with the rise of antireligious totalitarian movements in Europe, indicated loss of influence. Church officials complained that, even when membership was rising, golf and the automobile kept people away from services. Some saw the answer in interdenominational unity. Several Lutheran bodies drew closer together in 1931, and the Congregational and Christian churches were joined in that year. Another union established the Evangelical and Reformed Church in 1934; and in 1939 a great merger united 8,000,000 Methodists.

In the depression, revenues fell off; and the crisis led many clergymen to reconsider their views on social questions. The revitalization of the social gospel was reflected in a poll of 20,000 ministers (1934). Almost three-fifths advocated a "drastically reformed capitalism," and nearly a third declared in favor of socialism. In the prosperous 1940's the stress was shifted from economic to spiritual matters; but many clergymen continued to advocate reform.

These years saw one of the last rounds in the battle between rising urban modernists and declining rural fundamentalists. The modernists reconciled the Bible with modern scientific thought by using figurative interpretations; the fundamentalists insisted on literal interpretation. When several southern states prohibited the teaching of evolution in publicly supported schools and colleges, many regarded the move as a confession that the tide had turned the other way. In 1925 the attention of the nation was turned to the trial in Dayton, Tennessee, of John Scopes, a high school biology instructor who admitted having taught evolution in violation of state law. Clarence Darrow defended Scopes, while William Jennings Bryan supported the prosecution. A jury of rural Tennesseans found Scopes guilty (a higher court threw out the case on a technicality). But the public in general felt that Bryan's showing had been less than effective. The fundamentalists kept up the fight, even founding a William Jennings Bryan University in Dayton. The modernists, however, were gaining ground.

As always, there were new religious groups. Notable were the Churches of God, Pentecostal Assemblies, and Evangelical Associations, groups that used emotional appeals no longer stressed by the older sects. Most of the rising churches appealed primarily to the lower-income groups; but the Oxford or Buchmanite movement tried to fit the evangelical approach to the needs of upper-class citizens.

With the virtual cessation of immigration, the Roman Catholic Church grew less rapidly than before. The 1920's, which brought immigration restriction legislation, also brought the anti-Catholic Ku Klux Klan. There were additional attacks when a Catholic, Alfred E. Smith, ran for President in 1928. Nevertheless, the Catholic Church continued to grow, and consolidated its position in a growing system of parochial schools and other institutions. By the 1930's and 1940's, Catholic leaders were increasingly outspoken. They launched a campaign to "clean up" the movies; and their Legion of Decency became a strong influence in Hollywood. Members of the hierarchy, and Catholic laymen as well, attacked writings deemed hostile to their cause. The *Nation* was barred from New York City high school libraries because of a series of anti-Catholic articles by Paul Blanshard. By mid-century, Catholic spokesmen were demanding increased government aid to parochial schools, as for bus transportation to school and for health services. And Catholic officials were giving more attention to small towns and rural areas, where Catholicism had been feeble in the past.

Education

Education advanced rapidly after World War I. By the mid-1920's half the children of high school age were in school; state legislatures lengthened the school year and extended compulsory attendance through the sixteenth year. Institutions of higher learning enrolled one-eighth of the young people of college age by 1925, a fourth after World War II. Illiteracy retreated. Adult education expanded. The workers' education movement became important. Educational radio programs multiplied; and the public bought books designed to give a taste of mathematics, philosophy, or history.

The other side? Many farm children, especially in the South, did not attend high school because of economic pressure or lack of facilities. Low salaries meant substandard teachers for many grade schools. Some saw a remedy in federal subsidies. After World War II, President Truman urged such action. The question bogged down, however, over states' rights and segregation, then over parochial school issues.

The increase in school attendance raised problems. Some said that mass education put a premium on mere accumulation of credits. Others said the solution lay in deëmphasizing traditional subjects in the schools and stressing vocational and social education providing training for work, marriage, and citizenship. John Dewey's learning-by-doing and learning-for-living had influence. Even more important were the requirements of industrial society, and the fact that most high school students would not go on to college.

On the college level, many were dissatisfied with curriculums which reflected the pressure for specialization. A few small colleges, such as Bennington, adopted individualized programs that stressed student initiative. Under Robert Hutchins, the University of Chicago moved away from the elective system. Hutchins considered a core of knowledge indispensable to every educated person, and insisted on study of the great books of Western civilization. By the 1940's, many colleges were experimenting with "general education," especially for freshmen and sophomores. The elective system, however, held its own. So did the trend toward specialization.

The depression hit education very hard. Many schools could not pay their teachers, and closed their doors or shortened their terms. Outworn equipment was not repaired; and teachers' salaries, never high, sank to ever lower levels. Research suffered in many centers of higher learning. But there were bright points. Students were more serious than before. National Youth Administration subsidies enabled many high school and college students to continue their studies; and enrollment mounted. When prosperity returned, during World War II, the draft cut into totals. Colleges kept open by teaching girls and by special military training units. The regular job was resumed at war's end, but under difficulties, as veterans subsidized under the G.I. Bill of Rights doubled enrollment overnight.

By 1950 the veteran load was leveling off. There were indications, however, that college enrollment would in the long run increase. Nineteenth-century Americans considered a grade school education desirable. By 1920 the general goal was high school; and by 1950 parents and employers were considering college training a must. Opportunities were increasing, with the establishment of new municipal four-year and junior colleges and state university extension centers.

On the graduate level American education made great progress. Money was poured into libraries and laboratories. No longer was it necessary for Americans seeking specialized training to go abroad. Opposition to totalitarianism brought hundreds of outstanding scholars to the United States. This enhanced the prestige of American universities. European, Latin-American, and Oriental students now came to study in America.

The atomic age posed serious problems for scholars. Need for secrecy limited the free exchange of scientific information. No less real was the problem of preventing specialization from undermining a broad approach to man and his environment. Most serious of all was the necessity for continuing to expand frontiers in a period of crisis.

Meantime, secondary and primary schools faced problems of space and personnel. Depression, the declining birth rate, and World War II slowed school construction from 1930 to 1945; and many teachers quit because of poor pay. The increasing birth rate created a crisis by 1950. Despite a reluctance to raise taxes, and despite disapproval of teacher strikes, citizens felt that something must be done. Teachers' salaries were increased—not fast enough, unfortunately, in view of price inflation—and new school buildings were constructed. The trend was toward rambling, one-story construction, with emphasis on light and air.

Philanthropy and the Arts and Sciences

Since theirs was the wealthiest nation, Americans acquired abroad the reputation for being money-minded. Yet no people were more generous in supporting churches, schools, welfare organizations, and the arts and sciences. Americans also aided stricken areas abroad, as in the Japanese earthquake of 1923 and when, after World War II, Americans sent C.A.R.E. packages to those in want in Europe.

After World War I the zeal for private collecting in the fine arts gave way to interest in supporting art and science for the public benefit. Wealthy men continued to play the chief role. Motives varied: social conscience, quest for fame, a desire to avoid income taxes. Large gifts were now made to art institutes, museums, symphony orchestras—institutions calculated to improve public taste and encourage native contributions. Businessmen also used their influence to secure municipal aid for orchestras and libraries. Thus the city government assumed upkeep of the New York Public Library, an institution made possible by the earlier merger of three great private collections.

Higher institutions also received gifts. True, seven-eighths of college and university income came from tuition and government sources in 1950. But private funds were highly significant, especially since much of this money went to large universities equipped to do basic research.

In 1900 there were practically no large private foundations subsidizing research or welfare work. By 1950 there were 150 such organizations in the natural sciences, humanities, and social sciences. Medicine and public health led the way. The giant was the Rockefeller Foundation, which by 1940 had handed out a third of a billion dollars. Notable for its wide range of interests, this body spent abroad as well as at home, to aid medical education and other activities. The Ford Foundation, which got under way in 1950–51, promised to be an even more impressive organization.

At first foundation support was accepted with enthusiasm. Later, criticism arose. It was said that foundation officers were sometimes ill-informed, or played favorites. Many feared that foundations might exercise too much influence over universities. Nevertheless, foundations stimulated research and welfare work between 1910 and 1940, when large-scale government aid was not yet available.

Science and the Government

During World War I, a National Research Council had directed public and private investigations. After the armistice in 1918, the Council continued as a quasi-public body but avoided dependence on government funds, to maintain freedom from bureaucratic control. It established a fellowship program for training scientists; it initiated research programs which were subsidized by foundations. In other words, it coördinated the natural science research interests of federal bureaus, corporations, and the universities. Somewhat similar work was done in the humanities by the American Council of Learned Societies, in the social sciences by the Social Science Research Council.

When the crash of 1929 forced the government to weigh all possible means of recovery, President Roosevelt appointed a Science Advisory Board (1934). It reported that less than one-half of one percent of the budget went to research and that there was much duplication of effort.

From this time forward, government research appropriations soared. By 1937, 120 federal agencies were doing research; and federal research expenditures reached an eighth of a billion dollars a year. This was more than the research budget of foundations or universities, though not as much as was expanded by corporations. Most of the federal funds was spent on applied science, more than two-thirds of it on natural science and technology. The Department of Agriculture continued to lead. A Bankhead-Jones Act of 1935 authorized the department to set up regional laboratories and match state funds for development of state experiment stations. Some feared that red tape would reduce efficiency in government research projects. But government scientists made impressive records; and excellent results were obtained when government and university scientists worked in coöperation.

Science and World War II

Basic science had suffered in Germany under the Nazis, but engineering skills had remained high. Germany was ahead of Britain and America in development of jet planes, guided missiles, and supersubmarines. Much depended on whether Americans and their allies could meet or outdo German achievements. Thus science was a central factor in the war effort, more so than in any earlier conflict.

When it became apparent that the job was too vast for the National Research Council, President Roosevelt appointed a National Defense Research Committee to direct war research in the physical sciences and technology, and a Committee on Medical Research for that field. Combined, these committees were known as the Office of Scientific Research and Development (O.S.R.D.). Research was done in university, corporation, and government laboratories, O.S.R.D. providing grants to cover costs. Out of these studies emerged improved tanks, "walkie-talkies," radar, the proximity fuse, fast fighter planes, giant bombers. Also insecticides like D.D.T., and more reliable vaccines. Remarkable advances were also made in medical treatment, as in the large-scale production of penicillin and the isolation of blood derivatives for the handling of shock and hemorrhage. As a result of such progress, the army death rate from disease declined from the 1917 figure of 14 per thousand to .6; and this though many troops served in the tropics. Of wounded men who received medical attention and who did not die almost instantly, 97 percent survived, an amazing record.[1]

The major technologic achievement of the war was the atomic bomb. The principles of atomic fission were worked out before World War II. There ensued a race of physicists on both sides, to determine which could first apply these principles to manufacture of a super bomb. Americans, aided by Allied scientists, had two advantages: (1) the old flair for engineering stages of development, and (2) unique resources in both money and materials. Some $2,000,000,000 was spent by the supersecret Manhattan Project on a vast coördinated development which involved many scientific teams. As a result, atomic bombs were exploded over Hiroshima and Nagasaki, Japan, in August, 1945, with terrifying results (over 150,000 persons killed).

The A-bomb affected the public profoundly. Physicists involved in the bomb research acquired a prestige greater than that enjoyed by commanding generals during war. ("The 'absent-minded professors' with their theories . . . ," said one writer, "overnight donned the tunic of Superman.") Americans had always admired those who could get results; and in this case, the most abstract physics produced the most practical consequences. The atom bomb certainly "worked." Basic science might be feared; but it could never again be disdained.

Actually, the bomb only accentuated a popularizing process already under way. Advances in research and their application had made a strong impression on the public after World War I. Newspapers began using science reporters in the 1920's; and citizens read more about the "wonders of modern science." Radio helped, too; and millions saw such motion pictures as Madame Curie. Then war research further impressed the public. Everyone heard of radar and penicillin, as well as The Bomb.

Advances in the Natural Sciences

Americans "discovered" physics through the appearance of commercial radio, the talkies, television. Some inkling also reached the public of a revolution in theoretical physics, a new principle of "relativity" in the relations of space, time, energy, and matter. The chief figure here was the German Albert Einstein, who fled to America from the Nazi regime in the 1930's. It testified to the growing awe for basic science

---

[1] It was more difficult to handle those who became mental casualties under strain of combat or even in camp. Their type of illness was more clearly recognized than before, and progress was made in psychiatric treatment of milder forms. Serious cases, however, had to be assigned to veterans' hospitals, where many linger as tragic reminders of the horrors of war and present inability to cure the so-called psychoses.

that this leader became something of a popular hero here, among millions who could not comprehend his theories.

Clearly physics was no longer chiefly concerned with the relatively superficial behavior of bodies of matter and forms of energy like heat and electricity. Research had invaded the interior of atoms, where a whole new microcosm was revealed. Atoms, it was found, were made up of charged electrons and other particles, which moved in a minute universe of their own. The seeming solidity of bodies disappeared, since all were made up of these largely empty atomic units. The old distinction between matter and energy was breaking down.

So, too, were distinctions between physics and chemistry. By redistributing particles in atoms of one element, scientists could change it into another element—a miracle of which the alchemists had dreamed. The internal universe of the atom was held together by a tremendous amount of energy, far greater than that which bound together the whole atoms in the molecules of a chemical combination. Hence when a single atom was split apart, as in the bomb, it released a gigantic explosion. There were vast possibilities here for peace as well as war. No other source of energy promises so much for the power engines of the future. It will take time, though, before this greatest force—locked up in the smallest bodies—can be safely harnessed.

In chemistry proper, the most notable advances were in synthetic research. It now was possible to put together compounds unknown to nature, taking over, as it were, where nature left off. Using hydrocarbons, organic chemists could make whole series of dyes and other articles. Down to World War I, this was largely a German story; but Americans played a leading part after wartime seizure of enemy patents. The American leader, Du Pont (formerly a power-making concern) became one of the world's great producers of chemical products—everything from paint to textiles, for creative chemistry was unfolding a new synthetic world of plastics.

In the biologic fields, there were major advances in genetics (the science of heredity) and medicine. Mendel, an Austrian, had earlier discovered that certain qualities in crossed species were inherited according to an exact pattern in descendants. Experimenting with fruit flies, the American biologist Thomas H. Morgan showed that hereditary characteristics such as eye color depend on certain factors (genes) in the germ cells. Plant and animal breeding began to be relatively exact, applied sciences.

Medical research had developed vaccines against some infectious diseases (e.g., typhoid fever) even before 1910. But no bacteria were found responsible for other infections, such as influenza and yellow fever. Presently it was discovered that these diseases were caused by minute organisms known as viruses. But, since viruses could not be cultivated outside the animal or human host, it was difficult to prepare vaccines against them. Then, in the late 1930's, new synthetic drugs coming out of German laboratories—sulfonamides, or "sulfa drugs"—combated such infectious diseases as pneumonia. Soon after, another type of drug, the antibiotics, suddenly displayed great promise. These involved a principle recognized by Pasteur, that one organism could be set against another. English scientists found that a certain mold, penicillin, produced a substance destructive to many bacteria. Penicillin combated more infections than sulfa and seemed less toxic in its aftereffects. The war period also saw the development of vaccines against such virus diseases as influenza and yellow fever.

Meanwhile, biochemists traced serious malnutritional diseases, such as pellagra (widespread in the South), to lack of certain vitamins. Prevention or cure was possible if the vitamins were supplied. No less important was growing knowledge of the role of hormone substances produced by certain glands. It was found that diabetics could be kept in health by insulin, a cattle gland product. And pernicious anemia could be controlled by eating liver.

There was no such success in treating the degenerative or chronic diseases. As infectious diseases came under control, more people survived into old age. Since cancer and heart conditions take their greatest toll in later years, the incidence of these increased. At the present time, therefore, medical research is concentrating much of its attention on degenerative disorders.

The Social Sciences

Down to 1930, basic work in the social sciences had little application to practical problems. University men did not wish to be confused with the politicians and welfare workers; and they were too busy working on principles to give heed to immediate issues. Gradually, however, principles were applied to practice. Government and business employed social science specialists, especially after the crash of 1929. Economists advised banks, industries, and labor unions. Sociologists were consulted by courts and prison officials. Experts were taken into government (Roosevelt's brain trust, for example). Business leaders found it worth while to spend money both on science laboratories and on business research (studying production, marketing, advertising).

The influence of social scientists on courts, parole boards, and welfare organizations was one of objectivity and exactitude. Instead of citing horrible examples, social scientists marshaled statistics and appealed to reason. In this manner they sought to overcome popular superstitions or prejudices in social matters, much as natural scientists had earlier overcome suspicions about nature.

Trends in American social science had few counterparts abroad. Social thought in Europe continued to be largely of the armchair, philosophic sort, which had flourished in America also before 1900. Europeans were preëminent as theorists; but many of them neglected to check theory by systematic and controlled observations. Their work, therefore, had little value for the actual direction of business or government. Hence after World War II, Europe had few systematically trained experts. By 1950, however, a number of nations had set up social science institutes to produce needed personnel.

Some Europeans still view American social science as another scheme for getting merely practical results. But in social science, as in certain natural sciences, American research was by 1950 equal to or in advance of that in most European countries. After three centuries of colonial dependence, America had finally become outstanding in natural and social science as well as in technology.

Cultural Maturity: The Fine Arts

In the fine arts, too, the United States forged ahead after World War I. In some fields (as in abstract art) Americans continued to follow Old World styles. But Europeans as well as Americans acknowledged that the United States had come into its own in the creative arts. Each decade had special characteristics. The prosperity of the 1920's made possible a widespread patronage of the arts and led also to much satirizing of materialism and conformity. The depression of the 1930's brought expatriates home and led many intellectuals to discover for the first time the richness and promise of America. These years also saw the first major effort of the government to support the arts. The 1940's brought new advances, and by mid-century many called America the cultural center of Western civilization.

New government buildings of the 1920's and 1930's still followed the Greco-Roman form. But even classical structures reflected (especially in the interiors) the conviction that form must be related to function. The functionalist school, represented by Frank Lloyd Wright, William Lescaze, and others, was making steady gains. The modern style found much favor in domestic buildings. Factories and hospitals adopted it; so did the Nebraska state capitol. The Chicago World's Fair of 1893 had popularized the classical style. New expositions reflected changing attitudes. The Chicago Century of Progress (1933) and New York World of Tomorrow (1939) featured the dominance of machine civilization, presenting curious-shaped but functional structures.

The idea of efficient use led to city and state planning. Planners developed highways that connected the hearts of cities with suburban areas. Zoning restrictions became general. Slum clearance was discussed in many cities, tried in a few. Highways were improved; and a few areas experimented with roadside parks and anti-billboard drives.

To insure sufficient light, New York in 1916 required that the upper reaches of skyscrapers be set back from the street. This led to a variety of designs which relieved the boxlike regularity of lines. A reaction also set in against the tendency to increase the height of skyscrapers. New York City's Empire State Building reached a hundred stories; but such gargantuan structures yielded less return on investment than did more modest buildings. As traffic became congested, planners proposed decentralization of business in the interest of convenience. One result was the rise of suburban shopping centers.

Rockefeller Center in New York was one of many building units to adopt mural decorations in the modern manner. During the depression, when the government put up federal buildings as part of relief and pump-priming efforts, well-known artists were employed to decorate these structures. The painters, who included Rockwell Kent and Boardman Robinson, chose themes reflecting the new social consciousness: bread lines, mobs, dust bowls, erosion. The same tendency was apparent in the work of needy painters supported by the Federal Arts Project after 1935.

Sculpture also responded to the new tendencies. The Rockefeller Center forecourt featured an Atlas modern in technique and spirit. Chicago's Field Museum commissioned Malvina Hoffmann to model figures to show variations among ethnic groups of the human race. Many younger sculptors followed modernist painters in striving for angular lines, and the power, bewilderment, and despair of modern life.

In painting, the abstractionists continued to be strong. But regionalism also prospered. Most regionalists chose homely themes and stressed social significance. They painted eroded hillsides, ramshackle farmhouses besmirched with dust storms, impoverished sharecroppers. Some critics claimed that the regionalists reverted to European genre painting and failed to catch the meaning of the machine age. But there was something genuinely American in the simplicity and strength of Grant Wood of Iowa, Thomas Hart Benton of Missouri, John Steuart Curry of Kansas and Wisconsin. The regionalists increased popular interest in painting. Museum directors coöperated, changing the art gallery from a morguelike hall into a dynamic agency for community education.

In music, Deems Taylor, working in the classical tradition, achieved acclaim with his opera *The King's Henchman*. Jerome Kern carried on the Victor Herbert tradition of light opera. Some hailed jazz and its variants as contributions to serious music. Paul Whiteman won favorable notice when he took his jazz band to Europe, and when he presented a New York program in 1924 with all the trappings of a classical concert. The program included George Gershwin's *Rhapsody in Blue*, which at once kindled interest. In other works, Gershwin made use of Negro themes.

Interest in native compositions did not make Americans indifferent to the classics, or to the works of Europe's modern composers. In operatic and symphonic circles, American music received far less attention than did Old World compositions. European musicians were welcome, as visitors or as refugees from totalitarianism (Bruno Walter, Arturo Toscanini). Sale of classical records increased enormously, partly because of better music training in the schools. Partly, too, because of the availability of good music on the radio, though this was often drowned out by commercials.

Depression accentuated the economic problems of musicians. Unfortunately, the crash of 1929 coincided with the coming of talking pictures, which enabled movie exhibitors to get along without "living music." At the same time, night clubs closed for lack of patronage; and hard times made it difficult for some philanthropists to support symphony organizations. The government finally stepped in with a Federal Music Project. Hundreds of orchestras now gave free concerts; thousands of Americans heard good music at first hand. Musicians recorded folk songs from old people whose children did not sing these forms.

The dance also reflected the trends of the times. Public interest grew in popular forms and in more serious efforts. In the World War I era, Isadora Duncan sponsored a sort of classical revival. In the next generation there was much interest in the modern dance, as developed by Martha Graham and others. Here were seen many of the influences present in modernist paintings and sculpture.

Cultural Maturity: The Theater and Movies

With the coming of talking pictures in the late 1920's, many predicted death for Shakespeare's stage. "Opera houses" became movie palaces. Broadway actors were snapped up by Hollywood; the depression made it hard to get backers for plays. But the theater showed vitality. Untroubled by the censorship problems that beset Hollywood, playwrights could deal frankly with current problems. The stage retained prestige, and established movie actors added to their reputations by appearing in Broadway productions. Friends of the drama were, however, worried about the decline in road business: would the theater become merely a New York institution?

Even here, there were hopeful signs. The depression-inspired Federal

Theater Project gave Americans everywhere a chance to see stage plays. As depression lifted, there was an upswing in summer stock. Colleges improved their theater work; some sponsored regional drama. This effort may be compared with that of the regional painters.

Far greater, however, was the influence of motion pictures. Movies influenced fashions and speech, molded ideas about history, diet, morals, and diplomacy. Attendance dropped during the early 1930's, in spite of frantic efforts of exhibitors (reduced rates, double features, bank nights, free dishes). But recovery brought even bigger numbers than before.

On the technologic side, movies improved rapidly after World War I, with the shift from silent to talking pictures, the coming of color films, and so on. Less can be said on the story side. Movie magnates aimed their product, apparently, at children and at adults with twelve-year-old mentality. Concern over censorship made producers afraid of offending anybody, with insipid results. But Hollywood did do well in comedy and suspense; and by the 1940's some producers were tackling adult themes.

Movie makers adjusted their product to the times. In World War I they worked with the C.P.I. on anti-German films. In the gay 1920's they treated flaming youth. Escapist movies were popular during the depression; but Hollywood did try social themes (*Tobacco Road, Grapes of Wrath*). Early in the 1930's, when the public opposed involvement in European affairs, there were many antiwar pictures, such as *All Quiet on the Western Front*. As opinion against Germany mounted in the later 1930's, Hollywood turned out anti-Nazi films. In World War II, the industry helped maintain morale, and made movies praising America's allies (*Mrs. Miniver*, which dealt with England, and *Song of Russia*). During the postwar years Hollywood joined the antidiscrimination crusade; and the cold war with Russia brought forth anticommunist films.

Cultural Maturity: Literature

In letters, as in painting, there was a trend toward regionalism. This trend was promoted by the depression era's Federal Writers Project, which collected folklore and prepared state guides. Among the more important regionalists were Robert Frost and Edwin Arlington Robinson, poets who described a decaying New England. But the real center of literary regionalism was the South. Many wrote romantically of slavery days (Margaret Mitchell, for example, in *Gone With the Wind*). Allen Tate and other Southern Agrarians belittled machine civilization and idealized bygone southern agrarianism. More telling was the work of William Faulkner and Erskine Caldwell, who wrote of poor whites and Negroes, commercialism and decay. Negro writers also entered the field—

Richard Wright's *Native Son* described the prejudice and oppression that warped the personalities of many colored people. Such writings were in sharp contrast with the older presentations of Negroes by Joel Chandler Harris.

Many writers of the 1920's were influenced by behavioristic psychology and Freudian psychoanalysis. In *Winesburg, Ohio* Sherwood Anderson shocked many readers with his frank revelations of sex drives. F. Scott Fitzgerald wrote of the disillusioned, "lost" generation. Ernest Hemingway, leader of the hard-boiled school, used quick, vernacular dialogue to describe the violence and the excesses of near-derelicts (*The Sun Also Rises*). Thomas Wolfe wrote powerful, uneven novels of restless seeking and frustration. In drama, Eugene O'Neill's *Emperor Jones* described the mental collapse of a dictator who succumbed to his own neurotic fears. In *Strange Interlude*, O'Neill's characters reveal hidden thoughts through the old device of the aside. Among poets, Edna St. Vincent Millay wrote sensual lyrics; Robinson Jeffers expressed Freudian concepts in violent verses about frustration, aberrations, and death.

Many of these writers voiced dissatisfaction with the business-minded decade in which they lived. So did Sinclair Lewis, whose novels indicated his objections to commercialism in American life (*Main Street, Elmer Gantry*). A stronger condemnation of the machine age was *The Waste Land* by the poet T. S. Eliot (1922). Eliot considered America commercial, vulgar, and intellectually barren; expatriating himself, he went to England, and espoused monarchy, Anglo-Catholicism, and classicism. Another expatriate poet was Ezra Pound, who repudiated democratic capitalism altogether and became a World War II propagandist for Mussolini's fascism. (Being declared insane, he escaped trial for treason in the postwar years.)

The depression of the 1930's changed American letters. It no longer sufficed to talk as F. Scott Fitzgerald did of disillusionment; nor could one follow T. S. Eliot in giving way to fashionable despair. Ernest Hemingway, who had led the chorus of disillusionment in the 1920's, found values worth defending when fascism threatened Europe (*For Whom the Bell Tolls*). Edna St. Vincent Millay shifted from erotic verses to protests against economic ills. Sinclair Lewis turned from satirizing business to treating social welfare work (*Ann Vickers*) and warning against the evils of dictatorship (*It Can't Happen Here*).

In the prosperous 1920's many intellectuals felt discouraged. The depressed 1930's brought them hope, for it reaffirmed their belief in democracy. Among poets, Archibald MacLeish and Carl Sandburg asserted the positive values of social democracy. The migratory workers in *Grapes of Wrath* suffered unbelievable hardships without losing hope. And their creator, John Steinbeck, rejecting the aloof attitude of Mencken, looked on his humble characters with a touch of admiration.

World War II brought new war books. Several were distinguished: *A Bell for Adano*, in which John Hersey wrote of military government in Italy (even more telling was Hersey's reportorial account of the A-bomb, *Hiroshima*); Norman Mailer's *Naked and the Dead*, a vulgar, hard-hitting book about the war against Japan; *Mr. Roberts*, in which Thomas Heggen wrote engagingly of the noncombat side of the Pacific war. Most of these books were marked by realism, and by an all-pervading democratic spirit. The same spirit brought postwar books about discrimination against minorities. It was impressive, too, to see writers who had earlier used Marxian approaches reject these and work within the main stream of American democratic reform (John Dos Passos, Richard Wright).

At mid-century, many writers were uncertain as to their goals. There was a revival of interest in Fitzgerald, spokesman of disillusion and despair. Authors who refused to succumb to such views headed the other way, and sought certainty. *Peace of Mind* (by a rabbi) and *Peace of Soul* (by a Catholic churchman) were high on nonfiction best-seller lists; and novelists too were seeking firm ground in the atomic age.

American Culture and the Rest of the World

Down to World War I, American imports of European capital, labor, and knowledge were more impressive than America's influence abroad. The situation gradually changed. By 1950, many regarded the United States as the economic, military, and cultural center of Western civilization. The shift inevitably altered the images of America overseas.

American military power impressed Europeans even before World War I. Alfred T. Mahan's writings on sea power received wide attention, as did American naval construction. The American reinforcement of the Allies in 1917–18 and the disruption of the European economy in World War I led many to call the United States the most powerful nation on earth. Great powers are more likely to be admired than loved; and debtors seldom like creditors. Uncle Sam was now pictured as Uncle Shylock, laden with moneybags and machine guns. Americans contributed generously to postwar relief, even in Soviet Russia. But Europeans were in no mood to be grateful. They felt that America was wrong to insist on repayment of war debts of the Allies to the United States Treasury. Criticism mounted when the United States junked Wilson's program for American leadership in the postwar world. American immigration restriction aroused resentment. European visitors to the United States took back reports of Ku Klux Klan bigotry. They pictured a machine culture lacking spiritual depth. They told of crime waves and riotous spending.

Europeans also encountered denunciations of American civilization in the writings of such Americans as F. Scott Fitzgerald, Sinclair Lewis, and John Dos Passos. American movies convinced many Europeans that Americans were degenerate, comfort-loving, excessively conscious of sex and sports, preyed on by corrupt politicians and ruthless gangsters. American tourists struck many Europeans as wasteful and patronizing. Such images of American civilization encouraged Italian Fascists and German Nazis to assert that America was soft and corrupt, and would fall as Rome had fallen before the new vigor of a hard, aggressive Europe.

But there was another side. Europeans admitted that the new American writers had to be taken seriously. American jazz, fashions, and sports intrigued millions. American technology interested business leaders of western Europe and the secretive men in Moscow. Manufacturers invited American efficiency engineers to reorganize their antiquated plants. Soviet Russia employed 1500 American technicians to push the first Five-Year Plan. (The idea was to adopt American technology without adopting the capitalism in which this technology had developed.)

Latin-American writers also berated Yankee imperialism, commercialism, and materialism. This image prevailed even after Presidents Hoover and Roosevelt abandoned the older type of Caribbean imperialism in favor of a Good Neighbor Policy. Nazi and Communist propagandists in Latin America kept suspicions alive. Many Chinese and Indian intellectuals also regarded the United States as a nation intoxicated by power. But American influence on China was marked. For a century American merchants and missionaries had helped Europeans undermine the old Chinese culture. Chinese who studied in America from 1872 on took back concepts of individual freedom; also something of modern medicine, industry, and technology. These returned students (together with many trained in Europe) attacked Chinese conceptions of a feudal economy and a patriarchal family. The "new" China of the 1920's made some show of modeling its educational system on the ideas of John Dewey. And American missionaries, educators, physicians, and businessmen in the Far East continued to picture the United States as a land more powerful through a technology which China needed. Japan had shown the way, for Japanese had gone to school to America . . . and now threatened American policies in the Orient.

Though the depression of the 1930's was world-wide, it seemed to some to vindicate indictments of American inadequacy. The economic isolationism of the early New Deal appeared to indicate that the United States did not mean to challenge totalitarianism. But the militancy of American re-form measures encouraged liberals. The Tennessee Valley Authority espe-cially excited the imagination of peoples in economically backward areas.

Once danger of involvement in World War II became apparent, Frank-lin D. Roosevelt set out to dispel the hostility of Latin America toward the United States. The Good Neighbor Policy was broadened in 1938 by a cultural-relations program—one of the first formal efforts to use cultural re-lations as an instrument of American policy. American libraries were estab-lished in Latin America. Visiting scholars, artists, and educators from the United States served to correct the old view of the Yankee republic as a cultural desert. This program was expanded during World War II. An Office of War Information stressed the idealistic aims of America. Radio broadcasts, continued after the war (Voice of America), outdid the propa-ganda efforts of the C.P.I. in World War I.

Victory in World War II heightened American prestige. American lit-erature, art, music, and science enjoyed a reputation comparable to that of Europe before World War I. American books and movies publicized the United States as never before. American technology achieved an astonish-ing reputation; in 1948 50,000 foreigners journeyed to the United States to learn the secrets of American "know-how."

Concentrating on military and economic programs (e.g., Truman Doc-trine and Marshall Plan), Congress was reluctant to vote funds for the Voice of America and the cultural-relations activities of the State Depart-ment. Even so, these activities were sufficiently effective to alarm the Rus-sians. Money realized by the sale of surplus war equipment enabled the United States to provide Fulbright awards, under which scholars presented the nation's cause abroad. In 1949, President Harry Truman proposed step-ping up a long-active program of technical assistance to underdeveloped areas. By 1951 Congress was supporting this Point Four program.

Soviet Russia and her disciples spared no pains to publicize a false image of America. That image resembled Nazi pictures of an America temporarily prosperous but destined to collapse. Soviet propaganda stressed the denial of full equality to American Negroes, and the power of business and the military. The United States was further charged with an imperialistic de-sign to keep the world in bond to Wall Street. This, Communists cried, was the meaning behind military aid programs (Truman Doctrine, Atlantic Pact) and the Marshall Plan for economic aid.

Western Europeans who rejected Soviet propaganda were more friendly to America. But there, too, and in Latin America and elsewhere, the United States was frequently criticized. Americans had not yet adequately ex-plained their culture or their goals to others; this major task still lay ahead.

26

Political Trends

In American political history, the major parties often move in the same direction. As the public shifts, as special interest groups change, political leaders readjust their appeals.

From the 1870's to the 1890's, both Republican and Democratic parties were conservative. Republicans like Benjamin Harrison and Democrats like Cleveland were pro-business and anti-labor, favored hard money, avoided the farm question, and steered clear of most social and economic reforms.

After the rise of Bryan the major parties shifted. Republicans and Democrats alike espoused the progressive movement between 1900 and 1917. Theodore Roosevelt Republicans joined Wilson Democrats in working for the farmer and laborer and against big business.

With World War I, the parties turned again to a conservative position. This was the pattern from 1917 to 1929. Few reform laws were adopted in this dozen years. The farmers and laborers, who had been courted by the progressives, were looked on with less favor than before. Corporations which the progressives had attacked were now treated gently.

The stock market crash of 1929 ended this era and brought new demands for progressive legislation. The New Deal laws of 1933–38 were the result. Although pushed through chiefly by Democrats, the New Deal statutes were generally endorsed in Republican platforms, for the depression had made both major parties reform-conscious. And, as in World War I, the reform impulse died down in both parties during and after World War II.

Postwar Reaction

Republicans occupied the White House after World War I (Warren G. Harding, 1921–23; Calvin Coolidge, 1923–29; Herbert Hoover, 1929–33). Many, therefore, associated the conservative trend of those years with Republican leadership. Actually, both major parties were involved. The progressive movement ended, and conservative ascendancy began, under the Democrat Woodrow Wilson. The New Freedom reforms were enacted during Wilson's first term (1913–17). In his second (1917–21) Wilson concentrated on the war. Businessmen who directed the war effort changed the tone of the administration; and the influence of Bryan progressives gave way to that of antilabor Democrats like Attorney General A. Mitchell Palmer of Pennsylvania and conservative Southerners like Senator John Sharp Williams of Mississippi. After 1917, the necessities of war production led the government to set aside the antitrust laws and to promote rather than oppose coöperation among industrial giants.

Simultaneously, war feeling and Russia's Bolshevik revolution turned Americans against radicals, who were regarded as pacifists or revolutionaries. In the excitement, many citizens also turned against liberals, labor, and the whole progressive tradition. There was general dissatisfaction with wartime government controls. The progressives had long favored government activity in the economic field; but the unpopularity of war controls brought a reaction against such activity.

Under Theodore Roosevelt and Robert M. La Follette, progressives had greatly influenced the Republican party after 1900. The party split of 1912 saw the conservatives recapture the Republican machine. This they retained even after the Roosevelt progressives returned to the fold in 1916. Roosevelt himself, like Wilson, lost much of his interest in reform during World War I (he died in 1919). Some progressive Republicans kept up the fight —La Follette, for example, and George W. Norris. A number of these men, however, were suspect because of their opposition to American entry into World War I. Many were old and discouraged; and, given the temper of the times, they had difficulty attracting young recruits to carry on their work.

In the progressive era (1901–17) the Supreme Court had gradually come to reflect the progressive spirit. In the Northern Securities decision of 1904, the judges had supported Roosevelt's trust busting. In later cases, the Court upheld state social legislation—as in Muller vs. Oregon (1908) and Bunting vs. Oregon (1917), both concerning laws limiting hours of labor. Then came a shift. By the end of World War I, the Court seemed unwilling to break up big business combinations. In the United Shoe Machinery case (1918) and United States Steel decision (1920), the judges held that trusts should be judged, not by their intent to monopolize, but by their effects on the economy. In other words, the courts would decide whether a specific combination was desirable or undesirable. Such rulings broke down enforcement of the Sherman and Clayton Antitrust acts.

The courts also aided business by antilabor rulings. Despite the Clayton Act's supposed prohibition of injunctions in labor disputes, a federal district court broke a nation-wide railroad strike in 1922 by a sweeping injunction. Antitrust laws were enforced against unions, not against business. (Compare Industrial Association of San Francisco vs. U. S., 1925, with Bedford Cut Stone Co. vs. Journeyman Stone Cutters Association, 1927). And the courts struck down social legislation. The Supreme Court twice wrecked Congressional efforts to eliminate child labor. In Hammer vs. Dagenhart (1918), the judges held unconstitutional a law prohibiting interstate commerce in products of child labor. In Bailey vs. Drexel Furniture Company (1922), the Court threw out a statute levying a prohibitory tax on articles produced by children. The justices also declared unconstitutional a Congressional act fixing minimum wages for women and children workers in the District of Columbia (Adkins vs. Children's Hospital, 1923). Decisions were rarely unanimous. There were liberal judges, just as there were progressives in the major parties. Oliver Wendell Holmes, appointed by Republican President Theodore Roosevelt, was one; Louis Brandeis, appointed by Democratic President Wilson, was another. But control rested with the conservatives—Democrats like J. C. McReynolds, a Wilson appointee, Republicans like ex-President Taft, whom Harding made Chief Justice in 1921.

Republican Triumph (1920)

There was a sharp contest for the Republican presidential nomination in 1920, for it was generally assumed that this nomination meant election. General Leonard Wood (the presumed heir of Roosevelt) and Frank O. Lowden of Illinois were powerfully backed. Among other hopefuls was one progressive, Hiram Johnson, Roosevelt's running mate in 1912. But this was no day for progressives; the convention turned instead to a conservative, Warren G. Harding of Ohio, who had been a small-town editor and businessman, then an average sort of Senator. His running mate was Governor Calvin Coolidge, of Massachusetts, also conservative, and known chiefly for his opposition to the Boston police strike.

In the campaign Harding and Coolidge avoided the ticklish League of Nations issue. On domestic matters their slogan was "Back to Normalcy," which meant a relaxation of wartime controls, not a return to prewar progressive reform. The return was rather to the McKinley days, when the government had aided business but had otherwise avoided interfering with economic trends.

With the Republicans taking such a stand, the Democrats could have featured a progressive program. After a bitter convention struggle, the party nominated James M. Cox, who had a reform record as governor of Ohio. Second place went to Assistant Secretary of the Navy Franklin D. Roosevelt, a cousin of T. R. The family name suggested progressivism; and young F. D. R. had shown interest in reform as a New York State senator before World War I. But, instead of attempting to revive the progressive movement, Cox and Roosevelt emphasized the League of Nations question. This fitted in with Wilson's wishes and party policy; the Democratic platform of 1920 called for few reforms.

Those who wanted reform could turn to a new Farmer-Labor party, which ran P. P. Christensen of Utah for President. The Socialists again nominated Eugene V. Debs, then in prison for violation of the Espionage Act. The Farmer-Labor ticket did poorly, save in the state of Washington. Debs polled the largest vote of his five campaigns, but his percentage of the total was less than in 1912. The Socialists were heading downhill.

Cox also made a disappointing showing. The public cared little for the League issue; citizens were tired of the war, tired of war controls, tired of Wilson; and voters blamed the Democrats for the hard times of 1920. Harding won by a landslide, polling nearly twice as many votes as Cox (16,000,000 against 9,000,000). The Republicans carried the Northeast, Middle West, mountain states, and Pacific coast; and they cut into the normally Democratic South, winning Maryland, Oklahoma, and Tennessee.

Government to Help Business

In Harding's administration (1921–23), Congress created Federal Intermediate Credit banks for farmers; and federal highway appropriations also helped rural sections. Harding asked the steel industry to cut the working day; and he favored immigration restriction, which was desired by workingmen. But the administration gave much more attention to helping business. The theory was that if business prospered, workers and farmers would profit, too.

The Fordney-McCumber Tariff (1922) restored the high rates that had been a Republican tradition since the Civil War. High duties did not help all producers. Manufacturers of electrical equipment, machine tools, and motors could have held their domestic markets had there been no tariff at all. Lower duties would have increased foreign commerce and widened export markets for such efficient manufacturers (also for farm products). But tariff protection was needed by those who produced woolen clothing, shoes, sugar, and handmade luxuries. Americans active in these industries were too well represented in Congress to permit tariff reduction.

Among the "help business" features of the Fordney-McCumber Tariff of 1922 was a sharp increase in duties on chemicals, dyes, laces, and toys. Formerly purchased from Germany, these articles were now produced at home by war-created "infant industries," many of which operated under confiscated German patents. The law also extended the principle of flexibility, which had figured incidentally in earlier tariffs. On recommendation of the Tariff Commission, the President could raise or lower duties by as much as 50 percent, when necessary to equalize differences in production costs here and abroad. The trend of the times can be seen in Commission recommendations and the action taken by President Harding and his successor. Duties were lowered on a few minor items (paintbrush handles, for example). Rates were raised on such major items as chemicals, pig iron, and dairy products.

Results were disappointing. European countries raised rates in reprisal and otherwise discriminated against American products. American exporters, therefore, had difficulty building trade. Yet when the crash of 1929 brought a new crisis, Congress further increased rates (Hawley-Smoot Tariff, 1930). This in turn brought new reprisals.

The "help business" program also concerned finance. Prior to World War I the United States had been a major debtor. A surplus of exports had helped meet debt payments. Then the war suddenly made America an international creditor, European nations having borrowed heavily from private American investors and the United States Treasury. In the long run, these war debts could be paid only in gold or goods. Since gold was scarce —and largely in America—payment had to be in goods. But such payment would mean a surplus of imports over exports, which protectionists did not desire. The answer was found in more lending. Americans bought foreign bonds and invested in economic enterprises overseas. Europeans and Latin Americans used part of the money thus provided to pay interest on earlier loans, part to buy American products. But what would happen to American trade when Americans stopped lending? And how could foreign governments repay old loans when new lending became impossible? In the 1920's few Americans asked these questions. Foreign bonds yielded a good return, and stimulated the sale of goods abroad. Most citizens were willing to let it go at that.

Government policy fitted in with this attitude. The $10,000,000,000 in war debts owed by the Allies to the Treasury presented the first problem. Arrangements were made for very gradual repayment over long periods. Except for Britain, the interest rate was negligible. Under this plan, debt payments would interfere only slightly with the ability of foreign nations to make payments on new private loans. European governments were thus encouraged to float bond issues on Wall Street and buy American goods with part of the proceeds.

Simultaneously, Department of Commerce agents scoured the earth in search of opportunities for American traders and investors. Herbert Hoover, Secretary of Commerce from 1921 to 1929, pushed the policy with vigor. And the State Department, under Charles Evans Hughes, offered advice to bankers on foreign issues. The implication was that, in Latin America at least, the government would look after the safety of the investment. On this basis Wall Street urged loans on weak foreign governments. The result was misuse of money, leaving poor nations with large debts and few improvements. After the crash of 1929, many of these loans went into default.

Domestic policies were also geared to needs of capital investment. Andrew W. Mellon, whose business empire included the Aluminum Company of America, presided over the Treasury from 1921 to 1932. Mellon believed that businessmen should be allowed to accumulate large sums. (This money would go into new enterprises and build the nation.) He accordingly urged and obtained reduction of taxes on corporate profits and large incomes. Further aid to business was provided by Hoover's Commerce Department, which gathered information and gave useful advice to businessmen. Hoover urged industrialists to standardize sizes and types, so as to reduce the varieties of paving blocks, milk bottles, and typewriter ribbons. He also encouraged formation of trade associations to maintain uniform prices and practices; he favored ordered and stabilized, rather than completely free, competition. At first the Supreme Court ruled that much trade association activity ran counter to the Sherman Antitrust Act. But by 1925, as in the Maple Flooring Manufacturers' Association case, the judges took a kindlier view of industrial coöperation through trade associations.

From Harding to Coolidge

President Harding was a handsome man, popular with the public because of his amiable, easygoing manner. Long in politics, the President knew how to handle most political situations. But Harding lacked a penetrating mind; and he was lamentably weak in judging associates. When guided by party managers, he selected able men for key positions—Taft, Hughes, Mellon, Hoover. Frequently, however, Harding was steered and betrayed by personal friends, who used their influence with the President to fleece the government. The resulting scandals were like those of the Grant era. At the center of the stage was an Ohio gang, headed by Harry M. Daugherty, a corruptionist whom Harding made Attorney General. Alcohol permits were illegally sold through Daugherty's Justice Department. The Alien Property Custodian, Thomas Miller, and the director of the Veterans' Bureau, Charles Forbes, both went to prison for misusing their positions.

Most spectacular of all was Teapot Dome. Government oil lands at Teapot Dome, Wyoming, and Elk Hills, California, were leased to favored individuals without proper bidding. The favored oil magnates, Edward L. Doheny and Harry F. Sinclair, "lent" large sums to Secretary of the Interior Albert B. Fall, who arranged the leases. (Fall, like Daugherty, was one of Harding's personal friends.) A Senate investigation by Thomas J. Walsh of Montana uncovered the facts; and eventually Fall and Sinclair went to jail, for short terms.

Had Harding lived on into the campaign year of 1924, his party might have found Teapot Dome a heavy load to bear. But Harding died (August, 1923) before the scandals reached the public ear. He was succeeded by his Vice-President, Calvin Coolidge, who served out Harding's term and one of his own (1923–29). Coolidge was not connected with the Harding scandals; and it was hard to blame him for the faults of his predecessor. Harder when Coolidge eased suspected persons out of the government, and said that the guilty should be punished. This, combined with public indifference, saved the Republicans.

A native Vermonter, Coolidge was a taciturn person, short on qualities of leadership. He rose in Massachusetts politics by being a regular party man who made no enemies. As President, he often spoke in platitudes, or not at all ("Silent Cal," "Keeping Cool with Coolidge"). But Coolidge did not lack a program. Even more than Harding, he developed policies that aided big business. National prosperity, in Coolidge's view, was related to the success and leadership of industrialists and financiers like Secretary of the Treasury Mellon and Coolidge's college classmate, Dwight Morrow, a Morgan partner whom the President sent on a diplomatic mission to Mexico.

To protect business, Coolidge opposed anything that smacked of government ownership or regulation. He killed with a pocket veto Senator Norris' resolution for government development of water-power resources at Muscle Shoals, Tennessee (1928). He wrecked chances for subsidies to farmers by vetoing the McNary-Haugen bills (1927, 1928). He appointed friends of big business to commissions created to investigate business—the Tariff Commission, Interstate Commerce Commission, Federal Trade Commission. But for Senate opposition, he would have given the Attorney Generalship to Charles B. Warren. The Attorney General enforces antitrust legislation; Warren was a businessman apparently hostile to such legislation. Under William E. Humphrey, a Coolidge appointee, the Federal Trade Commission shifted from investigation of unfair practices to support of business combinations through trade associations.

Like Harding, Coolidge favored American investment overseas. He also said he would protect American lives and property anywhere on earth.

When Mexico cracked down on foreign oil and mining interests, Coolidge and his Secretary of State, Frank B. Kellogg, made it plain that they would use force if necessary to protect every interest of every American investor. Mexico thereupon backed down (1927).

On the whole, Coolidge seems to have approved of stock market speculation. In 1927–28, his administration helped keep this speculation going by an easy credit policy (by holding down the Federal Reserve rediscount rate). Meantime, however, Coolidge favored economy in government, and sometimes spent less than Congress appropriated. The President's Yankee frugality was involved here—Coolidge saved part of his own presidential salary. Then, too, stress on economy provided a good contrast with the waste and corruption of the Harding regime. Finally, economy in government made it possible to put through Mellon's program of cutting taxes on upper-bracket incomes.

Since the public was pro-business in the 1920's, Coolidge's policies were well received. The President pleased labor by signing the restrictive immigration law of 1924. He favored highway appropriations partly in the interest of farmers; and, though he opposed farm subsidies, he stood for high protective duties on agricultural products.

The La Follette Campaign (1924)

The Republicans of course nominated Coolidge in 1924. His running mate was Charles G. Dawes, a Chicago financier. Dawes symbolized the prosperity decade's admiration for men of wealth. In other periods, nominating a banker for high office would have been politically unwise; in the 1920's, it was good politics.

As in 1920, the Democrats could have challenged their opponents by naming an anti-big-business candidate. The Democratic party, however, was badly split, wet against dry, North against South, urban against rural. In the 1924 convention there was a bitter fight between the factions, which were headed by Alfred E. Smith of New York and William Gibbs McAdoo of California. After 103 weary ballots, the delegates turned to John W. Davis. Originally a West Virginian, Davis had become a conservative New York corporation lawyer. There was a lingering suggestion of progressivism in the nomination of William Jennings Bryan's brother Charles for Vice-President. But the Democrats, like the Republicans, had taken the conservative side.

The major-party trend toward business leadership dissatisfied old progressives; also certain farm and labor groups. After the collapse of the Farmer-Labor party of 1920, the railway brotherhoods led in forming a Conference for Progressive Political Action, which launched a new third party in 1924.

For President, the Progressives nominated a Republican, Robert M. La Follette; for Vice-President, a Democrat, Senator Burton K. Wheeler of Montana. The La Follette forces counted heavily on rural voters who had been Farmer-Laborites, or supporters of the Nonpartisan League or the earlier progressive movement. Labor was also in the picture; the American Federation of Labor backed the Progressives. La Follette also had the backing of the Socialists; but he specifically repudiated an offer of Communist support.

In his campaign, La Follette attacked monopoly, proposed curbing the courts, favored government ownership of railroads and water power. He demanded more rights for farmers and workers, called for tariff reduction, opposed the Mellon program of reducing taxes on high incomes. But somehow La Follette's campaign lacked the fire of the old progressive contests. This was in part a matter of age. Many Progressives of 1924 were old and tired; La Follette would die soon after the election. Attitudes were no less important. Back in the Bryan-Roosevelt era, the progressives had expected to usher in the golden age. World War I and its aftermath had brought disillusion to some; and it was difficult for a progressive to be optimistic in the business-dominated 1920's.

Coolidge won. Prosperity, the President's popularity, the weakness of the opposition brought a smashing victory. Except for Wisconsin, which went to its native son, La Follette, Coolidge carried every state outside the solid South. He lost Tennessee and Oklahoma, which Harding had captured in 1920; but he won in Kentucky. He carried nearly three-quarters of the electoral votes and had a clear majority of the popular total (54 percent, against 29 percent for Davis, 17 percent for La Follette).

Another Republican Victory (1928)

Coolidge's success led many Republicans to hope that he would run again in 1928. Democrats and progressive Republicans objected, saying this would violate the third-term tradition set by Washington, Jefferson, and Jackson. Regular Republicans replied that another term would not be Coolidge's third; he had served out half of Harding's time but only one term of his own. But Coolidge did not "choose to run." So the Republicans named Herbert Hoover of California for President in 1928. Senator Charles Curtis, a conservative Kansan, was nominated for Vice-President.

A self-made man, Hoover had become a successful mining engineer and promoter. World War I saw him directing relief in Belgium, then serving as Wilson's Food Administrator. His record as Secretary of Commerce made him a logical candidate for President. Progressive Republicans complained that Hoover was too conservative; professional politicians said he was a political amateur, who would blunder if placed in the White House. Others felt that Hoover was stiff and colorless. But he was nominated. In the 1928 campaign he stressed prosperity, which he ascribed to the Republican policy of not interfering with business. Hoover's term was "rugged individualism," suggesting the American traditions of individualism and liberty. Under business leadership, Hoover said, Americans could expect continued prosperity. As for the farmers, Hoover would have them combine for marketing, somewhat as other businessmen had combined in trade associations.

In 1928 the Democrats nominated Governor Alfred E. Smith of New York. Many southern Democrats objected to Smith as an urban, northern, Catholic wet (antiprohibition). Some found Smith's Tammany connections objectionable; others disliked his harsh voice and pronunciation. But Smith had drawing power in the industrial states. This was important, for the Democrats could not hope to regain office without northern city votes. So Smith was nominated; and the ticket was "balanced" by giving second place to Senator Joseph T. Robinson, who was Protestant and dry, and came from the southern, rural state of Arkansas.

As governor, Al Smith had frequently backed progressive measures. As presidential candidate, he adopted a pro-business line. Smith did favor government activity in the utility field. This, said Hoover, was the road to "state socialism." But Smith replied, and with some reason, that business had nothing to fear from him. Was not his campaign manager, J. J. Raskob, a Wall Street financier? Once more, then, the major parties were pursuing a like course. This time, though, there was no Progressive opposition. The chief protest organization, Norman Thomas' Socialist party, was extremely feeble. It drew only 270,000 votes, less than a third of Debs' strength in 1912, when the total vote was half that cast in 1928. War, postwar repression, divisions, secessions, and purges had crippled the Socialists; and, after Debs' death, the party had no leader with his popular appeal. In Europe, labor endorsed socialism; in America, the unions were antisocialist. And prosperity made other citizens reluctant to consider any major reorganization of the economy.[1]

The 1928 campaign closed with a resounding Republican victory. Smith

---

[1] Even feebler than the Socialists were two other left-wing parties: the old and militant (but microscopically small) Socialist Labor party, which traced its origin back to Daniel DeLeon; and the Communists, who called themselves Workers in 1924 and 1928. The American Communists had broken away from the Socialists in the World War I era. Unlike the Socialists, the Communists were unwilling to put much faith in the ballot. The Communist presidential candidates—first William Z. Foster, then Earl Browder—gained from 1924 to 1932, then declined. In their peak year, 1932, they polled about one-fourth of one percent of the total vote.

made a good showing in the popular vote but carried only eight states out of forty-eight. Hoover won the North and West, and cut deeply into the Democratic South. Florida, Texas, North Carolina, and Virginia all went Republican in a presidential race for the first time since Reconstruction. They did so, apparently, because of Smith's religion and his opposition to prohibition (which Hoover labeled a noble experiment). The normally Democratic border states all supported Hoover: Maryland, Kentucky, Tennessee, Oklahoma. On the other hand, Smith's urban and Catholic connections and wet views gave him the usually Republican states of Massachusetts and Rhode Island.

Political Techniques and Political Power

In the 1920's interested Americans could learn a good deal about politics. Radio took citizens inside convention halls; the interminable Democratic convention of 1924 was a turning point in radio history. Newsreels and improved newspaper photography gave citizens a chance to see the country's leaders. The automobile and sound truck enabled candidates to cover every hamlet. Simultaneously, state governments required schools to introduce civics courses; and political science became an important part of collegiate instruction.

Even so, interest lagged. The new guiding star was business; many looked at the financial pages before they read the political news. Improved recreational opportunities (motoring, sports, movies) turned attention away from politics. The major parties were so much alike as to create indifference; and most politicians ducked the interesting issues (Teapot Dome, prohibition, the Ku Klux Klan).

Given public apathy, control generally rested with political machines and pressure groups. City machines were alike, whether run by Republicans (Philadelphia, Chicago) or Democrats (Jersey City, New York, Kansas City). Many local bosses took bribes, protected gambling and the liquor traffic, rigged assessments to reward friends and punish enemies. Too often candidates for local office were incompetent or corrupt. Tammany's Jimmy Walker got by on looks and wisecracks (not much of a mayor, politicians said, but what a candidate!). Chicago's Big Bill Thompson tried superpatriotism, said that he intended to keep British influence out of Illinois.

At state and national capitals, public indifference gave great influence to lobbyists. Few Americans had as much power as Joseph Grundy of the Pennsylvania Manufacturers' Association. William B. Shearer, representing munitions makers, helped wreck disarmament negotiations. Wayne B. Wheeler of the Anti-Saloon League cracked the whip over Congressmen from rural areas. No less powerful were representatives of war veterans. The

American Legion was never so strong as the G.A.R. had been in the late nineteenth century; but it persuaded Congress to pass a soldiers' bonus bill over a Coolidge veto in 1924, and a measure providing for immediate payment of the bonus over Franklin D. Roosevelt's veto twelve years later. Even more significant was the development of a strong farm lobby. Though largely unsuccessful in the 1920's, this group was ready for decisive action in the 1930's. Labor's lobby helped put over immigration restriction in 1924; but it too was less influential than it would be later.

The progressive era and World War I had seen trends toward centralization of political power. Despite reduction in federal expenses in the 1920's, the central government retained its position of influence. The decade saw a shift from regulation to encouragement of business. But the encouragement, like the regulation, came from Washington rather than the state capitals. Thanks to Wilson's New Freedom, the federal government had increased its activities in finance, agricultural education, highway building. Coolidge economy did not end this work. Meantime, federal power increased in law enforcement. Prohibition was one factor. The automobile was another, for, under the Dyer Act of 1920, federal officers could enter a case if a suspect drove a stolen car across a state line. The changing pattern was indicated by the increasing reliance of state and local officials on the fingerprint files and scientific laboratories of the FBI.

The Constitution calls for separation of executive, legislative, and judicial powers, with the various branches related to each other by checks and balances. Within this structure, Congress had asserted its influence after the Civil War. But presidential power had increased rapidly under Theodore Roosevelt and Wilson. Not content to administer, these Presidents had proposed new legislation and used control of patronage to advance their ideas. In addition, Congress had delegated vast powers to the President during World War I.

Beginning in 1919, there was a sharp reaction against White House power. It was partly a matter of a Republican Congress checking a Democratic President (as in Senate rejection of the League). Also in the picture was Wilson's illness, and a natural desire of Congressmen to regain lost prestige. Then, in 1920, Lodge, Reed Smoot, and other Senators selected Harding as Republican nominee because they considered the Ohioan a second-rater whom they could control.

Legislation followed the same line. In 1921, while establishing the budget system, Congress specified that the Comptroller General (an accounting and auditing official) could never be discharged by any President. This was in sharp contrast to the wartime delegation of powers to the Chief Executive. No longer did Congress wait for the President to propose policy.

Instead, it went ahead on farm, tariff, and veterans' legislation. Presidents could veto bills if they desired—as Coolidge did with the McNary-Haugen measures. But the White House did not provide the leadership of earlier years.

In former days, presidential ineffectiveness had often been related to control of Congress by the opposition party. Harding and Coolidge, however, were Republican Presidents in a decade of Republican Congresses. Yet neither could control the legislative branch. Coolidge, the more capable of the two, met many defeats at the hands of Congress. The House and Senate passed bills which Coolidge did not like, refused to enact legislation the President desired. Coolidge vetoes were overridden, presidential appointments were turned down. In the case of Charles B. Warren, Coolidge was so irritated by Senate rejection that he resubmitted the appointment. The Senators thereupon rejected Warren by a larger margin.

When Hoover became President in 1929, he showed some signs of developing executive leadership. Congress followed to the extent of accepting some Hoover farm proposals, in the Agricultural Marketing Act of 1929. The House and Senate, though, would not listen to the President on tariff. Instead, they passed the spectacularly high Hawley-Smoot Tariff of 1930, which Hoover disapproved (though he did sign the bill). As depression deepened, Hoover lost prestige, and his efforts to control Congress were thus further weakened. Then, after the election of 1930, the Democrats won control of the House; and they, of course, showed little disposition to follow the lead of a Republican Chief Executive. Hence presidential power remained low—until another Roosevelt burst on the national scene.

The Great Depression (1929–39)

Though unexpected and spectacular, the New York stock market crash of 1929 did not at first seem very serious. Presently, however, it became apparent that stocks would not make a quick recovery. Instead, they sagged to new lows. Business was dull, wages and farm prices fell, exports dropped because of depression abroad. Unable to sell goods, manufacturers reduced production; and unemployment soared. In 1931, the economy of central Europe collapsed. International payments went into general default. The New York bond market then broke, and banks began to fail. Americans found themselves in the worst depression of their history.

By 1932 industrial production and money income stood at barely half the 1929 levels. Yet interest due on long-term debts (mortgages and bonds) had fallen less than 5 percent; and state and local taxes had increased. As a result, taxes claimed a third of the national income in 1932; and the claims of creditors erased corporation profits and drove property owners to the wall. Meantime, prices and production had fallen so unevenly that the economy was out of balance. By cutting production 80 percent, farm machinery companies had kept prices near the 1929 level. But farmers, unable to curtail production, saw their prices drop 60 percent. By early 1933, the jobless exceeded 15,000,000, about a third of all normally employed workers. Many of the unemployed took to wandering in quest of work, piling their worldly possessions on antiquated automobiles. Tens of thousands lived, if that is the word, in wretched tent-and-shanty camps ("Hoovervilles") on the fringes of American cities. Others doubled up in already overcrowded tenements or added to the desperate farm problem by returning to the land. Evicted farmers, refugees from the dust bowl, bankrupt small businessmen, and professional people who could not find work swelled the ranks of the jobless.

Private charity could not handle such a load; the soup-kitchen approach was simply not enough. Support of the unemployed therefore fell on local governments which could or would not assume the full burden. With taxes in arrears and revenues drying up, some cities went bankrupt and failed even to carry on normal functions. In Atlantic City the courts suspended civil suits because they lacked money to pay jurors. Los Angeles put its zoo up for auction. Chicago discontinued many municipal services and failed to pay its schoolteachers. Many destitute citizens received as little as four cents' worth of food a day; some were given nothing at all.

In spite of unemployment and deep distress, the Socialists and Communists gained very few adherents. Weak leadership in leftist parties was one explanation. More important was the traditional American rejection of Marxist approaches. Even in crisis, long-held philosophies of life are not lightly cast aside. In like fashion, the overwhelming majority of Americans refused to listen to suggestions from the extreme right. There was little response when *Vanity Fair*, an upper-crust monthly, and *Liberty*, a mass-circulation weekly, suggested that Hoover assume dictatorial power. Nor did the public respond favorably when Lawrence Dennis, Fritz Kuhn, and other fascist-minded "leaders" raised their banners. The only substantial success in this category was that of Huey Long, who established something like a dictatorship while governor of Louisiana. Moving to the Senate, Long launched a national share-the-wealth movement, with dazzling slogans ("Every Man a King"). But Long had made little headway when he was assassinated in 1935.

There was passing interest, but no more, in Technocracy, a half-thought-out scheme under which engineers were to solve problems with money representing productive energy. Elderly people became interested in Dr.

Francis E. Townsend, who favored large pensions for "senior citizens." (This would help the aged, Townsend said, and bring recovery by forcing money into circulation.) As in the days of Bryan, inflation attracted farmers burdened by low prices and fixed debt payments. Senator Elmer Thomas of Oklahoma, a greenbacker, was their principal spokesman. Senator Burton K. Wheeler, from Montana, revived the free-silver crusade (inflation-through-bimetallism). The idea was to raise prices and confer special benefits on the silver-producing states, including Wheeler's own. From urban Detroit, Father Coughlin also attacked gold, which he linked to Wall Street and international bankers. Labor spokesmen favored share-the-work proposals, including the thirty-hour week. Gerard Swope of General Electric and the United States Chamber of Commerce proposed setting aside the antitrust laws and letting trade associations eliminate competition and arbitrarily increase prices.

The Hoover Policies (1929–33)

Like most Americans, President Herbert Hoover failed to foresee the severity of the depression in 1929. His first effort, therefore, was to assure the public that all would soon be well. This was a speculative downturn, Hoover announced; the nation's "fundamental business" of production and distribution remained sound. Other officials were equally optimistic, and claimed that prosperity would be back in thirty, sixty, or ninety days. (Later, foes of Hoover would publish a collection of such statements as a book entitled *Oh, Yeah?*)

Hoover next turned to the industrialists and financiers with whom he had coöperated in the 1920's. Walter S. Gifford, Henry Ford, and others were called to the White House and urged to maintain wages and continue production. This might reassure the public, end hoarding, and cushion the shock of reduced purchasing power. But businessmen felt that cutbacks were necessary; and the public was in no mood to be reassured.

Hoover then tried other methods. His Federal Farm Board bought farm surpluses in a vain effort to hold up prices. The Federal Reserve Banks pumped money into financial markets by buying United States bonds from banks and other investors. The administration also tried to stimulate recovery by a public works program, which included the Boulder (then Hoover) Dam on the Colorado River. Taken together, these measures went beyond all earlier government efforts to end depressions. But in years of world collapse this was not enough.

Deciding that further steps were necessary, Hoover and Congressmen of both parties coöperated in creating the Reconstruction Finance Corporation (1932). In the Hoover period most RFC loans went to banks and railroads. In the President's judgment, such loans would protect the economy at key points; and the benefits would penetrate down to the people by a kind of percolator process. Hoover also approved of a law that established home loan banks to lend money on household mortgages. But he was against direct aid to agriculture and labor. Too expensive, he said; and for the same reason, the United States could not take over the relief burden from local communities. Even without such expenditures, there were mounting deficits; and Hoover considered a balanced budget a necessity.

The Hoover program stressed government coöperation with business. In the 1920's, such coöperation had struck Americans as desirable. In depression, citizens were not so sure. Business leadership was questioned when it became evident that bankers and industrialists were as confused as other Americans. And the trend was accelerated when Congressionally sponsored Pecora and Black investigations examined business practices in the old progressive manner.

Seizing their opportunity, the Democrats launched a smear-Hoover campaign. This was directed by a capable publicist, Charles Michelson, who wrote speeches for Democratic Congressmen, prepared material for radio, fed copy to the daily and weekly press. In this copy, Hoover was blamed for the depression; for failing to propose stock market reform; for the Hooverville shanty towns. He was denounced for proposing a sales tax, which would bear most heavily on low-income groups. He was attacked for using troops to disperse veterans who had come to Washington demanding immediate payment of the bonus voted back in the Coolidge period.

Replying, Hoover partisans said that the Democrats were "playing politics with human misery." Administration spokesmen rightly asserted that Hoover had been active, that he, first among Presidents, had recognized the government's direct responsibility for the national economic welfare. (This would be a cornerstone of future federal policy.) But Hoover had done too little, too late. And, since Republicans had claimed credit for prosperity, the public naturally blamed them for depression.

Presidential Election of 1932

It was clear, then, that Hoover would be defeated for reëlection in 1932. The Democratic nomination thus seemed tantamount to election. There was, in consequence, a scramble for the job. Al Smith wanted to run again; John Garner of Texas and Cordell Hull of Tennessee were other hopefuls; but the nomination went to Franklin D. Roosevelt.

A well-to-do member of a famous family, Roosevelt had been educated on two continents. After serving as Assistant Secretary of the Navy under

Wilson, he had been defeated for the vice-presidency in 1920. Soon afterward, he was crippled by poliomyelitis. Nonetheless, he remained in politics, and succeeded Al Smith as governor of New York. His gubernatorial record included a run-in with Tammany, which strengthened him throughout the country. His cause was further advanced by an able political manager, James A. Farley; and Roosevelt's name helped, as did his location in a strategically important state. The Hearst-Garner forces came in when Garner was offered the vice-presidential nomination; and Roosevelt was named for President.

In later years, F. D. R. would be known for his personality, **bold experimentation**, and aggressive leadership. But these factors did not figure in the 1932 campaign. Roosevelt talked persuasively, but vaguely, of a "New Deal." He promised to be less bound by precedent than Hoover, less afraid to expand the power of the federal government, more of a humantiarian. He spoke against prohibition (Hoover hedged), endorsed tariff reciprocity, and talked of cutting government expenses. On the whole, though, he confined his efforts to attacks on the incumbent administration. That was enough. Voting against Hoover, rather than for Roosevelt, the people gave the Democrats a solid victory. The popular vote was 23,000,000 against 16,000,000. Roosevelt carried the South and West and much of the East. Hoover led only in Pennsylvania, Delaware, and four New England states.

Franklin D. Roosevelt, President (1933–45)

When Franklin D. Roosevelt was inaugurated as President in March, 1933, he had no strong convictions regarding long-run policies. His was a trial-and-error approach, involving experiments with new uses of federal power. He was basically influenced by the apparent needs of the economy. His policies were radical in departure from nineteenth-century precedents. They were not radical, however, in the sense of threatening the overthrow of capitalism. First and last, F. D. R. believed in the capitalist economy. He saw his New Deal as a program of preserving and improving the existing economy, so that Americans would not turn to extreme measures.

Specifically, Roosevelt and his brain trust of 1933 favored immediate *relief*. This involved feeding the hungry and seeing that citizens did not lose their homes, farms, and businesses. The second need was for *recovery*. Business and agriculture were stranded on the rocks of capital overhead, during an ebbing tide of purchasing power. In earlier depressions, the practice had been to cut down the rocks—liquidate bonds and mortgages through bankruptcies and foreclosures. Roosevelt preferred to raise the level of purchasing power, by distributing relief payments to the unemployed and to farmers, by promoting public works, and by raising prices through trade agreements and currency management. The government could then turn to reform, so that the economy would not again face so serious a crisis.

The Hundred Days (1933)

The first challenge was the complete collapse of the banking system. Confidence in banks, shaken by failures, was further weakened by revelations of the Senate Banking Committee in the winter of 1932–33. Committee hearings indicated that many leading financiers had been more interested in profits for their companies than in the safety of the funds entrusted to their care. Concerned, depositors withdrew their savings, often in the form of gold, and hoarded their money in safe-deposit boxes and closets. The weakened banking structure could not stand the strain. Beginning with Nevada (October, 1932), state authorities declared bank "holidays," during which payments to depositors were suspended. With the closing of Detroit's banks in February, 1933, there was an acute crisis. In the early morning of March 4, 1933, the day of Roosevelt's inauguration, the governors and incoming President coöperated to extend the bank holiday to all banks in the nation.

Later that day, Roosevelt said in his inaugural address that "the only thing we have to fear is fear itself—needless, unreasoning, unjustified terror which paralyzes needed efforts to convert retreat into advance." This note explained the rapid action of the following weeks. Conservatives were too disturbed by the crisis to resist innovation. For a hundred days, all but die-hards gave way before the Roosevelt leadership. Had the President believed in the socialism favored by western Eurpoean Social Democrats, he could perhaps have had his way. As an example, he could probably have nationalized the banks. Instead, Roosevelt developed a relief-and-recovery program, based on meeting the emergency rather than overhauling the economy.

First on the agenda was the banking problem. Acting under extraordinary powers voted him by Congress, Roosevelt looked into the affairs of all closed banks. Solvent institutions were permitted to reopen. After passage of the Glass-Steagall Banking Act of June, 1933, individual deposits were guaranteed by the government, through a Federal Deposit Insurance Corporation (FDIC). To curb speculation, security affiliates were divorced from commercial banks. Hoarding of specie was prohibited, citizens being required to sell their gold to the Treasury.

These were but a few of many measures adopted from March to June, 1933. Relief was provided for the needy. A Federal Emergency Relief Administration (FERA), under Harry Hopkins, took relief out of the hands of state and local governments. A Civilian Conservation Corps (CCC) gave jobs to a quarter-million young men from relief rolls and a few veterans of World War I. The Public Works Administration (PWA), under Secretary of the Interior Harold Ickes, was also expected to provide employment. So were the NRA (National Recovery Administration) codes, which were based on the shorter-hour, spread-the-work concept.

Relief for the farmer came in several ways. An Emergency Farm Mortgage Act enabled farmers who faced foreclosure to have their mortgages taken over by the federal government. To facilitate all lending operations, the government's farm loan agencies were brought together in a Farm Credit Administration (FCA), first headed by Henry Morgenthau, Jr. The AAA (Agricultural Adjustment Administration), directed by Secretary of Agriculture Henry Wallace, paid for immediate reduction of output. After 1933, cuts were to be achieved by reducing acreage under cultivation. But, since land was already planted when the program began in 1933, the first-year cuts involved plowing under cotton, and even killing little pigs.

Other groups also obtained relief. The Home Owners' Loan Corporation (HOLC) helped hard-pressed owners of residential property, and mortgage holders, too. An expanded RFC (Reconstruction Finance Corporation), headed by Jesse Jones, kept large and small businessmen from going to the wall. Depressed mining areas were benefited by a silver-buying program and higher prices for gold.

Besides providing relief, the legislation of the Hundred Days was directed toward economic recovery. Often the goals overlapped. Payments to the unemployed (FERA) and farmers (AAA) were designed both for relief and to increase the purchasing power necessary for recovery. PWA construction projects meant employment. Their more important purpose, though, was to stimulate recovery. The theory was that government spending would prime the pump, set things going in iron and steel and in the building industry. And Roosevelt took the country off the gold standard partly in hopes of recovering foreign markets (countries with depreciated currencies are at an advantage in international trade).

Roosevelt put even greater emphasis on raising prices; this was the central feature of his recovery program. The AAA crop-reduction plan was, basically, an attempt to boost farm prices. The price-fixing provisions of Hugh Johnson's NRA codes were designed to do the same in industry and merchandising. Monetary policy aimed in the same direction. F. D. R. disapproved of all-out inflation. Though authorized to issue unsupported greenbacks, under AAA legislation, he did not do so. To please the mining states—strong in the Senate—he had the Treasury buy huge quantities of silver above the market value. Yet he refused to endorse bimetallism, or free-silver inflation. He did, however, favor controlled inflation, through reduction of the gold content of the dollar. During 1933 he used authority granted him by Congress to change the price of gold at frequent intervals. This was in accordance with the advice of Professor George Warren of Cornell University, who maintained that prices could be controlled by such a policy. But results were disappointing, and in 1934 Roosevelt pegged gold at just over 59 percent of its old value.

Republicans and conservative Democrats disapproved of Roosevelt's monetary experiments. On the whole, though, these groups grudgingly accepted the legislation of the Hundred Days. Conservative farm leaders admitted that the AAA helped agriculture in a desperate crisis. Conservative businessmen found much of the NRA acceptable (the whole scheme closely followed proposals of the Chamber of Commerce and General Electric's Gerard Swope).

In those early New Deal days, criticism came rather from the left. Socialists and a few major-party reformers felt that Roosevelt had erred in not inaugurating government ownership (say of banks and railroads). Many more complained that the laws passed in the Hundred Days pointed to no permanent solution of economic problems. In other words, by stressing relief and recovery, Roosevelt had neglected reform.

Answering, F. D. R. said that first things must come first, and that relief and recovery legislation contained reform elements. Notably, the new statutes established the vital principle that the government would supply aid in an emergency. The CCC advanced the cause of reforestation. PWA supplied irrigation dams and needed highways. NRA eliminated child labor in industry, banned unfair business practices, and (Section 7a) guaranteed workers the right to organize. AAA pointed toward better agricultural planning, as in taking submarginal lands out of production. FDIC was an important step forward. The separation of banks from security affiliates was another reform; and a new Securities and Exchange Commission (SEC) gained some control over Wall Street.

One new agency stood alone—the Tennessee Valley Authority (TVA). During World War I, the government had built a plant for chemical fixation of nitrogen, at Muscle Shoals on the Tennessee River. After the war, Senator George W. Norris, a progressive Republican, strove perennially to convert this into a government-run electric power plant. Twice he succeeded in getting the necessary legislation through Congress, only to meet vetoes by Coolidge (1928) and Hoover (1931), who denounced the proposal as socialistic. So, in a sense, it was. Roosevelt, however, gave Norris his support.[2] He did this, not because of doctrine, but because of the practical gains which he felt would come from a TVA program.

Linked to a rural electrification drive, TVA did a great deal to aid the inhabitants of the Tennessee Valley. Since it was limited to one region, advanced conservation, and helped depressed farmers, the program aroused less controversy than might have been expected from so fundamental a deviation in policy. Still, there was strong opposition, from conservative politicians and businessmen, and especially from the utilities (notably Wendell Willkie's Commonwealth and Southern). Many were disturbed when Norman Thomas called TVA the first flower of American socialism. Roosevelt nevertheless went ahead, and talked of launching Columbia, Missouri, and Arkansas Valley authorities. In fact, these extensions of the program were postponed; and TVA remained unique to the end of the Roosevelt era.

The Opposing Forces

During the Hundred Days, F. D. R. sought support from everyone—business, labor, and agriculture, producer and consumer, conservative and radical. But, as time went on, the administration's more conservative support melted away. Businessmen and professional people worried about government deficits and growth of the federal bureaucracy. Equally disturbing was the increase in forms to be filed with government agencies. Small businessmen did not like the NRA codes, many of which were drawn up by big business. Financiers disliked Roosevelt's monetary policy and felt that the SEC (by checking speculation) would impede recovery. Utility spokesmen were alarmed about TVA and administration opposition to holding companies. Industrialists felt the New Dealers were doing too much for labor and the farmer.

While business drifted away, Roosevelt picked up support from other quarters. Farmers in every state recognized that they were being helped by AAA. Labor leaders were enthusiastic, for Section 7a of NRA built union membership. The relief situation led lower-income groups to regard F. D. R. as their champion.

Conservative officeholders now faded out of the picture. Lewis Douglas, a businessman whom Roosevelt had appointed Budget Director, quit because he disapproved of deficit financing. Conservative brain trusters like Raymond Moley were eased out. Hugh Johnson, administrator of the business-inspired NRA, stayed on until the Supreme Court killed his agency; but he was unhappy to see business and government drifting apart. So were

---

[2] Norris also fathered the Twentieth ("lame duck") Amendment, added to the Constitution in 1933. Before this, federal officeholders defeated in November had served until March. Now they leave office in January.

other conservatives, including Vice-President Garner and James A. Farley, who was Postmaster General and chairman of the Democratic National Committee.

Meanwhile, liberal advisers told Roosevelt that he would fare best if he relied on labor and agriculture rather than on business, and if he stressed reform as well as recovery. This advice came from young brain trusters like Thomas Corcoran and Benjamin Cohen; long-time friends like Secretary of Labor Frances Perkins and Henry Morgenthau (who moved from FCA to the Treasury Department); Harry Hopkins, who headed government relief and later became confidential White House adviser; Secretary of Agriculture Henry Wallace; Senators like Hugo Black and Robert Wagner.

Conservative opposition to Roosevelt gradually became organized. Business associations and metropolitan newspapers talked about individual liberty *versus* government control. Many also argued against Rooseveltian legislation on the ground of states' rights. Similar in tone were statements of the National Association of Manufacturers, now well backed by big business. The Du Ponts joined such antiadministration Democrats as Al Smith in a Liberty League. Politicians in this combination talked of states' rights and called themselves Jeffersonian Democrats. Most of them, though, were pro-big business. Criticism of Roosevelt also mounted in the South, where conservatives were worried about Roosevelt's ties with labor and the Negro vote. Eugene Talmadge of Georgia and other southern politicians also complained that F. D. R. was building a national machine; that federal influence would soon make it impossible for local politicians to run their state Democratic organizations.

The average citizen was less worried than the well-to-do about unbalanced budgets and government control of the economy. Nor were most Americans impressed when N.A.M. and the Du Ponts talked about the threat to liberty. To millions, freedom in depression meant freedom to look for jobs that did not exist. Not a few were willing to exchange a little liberty for a bit of security.

A Second Term

In 1934, the Democrats carried the mid-term elections. In 1936, the administration did even better. The Republicans nominated Governor Alfred M. Landon of Kansas for President, Frank Knox a Chicago publisher, for Vice-President. An oilman who favored economy in politics, Landon was a "Kansas Coolidge." He and his running mate were, however, devoid of popular appeal; and their platform echoed that of the opposition. The Liberty League and a few disgruntled Democrats, including Al Smith, backed Landon; but Roosevelt, with 27,000,000

votes, ran 11,000,000 ahead of his opponent. Landon carried only Maine
and Vermont; forty-six states went for Roosevelt. This was the most striking electoral-college victory since the introduction of popular voting into
presidential contests. Local races went the same way. In Congress the Republicans reached their lowest level since the Civil War, with barely a fifth
of the seats.

Roosevelt's triumph of 1936 was a victory of lower-income groups over
the well-to-do. During the campaign, the *Literary Digest* polled citizens
who owned automobiles and telephones. The result was overwhelmingly
pro-Landon; so the editors predicted Roosevelt's defeat. This prediction
helped kill the *Digest* (it was limping anyway). Had the magazine also
polled Americans who owned neither cars nor phones, it would have found
a different current running in the land.

Noting the class division, some said that Roosevelt, a rich man, was a
"traitor to his class." Others saw peril to the republic in an alignment of
rich against poor. Yet the 1936 result was no triumph for radicals. Roosevelt had consistently defended the existing economic system. The Socialists, Communists, Socialist Laborites all refused to support the President.

Others, too, felt that Roosevelt had not gone far enough: Gerald L. K.
Smith, who claimed the remnants of Huey Long's share-the-wealth move-
ment; Dr. Townsend of the old-age Townsend Plan; Father Coughlin's
"Social Justice" cohorts; and many farm inflationists. Combining, these
groups nominated for the presidency Congressman William Lemke, a
North Dakota Republican who had been active in the Nonpartisan League.
Citizens could vote for Lemke (Union), Norman Thomas (Socialist), Earl
Browder (Communist), or J. W. Aiken (Socialist Labor). But Lemke re-
ceived fewer than 900,000 votes, less than a thirtieth of Roosevelt's total.
The Marxist parties fared even more poorly, all doing less well than in 1932.
While spurning Liberty League conservatism, Americans even more deci-
sively rejected those who wanted to go beyond the New Deal.

The Court Fight (1937)

By 1936 the voters had ousted most Con-
gressmen and administrators of the pre-1929 era. But the Supreme Court
remained unchanged. The justices who had ruled against labor, against social legislation, and for big business in the 1920's had appointments for life.
As late as 1936, when Roosevelt carried all states but two, a majority of the
Court was anti-Roosevelt. A liberal minority felt that most laws passed in
the Hundred Days and after could be declared constitutional (Justices
Louis D. Brandeis, Harlan F. Stone, Benjamin N. Cardozo, Chief Justice
Charles Evans Hughes). The majority disagreed, and held that most New

Deal legislation was unconstitutional (Justices J. C. McReynolds, Willis Van Devanter, Pierce Butler, George Sutherland, Owen J. Roberts). Since the Court had expressed a variety of views through the years, there were precedents on both sides; all depended on the social philosophy of each judge.

Decisions were not all adverse. The Court upheld Roosevelt's monetary legislation, including the act of 1933 that voided the clause in private contracts calling for payment of debts in gold (Gold Clause cases, 1935). In U. S. vs. Curtiss-Wright Export Corporation (1936), involving arms embargoes, the Court ruled that Congress could delegate sweeping powers to the President in foreign affairs. And the judges stated, in the Ashwander decision (1936), that it was constitutional for TVA to sell electric power.

Meanwhile, however, the Court declared unconstitutional several major New Deal statutes. The decisions often stressed limitations of the power of Congress under the interstate commerce clause of the Constitution. In 1935, the justices threw out a Railroad Retirement Act and the Frazier-Lemke Farm Bankruptcy Act, and curbed the President's power to discharge members of independent commissions. (Roosevelt had dismissed the ultraconservative William E. Humphrey, Coolidge-appointed chairman of the Federal Trade Commission.) Then, in a unanimous decision in the Schechter Poultry case, the judges ended the NRA codes, holding that Congress could not delegate lawmaking powers to the President.

The next year, 1936, the Court invalidated a Municipal Bankruptcy Act and Roosevelt's farm program (six justices holding, in the Hoosac Mills case, that AAA processing taxes interfered with the rights of states). Yet the Court checked state action, too. The Morehead decision (1936) invalidated a New York law establishing minimum wages for women and children. As Roosevelt remarked, there seemed to be a "twilight zone" in which neither federal nor state governments could legislate.

The administration tried rewriting laws to meet Court objections. New railroad-pension and farm-mortgage acts ultimately survived judicial examination; but the Guffey Coal Act, an NRA-type statute rewritten in hopes of satisfying the judges, was declared unconstitutional in 1936. What to do? Roosevelt could wait for conservative judges to die. Four of the five were over seventy. But judges often live to a ripe old age; all these five lasted until late in 1939, and two outlived Roosevelt. And the President, encouraged by his 1936 victory, felt strong enough to move against the "horse-and-buggy" justices.

F. D. R. might have denounced the doctrine of judicial review and the right of a court to overthrow legislative acts by 5-to-4 decisions. But Roosevelt wanted quick, practical results. He therefore turned early in 1937 to the method used by Lincoln—increasing the size of the Court so that the administration, by new appointments, could have a favorable majority. Roosevelt approached the matter indirectly, indicating that elderly judges were inefficient and asking Congress for authority to make an additional appointment (up to six) when any Supreme Court justice over seventy refused to retire.

Since the Democrats had control of Congress, F. D. R. expected victory. But there was unexpected opposition; and the Senate Judiciary Committee reported adversely. Through the years, Americans had developed great respect for the Supreme Court. This was true of the legal profession in particular—and most Congressmen are lawyers. Republicans seeking an issue denounced "court packing" with enthusiasm. Conservative Democrats who had long disapproved of Roosevelt, but had been bound to him by patronage, now ventured to sound off against this proposal. Elderly liberals were offended by the accent on age. (Was not the liberal Brandeis the oldest justice?) The opposition also included Congressmen who felt that the executive had grown too strong. If the legislative branch resisted, it might regain lost prestige, while protecting the judiciary.

Before the issue was decided, the judges themselves acted. After months of voting against New Deal statutes, the Court began upholding such measures. In National Labor Relations Board vs. Jones & Laughlin Steel Corporation (1937), the Court affirmed the constitutionality of the Wagner Act of 1935, which reasserted and extended the labor guarantees of Section 7a of NRA. At the same time, in the West Coast Hotel Company case, the justices approved a Washington state law fixing minimum wages for women and children. This reversed the Morehead ruling of 1936. Justice Roberts was the cause. Down to 1937, he voted with the older conservatives, helping them strike down New Deal legislation, 5–4. In 1937 Roberts shifted, and laws were upheld, 5–4. The new situation, of course, made many feel that judicial reorganization was now unnecessary.

The Judiciary Reform Act of 1937 contained little of what Roosevelt desired. The statute did, however, raise retirement pay for Supreme Court justices. Under its provisions, one conservative resigned in 1937, one in 1938, one in 1939. Roosevelt replaced them with liberals. With Roberts' shift, this meant that the Court now vigorously upheld New Deal legislation. The justices, in fact, emphasized "presumption of constitutionality," and overthrew Congressional legislation only on the rarest of occasions. The Court retained importance, especially with reference to civil rights; but it no longer opposed social legislation.

Roosevelt partisans said that, though whipped in battle, they had won the campaign. Nonetheless, the Court fight represented a real setback for the administration. The economic recession of 1937 was a further disappointment; and many said that F. D. R. had passed his peak. Irritated, Roosevelt announced a purge of some Democratic Congressmen who had fought the administration. That is, he tried to prevent the renomination in 1938 of such conservatives as Senators Walter George of Georgia and Millard Tydings of Maryland. But the purge was a failure. Much as they liked Roosevelt, Democratic voters did not want to have him interfere in state contests. And the purge, like the Court plan, looked to many like an effort of the executive to dominate another branch of the government.

The Permanent New Deal

By 1938, the New Deal had taken on permanent form. The legislation of the Hundred Days in 1933 had been hastily framed. Bit by bit it was modified and extended. As early as 1935, the President had said that his basic program had reached "substantial completion." This statement proved premature, for the 1937 recession spurred Roosevelt on to new action. But 1938 saw the end of the advance.

The direct relief of FERA met the emergency, then gave way to work relief. When PWA failed to furnish as many jobs as anticipated, Harry Hopkins organized a Civil Works Administration (1933–35), for jobs-in-a-hurry. Since many CWA projects were trivial, there were complaints about "boondoggling." So in 1935 PWA and CWA gave way to a Works Progress Administration, which lasted on into World War II. WPA had interesting sidelights—white-collar and fine-arts projects, aid for students (National Youth Administration). Basically, though, it was a construction agency which built roads, post offices, and the like. The liquidation of WPA (and NYA and CCC) in 1944 did not rule out the possibility of relief-through-public-works in later emergencies; but it was hoped that social security would reduce the need. Public works reduced but never eliminated the need for direct relief. This was turned back to the states and localities, with the federal government helping. Two interesting experiments were a school-lunch program and a food-stamp plan. The latter enabled families on relief to obtain surplus commodities, say citrus fruits, enriching their diet and at the same time relieving overproduction.

These were temporary projects. Social security (1935, expanded in 1938) was permanent. It provided federal agents for old-age assistance, mothers' and orphans' benefits, aid to the handicapped; also unemployment insurance and retirement programs, handled through the states and financed by employee and employer contributions. Amounts were small, coverage limited largely to industrial workers. Still, it was a beginning, and involved recognition of the government's duty to prevent acute distress and provide a measure of security in an age of declining individual opportunity.

Recovery was a major aim of the monetary legislation of the Hundred

SOME FEDERAL ACTIVITIES IN 1910

● National Monuments
■ National Parks
▨ National Forests

100   300   500
Miles

1

NATIONAL PARKS, MONUMENTS AND FORESTS
1940

● National Monuments
■ National Parks
▨ National Forests

100   300   500
Miles

2

These maps indicate a few of the fields in which the federal government now operates. By 1910, Presidents Theodore Roosevelt and Taft had launched a conservation program (Map 1). This program was greatly expanded in the years that followed, Franklin D. Roosevelt having particular interest in the national parks, monuments, and forests (Map 2).

The United States highway program was begun in Wilson's administration, with grants to the states. This development came into its own in the

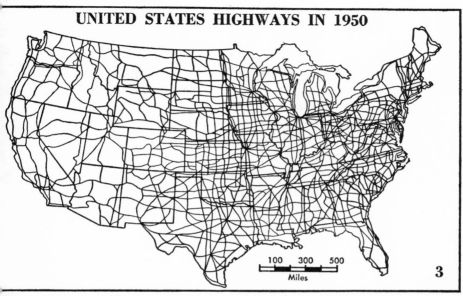

UNITED STATES HIGHWAYS IN 1950

100   300   500
Miles

3

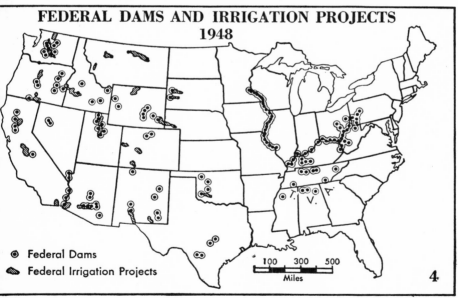

FEDERAL DAMS AND IRRIGATION PROJECTS
1948

◉ Federal Dams
◅ Federal Irrigation Projects

100   300   500
Miles

4

1920's, and was further extended during the depression, under Hoover and Roosevelt (Map 3). Federal interest in irrigation began in the early days of the century, expanding after small beginnings. Since the 1920's, the national government has also constructed dams for flood control, notably in the Mississippi Valley. Finally, the creation of the Tennessee Valley Authority in 1933 saw the United States using dams for power purposes.

Days, and the NRA, PWA, and AAA. In 1934 the administration added the Reciprocal Trade Agreements Act, which authorized the President to cut tariff duties as much as 50 percent, in return for concessions abroad. The plan was to promote exports, contributing to domestic recovery and, by building international commerce, aiding world recovery. Government loans to foreign countries, through the Export-Import Bank, fitted the same pattern.

For a time it looked as though the domestic recovery program would work. Prices, production, and employment rose from 1933 to 1937. Pleased, Roosevelt felt the recovery job was done, and that he could have a balanced budget. Disabused by the 1937 recession, he tried new recovery efforts. These included establishment of minimum wage rates for labor, under the Fair Labor Standards Act of 1938; new legislation to raise farm prices, the permanent AAA of 1938; increased WPA activity; federal aid for housing construction. The last came through the United States Housing Authority, set up in 1937 to promote slum clearance. (A Federal Housing Authority, 1934, aided middle-class residential building.)

Roosevelt also considered stimulating competition as a means of reviving business activity. This was the exact opposite of the 1933–35 NRA principle of coöperation and elimination of competition. Here F. D. R. was influenced by William O. Douglas and Thurman Arnold and by findings of a Congressionally appointed Temporary National Economic Committee, which investigated concentration of economic power. Pushing along this line, Roosevelt launched antitrust suits against some of the largest combinations.

All these things yielded less recovery than was desired. Ten years after the crash of 1929 there were 7,000,000 unemployed; it took defense orders to restore full employment and production. But the recovery efforts at least demonstrated that the government would in the future try to pull the country out of depressions.

At first F. D. R. had put little stress on reform. But he did tighten government control over the stock market in 1934, enabling the Securities and Exchange Commission to protect the public against fraud and uncontrolled speculation. In 1935 a new Banking Act gave the Federal Reserve Board power to regulate stock market margins. A Public Utility Holding Company Act of 1935 forbade the pyramiding by which Samuel Insull and others had built great power empires with small investments.

Regulation touched many other fields. A Federal Communications Commission (1934) regulated radio. A United States Maritime Commission (1936) and a Civil Aeronautics Board (1938) were set up; and the I.C.C. was given new authority, over buses, trucks, and water carriers. Pure food and drug legislation was extended—to cosmetics, for instance; and the government stepped up its regulation of advertising. Other legislation helped independents against chain stores, a Miller-Tydings Act (1937) specifying that state-sponsored agreements against price cutting were not violations of federal antitrust laws.

The New Deal also increased taxes on higher-level incomes. Roosevelt took a "soak-the-rich" position in 1935, partly because of public response to Huey Long's share-the-wealth plan. Late in 1935, Congress increased levies on high incomes and on profits of large corporations.

In planning for agriculture, Roosevelt first aimed at raising farm prices. But the President (like his cousin Theodore) was also interested in conservation. This was seen in the CCC; also in campaigns against erosion and for flood control. When the Supreme Court invalidated the first AAA in 1936, Roosevelt brought in Soil Conservation and Domestic Allotment, a plan to pay farmers for improving their land. This in 1938 gave way to a permanent AAA, which stressed conservation of soil as well as high-level prices (the latter to be achieved through crop loans and price support). Crop insurance for wheat, later cotton, was included. No less important were improved credit facilities and the work of the Rural Electrification Administration.

Roosevelt was also interested in farmers on submarginal land, in sharecroppers and other tenants, and in agricultural laborers. A few were aided through TVA. A Bankhead-Jones Act of 1937 helped some tenants and farm hands become owners. Experiments with resettlement, subsistence, and coöperative agriculture were combined in a Farm Security Administration in 1937. But FSA met criticism, was always starved for funds, and was killed in 1947. The New Deal helped agriculture; but the help was least striking among those who most needed aid.

The success of organization drives under NRA and the Wagner Act made organized labor increasingly important; and labor voted for Roosevelt. The President was disturbed by jurisdictional conflicts (A.F. of L. versus C.I.O.); and he had his troubles with John L. Lewis. Yet F. D. R. remained pro-labor. His legislative record in the field culminated in the Fair Labor Standards Act of 1938, which fixed minimum wages and maximum hours.

End of the New Deal

Important New Deal acts were passed in 1938: the new AAA; the Fair Labor Standards Act; improved social security. That, however, was the end. Much remained undone; but the movement slowed down and stopped. There were various reasons. Roosevelt was a moderate, and felt that after the successes of 1938 he should go easy for a time. In addition, the President received a serious setback when his purge failed in 1938. More important was the international crisis. Roosevelt turned attention away from domestic problems, as Wilson had a generation earlier. In diplomatic affairs, Roosevelt needed support of southern Democrats, who were more likely to assist if F. D. R. dropped domestic reform. Roosevelt also wanted backing from anti-New Deal Republicans in the Northeast. Needing aid of industrialists for war production, he was unable to continue his antitrust campaign. Needing efficient executives in government, he turned to big business administrators.

What did the New Deal accomplish? It did not produce full employment in peacetime, despite an increasing national debt ($3,000,000,000 added yearly in the 1930's). It did not check the growth of big business; it only slightly alleviated urban and rural slum conditions. But it established federal unemployment relief and old-age pensions. It insured small savings, curbed speculation, protected investors. It aided agriculture and promoted conservation. It stimulated home building and ownership. It changed a weak labor movement into one of the world's strongest. It established the principle of federal responsibility for the general economic welfare.

A Third Term and a Fourth Term

After hesitation, or appearance of hesitation, Roosevelt agreed to run for a third term in 1940. Some who opposed this were concerned about the tradition against a third term,[3] or the danger of entrenched executive power. Other objectors had their own presidential ambitions, or just wanted to get rid of Roosevelt.

Democrats critical of the third-term idea included James Farley, John Garner, and, for a time, Cordell Hull—conservatives hostile toward much of Roosevelt's New Deal. Backing Roosevelt were such New Deal Democrats as Harold Ickes, Harry Hopkins, and Henry Wallace; also machine Democrats who considered F. D. R. the candidate most likely to win. The link of the 1940 ticket with the New Deal was further seen in the vice-presidential nomination. At Roosevelt's insistence, this went to Wallace, Garner having decided not to run again.

In 1940, the Republicans nominated Wendell Willkie of Indiana, an ex-Democrat and a relative newcomer to politics. As a businessman who had

---

[3] After Roosevelt's death the third term tradition was written into the Constitution, a Twenty-Second Amendment (1951) specifying that no person may be elected President more than twice. A Vice-President succeeding to the presidency because of death and serving more than half the term of his predecessor could be elected to only one "term of his own." The amendment did not apply to the President in office in 1951, Truman.

fought TVA, Willkie was backed by utility interests. But he also was popular with the Republican rank and file, which had long been looking for a fresh personality. Since Willkie and Roosevelt agreed on most foreign questions (both were internationalists), the campaign centered on domestic issues. Roosevelt was known for the New Deal, Willkie for opposition to it. Nevertheless, Willkie indicated approval of most Rooseveltian measures, insisting, however, that Republicans could do these things better.

A good campaigner, Willkie picked up midwest farm support and bid for labor backing (he got John L. Lewis, little more). In the end Willkie ran 5,000,000 votes ahead of Landon's 1936 total, while Roosevelt dropped a half-million. This cut in half the margin between Democrats and Republicans. But it left Roosevelt ahead, 27,000,000 to 22,000,000. The President had five-sixths of the electoral vote. Willkie carried ten states, adding eight midwest states to faithful Maine and Vermont. The victory centered on the President's personality and political skill; effectiveness of Democratic machines; a critical international situation. Most important of all was a still-general approval of Roosevelt's domestic record.

In 1944 Roosevelt sought a fourth term. By then the United States was a belligerent. A wartime President assumes new stature as Commander in Chief; and citizens are reluctant to change leadership in a military emergency. Roosevelt had other points of strength in 1944. With the leveling off of the New Deal, conservative Democrats (as in the South) were less hostile than previously. Further to placate this group, the President dropped Vice-President Henry Wallace from the ticket and substituted Senator Harry S. Truman of Missouri. Truman had voted for New Deal measures and was approved by labor; but, unlike Wallace, he was not disliked by conservatives. The conservatives, however, did not run the whole show. A basic element in F. D. R. strength was the Political Action Committee (P.A.C.), a labor-sponsored agency.

To oppose Roosevelt in 1944 the Republicans turned to Governor Thomas E. Dewey of New York. Like Willkie, Dewey took care not to attack the aid-to-labor, aid-to-agriculture approach of the New Deal. He did, though, carry on a spirited campaign and made a good impression on the electorate. Roosevelt's total dipped a million and a half, to below 26,000,-000 (partly because state laws made it difficult for many in uniform to cast votes). With 22,000,000, Dewey polled about the same vote as Willkie— a little more in the South and Far West, a little less in the Middle West and East. Save for Michigan, Dewey carried all the states that had gone for Willkie; and he added Wisconsin, Ohio, and Wyoming. But Roosevelt won, with four-fifths of the electoral votes. Again the public had backed the father of the New Deal.

27

World Horizons

Retreat from Wilsonian Internationalism

During World War I, Wilson and his spokesmen said that Americans believed in national self-determination and international organization, and were convinced that a threat to peace in any part of the world was a threat to democracy everywhere. In advancing such views, Wilson was ahead of public opinion at home. Popular attitudes change slowly. Though Americans recognized their world-power position, they were not yet persuaded that developments in distant lands necessarily affected the American domestic pattern. For this and other reasons they reacted against Wilsonian internationalism when it was discovered that the armistice of 1918 meant problems as well as triumph. The Senate rejected the League of Nations and a Wilsonian proposal for an Anglo-French-American alliance; also membership in the Permanent Court of International Justice (World Court), although this was favored by Presidents Wilson, Harding, Coolidge, Hoover, and F. D. Roosevelt.

Withdrawal was military, too. Popular pressure caused the administration to bring American soldiers and sailors home quickly. That is, few citizens felt that American strategic interests necessitated active participation in the occupation of the Central Powers, or the working out of European boundary lines. In like fashion, few Americans favored the Allied and American intervention in north Russia and Siberia (1918–20). Though strongly anti-Soviet, most Americans thought of Archangel and Vladivostok as remote and unimportant. The Senate flatly rejected Wilson's proposal that the United States take on an Armenian mandate. Doing so would have built a strategic interest in the eastern Mediterranean, far beyond the American zone of security. As generally viewed, this security zone centered on the Panama Canal. It included much of the Western Hemisphere, but not Europe, Africa, or Asia. The line from Alaska to Hawaii was important; but most strategists wrote off the Philippines as difficult to defend. Thus defined, American strategic interest did not call for a large army or for completion of Wilson's navy-second-to-none. So Congress cut the army almost to zero, and the United States advocated naval disarmament.

The United States also retreated on the ideological front. The C.P.I. was closed out and had no immediate successor. In so far as American ideas were set forth overseas, it was mainly through private channels (books, movies, statements of businessmen and engineers). Wilsonians complained that all their work had been in vain. Americans had scrapped Wilson's diplomacy, his strategy, his ideological campaign. Wilson's successors even quarreled with America's old partners, France and Britain, over war debts and oil. In addition, they set aside the concept of self-determination by announcing that Philippine independence was to be postponed.

Return to Economic Emphasis

But the United States had not turned its back on the world. From the 1880's on, American influence overseas had been tied to economic expansion; strategic, diplomatic, and ideological considerations had been subordinate to commercial and financial factors. Then came Wilson, who relegated economic matters to secondary place and put the accent on principles like democracy and self-determination, and on the military force and diplomatic arrangements needed to support principles. On rejection of the Wilsonian program, the economic note again became dominant, remaining so through the prosperous 1920's and on into the depression. In the World War II era, an effort would be made to combine economic expansion with the Wilsonian program of international organization, world strategy, and American ideological leadership.

World War I boomed American exports. Postwar policy makers tried to retain this profitable business. There were difficulties. Much of the war exporting had been financed by the Treasury, which stopped lending money to foreign governments soon after the war. During World War I, Americans had captured Latin-American markets which Britain could not supply. In the 1920's, the British (and Germans, too) came back into the market. Along the same line, the wartime shipping crisis had led the Allies to buy food from American producers rather than from distant countries. After the armistice, tariff-connected exchange complications made it more convenient for Europe to buy from countries other than the United States.

Even so, American exports remained high from 1919 to 1929. Under the Webb-Pomerene Act (1918) American manufacturers and farmers could combine for foreign operations without violating antitrust laws. Nor did the government object when General Electric, Standard Oil, and other concerns made deals with international cartels. The State Department did object, though, when the British and Dutch used their monopolistic position in southeast Asia to run up the price of natural rubber. In this case, American diplomats assisted Henry Ford and Harvey Firestone in rather unsuccessful efforts to develop plantations in the Brazilian Amazon and Liberia.

The government, in fact, helped all Americans who wanted to invest money abroad. Such investments meant prestige; and they furnished dollars with which foreigners could buy American products. Direct investments included sales and service plants (Otis elevators, Underwood typewriters); branch factories (General Motors, Goodyear); branch banks (permitted under the Federal Reserve Act); mineral properties (Mellon, Guggenheim); cables and land communications (Western Union, and the foreign arm of A.T. & T.); utilities, railroads, movies. American diplomats helped the United Fruit Company carve out a banana-sugar-coffee-railroad-steamship empire in Central America and the West Indies. Congress voted a large sum to make Colombia forget the Panama affair (and grant concessions to American oil companies). The government subsidized Juan Trippe's Pan American air lines, and used diplomatic influence to help Trippe beat out the Germans.

Investments included loans to foreign governments. That is, investment bankers floated foreign bond issues on Wall Street. This added to American trade and prestige. Frequently, though, the money was loaned to unsound governments, which meant ultimate loss to American investors. Often, too, loans supported antidemocratic regimes, like those of Machado in Cuba and Leguia in Peru. The American government could have discouraged such lending; but Washington ruled against few issues.

When Americans had trouble overseas, the government lent aid. Gunboats helped Standard Oil and other American companies during the Chinese civil war of the mid-1920's. The State Department used pressure when France discriminated against American products, in retaliation for the high duties of the Fordney-McCumber Tariff. Even greater insistence helped American corporations land Arabian oil concessions, despite Anglo-French opposition. When Mexico launched campaigns against foreign investors Harding and Coolidge forced the Mexicans to back down. (Anti-Mexican feeling in the United States was increased by the hostile attitude of Mexico toward the Catholic Church.) Marines remained in Nicaragua and Haiti to protect investments and to guard approaches to the Panama Canal. The Nicaraguan venture took a bad turn in the 1920's, when an anti-Yankee politician, Sandino, led a guerrilla campaign against the marines. But, though unable to catch Sandino, the United States remained in occupation.

Depression Diplomacy

When the stock market broke in 1929, Americans stopped buying foreign bonds. This created crises in countries where governments had grown accustomed to meeting old obligations by borrowing more. Areas producing raw materials (southeast Asia and Latin America) had been hit by a reduction of orders even before the market collapse. The result was widespread distress. Governments fell. Trade dwindled; American foreign commerce declined by two-thirds. Exchange controls became universal, and Americans with funds abroad could not transfer them home. Foreign bonds went into default—a factor in the New York bond market collapse of 1931, which led to bank failures.

After 1929, Germany could not obtain funds from Wall Street. She could not, therefore, meet reparations payments to the Allies, who, in turn, could not pay war debts owed to the United States. President Hoover arranged a one-year moratorium on reparations and war debts in 1931; but this came too late to save the sagging economy of central Europe. In 1932 the Allies canceled German reparations and hoped the United States would cancel the war debts. When America refused, war debts went into default.

In this crisis, some Americans wanted to ignore developments abroad and concentrate on domestic matters. The Hawley-Smoot Tariff of 1930 was designed to protect the home market, no matter what happened overseas. The voting of independence to the Philippines in the early 1930's also reflected the desire of many Americans to wash their hands of overseas operations and keep home opportunities for Americans.

This spirit continued after Hoover left office (1933). F. D. R. broke up the World Economic Conference at London in 1933, when he sent word that he could not coöperate in international efforts to stabilize the currency. Roosevelt felt that he must be free of international controls, so that he could meet the domestic crisis by adjusting prices as he chose. Somewhat the same outlook was seen in the early AAA. Many felt that American agriculture could no longer rely on foreign markets and should cut acreage so as to readjust production to home consumption. Others favored getting out of international finance; a Johnson Act of 1934 prohibited war debt defaulters from borrowing money in the United States.

Despite sentiment for economic isolation, the Roosevelt administration never officially endorsed this approach to depression problems. Rather, there were determined efforts to recapture lost markets. Some of these efforts rested on good will. By 1929 the United States was losing as much as it gained by use of strong-arm methods south of the Rio Grande. President

Hoover and Secretary of State Henry L. Stimson, therefore, moved away from force diplomacy. Hoover made a good-will tour of Latin America while President-elect (1929). After inauguration he scrapped the Theodore Roosevelt Corollary of the Monroe Doctrine, which justified intervention practices (Clark Memorandum, made public in 1930). He also withdrew marines from Nicaragua. Roosevelt and Secretary of State Cordell Hull extended this policy. Roosevelt coined the "Good Neighbor" term, and pushed Good Neighbor propaganda. He withdrew troops from Haiti. He abrogated the Platt Amendment, which had given the United States rights of intervention in Cuba. He agreed to cancel similar rights in Panama. Roosevelt personally attended a Pan-American conference at Buenos Aires (1936). At this conference the United States agreed that the Monroe Doctrine, long a United States policy, should thereafter be run by and for all New World republics.

The Hoover-Roosevelt approach did not mean abandonment of interests in Latin America. Rather it was an effort to build greater interests. When crises arose, the United States could still handle the situation, by using economic instead of military pressure. When Cuba (under Dr. Grau San Martin) set out to confiscate foreign properties in 1933, the United States talked sugar quotas instead of sending in marines. Since Cuban prosperity rested on sales of sugar to the United States, the Grau government fell, and confiscation stopped.

When President Cárdenas took over foreign holdings, including American-owned oil wells (1937), the United States reduced purchases of Mexican silver, then insisted that Mexico pay a fair price for the expropriated properties. This was less vigorous than the Coolidge policy; Roosevelt desired to protect American interests without hurting Mexican reform. American officials also feared that a crackdown might drive Mexico into the arms of fascists or Communists. (The oil dispute was finally settled, amicably, during World War II.)

Depreciation of the currency (1933), primarily a device to raise domestic prices, was also designed to help American trade. So was the creation of the Stabilization Fund (1935), which enabled the government to control exchange rates. In a further attempt to build trade, Congress passed the Reciprocal Trade Agreements Act (1934, several times renewed). The President could now reduce tariff duties by 50 percent or less, in return for concessions abroad. When a concession was given to one foreign country, it was extended to all nations with which the United States had most-favored-nation agreements. In turn, foreign nations were to give American goods all the advantages given to products from any other nation. Secretary

Hull hoped this would break down tariff barriers and, by increasing world trade, contribute to world peace.

Finance being as important as trade, the United States established an Export-Import Bank system. During depression, American investors could not lend money abroad. Yet foreign countries needed funds; and if they had them, they might buy American goods, or unfreeze American credits. The government therefore decided to extend credit through official channels.

In the 1930's trade recovery was painfully slow; and finance limped even more. Currency depreciation brought no permanent advantage, for Nazi Germany and other countries went far beyond the United States in manipulation of exchange. While the good-will offensive yielded some return, one could not eliminate old prejudices overnight. On top of that, countries that had been badly burned on Wall Street loans were reluctant to borrow further, either from New York financiers or from the Export-Import Bank. The reciprocal trade agreements worked, but only within narrow limits. The administration made few far-reaching concessions, for fear of offending special interests. Besides, the high Hawley-Smoot Tariff remained in effect. Even with substantial cuts, rates were still heavy.

Working with France and England

When World War II broke out in 1939, Americans were sympathetic with the British and French, as in World War I. Anglo-American-French coöperation therefore emerges as a long-range fact of great importance.

Not that all went well on every occasion. After World War I, coöperation gave way to conflict. French intellectuals joined Latin-American scholars in attacking America as a nation without a soul. There was bad feeling on war debts. France developed a quota system directed especially against the United States. The British and French tried to squeeze American companes out of Near East oil. There was sharp Anglo-American competition in trade and money markets. London bankers resented hearing Americans say that New York had become the financial center of the world. Americans answered that Britain was a nation in decay.

Despite conflict, traditional friendships were kept alive by travel, exchange of students and scientific information, literary and fine-arts bonds. More basic was the fact that all three powers were satisfied nations, with large interests to defend: colonies, spheres of influence, world trade and investments. No one of the three wanted further territory. All were "have" nations, with every reason to hold back the nations that felt dissatisfied with the World War I peace settlement (Germany, Soviet Russia, Italy, Japan). Hence it was often possible for the United States, France, and Britain to work out common solutions.

In the Far East, these three nations were rivals but were agreed in suspicion of rising Japan. At the end of World War I, all three joined Japan in sending troops into the Vladivostok area. The English, French, and American forces went partly to make sure that the Japanese did not establish themselves permanently in eastern Siberia. At the Washington Disarmament Conference of 1921–22, Japan sought but did not obtain the right to have capital-ship strength equal to that of the United States and Britain (the final ratio was 5:5:3). The Japanese were persuaded to sign a Nine-Power Treaty recognizing the open door and guaranteeing Chinese territorial integrity; also a Four-Power Treaty (United States, Britain, France, and Japan) calling for consultation in case of aggressive action. The twenty-year-old Anglo-Japanese alliance was terminated, as was the five-year-old Lansing-Ishii agreement, in which the United States had unwittingly recognized Japanese special interests in China.

At this same conference, France opposed Italy's bid for naval power. France, however, was more interested in guarding against the rise of her old enemy, Germany. Here chief reliance was on the Versailles Treaty (which had disarmed Germany) and the League of Nations. In addition, France, Britain, and others created the Locarno system, designed to prevent future German aggression. The United States did not sign the Locarno treaties, but it did join France in working out the Kellogg-Briand Peace Pact, signed by most of the nations in the world in 1928. Signatories agreed not to wage aggressive war; that is, the treaty was in line with the thinking of France, Britain, and the United States, nations interested in keeping things as they were.

The Russian Question

Western leaders expected the Bolsheviks to collapse soon after the Revolution of November, 1917. But they did not; and through the next decade the Soviet Union was regarded with suspicion in Paris, London, and Washington. France and Britain did not welcome the Russians into their League of Nations; and American Presidents, who had the recognition power, pointedly refused to have diplomatic relations with Moscow.

Anti-Russian sentiment, strong in the United States in tsarist days, became stronger after 1917. The average American approved of White House refusal to recognize the existence of the Soviet Union, from 1917 to 1933. At first recognition was urged by a few businessmen, by some intellectuals and liberal politicians (notably Senator William E. Borah of Idaho), and by Socialists and Communists. But by the 1920's, most financiers and manufacturers opposed recognition. One factor was the ideological conflict between communism and capitalism; another was Soviet refusal to assume the debts of earlier Russian regimes. Also against diplomatic contacts were Catholic and other church groups, disturbed over the antireligious aspects of communism. Nonrecognition was further approved by labor leaders, who followed in Gompers' anti-Marxian tradition and were concerned about Communist infiltration into American labor organizations.

Attitudes changed in the depression; there was little objection when Franklin D. Roosevelt extended recognition to the Soviet Union in 1933. With foreign trade at disastrous lows, the Russian market beckoned. The Russian debt attitude seemed less serious, now that dozens of countries were in default. And Russia appeared, for the moment, to be concentrating on domestic rather than foreign ventures. She thus seemed less menacing than Japan, Italy, and Germany, which were pushing outward. The Russians, in fact, seemed willing to join Americans, Britishers, and Frenchmen in maintaining the status quo.

Notwithstanding these trends, Russia and America did not become friends. During the 1930's Communists all over the world offered to cooperate with Socialists and liberals in antifascist "popular fronts." Such combinations were formed from France to Chile; but not in the United States, where there was deep doubt as to Russian motives. The Norman Thomas Socialists refused to work with Earl Browder; and President Roosevelt repeatedly said he wanted no aid from Communists. Nor was dislike one-sided. Soviet agents everywhere denounced American capitalism and the American government.

Rise of the Axis

Depression made dissatisfaction acute in Germany, Italy, and Japan; and the political leaders of these nations set out to improve their positions. All tried trade promotion ("We must export or die," said Adolf Hitler, who came to power in Germany in 1933). In addition, Italy and Germany carried on propaganda drives in Europe and South America, while Japan did the same in the Orient. Then came force. Japan invaded China's Manchurian provinces in 1931, establishing the puppet empire of Manchukuo. Next she pressed on into adjacent provinces, and in 1937 carried war into the heart of China. Meanwhile, Mussolini conquered the African kingdom of Ethiopia (1935). The Italian dictator then joined Hitler in helping the rebel Franco win the Spanish civil war (1936–39). Simultaneously, Hitler reoccupied the demilitarized Rhineland and began a heavy armament program. In 1938 he annexed Austria, and demanded that Czechoslovakia cede her German-speaking Sudeten territory to Germany. (This was arranged in the Munich settlement of 1938.) Hitler next took Czechoslovakia (1939). By then the three chief fascist powers were moving together, forming what became a formal Berlin-Rome-Tokyo Axis in 1940.

President Hoover and Secretary of State Stimson were disturbed when Japan invaded Manchuria in 1931. But what could they do? Hoover had little public support. Most Americans had no interest in the Orient. Times being bad, few businessmen wanted to boycott Japan, America's best Oriental customer. The Navy, cut by international agreement and economy drives, was not ready for action. Anyway, Americans disapproved of military pressure, as did France and England. So action was limited to protest —announcement that the United States would not recognize territorial changes achieved by force. This Hoover-Stimson doctrine involved neither economic nor military force, merely moral pressure. But it represented American leadership of a sort; and it drew the United States closer to the League of Nations, which endorsed the nonrecognition principle.

The doctrine displeased but did not stop Japan. American businessmen and missionaries were not welcome in areas under Japanese control. Reasonably coöperative at the London Naval Conference of 1930, Japan would thereafter agree to no limitations. Japanese propaganda agents publicized American exclusion of Orientals and Anglo-French mistreatment of the darker races.

Meantime, Hjalmar Schacht, Hitler's financial wizard, used barter and currency deals to cut into United States markets in Latin America. Germans piloted planes for German-dominated air lines within striking distance of the Panama Canal. And Hitler's propaganda was directed in part against the United States.

"Stay Out This Time"

By 1935, sentiment against Japan and Germany was rising in the United States; and there was great sympathy for the victims of fascism, including the persecuted Jews of Germany and the Chinese and Ethiopians. But, above all, Americans wanted to stay out of war. *All Quiet on the Western Front* and other pacifist movies were popular; so were books that condemned American entry into World War I. Senator Gerald P. Nye's investigation of the munitions industry presented munitions makers as merchants of death and suggested that Wall Street bankers had tricked America into declaring war in 1917.

The desire to "stay out this time" produced the neutrality laws of 1935–

37. Belligerents were forbidden to raise money in the United States, directly or under guise of humanitarian activity. American vessels were prohibited from entering war zones. Americans were warned against (later prohibited from) traveling on belligerent ships. The laws barred sale of arms and ammunition to belligerents. Sale of other articles was permitted but, for a time, was limited by a cash-and-carry clause. All provisions applied to any and all belligerents.

Those who favored these laws called themselves noninterventionists. Their opponents called them isolationists. Most noninterventionists opposed American participation in international organizations. Some were anti-British; a very few were pro-German. Most were favorable to Britain and hostile to Germany—but anxious to avoid close friendship or conflict with either side. Although most pacifists were isolationist, nonintervention leaders were antipacifist, feeling that an isolated America would need powerful defenses. Isolationist Congressmen voted for heavy naval appropriations in the 1930's. They also favored close ties with Latin America, since they saw isolation as hemispheric rather than merely national. The noninterventionists were particularly strong in the Middle West. Their most effective spokesmen were United States Senators Nye from North Dakota; Robert M. La Follette of Wisconsin (son of the old progressive); Burton K. Wheeler of Montana; Robert A. Taft of Ohio; Arthur H. Vandenberg of Michigan; Bennett Champ Clark of Missouri. Wheeler and Clark were Democrats, the others Republican.

The Roosevelt Position

Opposing isolationism were citizens called internationalists by their friends, interventionists by their foes. Weak in 1930, the internationalists gained during the decade, especially in the South and on the Atlantic and Pacific coasts. This group held that the United States could not avoid choosing sides. American coöperation with England and France might cause the Axis to back down; and if war came, coöperation with the Anglo-French group was essential to prevent Axis domination of areas vital to American economy, defense, and democracy. This was the view of such Republicans as Henry L. Stimson (Hoover's Secretary of State), Frank Knox (candidate for Vice-President, 1936), and Wendell L. Willkie (presidential nominee, 1940). On the Democratic side, support was stronger still, for it included Secretary of State Hull and President Roosevelt.

In World War I, F. D. R. had been a Wilsonian internationalist, a pro-British advocate of the League of Nations. Practical politics later caused him to shift a little. Thus, while seeking his first presidential nomination in

1932, he said he did not favor American membership in the League. As President he refused to work with other nations in the London Economic Conference (1933). He favored but did not actively insist on American membership in the World Court. He endorsed the pacifist-and-isolationist-sponsored Nye investigation. He signed the neutrality laws of 1935–37 and asked that they be extended to cover the Spanish civil war. Roosevelt here seemed to be standing with the noninterventionists. But gradually he made it clear that he stood on the other side, with those who favored close coöperation with the French and British.

First came economic coöperation. Roosevelt made reciprocal trade agreements with Britain, France, British dominions, and such allies of France as Czechoslovakia; also with Latin-American nations, partly as a means of fighting Hitler's barter deals. But no agreements were made with Axis states. Negotiations with Italy ended when Mussolini invaded Ethiopia. Because of discrimination against American trade, Japan was denied most-favored-nation treatment in American markets; and products from German and German-controlled countries were placed on a penalty level. When the reciprocal trade system was authorized (1934), Hull had said it would develop trade everywhere and contribute toward world peace. Presently, however, it became a device to strengthen the Anglo-French combination for a showdown with the Axis. Along the same line, Roosevelt arranged an Anglo-American cotton-for-rubber swap and persuaded Latin-America to condemn Nazi trade methods (Lima Declaration, 1938). Export-Import Bank loans were used to fight Hitler exchange deals. The $2,000,000,000 Stabilization Fund (1935) tied the dollar to the pound and franc—but not to the mark, lira, or yen.

As hopes for limitation of armaments faded, a great arms race ensued. In 1934, Japan gave notice of the end of the Washington naval treaty of 1922. At a London conference of 1935–36, Japan and Italy refused to sign any agreement. France, Britain, and the United States therefore joined in a treaty which, though weak, drew these states together and paved the way for exchange of naval information.

Diplomatic coöperation followed. Roosevelt worked with the British and French in the Ethiopian crisis of 1935, when the League of Nations voted economic sanctions against Italy. When Japan bombarded unfortified Chinese cities after 1937, the United States, France, and Britain sent identical protests. Roosevelt supported the Anglo-French policy of nonintervention in the Spanish civil war.[1] At the Evian conference American diplo-

---

[1] The hope was that if Britain, France, and America refrained from aiding the Loyalists, the Axis might reduce aid to Franco. But Hitler and Mussolini kept on helping Franco, who won. Since Russia gave help to the Loyalists, and since some Loyalists were

mats worked with the French, British, and other countries in unsuccessful efforts to help Jewish and other refugees from fascist states. In the Munich crisis of 1938, Roosevelt again backed French-English policy. This meant appeasing Hitler, in line with the views of British Prime Minister Neville Chamberlain. Appeasement had grave defects. To Roosevelt, however, the choice was not between appeasing and challenging Hitler. It was a matter of supporting or abandoning the French and English in their efforts (however ineffective) to hold back the Axis.

Roosevelt was against aggression, which he defined as the crossing of frontiers. As he came to doubt the effectiveness of paper promises, he publicly suggested that peace-loving nations combine against aggressors (quarantine speech, Chicago, October, 1937). Hence, F. D. R. felt that the neutrality laws of 1935–37, should have authorized the President to discriminate between aggressors and victims, to bar sale of war materials to attacking nations while permitting trade with the attacked.

Feeling that such discrimination might take the United States into war, Congress insisted that prohibitions be levied against all belligerents. The laws did, however, require a presidential proclamation before the provisions could be effective. Roosevelt issued such a proclamation in the Italo-Ethiopian conflict of 1935. Since the United States traded little with Ethiopia, enforcement of the Neutrality Act would do little harm to that victim of aggression. The prohibitions would, however, reduce commerce with the aggressor, Italy. But in 1937, when Sino-Japanese hostilities were resumed, Roosevelt issued no proclamation; and the neutrality law did not go into effect. By not applying the statute, the President made it possible for Japan to buy American oil and scrap iron. But he also enabled hard-pressed China to secure desperately needed American supplies and credit.

At the end of 1937, a Japanese military force attacked the *Panay*, a United States gunboat in Chinese waters. Moving pictures and other evidence clearly established Japanese guilt. Yet there was no demand for war —partly because the government of Japan offered apologies and damages, partly because Americans did not want war. Noting this sentiment, anti-interventionist Congressmen pushed the Ludlow Amendment. Louis Ludlow, an Indiana Democrat, wanted to change the Constitution to require a nation-wide referendum before Congress could declare war (except in case of actual invasion). Long buried, Ludlow's proposal was brought forward during the *Panay* crisis and was defeated only because

Communists, the situation was complicated by the issue of communism. Franco received support from the Vatican, which disliked the anticlerical record of the Loyalists. Roosevelt here followed his basic policy of working with Britain. He also satisfied isolationists who wanted to steer clear of all foreign disputes; and Catholic officials and laymen who opposed support of the Loyalists.

Roosevelt threw all the power of his administration into the fight. Roosevelt's triumph resembled Wilson's success in defeating the Gore-McLemore Resolution of 1916. Then, as in 1937, Congressmen were opposing the foreign policy of the pro-British Chief Executive. In both cases, key resolutions were voted down; and administration policy prevailed.

World War II (1939–45)

For a time, Soviet Russia worked with Britain, France, and the United States against the Axis. Coöperation, never satisfactory, broke down by the time of the Munich settlement (1938). In 1939, Hitler and Stalin came to terms. Hitler then invaded Poland (September 1, 1939), planning to divide that country with the Russians. As Poland's allies, Britain and France declared war against Germany. World War II had begun.

The United States stood by when Hitler's blitzkrieg (lightning war) overwhelmed Poland. Nor did America act when Russia received part of conquered Poland and snapped up the Baltic republics of Estonia, Lithuania, and Latvia. Russia then demanded key positions from Finland, and invaded that republic (1939–40). Despite heroic resistance, Finland was beaten, and forced to cede the territory Russia desired.

Meantime, so little happened on the western front that some spoke of a "phony war." But in the spring, 1940, Hitler's legions overran northern neutrals (Norway, Denmark, the Netherlands), then smashed through Belgium and Luxembourg into France. An evacuation at Dunkirk saved a substantial British force; but in June, 1940, France fell. Hitler could have occupied the whole republic. He chose, however, to leave a fragment of the country under French officials at Vichy. Full occupation would have caused the French colonies to break away. (The Dutch colonies refused to obey orders from the Nazi-occupied Netherlands and tied in with a Dutch government-in-exile in London.) Germany hoped Vichy could control the French colonies and fleet, perhaps in the interest of the Axis.

Hitler turned next to the British Isles. In the battle of Britain (1940–41) German bombers hammered at factories and cities, to set the stage for invasion. Submarines struck at Britain's vital trade lines. But Britain held up. The Royal Air Force did miracles; and Prime Minister Winston Churchill provided outstanding leadership.

As France fell in 1940, Italy entered the war on Germany's side. Mussolini then tried to control the Mediterranean, by driving into Egypt from Italian Libya and by invading Greece. (He had conquered Albania just before World War II.) Italian weakness and Greek resistance made these operations falter; and in spring, 1941, the Germans helped their Italian partners, smashing into Greece and Yugoslavia. Since Hungary, Bulgaria, Rumania, and Spain were coöperating with Berlin, Germany dominated western Europe. But, instead of consolidating his gains and concentrating on Britain, Hitler chose to invade Russia (June, 1941). This decision to fight on two major fronts at once was a major miscalculation.

In June, 1941, Japan was in the fourth year of her war with China. Fighting both Nationalists and Communists, Japanese forces had gone far into the interior. Initial conquest was less difficult than occupation, which was marked by quiet resistance and guerrilla operations. Japan nonetheless hoped to complete her victory in China and secure other areas. When France fell, Japan moved into French Indo-China. Even more tempting were the markets, oil, tin, and rubber of British Malaya, Netherlands East Indies, French Pacific islands, and American Philippines. Deciding that these regions could be occupied more easily if the United States Navy were out of the way, Japan attacked the American fleet at its Pearl Harbor base, in Hawaii, December 7, 1941. After this, the United States became a full-fledged participant in the war.

Helping Britain

Between September, 1939, and December, 1941, the United States was not a belligerent. Neither, however, was she strictly neutral. President Roosevelt did proclaim neutrality in 1939, and announced that the neutrality law was in effect. The United States also joined Latin America in a Declaration of Panama, establishing a 300-mile neutrality belt around the Americas. Belligerents were ordered not to fight within this zone, which was to be protected by a Neutrality Patrol. Meantime, however, the United States helped Britain and France. At White House request, Congress in the fall of 1939 modified the neutrality legislation of 1939 so as to permit the sale of arms and ammunition to belligerents.

The plain intention was to help the Anglo-French team. Theoretically, Germany, Italy, and Japan could now buy arms in the United States. Actually, they could not, because of administration pressure and because businessmen, like other Americans, were anti-Axis. Britain and France could and did buy planes and other equipment. This increased American trade and helped what most Americans considered the "right side." For, as Hitler advanced, more and more Americans came to feel that a Nazi or Nazi-Soviet triumph would hurt American trade and investment; would threaten American security; would constitute a challenge to American ideals and values.

In the first winter of war (1939–40), Americans were more anti-Soviet than anti-Nazi. Russia's attack on Finland brought to the surface traditional anti-Russian and anticommunist sentiment. There was sympathy for the underdog and special fondness for Finland, the one European nation that had continued to make payments on governmental war debts. There were concerts and dances for Finnish relief; and Congress discussed aid. But it was too little, too late; Finland went down.

Hitler's spring offensive in 1940 led Roosevelt to act without waiting for Congress. He begged France to keep on fighting, promising aid. He transferred rifles to the British. (To maintain appearance of neutrality, the rifles were transferred to a private company, then to Britain.) The United States joined Latin-American republics in announcing that no European colony in the New World could change hands (Declaration of Havana, summer of 1940, authorizing the United States Navy to prevent such transfer). Roosevelt also coördinated the defense plans of the United States (technically a neutral) with those of Canada (a belligerent).

In the fall of 1940, as the battle of Britain started, America and Britain worked out the destroyer deal. F. D. R. gave the British fifty World War I destroyers, serviceable for convoy duty. In return, Britain permitted the United States to build naval and air bases in British possessions in the New World (Newfoundland, for example, and Jamaica). Simultaneously, Churchill announced that if the British Isles fell, His Majesty's Navy would continue the fight in the Western Hemisphere. The destroyer deal was a great departure from—perhaps the end of—traditional American neutrality. Roosevelt acted on rather doubtful constitutional authority, during a presidential campaign. The opposition candidate, Willkie, favored the agreement but denounced the method. Roosevelt, however, lost little if at all by this act. The average American approved aid to Britain, knew neutrality was not what it had been, and wanted the bases. (The bases, incidentally, were another step on a long road. In 1900 Britain withdrew from the Panama area. In 1906 she took her Caribbean fleet home. Now she gave the United States strategic control even of British possessions.)

At this same time—in the presidential race of 1940—Roosevelt asked Congress for a peacetime draft. Congress reluctantly voted conscription, service for one year only and limited to the Western Hemisphere. The time limit was extended in 1941, before the year ran out. Some Democrats refused to go along, but some Republicans came to Roosevelt's assistance.

Deciding Foreign Policy

Granting that it was wise to help the British, had Roosevelt gone too far? Would his policy result in American involvement in war? Opposition came from conservative businessmen, who were distressed to see the Chief Executive gain power in the crisis. They were joined by liberal Democrats and Republicans and Norman Thomas Socialists, who wanted F. D. R. to concentrate on domestic reforms rather than foreign ventures. Farmers, laborers, and businessmen who produced for local markets were sometimes drawn into the movement. Anti-British sentiment survived among some Irish-Americans and German-Americans, and with midwest reformers who associated Britain with Wall Street money men. Some Italian-Americans were sorry to see Roosevelt take an anti-Italian stand. American fascists, of course, wanted to support Hitler; American Communists dropped their anti-Nazi crusade when Stalin signed with Hitler in 1939. (They picked it up again when the Russo-German pact was broken in 1941.) The chief noninterventionist organization was the America First Committee (1940–41). America First claimed it did not want pacifists, Communists, or fascists; that it favored large military expenditures, close relations with Latin America, and some aid for Britain. But not commitments that would lead to American participation in war. Under General Robert E. Wood (president of Sears, Roebuck), America First became very strong in the East and Middle West.

On the other side was the Committee to Defend America by Aiding the Allies. Better known as the White Committee, it was at first headed by William Allen White, the Kansas journalist. Avowedly pro-British, this Committee went beyond the President in favoring aid for anti-Axis countries. Many of those active in the group hoped that by helping Britain America could avoid participation in the war. Others came to believe that American entry was inevitable and should not be delayed. Like America First, the White Committee lobbied, held meetings, and issued pamphlets. Results were good, since most newspapers and radio commentators inclined toward this side; and Hollywood, dropping pacifist themes, featured the Nazi menace. Among advocates of full aid to Britain were businessmen who had interests in London or had lost trade and investments in Nazi-occupied territory; cotton growers and other farmers who sought world markets; laborers in industries that sold a good deal overseas. Also politicians who saw this as the coming issue and liberal Democrats and Republicans who felt that reform at home could not proceed until international conditions improved. Artists and intellectuals who had ties with England were in the picture. So were many members of immigrant groups: Polish-, Scandinavian-, Czech-, Greek-, Serbian-Americans. These blocs had special reasons for hating Hitler. Many German- and Italian-Americans were antifascist. Religious leaders were disturbed by Hitler policies: Jews especially, Protestants and Catholics as well. And Americans in general were affected by reports of Japanese and German outrages and tyranny.

The strength of the opposing sides was never clearly tested before the voters. Both presidential candidates in 1940 favored the draft, the destroyer deal, and aid to Britain. Both, however, felt it necessary to hedge a little in the interest of vote-getting. As election day approached, for instance, Roosevelt gave his pledge to the mothers of America that their sons would not fight in a foreign war.

Lend-Lease and the "Shooting War"

As the battle of Britain reached a critical stage, the British ran short of credit in the United States. In World War I they had raised necessary funds by private loans. This was impossible in World War II. Britain could not float loans on Wall Street because she was in default on her World War I debt (Johnson Act, 1934) and because she was a belligerent (Neutrality Act, 1937). Churchill therefore proposed that the American government provide the necessary aid. Adopting the idea, Roosevelt asked Congress to subsidize Britain and other foes of Germany. By becoming an "arsenal of democracy," Roosevelt said, the United States might stay out of war. Foes said it was the other way around, that Lend-Lease was a step toward American involvement in war.

Considering this the decisive issue, America First and other noninterventionist groups threw their full weight into the contest. And lost; Congress adopted Lend-Lease in March, 1941. Aid was immediately extended to Britain; and, after Hitler invaded Russia (June, 1941), to the Soviet, too. By the end of summer, Lend-Lease assistance was also flowing toward China.

Other commitments quickly followed. When Lend-Lease goods failed to reach the British Isles, because of German submarines, Roosevelt decided that the United States should guarantee delivery by convoying British ships. At first, protection was limited to American waters—the zone covered by the so-called Neutrality Patrol. By summer, 1941, American troops occupied Greenland and Iceland, islands theoretically under the king of Nazi-occupied Denmark. This enabled the United States Navy to protect British vessels on the North Atlantic route to Britain. By fall, 1941, American naval vessels were convoying British ships all the way to the British Isles and were supporting the British antisubmarine campaign. By then Roosevelt had frozen German and Italian credits (June, 1941). In November the President persuaded Congress to scrap more of the Neutrality Act of 1937, so as to permit American merchant vessels to enter war zones, that is, to deliver goods to Britain. As might have been expected, there were incidents. An American merchantman, the *Robin Moor*, was sunk in May, 1941. In September, the *Greer*, an American destroyer, exchanged fire with a U-boat (the destroyer was pursuing the submarine). In November, a hundred American lives were lost on the *Kearney* and *Reuben James*. As an administration spokesman said, the United States was in a "shooting war" on the Atlantic.

As in World War I, basic economic, strategic, and sentimental ties bound America to Britain. In addition, there was an expanding trade as in World War I, linking aid-to-Britain to American prosperity. In 1914–17, American citizens lent huge sums to the Allies. In 1939–41, the American government invested even larger amounts. Of great importance in both wars was the pro-British, anti-German attitude of high officials. Propaganda intensified attachment in both conflicts.[2] And in both cases incidents (ship sinkings, for example) influenced policy and public attitudes, dramatizing the strategic conflict between the United States and Germany.

The Atlantic Charter

In August, 1941, Roosevelt met Churchill at sea. Problems of coöperation were discussed, and the meeting produced a peace plan, the Atlantic Charter. It was strange, perhaps, for the head of a belligerent government to join the President of a nonbelligerent in preparing such a document. But, as all knew, the United States was committed to defeat of the Axis.

As a document showing Anglo-American coöperation, the Atlantic Charter was a success. As a peace plan, it was less impressive than Wilson's Fourteen Points. There was little stress on the League of Nations idea. Roosevelt and Churchill seemed to favor an Anglo-American peace, with disarmament of aggressor nations. There was no emphasis on neutral rights. National self-determination was endorsed, and the Charter called for trade promotion and social welfare activity. It approved two of the four freedoms set forth by Roosevelt a half-year earlier (freedom from fear and want) but ignored the other two (freedom of religion and speech).

Pearl Harbor

By this time Roosevelt had decided that further appeasement of Japan would merely lead to new demands. He had therefore frozen Japanese credits in the United States (July, 1941), thus ending Japanese-American trade. A month later, the United States ex-

---

[2] A British Library of Information in New York did effective work; and British control of the cables remained important in the radio age. Chinese publicists also had some influence, as did representatives of the Czech, Polish, Dutch, and other governments-in-exile. But propaganda only tightened existing bonds; it did not eliminate preëxisting prejudices. A German Library of Information in New York turned out striking documents in colloquial English; but this Nazi effort had no effect on the public.

tended Lend-Lease aid to China. In August and again in November, the United States urged Japan to abandon aggression and withdraw from areas already conquered. Japan replied by asking America to stop backing China —and by getting ready to strike. A special diplomatic mission acted as a cover for final preparations; and on December 7, 1941, Japan attacked Pearl Harbor. The attack inflicted heavy damage on the base, which was inexcusably ill prepared. But it also united Americans behind the government, as the United States formally declared war on Japan and on Japan's allies, Germany and Italy.

28

War and a Troubled

Peace

Producing for War

Though inadequately prepared for global warfare in December, 1941, the United States was more nearly ready than she had been in April, 1917. The President and Congress had been building a big navy since 1933. Land armaments had been increased after September, 1939, when Roosevelt had proclaimed a "limited national emergency"; especially after May, 1941, when the President had announced an "unlimited state of national emergency." Congress had voted a draft in 1940, and there were 2,000,000 men in uniform in December, 1941.

In organizing production, the administration brought businessmen into government, and worked closely with big business. Such giants as General Electric, General Motors, Ford, Du Pont, and U.S. Steel handled most of the war orders.[1] Antitrust suits gave way to the cost-plus system, which overcame business suspicion and guaranteed substantial profits. Authorities used government facilities (TVA, for instance) and financed construction of plants, ships, pipe lines, and emergency housing. The accent, however, was on private enterprise, government plants being run by private companies lest the cry of "socialism" make businessmen reluctant to coöperate. The government did not take over the railroads, telephones, and telegraph, as it had in World War I. And after 1945, the government set out to dispose of the war plants and housing which it had built during the conflict.

In many fields Roosevelt failed to profit from the mistakes of 1917–18. Instead of establishing centralized control at the start, the President and Congress created many overlapping agencies in 1940–41. After Pearl Harbor a War Production Board was created, under Donald Nelson of Sears, Roebuck. This was roughly the equivalent of Bernard Baruch's War Indus-

---

[1] The giants, of course, dealt with many small producers. A Smaller War Plants Corporation also tried to help lesser companies. The purposes were two: to achieve maximum production and win popular support for the war.

tries Board of World War I. Nelson was to supervise production, working in coöperation with the industries involved in war work.

The WPB did get results. The American industrial structure was converted to war production. Output lagged at first but was impressive by 1944. (The armed services had 8000 airplanes in December, 1941; 120,000 in 1945.) Production was both for American units and for America's allies (through the Lend-Lease administration, headed in 1941–43 by Edward R. Stettinius, Jr., formerly of U. S. Steel). At best, though, Nelson was no Baruch. He was finally eased out (1943), his authority, and more, being given to James F. Byrnes, who headed a new Office of War Mobilization after May, 1943. Byrnes was a politician, not a businessman; he had been Senator from South Carolina and a Supreme Court justice. As Director of War Mobilization he had powers so extensive that he was labeled "Assistant President." But this desirable concentration of authority came rather late.

Meantime, officials had engaged in many quarrels. Jesse Jones of the RFC publicly criticized as unbusinesslike methods used by Vice-President Henry Wallace's Board of Economic Warfare (which, among other things, obtained raw materials from Latin America). Reorganizations followed, leading eventually to the creation of the Foreign Economic Administration (FEA).

But many jobs were well done. An Office of Defense Transportation under Joseph Eastman handled the railroad problem efficiently. A War Shipping Administration headed by Admiral Emory S. Land set out to provide the ocean transportation needed in this global conflict. Despite sinkings, the American merchant marine more than trebled in the war era; and the United States emerged from the war as the largest shipping nation on earth. Another important figure was Rubber Administrator William Jeffers (of the Union Pacific Railroad). Japanese conquest of southeast Asia shut off the supply of plantation rubber in December, 1941. To protect America's small rubber stock pile, the government adopted tire and gasoline rationing and a thirty-five-mile speed limit for automobiles. A synthetic-rubber program helped see the nation through.

Organized labor supported the war effort. Sidney Hillman of the C.I.O. had high government positions (though his influence was less than that of the industrialists). Most problems were ironed out amicably, some through a War Labor Board. To assure efficient operation of war plants, some key workers were exempted from the draft; and Paul McNutt's War Manpower Commission froze men on the job. Strikes ("work stoppages") persisted, however, and Congress finally adopted a get-tough policy, passing the Smith-Connally War Labor Disputes Act over a presidential veto in 1943.

As in World War I, the government encouraged farmers to go into full production, thus reversing the cut-production trend of the depression. The selective service coöperated, allowing some workers to stay on the farm. Results were spectacular. Wheat production went above a billion bushels in 1944, for the first time since World War I (and stayed up thereafter). The price of farmland increased rapidly.

War Finance

World War II was phenomenally expensive. In one fiscal year, 1944–45, the United States spent over $100,000,000,000. The total exceeded $300,000,000,000, ten times the total for World War I. (Interest and pensions would make the final figure much higher.) The national debt went up at a rate of fifty billions a year after Pearl Harbor, to $250,000,000,000 in 1945. Yet there was little public complaint. Conservatives who had grumbled about $3,000,000,000 deficits in New Deal days had little to say against war deficits fifteen times that large. Perhaps the new figures were too large for comprehension. Perhaps, too, citizens had become accustomed to deficit financing. Of greater importance, however, was patriotic sentiment, plus the fact that business was doing well in the 1940's, and was working with rather than against the government.

In World War I, the government had met only a third of the bill out of taxes. In World War II, it was two-fifths (nearly half in 1944). Taxes were increased sharply on individual and corporation incomes. A new withholding system made the former seem less unpalatable. An excess-profits tax of 90 percent was designed to (but did not altogether) eliminate war profiteering. And there were all the usual wartime taxes on luxuries, with some new ones besides.

Borrowing was not difficult; the banks could provide all the money the government required. This type of financing, though, was inflationary, since it increased the amount of money in circulation. Bond buying by individuals had the opposite effect, reducing the money in circulation and keeping prices down. It was also felt that bond buying would increase patriotic zeal. Consequently, the government sold bonds and stamps through the radio, movies, churches, schools, and through pay-roll deduction plans. But only a fifth of the bonds went to small investors; two-thirds were purchased by banks.

It was necessary, therefore, to take other steps to check inflation. Among these was Roosevelt's hold-the-line proclamation of April, 1943, designed to freeze prices, rates, wages, and jobs. The day-by-day work was done by the Office of Price Administration, which set up a system of rationing, with ceiling prices for rents and consumers' goods. Despite widespread evasion of OPA regulations, the agency did hold down prices. One reason for success was the general willingness of consumers to coöperate. Another was the Congressional system of subsidizing processors. Finally, OPA was run in a fairly efficient manner by national and state officials and local ration boards. Three different persons took on the job of running the agency, the third administrator (Chester Bowles) being the most successful.

Civilians and the War

Some administration leaders felt that the civilian economy should be cut to the bone in wartime. Roosevelt and Congress decided otherwise; too severe a cutback would reduce farmer-labor-business incentive for full production. Hence it was decided that civilian needs and desires would not be totally neglected. But war production came first. Consequently, there were many shortages. Civilians found it almost impossible to get automobiles, apartments, Hershey bars, or nylon hosiery. There were restrictions on house construction and driving, heating fuel and intersectional sports events. It was hard to get a physician or repairman. Cigarettes, steaks, and toys were in short supply. Yet one could get the necessities and some luxuries. Restaurants, sports arenas, and motion-picture theaters prospered, though the fare was below peacetime standards.

Besides working, paying taxes, and buying bonds, civilians gave cash or time to the USO (United Service Organizations). Many worked for the Red Cross or served without pay on draft and ration boards. Early in the war, when there was talk of an Axis invasion, an Office of Civilian Defense organized volunteers to serve as plane spotters and air-raid wardens. This work lost its appeal after the enemy was thrown on the defensive.

As always in wartime, the normal freedom of the press was curtailed. The Director of Censorship, Byron Price, was a newspaperman with a preference for voluntary methods. Much military information was properly kept secret. Unfortunately, army and navy officials sometimes went far beyond security needs in withholding statements.

An Office of War Information, under the author and radio commentator Elmer Davis, was effective at home and abroad. But OWI was less important than George Creel's CPI. Davis was less aggressive than Creel. Besides, Congress limited the domestic operations of OWI, for fear it would be a publicity agency for Roosevelt. Finally, CPI had helped break down German morale in World War I by offering Germany an easy peace (Fourteen Points). This was impossible in World War II, for Roosevelt insisted on the unconditional surrender of Germany.

Immediately after Pearl Harbor, Japanese-Americans were driven from the Pacific coast. Most evacuees were citizens, and there was no sound ground for this violation of their rights. Otherwise, the government's civil rights record in World War II was better than in World War I. Individuals dangerous to the republic were of course put under restraint. Saboteurs sent in from Germany were executed after a legal trial, complete with an appeal to the Supreme Court. Some German Bundists lost their citizenship. A few American fascists were jailed, a few fascist-type journals barred from the mails. But there was no wartime witch hunt. Conscientious objectors were treated better than in World War I. The harsh policy toward Japanese-Americans was modified during the war. Roosevelt announced (1942) that non-naturalized Italian-Americans were not to be considered enemy aliens. Such attitudes were possible because there was less opposition to the war than in 1917–18; perhaps also because Americans had developed more maturity of judgment.

Many civilians gave up that role for the duration. Following Britain's lead, the government accepted women volunteers, not only for nursing, but also for other noncombat jobs. Some 200,000 women went into uniform, as Wacs (army), Waves (navy), Spars (coast guard), or marines. The army and navy jumped from 2,000,000 in 1941 to 12,000,000 in 1945. The great majority came in through the selective service system, which was headed by General Lewis B. Hershey. Males from eighteen to sixty-five were enrolled, though the older age groups were not called. Standards of acceptance varied from time to time, according to the needs of the services. In addition, there were regional variations, partly because of the difficulty of interpreting orders from national headquarters, partly because of the original decision that the draft should be decentralized.

The government recognized its obligations to those it called to the colors. At the end of the war, the wife of a private was allotted $50 a month ($22 of this being from the private's $50 pay), plus $30 for one child, $20 for additional children. Soldiers were also guaranteed their old jobs on return from service. The G.I. Bill of 1944 provided additional benefits for veterans with special needs: improved hospitalization; unemployment compensation for a year; aid in finding a job (through the United States Employment Service); loans for business or residential housing; educational subsidies, for tuition, supplies, and subsistence, at college, vocational school, or in a job-training program.

The United Nations

In World War I the United States had declared war on only two of the Central Powers, and had refused to become an Ally. In World War II the United States declared war on all three major Axis powers (December, 1941); later also on Axis satellites. The American

Hitler had conquered much of western Europe in the two years before Pearl Harbor (December, 1941). In 1942 the Germans extended their control, driving far into Russia and making gains in the Mediterranean. But by the end of 1942, the tide had turned. Russia held at Stalingrad, Britain at El Alamein, and American troops landed in North Africa. In 1943, while Russia pushed the Nazis westward, the Anglo-American allies took Sicily, and landed on the Italian mainland. The King of Italy sued for peace; German troops, how-

DEFEATING THE AXIS POWERS
1942–1945
THE EUROPEAN THEATER

FINLAND

Leningrad

ESTONIA

LATVIA

LITHUANIA

Warsaw

ND

ROMANIA

A

BULGARIA

EECE

o Moscow

o Stalingrad

U. S. S. R.

CASPIAN SEA

BLACK SEA

TURKEY

SEA

El Alamein
Cairo o
EGYPT

Flannery

▓	Area Under Axis Control In Early 1942
░	Neutral States
□	Area Under Allied Control In Early 1942
←	Allied Advances
–·–·–·–	1939 Boundaries
⌐	Beach Heads

ever, fought on in Italy. Churchill favored moving north from the Mediterranean. Roosevelt, though, decided on a cross-channel invasion. The D-Day landing in Normandy (June, 1944) and the landing in southern France opened the last phase of the war. After a final thrust (Battle of the Bulge, winter of 1944–45), the German armies collapsed. Aerial bombardment of Nazi territory and Anglo-American control of the seas hastened the end.

republic also entered a formal alliance with other anti-Axis states (United Nations, January, 1942). This was the first alliance of the United States with a major power since the French alliance of 1778–1800. It was a military combination, binding the United States to Britain, Russia, China, and lesser nations. It was also an alliance for postwar purposes, for the United Nations agreed to work together on the peace settlement.

The formation of the UN also indicated the growing influence of the United States in Latin America. Most republics south of the Rio Grande quickly followed the United States into the war against the Axis. This reflected the strength of economic ties; also a feeling of insecurity in the air age. Perhaps, too, the Good Neighbor Policy of Hoover and Roosevelt had yielded some returns.

The Big Four of the United Nations were the United States, Great Britain, Russia, and China. Churchill and Roosevelt met frequently, as at Washington after Pearl Harbor, at Casablanca (1942), Quebec (1944). Roosevelt, Churchill, and Chiang Kai-shek met at Cairo in 1943 (Russia was not yet in the Far East war). Stalin, Churchill, and Roosevelt met at Teheran, in Iran, in 1943, and at Yalta in the Russian Crimea early in 1945. There were also dozens of special missions, and day-by-day contacts of diplomatic and military leaders all over the world.

Though one of the Big Four, China was not treated as an equal partner. Russia of course did not enter the Pacific war until after the collapse of Germany. Also, Moscow tended to favor the Chinese Communists, who held part of China and were bitter foes of the Nationalist government of Chiang Kai-shek. Britain and America thought better of Chiang but did not consider Chinese fighting forces strong enough to make much contribution to the winning of the war.

America, Britain, and Russia did not underrate each other; but coöperation was imperfect. The Russians were glad to get Lend-Lease aid but were reluctant to supply the Americans and British with exact information, or to let observers visit their front lines, or to provide facilities for shuttle-bombing operations. On the other side, the British and Americans made vital decisions without consulting the Russians. Churchill made no secret of his anti-Russian views, and his fears that the Soviet Union would emerge from the war as master of much of Europe.

Despite disagreements, the United States and Britain became and remained close partners. The tradition of Anglo-American coöperation helped. Intimate personal relations between Churchill and Roosevelt made for top-level harmony. No less important was the work of such other officials as the American Chief of Staff, General George C. Marshall, and organizations like the Joint Chiefs of Staff.

When Anglo-American coöperation had been established early in the century, Britain had been the stronger member of the combination. The pattern had changed by World War II, as Americans gradually came to realize. In 1942, Roosevelt was inclined to defer to Churchill not only in matters touching the British Empire (India, for instance) but also in questions involving such other areas as Italy, the Balkans, and the Near East. But by 1945 the British themselves made it plain that leadership had passed to the United States. America supplied the bulk of the fighting force in Anglo-American offensives; American officers had the top commands. American strength and the comparative weakness of Britain made it impossible for the United States to turn Mediterranean questions over to the British after the conquest of Italy; and on Pacific problems, Britain's own dominions, Canada and Australia, often tended to look to Washington rather than London. The new relationship irritated many Britishers, who did not like to see their nation playing a secondary role and feared that the United States lacked the experience and responsibility necessary for leadership. Many Americans were equally disturbed. Some felt that they were being "taken in," that the whole thing was a device to save British soldiers and taxpayers. Nevertheless, the trend continued through and after the war.

A Rio de Janeiro conference, after Pearl Harbor, indicated that Latin-America would coöperate with the United States. Roosevelt provided Latin-American governments with Lend-Lease aid. In return, these republics routed out Axis agents, supplied airfields, and increased production of needed raw materials. The State Department was unable to solve the Argentine question, or to remove Latin-American suspicion of the United States. There were complaints, too, that Lend-Lease supplies strengthened dictators, and thus were an antidemocratic force. But 1945 saw close coöperation on economic, military, and diplomatic levels, a coöperation that carried over into the days of peace.

Days of Defeat (1941–42)

Over 3000 American servicemen lost their lives at Pearl Harbor; hence many Americans felt that the United States should concentrate on Japan. Roosevelt, however, called Hitler the major foe and felt the Pacific was of secondary importance. Master plans thus gave chief attention to Europe.

With its striking power greatly reduced by Pearl Harbor losses, the United States could neither reinforce nor supply Douglas MacArthur's Filipino and American troops when Japan invaded the Philippines. The defenders nonetheless fought valiantly—under General MacArthur until he was ordered to Australia; then under General Jonathan Wainwright. Surrender became necessary on the Bataan peninsula in April, on the island of Corregidor in May, 1942. Meantime, the Japanese had taken over British Hong Kong, Singapore, and Burma (where American General Joseph Stilwell took a "hell of a beating"), had occupied Malaya and the British, French, and Netherlands East Indies. In June, 1942, Japan invaded the Aleutian Islands.

The news from Europe was no better. The United Nations could not establish a base in western Europe or organize large-scale bombing operations. To the east, the Nazis drove far into Russia. To the south, German and Italian troops under Erwin Rommel threatened the Suez Canal and the oil fields beyond. And on the Atlantic, the submarines were so effective that some felt the United States could not deliver the Lend-Lease supplies so desperately needed by Russia and Britain.

Taking the Offensive (1942–44)

At the end of 1942 the situation changed. Antisubmarine measures became effective; supplies and troops got through. Russian armies stopped the Germans at Stalingrad and began rolling back the Nazi tide. British General Bernard Montgomery held in Egypt (El Alamein), then drove Rommel back across Libya into French Tunisia. Allied bombers stepped up operations over the Continent.

Then, in November, 1942, Anglo-American forces under General Dwight D. Eisenhower landed in French North Africa. The Russians wanted America and Britain to invade western Europe and relieve German pressure on Russia by establishing a "second front" on the Continent. Churchill and Roosevelt, however, decided that a landing in France would cost many lives and might not serve the desired military purpose. They therefore operated further south, using 850 vessels to land 400,000 troops in Algiers-Oran-Casablanca. After a brief resistance, the French capitulated. Official orders were to resist; but Admiral Jean Darlan, the Vichy official on the ground, came to terms. Since Darlan and many of his followers were tarred with the brush of fascism, some Americans felt that this was practically dealing with the enemy. Eisenhower and Roosevelt, however, felt that the act was defensible: (1) the French stopped fighting, which saved American lives; (2) American troops were freed for action against the major enemy, Germany; (3) it was easier to negotiate with Darlan (and Henri Giraud, who took over when Darlan was assassinated) than with Charles de Gaulle, the difficult and unbending leader of the Free French, who opposed compromise with Vichy.

Established in French North Africa, Eisenhower pushed eastward, while Montgomery drove westward from Egypt. Pressed from both sides, Axis forces put up a vigorous fight in Tunisia, then gave up in Africa (1943). The Americans and British next invaded Sicily (July) and the foot of the Italian boot (September, at Salerno; another landing up the coast at Anzio in January, 1944).

When Sicily was invaded, King Victor Emmanuel tried to take Italy out of the war. Announcing Mussolini's resignation, he designated Pietro Badoglio as Premier. This posed a problem similar to that of Darlan. Should Americans deal with an Italian government that contained former fascists? As before, it was decided that negotiation would save the lives of American soldiers, and that the great enemy was, not Italy, but Germany. Badoglio and the king could not, however, deliver Italy to the Allies. The Germans stayed on, and bitterly contested the Allied advance. Rome was taken in June, 1944; but the Italian campaign dragged on into 1945.

Meanwhile, Allied bombers carried the fight to Germany. Round-the-clock bombing began in summer, 1943, Americans hammering targets by day, the Royal Air Force by night. These raids kept Hitler from expanding industrial production. Morale, too, was affected, leading Germany to launch an all-out air offensive against England early in 1944. When this failed, the United Nations had complete control of the skies. The Germans would try rockets in a final effort. But, with Russia pounding in from the east, the days of Nazi power seemed numbered by spring, 1944.

In the Pacific, too, the foe had been forced onto the defensive. The first American offensive—James Doolittle's Tokyo raid of April, 1942—was of little military value, though it may have helped Allied morale. But in the next month, Japan's southward movement was checked in the battle of the Coral Sea. This was a new-style naval engagement. All blows were struck by aircraft; the surface vessels did not sight each other. In June, 1942, land- and carrier-based planes inflicted heavy damage on the Japanese in the battle of Midway. Thereafter, though slowly, the United States moved forward, under Admiral Chester W. Nimitz and General MacArthur.

It was hard going, because of shortages of men and material, distances, the terrain, and fierce Japanese resistance. Nonetheless, army, navy, and marine forces moved ahead, pounding garrisons from the air, attacking supply lines, landing on beaches, fighting through jungles. Marines moved into Guadalcanal, in the Solomons, in summer, 1942—and held on, despite arrival of Japanese reinforcements. By February, 1943, the army had completed conquest of the island; and American forces were on their way to Tokyo. Late in 1943, while Allied troops were digging in in southern Italy, Americans invaded the Gilbert Islands. Despite preliminary air bombardment, there were heavy losses when the marines hit the beaches at Tarawa; but again the Japanese were routed out. With bases in the Gilberts, the

United States was ready to move against islands which the Japanese had held before Pearl Harbor—the Marshalls, Carolines, and Marianas—and to bid for repossession of such former American possessions as Guam and the Philippines.

Victory (1944–45)

What next? Churchill felt Britain and America should strike the "soft underbelly" of the Axis by advancing through Italy and the Balkans. This, among other things, would give the Anglo-American combination something to say about the postwar fate of southeast Europe. Stalin, as before, wanted the United States and Britain to land in western Europe. This would draw more Nazi soldiers away from the eastern front and would leave Russia dominant in the Balkans. Roosevelt cast the deciding vote, choosing Stalin's plan. Advice from American military leaders was the decisive factor. That is, invading Germany from the west looked easier than a movement from the south, across rugged country. Roosevelt, Churchill, and Stalin reached agreement at the Teheran Conference, and on June 6, 1944 (D-day), came the landing, in Normandy, the largest military operation in American history.

General Eisenhower, as supreme commander, had nearly 3,000,000 men available, mostly American and British (including Canadian). He had 4000 ships, 15,000 planes. After air bombardment, troops were landed along a sixty-mile beachhead. Fearing a second landing elsewhere, the Germans did not throw their full weight against the landing forces. But there was bitter fighting along the shore, more as the Allies moved inland. Using cover afforded by the hedgerows of Normandy, the Germans contested every inch of ground. But summer brought victory in France, as troops under the British General Montgomery and the American Generals Omar Bradley and George S. Patton, Jr., forced the Germans back. Paris was liberated, partly owing to the efforts of the French underground; and another landing in southern France wound up the job.

With the Russians reaching Prussia (fall, 1944), many felt the war was over. Then German Field Marshal Karl von Rundstedt counterattacked in the Belgian Ardennes sector, throwing 300,000 men at a weak point in the Allied line (battle of the Bulge, December, 1944–January, 1945). This engagement cost the United States a dozen times as many casualties as the attack upon Pearl Harbor. But it was the Nazis' dying gasp. By March, 1945, Americans had crossed the Rhine; and in May, 1945, after Hitler's suicide, Germany surrendered.

Japan was also near the end. In summer, 1944, the United States obtained a foothold in the Marianas, after a bloody battle on Saipan. Guam was reoccupied; and in the fall Americans moved into the Philippines, where Admiral William F. Halsey smashed Japanese naval power. American troops landed first on Leyte, then (early 1945) on Luzon. Manila fell in February, 1945. Americans suffered heavy loss at Iwo Jima and on Okinawa (invaded in April, 1945). These victories, however, enabled the United States to begin saturation bombing of the Japanese mainland.

At the same time, Allied forces under Stilwell were reoccupying Burma. And, as Germany fell, Russia prepared to attack Japanese positions in Manchuria and Korea. Military men judged that Russian aid would save the United States hundreds of thousands of casualties. Roosevelt, Churchill, and Stalin made the arrangements at the Yalta Conference of February, 1945; and these were confirmed by Roosevelt's successor Truman at the Potsdam Conference in July. In return for aid, Russia was to receive the Kurile Islands, southern Sakhalin, and strategic control over Manchuria. Russia entered the war on August 9, 1945.

As it turned out, the United States did not need Russian aid in the Far East. The atomic bomb was tested in Los Alamos, New Mexico, on July 16, 1945, one day before the opening of the Potsdam Conference. On August 6 an atomic bomb was dropped on Hiroshima, Japan; another on Nagasaki August 9. Near defeat before the bombs were dropped, Japan now offered to surrender, stipulating, however, that Emperor Hirohito should retain his crown. Since Japan had gone to war in December, 1941, under an imperial rescript, dealing with Hirohito was like dealing with the king of Italy. Again, however (as in use of the atomic bomb), a major consideration was saving lives of American soldiers. In addition, a quick conclusion of the war might check Russian advances. So, without giving assurances that Hirohito could continue permanently as emperor, the United States accepted the Japanese offer. A formal surrender was signed on the battleship *Missouri* on September 2, 1945; and the fighting phase of World War II was over.

Truman, Postwar President

Franklin D. Roosevelt was not alive when World War II ended; worn out by years of service, he died in April, 1945, and was succeeded by Harry S. Truman. After Roosevelt, any President might have seemed less than forceful. Citizens tended to regard the new Chief Executive with sympathy rather than admiration. Truman was a self-made man who fought in World War I, failed in business, then became a Democratic politician in Missouri. Ability, plus ties with Kansas City's Pendergast machine, took Truman to the Senate (1934), where he voted with his party. During World War II he received notice for investigating

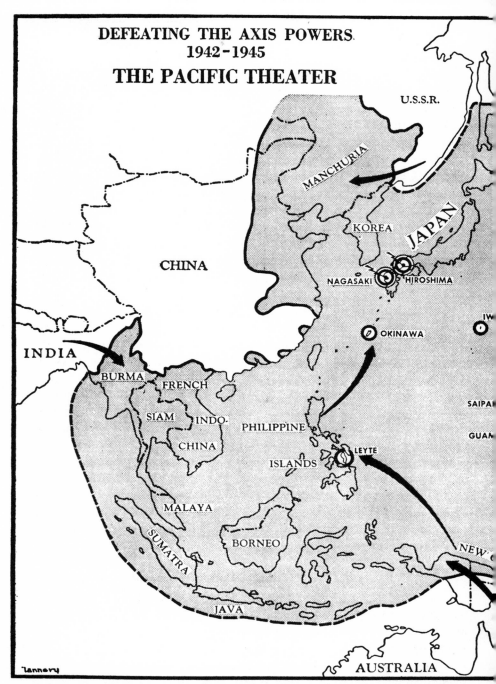

DEFEATING THE AXIS POWERS
1942-1945
THE PACIFIC THEATER

U.S.S.R.

MANCHURIA

KOREA

JAPAN

CHINA

NAGASAKI   HIROSHIMA

OKINAWA

IW

INDIA

BURMA

FRENCH

SAIPAN

SIAM   INDO-

GUAM

CHINA

PHILIPPINE

LEYTE

ISLANDS

MALAYA

SUMATRA

BORNEO

NEW

JAVA

AUSTRALIA

Lannery

In Europe, Anglo-American advances were aided by Russian pressure from the other side; but Russia did not enter the Far East war until the very end. China kept many Japanese troops engaged, but was not effective on offense. Since European operations had priority, allied forces in the Pacific were short of men and supplies, especially in the early part of the war. Moreover, the distances were greater than in Europe.

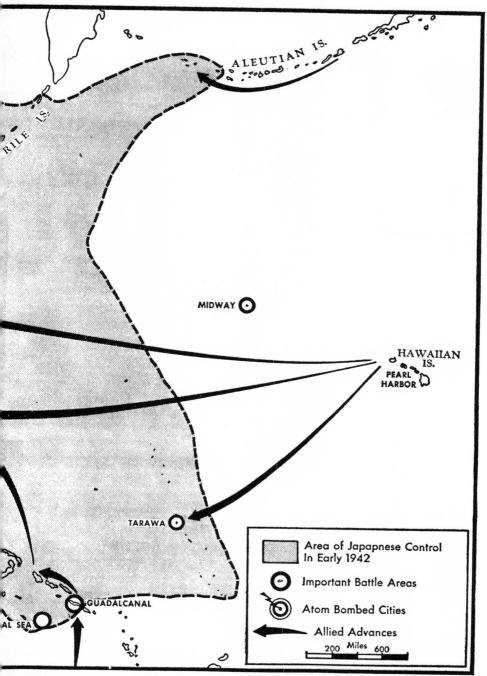

	Area of Japapnese Control In Early 1942
	Important Battle Areas
	Atom Bombed Cities
	Allied Advances

200 Miles 600

Nevertheless, Americans checked Japan in 1942 (Coral Sea, Midway), then began the long push to Tokyo. Guadalcanal was invaded in 1942, Tarawa in 1943, Saipan, Guam, and Leyte (in the Philippines) in 1944, Iwo Jima and Okinawa in 1945. By 1944–45, the United States and her allies were moving back into Burma. The use of the atom bomb against Japan (August, 1945) then brought the war to a close.

war plants; and when Henry Wallace was dropped from the Roosevelt ticket in 1944, Truman was named for Vice-President. Machine backing and support from labor and from Roosevelt won him the post.

There was some evidence in 1945 and 1946 that Truman was more conservative than the prewar Roosevelt. Truman picked conservative advisers; and Roosevelt New Dealers left the administration. (Ickes, Secretary of the Interior since 1933, resigned in 1946.) Truman favored universal military service; and he took an antilabor attitude in the railroad strike of 1946. Such policies were in tune with the times, for postwar trends were to the right. Truman, however, seemed offhand and ineffective in his first years in office. After seeming to oppose continuance of wartime controls, he fought for OPA in 1946. When Congress refused to coöperate, the President vetoed one unsatisfactory bill, then accepted a similar one. When this statute worked badly, Truman ended price ceilings, save for rental properties. Prices then rose rapidly.

Truman's apparent ineffectiveness helped the Republicans win the Congressional election of 1946. Another factor was general dislike for wartime government controls (as in "back-to-normalcy" sentiment after World War I). The Republican-controlled Eighticth Congress (1947–49) was conservative, refusing to extend social security or do much for the farmers, and passing the Taft-Hartley Act, which put curbs on labor. As Congress shifted right, Truman moved left, backed labor and aid-to-farmers, talked of broader social security, federal help to housing, civil rights for Negroes. (All this he would eventually term the Fair Deal.)

The Election of 1948

Considering Truman a weak candidate, several Democratic managers tried to have him set aside in the 1948 convention. Active here were the Americans for Democratic Action, who included some Roosevelt New Dealers. But the A.D.A. was short of practical politicians and could find no suitable candidate; so Truman was nominated for President, with Senator Alben Barkley of Kentucky as his running mate.

Few felt that Truman could win. His own party managers gave him little backing, and concentrated on local contests. Southern Democrats considered the President's civil-rights position a challenge to states' rights and white supremacy. Some of these southern Democrats stayed with Truman; others ran a Dixiecrat presidential candidate in 1948, Governor J. Strom Thurmond of South Carolina. On the other side, Henry Wallace ran on a Progressive ticket. Wallace wanted to push domestic reform faster than did Truman, and disapproved of Truman's policy of getting tough with Russia. This Democratic division seemed to spell Republican victory in 1948. After a spirited contest, the Republican presidential nomination went to Governor Thomas E. Dewey of New York. When opposing Roosevelt in 1944 Dewey had campaigned vigorously. In 1948 he felt so sure of victory that he avoided issues and confined himself to platitudes. Substantially his only pledge was to preserve existing foreign policy.

Threatened with defeat, the hitherto ineffective Truman toured the country, meeting the people as an "average man" (Dewey was stiff and formal). Seeking farm and labor votes, the President denounced the Eightieth Congress and declared for welfare legislation. Oddly, the secessions from the Democratic party helped Truman. The Thurmond opposition made many feel that Truman was a real liberal, not a Dixiecrat reactionary. Wallace's candidacy convinced many that the President was no radical, and could be trusted.

Straw votes indicated a Dewey victory; but Truman won. The Dixiecrats carried South Carolina, Louisiana, Alabama, Mississippi. Most southern Democrats, however, avoided a regional ticket that had no chance of winning national success or patronage. Wallace faded fast. Unlike La Follette in 1924, Wallace accepted Communist support. Many therefore concluded that the Progressives were Communist-controlled. Wallace polled 1,150,000 votes—less than Thurmond, only a few more than Lemke, the forgotten Union candidate of 1936. Wallace ran best in New York, where he took enough votes away from Truman to give the state to Dewey. But Truman carried Ohio, Iowa, Wisconsin, and Colorado, which Roosevelt had lost in 1944. Labor remembered that a Republican Congress had passed the Taft-Hartley Act over Truman's veto. Farmers knew that the Democrats were more committed to farm support than the Republicans.

Truman's victory was a narrow one. Not since 1916 had a victor run so few votes ahead of the other major-party nominee (2,000,000 in a total of 49,000,000). Not since 1888 had a victor received so small a majority in the electoral college. Only once before (1916) had a victor lost the two most populous states, New York and Pennsylvania. Truman's victory seemed like a great triumph mainly because the experts had predicted a Dewey landslide. Yet in a way the outcome was impressive. In winning their fifth straight presidential race, the Democrats had shown that most farmers and union workingmen had become "normally Democratic." Truman had won even while losing over a million Democratic votes to Wallace and Thurmond.

The Campaign of 1952

How, then, could the Republicans ever win a national election? Some Republicans said Landon, Willkie, and Dewey had erred in echoing New Deal Democrats. Victory might come if Republicans dropped the "me, too" policy and became frankly conservative, under such a leader as Senator Robert Taft of Ohio. Launching his campaign early, Taft long led in the race for the Republican nomination for 1952. Many Republicans, however, felt that Taft lacked the color needed to attract the independent vote. Gaining ground at the end, these Republicans secured the nomination for General Dwight D. Eisenhower in July, 1952, with Senator Richard Nixon of California as his running mate.

The Democrats also had their problems. They found it easier to win elections than to agree as to a legislative program. Conservative southern Democrats often joined conservative northern Republicans to defeat presidential proposals. Truman managed to get military and foreign-aid appropriations during his second term (1949–53), but his Fair Deal domestic reform program bogged down. Bureau of Internal Revenue and other scandals hurt the party in power, and Truman did not do a good job of cleaning house. The President's popularity declined, and he was badly beaten by Senator Estes Kefauver in the New Hampshire presidential-preference primaries in March, 1952. Even so, Truman could easily have won the Democratic nomination in 1952. He decided, however, not to run. In the resulting scramble for delegates, Kefauver was the popular favorite in the primaries. But, being unacceptable to Truman and other party leaders, the Senator from Tennessee lost out in the convention. The nomination went to Governor Adlai E. Stevenson of Illinois, Senator John Sparkman of Alabama being named for vice-president.

Minor party strength being almost zero, it was a two-party race. Stevenson won prestige in the campaign, but aroused little popular enthusiasm. He, Truman, and other Democrats stressed prosperity; Americans normally favor the incumbents in years of full employment and high prices. Prosperity, however, was accompanied by heavy taxes, inflation, and the Korean war. The Republicans stressed this, and said Truman had bungled the problems of corruption and Communism. This impressed many voters. Others were attracted by the fame and personality of Eisenhower ("I Like Ike"). The result was a Republican landslide. Eisenhower swept the Northeast and Middle West, won the Rocky Mountain and Pacific coast states, and cut into the solid South. He captured Texas, Virginia, and Florida, and nearly carried South Carolina. The Democrats fared better in House and Senate races, but lost control of both houses of Congress. It was evident that the age of Democratic domination—the age of Franklin D. Roosevelt—was ended.

Bipartisan Foreign Policy

During World War II, many administration leaders feared a repetition of the World War I pattern, with America pulling out of Europe in the postwar era. To guard against this, Franklin

D. Roosevelt tried a bipartisan approach to foreign policy and took leading Senators into his confidence. (Wilson had offended Republicans by working only through Democrats, and had irritated Senators by ignoring them.) As early as 1940 two Republicans were taken into the cabinet (Henry L. Stimson as Secretary of War, Frank Knox as Secretary of Navy). Republican as well as Democratic votes were needed for the draft, repeal of neutrality legislation, and other administration proposals. Later, Roosevelt sponsored a world tour by Wendell Willkie, his opponent in the 1940 presidential contest. A bipartisan agreement kept foreign policy out of the wartime presidential campaign of 1944.

At the peacemaking stage Roosevelt had United States Senators of both parties participate in the negotiations (Senator Tom Connally of Texas, Democratic chairman of the Foreign Relations Committee, and Senator Arthur Vandenberg of Michigan, ranking Republican member). Results were satisfactory. The Senate raised no objection to American membership in the United Nations (1945). Congress provided funds for European relief and recovery (United Nations Relief and Rehabilitation Administration, 1943–46; the Marshall Plan after 1947); for economic aid to America's chief ally, Britain (a loan of 1947); for military aid programs (Greece and Turkey, the Truman Doctrine, 1947; North Atlantic Pact, 1949); for postwar propaganda (the State Department's Voice of America); for an overseas development program (technological aid, Point Four, 1950). Diplomatic issues were played down in 1948, except for Henry Wallace, who opposed the anti-Russian attitude of both major parties.

The bipartisan program was not perfect. Senators—Republicans especially—complained that the executive made basic decisions without consulting the Senate, as at Teheran, Yalta, and Potsdam. What was more, agreements among the Big Three were not submitted to the Senate. Republicans said that the administration should, but did not, consult them before announcing new policies (Truman Doctrine, Point Four). The Democrats, in turn, said their opponents made political capital out of questions involving national interest. Some independents complained that the bipartisan policy gave the public little voice in foreign policy, that everything was decided in Washington.

In 1950, Republican Senator Joseph R. McCarthy of Wisconsin made sensational charges as to Communists in the State Department. Since McCarthy offered accusation without proof, many Republicans were reluctant to support him, the more so since the Truman administration was strongly anti-Communist. Others backed McCarthy, because they believed some of his statements, or hoped to embarrass Truman or break the bipartisan foreign policy. McCarthy won reëlection to the Senate in 1952, but ran far behind his ticket.

By then, the United States was fighting Communists in Korea. Many Republicans were sharply critical of Truman's Far East policy, especially after the President relieved General MacArthur from his command (April, 1951). Others complained when, early in 1951, Truman claimed constitutional authority to send additional troops to Europe without consulting Congress. If the Republicans had been united they would probably have launched an all-out attack. They were, however, divided. Some, like ex-President Hoover, favored concentration on continental defense. Others, including Dewey, felt America should continue active in Europe. Eisenhower favored the Dewey, as against the Hoover, point of view, as was shown in his choice of John Foster Dulles for Secretary of State.

Occupation Policy

At the end of World War II Germany and Austria were divided into French, English, American, and Russian zones. North Korea was to be occupied by Soviet Russia, South Korea and Japan by the United States.

Soviet Russia had a definite occupation policy. First, she took goods— machinery from Manchuria, minerals from eastern Germany. Second, she reorganized each occupied area, working through local Communists. The United States had no such clear policy. During the war, Roosevelt for a time favored a Morgenthau Plan, designed to close factories and reduce Germany to agricultural status. Churchill approved this plan; but when Secretary of State Hull and Secretary of War Stimson attacked the proposal, it was set aside. Yet nothing very definite was substituted. In Japan, General MacArthur was given a free hand. In Europe, the military took charge, later giving way to a civilian administration. Occupation officials and troops were inadequately trained, inadequately supervised; hence there was much confusion, and some corruption.

At first, emphasis was on punishment. This was natural, considering war feeling and Axis mistreatment of prisoners. Resulting war trials were, however, not altogether satisfactory. Questionable legal methods were used in the trial of Japanese general Yamashita. This trial, and most of those in Europe, centered on war atrocities. At the Nuremberg trials of Goering and other Nazis, the Allies used the broader charge of waging aggressive war. Convictions were obtained; but, since judges were from the victor nations, it could hardly be said that the principle was established in international law.

Punishment was gradually deëmphasized. Instead of dismantling factories and restricting occupied populations, America used encouragement and aimed at expanded production. The reasons were various:

1. When repression was used, occupation was expensive and difficult; if encouraged, defeated states were coöperative and more nearly self-supporting.

2. Punishment held down output. American officials came to feel that Germany must again become a great producer in the interest of world recovery.

3. Russia and America came into conflict in 1946. American occupation officials then prepared to build up Japan and western Germany as bulwarks against an advancing Russia.

International Organization

Early in World War II, Roosevelt was doubtful as to the value of a postwar league of nations. He was more optimistic by 1945. Meantime, in 1944, anti-Axis powers had had discussions at Dumbarton Oaks (political) and Bretton Woods (economic). A San Francisco conference (1945), held after Roosevelt's death, perfected the United Nations organization. UN headquarters would be in New York, which helped Americans feel a deeper interest in the UN than in the League of Nations. Also indicating the new viewpoint was the House passage of the Fulbright Resolution in 1943, favoring an organization "with power adequate to establish and maintain a just and lasting peace."

UN had limitations. Both Soviet Russia and the United States insisted that major states have veto power. Hence the future of the world depended not so much on UN as on the ability of the United States, Britain, France, and Russia to get along with each other.

The UN won limited successes, as in Palestine. Presently, however, the UN became a sort of forum in which America and Russia denounced each other. Perhaps something was gained by airing such questions. Perhaps not. But the UN did increase American attachment to international organizations. Backed by Latin America, the British Empire, and western Europe, the United States could outvote Russia and her satellites. To escape defeat, Russia used the veto. Americans therefore regarded themselves as the defenders and the Russians as the foes of international organization.

On occasion, the United States by-passed the UN, as in announcing the Truman Doctrine. Generally, however, Americans showed a desire to work through international organization. In a government-sponsored Baruch plan (1946), the United States offered to turn its information on atomic energy over to an international body with authority to end atomic warfare and to inspect and control civil uses of atomic energy. Russian opposition (on inspection) prevented adoption. Nonetheless, the plan was an American offer to yield sovereignty and work on an international plane. The close coöperation of UN and United States in the Korean crisis of 1950–52 further illustrated this point.

Military Influence

Significantly, Congress decided that atomic secrets should be controlled by the government, not by private industry; and by civilians, not the military. The Atomic Energy Commission thus developed the hydrogen bomb (1952). And, although most military leaders supported Truman's request for universal military service, Congress did not immediately agree. Nor did voters show much interest in General Mac-Arthur's candidacy in 1948 (Wisconsin presidential-preference primary).

Still, military influence was strong. The public listened with respect to statements by admirals and generals and hailed MacArthur as a hero when he returned home in 1951. Roosevelt and Truman held the professional military in high esteem and sent military men on diplomatic missions. In 1947 Truman made General Marshall Secretary of State, the first professional military man to be so named. (Marshall resigned in 1948; he was Secretary of Defense 1950–51.) Both Democrats and Republicans considered Eisenhower possible presidential timber in 1948. The general refused to run; but after he became head of North Atlantic Treaty forces in Europe (1951) he was urged again for 1952. He finally agreed to run, and won the Republican nomination in July, 1952, and a landslide victory in November.

Military appropriations remained high after World War II and were further increased after fighting began in Korea in 1950. For increased efficiency, Congress overhauled the military establishment in 1947, creating a Department of Defense. Under the Secretary of Defense were Secretaries for the Army, Navy, and Air. The new setup did not work very well at first, and in 1949 navy officers openly complained that their branch was mistreated. A National Security Council (1947) gave the Defense Department a large voice in diplomatic decisions. A higher pay scale drew enough volunteers to take care of military man-power needs after 1945. But when actual fighting began (Korea, summer, 1950) draft calls were resumed.

Cold War with Russia

Hope for postwar coöperation faded as the Soviet Union and United States differed over peace treaties (those for Italy and four lesser states were concluded in 1946; but not for Germany, Austria, or Japan). Further difficulties arose when Russia failed to allow in eastern Europe the free elections which Stalin had agreed upon at Yalta. Nor would Russia permit Russian-occupied North Korea to join American-occupied South Korea—the latter, under UN auspices, became the Republic of Korea in 1948. Secretary of State James F. Byrnes sought a solution in 1946, proposing that Russia and America join Britain and France in a four-power treaty to hold Germany down for a generation. Russia declined, and in 1947 the Soviet Union and her satellites refused to accept Marshall Plan aid.

By then, America was trying to "contain" Russia. The stopgap relief program of UNRRA was replaced by the Marshall Plan (1948). Under this program, an Economic Cooperation Administration supplied American goods to Europe. The idea was to stimulate European recovery; to keep western Europe from moving into the Soviet orbit; to revive world trade; to help Latin America; and to maintain full employment and full farm and factory production in the United States. Besides ECA, the United States made a special loan to Britain ($3,750,000,000) and helped finance a World Bank (International Bank for Reconstruction and Development), which also provided aid.

Along with economic help went military aid. Communist advance in the Balkans threatened Greece by 1947. Victory would give Russia control of the Straits, which were under Turkish rule; this in turn would endanger Anglo-American control of Near East oil and of the Mediterranean. President Truman therefore asked for military aid for Greece and Turkey (Truman Doctrine). Congress coöperated, and the United States provided equipment and military advisers who helped check the Greek Communists. The program was already becoming effective when (1948) Marshal Tito, Communist dictator of Yugoslavia, quarreled with Moscow and became less unfriendly to the United States. Thus Russian advance had for the time been checked in southeast Europe.

In June, 1948, Russia blocked approaches to Berlin. Britain, France, and the United States had zones in the German capital; but Berlin was surrounded by Russian-occupied territory. Instead of yielding, Britain and America organized a Berlin airlift and sent in food and fuel by air. Over 2,000,000 tons of supplies were shipped in on 250,000 flights. The operation was expensive, but successful, for Russia lifted the blockade (fall, 1949).

In June, 1948, the Senate adopted a Vandenberg Resolution, favoring regional military alliances. In 1949, an Atlantic Pact established a ten-year military alliance or mutual defense agreement, linking the United States with Canada, Britain, France, Italy, Belgium, the Netherlands, Luxembourg, Norway, Denmark, Iceland, Portugal. By 1950, Congress was appropriating funds for military assistance to members of this alliance; also for Greece and Turkey, and for Asiatic friends, including Iran, Nationalist China, Korea, and the Philippine Islands. Another program provided "arms for the Americas." Worked out in the Rio Pact of 1947, and later, this embraced coöperation in the face of possible danger; standardization of equipment; arms assistance; and a general anti-Communist stand.

The economic and military program was to be tied to an ideological offensive. Since Russia actively propagandized all over the world, it was logical that the United States should reply. This the State Department did through cultural attachés, printed material, and short-wave radio programs (Voice of America). Congressional suspicion kept this work from becoming as effective as other parts of the check-Russia program. More effective, perhaps, was the exchange of scholars and students, partly financed by the government (Fulbright grants, using money realized by sale of surplus war equipment overseas). Also significant were unofficial bodies, such as the International Confederation of Free Trade Unions, formed in 1949 after the World Federation of Trade Unions came under Communist influence.

Conflict in Asia

American efforts helped turn the tide against communism in western Europe; but Russia won a crushing victory when in 1949 the Chinese Communists defeated the Chinese Nationalists and drove Chiang Kai-shek to Formosa. In 1931, when Japan invaded Manchuria, the Chinese Nationalists controlled most of China; the Communists held only a small region. After the Japanese invasion of 1937, Chinese Nationalists and Communists both fought the invader. Lend-Lease aid was sent to the Nationalists; the Roosevelt administration hoped, however, that the Nationalists and Communists could serve together under American General Stilwell. Stilwell, though, quarreled with Chiang and was recalled; and the Nationalists and Communists did not combine.

After World War II, General Marshall went to China, hoping to bring Nationalists and Communists together in a coalition government, using also a middle group of American-trained Chinese liberals. Failing, Marshall returned home to become Secretary of State in 1947, convinced that the China situation was close to hopeless (the Chinese Communists were pro-Russian, the Chinese Nationalists corrupt and undemocratic). Most Americans cared little about the Far East. Congress voted the Chinese· Nationalists some Marshall Plan aid, and later some military assistance. The sums, though, were small, the problem great.

When Nationalist China fell, there was concern lest communism spread further in the Orient—into Indo-China and Tibet, threatened by Chinese Communists; into the Republic of the Philippines, where Communist-influenced "Huks" fought a conservative government; into the Republic of Korea, from which American troops were withdrawn in 1949; into other areas where Communists were active: Iran, Siam, Malaya, newly freed Indonesia, India, and Burma.

When Russian-trained and Russian-equipped North Korean troops crossed the 38° parallel and invaded South Korea in June, 1950, President Truman had General Douglas MacArthur use air, naval, and ground forces against the invaders. This action was endorsed by virtually every Congressman, and by the general public. Significantly, too, Britain gave the United States support, as did the United Nations. At first forced back, almost into the sea, the UN forces (chiefly Americans and South Koreans) pushed the North Koreans back in the fall of 1950. Confidence was high when the Americans crossed the 38° parallel and pressed to the Manchurian border. But then (November, 1950) Chinese Communist troops entered Korea. After falling back, the UN forces advanced again in the new year, and they held against a new Chinese offensive in May, 1951. Although forbidden to bomb China (for fear Russia would enter the war), the UN forces inflicted heavy losses on their foes. UN losses were smaller, but American casualties were 115,000 by August, 1952, including 20,000 known dead.

In April, 1951, President Truman relieved Douglas MacArthur as occupation chief in Japan and UN commander in Korea. MacArthur disagreed with the administration on strategy (he wanted to carry the war to China by air) and openly criticized the Roosevelt-Truman Europe-first policy and failed to obey some orders from superiors. The public gave MacArthur a magnificent reception on his return to the United States, and the general became active in Republican circles. There was little indication, however, that the MacArthur question would greatly affect policy.

With both sides desiring to end hostilities, truce negotiations began in June, 1951. Talks continued for more than a year, but without ending the fighting, or solving the problems involved.

Problems at Home

As feeling against Russia increased, Americans regarded Communists with growing hostility.[2] Congress and the President launched investigations. Some government officials were dropped or resigned after loyalty checks. The Justice Department issued lists of "subversive organizations," groups founded or used by Communists. The

---

[2] Early in World War II, when Stalin was working with Hitler, Roosevelt moved against American Communists; Earl Browder went to prison for passport fraud. American Communists were then denouncing Roosevelt as an imperialist. (After Russia was invaded, they called the conflict a "people's war.") Browder (now out of jail) supported the war effort after Pearl Harbor, saying Communists and capitalists could coöperate. The party line changed again after the war. Browder was deposed for his coöperation stand, and the American Communists (under William Z. Foster and Eugene Dennis) became violently opposed to capitalism and American foreign policy.

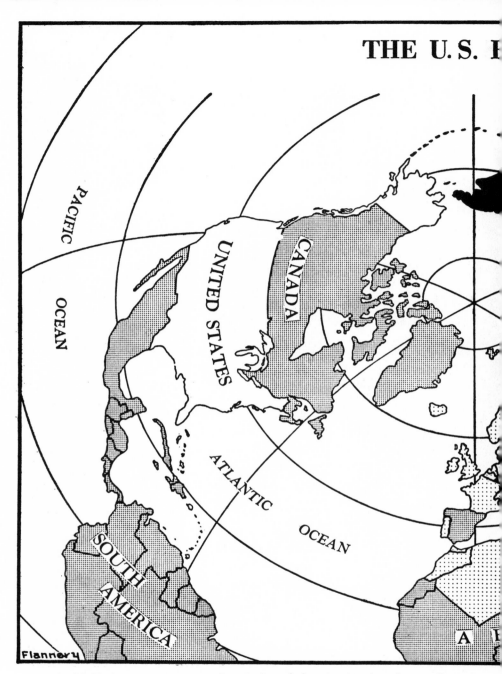

PACIFIC

OCEAN

UNITED STATES

CANADA

ATLANTIC

OCEAN

SOUTH

AMERICA

Flannery

A

In 1945, American policy makers believed that Russian-American coöperation was desirable and possible. Soon thereafter conflicts put these two powers into separate camps. Areas of friction included the Middle East, the Balkans, occupied Germany, and the Far East.

In the Cold War, both sides used economic, military, and propagandist
weapons. The Russians appealed to peasants in satellite states by breaking
up the large estates. Russian experts trained satellite armies, and the Soviet
Union provided military equipment. Meantime, Moscow carried on a well-

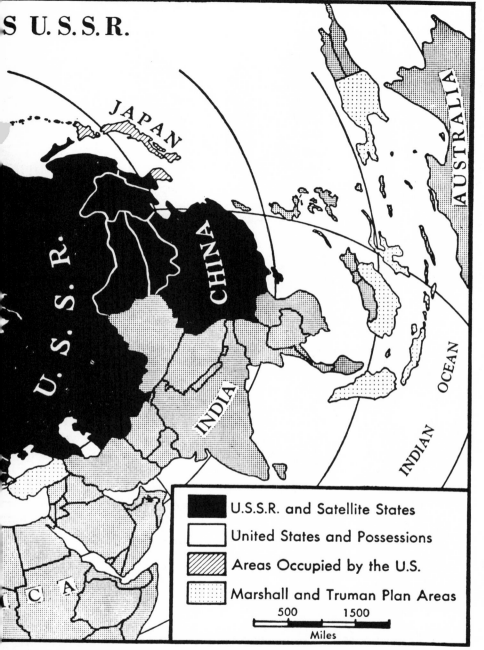

S U.S.S.R.

JAPAN

AUSTRALIA

CHINA

U. S. S. R.

INDIA

OCEAN

INDIAN

C A

U.S.S.R. and Satellite States

United States and Possessions

Areas Occupied by the U.S.

Marshall and Truman Plan Areas

500   1500

Miles

organized world propaganda campaign. The United States provided economic aid for its allies, notably through the Marshall Plan; also in a large
loan to Britain. On the military side, the American republic gave military
advice and supplies to Greece and Turkey under the Truman Doctrine; and
with the signing of the North Atlantic Pact, embarked on a military-aid program for western Europe. Similar aid was to be given to coöperating states
in the Middle and Far East, e.g., Iran and the Philippines. The Voice of America represented the publicity approach.

Taft-Hartley Act required labor leaders to swear they were not Communists. There were convictions for perjury (Harry Bridges, longshoreman leader; Alger Hiss, formerly a State Department official); for contempt in refusing to answer questions asked by Congressional investigators (ten Hollywood writers, among others); espionage (Judith Coplon, a Justice Department employee, and Valentin Gubitchev, a Russian employed by the United Nations); violation of the Smith Act, i.e., plotting to overthrow the government (Eugene Dennis and thirty other Communist leaders by August, 1952). Americans were particularly disturbed to hear of spy activities. In 1951 Julius Rosenberg and his wife, both Americans, were sentenced to death for wartime espionage—they helped supply Russia with information about the atomic bomb. (Russia achieved an atomic explosion in 1949.)

Meantime, the C.I.O. expelled Communist-dominated unions (1949–50) and set up new unions to take over the field. There were campaigns to get Communists out of religious and veterans' organizations and minority-group associations. The Regents of the University of California required employees to swear that they were not Communists. A flood of books by former Communists recited the evils of communism. Hollywood turned out anticommunist movies. *The Iron Curtain* and *I Was a Communist for the FBI* were in sharp contrast with *Mission to Moscow* and *Song of Russia*, pro-Soviet pictures produced in the war years, when Russia and America were coöperating.

The public fully endorsed the efforts of the FBI to round up Russian spies. The great majority of Americans also approved of the bipartisan anti-Russian foreign policy (after 1946) and the steps taken against Communists in unions and other American organizations. At the same time, many were disturbed by the tendency of some anticommunists to identify everything they disliked with Russia. Unscrupulous politicians gained the spotlight by making reckless charges. Ultraconservative newspaper columnists and radio commentators suggested that Socialists and Communists were virtually identical, and that Socialists included all who advocated public housing or socialized medicine. David Lilienthal and other loyal officials were so much harassed by investigations that many able citizens were reluctant to enter public employment. Strong foes of communism and of Russian expansion were denounced as "Reds"—religious leaders with liberal beliefs, C.I.O. and A.F. of L. officials, liberal intellectuals. With talk of teachers' oaths, some wondered if academic freedom was in danger. Communists eliminated civil liberties and insisted on conformity in areas under their control. Were Americans moving in the same direction?

Fortunately, the tradition of civil liberties was very strong in the United

States. There were other hopeful signs. Labor was crushed after World
War I; it held its own after World War II. Minority groups suffered after
1918; the years after 1945 brought a strong, partially successful drive against
discrimination. Postwar reactions turned Americans against international
coöperation by 1920; at mid-century, by contrast, citizens were generally
favorable toward UN. Associating reform with radicalism, Americans had
turned away from the progressive movement after World War I; and both
major parties had become very conservative. The politicians of 1952 may
have lacked the crusading zeal of earlier days; but few favored wiping out
the social legislation of the past two decades.

By 1952, the United States was moving into large-scale war production.
As in World Wars I and II, the government relied heavily on the larger
manufacturers and brought big businessmen into the government. The key
figure in war production from 1950 to 1952 was Defense Mobilizer
Charles E. Wilson, formerly of General Electric. Labor, however, was
strong; Wilson quit his job when Truman favored an increase in wages for
steel workers in April, 1952. By then, war production had brought full
employment and prosperity; but it had also brought high prices. An office
of Price Stabilization tried to meet this situation, but neither Congress nor
the President seemed able to resist farmer-labor-business pressures for
higher prices.

A Better World?

As they entered the second half of the
twentieth century, Americans were enjoying great material prosperity.
National income was over $200,000,000,000 a year. Employment was high,
around 60,000,000. Farmers were doing well, workingmen were obtaining
a measure of security. Improved educational opportunities enabled an increasing number of Americans to enter the professions. Business earnings
were at peak levels. Americans had more mechanical conveniences, cultural
opportunities, and leisure than before. Women and minority groups met
with less discrimination than in earlier periods. Americans were learning
to conserve natural resources. Their republic had more naval and economic
power than any other nation; and America was a great scientific and cultural
center. If atomic energy could be put to peacetime use, greater gains might
lie ahead.

Yet, in midst of plenty, Americans were worried about the future. The
rise of Russia, the threat of atomic war bore heavily upon Americans in an
age when isolation had become impossible. Domestic prosperity no longer
seemed enough; no nation appeared secure while distress and want haunted
other sections of the globe. Even at home, all was not well. Prosperity

depended in part on exports for which foreign countries could not pay; and on an armament program which increased an already staggering tax burden. The individualism and opportunity of an earlier America seemed to have faded; some felt the nation had suddenly grown old. Despair became fashionable in intellectual circles. No longer did Americans speak of the inevitability of progress. Rather they talked of an uncertain future.

In earlier generations, Americans had been overoptimistic. Now they were overpessimistic. There were problems, certainly. But, in facing these problems, Americans had a great store of natural resources; a large, prosperous, relatively homogeneous population; a deep attachment to democracy; ability to meet crises and adjust to change; organizing talent; a critical spirit; an abiding faith in education. And Americans still believed in themselves. Their ancestors had conquered the wilderness and built a great republic. Looking forward, Americans saw signs of trouble and sometimes felt disheartened. Deep down, however, they believed their land would prosper in the future as in the past, were certain that the history of the American republic was just beginning to unfold.

Significant Dates in
American History

1000 Leif Ericson's Vinland settlement

1492 First voyage of Columbus

1493 Papal line of demarcation

1497 Cabot reaches North American mainland for England

1509 Spain settles Puerto Rico, first permanent European settlement, present U. S. territory

1513 Ponce de Leon explores Florida for Spain

1524 Verrazano explores North American coast for France

1534–36 Cartier explores St. Lawrence for France

1539–42 De Soto (Spanish) explores interior present U. S., discovers Mississippi River

1540–41 Coronado (Spanish) explores present U. S., New Mexico to Kansas

1564 Spain settles Philippines

1565 Spain settles St. Augustine, Fla., first permanent European settlement, present U. S.

1587 Raleigh's Roanoke Island settlement, the "lost colony"; Virginia Dare, first English child born in America

1588 England defeats Spanish Armada

1598 Spain settles New Mexico (Santa Fe, 1605)

1603–25 James I, first Stuart King of England

1606 London and Plymouth Companies authorized to start colonies

1607 London Company establishes Jamestown colony in Virginia

1608 French settle Quebec

1609 Exploration, Hudson River (Hudson, for Dutch), Lake Champlain (Champlain, for French)

1609–10 "Starving time" in Jamestown

1612 John Rolfe plants tobacco in Virginia

1619 House of Burgesses, Virginia (beginning representative government); Negro slaves introduced, Virginia

1620 Pilgrims found Plymouth colony; Mayflower Compact

1621 Pilgrims obtain grant from Council for New England

1622 Council for New England grants Maine to Gorges and Mason

1623 Thanksgiving Day celebrated by Pilgrims

1624 Dutch found New Netherland; Virginia made royal colony

1625–49 Charles I, King of England

1629 Council for New England grants New Hampshire to Mason; Massachusetts Bay Company chartered; patroon system started, New Netherland

1632 Lord Baltimore obtains Maryland charter

1633 Dutch establish themselves in Connecticut

1634 English settle in Connecticut, Maryland; Harvard College founded

1636 Roger Williams founds settlement in Rhode Island

1637 Pequot War against Indians, Connecticut; trial of Anne Hutchinson, Massachusetts

1638 English found New Haven colony; Swedes settle on Delaware (New Sweden), build log cabins

1639 Fundamental Orders of Connecticut, first written constitution creating government in present U. S.

1640–60 Puritan Revolution, England (Charles I beheaded, 1639; Cromwell Lord Protector, 1653–58)

1641 Massachusetts takes over New Hampshire

1643 New England Confederation formed (to 1684)

1644 Saybrook (founded 1635) added to Connecticut; Rhode Island gets charter; Indians driven from Virginia coastal plain

1647 Massachusetts public school law

1649 Maryland Toleration Act

1651 Navigation Act (others 1660, 1662, 1663, 1670, 1673, 1696)

1652–54 First Anglo-Dutch war (others 1664–67, 1672–74)

1654 Dutch driven from Connecticut; English settle North Carolina; Toleration Act repealed in Maryland

1655 Dutch take over New Sweden

1657 Baltimore regains control, Maryland; Toleration Act restored

1660 Stuart Restoration in England (Charles II, 1660–85)

1662 Connecticut gets royal charter, uniting Connecticut and New Haven

1663 Charter for Carolinas

1664 English take New Amsterdam and Delaware from Dutch; New Amsterdam granted to Duke of York, who rules part (New York), grants part to friends (New Jersey)

1666 Denmark colonizes Virgin Islands

1670 English settle South Carolina

1673 Dutch recapture New York (returned to England, 1674); Marquette and Joliet explore Mississippi River for France

1675 Lords of Trade become royal advisers on colonial affairs

1675–78 King Philip's Indian War, New England

1676 Nathaniel Bacon's rebellion, Virginia

1679 New Hampshire becomes royal colony

1681 Pennsylvania granted to William Penn

1681–87 LaSalle develops French claims, Mississippi valley

1682 First Spanish, French settlements in Texas; Delaware granted to Penn; Penn settles Pennsylvania

1684 Massachusetts made royal colony

1685 New York becomes royal colony when Duke of York becomes James II

1686–89 Dominion of New England (effort to consolidate royal power in colonies)

1688 Glorious Revolution in England deposes James II, establishes rule of Parliament

1689 Uprising in Maryland; Jacob Leisler's uprising in New York (executed, 1691); William and Mary rule in England (Mary to 1694, William to 1702)

1689–97 King William's War

1691 Maryland becomes royal colony (to 1715); Plymouth joined to Massachusetts

1692 Salem witchcraft trials

1692–94 Pennsylvania and Delaware temporarily royal colonies

1693 William and Mary College founded

1696 King William gives Board of Trade colonial powers

1699 Wool Act; French settle Louisiana

1701 Yale College founded

1701–13 Queen Anne's War (War of Spanish Succession); (Anne's reign, 1702–14)

1702 New Jersey becomes royal colony

1704 First American newspaper, *Boston News Letter*

1705 Parliament votes bounties on naval stores

1706 Rice, naval stores, molasses become enumerated articles

1712 Slave uprising, New York; Carolina divided

1714–27 George I founds Hanoverian line in England

1716 Permanent settlement of Texas by Spain

1717–20 John Law's Mississippi Bubble (unsuccessful French effort to develop Louisiana rapidly)

1718 French establish New Orleans

1719 South Carolina becomes royal colony

1721 Inoculation against smallpox introduced into colonies; first marine insurance issued, Philadelphia

1722 Additional articles, e.g., beaver, on enumerated list

1727–60 George II's reign

1729 North Carolina made royal colony

1732 Hat Act; Georgia granted to Oglethorpe and others; Philadelphia almshouse completed

1733 Molasses Act

1734 Jonathan Edwards' Northampton revival helps stir Great Awakening

1735 Zenger acquitted in free-press trial, New York

1741 Slave uprising, New York

1744 Eliza Lucas Pinckney introduces indigo culture; American Philosophical Society formed

1744–48 King George's War (War of Austrian Succession)

1746 Princeton College founded

1748 Parliament votes indigo bounty; first Lutheran synod in America, Pennsylvania

1749 Founding of academy which becomes University of Pennsylvania

1750 Iron Act

1751 Georgia becomes royal colony

1752 Franklin's lightning rod experiment; Pennsylvania Hospital founded (first modern hospital in colonies); first fire insurance company, Philadelphia

1753 Post office organized for colonies

1754 Albany Congress; Albany Plan of Union; King's College founded (Columbia)

1754–63 French and Indian War (Seven Years War), Braddock's defeat, 1755; British take Louisbourg, Fort Duquesne (Pittsburgh), 1758; Quebec, 1759, Montreal, 1760

1760–1820 George III, King of England

1762 France cedes Louisiana to Spain

1763 Pontiac's rising; Proclamation Line

1763–67 Mason and Dixon line surveyed

1764 Sugar Act; Paper Money Act; Paxton boys march on Philadelphia; founding of St. Louis; Brown College founded

1765 Stamp Act; Quartering Act; Stamp Act Congress

1766 Stamp Act repealed; Queen's College (Rutgers) founded; first permanent theater in colonies, Philadelphia

1767 Townshend Acts; first American play (Godfrey's *Prince of Parthia*) performed

1768 Non-importation agreements

1769 Spain settles California; Dartmouth College founded; first settlement of Tennessee (Watauga)

1770 Boston Massacre; Townshend Acts repealed, except on tea

1771 North Carolina Regulators rise

1773 Tea Act; tea ship burned, Annapolis; Boston Tea Party

1774 First Continental Congress; Intolerable Acts; first settlement in Kentucky (Harrodsburg)

1775–83 American Revolution

1775 Battles of Lexington, Concord (April); Patriots take Ticonderoga (May); Bunker Hill (June); Washington takes command (June); Patriots invade Canada (July–Dec.); first antislavery society, Philadelphia; Daniel Boone cuts Wilderness Road through Cumberland Gap

1776 British evacuate Boston (March), but take New York (battle of Long Island, Aug.); Washington retreats into Pennsylvania, returns to take Trenton (Dec.); British take Newport, R. I. (Dec.); Congress declares independence (July); secret French aid; Virginia abolishes entail, adopts Declaration of Rights; Delaware ends importation of slaves; Spain settles San Francisco

1777 British defeat Washington at Brandywine, take Philadelphia (Sept.), but Americans beat British at Bennington, Oriskany (Aug.), and force Burgoyne to surrender (Saratoga, Oct.); Washington winters at Valley Forge (1777–78); Congress adopts Stars-and-Stripes, approves Articles of Confederation; Vermont abolishes slavery and adopts manhood suffrage

1778 Steuben drills Washington's army; Greene as Quartermaster General; France recognizes American independence; Franco-American alliance (Feb.); Clark begins western campaign, takes Kaskaskia (July); British evacuate Philadelphia (June), begin southern campaign, taking Savannah (Dec.); Indian-Tory massacres of Patriots, Wyoming Valley, Pa. (July), Cherry Valley, N. Y. (Nov.)

1779 Clark takes Vincennes (Feb.); British evacuate Newport (Oct.); Sullivan expedition against Indians; British win victories, Georgia; Spain enters war; Anglican Church disestablished, Virginia

1780 British take Charleston (May); Patriots beaten at Camden, S. C. (Aug.) but win at Kings Mountain, N. C. (Oct.); Arnold's treason; Pennsylvania votes gradual emancipation; Transylvania College founded, Kentucky, first west of mountains; Dutch forced into war by British

1781 Robert Morris becomes Superintendent of Finance; Cornwallis drives Americans across North Carolina (Jan.–March), but surrenders after siege of Yorktown (Sept.–Oct.); Articles of Confederation go into effect; Bank of North America chartered by Congress

1781–89 Confederation era

1782 British evacuate Savannah (July), Charleston (Dec.); preliminary peace treaty (Nov.)

1783 Final peace treaty (Sept.); Massachusetts Supreme Court rules that 1780 state constitution ended slavery; Protestant Episcopal Church organized; Order of Cincinnati formed; Webster's *Spelling Book*

1784 Tennessee settlers try to organize state of Franklin; New Hampshire ends slavery; Rhode Island, Connecticut adopt gradual emancipation; Methodist Episcopal Church organized; first daily newspaper started (*Pennsylvania Packet and Daily Advertiser*); American trade with China begins; first permanent Russian settlement in Alaska; Morse's first geography text

1785 Virginia ends primogeniture; University of Georgia founded; Survey Bill (Land Ordinance of 1785)

1786 Virginia Statute of Religious Freedom; Congress rejects Jay-

Gardoqui agreement; Shays' rebellion, Massachusetts (Aug.); Annapolis Convention calls Constitutional Convention (Sept.)

1787 Congress adopts Northwest Ordinance (July), sells much land to Ohio Co. (Oct.); Constitutional Convention in Philadelphia (May–Sept.); Congress submits Constitution to state conventions (Sept.); Delaware first to ratify (Dec.); first prison reform society, Philadelphia; first Shaker society, New York

1788 Ratification struggle; Constitution adopted (New Hampshire, ninth to ratify, June 21)

1789 Government under Constitution launched; first presidential election (Jan.); Congress organized, Washington inaugurated as President (April); Tariff Act; Cabinet system; Judiciary Act; North Carolina ratifies (twelfth state); University of North Carolina founded

1789–1801 Federalist era

1790 First census; Rhode Island ratifies (thirteenth state); patent and copyright laws; capital shifted to Philadelphia from New York, for decade; Funding Act, funding domestic and foreign debt and assuming state debts; first Catholic bishop for U. S.; Harmar fails against Indians; Slater enters textile industry in Rhode Island

1791 Congress charters first Bank of United States; excise tax voted; statehood for Vermont (fourteenth); St. Clair fails against Indians; Hamilton's Report on Manufacturers; Bill of Rights added to Constitution (Amendments I–X)

1792 Mint established; coinage system based on gold and silver, valued in ratio 15:1; New York stock exchange formed; Kentucky admitted to union; Presbyterian-Congregationalist Plan of Union for missions (to 1837)

1793 Fugitive Slave law; American neutrality proclaimed, Wars of French Revolution; Genet mission; Whitney's cotton gin; Philadelphia yellow fever epidemic

1794 Neutrality Act; Whiskey Rebellion; Wayne defeats Ohio Indians, Fallen Timbers; Jay Treaty signed with Britain

1795 Senate accepts Jay Treaty; Wayne's Treaty of Greenville with Indians; Yazoo land fraud; Pinckney Treaty with Spain (ratified, 1796)

1796 Land Law; Tennessee admitted to union; Congress encourages road building (Zane's Trace); Washington's Farewell Address; Adams elected President (71 electoral votes, to 68 for Jefferson, who becomes Vice-President)

1798 Amendment XI to Constitution (right to sue states); Navy Department organized; XYZ affair leads to undeclared war with France; Alien and Sedition Acts; opposition expressed, Kentucky and Virginia Resolutions (1798–99); Whitney's interchangeable-parts system

1798–1800 Undeclared war with France

1799 New York adopts gradual emancipation (emancipation achieved, 1827)

1800 Land Law; Washington, D. C., becomes capital; Library of Congress founded; France and U. S. end conflict, cancel alliance of 1778; Spain cedes Louisiana to France; Adams (Federalist) beaten for reëlection (65–73 electoral votes) by Republican candidates, Jefferson and Burr

1801 Jefferson-Burr contest; House names Jefferson President; Marshall appointed Chief Justice by Adams (to death, 1835); Judiciary Act increases judgeships; Adams appoints "midnight judges"; war with Tripoli (to 1805)

1801–25 Jeffersonian era ("Virginia dynasty" in White House)

1802 Congress repeals Judiciary Act of 1801, drops excise taxes; Military Academy founded, West Point; first municipal water supply, Philádelphia; right of deposit withdrawn, New Orleans

1803 Marbury vs. Madison (judicial review); statehood for Ohio; Congress agrees to use part of public-land-sale income for road building; purchase of Louisiana from France

1804 Land Law; New Jersey adopts gradual emancipation; Burr-Hamilton duel; Amendment XII (election of President); Jefferson reëlected easily (162 electoral votes, 14 for C. C. Pinckney, Federalist)

1804–06 Lewis and Clark explore Far West

1805 Justice Chase acquitted in impeachment trial; first Rappite community, Pennsylvania

1807 Burr acquitted in treason trial; Fulton demonstrates practicality of steamboat; Vermont separates church and state; first agricultural town fair, Pittsfield, Mass.; *Chesapeake* and *Leopard* affair leads to adoption of Embargo (Dec., 1807—March, 1809); importation of slaves prohibited (as of Jan. 1, 1808)

1808 American Fur Company organized; Madison (Jeffersonian) elected President over C. C. Pinckney (Federalist), 122–47 electoral votes

1809 Non Intercourse (with Britain and France) substituted for Embargo

1810 Macon's Bill No. 2 (another effort to deal with neutral trade question); Congress authorizes construction of Cumberland (National) Road; Fletcher vs. Peck (sanctity of contracts); Madison proclaims annexation of West Florida; American Board of Commissioners for Foreign Missions organized

1811 Charter of first Bank of United States expires; George Mathews unsuccessfully invades East Florida; Harrison fights Tecumseh's braves at Tippecanoe; Astor locates fur trading post in Oregon (Astoria, mouth of Columbia); War Hawks win control of Congress; great earthquake, southeast Missouri

1812–15 War of 1812

1812 Louisiana admitted to union; Adoniram Judson launches missionary work in Orient; Congress declares war against Britain (June); Americans surrender Detroit (Aug.); Americans fail in efforts to take Canada, defeated at Queenstown Heights (Oct.); Madison re-elected President, 128–89 electoral votes, over DeWitt Clinton (Federalist)

1813 British blockade American coast; Americans take Mobile (April), raid York (Toronto, April), win battles of Lake Erie (Sept.) and Thames (Oct.)

1814 Banks outside New England suspend specie payments; Jackson defeats Creeks at Horseshoe Bend (March); drawn battle at Lundy's Lane (July); English take Washington (Aug.) but are repulsed at Baltimore (Sept.); British invasion checked at Lake Champlain (Sept.); peace treaty signed at Ghent (Dec. 14); Hartford Convention (Dec. 15, 1814—Jan. 5, 1815)

1815 Battle of New Orleans (Jan.); Treaty of Ghent ratified (Feb.); Treaty with Algiers ends troubles with Barbary states; *North American Review* founded

1816 Boston Manufacturing Company combines all operations in making cotton cloth under one roof; Martin vs. Hunter's Lessee (national supremacy over state courts); second Bank of United States chartered; protective tariff adopted; Monroe elected President, 183–34 electoral votes, over Rufus King (Federalist); statehood for Indiana; first American savings bank, Boston; American Colonization Society, American Bible Society organized; Russian-American Company establishes trading post in California (Fort Ross, Bodega Bay)

1817 Madison vetoes Bonus Bill (internal improvements); Rush-Bagot agreement with Britain; construction begins on Erie Canal; troubles with Seminoles, Jackson authorized to handle problem; statehood for Mississippi; New Hampshire separates church and state; John Stevens obtains first American railway charter; Gallaudet opens first school for deaf, Connecticut

1818 Black Ball line begins regular trans-Atlantic service; Cumberland (National) Road opened to Wheeling; Jackson invades Spanish Florida, defeats Seminoles, hangs two Britishers; Anglo-American treaty, joint occupation of Oregon; Illinois becomes state; Connecticut separates church and state

1819–21 Depression, following Panic of 1819

1819 Transcontinental Treaty with Spain signed (cession of Florida; ratified 1821); Dartmouth College case; McCulloch vs. Maryland (on national bank); Missouri debate begins; Alabama becomes state

1820 Missouri Compromise; statehood for Maine; Land Law (hundred-dollar farms); foreign slave trade made piracy; American missionaries to Hawaii; Dedham decision (Unitarian church property); Monroe reëlected without opposition, 231–1 electoral vote

1821 Statehood for Missouri; Florida annexed; Spanish officials in Mexico grant Moses Austin large tract of land in Texas; Russian ukase, effort to control Pacific coast north of 51°

1822 U. S. recognizes independence of Latin American republics; Monroe vetoes Cumberland tolls bill; slave uprising, South Carolina; American Colonization Society founds Liberia

1823 Mexico confirms Austin grant; Monroe Doctrine

1824 Gibbons *vs.* Ogden (interstate commerce); minor revision of tariff; Jedediah Smith opens Oregon Trail as trade route; Russian-American treaty sets 54° 40′ Alaska boundary; Rensselaer Polytechnic Institute opens (engineering education); last Congressional caucus nomination for President (Crawford); electoral deadlock in election, Jackson 99, J. Q. Adams 84, Crawford 41, Clay 37

1825 House names Adams President; Erie Canal opened; organization of American Tract Society, American Sunday School Union, American Unitarian Association; Owen launches New Harmony experiment

1826 National Academy of Design, American Temperance Society, American Home Missionary Society founded; Josiah Holbrook launches lyceum movement; John Stevens demonstrates practicality of steam railroad

1827 Harrisburg high-tariff convention

1828 Tariff of Abominations; construction begins, Baltimore and Ohio Railroad; Webster's dictionary published; organization of American Peace Society, General Union for Promoting Observance of Christian Sabbath; and Workingmen's party, Philadelphia; Jackson elected President, 178 electoral votes (83 for Adams)

1829 Postmaster General given Cabinet rank; spoils system in operation; first American missionary to China

1830 Webster-Hayne debate; Church of Latter-Day Saints organized (Mormons); Jackson's "federal union" toast; Jackson's Maysville Road veto; Indian Removal Act, to move tribes west of Mississippi; first American-built locomotive (Peter Cooper's "Tom Thumb")

1831 Garrison's *Liberator* commences publication; Cabinet breakup, involving Peggy Eaton affair; Nat Turner's slave insurrection; first national political convention (Anti-Masonic Party)

1832 Black Hawk War; cholera epidemic, New York; Jackson vetoes recharter of second Bank of United States; Tariff of 1832; South Carolina convention adopts Nullification Ordinance (Nov.), Jackson answers with proclamation against nullification (Dec.); Jackson (Dem.) reëlected, 219 electoral votes, Clay (Whig) 49, John Floyd (Whig) 11, William Wirt (Anti-Mason) 7; Russian-American commercial treaty signed; Disciples of Christ (Christian Church) formally organized; S. G. Howe opens Massachusetts School for Blind (later Perkins Institute); first clipper ship, *Ann McKim* of Baltimore

1833 Compromise tariff and Force Bill; South Carolina rescinds Nullification Ordinance; Massachusetts separates church and state (last state to do so); first penny newspaper, *New York Sun*; Jackson begins withdrawal of government deposits from Bank of United States, deposits money in "pet banks"; American Antislavery Society formed; Oberlin College founded (admits Negroes and women); first tax-supported free public library, Peterboro, N. H.

1834 Senate censures Jackson for withdrawing deposits from Bank of United States; gold:silver ratio changed to 16:1; Seminole War begins (to 1842); McCormick's reaper

1835 National debt paid off; Charleston, S. C., citizens seize and burn abolition literature; local postmasters authorized to refrain from delivering such material; Garrison suffers mob violence in Boston; great New York fire; Texas Revolution begins

1836 Texas declares independence from Mexico; battles of Alamo (March), San Jacinto (April); House of Representatives adopts gag rule, to table antislavery petitions; Congress votes to distribute surplus to states; statehood for Arkansas; Jackson's Specie Circular; Van Buren (Dem.) elected President, 170 electoral votes, Whigs scatter 124 (Harrison 73, Hugh White 26, Webster 14, Willie Mangum 11); no majority in vice-presidential contest

1837 Senate chooses Richard M. Johnson (Dem.) Vice-President; Michigan becomes state; 1834 censure of Jackson expunged from Senate journal; U. S. recognizes Texan independence; first general incorporation law, Connecticut; nativist riot, Massachusetts; abolitionist editor E. P. Lovejoy killed by mob, Alton, Ill.; Massachusetts creates state Board of Education (Horace Mann secretary)

1837–43 Depression, following Panic of 1837

1838 First all-steam-power crossings of Atlantic; Massachusetts fifteen-gallon law (to limit liquor sales)

1839 Aroostook War (Maine boundary); Goodyear vulcanization of rubber

1840 Ten-hour day for federal workers; Independent Treasury established (dropped, 1841); Log Cabin campaign, Harrison (Whig) defeats Van Buren (Dem.), 234–60 electoral votes, J. G. Birney (Liberty) drawing very small popular vote

1841 On death of Harrison (April), Tyler is first Vice-President to become President; vetoes Bank charter; Preëmption Act; Russians leave California; Fanny Elssler's tour introduces Americans to ballet

1842 Dorr Rebellion, Rhode Island (demand for broader suffrage); Webster-Ashburton Treaty (Maine boundary); Dr. C. W. Long uses ether as anaesthetic (not publicized); Prigg *vs.* Pennsylvania (fugitive slaves); Commonwealth *vs.* Hunt (right to organize); Whig tariff raises rates; Oregon trail becomes emigrant route; New York Philharmonic Society organized; Christy's Minstrels formed; Brook Farm experiment begins

1843 Fourierist North American Phalanx experiment, Red Bank, N. J.; Dorothea Dix memorial on care of insane

1844 Senate rejects Texas annexation treaty; first treaty with China; Morse's telegraph commercial success; Dr. Horace Wells uses laughing gas as anaesthetic; Brook Farm becomes Fourierist; Evans forms National Reform Association; Baptists divide on slavery; House ends gag rule on abolition petitions; Polk (Dem.) defeats Clay (Whig) for President (170–105 electoral votes)

1845 Statehood for Florida; Texas annexed. comes in as state; Methodists split on slavery; Congress votes postal subsidy for steamships (to 1858)

1846–48 War with Mexico

1846 Polk's war message (May); Bear Flag revolt in California (June); Kearney's expedition (June–Dec.); start Mormon trek west; Oregon treaty with Britain; Walker Tariff cuts rates; Independent Treasury permanently adopted; Wilmot Proviso first introduced; Smithsonian Institution established; Howe patents sewing machine; Hoe invents rotary printing press; Dr. W. T. G. Morton public demonstration of ether as anaesthetic; treaty with Colombia to protect transit across Panama; statehood for Iowa

1847 Battle of Buena Vista (Feb.); Scott lands at Vera Cruz (March), defeats Mexicans at Cerro Gordo (April), takes Mexico City (Sept.); Oneida Community formed; collapse of Brook Farm; New Hampshire ten-hour law for factory workers; American Medical Association organized

1848 Gold discovered in California; treaty of peace with Mexico (Guadalupe Hidalgo); statehood for Wisconsin; Women's Rights convention, Seneca Falls, N. Y. (Declaration of Rights); Associated Press founded; American Association for Advancement of Science organized; pioneer department store, A. T. Stewart, New York; European revolutions affect U. S.; Taylor (Whig) defeats Cass (Dem.), 163–127 electoral votes; new Free Soil party shows strength at polls (Van Buren presidential candidate)

1849 Department of Interior organized; safety pin patented (Walter Hunt); California Gold Rush

1850 Compromise of 1850: Fugitive Slave law, popular sovereignty for New Mexico, Utah, slave trade ended in District of Columbia, statehood for California; southern secession discussed, Nashville Convention (June) and Georgia Platform (Dec.); Taylor dies, Fillmore becomes President (Sept.); first federal land grants for railroads (Illinois Central); Jenny Lind's tour; Massachusetts Board of Health organized; Order of Star Spangled Banner started (nativist); Lopez filibuster to Cuba (to 1851)

1851 Maine prohibition law; Y.M.C.A. organized in U. S.; Kossuth visit (to 1852)

1852 Uncle Tom's Cabin published; Massachusetts compulsory school attendance law; American Society of Civil Engineers (oldest engineering organization) formed; Pierce (Dem.) defeats Scott (last Whig candidate for President) 254–42 electoral votes; J. P. Hale (Free Soil) makes poor showing

1853 Gadsden Purchase from Mexico (ratified 1854)

1854 Perry "opens" Japan; first Japanese-American treaty (ratified 1855); Kansas-Nebraska Act; Anthony Burns fugitive slave rescue; New England Emigrant Aid Company founds Lawrence, Kan.; competing proslavery settlements; reciprocity with Canada (to 1866); Ostend Manifesto (demand for Cuba); beginnings of Republican party (Ripon, Wis., meeting, Feb.; Jackson, Mich., meeting, July; anti-Nebraska combination in Congress); Know Nothings (Americans) reach peak, carry Massachusetts

1855 "Bleeding Kansas," rival governments; Walker's first Nicaraguan filibuster; Amana Society locates in Iowa; Walt Whitman's *Leaves of Grass*

1856 Formal organization Republican party (Feb.); Sumner-Brooks affair; sack of Lawrence by proslavery forces; John Brown murders proslavery men on Pottawatomie; President Pierce establishes military law in Kansas; Buchanan (Dem.) wins presidential election, 174 electoral votes (114 for Fremont, Rep., 8 for Fillmore, American)

1857 Tariff Act, some reductions; Dred Scott decision; Panic of 1857; federal government's armed conflict with Mormons in Utah (to 1858); proslavery forces in Kansas prepare Lecompton Constitution; William Kelley's steel process; Currier & Ives begin business; National Health Association formed; Helper's *Impending Crisis*

1858 Despite Buchanan's support, Lecompton Constitution rejected; statehood for Minnesota; Lincoln-Douglas debates; Atlantic cable laid (functions three weeks only); sectional split, Presbyterian Church; gold discovered, Pike's Peak (gold rush, 1859); National Association of Baseball Players formed; Pullman's sleeping car; first evaporated-milk plant (Gail Borden)

1859 Statehood for Oregon; oil strike at Titusville, Pa.; silver in Nevada (Comstock Lode); Virginia raid, trial, execution of John Brown; Great Atlantic and Pacific Tea Company started (beginnings of chain stores)

1860 Pony express (to 1861); Democrats split, and Lincoln (Rep.) wins presidential election, 180 electoral votes, 72 for Breckinridge (Dem.), 39 for Bell (Const. Union), 12 for Douglas (Dem.); South Carolina secedes

1861–65 Civil War

1861 Kansas admitted as free state (Jan.); Peace Convention (Feb.); Confederate States formed, Davis made President, call for volunteers (Feb.); Morrill Tariff (March 2); Lincoln inaugurated (March 4), decides to supply Fort Sumter; Sumter fired on, surrenders (April 12, 14); Lincoln calls for volunteers (April 15);

blockade organized; Confederates win first battle of Bull Run (July); higher taxes, including income tax; Confederate specie loan from banks; "Trent" affair; French invasion of Mexico

1862 Union takes Forts Henry, Donelson (Feb.), New Orleans (April); *Merrimac* vs. *Monitor* (March); Jackson's Valley campaign (March–May); McClellan's Peninsular campaign (March–July, ending in Seven Days battles); Shiloh (April); second battle of Bull Run (Aug.); battles of Antietam (Sept.), Fredericksburg (Dec.); Anglo-American treaty on slave trade (April); Dept. of Agriculture formed, Homestead Act (May); Union Pacific Railroad chartered (July); Morrill Land-Grant Act (July); Union Confiscation Act (July); Union greenbacks authorized (July); Confederates adopt conscription (April); slavery abolished, District of Columbia (April); preliminary Emancipation Proclamation (Sept.)

1863 Battles of Chancellorsville (May), Gettysburg (July); siege of Vicksburg (May–July); battle of Chattanooga (Nov.); Union establishes National Banking system (reorganized, 1864); Union conscription (March; draft riots, July); West Virginia enters union; Lincoln's 10% reconstruction plan (Dec.); higher taxes, e.g., Confederate taxes in kind; repressive measures, Vallandigham expelled from Union

1864 Grant in command Union armies (March); battle of Wilderness (May); Sherman marches through Georgia, battle of Atlanta (July), occupies Atlanta (July), Savannah (Dec.); battle of Nashville (Dec.); Lincoln's pocket veto of Wade-Davis bill (July); Wade-Davis Manifesto (Aug.); contract labor law; Nevada admitted to union; Republican radicals try to drop Lincoln, nominate Fremont in April; but Lincoln renominated, runs as Union candidate, wins over McClellan (Dem.), 212 electoral votes to 21; Congress (Dec.) does not accept Lincoln-plan reconstructed southern governments

1865 Sherman takes Charleston, Wilmington (Feb.); Lee surrenders at Appomatox (April 9), other Confederate forces surrender from April to June; Lincoln assassinated (April 14); Johnson becomes President, adopts Lincoln's moderate-reconstruction plan; Amnesty Proclamation (May 29); Congress rejects Johnson's southern governments (Dec.); Amendment XIII ends slavery (Dec.); Ku Klux Klan organized in Tennessee (organization perfected 1867)

1865–77 Reconstruction era

1866 Congress passes Freedman's Bureau and Civil Rights bills over Johnson's vetoes; 10% tax destroys state bank notes; Fenian raids into Canada; Atlantic cable completed; National Labor Union organized; Radical Republicans win Congressional election; Grand Army of the Republic organized

1867 Tenure of Office and three Reconstruction Acts passed over Johnson's vetoes; President dismisses Secretary of War Stanton, in defiance of Tenure of Office Act; purchase of Alaska; Midway annexed; Howard University founded; Grange (Patrons of Husbandry) organized; statehood for Nebraska

1868 Impeachment trial of Johnson; readmission of "reconstructed" southern states; Congress establishes 8-hour day for federal workers; Amendment XIV (reconstruction); Burlingame treaty with China (protects immigration); Sholes' typewriter; Grant (Rep.) elected President, 214–80 electoral votes over Seymour (Dem.); Democrats endorse Ohio Idea (Pendleton's money plan)

1869 Black Friday (Sept. 24, attempt of Gould and Fisk to corner gold); Massachusetts sets up Railway Commission; second class mailing privileges for periodicals; Wyoming Territory grants woman suffrage; Westinghouse air brake; organization of Knights of Labor, Prohibition Party, National and American Woman Suffrage Associations (these two united, 1890); first intercollegiate football game, Rutgers beats Princeton

1870 Amendment XV (Negro suffrage); Senate rejects Dominican annexation treaty; Legal Tender cases (1870–71); Standard Oil Company incorporated; first Negro Congressmen

1871 Treaty of Washington with Britain (*Alabama* claims, etc.); Ku Klux Act; first Granger law, to regulate railroads, Illinois; Tweed Ring exposed; Chicago fire; Wisconsin forest fire, Pestigo; Metropolitan Museum of Art opened; Barnum opens his circus

1872 Mining Act; income tax repealed; Credit Mobilier scandal breaks; Labor Reform movement; Grant wins reëlection, 286 electoral votes to 66 (Greeley, Dem. and Liberal Rep.); American Public Health Association formed; Montgomery Ward pioneers mail-order store business

1873 "Crime of '73," demonetization of silver; Timber Act; Coal Act; Salary Grab; Janney's car coupler; Glidden's barbed wire demonstrated; failure of Jay Cooke leads to Panic of 1873

1873–79 Depression following Panic of 1873

1874 Whiskey Ring broken; Massachusetts 10-hour law for women and children; Chautauqua movement launched; Hungarian methods introduced into Minneapolis flour mills; W.C.T.U. organized; tennis introduced from England

1875 Civil Rights Act; Hawaiian reciprocity treaty; gold discovered in Black Hills

1876 Philadelphia Centennial Exposition; statehood for Colorado; Greenback Party organized; disputed presidential election, Hayes (Rep.) vs. Tilden (Dem.); Tilden has popular majority, 22 electoral votes in dispute; Bell's telephone; Granger cases, upholding state right to regulate railroads; Custer's last stand; Johns Hopkins founded, research emphasis; American Library Association

1877 Congress decides that Hayes won 1876 election, 185–184 electoral votes; Hayes withdraws last federal troops from South (end of

Reconstruction); execution of Molly Maguire leaders (coal mine labor terrorists); great wave of strikes, coal, railroad, etc.; federal troops used against strikers; Desert Land Act; Elmira, N. Y., Reformatory, special treatment young lawbreakers; Edison's phonograph; Society of American Artists

1878 Bland-Allison Act, passed over presidential veto; treaty with Samoa (coaling station); Timber and Stone Act; yellow fever epidemic in South

1879 Hayes vetoes Chinese exclusion bill; Civil War pensions increased; resumption of specie payments; Standard Oil trust formed; F. W. Woolworth starts five-and-ten-cent store business; Church of Christ, Scientist, organized; Edison demonstrates practical electric light

1880 Chinese exclusion treaty; Garfield (Rep.) defeats Hancock (Dem.), 214–155 electoral votes; popular vote very close; first manual training school, St. Louis; Northwestern Alliance formed

1881 Garfield assassinated (July 2, dies Sept. 19); Arthur becomes President; organization of American Red Cross, National Civil Service Reform League; first Carnegie library gifts; Star Route frauds exposed

1882 Congress excludes Chinese, convicts, paupers, and votes head tax for immigrants; U. S. helps "open" Korea (first treaty ratified, 1883); first trust company organized, New York; Sprague's trolley; Knights of Columbus organized; French try to construct Panama canal

1883 Pendleton Civil Service Reform Act; Civil Rights cases; Brooklyn Bridge completed; first skyscraper, Jenney's Home Insurance Building, Chicago; Metropolitan Opera House opened; Congress begins to build new Navy; Pulitzer buys New York *World*; standard time adopted; minor panic

1884 U. S. obtains Pearl Harbor rights from Hawaii; Mergenthaler's linotype; S. S. McClure starts syndicated-features agency; Knights of Labor win Union Pacific strike; Democrats win first presidential election since Civil War, Cleveland beating Blaine (Rep.), 219–182 electoral votes

1885 Importation of contract labor prohibited; Rock Springs, Wyoming, massacre of Chinese; Knights of Labor win Wabash strike

1886 Knights lose Missouri Pacific strike; Haymarket riot; American Federation of Labor formed; Statue of Liberty dedicated; Wabash case (limiting state control of railroads); safety bicycle; Presidential Succession Act (Cabinet members instead of President *pro tem* of Senate follows Vice-President)

1887 Interstate Commerce Commission established; Dawes Act (Indians); Hatch Act (experiment stations); American Protective Association; first school for librarians at Columbia; Cleveland demands tariff reform

1888 Australian ballot introduced into U. S.; American Sabbath Union formed; great blizzard; Kodak roll film introduced (George Eastman); though wins popular plurality, Cleveland beaten for reëlection by Benjamin Harrison (Rep.), 233–168 electoral votes

1889 Cabinet rank for Department of Agriculture; Omnibus states admitted to union (Dakotas, Montana, Washington); Anglo-German-American treaty on Samoa; first state anti-trust laws; New Jersey passes holding company bill; first Pan-American conference (1889–90); Oklahoma land rush; Society of Christian Socialists organized; Minnesota Rate case; Johnstown, Pa., flood; last bare-knuckle championship prize fight (Sullivan-Kilrain); Southern Alliance organized

1890 "Czar" Reed's billion dollar Congress; Reed's Rules (for tight control of House); Civil War pensions increased; river and harbor bills, etc., to spend surplus; Sherman Anti-Trust Act; Sherman Silver-Purchase Act; McKinley Tariff; big Navy bill; Lodge's Force Bill (not passed); statehood for Idaho, Wyoming; New York corrupt practices act (campaign expenses); Republicans lose midterm elections

1891 Forest Reserve Act; Ocean Mail Subsidy Act; International Copyright law; 11 Italians lynched, New Orleans; conflict with Chile when American sailors are attacked on shore; basketball invented; zipper patented

1892 People's Party (Populists) organized; Socialist Labor Party formed; Cleveland (Dem.) defeats Harrison (Rep.) for presidency, 277–145 electoral votes, Weaver (Populist) polling 1,000,000 votes (8.7%) and 22 electoral votes; Prohibition Party reaches its peak vote in this campaign (264,000); Homestead strike

1893 Hawaiian annexation treaty fails to get Senate approval; Frederick Taylor becomes first specialist in scientific management; Chicago World's Fair (Columbian Exposition); Edison's motion picture machine; first successful American gasoline-powered automobile (Duryea brothers); Altgeld pardons anarchists; Panic of 1893; Sherman Silver-Purchase Act repealed; Anti-Saloon League formed

1893–96 Depression following Panic of 1893

1894 Wilson-Gorman Tariff, includes income tax; Pullman strike, Cleveland intervenes; Coxey's march on Washington; Democrats lose midterm elections; Simon Lake's even-keel submarine

1895 Dispute with Britain over Venezuelan boundary ("Olney Doctrine"); Cuban insurrection begins; Supreme Court limits Sherman Anti-Trust Act (E. C. Knight case), except on labor (Debs case), and rules out income tax (Pollock vs. Farmers' Loan); National Association of Manufacturers organized; Hearst buys *New York Journal*; Niagara Falls harnessed

1896 Statehood for Utah; final amnesty for Confederate officers; U. S. participates in Olympic Games; McKinley (Rep.) defeats Bryan

(Dem., Populist), 271–176 electoral votes; Gold Democrats also in field

1897 Dingley Tariff Act; Maximum Freight Rate decision limits I.C.C.; Sam ("Golden Rule") Jones first reform mayor (Toledo); first subway, Boston

1898 De Lome letter and *Maine* sinking help bring on war with Spain (April), Teller Amendment defines aims (no annexation of Cuba); battles of Manila Bay (May), Santiago (July), invasion of Cuba (June–Aug.), U. S. takes Guam (June), Puerto Rico (July–Aug.), Manila (Aug.); armistice agreement (Aug.), peace treaty of Paris (Dec.); Cuba occupied to 1902; Anti-Imperialist League organized; American Asiatic Association organized; South Dakota adopts referendum

1899 Struggle over ratification of peace treaty; Senate approves treaty (Feb.); Filipino insurrection (1899–1902); final adjustment of Samoan question; Open Door notes; Hague conference; Addyston Pipe case (on pools)

1900 Gold Standard Act; first Hay-Pauncefote Treaty; Foraker Act (for Puerto Rico); troops in China (Boxer revolt); establishment of General Electric research laboratory; Galveston hurricane and tidal wave (produces commission form of government); conquest of yellow fever, Dr. Walter Reed; Davis Cup international tennis competition begins; National Civic Federation formed; Social Democratic (Socialist) Party founded; McKinley defeats Bryan again, 292–155 electoral votes

1901–17 Progressive era

1901 McKinley shot, Sept. 6, dies Sept. 14, succeeded by Roosevelt; Platt Amendment for Cuba; Insular cases; Boxer indemnity; second Hay-Pauncefote Treaty; U. S. Steel Company formed; Taylor and White method of treating high speed tool steel

1902 Newlands Reclamation Act; coal strike, Roosevelt helps settle; Chinese exclusion made permanent (repealed 1943); reciprocity with Cuba; organization of Navy League, American Society of Equity, Farmers Union

1903 Elkins Act (on rebates); establishment of Bureau of Corporations; Dept. of Commerce and Labor created; Wisconsin direct primary act; Army General Staff set up; Hay-Herran Treaty rejected by Colombia; U. S. intervention in Panama; Hay-Bunau-Varilla Treaty with Panama for Canal; Alaska boundary settled; Wrights fly at Kittyhawk; *Great Train Robbery*, first feature movie

1904 Northern Securities case; Roosevelt intervenes in Dominican Republic, announces Roosevelt Corollary to Monroe Doctrine; Roosevelt elected President over Parker (Dem.), 336–140 electoral votes

1905 Supreme Court rules out New York social legislation (limitation on hours), Lochner vs. U. S.; New York insurance investigations begin; I.W.W. organized; Japanese and Korean Exclusion League formed; first movie theater, McKeesport, Pa.; Rotary Club founded; muckraking activity (*McClure's*, etc.)

1906 Meat Inspection, Pure Food and Drug Acts; Hepburn Act and Employers' Liability Act (railroads); reoccupation of Cuba (to 1910); Britain withdraws fleet from Caribbean; trouble with Japan over segregation in San Francisco schools; San Francisco earthquake and fire

1907 Minor panic; Navy sent around world (to 1909); Oklahoma admitted as state; second Hague conference; DeForest's vacuum radio tube; negotiation of Gentlemen's Agreement with Japan on immigration (completed 1908)

1908 Aldrich-Vreeland Act (currency); Danbury Hatters case (bars secondary boycotts); Muller *vs.* Oregon (upholding Oregon ten-hour-law for women); governors' conference on conservation; Oregon adopts recall; Root-Takahira agreement with Japan; part of Boxer indemnity returned; FBI set up; Federal Council of Churches founded; Taft wins presidential election, 321–182 electoral votes over Bryan

1909 Payne-Aldrich Tariff; Taft adopts dollar diplomacy, helps American bankers get into China (Hukuang loan); Robert E. Peary reaches North Pole; Ford's Model T marketed; National Association for Advancement of Colored People founded

1910 Successful revolt against Speaker Cannon; Mann-Elkins Act (railroad regulation); Fundamentalists present their basic argument (*Fundamentals*); World Peace Foundation and Carnegie Endowment for International Peace founded; Pinchot dismissed by Taft (Ballinger-Pinchot controversy)

1911 Organization of National Republican Association launches movement against Taft; Supreme Court orders dissolution of Standard Oil, but also establishes "rule of reason"; reciprocity with Canada fails (Canada rejects); American proposal for neutralization of Manchuria fails; U. S. abrogates 1832 treaty with Russia because of Russian mistreatment of Jews; Taft vetoes bills reducing tariff rates; C. F. Kettering invents self-starter for autos

1912 Statehood for New Mexico (47th) and Arizona (48th); I.W.W. wins Lawrence textile strike; Massachusetts sets minimum wages for women and children; Pujo investigation of banking begins; marines occupy Nicaragua (to 1933, except for 1925–26); Republican split gives Wilson victory in presidential election, 435 electoral votes–88 (Roosevelt, Progressive)–8 (Taft, Republican); popular vote 6,000,000–4,000,000–3,500,000. Socialists, with 900,000 (Debs) reach their peak in percentage of total vote; Congress sets up parcel post (effective 1913)

1913 Amendments XVI (income tax) and XVII (direct election of Senators); Department of Commerce and Labor divided into two departments; Railroad Valuation Act (on rate-making); Wilson's **"New Freedom"**: Underwood Tariff, Federal Reserve Act; California bars aliens from landholding (causes trouble with Japan); Wilson's Mobile address (friendship for Latin America); but quarrels with Mexico; Armory Show in New York, modern art; Federal League challenges baseball "monopoly" (to 1915); establishment of Rockefeller Foundation which aids research; peak year for immigration

1914–18 World War I (U. S. participates, 1917–18)

1914 Smith-Lever Act; Federal Trade Commission Act; Clayton Anti-Trust Act; Panama Canal Tolls Act repealed; Canal opened (Aug.); occupation of Vera Cruz (April–Nov.); Bryan-Chamorro treaty with Nicaragua; U. S. neutral in World War I (Aug.) but allows short-term credit for belligerents; preparedness movement launched, National Security League organized; Ford adopts $5-day minimum; Colorado Fuel & Iron strike leads to use of company union; American Association of University Professors organized

1915 LaFollette Seamen's Act; *Lusitania* sinking; Wilson sends *Lusitania* notes; Secretary of State Bryan resigns in disagreement over these; U. S. allows long-term loans to belligerents (i.e., sale of bonds in U. S.); organization of League to Enforce Peace (pro-Ally, pro-League of Nations); Ford Peace Ship (effort to end war); Colonel House's missions to Europe; organization of Non-Partisan League, and of new Ku Klux Klan; Griffith's *Birth of a Nation*; Supreme Court declares grandfather clause unconstitutional (Negro suffrage), and voids state law barring yellow dog contracts; U. S. occupies Haiti (to 1934)

1916 Federal Highway Act (aid to states for road building); Farm Loan Act; National Park Service created; Jones Act promises independence to Philippines; Adamson Act (8-hour day railroads); Gore-McLemore resolution (barring travel on belligerent ships) defeated by administration pressure; after Wilson ultimatum, Germany gives Sussex pledge against unrestricted submarine warfare; Wilson converted to preparedness (Navy "second to none"); Council of National Defense, National Research Council organized; Pershing chases Villa in Mexico; occupation of Dominican Republic (to 1924); purchase of Danish West Indies (Virgin Islands); Wilson reëlected, 277–254 electoral votes over Hughes (Rep.), close popular vote (9,000,000–8,500,000); first woman elected to Congress (Jeanette Rankin, Montana); Wilson appeals for peace without victory

1917 Germany resumes unrestricted submarine warfare, U. S. breaks diplomatic relations (Feb.); filibuster defeats Armed Merchant Ship bill, but Wilson authorizes arming, executive order (March); Zimmermann note released by U. S.; Congress declares war (April 6); Liberty Loan; Committee on Public Information organized (April); Selective Service (May); Espionage Act (June); Pershing in France (June); War Industries Board created (July); Lever Act (control food, fuel, Aug.); increased taxes (War Revenue Acts); Trading-with-Enemy Act (Oct.); first American combat (Oct.); Lansing-Ishii agreement (Nov.); government seizes railroads (Dec.); Smith-Hughes Act (vocational education); Jones Act (Puerto Rico); immigration act passed over veto, literacy test, and excludes most Asiatics; Bunting vs. Oregon, upholds state limitation working hours; race riot, East St. Louis; organization American Birth Control League; U. S. recognizes new government after first Russian Revolution (March), not after second (Nov., Bolshevik Revolution)

1918 14 Points (Jan.); seizure telephone, telegraph (Jan.); more power for War Industries Board (March); National War Labor Board (March); Webb-Pomerene Act (exporters exempted from anti-trust); Overman and Sedition Acts (May); American troops in action (second Marne, spring, St. Mihiel, Sept., Meuse-Argonne, fall); Student Army Training Corps (Oct.); American troops in North Russia (to May, 1919); Siberia (April, 1920); Hammer vs. Dagenhart rules out child labor law; Republicans win Congressional elections (Nov. 5); Armistice (Nov. 11); influenza epidemic

1919 Versailles Treaty considered, rejected by Senate; Victory loans; Amendment XVIII (prohibition) adopted; race riots, Washington, Chicago; strikes (Boston police, Sept., coal, Nov., steel, Sept.–Jan. 1920; fail); National Industrial Conference fails; Socialist Congressman Berger unseated by House; Communist Party organized; first tabloid newspaper, *New York Daily News*; American Legion launched

1920 Amendment XIX (woman suffrage) adopted; Transportation Act, returns railroads to private owners (despite Plumb Plan); Dyer Act (car theft); Jones Merchant Marine Act; Senate again rejects Versailles Treaty, also rejects Armenian mandate, will not consider British-French-American alliance; Palmer raids, Wall St. bombing; American Farm Bureau Federation organized; beginning of commercial radio broadcasting; Harding and Coolidge (Rep.) landslide victory over Cox and F. D. Roosevelt (Dem.), 404–127 electoral votes, 16,000,000–9,000,000; Socialists get 920,000, a Farmer-Labor ticket 265,000; Supreme Court holds U. S. Steel not illegal monopoly

1921 Emergency tariff; budget established; official end, war with Germany, Austria, Hungary; treaty with Colombia to reëstablish good relations; Washington Conference (to 1922, naval limitation, peace in Pacific); Ford's *Dearborn Independent* promotes anti-Semitism (Ford later disavows); farm bloc formed; short depression

1922 Fordney-McCumber Tariff; Bailey vs. Drexel Furniture, ruling out prohibition of child labor

1923 End of American occupation of Germany; Federal Intermediate Credit banks established; Adkins vs. Children's Hospital, voids minimum wage law for women, D. C.; investigation of Teapot Dome begins; Harding dies, Coolidge President (Aug.)

1924 Soldiers' bonus, over veto; Immigration Act, quota system and Japanese exclusion; Rogers Act improves Foreign Service; tax cuts; Veterans' Bureau scandals; troops out of Dominican Republic; Coolidge (Rep.) wins presidency, 382–136 electoral votes, over J. W. Davis (Dem.); LaFollette (Prog.) 13 electoral votes (popular 16,000,000–8,000,000–5,000,000); Communists run candidate for first time (36,000 votes); Steenbok, Vitamin D by irradiation

1925 Scopes evolution trial; Air Mail Commerce Act (another, 1926), subsidizing airlines; Maple Flooring case, approving trade associations; conflict with Mexico over oil (to 1927)

1926 Florida land boom (bursts, 1927); marines return to Nicaragua after a few months' absence, remain till 1933

1927 McNary-Haugen veto; Nixon vs. Herndon, on exclusion of Negroes from primaries; execution of Sacco and Vanzetti; great Mississippi River flood; Lindbergh's flight to Paris; Tunney defeats Dempsey second time, largest gate in boxing history; Federal Radio Commission given control of radio; Geneva Naval Disarmament conference fails

1928 Second McNary-Haugen veto; Jones-White Merchant Marine Act; Muscle Shoals bill (public power) killed by pocket veto; Kellogg-Briand Peace Pact; Hoover (Rep.) defeats Smith (Dem.), 444–87 electoral votes; popular vote 21,000,000 to 15,000,000; minor party vote negligible; Hoover's good-will tour of Latin America begins; first all-talking moving picture

1929 Agricultural Marketing Act; national origins system becomes effective for immigration restriction (terms of 1924); New York Stock Market crash (Oct.)

1929–39 "The great depression"

1930 Hawley-Smoot Tariff raises rates; London Naval Conference; Clark Memorandum on Monroe Doctrine published (drops Roosevelt Corollary); drought in South and Midwest adds to woes of depression; increased appropriations for public works; Democrats win midterm elections

1931 Defaults on foreign bonds; New York Bond Market collapses; marked increase in bank failures; Hoover Moratorium (to 1932); Muscle Shoals bill vetoed; bonus loan bill passed over veto; Japan invades Manchuria, Hoover-Stimson non-recognition doctrine; Empire State Building; Al Capone convicted, income tax evasion

1932 Reconstruction Finance Corporation established; failure World Disarmament Conference; bonus army evicted from Washington; Norris-LaGuardia Anti-Injunction Act; bank holidays start (Nevada, Oct.); defaults on war debts owed to U. S.; Roosevelt (Dem.) elected President, 472 electoral votes to 59 (Hoover, Rep.), popular vote 23,000,000–16,000,000

1933–45 Roosevelt era (FDR as President)

1933 Amendments XX (lame duck, Feb.), XXI (ending prohibition, Dec.); marines leave Nicaragua (Jan.); Michigan bank holiday

(Feb.) then national crisis; FDR makes bank holiday national (March 5); first New Deal laws, Hundred Days, March–June (Emergency Banking Act; Glass-Steagall Act, creating FDIC; U. S. off gold standard; Gold Repeal Resolution cancels gold clause in contracts; Economy Act cuts government workers' pay; Federal Emergency Relief Act, creating FERA; Agricultural Adjustment Act, creating AAA; National Industrial Recovery Act, creates NRA and PWA; Securities Act; Farm Credit Act, consolidating many agencies in FCA; Tennessee Valley Authority Act, creating TVA; Home Owners' Refinancing Act, creates HOLC; Forestation Act, sets up Civilian Conservation Corps (CCC); Emergency Farm Mortgage Act); World Economic Conference fails as FDR rejects international currency stabilization plan; U. S. recognizes U. S. S. R.; American pressure on Cuba; Civil Works Administration (CWA) created by executive order for quick jobs (Nov.)

1934 Gold Reserve Act devalues gold; Securities and Exchange Act (creates SEC); Export-Import Bank set up; Silver Purchase Act; Farm Mortgage Refinancing Act; Frazier-Lemke Farm Bankruptcy Act; establishment of National Labor Relations Board (NLRB), Federal Communications Commission (FCC), Federal Housing Authority (FHA); Railroad Retirement Act; Indian Reorganization Act; Taylor Grazing Act (for public lands); Tydings-McDuffie Act (Philippine independence); end of Platt Amendment for Cuba; troops withdrawn from Haiti; Reciprocal Trade Agreements Act; Johnson Act, prohibiting loans to war-debt defaulters; U. S. joins International Labor Office; great dust storms and drought; many strikes, including general strike San Francisco; Liberty League formed to fight FDR; Father Coughlin launches Union for Social Justice; Townsend Plan proposed; air mail contracts cancelled

1935 Creation of Works Progress Administration (WPA, replaces CWA, PWA), Resettlement Administration (RA) for farmers, Rural Electrification Administration (REA), National Youth Administration (NYA); Wagner (National Labor Relations) Act; Motor Carrier Act; Social Security Act; Public Utility Holding Company Act; Guffey Coal Act; Bankhead-Jones Experiment Station Act; Revenue Act includes "soak-the-rich" principle; Supreme Court upholds devaluation (Gold Clause cases) but invalidates Railroad Retirement Act, NRA (Schechter case), Frazier-Lemke Farm Bankruptcy Act; Senate rejects World Court; Neutrality Act (no export of munitions to belligerents, no travel on belligerent ships), applied Italo-Ethiopian war; Stabilization Fund set up; London Naval Conference begins (fails, 1936)

1936 Robinson-Patman Act (fair price); Soldiers' bonus (over veto); Merchant Marine Act; Soil Conservation and Domestic Allotment (SCADA) as stopgap after Supreme Court invalidates AAA (Hoosac Mills case); Court also kills Municipal Banking, Guffey Coal, and New York Minimum Wage (Morehead case) Acts; upholds TVA (Ashwander case); Neutrality Act (no credits for belligerents); end of Platt Amendment type of control of Panama (treaty, Senate consents 1939); CIO unions suspended by AFL; sulfa drugs introduced into U. S.; FDR reëlected in landslide, 523–8 electoral votes, 28,000,000–17,000,000 over Landon (Rep.); Lemke (Union) draws only 880,000; FDR attends Buenos Aires conference, which makes Monroe Doctrine multilateral, ends intervention system; sit-down first tried

1937 Sit-down leads to victory in General Motors strike, but is widely denounced and generally abandoned (declared illegal 1939); Republic Steel strike; FDR recommends reform of Supreme Court (Jan., "court-packing" plan); gets less than requested (Judiciary Reform Act, Aug.), but Supreme Court reverses stand on New Deal, upholds state minimum-wage law (West Coast Hotel case), Wagner Act (NLRB vs. Jones & Laughlin), Social Security; and conservative judges retire; Bankhead-Jones Farm Tenancy Act; Congress creates U. S. Housing Authority (USHA), Farm Security Administration (FSA); Neutrality Act extended to cover Spanish Civil War (in which U. S. follows British non-intervention policy); cash-and-carry plan; Neutrality Act not applied when Japan again invades China; FDR's Quarantine speech; Panay attacked by Japanese, Japan apologizes; Ludlow resolution (popular vote on war) gains popularity, beaten by administration pressure (Jan., 1938); recession brings resumption of government spending on public works, etc.; DuPont develops nylon

1938 Permanent AAA; Civil Aeronautics Act (creates CAB); Federal Food, Drug & Cosmetic Act; Fair Labor Standards (Wages & Hours) Act; Social Security extended; Roosevelt fails in purge within Democratic party; oil expropriation controversy with Mexico (to 1942); FDR peace plea to Hitler at Munich (U. S. backs Chamberlain appeasement); Declaration of Lima (Pan-American solidarity); CIO forms permanent organization

1939 Food Stamp plan; Hatch Act (extended 1940), federal employees to keep out of politics; NLRB vs. Fansteel Metallurgical Corp. bars sit-down strikes; Methodist reunion; U. S. declares neutrality in World War II, but modifies Neutrality Act by ending arms embargo (cash-&-carry had expired); Panama Declaration for Pan-American unity in war; sympathy but little aid for Finland in Russo-Finnish war (1939–40)

1939–45 World War II, U. S. acknowledged belligerent 1941–45

1940 Battle of the Committees (America First vs. White Committee); FDR freezes assets of German-conquered areas; Cabinet changes bring in Republicans, Stimson, Knox (June); hoping to stave off fall of France, FDR offers aid (June), but recognizes Vichy regime after France collapses; transfer of small arms to Britain; Act of Havana, to prevent transfer of territories to Axis; U. S. and Canada joint defense plans; destroyer deal with Britain (Sept.); Export Control Act (July), leads to embargo on scrap iron to Japan (Oct.);

Alien Registration Act (June); Selective Service Act (Sept.); despite third-term tradition, Democrats renominate FDR, elected 449–82 electoral votes over Willkie (Rep.), 27,000,000–22,000,-000; Political Action Committee (P.A.C.) active in campaign; Roosevelt makes "arsenal of democracy" plea

1941 Four Freedoms speech (Jan.); creation of Office of Production Management (OPM, Jan.), Office of Price Administration (OPA, April), Office of Civilian Defense (May), Fair Employment Practice Committee (FEPC), Office of Scientific Research & Development (June); Lend-Lease adopted (March), extended to Russia as well as Britain after German invasion of Russia (June); Axis credits frozen (June–July); unlimited emergency declared (May); Iceland occupied (July); Atlantic Charter (Aug.); Selective Service extended (Aug.); convoy system established, with shoot-on-sight order by Sept.; incidents of *Robin Moor* (May), *Greer* (Sept.), *Kearney, Reuben James* (Oct.); Neutrality Act revised to allow merchant ships to enter combat zones (Nov.); Dutch Guiana occupied (Nov.); final negotiations with Japan (Nov.–Dec.), Pearl Harbor attacked (Dec.), war declared on Axis powers; after declaration, creation of Office of Defense Transportation, Office of Censorship; new Defense Act extends age limits for draft (further extended, Nov., 1942); Roosevelt-Churchill decision to emphasize European front

1942 United Nations alliance (Jan.); Rio conference, hemispheric solidarity; Emergency Price Control Act authorizes ceilings; War Production Board (WPB, Jan.), War Shipping Administration (Feb.), War Manpower Commission (April), Office of War Information (OWI, June), Office of Economic Stabilization (Oct.); relocation of West Coast Japanese; women enlisted (WAC, WAVE, etc.); rationing (gas, rubber, coffee) begins; anti-inflation legislation (Oct.), freezing wages and prices; end of CCC, NYA, WPA; Combined Chiefs of Staff, Britain–U. S.; Japan takes Philippines (Bataan, April; Corregidor, May); Japan checked at Coral Sea (May), Midway (June); Americans land on Guadalcanal (Aug., fighting to Feb., 1943); North African campaign (Nov., 1942—May, 1943)

1943 Conferences at Casablanca (Jan.), Cairo, Teheran (Nov.–Dec.); move into Sicily (July), Italian mainland (Salerno, Sept.); King of Italy surrenders (Sept.); Allied victories in New Guinea, Solomons, Gilberts; Office of War Mobilization (May) at last coördinates war effort; Smith-Connally War Labor Disputes Act, over veto; withholding tax (June); rationing extended (meat, shoes, etc.); government takes over coal mines; race riots, Detroit; Chinese exclusion repealed; Fulbright Resolution, House, favors international organization; United Nations Relief and Rehabilitation Administration created (UNRRA, to 1946)

1944 American victories in Marshalls, Carolinas, Marianas (Saipan, Guam, June–July), invasion of Philippines, battle of Leyte Gulf (Oct.–Dec.); Anzio beachhead in Italy (Jan.), Rome taken (June);

D-Day landing in Normandy (June), Paris taken (Aug.), Belgium (Sept.); Germany invaded (Sept.); battle of Bulge (Dec.); Bretton Woods conference (July), Dumbarton Oaks (Aug.–Oct.); Smith vs. Allwright (Democratic primaries must admit Negroes); bipartisan foreign policy agreed on; FDR elected to fourth term over Dewey (Rep.), 432–99 electoral votes, 26,000,000–22,000,000

1945 Battle of Bulge ends (Jan.), crossing of Rhine (March), Germany surrenders (VE day, May 8); invasion of Luzon (Jan.), Manila taken (Feb.); fighting on Iwo Jima (Feb.–March), Okinawa (April–June); atom bomb tested (July), used on Hiroshima, Nagasaki (Aug.) and Japan surrenders (VJ day, Sept. 2); Roosevelt dies (April 12), Truman President; conferences at Yalta (Feb.), San Francisco (April–June), Potsdam (July); Senate approves UN charter (July); occupation of Japan, South Korea, Germany, Austria, Italy; war crime trials begin; Truman ends gas rationing, Lend-Lease (Aug.), food rationing (Nov.); wave of strikes; New York chosen as site UN

1946 UN begins to operate; US joins United Nations Educational, Scientific and Cultural Organization (UNESCO), World Court; U. S. coöperation with Russia gives way to conflict; Wallace dropped from Cabinet (Sept.) when criticizes Byrnes' get-tough-with-Russia policy; many strikes, Truman uses war powers to seize railroads (March), coal mines (May), urges get-tough-with-labor policy in rail strike (May), later shifts ground; John L. Lewis and United Mine Workers fined for defying injunction (Dec., ends strike); OPA weakened by Congress, price controls end, except rent, sugar, rice (Nov.); marked inflation; Atomic Energy Commission created (Aug.) for civilian control of atomic power; Philippine independence; Marshall's mission to China; Republicans win midterm elections; Truman proclaims end of hostilities, World War II (Dec. 31)

1947 Truman Doctrine for Greece and Turkey (March), Congress votes funds (May); Marshall Plan proposed (June), plans made in Europe with Russian bloc not participating, Congress votes funds (Dec.); National Security Act, combines Army and Navy in new Department of Defense; National Security Council set up, increased influence for military in policy decisions; U. S. turns Korean question over to UN; end of World War II rationing (sugar) and most war statutes; Taft-Hartley Act passed over veto; Rio conference on hemisphere defense; evacuation of Italy; mines restored to owners; Truman orders loyalty checks on federal employees; House Committee on Un-American Activities active, Hollywood probe; increased self-rule for Puerto Rico

1948 Foreign Assistance Act starts European Recovery Program (ERP), sets up Economic Coöperation Administration (ECA); Vandenberg Resolution passed (favors military alliances); Berlin airlift (June, 1948—Sept., 1949); Displaced Persons Act; tax cuts, over veto; 70-group air force provided for; installment credits introduced;

Alger Hiss indicted (convicted, 1950); Ada Sipuel case (segregation in higher education); Truman elected President in close contest, 303–189 electoral votes over Dewey (Rep.), 24,000,000–22,000,-000, Thurmond (Dixiecrat) getting 39 electoral, 1,170,000 popular votes; Wallace (Progressive), 1,160,000 votes

1949 North Atlantic Pact (April); Truman proposes Point Four program; U. S., Britain, France join their West German zones; eleven Communists convicted under Smith Act; Housing Act (aid to lower-income groups); Minimum Wage Act raises hourly minimum from 40¢ to 75¢; D. C. Covenant cases (housing segregation agreements unenforceable)

1950 U. S. withdraws representation from China, Communists having taken over; North Korea invades South (Republic of) Korea (June), Truman announces U. S. support of South Koreans, UN Security Council supports U. S.; Selective Service extended; Defense Production Act (priorities, etc., Sept.); Internal Security Act (registration of Communists); China supports North Korea (Nov.), Truman declares national emergency (Dec.); McCarthy's charges as to Communists in government; National Council of Churches formed (old Federal Council, enlarged)

1951 Production increased under direction of Defense Mobilizer Wilson; but Office of Price Stabilization, Economic Stabilizer, and Wage Stabilization Board fail to hold price line, because of insufficient powers and pressure for wage and price increases; Amendment XXII (no third term for Presidents); Rosenbergs convicted of espionage; Fulbright investigation shows influence peddling in RFC; Kefauver investigation reveals gangster-politics ties; King investigation unearths tax scandals; sports scandals, e.g., basketball; MacArthur removed for insubordination, triumphal reception in U. S. but limited support for his views; Congress investigates past China policy; Korean truce talks start; North Atlantic Treaty Organization set up

1952 More tax scandals; McCarran Internal Security, Immigration Acts; Defense Mobilizer Wilson quits; Truman seizes steel mills during labor dispute (April), Supreme Court overrules (June), strike ended (July) with pay and price increases; Supreme Court upholds New York State released time for religious training; but bars movie censorship on religious subjects (*Miracle* case); racial tension, but federal and state governments crack down on Ku Klux Klan; Japanese peace treaty; mutual defense pacts with Japan, Australia, New Zealand, Philippines; Truman refuses another nomination, Stevenson (Dem.) defeated by Eisenhower (Rep.), 442–89 electoral votes; first hydrogen bomb exploded

Constitution of the United States
and
Presidents of the United States

Constitution of the United States

We the People of the United States, in Order to form a more perfect Union, establish Justice, insure domestic Tranquility, provide for the common defence, promote the general Welfare, and secure the Blessings of Liberty to ourselves and our Posterity, do ordain and establish this Constitution for the United States of America.

ARTICLE I.

Section 1. All legislative Powers herein granted shall be vested in a Congress of the United States, which shall consist of a Senate and House of Representatives.

Section 2. The House of Representatives shall be composed of Members chosen every second Year by the People of the several States, and the Electors in each State shall have the Qualifications requisite for Electors of the most numerous Branch of the State Legislature.

No Person shall be a Representative who shall not have attained to the Age of twenty-five Years, and been seven Years a Citizen of the United States, and who shall not, when elected, be an Inhabitant of that State in which he shall be chosen.

Representatives and direct Taxes shall be apportioned among the several States which may be included within this Union, according to their respective Numbers, which shall be determined by adding to the whole Number of free Persons, including those bound to Service for a Term of Years, and excluding Indians not taxed, three fifths of all other Persons.[1] The actual Enumeration shall be made within three Years after the first Meeting of the Congress of the United States, and within every subsequent Term of ten Years, in such Manner as they shall by Law direct. The Number of Representatives shall not exceed one for every thirty Thousand, but each State shall have at Least one Representative; and until such enumeration shall be made, the State of New Hampshire shall be entitled to chuse three, Massachusetts eight, Rhode-Island and Providence Plantations one, Connecticut five, New-York six, New Jersey four, Pennsylvania eight, Delaware one, Maryland six, Virginia ten, North Carolina five, South Carolina five, and Georgia three.

When vacancies happen in the Representation from any State, the Executive Authority thereof shall issue Writs of Election to fill such Vacancies.

The House of Representatives shall chuse their Speaker and other Officers; and shall have the sole Power of Impeachment.

---

[1] Modified by Amendment XIV, Section 2, and by Amendment XVI.

Section 3. The Senate of the United States shall be composed of two Senators from each State, [chosen by the Legislature thereof,]² for six Years; and each Senator shall have one Vote.

Immediately after they shall be assembled in Consequence of the first Election, they shall be divided as equally as may be into three Classes. The Seats of the Senators of the first Class shall be vacated at the Expiration of the second Year, of the second Class at the Expiration of the fourth Year, and of the third Class at the Expiration of the sixth Year, so that one-third may be chosen every second Year; [and if Vacancies happen by Resignation, or otherwise, during the Recess of the Legislature of any State, the Executive thereof may make temporary Appointments until the next Meeting of the Legislature, which shall then fill such Vacancies.]²

No Person shall be a Senator who shall not have attained to the Age of thirty Years, and been nine Years a Citizen of the United States, and who shall not, when elected, be an Inhabitant of that State for which he shall be chosen.

The Vice President of the United States shall be President of the Senate, but shall have no Vote, unless they be equally divided.

The Senate shall chuse their other Officers, and also a President pro tempore, in the Absence of the Vice President, or when he shall exercise the Office of President of the United States.

The Senate shall have the sole Power to try all Impeachments. When sitting for that Purpose, they shall be on Oath or Affirmation. When the President of the United States is tried, the Chief Justice shall preside: And no Person shall be convicted without the Concurrence of two thirds of the Members present.

Judgment in Cases of Impeachment shall not extend further than to removal from Office, and disqualification to hold and enjoy any Office of honor, Trust or Profit under the United States: but the Party convicted shall nevertheless be liable and subject to Indictment, Trial, Judgment and Punishment, according to Law.

Section 4. The Times, Places and Manner of holding Elections for Senators and Representatives, shall be prescribed in each State by the Legislature thereof; but the Congress may at any time by Law make or alter such Regulations, except as to the Places of chusing Senators.

The Congress shall assemble at least once in every Year,³ [and such Meeting shall be on the first Monday in December,] unless they shall by Law appoint a different Day.

Section 5. Each House shall be the Judge of the Elections, Returns and Qualifications of its own Members, and a Majority of each shall constitute a Quorum to do Business; but a smaller Number may adjourn from day to day, and may be authorized to compel the Attendance of absent Members, in such Manner, and under such Penalties as each House may provide.

Each House may determine the Rules of its Proceedings, punish its Members for disorderly Behavior, and, with the Concurrence of two thirds, expel a Member.

Each House shall keep a Journal of its Proceedings, and from time to time

---

² Superseded by Amendment XVII.
³ Superseded by Amendment XX, Section 1.

publish the same, excepting such Parts as may in their Judgment require Secrecy; and the Yeas and Nays of the Members of either House on any question shall, at the Desire of one fifth of those Present, be entered on the Journal.

Neither House, during the Session of Congress, shall, without the Consent of the other, adjourn for more than three days, nor to any other Place than that in which the two Houses shall be sitting.

Section 6. The Senators and Representatives shall receive a Compensation for their Services, to be ascertained by Law, and paid out of the Treasury of the United States. They shall in all Cases, except Treason, Felony and Breach of the Peace, be privileged from Arrest during their Attendance at the Session of their respective Houses, and in going to and returning from the same; and for any Speech or Debate in either House, they shall not be questioned in any other Place.

No Senator or Representative shall, during the Time for which he was elected, be appointed to any civil Office under the Authority of the United States, which shall have been created, or the Emoluments whereof shall have been encreased during such time; and no Person holding any Office under the United States, shall be a Member of either House during his Continuance in Office.

Section 7. All Bills for raising Revenue shall originate in the House of Representatives; but the Senate may propose or concur with Amendments as on other Bills.

Every Bill which shall have passed the House of Representatives and the Senate, shall, before it become a Law, be presented to the President of the United States; If he approve he shall sign it, but if not he shall return it, with his Objections to that House in which it shall have originated, who shall enter the Objections at large on their Journal, and proceed to reconsider it. If after such Reconsideration two thirds of that House shall agree to pass the Bill, it shall be sent, together with the Objections, to the other House, by which it shall likewise be reconsidered, and if approved by two thirds of that House, it shall become a Law. But in all such Cases the Votes of both Houses shall be determined by Yeas and Nays, and the Names of the Persons voting for and against the Bill shall be entered on the Journal of each House respectively. If any Bill shall not be returned by the President within ten Days (Sundays excepted) after it shall have been presented to him, the Same shall be a Law, in like Manner as if he had signed it, unless the Congress by their Adjournment prevent its Return, in which Case it shall not be a Law.

Every Order, Resolution, or Vote to which the Concurrence of the Senate and House of Representatives may be necessary (except on a question of Adjournment) shall be presented to the President of the United States; and before the Same shall take Effect, shall be approved by him, or being disapproved by him, shall be repassed by two thirds of the Senate and House of Representatives, according to the Rules and Limitations prescribed in the Case of a Bill.

Section 8. The Congress shall have Power To lay and collect Taxes, Duties, Imposts and Excises, to pay the Debts and provide for the common Defence and general Welfare of the United States; but all Duties, Imposts and Excises shall be uniform throughout the United States;[4]

---

[4] Modified by Amendment XVI.

To borrow Money on the credit of the United States;

To regulate Commerce with foreign Nations, and among the several States, and with the Indian Tribes;

To establish an uniform Rule of Naturalization, and uniform Laws on the subject of Bankruptcies throughout the United States;

To coin Money, regulate the Value thereof, and of foreign Coin, and fix the Standard of Weights and Measures;

To provide for the Punishment of counterfeiting the Securities and current Coin of the United States;

To establish Post Offices and post Roads;

To promote the Progress of Science and useful Arts, by securing for limited Times to Authors and Inventors the exclusive Right to their respective Writings and Discoveries;

To constitute Tribunals inferior to the supreme Court;

To define and punish Piracies and Felonies committed on the high Seas, and Offences against the Law of Nations;

To declare War, grant Letters of Marque and Reprisal, and make Rules concerning Captures on Land and Water;

To raise and support Armies, but no Appropriation of Money to that Use shall be for a longer Term than two Years;

To provide and maintain a Navy;

To make Rules for the Government and Regulation of the land and naval Forces;

To provide for calling forth the Militia to execute the Laws of the Union, suppress Insurrections and repel Invasions;

To provide for organizing, arming, and disciplining the Militia, and for governing such Part of them as may be employed in the Service of the United States, reserving to the States respectively, the Appointment of the Officers, and the Authority of training the Militia according to the discipline prescribed by Congress;

To exercise exclusive Legislation in all Cases whatsoever, over such District (not exceeding ten Miles square) as may, by Cession of particular States, and the Acceptance of Congress, become the Seat of the Government of the United States, and to exercise like Authority over all Places purchased by the Consent of the Legislature of the State in which the Same shall be, for the Erection of Forts, Magazines, Arsenals, dock-Yards, and other needful Buildings;—and

To make all Laws which shall be necessary and proper for carrying into Execution the foregoing Powers, and all other Powers vested by this Constitution in the Government of the United States, or in any Department or Officer thereof.

Section 9. The Migration or Importation of such Persons as any of the States now existing shall think proper to admit, shall not be prohibited by the Congress prior to the Year one thousand eight hundred and eight, but a tax or duty may be imposed on such Importation, not exceeding ten dollars for each Person.

The privilege of the Writ of Habeas Corpus shall not be suspended, unless when in Cases of Rebellion or Invasion the public Safety may require it.

No Bill of Attainder or ex post facto Law shall be passed.

No capitation, or other direct, Tax shall be laid unless in Proportion to the Census or Enumeration herein before directed to be taken.[5]

No Tax or Duty shall be laid on Articles exported from any State.

No Preference shall be given by any Regulation of Commerce or Revenue to the Ports of one State over those of another: nor shall Vessels bound to, or from, one State, be obliged to enter, clear, or pay Duties in another.

No Money shall be drawn from the Treasury, but in Consequence of Appropriations made by Law; and a regular Statement and Account of the Receipts and Expenditures of all public Money shall be published from time to time.

No Title of Nobility shall be granted by the United States: And no Person holding any Office of Profit or Trust under them, shall, without the Consent of the Congress, accept of any present, Emolument, Office, or Title, of any kind whatever, from any King, Prince, or foreign State.

Section 10. No State shall enter into any Treaty, Alliance, or Confederation; grant Letters of Marque and Reprisal; coin Money; emit Bills of Credit; make any Thing but gold and silver Coin a Tender in Payment of Debts; pass any Bill of Attainder, ex post facto Law, or Law impairing the Obligation of Contracts, or grant any Title of Nobility.

No State shall, without the Consent of the Congress, lay any Imposts or Duties on Imports or Exports, except what may be absolutely necessary for executing its inspection Laws: and the net Produce of all Duties and Imposts, laid by any State on Imports or Exports, shall be for the Use of the Treasury of the United States; and all such Laws shall be subject to the Revision and Control of the Congress.

No State shall, without the Consent of Congress, lay any duty of Tonnage, keep Troops, or Ships of War in time of Peace, enter into any Agreement or Compact with another State, or with a foreign Power, or engage in War, unless actually invaded, or in such imminent Danger as will not admit of delay.

ARTICLE II.

Section 1. The executive Power shall be vested in a President of the United States of America. He shall hold his Office during the Term of four Years, and, together with the Vice President, chosen for the same Term, be elected, as follows

Each State shall appoint, in such Manner as the Legislature thereof may direct, a Number of Electors, equal to the whole Number of Senators and Representatives to which the State may be entitled in the Congress: but no Senator or Representative, or Person holding an Office of Trust or Profit under the United States, shall be appointed an Elector.

[The Electors shall meet in their respective States, and vote by Ballot for two Persons, of whom one at least shall not be an Inhabitant of the same State with themselves. And they shall make a List of all the Persons voted for, and of the Number of Votes for each; which List they shall sign and certify, and transmit sealed to the Seat of the Government of the United States, directed to the President of the Senate. The President of the Senate shall, in the Presence of the Senate and House of Representatives, open all the Certificates, and the Votes shall then be counted. The Person having the greatest Number of Votes

---

[5] Modified by Amendment XVI.

shall be the President, if such Number be a Majority of the whole Number of Electors appointed; and if there be more than one who have such Majority, and have an equal Number of Votes, then the House of Representatives shall immediately chuse by Ballot one of them for President; and if no Person have a Majority, then from the five highest on the List the said House shall in like Manner chuse the President. But in chusing the President, the Votes shall be taken by States, the Representation from each State having one Vote; A quorum for this Purpose shall consist of a Member or Members from two-thirds of the States, and a Majority of all the States shall be necessary to a Choice. In every Case, after the Choice of the President, the Person having the greatest Number of Votes of the Electors shall be the Vice President. But if there should remain two or more who have equal Votes, the Senate shall chuse from them by Ballot the Vice President.][6]

The Congress may determine the Time of chusing the Electors, and the Day on which they shall give their Votes; which Day shall be the same throughout the United States.

No Person except a natural born Citizen, or a Citizen of the United States, at the time of the Adoption of this Constitution, shall be eligible to the Office of President; neither shall any Person be eligible to that Office who shall not have attained to the Age of thirty-five Years, and been fourteen Years a Resident within the United States.

In Case of the Removal of the President from Office, or of his Death, Resignation or Inability to discharge the Powers and Duties of the said Office, the same shall devolve on the Vice President, and the Congress may by Law provide for the Case of Removal, Death, Resignation or Inability, both of the President and Vice President, declaring what Officer shall then act as President, and such Officer shall act accordingly, until the Disability be removed, or a President shall be elected.[7]

The President shall, at stated Times, receive for his Services, a Compensation, which shall neither be encreased nor diminished during the Period for which he shall have been elected, and he shall not receive within that Period any other Emolument from the United States, or any of them.

Before he enter on the Execution of his Office, he shall take the following Oath or Affirmation:—"I do solemnly swear (or affirm) that I will faithfully execute the Office of President of the United States, and will to the best of my Ability, preserve, protect and defend the Constitution of the United States."

Section 2. The President shall be Commander-in-Chief of the Army and Navy of the United States, and of the Militia of the several States, when called into the actual Service of the United States; he may require the Opinion in writing, of the principal Officer in each of the executive Departments, upon any subject relating to the Duties of their respective Offices, and he shall have Power to Grant Reprieves and Pardons for Offenses against the United States, except in Cases of Impeachment.

He shall have Power, by and with the Advice and Consent of the Senate, to make Treaties, provided two-thirds of the Senators present concur; and he shall nominate, and by and with the Advice and Consent of the Senate, shall

[6] Superseded by Amendment XII.
[7] Amended by Amendment XX, Sections 3, 4.

appoint Ambassadors, other public Ministers and Consuls, Judges of the supreme Court, and all other Officers of the United States, whose Appointments are not herein otherwise provided for, and which shall be established by Law: but the Congress may by Law vest the Appointment of such inferior Officers, as they think proper, in the President alone, in the Courts of Law, or in the Heads of Departments.

The President shall have Power to fill up all Vacancies that may happpen during the Recess of the Senate, by granting Commissions which shall expire at the End of their next Session.

Section 3. He shall from time to time give to the Congress Information of the State of the Union, and recommend to their Consideration such Measures as he shall judge necessary and expedient; he may, on extraordinary Occasions, convene both Houses, or either of them, and in Case of Disagreement between them, with Respect to the Time of Adjournment, he may adjourn them to such Time as he shall think proper; he shall receive Ambassadors and other public Ministers; he shall take Care that the Laws be faithfully executed, and shall Commission all the Officers of the United States.

Section 4. The President, Vice President and all civil Officers of the United States, shall be removed from Office on Impeachment for, and Conviction of, Treason, Bribery, or other high Crimes and Misdemeanors.

ARTICLE III.

Section 1. The judicial Power of the United States, shall be vested in one supreme Court, and in such inferior Courts as the Congress may from time to time ordain and establish. The Judges, both of the supreme and inferior Courts, shall hold their Offices during good Behaviour, and shall, at stated Times, receive for their Services a Compensation which shall not be diminished during their Continuance in Office.

Section 2. The judicial Power shall extend to all Cases, in Law and Equity, arising under this Constitution, the Laws of the United States, and Treaties made, or which shall be made, under their Authority;—to all Cases affecting Ambassadors, other public Ministers and Consuls;—to all Cases of admiralty and maritime Jurisdiction;—to Controversies to which the United States shall be a Party;—to Controversies between two or more States;—between a State and Citizens of another State;—between Citizens of different States;—between Citizens of the same State claiming Lands under Grants of different States, and between a State, or the Citizens thereof, and foreign States, Citizens or Subjects.

In all Cases affecting Ambassadors, other public Ministers and Consuls, and those in which a State shall be Party, the supreme Court shall have original Jurisdiction. In all the other Cases before mentioned, the supreme Court shall have appellate Jurisdiction, both as to Law and Fact, with such Exceptions, and under such Regulations as the Congress shall make.

The Trial of all Crimes, except in Cases of Impeachment, shall be by Jury; and such Trial shall be held in the State where the said Crimes shall have been committed; but when not committed within any State, the Trial shall be at such Place or Places as the Congress may by Law have directed.

Section 3. Treason against the United States, shall consist only in levying War against them, or in adhering to their Enemies, giving them Aid and Comfort. No Person shall be convicted of Treason unless on the Testimony of two Witnesses to the same overt Act, or on Confession in open Court.

The Congress shall have Power to declare the Punishment of Treason, but no Attainder of Treason shall work Corruption of Blood, or Forfeiture except during the Life of the Person attainted.

ARTICLE IV.

Section 1. Full Faith and Credit shall be given in each State to the public Acts, Records, and judicial Proceedings of every other State. And the Congress may by general Laws prescribe the Manner in which such Acts, Records and Proceedings shall be proved, and the Effect thereof.

Section 2. The Citizens of each State shall be entitled to all Privileges and Immunities of Citizens in the several States.

A person charged in any State with Treason, Felony, or other Crime, who shall flee from Justice, and be found in another State, shall on Demand of the executive Authority of the State from which he fled, be delivered up to be removed to the State having Jurisdiction of the Crime.

No Person held to Service or Labour in one State, under the Laws thereof, escaping into another, shall, in Consequence of any Law or Regulation therein, be discharged from such Service or Labour, but shall be delivered up on Claim of the Party to whom such Service or Labour may be due.

Section 3. New States may be admitted by the Congress into this Union; but no new State shall be formed or erected within the Jurisdiction of any other State; nor any State be formed by the Junction of two or more States, or Parts of States, without the Consent of the Legislatures of the States concerned as well as of the Congress.

The Congress shall have Power to dispose of and make all needful Rules and Regulations respecting the Territory or other Property belonging to the United States; and nothing in this Constitution shall be so construed as to Prejudice any Claims of the United States, or of any particular State.

Section 4. The United States shall guarantee to every State in this Union a Republican Form of Government, and shall protect each of them against Invasion; and on Application of the Legislature, or of the Executive (when the Legislature cannot be convened) against domestic Violence.

ARTICLE V.

The Congress, whenever two-thirds of both Houses shall deem it necessary, shall propose Amendments to this Constitution, or, on the Application of the Legislatures of two-thirds of the several States, shall call a Convention for proposing Amendments, which, in either Case, shall be valid to all Intents and Purposes, as part of this Constitution, when ratified by the Legislatures of three-fourths of the several States, or by Conventions in three-fourths thereof, as the one or the other Mode of Ratification may be proposed by the Congress; Provided that no Amendment which may be made prior to the Year One thousand eight hundred and eight shall in any Manner affect the first and fourth

Clauses in the Ninth Section of the first Article; and that no State, without its Consent, shall be deprived of its equal Suffrage in the Senate.

ARTICLE VI.

All Debts contracted and Engagements entered into, before the Adoption of this Constitution, shall be as valid against the United States under this Constitution, as under the Confederation.

This Constitution, and the Laws of the United States which shall be made in Pursuance thereof; and all Treaties made, or which shall be made, under the Authority of the United States, shall be the supreme Law of the Land; and the Judges in every State shall be bound thereby, any Thing in the Constitution of Laws of any State to the Contrary notwithstanding.

The Senators and Representatives before mentioned, and the Members of the several State Legislatures, and all executive and judicial Officers, both of the United States and of the several States, shall be bound by Oath or Affirmation, to support this Constitution; but no religious Test shall ever be required as a Qualification to any Office or public Trust under the United States.

ARTICLE VII.

The Ratification of the Conventions of nine States shall be sufficient for the Establishment of this Constitution between the States so ratifying the Same.

DONE in Convention by the Unanimous Consent of the States present the Seventeenth Day of September in the Year of our Lord one thousand seven hundred and Eighty seven and of the Independence of the United States of America the Twelfth. In Witness whereof We have hereunto subscribed our Names.[8]

Amendments

ARTICLE I [first ten Amendments in force, December, 1791].

Congress shall make no law respecting an establishment of religion, or prohibiting the free exercise thereof; or abridging the freedom of speech, or of the press; or the right of the people peaceably to assemble, and to petition the Government for a redress of grievances.

ARTICLE II.

A well regulated Militia, being necessary to the security of a free State, the right of the people to keep and bear Arms, shall not be infringed.

ARTICLE III.

No Soldier shall, in time of peace, be quartered in any house, without the consent of the Owner, nor in time of war, but in a manner to be prescribed by law.

ARTICLE IV.

The right of the people to be secure in their persons, houses, papers, and effects, against unreasonable searches and seizures, shall not be violated, and

---

[8] Declared in effect March 4, 1789.

no Warrants shall issue, but upon probable cause, supported by Oath or affirmation, and particularly describing the place to be searched, and the persons or things to be seized.

ARTICLE V.

No person shall be held to answer for a capital, or otherwise infamous crime, unless on a presentment or indictment of a Grand Jury, except in cases arising in the land or naval forces, or in the Militia, when in actual service in time of War or public danger; nor shall any person be subject for the same offence to be twice put in jeopardy of life or limb; nor shall be compelled in any criminal case to be a witness against himself, nor be deprived of life, liberty, or property, without due process of law; nor shall private property be taken for public use, without just compensation.

ARTICLE VI.

In all criminal prosecutions, the accused shall enjoy the right to a speedy and public trial, by an impartial jury of the State and district wherein the crime shall have been committed, which district shall have been previously ascertained by law, and to be informed of the nature and cause of the accusation; to be confronted with the witnesses against him; to have compulsory process for obtaining witnesses in his favor, and to have the Assistance of Counsel for his defence.

ARTICLE VII.

In suits at common law, where the value in controversy shall exceed twenty dollars, the right of trial by jury shall be preserved, and no fact tried by a jury, shall be otherwise reexamined in any Court of the United States, than according to the rules of the common law.

ARTICLE VIII.

Excessive bail shall not be required, nor excessive fines imposed, nor cruel and unusual punishments inflicted.

ARTICLE IX.

The enumeration in the Constitution, of certain rights, shall not be construed to deny or disparage others retained by the people.

ARTICLE X.

The powers not delegated to the United States by the Constitution, nor prohibited by it to the States, are reserved to the States respectively, or to the people.

ARTICLE XI [in force January, 1798].

The Judicial power of the United States shall not be construed to extend to any suit in law or equity, commenced or prosecuted against one of the United States by Citizens of another State, or by Citizens or Subjects of any Foreign State.

ARTICLE XII [in force September, 1804].

The Electors shall meet in their respective states and vote by ballot for President and Vice President, one of whom, at least, shall not be an inhabitant of the same state with themselves; they shall name in their ballots the person voted for as President, and in distinct ballots the person voted for as Vice President, and they shall make distinct lists of all persons voted for as President, and of all persons voted for as Vice President, and of the number of votes for each, which lists they shall sign and certify, and transmit sealed to the seat of the government of the United States, directed to the President of the Senate;—The President of the Senate shall, in presence of the Senate and House of Representatives, open all the certificates and the votes shall then be counted;—The person having the greatest number of votes for President, shall be the President, if such number be a majority of the whole number of Electors appointed; and if no person have such majority, then from the persons having the highest numbers not exceeding three on the list of those voted for as President, the House of Representatives shall choose immediately, by ballot, the President. But in choosing the President, the votes shall be taken by states, the representation from each state having one vote; a quorum for this purpose shall consist of a member or members from two-thirds of the states, and a majority of all the states shall be necessary to a choice. And if the House of Representatives shall not choose a President whenever the right of choice shall devolve upon them, before the fourth day of March next following, then the Vice President shall act as President, as in the case of the death or other constitutional disability of the President. The person having the greatest number of votes as Vice President, shall be the Vice President, if such number be a majority of the whole number of Electors appointed, and if no person have a majority, then from the two highest numbers on the list, the Senate shall choose the Vice President; a quorum for the purpose shall consist of two-thirds of the whole number of Senators, and a majority of whole number shall be necessary to a choice. But no person constitutionally ineligible to the office of President shall be eligible to that of Vice President of the United States.

ARTICLE XIII [in force December, 1865].

Section 1. Neither slavery nor involuntary servitude, except as a punishment for crime whereof the party shall have been duly convicted, shall exist within the United States, or any place subject to their jurisdiction.

Section 2. Congress shall have power to enforce this article by appropriate legislation.

ARTICLE XIV [in force July, 1868].

Section 1. All persons born or naturalized in the United States, and subject to the jurisdiction thereof, are citizens of the United States and of the State wherein they reside. No State shall make or enforce any law which shall abridge the privileges or immunities of citizens of the United States; nor shall any State deprive any person of life, liberty, or property, without due process of law; nor deny to any person within its jurisdiction the equal protection of the laws.

Section 2. Representatives shall be apportioned among the several States according to their respective numbers, counting the whole number of persons in each State, excluding Indians not taxed. But when the right to vote at any election for the choice of electors for President and Vice President of the United States, Representatives in Congress, the Executive and Judicial officers of a State, or the members of the Legislature thereof, is denied to any of the male inhabitants of such State, being twenty-one years of age, and citizens of the United States, or in any way abridged, except for participation in rebellion, or other crime, the basis of representation therein shall be reduced in the proportion which the number of such male citizens shall bear to the whole number of male citizens twenty-one years of age in such State.

Section 3. No person shall be a Senator or Representative in Congress, or elector of President and Vice President, or hold any office, civil, or military, under the United States, or under any State, who, having previously taken an oath, as a member of Congress, or as an officer of the United States, or as a member of any State legislature, or as an executive or judicial officer of any State, to support the Constitution of the United States, shall have engaged in insurrection or rebellion against the same, or given aid or comfort to the enemies thereof. But Congress may by a vote of two-thirds of each House, remove such disability.

Section 4. The validity of the public debt of the United States, authorized by law, including debts incurred for payment of pensions and bounties for services in suppressing insurrection or rebellion, shall not be questioned. But neither the United States nor any State shall assume or pay any debt or obligation incurred in aid of insurrection or rebellion against the United States, or any claim for the loss or emancipation of any slave; but all such debts, obligations and claims shall be held illegal and void.

Section 5. The Congress shall have power to enforce, by appropriate legislation, the provisions of this article.

ARTICLE XV [in force March, 1870].

Section 1. The right of citizens of the United States to vote shall not be denied or abridged by the United States or by any State on account of race, color, or previous condition of servitude.

Section 2. The Congress shall have power to enforce this article by appropriate legislation.

ARTICLE XVI [in force February, 1913].

The Congress shall have power to lay and collect taxes on incomes, from whatever source derived, without apportionment among the several States, and without regard to any census or enumeration.

ARTICLE XVII [in force May, 1913].

The Senate of the United States shall be composed of two Senators from each State, elected by the people thereof, for six years; and each Senator shall have one vote. The electors in each State shall have the qualifications requisite for electors of the most numerous branch of the State legislatures.

When vacancies happen in the representation of any State in the Senate, the executive authority of such State shall issue writs of election to fill such vacancies: *Provided,* That the legislature of any State may empower the executive thereof to make temporary appointments until the people fill the vacancies by election as the legislature may direct.

This amendment shall not be so construed as to affect the election or term of any Senator chosen before it becomes valid as part of the Constitution.

ARTICLE XVIII [in force January, 1920; superseded by Amendment XXI].

After one year from the ratification of this article the manufacture, sale, or transportation of intoxicating liquors within, the importation thereof into, or the exportation thereof from the United States and all territory subject to the jurisdiction thereof for beverage purposes is hereby prohibited.

The Congress and the several States shall have concurrent power to enforce this article by appropriate legislation.

This article shall be inoperative unless it shall have been ratified as an amendment to the Constitution by the legislatures of the several States, as provided in the Constitution, within seven years from the date of the submission hereof to the States by the Congress.

ARTICLE XIX [in force August, 1920].

The right of citizens of the United States to vote shall not be denied or abridged by the United States or by any State on account of sex.

Congress shall have power to enforce this article by appropriate legislation.

ARTICLE XX [in force February, 1933].

Section 1. The terms of the President and Vice President shall end at noon on the twentieth day of January, and the terms of Senators and Representatives at noon on the third day of January, of the years in which such terms would have ended if this article had not been ratified; and the terms of their successors shall then begin.

Section 2. The Congress shall assemble at least once in every year, and such meeting shall begin at noon on the third day of January, unless they shall by law appoint a different day.

Section 3. If, at the time fixed for the beginning of the term of the President, the President-elect shall have died, the Vice President-elect shall become President. If a President shall not have been chosen before the time fixed for the beginning of his term, or if the President-elect shall have failed to qualify, then the Vice President-elect shall act as President until a President shall have qualified; and the Congress may by law provide for the case wherein neither a President-elect nor a Vice President-elect shall have qualified, declaring who shall then act as President, or the manner in which one who is to act shall be selected, and such person shall act accordingly until a President or Vice President shall have qualified.

Section 4. The Congress may by law provide for the case of the death of any of the persons from whom the House of Representatives may choose a President whenever the right of choice shall have devolved upon them, and for the case of the death of any of the persons from whom the Senate may choose a Vice President whenever the right of choice shall have devolved upon them.

Section 5. Sections 1 and 2 shall take effect on the 15th day of October following the ratification of this article.

Section 6. This article shall be inoperative unless it shall have been ratified as an amendment to the Constitution by the legislatures of three-fourths of the several States within seven years from the date of its submission.

ARTICLE XXI [in force December, 1933].

Section 1. The eighteenth article of amendment to the Constitution of the United States is hereby repealed.

Section 2. The transportation or importation into any State, Territory, or possession of the United States for delivery or use therein of intoxicating liquors, in violation of the laws thereof, is hereby prohibited.

Section 3. This article shall be inoperative unless it shall have been ratified as an amendment to the Constitution by conventions in the several States, as provided in the Constitution, within seven years from the date of the submission hereof to the States by the Congress.

ARTICLE XXII [in force February, 1951].

No person shall be elected to the office of the President of the United States more than twice, and no person who has held the office of President, or acted as President, for more than two years of a term to which some other person was elected President shall be elected to the office of President more than once.

But this Article shall not apply to any person holding the office of President when this Article was proposed by Congress, and shall not prevent any person who may be holding the office of President, or acting as President, during the term within which this Article becomes operative from holding the office of President or acting as President during the remainder of such term.

Presidents of the United States

Name	State	Political Party	Years as President
George Washington	Virginia	Federalist	1789–1797
John Adams	Massachusetts	Federalist	1797–1801
Thomas Jefferson	Virginia	Jeffersonian	1801–1809
James Madison	Virginia	Jeffersonian	1809–1817
James Monroe	Virginia	Jeffersonian	1817–1825
John Quincy Adams	Massachusetts	Jeffersonian	1825–1829
Andrew Jackson	Tennessee	Democrat	1829–1837
Martin Van Buren	New York	Democrat	1837–1841
William Henry Harrison	Indiana	Whig	1841*
John Tyler	Virginia	Whig	1841–1845
James Knox Polk	Tennessee	Democrat	1845–1849
Zachary Taylor	Louisiana	Whig	1849–1850*
Millard Fillmore	New York	Whig	1850–1853
Franklin Pierce	New Hampshire	Democrat	1853–1857
James Buchanan	Pennsylvania	Democrat	1857–1861
Abraham Lincoln	Illinois	Republican	1861–1865*
Andrew Johnson	Tennessee	Republican	1865–1869
Ulysses Simpson Grant	Illinois	Republican	1869–1877
Rutherford Birchard Hayes	Ohio	Republican	1877–1881
James Abram Garfield	Ohio	Republican	1881*
Chester Alan Arthur	New York	Republican	1881–1885
Grover Cleveland	New York	Democrat	1885–1889
Benjamin Harrison	Indiana	Republican	1889–1893
Grover Cleveland	New York	Democrat	1893–1897
William McKinley	Ohio	Republican	1897–1901*
Theodore Roosevelt	New York	Republican	1901–1909
William Howard Taft	Ohio	Republican	1909–1913
Woodrow Wilson	New Jersey	Democrat	1913–1921
Warren Gamaliel Harding	Ohio	Republican	1921–1923*
Calvin Coolidge	Massachusetts	Republican	1923–1929
Herbert Hoover	California	Republican	1929–1933
Franklin Delano Roosevelt	New York	Democrat	1933–1945*
Harry S. Truman	Missouri	Democrat	1945–1953
Dwight D. Eisenhower	New York	Republican	1953–

* Died in office.

Bibliography

Basic reference works include the Dictionary of American Biography (20 vols., 1928–36); Dictionary of American History (5 vols., 1940); Encyclopaedia of the Social Sciences (15 vols., 1930–35). See also H. P. Beers, Bibliographies in American History (1938).

No one should miss C. A. and M. R. Beard, Rise of American Civilization (1933). The best longer histories are Edward Channing, History of the United States (6 vols., to 1865, 1927–30); the American Nation series (28 vols., 1904–18); the Chronicles of America (50 short vols., 1918–21); J. B. McMaster, History of the People of the United States (8 vols., covering 1783–1865, 1931–38); the History of American Life, edited by A. M. Schlesinger and D. R. Fox (13 vols., 1927–48). A new Economic History of the United States is to be 9 volumes.

Merle Curti, Growth of American Thought (1943), concerns ideas. See also C. A. and M. R. Beard, American Spirit (1942); Joseph Dorfman, Economic Mind (1946–49); R. H. Gabriel, Course of American Democratic Thought (1940); Gustavus Myers, History of American Idealism (1925); R. G. Gettell, History of American Political Theories (1929); Merle Curti, Peace or War (peace movement, 1936); H. Koht, American Spirit in Europe (1949); D. F. Bowers, Foreign Influences on American Life (1944). Literary materials are stressed in V. L. Parrington, Main Currents in American Thought (3 vols., 1939). And see the 3-volume Literary History of the United States (1948); Cambridge History of American Literature (4 vols., 1931); F. L. Mott, American Journalism (1941), his History of American Magazines (3 vols., 1938), his Golden Multitudes (best sellers, 1947); Michael Kraus, History of American History (1937).

For religious history, see W. W. Sweet, Story of Religions in America (1930); Theodore Maynard, Story of American Catholicism (1941); T. C. Hall, Religious Background of American Culture (1930); A. P. Stokes, Church and State in United States (3 vols., 1950). E. P. Cubberly, Public Education (1934), and E. W. Knight, Education in the United States (1941), are standard. Note Thomas Woody, History of Women's Education (1929); Merle Curti, Social Ideas of American Educators (1935); H. K. Beale, History of Freedom of Teaching in American Schools (1941). A. W. Calhoun, Social History of the American Family (3 vols., 1917–19), is a pioneer study. And see W. C. Langdon, Everyday Things (1937); F. R. Dulles, America Learns to Play (1940); Dixon Wecter, Saga of American Society (1937).

For science there are Bernard Jaffe, Men of Science (1944); W. B. Kaempffert, Popular History of American Invention (1924); F. R. Packard, History of Medicine in the United States (1932); R. H. Shryock, Development of Modern Medicine (1936). For fine arts, O. W. Larkin, Art and Life in America (1949); J. M. Fitch, American Building (1948); T. E. Tallmadge, Story of Architecture in America (1936); Lewis Mumford, Sticks and Stones (1934); Suzanne LaFollette, Art in America (1929); Holger Cahill, American Folk Art (1933); Alan Burroughs, Limners and Likenesses (1936); Lorado Taft, History of American Sculpture (1930); J. T. Howard, Our American Music (1941).

One-volume American economic histories include those by H. F. Williamson (ed., 1944), C. W. Wright (1941), F. A. Shannon (1940), R. C. McGrane (1942), E. C. Kirkland (1951), A. C. Bining (1943), J. A. Barnes (1949), H. U. Faulkner (1943), Broadus and L. P. Mitchell (1947), D. L. Kemmerer and E. L. Bogart (1943). For interpretation, read T. C. Cochran and William Miller, *Age of Enterprise* (1942); L. M. Hacker, *Triumph of American Capitalism* (1940). For special fields, W. J. Shultz and M. R. Caine, *Financial Development of the United States* (1937); Sidney Ratner, *American Taxation* (1942); Joseph Schafer, *Social History of American Agriculture* (1936); F. W. Taussig, *Tariff History of the United States* (1931); Carnegie Institution studies by P. W. Bidwell and J. I. Falconer (northern agriculture, 1925), L. C. Gray (southern agriculture, 1933), V. S. Clark (manufacturing, 1929), E. R. Johnson (foreign and domestic commerce, 1922), B. H. Meyer (transportation, 1917). Clark and Johnson go beyond 1900; the others stop at 1860.

F. R. Dulles, *Labor in America* (1949), covers the whole field; and see J. R. Commons, *History of Labour in the United States* (4 vols., 1935–36). For immigration, M. L. Hansen, *Atlantic Migration* (1940) and *Immigrant in American History* (1940); Carl Wittke, *We Who Built America* (1939); Ralph Wood, *Pennsylvania Germans* (1942); Oscar Handlin, *The Uprooted* (1951), are good. See also C. G. Woodson, *Negro in Our History* (1941); J. H. Franklin, *From Slavery to Freedom* (1947).

Everyone should know F. J. Turner's interpretation of the significance of the frontier, in his *Frontier in American History* (1921). There are histories of the frontier by R. E. Riegel (1930), R. A. Billington (1949), L. R. Hafen and C. C. Rister (1941), F. L. Paxson (1924). R. M. Robbins, *Our Landed Heritage* (1942); B. H. Hibbard, *History of Public Land Policies* (1939); A. M. Sakolski, *Great American Land Bubble* (1932), deal with land policy.

For sectionalism, read F. J. Turner, *Significance of Sections in American History* (1932). A multi-volume *History of the South* is now appearing (1947–   ). Note W. B. Hesseltine, *South in American History* (1943); Clement Eaton, *History of the Old South* (1949); F. B. Simkins, *South, Old and New* (1947). J. T. Adams has 3 volumes on New England to 1850 (1927); and see J. W. Caughey's history of the Pacific coast (1938) and O. O. Winther's *Great Northwest* (1947). State and city studies include the *History of the State of New York* (10 vols., 1933–37); a new *History of the State of Ohio* (6 vols., 1941–   ); B. L. Pierce, *Chicago* (1937–   ); Blake McKelvey, *Rochester* (1938). E. C. Semple, *American History and Its Geographic Conditions* (1933), and A. P. Brigham, *Geographic Influences in American History* (1903), are useful, as is C. O. Paullin, *Atlas of the Historical Geography of the United States* (1932). See also A. B. Hulbert, *Soil* (1930); Seymour Dunbar, *History of Travel in America* (1937); Isaiah Bowman, *Forest Physiography* (1911); A. B. Hulbert (ed.), *Historic Highways* (16 vols., 1902–05); new *American Trails* (1947–   ) and *American Lakes* (1944–   ) series. For pictures, R. H. Gabriel (ed.), *Pageant of America* (15 vols., 1925–29); J. T. Adams (ed.), *Album of American History* (5 vols., 1944–49).

Important for political history are W. E. Binkley, *American Political*

Parties (1943); Richard Hofstadter, *American Political Tradition* (1948); Edward Stanwood, *History of the Presidency* (2 vols., 1916). Constitutional history is treated by A. H. Kelly and W. A. Harbison (1948), C. B. Swisher (1943), A. C. McLaughlin (1936), H. C. Hockett (1938). And note Charles Warren, *Supreme Court* (2 vols., 1937); L. B. Boudin, *Government by Judiciary* (2 vols., 1932); Willard Hurst, *Growth of American Law* (1950). There are one-volume diplomatic histories by T. A. Bailey (1950), S. F. Bemis (1950), L. E. Ellis (1951), R. W. Van Alstyne (1944). See also S. F. Bemis (ed.), *American Secretaries of State* (10 vols., 1927–29); M. W. Graham, *American Diplomacy in International Community* (1948); C. A. Beard, *Idea of National Interest* (1934). O. H. Spaulding, *United States Army* (1937), and C. S. Alden and Allan Westcott, *United States Navy* (1945), stress engagements. For policy, read H. H. and Margaret Sprout, *Rise of American Naval Power* (1939); Lovis Smith, *American Democracy and Military Power* (1952).

For source material, there are H. S. Commager, *Documents of American History* (1948); L. M. Hacker and H. S. Zahler, *Shaping of American Tradition* (1947); Merle Curti, Willard Thorp, and Carlos Baker, *American Issues* (1941); new series prepared at Chicago (*People Shall Judge*, 1949), Amherst (*Problems in American Civilization*, 1949), Yale (*Select Problems in Historical Interpretation for American History*, (1949). Donald Sheehan, *Making of American History* (1950), reprints historians' essays. There are special collections of sources for economic history (Felix Flugel and H. U. Faulkner, 1929), diplomatic history (R. J. Bartlett, 1947), religious history (P. G. Mode, 1921), agricultural history (L. B. Schmidt and E. D. Ross, 1925), labor and industry (J. R. Commons, 1910–11), westward movement (I. F. Woestemeyer and J. M. Gambrill, 1939). See also A. B. Hart, *American History Told by Contemporaries* (1897–1929); and travelers' accounts: Allan Nevins, *America Through British Eyes* (1948), and Oscar Handlin, *This Was America* (1949).

Part I (1607–1763)

(Books given above will not be listed again.)

There are excellent one-volume surveys of the colonial era by C. P. Nettels (1938), Max Savelle (1942), O. P. Chitwood (1931), E. B. Greene (1935), L. B. Wright (1947). For more detail, H. L. Osgood, *American Colonies* (7 vols., 1904–30); C. M. Andrews, *Colonial Period* (4 vols., 1934–38); L. H. Gipson, *British Empire Before the American Revolution* (1936–). For special areas, T. J. Wertenbaker, *Old South* (1942), *Middle Colonies* (1938), *Puritan Oligarchy* (1947); W. F. Craven, *Southern Colonies in the Seventeenth Century* (1949).

Clark Wissler, *American Indian* (1938), is good, as are Paul Radin, *Story of the American Indian* (1937); Ellsworth Huntington, *Red Man's Continent* (1921); John Collier, *Indians of the Americas* (1947). On the colonial era are G. T. Hunt, *Wars of the Iroquois* (1940); H. H. Peckham, *Pontiac and the Indian Rising* (1947). For later policy, G. D. Harmon, *Sixty Years of Indian Affairs, 1789–1850* (1941); L. B. Priest, *Uncle Sam's Stepchildren,*

1865–87 (1942). See also Charles Hamilton (ed.), *Cry of the Thunderbird* (1950).

E. P. Cheyney, *European Background of American History* (1904), is useful. For colonization, see Halldor Hermannsson, *Problem of Wineland* (1936); H. E. Bolton and T. M. Marshall, *Colonization of North America* (1920); H. I. Priestley, *Coming of the White Man* (1929); *Cambridge History of the British Empire*, Vol. I (1929); E. G. Bourne, *Spain in America* (1904); R. G. Thwaites, *France in America* (1905); H. E. Bolton, "Epic of Greater America," *Wider Horizons of American History* (1939).

Economic history: C. P. Nettels, *Money Supply of the American Colonies Before 1720;* R. B. Morris, *Government and Labor in Early America* (1946); Lyman Carrier, *Beginnings of Agriculture in America* (1923); R. M. Tryon, *Household Manufactures* (1917); A. E. Smith, *Colonists in Bondage* (1947); B. W. Bond, *Quit-Rent System* (1919); R. G. Albion, *Forests and Sea Power* (1926); L. K. Mathews, *Expansion of New England, 1620–1865* (1909); V. W. Crane, *Southern Frontier, 1670–1732* (1929); A. O. Craven, *Soil Exhaustion in Virginia and Maryland, 1606–1860* (1926); E. A. J. Johnson, *American Economic Thought in the Seventeenth Century* (1932).

Religious history: W. W. Sweet, *Religion in Colonial America* (1942); E. B. Greene, *Religion and the State* (1941); Sister M. R. Ray, *American Opinion of Roman Catholicism in the Eighteenth Century* (1936); A. V. Goodman, *American Overture* (Jews, 1947); F. J. Klingberg, *Anglican Humanitarianism in Colonial New York* (1940); H. M. Morais, *Deism in Eighteenth Century America* (1934); W. M. Gewehr, *Great Awakening in Virginia* (1930); L. B. Wright, *Religion and Empire* (1943); R. M. Jones, *Quakers in the American Colonies* (1911). New England Puritanism has attracted many: H. W. Schneider (1930), Perry Miller (1939), S. E. Morison (1936), R. B. Perry (1944), Joseph Haroutunian (1932).

Social and intellectual life: T. J. Wertenbaker, *First Americans* (1929); J. T. Adams, *Provincial Society* (1938); Max Savelle, *Seeds of Liberty* (1948); Carl Bridenbaugh, *Cities in the Wilderness* (1938); Michael Kraus, *Intercolonial Aspects of American Culture* (1928); L. W. Labaree, *Conservatism in Early American History* (1948); Edward Eggleston, *Transit of Civilization* (1901); M. W. Jernegan, *Laboring and Dependent Classes in Colonial America* (1931); S. E. Morison, *Harvard College in the Seventeenth Century* (1936); C. M. Andrews, *Colonial Folkways* (1921); M. S. Benson, *Women in Eighteenth Century America* (1935); A. M. Earle, *Home Life in Colonial Days.* Fiske Kimball treats colonial architecture (1927), J. T. Flexner colonial painters (1947).

For science and medicine: Theodore Hornberger, *Scientific Thought in American Colleges, 1638–1800* (1945); I. B. Cohen, *Benjamin Franklin's Experiments* (1941); J. T. Flexner, *Doctors on Horseback* (1939); P. M. Ashburn, *Ranks of Death* (1947); St. J. R. Childs, *Malaria and Colonization in the Carolina Low Country, 1526–1696* (1940).

Political institutions and conflicts: R. B. Morris, *Studies in the History of American Law* (1930); A. E. McKinley, *Suffrage Franchise in the Thirteen Colonies* (1905); J. F. Sly, *Town Government in Massachusetts* (1930); Irving Mark, *Agrarian Conflicts in Colonial New York* (1940); G. A. Cribbs,

Frontier Policy of Pennsylvania (1919); D. L. Kemmerer, Path to Freedom (New Jersey, 1940); W. R. Shepherd, Proprietary Government in Pennsylvania (1896); N. D. Mereness, Maryland as a Proprietary Province (1901); W. A. Schaper, Sectionalism and Representation in South Carolina (1901); J. S. Bassett, Regulators of North Carolina (1895); T. J. Wertenbaker, Torchbearer of the Revolution (Bacon, 1940); L. B. Wright, First Gentlemen of Virginia (1940).

Relations with Britain: C. M. Andrews, Colonial Self-Government (1904); L. W. Labaree, Royal Government in America (1930); G. L. Beer, Origins of the British Colonial System (1908) and Old Colonial System (1932); L. A. Harper, English Navigation Laws (1939); A. C. Bining, British Regulation of the Colonial Iron Industry (1933); V. F. Barnes, Dominion of New England (1923).

There are biographies of Columbus (S. E. Morison, 1942), James Oglethorpe (A. A. Ettinger, 1932), William Penn (S. G. Fisher, 1932; Bonamy Dobree, 1932, Roger Williams (S. H. Brockunier, 1940; J. E. Ernst, 1932), Jonathan Edwards (O. E. Winslow, 1940; H. B. Parkes, 1930), Benjamin Franklin (V. W. Crane, 1936; Bernard Fay, 1929; Carl Van Doren, 1938), Alexander Spotswood (Leonidas Dodson, 1932), Cotton Mather (R. P. and Louise Boas, 1928), Eliza Lucas Pinckney (H. H. Ravenel, 1909), John Peter Zenger (Livingston Rutherford, 1904), Sir William Johnson (Arthur Pound, 1930), "King" Carter (Louis Morton, 1941).

Part II (1763–1815)

Parts of this period are covered by J. C. Miller, Origins of American Revolution (1943) and Triumph of Freedom (1948). Histories of the Revolution have been written by C. H. Van Tyne (1905, 1929), W. E. H. Lecky (1898), S. G. Fisher (1908), G. O. Trevelyan (1899–1907). M. M. Jensen, New Nation (1950); A. C. McLaughlin, Confederation and Constitution (1905); J. S. Bassett, Federalist System (1906); Edward Channing, Jeffersonian System (1906); Henry Adams, History of the United States During the Administrations of Jefferson and Madison (9 vols., 1909–11), are important.

For social history there are E. B. Greene, Revolutionary Generation (1943); J. A. Kraut and D. R. Fox, Completion of Independence (1944); J. F. Jameson, American Revolution Considered as a Social Movement (1926); Allan Nevins, American States During and After the Revolution (1924). For slavery, M. S. Locke, Antislavery in America, 1619–1808 (1901); W. E. B. DuBois, Suppression of the African Slave Trade (1896). And see S. D. McKee, Labor in Colonial New York (1935).

Separation of church and state: H. J. Eckenrode (Virginia, 1910), R. C. Strickland (Georgia, 1939). Also on religion: A. M. Baldwin, New England Clergy and the American Revolution (1928); C. C. Cleveland, Great Revival in the West (1916); W. B. Posey, Development of Methodism in the Old Southwest (1933); O. W. Elsbree, Rise of the Missionary Spirit in America, 1790–1815 (1928); G. A. Koch, Republican Religion (1933). On education: A. O. Hansen, Liberalism and American Education in the Eighteenth Century (1926); J. J. Walsh, Education of the Founding Fathers (1935).

Cultural trends: M. C. Tyler, Literary History of the American Revolution

(1897); Leon Howard, Connecticut Wits (1943); H. M. Jones, America and French Culture, 1750–1848 (1927); Bernard Fay, Revolutionary Spirit in France and America (1927); E. P. Link, Democratic-Republican Societies (1942); J. L. Mesick, English Traveller in America, 1783–1835 (1922); C. M. Wiltse, Jeffersonian Tradition (1935); E. T. Mudge, Social Philosophy of John Taylor of Caroline (1939); I. W. Riley, American Philosophy, Early Schools (1907).

Economic developments: R. A. East, Business Enterprise in the American Revolutionary Era (1938); V. D. Harrington, New York Merchant on the Eve of the Revolution (1935); Leila Sellers, Charleston Business on the Eve of the American Revolution (1934); J. G. B. Hutchins, American Maritime Industries and Public Policy, 1789–1914 (1941); C. J. Bullock, Finances of the United States from 1775 to 1789 (1895); Fritz Redlich, Molding of American Banking (1940). State studies are useful: Oscar and M. F. Handlin, Commonwealth: Massachusetts, 1774–1861 (1947); Louis Hartz, Economic Policy and Democratic Thought: Pennsylvania, 1776–1860 (1948); M. B. Jones, Vermont in the Making (1939); R. F. Upton, Revolutionary New Hampshire (1936); R. J. Purcell, Connecticut in Transition (1918); T. C. Cochran, New York in Confederation (1932); H. J. Eckenrode, Revolution in Virginia (1916); T. P. Abernethy, From Frontier to Plantation in Tennessee (1932); S. J. and E. H. Buck, Planting of Civilization in Western Pennsylvania (1939); N. H. Sonne, Liberal Kentucky (1939); L. P. Kellogg, British Regime in Wisconsin and the Northwest (1935).

Technological progress: J. V. Roe, English and American Tool Makers (1926); A. P. Usher, History of Mechanical Inventions (1929); J. T. Flexner, Steamboats Come True (1944).

Westward movement: P. J. Treat, National Land System, 1785–1820 (1910); A. B. Hulbert, Paths of Inland Commerce (1921); P. D. Jordan, National Road (1948); Archibald Henderson, Conquest of the Old Southwest (1920); B. A. Hinsdale, Old Northwest (1899); B. W. Bond, Civilization of the Old Northwest (1934).

Relations with Britain: C. H. Van Tyne, Causes of the War of Independence (1922); C. M. Andrews, Colonial Background of the American Revolution (1931); G. L. Beer, British Colonial Policy, 1754–65 (1907); Reginald Coupland, American Revolution and the British Empire (1930); P. G. Davidson, Propaganda and the American Revolution (1941); C. H. McIlwain, American Revolution (1923); R. L. Schuyler, Parliament and the British Empire (1929); C. W. Alvord, Mississippi Valley in British Politics (1917); C. H. Metzger, Quebec Act (1936); A. M. Schlesinger, Colonial Merchants and the American Revolution (1918); T. P. Abernethy, Western Lands and the American Revolution (1937); W. A. Brown, Empire or Independence (1941); C. L. Becker, Declaration of Independence (1942); C. H. Van Tyne, Loyalists in the American Revolution (1929); state studies by C. A. Barker (Maryland, 1940), C. H. Lincoln (Pennsylvania, 1901), E. A. Bailey (Connecticut, 1920).

Diplomacy: A. B. Darling, Our Rising Empire (1940); S. F. Bemis, Diplomacy of the American Revolution (1935); A. P. Whitaker, Spanish-American Frontier, 1783–95 (1927) and Mississippi Question, 1795–1803 (1934); J. W. Pratt, Expansionists of 1812 (1936); A. L. Burt, United States, Great Britain and British North America (1940); L. M. Sears, Jefferson and the Embargo (1927).

Nationalism: Merle Curti, Roots of American Loyalty (1946); J. F. Rippy and Angie Debo, Historical Background of the American Policy of Isolation (1924); E. F. Humphrey, Nationalism and Religion in America, 1774–1789 (1924).

Military history: F. V. Greene, Revolutionary War (1911); C. K. Bolton, Private Soldier Under Washington (1902); L. C. Hatch, Administration of the American Revolutionary Army (1904); C. O. Paullin, Navy of the American Revolution (1906); Bernhard Knollenberg, Washington and the Revolution (1940); J. W. Fortescue, History of the British Army (13 vols., 1899–1930); C. P. Lucas, Canadian War of 1812 (1906); A. T. Mahan, Sea Power in the War of 1812 (1905).

For political struggles: C. A. Beard, Economic Interpretation of the Constitution (1913) and Economic Origins of Jeffersonian Democracy (1927); E. C. Burnett, Continental Congress (1941); M. M. Jensen, Articles of Confederation (1940); Max Farrand, Fathers of the Constitution (1921) and Framing of the Constitution (1936); Carl Van Doren, Great Rehearsal (1948); O. G. Libby, Geographical Distribution of the Vote on the Federal Constitution (1894); C. G. Bowers, Jefferson and Hamilton (1925) and Jefferson in Power (1936); J. C. Miller, Crisis in Freedom (1951); D. R. Fox, Decline of Aristocracy in the Politics of New York (1919); E. S. Corwin, John Marshall and the Constitution (1921); W. A. Robinson, Jeffersonian Democracy in New England (1916); H. C. Hockett, Western Influence on Political Parties to 1825 (1917).

Biographies: J. J. Astor (K. W. Porter, 1931), Robert Morris (E. P. Oberholtzer, 1903), John Stevens (A. D. Turnbull, 1928), Dr. Benjamin Rush (Nathan Goodman, 1934), John and William Bartram (Ernest Earnest, 1940), Bishop Carroll (Peter Guilday, 1922), Bishop Asbury (Herbert Asbury, 1927), Philip Freneau (S. E. Forman, 1902), Joseph Dennie (H. M. Ellis, 1915), William Dunlap (O. S. Coad, 1917), H. H. Brackenridge (C. M. Newlin, 1932), Daniel Boone (R. G. Thwaites, 1903), George Rogers Clark (J. A. James, 1928), William Henry Harrison (Freeman Cleaves, 1939), Anthony Wayne (T. A. Boyd, 1929), James Wilkinson (J. R. Jacobs, 1938), John Paul Jones (Mrs. Reginald De Koven, 1913), John Adams (Gilbert Chinard, 1933), Samuel Adams (R. V. Harlow, 1923; J. C. Miller, 1936), Ethan Allen (John Pell, 1929), Ira Allen (J. B. Wilbur, 1928), Aaron Burr (S. H. Wandell and Meade Minnigerode, 1927), John Hancock (H. S. Allen, 1948), John Jay (Frank Monaghan, 1935), Alexander Hamilton (Nathan Schachner, 1946), James Madison (Irving Brant, 1941–   ), John Randolph (W. C. Bruce, 1939), Thomas Jefferson (Gilbert Chinard, 1939; Dumas Malone, 1948–   ; Marie Kimball, 1943–   ), George Washington (J. C. Fitzpatrick, 1933; D. S. Freeman, 1948–   ), Adams family (J. T. Adams, 1930), Lee family (B. J. Hendrick, 1935), Lowell family (Ferris Greenslet, 1946).

Part III (1815–1850)

For the period as a whole, see F. J. Turner, Rise of the New West, 1819–1829 (1906), and his United States, 1830–50 (1935).

Economic history: W. B. Smith and A. H. Cole, *Fluctuations in American Business, 1790–1860* (1935); R. C. McGrane, *Panic of 1837* (1924) and *Foreign Bondholders and American State Debts* (1935); D. R. Dewey, *State Banking* (1910); H. E. Miller, *Banking Theories Before 1860* (1927); H. M. Fletcher, *History of Economic Theory, 1820–66* (1928); R. C. H. Catterall, *Second Bank of the United States* (1903); M. G. Myers, *New York Money Market* (1931).

Transportation: U. B. Phillips, *History of Transportation in the Eastern Cotton Belt to 1860* (1908); E. C. Kirkland, *Men, Cities and Transportation* (New England, 1948); L. H. Haney, *Congressional History of Railways to 1850* (1910); A. F. Harlow, *Old Towpaths* (1926); W. S. Sanderlin, *Great National Project* (1947); L. D. Baldwin, *Keelboat Age* (1941); G. M. Capers, *Memphis* (1939); W. J. Petersen, *Steamboating on the Upper Mississippi* (1937); R. G. Albion, *Rise of New York Port* (1939) and *Square Riggers on Schedule* (1938); A. H. Clark, *Clipper Ship Era* (1910).

Business history: A. H. Cole, *American Wool Manufacture* (1926); C. F. Ware, *Early New England Cotton Manufacture* (1931); Kathleen Bruce, *Virginia Iron Manufacture in the Slave Era* (1930); N. J. Ware, *Industrial Worker, 1840–60* (1924); Edith Abbott, *Women in Industry* (1910); Hannah Josephson, *Golden Threads* (1949).

Agriculture: W. C. Neely, *Agricultural Fair* (1935); A. L. Demaree, *American Agricultural Press, 1819–60* (1941); Leo Rogin, *Introduction of Farm Machinery* (1931); D. M. Ellis, *Landlords and Farmers* (Hudson-Mohawk, 1946); J. P. Pritchett, *Red River Valley, 1811–49* (1942).

Westward movement: R. G. Wellington, *Political and Sectional Influence of Public Lands, 1828–42* (1914); L. E. Atherton, *Pioneer Merchant* (1939); Everett Dick, *Vanguards of Frontier* (1941); C. L. Goodwin, *Trans-Mississippi West, 1803–53* (1922); H. M. Chittenden, *American Fur Trade of the Far West* (1936); Katharine Coman, *Economic Beginnings of the Far West* (1925); L. H. Creer, *Founding of an Empire* (1947); Grant Foreman, *Indian Removal* (1932); R. C. Buley, *Old Northwest, 1815–40* (1950).

The South: C. S. Sydnor, *Development of Southern Sectionalism, 1819–48* (1948); W. E. Dodd, *Cotton Kingdom* (1921); R. S. Cotterill, *Old South* (1939); F. P. Gaines, *Southern Plantation* (1924); studies of slavery in Georgia (R. B. Flanders, 1933), Mississippi (C. S. Sydnor, 1933), Louisiana (V. A. Moody, 1924), Missouri (H. A. Trexler, 1914), North Carolina (R. H. Taylor, 1920); J. C. Robert, *Tobacco Kingdom* (1938); Herbert Weaver, *Mississippi Farmers* (1945); U. B. Phillips, *American Negro Slavery* (1918) and *Life and Labor in the Old South* (1929); Frederic Bancroft, *Slave Trading in the Old South* (1931).

Reforms: A. F. Tyler, *Freedom's Ferment* (1944); Merle Curti, *Learned Blacksmith* (1937) and *American Peace Crusade* (1929); W. F. Galpin, *Crusading for Peace* (1933); K. H. Porter, *History of Suffrage* (1918); E. C. Stanton and others, *History of Woman Suffrage* (1889–1922); J. A. Krout, *Origins of Prohibition* (1925).

Abolitionists: A. D. Adams, *Neglected Period of Antislavery, 1808–31* (1908); G. H. Barnes, *Antislavery Impulse* (1933); Jesse Macy, *Antislavery Crusade* (1921); D. L. Dumond and G. H. Barnes (eds.), *Weld-Grimké Let-*

ters (1934); E. L. Fox, *American Colonization Society* (1919); W. H. Siebert, *Underground Railroad* (1898); R. B. Nye, *Fettered Freedom* (1949).

Transcendentalism is treated by O. B. Frothingham (1903) and H. C. Goddard (1908); Arthur Christy, *Orient in American Transcendentalism* (1932); R. V. Wells, *Three Christian Transcendentalists* (1943). See also A. A. Ekirch, *Idea of Progress in America, 1815–60* (1944); F. O. Matthiessen, *American Renaissance* (1941); George Boas, *Romanticism in America* (1940); Van Wyck Brooks, *Flowering of New England, 1815–65* (1936); Clement Eaton, *Freedom of Thought in the Old South* (1940).

Religion: C. B. Goodykoontz, *Home Missions on the American Frontier* (1939); Albert Post, *Popular Freethought, 1825–50* (1943); R. A. Billington, *Protestant Crusade* (1938); J. N. Norwood, *Schism in the Methodist Episcopal Church* (1923).

Education: Paul Monroe, *Founding of the American Public School System* (1940); D. G. Tewksbury, *Founding of American Colleges* (1932); B. A. Hinsdale, *Horace Mann and the Common School Revival* (1898); E. W. Knight, *Public Education in the South* (1922); S. L. Jackson, *American Struggle for Free Schools* (1941); C. G. Woodson, *Education of the Negro Prior to 1861* (1915).

Science and invention: Holland Thompson, *Age of Invention* (1921); R. S. Burlingame, *March of the Iron Men* (1938); E. W. Byrn, *Progress of Invention in the Nineteenth Century* (1900); George Iles, *Leading American Inventors* (1912); R. H. Shryock, *American Medical Research* (1947); D. J. Struik, *Yankee Science in the Making* (1948); P. C. Ricketts, *History of Rensselaer Polytechnic Institute* (1934); T. C. Johnson, *Scientific Interests in the Old South* (1936); R. H. Shryock (ed.), *Letters of Richard D. Arnold, M.D.* (1929); J. S. Chambers, *Conquest of Cholera* (1938); H. B. Shafer, *American Medical Profession, 1783–1850* (1936).

C. R. Fish, *Rise of the Common Man* (1937) is social history; and see G. W. Pierson, *Tocqueville and Beaumont in America* (1938); Carl Wittke, *Tambo and Bones* (1930); Jennie Holliman, *American Sports, 1785–1935* (1931); N. I. White, *American Negro Folk Songs* (1928); Samuel Isham and Royal Cortissoz, *History of American Painting* (1936).

Political history: George Dangerfield, *Era of Good Feelings* (1952); A. M. Schlesinger, Jr., *Age of Jackson* (1945); William McDonald, *Jacksonian Democracy* (1906); C. G. Bowers, *Party Battles of the Jackson Period* (1928); F. C. Shoemaker, *Missouri's Struggle for Statehood* (1916); C. S. Boucher, *Nullification Controversy* (1916); O. D. Lambert, *Presidential Politics 1841–44* (1936); A. C. Cole, *Whig Party in the South* (1913); G. R. Poage, *Henry Clay and the Whig Party* (1936).

Foreign relations: A. K. Weinberg, *Manifest Destiny* (1935); A. P. Whitaker, *United States and the Independence of Latin America* (1941); Dexter Perkins, *Hands Off* (1941); E. C. Barker, *Mexico and Texas, 1821–35* (1928); J. H. Smith, *Annexation of Texas* (1941) and *War with Mexico* (1919); Tyler Dennett, *Americans in Eastern Asia* (1922); F. R. Dulles, *Old China Trade* (1930); W. O. Scroggs, *Filibusters and Financiers* (1916); M. W. Williams, *Anglo-American Isthmian Diplomacy* (1916); Merle Curti, *Austria and the United States, 1848–52* (1926).

Biographies: R. W. Emerson (R. L. Rusk, 1949), Nathaniel Hawthorne (Robert Cantwell, 1948), A. B. Longstreet (J. D. Wade, 1924), James Fennimore Cooper (R. E. Spiller, 1931), Robert Dale Owen (R. W. Leopold, 1940), Lucretia Mott (L. C. M. Hare, 1937), Frances Wright (W. R. Waterman, 1924), Dorothea Dix (H. E. Marshall, 1937), William Lloyd Garrison (W. P. and F. J. Garrison, 1894), Gerrit Smith (R. V. Harlow, 1939), J. G. Birney (William Birney, 1890), Orestes Brownson (A. M. Schlesinger, Jr., 1939), Theodore Parker (H. S. Commager, 1936), Joseph Smith (F. M. Brodie, 1945), Cyrus McCormick (W. T. Hutchinson, 1930–35), S. F. B. Morse (Carleton Mabee, 1943), John Murray Forbes (H. G. Pearson, 1911), Charles Goodyear (P. W. Barker, 1940), Winfield Scott (C. W. Elliott, 1937), William Henry Harrison (J. A. Green, 1941), Zachary Taylor (Brainerd Dyer, 1946), Henry Clay (G. G. Van Deusen, 1937; Bernard Mayo, 1937–), Andrew Jackson (Marquis James, 1938; J. S. Bassett, 1931), Daniel Webster (C. M. Fuess, 1930), J. C. Calhoun (M. L. Coit, 1950; C. M. Wiltse, 1944–51), John Tyler (O. P. Chitwood, 1939), Martin Van Buren (H. P. Alexander, 1935), James K. Polk (E. I. McCormac, 1922), Sam Houston (Marquis James, 1935), Stephen F. Austin (E. C. Barker, 1910).

Part IV (1850–1877)

This era is covered by J. F. Rhodes, *History of the United States* (9 vols., 1893–1922), and a new multi-volume work by Allan Nevins (1944–). J. G. Randall, *Civil War and Reconstruction* (1937), is the best survey. For social history, see A. C. Cole, *Irrepressible Conflict, 1850–65* (1938), and Allan Nevins, *Emergence of Modern America, 1865–78* (1935). For secession, R. F. Nichols, *Disruption of American Democracy* (1948); K. M. Stampp, *And the War Came* (1950); A. O. Craven, *Coming of Civil War* (1942); U. B. Phillips, *Course of the South to Secession* (1939); G. F. Milton, *Eve of Conflict* (1934); R. R. Russel, *Economic Aspects of Southern Sectionalism* (1924); J. G. Van Deusen, *Economic Bases of Disunion in South Carolina* (1928); R. H. Shryock, *Georgia and the Union in 1850* (1926); H. H. Simms, *Decade of Sectional Controversy* (1942); M. J. White, *Secession Movement in 1847–52* (1916); J. T. Carpenter, *South as a Conscious Minority* (1930); Ollinger Crenshaw, *Slave States in the Election of 1860* (1945); R. H. Luthin, *First Lincoln Campaign* (1944); D. L. Dumond, *Secession Movement, 1860–61* (1931); W. E. Baringer, *A House Dividing* (1945); D. M. Potter, *Lincoln and His Party in the Secession Crisis* (1942).

Civil War military history is outlined by J. C. Ropes (1894) and J. F. Rhodes (1917); and see J. P. Baxter, 3d, *Introduction of the Ironclad Warship* (1933); B. I. Wiley, *Johnny Reb* (1943); Ella Lonn, *Desertion in the Civil War* (1928); D. S. Freeman, *Lee's Lieutenants* (3 vols., 1942–44); F. A. Shannon, *Organization and Administration of the Union Army* (1928); W. B. Hesseltine, *Civil War Prisons* (1930). Diplomacy is covered by F. L. Owsley, *King Cotton Diplomacy* (1931); E. D. Adams, *Great Britain and the American Civil War* (1925); Donaldson Jordan and E. J. Pratt, *Europe and the American Civil War* (1931).

The South: C. H. Wesley, *Collapse of Confederacy* (1937); F. L. Owsley,

States Rights in the Confederacy (1925); G. L. Tatum, *Disloyalty in the Confederacy* (1934); A. B. Moore, *Conscription and Conflict in the Confederacy* (1924); F. B. Simkins and J. W. Patton, *Women of the Confederacy* (1936); B. I. Wiley, *Southern Negroes, 1861–65* (1938).

The North: E. D. Fite, *Social and Industrial Conditions in the North During the Civil War* (1910); W. B. Hesseltine, *Lincoln and the War Governors* (1948); T. H. Williams, *Lincoln and the Radicals* (1941); J. G. Randall, *Constitutional Problems Under Lincoln* (1926); H. J. Carman and R. H. Luthin, *Lincoln and the Patronage* (1943); A. M. Davis, *Origin of the National Banking System* (1910); E. D. Ross, *Democracy's College* (1942); F. P. Summers, *Baltimore and Ohio During the Civil War* (1939); G. W. Dalzell, *Flight from the Flag* (1940); L. G. Vander Velde, *Presbyterian Churches and the Federal Union* (1932); R. M. Andrews, *Archbishop Hughes and the Civil War* (1934).

Reconstruction: H. K. Beale, *Critical Year* (1930); E. M. Coulter, *South During Reconstruction* (1947); C. G. Bowers, *Tragic Era* (1929); G. F. Milton, *Age of Hate* (1930); W. A. Dunning, *Reconstruction* (1907); W. E. B. DuBois, *Black Reconstruction* (1935). State monographs include W. L. Fleming (Alabama, 1905), T. S. Staples (Arkansas, 1923), W. W. Davis (Florida, 1913), C. M. Thompson (Georgia, 1915), W. M. Caskey (Louisiana, 1938), Ella Lonn (Louisiana, 1918), J. W. Garner (Mississippi, 1901), J. G. deR. Hamilton (North Carolina, 1906), R. H. Woody and F. B. Simkins (South Carolina, 1932), J. W. Patton (Tennessee, 1934), C. W. Ramsdell (Texas, 1910), H. J. Eckenrode (Virginia, 1904). See also R. W. Shugg, *Origins of Class Struggle in Louisiana* (1939); P. S. Peirce, *Freedman's Bureau* (1904); E. W. Knight, *Influence of Reconstruction on Education in the South* (1913); H. L. Swint, *Northern Teacher in the South, 1862–70* (1941); H. M. Bond, *Negro Education in Alabama* (1939); V. L. Wharton, *Negro in Mississippi, 1865–90* (1947); A. A. Taylor, *Negro in Tennessee, 1865–80* (1941); S. F. Horn, *Invisible Empire: Ku Klux Klan* (1939). For the North, see E. D. Ross, *Liberal Republican Movement* (1919); P. H. Buck, *Road to Reunion* (1937); C. V. Woodward, *Reunion and Reaction* (1951); Matthew Josephson, *Politicos, 1865–96* (1938).

Western expansion: J. W. Caughey, *Gold Rush* (1948); H. C. Hubbart, *Older Middle West, 1840–80* (1936); W. P. Webb, *Great Plains* (1931); A. F. Harlow, *Old Waybills* (1934); L. R. Hafen, *Overland Mail* (1926); Louis Pelzer, *Cattleman's Frontier* (1936); R. E. Riegel, *Story of Western Railroads* (1927); W. W. Belcher, *Economic Rivalry Between St. Louis and Chicago* (1947).

Biographies: R. E. Lee (D. S. Freeman, 4 vols., 1934–35), Stonewall Jackson (G. F. R. Henderson, 1900), W. T. Sherman (Lloyd Lewis, 1932), G. B. McClellan (W. S. Myers, 1934), D. G. Farragut (C. L. Lewis, 1943), Jefferson Davis (H. J. Eckenrode, 1923), Andrew Johnson (L. P. Stryker, 1929; R. W. Winston, 1928), Robert Toombs (U. B. Phillips, 1913), Edmund Ruffin (A. O. Craven, 1932), W. G. Brownlow (E. M. Coulter, 1937), Alexander H. Stephens (R. R. Von Abele, 1946), John Slidell (L. M. Sears, 1925), John Brown (O. G. Villard, 1910), Harriet Beecher Stowe (Forrest Wilson, 1941), J. C. Frémont (Allan Nevins, 1939), Thurlow Weed (G. G. Van Deusen, 1947), Carl Schurz (C. M. Fuess, 1932), Francis Lieber (Frank Freidel,

1948), Frederick Douglass (Benjamin Quarles, 1940), Thaddeus Stevens (R. N. Current, 1942), N. P. Banks (F. H. Harrington, 1948), Jay Cooke (H. M. Larson, 1936), U. S. Grant (W. B. Hesseltine, 1935), R. B. Hayes (H. J. Eckenrode, 1930), Boss Tweed (D. T. Lynch, 1927), Abraham Lincoln (A. J. Beveridge, 1928; N. W. Stephenson, 1922; J. G. Randall, 1945–   ).

Part V (1850–1896)

V. S. Clark, *History of Manufactures* (1929), is useful. See also Gustavus Myers, *History of the Great American Fortunes* (1910); Matthew Josephson, *Robber Barons* (1934); I. M. Tarbell, *Nationalizing of Business, 1878–98* (1936); B. J. Hendrick, *Age of Big Business* (1921); John Moody, *Masters of Capital* (1919); A. F. Burns, *Production Trends Since 1870* (1934). Area studies include books by Bayrd Still (Milwaukee, 1948), Charles Hirschfeld (Baltimore, 1870–1900, 1941), C. M. Green (Holyoke, 1939). Industry histories: carpets (A. H. Cole and H. F. Williamson, 1941), cotton textiles (M. T. Copeland, 1912), flour milling (C. B. Kuhlmann, 1929); and see T. C. Cochran, *Pabst Brewing Company* (1948), and H. M. Larson, *Guide to Business History* (1948). Oil has been treated by W. D. Lloyd, *Wealth Against Commonwealth* (1894); I. M. Tarbell, *History of the Standard Oil Company* (1904); P. H. Giddens, *Birth of the Oil Industry* (1938); C. C. Rister, *Oil! Titan of the Southwest* (1949). For trade and transportation, see E. R. Johnson, *History of the Domestic and Foreign Commerce of the United States* (1915); John Moody, *Railroad Builders* (1919); C. R. Fish, *Restoration of the Southern Railroads* (1919); J. B. Hedges, *Henry Villard and the Railways of the Northwest* (1930); P. W. Gates, *Illinois Central Railroad and Its Colonization Work* (1934). Frank Presbrey has written a history of advertising (1929); and see insurance company histories by S. B. Clough (1946) and Marquis James (1942). Cf. R. M. Hower's book on Macy's (1946) with T. D. Clark, *Pills, Petticoats and Plows* (1944, southern country store).

Finance: A. B. Hepburn, *History of the Coinage and Currency* (1903); R. W. Hidy, *House of Baring in American Trade and Finance* (1949); F. C. James, *Growth of Chicago Banks* (1938); R. A. Foulke, *Sinews of American Commerce* (1941); M. S. Wildman, *Money Inflation* (1905); D. C. Barrett, *Greenbacks and the Resumption of Specie Payments* (1931); F. P. Weberg, *Background of the Panic of 1893* (1929).

Labor: N. J. Ware, *Labor Movement in the United States, 1860–95* (1929); L. L. Lorwin, *American Federation of Labor* (1933); Samuel Yellen, *American Labor Struggles* (1936); Edward Berman, *Labor Disputes and the President* (1924); books on Molly Maguire riots (J. W. Coleman, 1936), Southwest railway strike of 1886 (R. A. Allen, 1942), Haymarket affair (Henry David, 1936), Pullman strike (Almont Lindsey, 1942), Coxey's march (D. L. McMurry, 1929).

Agriculture: F. A. Shannon, *Farmer's Last Frontier* (1945); A. C. True's books on agricultural research (1937), education (1929), extension work (1928); E. G. Nourse, *American Agriculture and the European Market* (1924); J. C. Malin, *Grassland of North America* (1947) and *Winter Wheat in the Golden Belt of Kansas* (1944); John Ise, *Sod and Stubble* (1938); J. G.

Thompson, *Rise and Decline of the Wheat Growing Industry in Wisconsin* (1909); H. M. Larson, *Wheat Market and the Farmer in Minnesota, 1858–1900* (1926); R. P. Brooks, *Agrarian Revolution in Georgia, 1865–1912* (1914); Meyer Jacobstein, *Tobacco Industry* (1907); R. B. Vance, *Human Factors in Cotton Culture* (1929); A. F. Raper and I. D. Reid, *Sharecroppers All* (1941).

The New South: Holland Thompson, *New South* (1921); P. A. Bruce, *Rise of the New South* (1905); Broadus Mitchell, *Rise of the Cotton Mills in the South* (1921) and *Industrial Revolution in the South* (with G. S. Mitchell, 1930); C. V. Woodward, *Origins of the New South* (1951).

The West: J. C. Parish, *Persistence of the Westward Movement* (1943); E. S. Pomeroy, *Territories and the United States, 1861–90* (1947); H. E. Briggs, *Frontiers of the Northwest* (1940); G. S. Dumke, *Boom of the Eighties in Southern California* (1944); E. N. Dick, *Sod-House Frontier* (1937). State studies: Oklahoma (E. E. Dale and M. L. Wardell, 1948), Nevada (E. M. Mack, 1936), Montana (J. K. Howard, 1944), Colorado (P. S. Fritz, 1941), California (J. W. Caughey, 1940). For land, see H. O. Brayer's work on Blackmore (1949); A. N. Chandler, *Land Title Origins* (1945); Reuben McKitrick, *Public Land System of Texas* (1918); P. W. Gates, *Wisconsin Pine Lands of Cornell University* (1943). For mining, T. A. Rickard, *History of American Mining* (1932); W. J. Trimble, *Mining Advance* (1914); Oscar Lewis, *Silver Kings* (1947). For law enforcement, Wayne Gard, *Frontier Justice* (1949); W. P. Webb, *Texas Rangers* (1935); F. H. Harrington, *Hanging Judge* (1951). For Indians, Southwest (E. E. Dale, 1949), Cheyenne (G. B. Grinnell, 1923), Apache (R. H. Ogle, 1940), Five Civilized Tribes (M. L. Wardell, 1938; Angie Debo, 1934; Grant Foreman, 1934). For grazing, E. S. Osgood, *Day of the Cattleman* (1929); O. B. Peake, *Colorado Range Cattle Industry* (1937); R. A. Clemen, *American Livestock and Meat Industry* (1923).

Intellectual trends: Richard Hofstadter, *Social Darwinism in American Thought* (1944); P. P. Wiener, *Evolution and the Founders of Pragmatism* (1949); H. W. Schneider, *History of American Philosophy* (1946); books on thought of William James (R. B. Berry, 1935), John Dewey (Sidney Hook, 1939; W. T. Feldman, 1934), Henry George (G. R. Geiger, 1933).

Social history: A. M. Schlesinger, *Rise of the City, 1878–98* (1927); R. O. Cummings, *American and His Food* (1941); Lloyd Lewis and H. J. Smith, *Oscar Wilde Discovers America* (1936).

Religion: F. X. Curran, *Major Trends in American Church History* (1941); W. E. Garrison, *March of Faith* (1933); A. I. Abell, *Urban Impact on American Protestantism, 1865–1900* (1943); C. H. Hopkins, *Rise of the Social Gospel, 1865–1915* (1940); Sidney Warren, *American Freethought, 1860–1914* (1943); H. J. May, *Protestant Churches and Industrial America* (1949); Stow Persons, *Free Religion* (1947); James Dombrowski, *Early Days of Christian Socialism in America* (1936); D. D. Williams, *Andover Liberals* (1941); Gustavus Myers, *History of Bigotry in the United States* (1943); T. H. A. LeDuc, *Pietry and Intellect at Amherst College* (1946).

A few important university histories: Wisconsin (Merle Curti and V. L. Carstensen, 1949), Pennsylvania (E. P. Cheyney, 1940), Johns Hopkins (J. C.

French, 1946), Mt. Holyoke (A. C. Cole, 1940), Catholic University (J. T. Ellis, 1946), C.C.N.Y. (S. W. Rudy, 1949), Iowa State (E. D. Ross, 1942), College of Charleston (J. H. Easterby, 1935), Duke (N. C. Chaffin, 1950), Vanderbilt (Edwin Mims, 1946), Dartmouth (L. B. Richardson, 1932), Wilberforce (F. D. McGinnis, 1941).

Literature: Oscar Cargill, *Intellectual America* (1941); W. F. Taylor, *Economic Novel* (1942); Van Wyck Brooks, *New England: Indian Summer* (1940).

Fine arts: David Ewen, *Music Comes to America* (1942); Sigmund Spaeth, *History of Popular Music in America* (1948). There are many books on painting (e.g., C. H. Caffin, 1907), sculpture (L. H. Dodd, 1936), architecture (T. F. Hamlin, 1926), music (L. C. Elson, 1904).

Invention: Roger Burlingame, *Engines of Democracy* (1940); W. B. Bennett, *American Patent System* (1943); H. N. Casson, *History of the Telephone* (1910); T. C. Martin and S. L. Coles, *Story of Electricity* (1919–22); Malcolm McLaren, *Rise of the Electrical Industry* (1943). Science: E. S. Dana, *Century of Science* (1918); J. G. Crowther, *Famous American Men of Science* (1937); Paul DeKruif, *Microbe Hunters* (1926); J. W. Fay, *American Psychology Before William James* (1939); histories of chemistry (E. F. Smith, 1914), entomology (H. B. Weiss, 1936), geology (G. P. Merrill, 1924).

Medicine: M. P. Ravenel, *Half-Century of Public Health* (1921); R. D. Leigh, *Federal Health Administration* (1927); G. C. Whipple, *State Sanitation* (1917); Albert Deutsch, *Mentally Ill in America* (1941).

For special immigrant groups: Scandinavians (K. C. Babcock, 1914), Swedes (A. B. Benson and Naboth Hedin, 1938), Norwegians (C. C. Qualey, 1938; T. C. Blegen, 1940), Irish (E. F. Roberts, 1931), Germans (A. B. Faust, 1927), Chinese (M. R. Coolidge, 1909), Poles (W. I. Thomas and Florian Znaniecki, 1930), Russians (Jerome Davis, 1922), Jews (Samuel Joseph, 1914; B. J. Hendrick, 1923; Peter Wiernik, 1912), Hungarians (Emil Lengyel, 1948), Ukrainians (Wasyl Halich, 1937), Italians (R. F. Foerster, 1919); and M. L. Hansen and J. B. Brebner, *Mingling of Canadian and American Peoples* (1940). On the Negro: B. G. Brawley, *Social History of the American Negro* (1921); W. F. Nowlin, *Negro in American National Politics* (1931).

Political history: E. P. Oberholtzer, *History of the United States* (5 vols., 1917–37); W. E. Binkley, *President and Congress* (1947); F. E. Haynes, *Third Party Movements* (1916); C. M. Destler, *American Radicalism, 1865–1901* (1946); E. B. Usher, *Greenback Movement* (1911); S. J. Buck, *Granger Movement* (1913); J. D. Hicks, *Populist Revolt* (1931); books on Tammany (Gustavus Myers, 1917; M. R. Werner, 1928), 1884 (H. C. Thomas, 1919), 1892 (G. H. Knoles, 1942), veterans (J. W. Oliver, 1917; Dixon Wecter, 1944).

Constitutional history: E. S. Corwin, *Court over Constitution* (1938) and *Twilight of the Supreme Court* (1934); C. O. Gregory, *Labor and the Law* (1946); B. F. Wright, *Growth of American Constitutional Law* (1942).

Biographies: J. D. Rockefeller (Allan Nevins, 1940; J. K. Winkler, 1929), Andrew Carnegie (B. J. Hendrick, 1932; J. K. Winkler, 1931), J. B. Duke (J. W. Jenkins, 1927; J. K. Winkler, 1942), Henry Clay Frick (G. B. M. Harvey, 1928), Abram Hewitt (Allan Nevins, 1935), the Merritts (Paul DeKruif,

1929), the Guggenheims (Harvey O'Connor, 1937), Cornelius Vanderbilt (W. J. Lane, 1942), Daniel Drew (Bouck White, 1910), Jim Fisk (R. H. Fuller, 1928), D. C. Gilman (Fabian Franklin, 1910), Mark Twain (A. B. Paine, 1912; Bernard DeVoto, 1932), William Dean Howells (O. W. Firkins, 1924), Walt Whitman (H. S. Canby, 1932), Edward Bellamy (A. E. Morgan, 1944), Horatio Alger (H. R. Mayes, 1928), Dwight Moody (Gamaliel Bradford, 1928), Mary Baker G. Eddy (L. P. Powell, 1930; E. S. Bates and J. V. Dittemore, 1930), Walter Rauschenbusch (D. R. Sharpe, 1942), Lester F. Ward (Samuel Chuggerman, 1939), William Graham Sumner (H. E. Starr, 1925), Thorstein Veblen (Joseph Dorfman, 1934), T. A. Edison (F. L. Dyer and T. C. Martin, 1929), George Westinghouse (H. G. Prout, 1921), Willard Gibbs (Muriel Rukeyser, 1942), William H. Welch (Simon and J. T. Flexner, 1931), J. M. Whistler (E. R. and Joseph Pennell, 1909), Thomas Eakins (Lloyd Goodrich, 1933), George Inness (Elizabeth McCausland, 1946), Augustus St. Gaudens (Royal Cortissoz, 1907), Theodore Thomas (C. E. Russell, 1927), H. H. Richardson (H. R. Hitchcock, 1927), Louis Sullivan (Hugh Morrison, 1935), James A. Garfield (R. G. Caldwell, 1936), Chester A. Arthur (G. F. Howe, 1934), Grover Cleveland (Allan Nevins, 1932), William McKinley (C. S. Olcott, 1916), J. G. Blaine (D. S. Muzzey, 1934), Czar Reed (W. A. Robinson, 1930), J. G. Carlisle (J. A. Barnes, 1931), Philetus Sawyer (R. N. Current, 1950), L. Q. C. Lamar (W. A. Cate, 1935), Henry M. Teller (Elmer Ellis, 1941), B. H. Hill (H. J. Pearce, 1928), Mark Hanna (Thomas Beer, 1929), W. J. Bryan (Paxton Hibben, 1929), James B. Weaver (F. E. Haynes, 1919), J. P. Altgeld (Harry Barnard, 1938), Tom Watson (C. V. Woodward, 1938), L. L. Polk (Stuart Noblin, 1949), Ben Tillman (F. B Simkins, 1944), Frances Willard (Mary Earhart, 1944), Elizabeth Cady Stanton (Alma Lutz, 1940), Henry Demarest Lloyd (Caro Lloyd, 1912), Frank Munsey (George Britt, 1935), Henry W. Grady (R. B. Nixon, 1943), Justice Field (C. B. Swisher, 1930), Chief Justice Waite (B. R. Trimble, 1939).

Part VI (1896–1919)

Twentieth-century American history is treated in books by O. T. Barck and N. M. Blake (1947), F. R. Dulles (1945), Harvey Wish (1945), D. L. Dumond (1945), Jeannette and R. F. Nichols (1939), H. B. Parkes (1943).

Roger Burlingame, *Backgrounds of Power* (1943), is on mass production; and see Harry Jerome, *Mechanization in Industry* (1934); R. C. Epstein, *Automobile Industry* (1928); J. W. Hammond, *Men and Volts* (1941). For bankers, see G. W. Edwards, *Evolution of Finance Capitalism* (1938); F. L. Allen, *Lords of Creation* (1935); Lewis Corey, *House of Morgan* (1930). On trusts, John Moody, *Truth About Trusts* (1904); H. W. Laidler, *Concentration of Control in American Industry* (1931); A. A. Berle and G. C. Means, *Modern Corporation* (1932); J. D. Clark, *Federal Trust Policy* (1931). On labor, M. R. Carroll, *Labor and Politics* (1923); L. S. Reed, *Labor Philosophy of Samuel Gompers* (1930); Edward Berman, *Labor and the Sherman Act* (1930); Felix Frankfurter and Nathan Greene, *Labor Injunctions* (1930); D. J. Saposs, *Left Wing Unionism* (1926); E. E. Witte, *Government in Labor Disputes* (1937). See also R. L. Garis, *Immigration Restriction* (1927).

For the life of the people, see H. U. Faulkner, *Quest for Social Justice, 1898–1914* (1937); Mark Sullivan, *Our Times* (1928–35); D. L. Cohn, *Good Old Days* (1940); Roger Butterfield, *American Past* (pictures, 1947). For the city, J. G. Thompson, *Urbanization* (1927); Lewis Mumford, *Culture of Cities* (1938); W. G. Ogburn, *Social Characteristics of Cities* (1937); compare J. W. Williams, *Our Rural Heritage* (1925).

Alfred Kazin, *On Native Grounds* (1942), and Lloyd Morris, *Postscript to Yesterday* (1947), are based on literary materials. For religion, read G. B. Smith (ed.), *Religious Thought* (1927); S. G. Cole, *History of Fundamentalism* (1931); F. H. Foster, *Modern Movement in American Theology* (1939); Maynard Shipley, *War on Modern Science* (1927). For education, A. E. Meyer, *Development of Education in the Twentieth Century* (1939); J. E. Russell, *Trend in American Education* (1922). For research interests, G. A. Weber's studies of Department of Agriculture bureaus; Paul DeKruif, *Hunger Fighters* (1928); C. M. Wilson, *Ambassadors in White* (1942); J. K. Hall and others, *One Hundred Years of American Psychiatry* (1944); C. E. A. Winslow, *Evolution and Significance of the Modern Public Health Campaign* (1935).

The progressive movement: John Chamberlain, *Farewell to Reform* (1932); Louis Filler, *Crusaders for American Liberalism* (1939); Matthew Josephson, *President Makers, 1896–1919* (1940); C. C. Regier, *Era of Muckrakers* (1932); G. E. Mowry, *Theodore Roosevelt and the Progressive Movement* (1946); K. W. Hechler, *Insurgency* (1940); R. B. Nye, *Midwestern Progressive Politics* (1951); William Diamond, *Economic Thought of Woodrow Wilson* (1943); Harold Zink, *City Bosses* (1930); C. W. Patton, *Battle for Municipal Reform* (1940).

State studies: Vermont (W. A. Flint, 1941), New Jersey (R. E. Noble, Jr., 1946), Oregon (A. H. Eaton, 1912), Wisconsin (Charles McCarthy, 1912; A. F. Lovejoy, 1941).

Issues: woman suffrage (C. C. Catt, 1926); initiative, referendum, recall (W. B. Munro, 1916); food and drug regulation (Stephen Wilson, 1942); conservation (A. E. Parkins and J. R. Whitaker, 1936; C. J. Hynning, 1939; also A. T. Mason, *Beauraucracy Convicts Itself* (1941). T. C. Blaisdell, Jr., has treated the Federal Trade Commission (1932); E. W. Kemmerer the Federal Reserve System (1950); A. F. Macdonald federal aid (1928); W. S. Holt the farm loan system (1924) and federal roads (1923).

Constitutional history: B. H. Meyer, *History of the Northern Securities Case* (1906); R. G. Fuller, *Child Labor and the Constitution* (1923); R. E. Cushman, *Independent Regulatory Commissions* (1941).

Diplomacy: J. W. Pratt, *Expansionists of 1898* (1935); A. F. Tyler, *Foreign Policy of Blaine* (1927); Scott Nearing and Joseph Freeman, *Dollar Diplomacy* (1925); Walter Millis, *Martial Spirit* (1931); J. E. Wisan, *Cuban Crisis as Reflected in the New York Press* (1934); W. S. Holt, *Treaties Defeated by the Senate* (1933); G. L. Kirk, *Philippine Independence* (1936); A. W. Griswold, *Far Eastern Policy of the United States* (1938); S. K. Stevens, *American Expansion in Hawaii* (1945); F. H. Harrington, *God, Mammon and the Japanese* (Korea, 1944); F. R. Dulles, *China and America* (1946); E. H. Zabriskie, *American-Russian Rivalry in the Far East, 1895–1914* (1946); S. F. Bemis,

Latin American Policy of the United States (1943); H. C. Hill, Roosevelt and the Caribbean (1927); D. C. Miner, Fight for the Panama Route (1940); L. M. Gelber, Rise of Anglo-American Friendship (1938); R. H. Heindel, American Impact on Great Britain, 1898–1914 (1940); W. E. Livezey, Mahan on Sea Power (1947); D. W. Mitchell, History of the Modern American Navy (1946); Merle Curti, Bryan and World Peace (1931).

Entry into World War I: Harley Notter, Origins of the Foreign Policy of Woodrow Wilson (1937); Charles Seymour, American Neutrality (1935); N. D. Baker, Why We Went to War (1936); Dexter Perkins, America and Two Wars (1944); C. H. Grattan, Why We Fought (1929); Walter Millis, Road to War (1935); C. C. Tansill, America Goes to War (1938); H. C. Peterson, Propaganda for War (1939). Participation in war: F. L. Paxson, American Democracy and the World War (3 vols., 1936–48); T. G. Frothingham, American Reinforcement (1927); J. G. Harbord (on army, 1936), W. S. Sims and B. J. Hendrick (on navy, 1920), Johnson Hagood (supply, 1927), W. D. Hines (railroads, 1928), W. C. Mullendore (food, 1941), L. P. Todd (education, 1945). Important are B. M. Baruch, American Industry in the War (1941); J. R. Mock and Cedric Larson, Words That Won the War (1939); J. R. Mock, Censorship, 1917 (1941); Zechariah Chafee, Free Speech in the United States (1941). For peace settlement, see D. F. Fleming, United States and the League of Nations (1932); T. A. Bailey, Wilson and the Peacemakers (1947).

Biographies: E. H. Harriman (George Kennan, 1922), J. J. Hill (J. G. Pyle, 1917), Elbert Gary (I. M. Tarbell, 1926), A. I. DuPont (Marquis James, 1941), J. P. Morgan (H. L. Satterlee, 1939; F. L. Allen, 1949), Frederick Taylor (F. B. Copley, 1923), John Mitchell (Elsie Gluck, 1929), Samuel Gompers (R. H. Harvey, 1935), Jane Addams (J. W. Linn, 1935), Seaman Knapp (J. C. Bailey, 1945), G. W. Goethals (J. B. and F. Bishop, 1930), George Washington Carver (Rackham Holt, 1943), Doctors Mayo (H. B. Clapsattle, 1941), Harvey C. Cushing (J. F. Fulton, 1946), Walter Reed (L. N. Wood, 1943), W. C. Gorgas (M. D. Gorgas and B. J. Hendrick, 1924), Booker T. Washington (B. J. Mathews, 1948), A. Lawrence Lowell (H. A. Youmans, 1948), Theodore Dreiser (R. H. Elias, 1948), Edith Wharton (Percy Lubbock, 1947), Frank Norris (Franklin Walker, 1932), Jack London (Irving Stone, 1938), Cardinal Gibbons (A. S. Will, 1922), W. R. Hearst (E. S. Bates and Oliver Carlson, 1936), Joseph Pulitzer (D. C. Seitz, 1924), W. S. Sims (E. E. Morison, 1942), Theodore Roosevelt (H. F. Pringle, 1931), William Howard Taft (H. F. Pringle, 1939), Woodrow Wilson (H. C. F. Bell, 1945; A. S. Link, 1947–), E. V. Debs (Ray Ginger, 1949), Joe Cannon (L. W. Busbey, 1927), George W. Norris (Alfred Lief, 1939), Nelson W. Aldrich (N. W. Stephenson, 1930), Walter Clark (A. L. Brooks, 1944), Carter Glass (Rixey Smith and Norman Beasley, 1939), Newton D. Baker (Frederick Palmer, 1939), John Sharp Williams (G. C. Osborn, 1943), Carrie Chapman Catt (M. G. Peck, 1944), E. M. House (A. D. H. Smith, 1940), Peter Norbeck (G. D. Fite, 1948), Elihu Root (P. C. Jessup, 1938), Chief Justice White (M. L. Klinkhamer, 1943), Chief Justice Fuller (W. L. King, 1950), Justice Brandeis (A. T. Mason, 1946), Justice Holmes (C. D. Bowen, 1944).

Part VII (Since 1919)

Economic history: George Soule, *Prosperity Decade* (1947); Broadus Mitchell, *Depression Decade* (1947); A. R. Burns, *Decline of Competition* (1936); David Lynch, *Concentration of Economic Power* (1946); Ferdinand Lundberg, *America's Sixty Families* (1937); Wendell Berge, *Cartels* (1944); T. W. Arnold, *Folklore of Capitalism* (1937); Lewis Corey, *Decline of American Capitalism* (1934); Merle Fainsod and Lincoln Gordon, *Government and the American Economy* (1948); A. E. Burns and D. S. Watson, *Government Spending and Economic Expansion* (1940); J. M. Clark, *Social Control of Business* (1939); M. F. Gallagher, *Government Rules Industry* (1934).

Industry: O. W. Knauth, *Managerial Enterprise* (1948); C. E. Merriam, *Public and Private Government* (1944); J. C. Bonbright and G. C. Means, *Holding Company* (1932); Twentieth Century Fund, *Power Industry and Public Interest* (1948); H. L. Smith, *Airways* (1942); N. R. Danielian, *A. T. & T.* (1939); E. D. Kennedy, *Automobile Industry* (1941); C. L. Dearing, *American Highway Policy* (1942); W. R. Maclaurin, *Invention and Innovation in the Radio Industry* (1949); F. T. Pecora, *Wall Street Under Oath* (1939); C. C. Chapman, *Development of American Business and Banking Thought, 1913–36* (1936).

Agriculture: W. P. Gee, *Place of Agriculture in American Life* (1930); Theodore Schultz, *Agriculture in an Unstable Economy* (1945); Carey McWilliams, *Factories in the Field* (1939); C. E. Lively and Conrad Taeuber, *Rural Migration* (1939). Sectional problems, H. W. Odom, *Way of the South toward the Regional Balance* (1947); W. P. Webb, *Divided We Stand* (1937).

Labor: R. R. R. Brooks, *When Labor Organizes* (1937); Edward Levinson, *Labor on the March* (1938); Herbert Harris, *Labor's Civil War* (1940); J. R. Walsh, *C.I.O.* (1937); C. E. Lindblom, *Unions and Capitalism* (1949); C. W. Mills, *New Men of Power* (1948); Stuart Jamieson, *Labor Unionism in American Agriculture* (1946).

Social history: P. W. Slosson, *Great Crusade and After, 1914–28* (1931); Dixon Wecter, *Age of the Great Depression, 1929–41* (1948); F. L. Allen, *Only Yesterday* (1931) and *Since Yesterday* (1940); Charles Merz, *Dry Decade* (1931); G. V. Seldes, *Years of the Locust* (1933); *Recent Social Trends* (1933); R. S. and H. M. Lynd, *Middletown* (1930) and *Middletown in Transition* (1937); H. F. Stearns (ed.), *Civilization in the United States* (1922) and *America Now* (1938); Malcolm Cowley, *Exile's Return* (1934); *I'll Take My Stand* (Southern Agrarians, 1930); David Spitz, *Patterns of Anti-Democratic Thought* (1949).

Literature: H. E. Luccock, *American Mirror* (1940); Leo Gurko, *Angry Decade* (1947); J. W. Krutch, *American Drama Since 1918* (1939).

Education: R. L. Kelly, *American Colleges and the Social Order* (1940); R. L. Duffus, *Democracy Enters College* (1936); R. F. Butts, *American Tradition in Religion and Education* (1950); J. M. O'Neill, *Religion and Education Under the Constitution* (1949).

Religion: J. A. Ryan, *Seven Troubled Years* (1937); F. S. Loescher, *Protestant Church and the Negro* (1948); H. P. Douglass and E. deS. Brunner, *Protestant Church as a Social Institution* (1935).

Research in World War II: J. P. Baxter, 3d, *Scientists Against Time* (1946); H. D. Smyth, *Atomic Energy for Military Purposes* (1945); Vannevar Bush, *Modern Arms and Free Men* (1949).

Medicine: H. E. Sigerist, *Medicine and Human Welfare* (1941); M. M. Davis, *America Organizes Medicine* (1941); E. C. Andrus and others, *Advances in Military Medicine* (1948); Albert Deutsch, *Shame of the States* (1948).

Minorities: H. P. Fairchild, *Race and Nationality as Factors in American Life* (1947); T. J. Woofter, *Races and Ethnic Groups in American Life* (1933); O. C. Cox, *Caste, Class and Race* (1948); M. R. Davie, *Refugees* (1947); Carey McWilliams, *Brothers Under the Skin* (1944), *North from Mexico* (1949), *Mask for Privilege* (1948), *Prejudice* (1944). On the Negro: Arnold Rose, *Negro in America* (1948); H. L. Moon, *Balance of Power* (1948); H. R. Cayton and G. S. Mitchell, *Black Workers and New Unions* (1939); B. H. Nelson, *Fourteenth Amendment and the Negro Since 1920* (1946); John Dollard, *Caste and Class in a Southern Town* (1937); C. S. Johnson, *Patterns of Negro Segregation* (1943); R. C. Weaver, *Negro Ghetto* (1948); C. G. Woodson, *Negro Professional Man* (1934); E. F. Frazier, *Negro Family* (1939); Gunnar Myrdal, *American Dilemma* (1944).

Civil liberties: J. P. Clark, *Deportation of Aliens* (1941); G. L. Joughlin and E. M. Morgan, *Legacy of Sacco and Vanzetti* (1948); George Seldes, *Witch Hunt* (1940); E. S. Corwin, *Total War and the Constitution* (1947).

Leisure: books by J. B. Nash (1940) and G. A. Lundberg (1934); L. M. Morris, *Not So Long Ago* (1949); *I Remember Distinctly* (1947); books on radio by E. P. J. Shurick (1946) and Francis Chase (1942); movies, L. C. Rosten (1941). See also Thomas Craven, *Modern Art* (1940); Jacques Schnier, *Sculpture in Modern America* (1948); Aaron Copland, *Our New Music* (1941); Grace Overmyer, *Government and the Arts* (1939); Willson Whitman, *Bread and Circuses* (1937).

Politics: S. H. Adams, *Incredible Era* (Harding, 1939); Karl Schriftgiesser, *This Was Normalcy* (1948); M. E. Ravage, *Story of Teapot Dome* (1924); M. M. Milligan, *Story of the Pendergast Machine* (1948); Wesley McCune, *Farm Bloc* (1943); E. P. Herring, *Group Representation Before Congress* (1929); Stuart Chase, *Democracy Under Pressure* (1945); V. O. Key, *Southern Politics* (1949); J. P. Clark, *Rise of a New Federalism* (1939); C. A. Patterson, *Presidential Government* (1947); books on the Nonpartisan League (A. A. Bruce, 1921; C. E. Russell, 1920) and on the La Follette campaign (K. C. McKay, 1947); R. A. Wilbur and Arthur Hyde, *Hoover Policies* (1937). On F. D. R.: Basil Rauch, *History of the New Deal* (1944); E. E. Robinson, *They Voted for Roosevelt* (1947); C. W. Stein, *Third Term Tradition* (1943); J. C. Brown, *Public Relief, 1929–39* (1940). Books on rural relief (C. C. Zim and N. L. Whetten, 1937), PWA (J. F. Isakoff, 1938), WPA (D. S. Howard, 1943), CCC (Kenneth Holland and F. E. Hill, 1942), NYA (Betty and E. K. Lindley, 1938), NRA (C. F. Roos, 1940; Hugh Johnson, 1937), AAA (E. G. Nourse, 1937). J. K. Galbraith and G. G. Johnson, Jr., *Economic Effects of Federal Public Works Expenditures, 1933–38* (1940); J. S. Davis, *On Agricultural Policy, 1926–38* (1939); H. I. Richards, *Cotton and the AAA* (1936). Books on TVA (D. E. Lilienthal, 1944; C. H. Pritchett, 1943); social security

(P. H. Douglas, 1936). The Court fight: E. M. Eriksson, *Supreme Court and the New Deal* (1940); M. L. Ernst, *Ultimate Power* (1937); Charles Warren, *Congress, Constitution and Supreme Court* (1935); R. H. Jackson, *Struggle for Judicial Supremacy* (1941); and see C. H. Pritchett, *Roosevelt Court* (1948); E. S. Corwin, *Constitutional Revolution, Ltd.* (1941).

Foreign relations: B. H. Williams, *Economic Foreign Policy of the United States* (1929); Ludwell Denny, *We Fight for Oil* (1928); D. F. Fleming, *United States and World Organization* (1938); T. A. Bailey, *Man in the Street* (1948); F. R. Dulles, *Road to Teheran* (1944); E. R. Stettinius, *Roosevelt and the Russians* (1949); T. A. Bailey, *America Faces Russia* (1950); W. A. Williams, *American-Russian Relations* (1952); H. H. and Margaret Sprout, *Toward a New Order of Sea Power* (1943); Merze Tate, *United States and Armaments* (1948); H. C. Engelbrecht and F. C. Hanighen, *Merchants of Death* (1934).

Entry into World War II: Basil Rauch, *Roosevelt from Munich to Pearl Harbor* (1950); Walter Millis, *This Is Pearl* (1947); Herbert Feis, *Road to Pearl Harbor* (1951); C. C. Tansill, *Back Door to War* (1952); C. A. Beard, *President Roosevelt and the Coming of the War* (1948). World War II: D. M. Nelson, *Arsenal of Democracy* (1946); E. R. Stettinius, *Lend-Lease* (1944); S. E. Harris, *Price and Related Controls* (1945); W. W. Wilcox, *Farmer in the Second World War* (1947); L. W. Koenig, *Presidency and the Crisis* (1944); W. F. Ogburn, *American Society in Wartime* (1943).

Biographies: Henry Ford (W. C. Richards, 1948; K. T. Sward, 1948), Andrew W. Mellon (Harvey O'Connor, 1933), Dwight Morrow (Harold Nicholson, 1935), George Eastman (C. W. Ackerman, 1930), John L. Lewis (J. A. Wechsler, 1944), Albert Einstein (Philipp Frank, 1947; Lincoln Barnett, 1948), the Wright brothers (J. R. McMahon, 1930; F. C. Kelly, 1943), Grant Wood (Darrell Garwood, 1944), Thomas Wolfe (P. H. Johnson, 1948), Bishop Cannon (Virginius Dabney, 1949), Chief Justice Stone (S. J. Konefsky, 1945), Justice Cardozo (J. F. Pollard, 1935), Calvin Coolidge (C. M. Fuess, 1940), Alfred E. Smith (H. F. Pringle, 1927), Huey Long (H. T. Kane, 1941), the Wallaces (Russell Lord, 1947), Wendell Willkie (M. E. Dillon, 1952). Frank Freidel has begun to publish his multivolume biography of Franklin D. Roosevelt; and see R. E. Sherwood, *Roosevelt and Hopkins* (1948), and the memoirs of Frances Perkins (1946), Mrs. Roosevelt (1949), Cordell Hull (1948), Henry L. Stimson (1948), James A. Farley (1948), and Raymond Moley (1939).

Abbott, Lyman, 548
Abolitionists, 199, 242, 246–251, 302, 309–310
Academic freedom, 496, 734
Academies, 158–159, 201
Adams, C. F., father, 314; son, 450
Adams, Henry, 502
Adams, John, Revolution, 98–99; President, 120, 126–127, 173; views, 125, 156, 163, 167
Adams, J. Q., Congressman, 251, 272; President, 264–268; Secretary of State, 278
Adams, Samuel, 78, 118
Adams, Samuel Hopkins, 519
Adamson Act, 533, 574
Addams, Jane, 518, 549
Addyston Pipe case, 465
Adet, French diplomat, 172
Adkins vs. Children's Hospital, 658
Adult education, 237–238, 412, 494–496
Advertising, 69, 224, 358, 374, 385–386, 439, 519, 595, 600–601
Africa, and Europe, 19, 21–22; slavery, 32–33, 232, 279, 289; World War II, 716–717
Agrarians, Southern, 611, 633, 651
Agricultural Adjustment Act (AAA), 614–615, 674–676, 679, 684–685, 691
Agricultural Marketing Act, 668
Agriculture, Indian and colonial, 3–6, 11, 22–26, 29–33, 59; to 1815, 131–142, 144, 148–150, 155; 1815–50 era, 187–201; 1850–96 era, 301–304, 324, 347, 353, 427–441; progressive era, 476–477, 533, 536, 541; since 1917, 550–551, 572–573, 604, 609–616, 659, 663, 668–669, 674–676, 679, 684–685, 687, 709, 722–723, 735
Agriculture, Department of, 194, 434, 436, 498, 528, 674
Aguinaldo, Emilio, 549–550
Aiken, J. E., 678
Air Power, 580, 696, 706, 717
See also Aviation
Alabama, 24, 228; economic activities, 141, 193, 196, 208, 216, 300, 371–372, 400; statehood, 190, 263; politics, 439, 723
Alabama, Confederate ship, 326 n.
Alamo, 282
Alaska, Indians, 3; Russians, 7; U. S. buys, 274, 279, 542; resources, 493, 528; government, 550–551; boundary, 563; World War II, 716
Albany, N. Y., key location and transportation, 24, 52, 207–208, 211–213; Plan of Union, 55

Aldrich, Nelson, 468, 520, 522, 526–527
Aldrich-Vreeland Act, 468
Aleutians, 716
Alien and Sedition Acts, 126–129, 266
Alien Property Custodian, 661
Allen, Ethan, 90, 164
Allen, Dr. Horace N., 539
Alliances, French, 95, 98, 170–173; opposition to any, 169–171, 173, 275, 563, 578–579, 585; formed, 714–715, 729–730
Allies (World War I), 565–570, 579–582
Allston, Washington, 241
Alsace-Lorraine, 581
Almy & Brown, manufacturers, 144, 219
Altgeld, J. P., 399, 516
Aluminum, 661
Amana Society, 248
Amendments to Articles of Confederation, 110–111; to Constitution, I–X, 119; XI, 125; XII, 126 n.; XIII, 343; XIV, 351, 460; XV, 351; XVI, 526, 531; XVII, 517, 526; XVIII, 511, 634–635; XIX, 487, 517–518, 576, 638; XX, 676 n.; XXI, 635; XXII, 686 n.
America First, 627, 703
American (magazine), 506
American Asiatic Association, 539, 552
American Association for Advancement of Science, 493
American Association of University Professors, 496
American Bible Society, 232
American Board of Commissioners for Foreign Missions, 232
American Colonization Society, 140–141, 247
American Council of Learned Societies, 644
American Expeditionary Forces (A.E.F.), 579–580
American Federation of Labor (A.F. of L.), early growth, 397–399; from 1896 to 1919, 471–472, 483, 526, 529, 551, 574, 577; since 1919, 604–608, 624, 664, 685, 735
American Home Missionary Society, 232
American League (baseball), 491–492
American Legion, 625, 667
American Mercury, 636, 652
American Party, 293, 315–316
American Peace Society, 247
American Philosophical Society, 71, 159
American Protective Association (A.P.A.), 408–409, 483, 510
American Protective League, 577
American Railway Union, 399